Dr. Effie Maclellan
Department of Edu
University of
Southbrae Dr
GLASGOW   G13 1PP
Tel:- 0141 950 3355
e-mail:- e.maclellan@strath.ac.uk

HANDBOOK OF

Classroom

Assessment

Learning, Achievement,
and Adjustment

This is a volume in the Academic Press
EDUCATIONAL PSYCHOLOGY SERIES

Critical comprehensive reviews of research knowledge, theories, principles, and practices

Under the editorship of Gary D. Phye

HANDBOOK OF
Classroom
Assessment
Learning, Achievement, and Adjustment

EDITED BY
Gary D. Phye
Department of Psychology
Iowa State University
Ames, Iowa

ACADEMIC PRESS

San Diego   *London*   *Boston*   *New York*   *Sydney*   *Tokyo*   *Toronto*

Background image © 1993 Color Bytes, Inc.
Inset image © 1995 PhotoDisc, Inc.

This book is printed on acid-free paper. ∞

Academic Press, Inc.
525 B Street, Suite 1900, San Diego, California 92101-4495, USA
http://www.apnet.com

Academic Press Limited
24-28 Oval Road, London NW1 7DX, UK
http://www.hbuk.co.uk/ap/

Library of Congress Cataloging-in-Publication Data

Handbook of classroom assessment : learning, achievement, and
  adjustment / edited by Gary D. Phye.
          p.   cm. -- (The educational psychology series)
    Includes bibliographical references and index.
    ISBN 0-12-554155-4 (case : alk. paper). -- ISBN 0-12-554156-2
(paper : alk. paper)
    1. Educational tests and measurements--United States--Handbooks,
manuals, etc.   2. Learning--Handbooks, manuals, etc.   3. Academic
achievement--United States--Handbooks, manuals, etc.   4. Educational
psychology--United States--Handbooks, manuals, etc.   I. Phye, Gary
D.   II. Series: Educational psychology.
  LB3051.H3198   1996
  371.2'6--dc20   96-41805
                                                                   CIP

PRINTED IN THE UNITED STATES OF AMERICA
96   97   98   99   00   01   BC   9   8   7   6   5   4   3   2   1

Contents

Contributors   xvii

Preface   xix

I

Assessment
Perspectives and Theory

1. LEARNING, ACHIEVEMENT, AND ASSESSMENT: CONSTRUCTS AT A CROSSROADS
Gregory J. Cizek

2. CLASSROOM ASSESSMENT:
A MULTIDIMENSIONAL PERSPECTIVE
Gary D. Phye

3. TEACHER ASSESSMENT LITERACY:
WHAT DO TEACHERS KNOW ABOUT ASSESSMENT?
Barbara S. Plake and James C. Impara

4. CLASSROOM ASSESSMENT AS INQUIRY
Robert C. Calfee and Walter V. Masuda

Contents

5. CLASSROOM ASSESSMENT OF REASONING STRATEGIES

Edys Quellmalz and Janita Hoskyn

6. ACADEMIC SELF-CONCEPT: BEYOND THE DUSTBOWL

Herbert W. Marsh and Rhonda Craven

7. ASSESSMENT OF SUBJECTIVE WELL-BEING DURING CHILDHOOD AND ADOLESCENCE

Timothy A. Bender

II

Standardized Assessment

8. ASSESSMENT DURING THE PRESCHOOL YEARS

Cheryl E. Sanders

9. THE ROLE OF STANDARDIZED ACHIEVEMENT TESTS
IN GRADES K–12

Tim Ansley

Assessment of Classroom Learning

10. A NEW VISION OF THE NATURE AND PURPOSES OF ASSESSMENT IN THE MATHEMATICS CLASSROOM

Frank K. Lester, Jr., Diana V. Lambdin, and Ronald V. Preston

11. ELEMENTARY SOCIAL STUDIES: INSTRUMENTS, ACTIVITIES, AND STANDARDS

Janet Alleman and Jere Brophy

12. AUTHENTIC ASSESSMENT IN SOCIAL STUDIES: STANDARDS AND EXAMPLES

Fred M. Newmann

13. FOREIGN LANGUAGES: INSTRUMENTS, TECHNIQUES, AND STANDARDS

Nancy C. Rhodes, Marcia H. Rosenbusch, and Lynn Thompson

14. A USER-FRIENDLY GUIDE TO ASSESSMENT IN VISUAL ARTS

Dennis Dake and John Weinkein

Developing Standards

17. THE NATIONAL ASSESSMENT OF
EDUCATIONAL PROGRESS
Albert E. Beaton

18. EPILOGUE:
CLASSROOM ASSESSMENT—LOOKING FORWARD
Gary D. Phye

Contributors

Numbers in parentheses indicate the pages on which the authors' contributions begin.

Janet Alleman (321), Department of Teacher Education, Michigan State University, East Lansing, Michigan 48824

Tim Ansley (265), University of Iowa, Iowa City, Iowa 52242

Albert E. Beaton (517), Boston College, Chestnut Hill, Massachusetts 02167

Timothy A. Bender (199), Psychology Department, Southwest Missouri State University, Springfield, Missouri 65804

Jere Brophy (321), Department of Teacher Education, Michigan State University, East Lansing, Michigan 48824

Robert C. Calfee (69), School of Education, Stanford University, Stanford, California 94305

Gregory J. Cizek (1), College of Education and Allied Professions, University of Toledo, Toledo, Ohio 43606

Rhonda Craven (131), University of New South Wales, St. George, Australia

Dennis Dake (417), Department of Art/Design, Art/Design College, Iowa State University, Ames, Iowa 50011

Joan L. Herman (491), CRESST, University of California, Los Angeles, California 90024

Janita Hoskyn (103), University of Arkansas, Little Rock, Arkansas 72227

James C. Impara (53), Department of Education, Psychology and Measurement, University of Nebraska, Lincoln, Nebraska 68588

Diana V. Lambdin (287), School of Education, Indiana University, Bloomington, Indiana 47405

Frank K. Lester, Jr. (287), School of Education, Indiana University, Bloomington, Indiana 47405

Brenda H. Loyd (481), School of Education, University of Virginia, Charlottesville, Virginia 22903

Douglas E. Loyd (481), School of Education, University of Virginia, Charlottesville, Virginia 22903

Herbert W. Marsh (131), School of Education, University of Western Sydney, Macarthur, Campbelltown, New South Wales 2560, Australia

Walter V. Masuda (69), Graduate School of Education, Division of Language and Literacy, University of California, Berkeley, California 94720

Fred M. Newmann (359), Center on Organization and Restructuring of Schools, University of Wisconsin, Madison, Wisconsin 53705

Gary D. Phye (33, 531), Psychology Department, Iowa State University, Ames, Iowa 50011

Barbara S. Plake (53), University of Nebraska, Lincoln, Nebraska 38588

Ronald V. Preston (287), Mathematics Department, East Carolina University, Greenville, North Carolina 27858

Edys Quellmalz (103), SRI International, Portola Valley, California 94025

Nancy C. Rhodes (381), Center for Applied Linguistics, Washington, DC 20037

Marcia H. Rosenbusch (381), National Foreign Language Research Center, Iowa State University, Ames, Iowa 50011

Cheryl E. Sanders (227), Metropolitan State College of Denver, Louisville, Colorado 80027

Brian M. Stecher (491), RAND Corporation, Santa Monica, California 90407

Lynn Thompson (381), Center for Applied Linguistics, Washington, DC 20037

John Weinkein (417), Department of Art/Design, Art/Design College, Iowa State University, Ames, Iowa 50011

Preface

Academic Press has a long and successful history of publishing the *Educational Psychology* series. New to this series are both myself as editor and handbooks as a type of publication within the series. The *Handbook of Classroom Assessment* is an effort to bridge the communication gap between theory and practice. Chapter authors are prominent authorities in their own areas of research and theory development. These individuals have been actively involved with the transformation of *theory* into *practice*. This commitment to providing a theoretically sound but practical basis for change is evident in the cogent ideas and practices provided in the chapters that follow.

The focus of this handbook is the classroom assessment of learning, achievement, and adjustment. These three areas of student growth and development are the focus of most assessment activities conducted in the classroom. However, assessment is more than simply testing as practiced in schools today.

In some classrooms, standardized achievement testing is conducted on a yearly basis. In these cases, the results are frequently used to demonstrate academic achievement for such educational units as schools and school districts. In some cases, the results are used to make decisions about individual students or serve as the basis for parent–teacher conferences. However, a yearly assessment does not provide a clear picture of what has been learned during the academic year. On the other hand, teacher-made tests are frequently used for grading students. In this respect, they reflect the progress of learning during the school year better than a single yearly assessment of achievement.

Effective classroom assessment practices include not only standardized achievement testing and the development of classroom tests for grading, but also formative and summative evaluations that are not part of the grading scheme. In other words, classroom assessment must be multidimensional. While academic learning and achievement are the primary targets of classroom assessment, the personal adjustment of individual students to the academic environment cannot be ignored.

The *Handbook of Classroom Assessment* is divided into four sections. Part I deals with assessment issues of pedagogical importance. Initially the reader is provided an overview of the dilemma assessment experts are facing in their attempts to meet the demands of the times. This is followed by a discussion of the multidimensional nature of assessment activities commonly found in the classroom. Next is a chapter devoted to a recent study of teacher assessment literacy in the United States. The second half of Part I is devoted to the topics of classroom assessment, such as inquiry, assessment of reasoning strategies, assessment of academic self-concept, and assessment of subjective well-being.

Part II is the smallest section in the handbook, covering preschool assessment and standardized achievement testing. Both chapters in this section are approached from the perspective of "what teachers should know" about the *use* of standardized instruments.

Part III is organized around the content areas of mathematics, social studies, foreign languages, and the visual arts. Assessment is approached from a developmental perspective. Features of special interest in this section are the activities and examples of classroom assessment used in the respective content areas. These examples provide valuable assistance for the classroom teacher seeking help in the development of authentic assessment activities.

Part IV is devoted to issues of interpretation. At the school level, a grading philosophy must be developed. This issue has been neglected in many discussions of classroom assessment. At the state level, accountability is an issue. Several states have mandated the use of portfolio assessment practices. The strengths and weaknesses of using portfolios for large-scale assessment are discussed with examples from recent statewide efforts. The last topic is the national assessment of educational progress. Is this a new level of assessment or are we simply becoming more aware of its existence?

I gratefully acknowledge the efforts of two persons responsible for providing the foundation for this effort. Allan J. Edwards was the originator and editor of the *Educational Psychology* book series for Academic Press until his recent retirement. I will strive to continue the tradition of scholarship he so successfully established. I also thank Nikki Levy, Senior Acquisitions Editor for Academic Press. Nikki's willingness to take a chance by publishing handbooks for a new audience (the educational professional in the field) facilitates my efforts as series editor.

Gary D. Phye

Memoriam

During the preparation of this volume, we lost a valued colleague and friend—Brenda Loyd. Brenda was developing the chapter on the philosophy of grading, coauthored with her husband Douglas, at the time of her death. For those who did not have the opportunity to know Brenda, I am providing a short biographical sketch, which in no way covers all her accomplishments. This is followed by an excerpt from a letter written to Douglas by a long-time friend and colleague—Gregory Cizek.

BRENDA LOYD

- B.A. Psychology (with honors), 1970, from University of Texas, Austin.
- M.A. Counseling Education, 1972, from University of Texas, Austin.
- Ph.D. Educational Measurement, Statistics, and Evaluation, 1980, from University of Iowa; emphasis in Educational and Mathematical Statistics, Applied and Theoretical Measurement, and Evaluation.
- Associate Director of Test Development at ACT in 1980–1981; Faculty at the Curry School of Education in 1981 at the University of Virginia.
- Coauthor of several test batteries, including the Test of Academic Proficiency, and contributor to the Iowa Tests of Basic Skills Primary Battery.
- GRE Board of Directors, technical committees for the states of Kentucky, Delaware, and New Jersey; technical committee for NAEP, ACE test review committee, NBPTS Technical Advisory Group.
- Secretary for Division D of AERA (1985); Assistant Program Chair for Division D (1992)
- In NCME, Chair of the Professional Development Committee (1987–1988); Chair of Training Presessions (1988); Program Cochair for annual meeting (1990); Chair of Budget and Finance Committee (1992–1995), Board of Directors (1991–1994); President-Elect of NCME (1994).

Honors and awards: UV Outstanding Teacher Award (1995); Virginia Educational Research Award (1983–1987, 1990); Charles Edward Clear Research Award from VERA (1987, 1990).

I guess all that I wanted to say is something that you know already. Brenda was an outstanding woman. In her profession, she was a woman of great knowledge, stature, and integrity. Her wisdom and expertise made her a leader. More than this, I knew Brenda as a gracious person. She was kind and forebearing. And, although many professional people simply don't care to discuss their families, Brenda would talk frequently about hers—a sign of her great love for her husband and her children and of the importance of her family in her life.

Brenda will be greatly missed.

Assessment

Perspectives and Theory

CHAPTER

1

Learning, Achievement, and Assessment: Constructs at a Crossroads

GREGORY J. CIZEK

University of Toledo, Ohio

It is a dynamic time for those involved in education: learning theorists, teachers, measurement specialists, and policy makers. Theories of learning are rapidly changing and influencing conceptions of appropriate instruction. It is also a pivotal era for those who design, implement, and are affected by innovations in assessment, including teachers, administrators, parents, students, and communities.

The fact that these changes are concurrent is not coincidental. Any educational reform effort that addressed only learning or assessment would necessarily be inadequate. However, periods of educational reform cause us to reflect on the essential purpose of education. When we (re)ask the question, "What is the purpose of education?" we are inevitably faced with defining outcomes. Is the purpose of education to encourage and facilitate the greatest achievement for each student? If so, what do we mean by *achievement*? Or, is the purpose of education to encourage learning, as both an immediate aim and a lifelong process? If so, what do we mean by *learning*?

Answering the question about the purpose of education also requires us to confront the question, "What is the purpose of *assessment*?" At first blush, the purpose of assessment would seem to be the measurement of learning or the demonstration of achievement. However, if it is now timely to reintroduce fundamental questions such as, "Are learning and achievement the

Handbook of Classroom Assessment

same thing?" it is equally worthwhile to re-examine the issue of the purpose of assessments.

This chapter provides some background and perspectives on these questions. It addresses three constructs in flux: learning, achievement, and assessment. The following sections are directed toward five objectives. First, a distinction is drawn between learning and achievement. Second, a conceptual definition of assessment is developed. Third, a new conceptualization of assessment is provided in which assessment is viewed as a special case of research design. Fourth, an organizing framework for assessment is provided that attempts to illustrate the practical relationships between learning, achievement, and assessment. Finally, suggestions for the future interplay between learning, achievement, and assessment are provided.

LEARNING AND ACHIEVEMENT: ARE THEY THE SAME?

The answer to the title question is easy: No. Although sometimes used interchangeably, learning and achievement are surely related; however, they differ in significant ways that have implications for both instruction and assessment. In this section, some definitions of learning and achievement will be presented and the differences between the two will be highlighted. In the following sections, some implications for instruction and assessment will be examined.

Learning: Constructing Cognitive Change

Mayer (1987) has described education in the following way: "Changing the learner's knowledge—manifested in changes in academic, motor, social, and personal behavior—is what education is all about" (p. 9).

Mayer's emphasis on changes in behavior as indicators of learning is not new. The process of learning has been fairly consistently defined since the early 1900s. Definitions offered in various places, especially in educational psychology textbooks, appear to retain much of E. L. Thorndike's early notions of learning as consisting of cognitive associations that result in observable changes in behavior (see, for example, Thorndike, 1931).

For example, a fairly recent work by Gagné (1970) provides a representative definition of learning that illustrates continuing references to change and behavior:

> Learning is a change in human disposition or capability, which can be retained, and which is not simply ascribable to the process of growth. The kind of change called learning exhibits itself as a change in behavior, and the inference of learning is made by comparing what behavior was possible before the individual was placed in a "learning situation" and what behavior can be exhibited after such treatment. (p. 3)

In the late 1970s, however, references to learning changed subtly to exclude reference to behavior and focus exclusively on cognitive change. For example, Wittrock defined learning as: "the term we use to describe the processes involved in changing through experience. It is the process of acquiring relatively permanent change in understanding, attitude, knowledge, information, ability, and skill through experience" (1977, p. ix).

Commenting on Wittrock's definition, T. L. Good and Brophy (1986) presaged that the exclusion of behavior would lead to new ways of measuring learning:

> Defined in this way, learning is an internal, cognitive event that cannot be equated with observable performance. It is true that learning produces changes in capacity for performance, and that we must observe changes in performance in order to infer that learning has occurred. . . . Nevertheless, the performance potential acquired through learning is not the same as its reproduction or application in any particular performance situation. (p. 134)

In summary, although the terms *achievement* and *learning* may have been used synonymously in the past, they are now distinct. Currently learning is viewed as a relatively permanent reorganization of cognitive structures, such as in the integration of existing schema, or the development of new schema. Learning occurs as a result of an individual's experience and the active construction of knowledge and processing of information. Accordingly, the kind of cognitive reorganization called *learning* would not simply be the result of maturation or development. Experiences that result in learning can be either internally initiated (e.g., reflection, thinking) or externally driven (e.g., the result of instruction, interaction with other students).

Achievement: Desired by All, Defined by Few

The exclusion of the aspect of performance from the changing definitions of learning has had conflicting results. First, the exclusion of observable performance from the definition of learning has meant that, as a construct, achievement must now stand on its own two feet: a stand-alone definition of achievement is required.

Achievement, especially academic achievement, is universally praised as a goal of American education. Programs are designed to enhance achievement; students are honored for high achievement; many tests covering school subject matter contain the word *achievement* in their titles; labels are assigned for over- and underachievement.

Ironically, however, the term *achievement* is described in few educational references. For example, a review of several educational psychology texts revealed that none actually attempted to define *achievement*. The general topic of achievement is often presented, though couched in references to achievement motivation, gender differences, or academic self-concept. Surprisingly, the term *achievement* is not even found in some dictionaries of education (see, e.g., Rowntree, 1982). Glaser and Silver (1994) observe, with understatement, that, compared to the basis for other purposes of testing, "the theory underlying the assessment of school achievement is less explicit" (p. 400).

One definition of achievement can be found in the *Dictionary of Education* (which is currently undergoing its first revision in over two decades). In this reference, achievement is defined as "(1) accomplishment or proficiency of performance in a given skill or body of knowledge; (2) progress in school" (C. V. Good, 1973, p. 7). *Academic achievement* is defined as "knowledge gained or skills developed in the school subjects, usually designated by test scores or by marks assigned by teachers, or by both" (p. 7).

Admittedly, the definitions in the *Dictionary of Education* are dated. Hindsight, however, permits some interesting observations. First, definition 1 does seem to point toward a notion of achievement that requires performance or demonstration. This is the key distinction between learning and achievement. As T. L. Good and Brophy (1986) noted "the performance potential acquired through learning is not the same as its reproduction or application in any particular performance situation" (p. 134).

Second, definition 2 highlights the ways that learning and achievement are *not* related. For example, as critics of what is called social promotion in schools argue, progress in school may be completely unrelated to performance. Also, learning is not a necessary condition for achievement to occur, as in successful performance that is due to luck, guessing, or cheating. And, the definition of academic achievement as "usually designated by test scores, marks" and so on, illustrates another distinction between achievement and learning: Performances and demonstrations of knowledge or skill acquisition can be ranked, graded, or certified; cognitive reorganization is usually not the object of normative or evaluative measurement.

Third, it is important to recognize that achievement is a fallible representation or indicator of learning. T. L. Good and Brophy (1986) observe that:

> [The] relationships between prior learning and subsequent performance are imperfect at best. The absence of a particular behavior does not mean that the person does not know anything about it, and the disappearance of a behavior observed in the past does not mean that it has been forgotten or that the ability to perform has been lost. (p. 134)

Far from being a hindrance to designing educational experiences and gauging their effectiveness, these imperfections in the relationship between learning and achievement are beneficial to encouraging sound educational practice. For example, an expansion of classroom concerns to focus more intensively on learning suggests that new models of the relationship between teaching and learning are vital (see Gallagher, 1994). Also, because the relationship between learning and achievement is not direct, it serves to highlight the inferential nature of all assessment. As a result, it will be essential to examine the interrelationships between learning, achievement, and assessment. Finally, because the distinction between learning and achievement has important implications for curriculum, these implications will be briefly explored in the following section.

LEARNING, ACHIEVEMENT, AND CURRICULUM

The distinction between learning and achievement just described provides a detailed, semantic perspective on a way to view recent evolution of educational theory and practice. The semantic differentiation may be sufficient to notice key differences between current notions of learning and achievement, but does not necessarily provide a link to instructional planning or student assessment. The following sections present a broad overview of these changing notions of learning, with implications for planning instruction and assessment.

Early Notions of Learning

A broad overview has been provided by Glaser (1984), who has chronicled theories for the teaching of thinking. Glaser begins tracing notions of thinking in American psychology by referencing "early associationistic theor[ies] of learning" (p. 93). According to Shepard (1991), the associationistic or behavioristic approaches to educational practice can be summarized in two principles:

> 1. Learning is seen to be linear, and sequential. Complex understandings can only occur by the accretion of elemental, prerequisite learnings . . . [and]
> 2. To facilitate learning, assessment should be closely aligned with instruction. Tests should exactly specify the desired behavioral outcomes of instruction and should be used at each learning juncture; that is, one should "test–teach–test". (pp. 6–7)

The early associationistic theories described by Glaser, Shepard, and others have been widely rejected as inadequate for representing thinking and knowledge acquisition (see, for example, Resnick & Resnick, 1992). Also, the early theories have been strongly criticized for their unwanted effects on teachers' instructional planning, students' learning, and measurement specialists' test construction practices.

Despite the criticisms, however, behavioristic teaching and testing practices have not been entirely abandoned. Shepard (1991) has suggested that the problem of lingering behavioristic influences may in large part be attributable to an elaborate web of relationships with psychometricians' beliefs at the center. She asserts that measurement specialists: (1) "are no longer psychologists conversant with changes in learning theories;" (2) "operate from implicit learning theories that . . . derive from behavioristic learning theory;" (3) hold "belie[fs] about learning [that] shape practice, including instructional practice;" and (4) represent "an entrenched technical community . . . unable to respond thoughtfully to legitimate criticisms of current tests" (p. 9).

Some of Shepard's assertions are probably correct. For example, others have documented the dissociation of educational measurement and educational psychology (cf. Anastasi, 1967; Glaser, Lesgold, & Lajoie, 1987) and the insularity of the technical community (see Cizek, 1990). However, her identification of psychometricians' beliefs as a mechanism for sustaining the hegemony of behavioristic instructional practices is probably misspecified. It is more likely that psychometricians actually have a *shared* training and experience with curriculum planners, teachers, and educational administrators vis-à-vis learning theories. As Cizek (1993b) has argued: "Criticism centering on the educational training of psychometricians [is] an indictment of the training of teachers generally. If Shepard *has* seen the enemy, it is all of us" (p. 5).

Current Notions of Learning

According to Glaser and Silver (1994), it is clear that new theories of learning were necessary, because "the behavioral theories of the mid-20th century that generated behavioral objectives . . . could not adequately describe complex processes of thought, reasoning and problem solving (p. 401). Glaser's chronology of the developments in learning theory concludes with the portent of a new age of learning theory. Glaser (1984) describes the new age as one in which "there is a new relationship between students and their subject matter, in which knowledge and skill become objects of interrogation, inquiry, and extrapolation" (p. 103).

Glaser (1984) envisioned a new line of research on learning with a focus on "the possession and utilization of an organized body of conceptual and procedural knowledge" (p. 97). And, a substantial body of research evidence on a variety of dimensions related to this vision has accumulated. For example, research has examined differences in expert and novice problem solving (Chi, Glaser, & Rees, 1982); inquiry-based instruction (Collins & Stevens, 1982); reciprocal teaching (Palincsar & Brown, 1984); cognitive scaffolding (Palincsar, 1986); and metacognition and cognitive monitoring (Flavell, 1979).

Collectively, incorporation of these aspects of newer notions of learning is sometimes referred to as *cognitive instruction*. Summarizing why cognitive instruction can be effective in the classroom, Reid and Stone (1991) contrast the roots of the cognitive perspective with behavioristic approaches. They observe that, with the cognitive approaches, "students are no longer regarded as empty vessels to be filled with knowledge. They are viewed as inherently active 'apprentice learners' . . . who benefit from participation . . . in goal-oriented, collaborative activities" (p. 8).

Current conceptions of learning view the learner as interacting with an external world that the learner actively engages, constructs, and interprets, bringing to bear prior knowledge, experiences, interests, and attitudes. Wolf, Bixby, Glenn, and Gardner (1991) have termed this new framework "an epistemology of mind" in which "learning at all levels involves sustained performances of thought and collaborative interactions of multiple minds and tools as much as the individual possession of information" (p. 48). Others have described the new cognitive paradigm by asserting that "learners become more competent not simply by learning more facts and skills, but by reconfiguring their knowledge; by 'chunking' information to reduce memory loads; and by developing strategies and models that help them discern when and how facts and skills are important" (Mislevy, Yamamoto, & Anacker, 1991, abstract).

Finally, some emerging notions of learning have insisted that external influences must be incorporated into theories of cognition (see, for example, Mishler, 1979). Bereiter (1990) has observed that "a persistent complaint against cognitive theories in general is that they are all 'in the head,' ignoring culture, history, economics, the environment, tools, parenting, and all such forces that shape our lives" (p. 604).

Along these lines, some theorists have begun to explore the role of these influences on student learning. One example of this perspective can be found in the work of Doll (1993), who explicates the possibilities of expanded notions of learning for curriculum construction. Doll suggests that curriculum be viewed as "a process—dialogic and transformative, based on the inter- or transactions peculiar to local situations" (p. 140). According to Doll, a curriculum should focus on the principles of (1) richness, in which the multiple layers of meaning or possible interpretations of events are explored; (2) recursion, in which the human capacity of repeated considerations with reflection is used to expand students' depth of understanding; and (3) relations, in which the interconnectedness between subject areas is explored as well as "those cultural or cosmological relations which lie outside the curriculum, but form a large matrix within which the curriculum is embedded" (p. 179).

EDUCATIONAL REFORM AND THE ROLE OF ASSESSMENT

Changing conceptions of learning, achievement, and curriculum have resulted in expanded notions of what constitutes real educational reform. Over the past several years, the comparatively dry enterprise of measuring student attainment of academic outcomes has become the focus of considerable attention as a mechanism for instigating changes in what and how students learn. Educational reformers have increasingly relied on assessment to attain their objectives, to substantiate their contentions, or to promote implementation of their innovations (cf. Airasian, 1988; Geiger, 1991; Heyneman & Ransom, 1990; National Commission on Testing and Public Policy, 1990).

Educational reformers are joined by lawmakers, who frequently incorporate an assessment framework or mandate an evaluation component into new legislation. At the center of the assessment revolution are teachers and those with concerns about the information needs of classroom teachers. Many researchers and practitioners consider assessment reform to be the very foundation of general educational reforms. For example, one leader in assessment reform efforts has highlighted the important role assessment must play in reforms, suggesting that "more important for school restructuring is the need to build local educator capacity and interest in quality assessment" (Wiggins, 1992, p. 33).

Recent, revived interest in assessment has exceeded reasonable predictions. From the national level to the local level, assessment innovations are being proposed and tested. Teachers are participating in professional development activities designed to enable them to better integrate assessment and instruction. An abundance of written materials, videotapes, special issues of journals, and conferences have been produced to provide guidance on implementing new ways of gathering information about students, such as portfolios and performance assessments.

Despite this wealth of information—or perhaps because of it—a conundrum has arisen. It used to be a simpler world, a world in which a test meant a number two pencil and an answer sheet. In such a world, *everyone* seemed to know what a test was and what it was for. Now, however, as the assessment world has expanded, there is considerable confusion about the purpose, role, and interpretation of assessments. In the rush to develop more authentic assessments, to promote alternatives to traditional assessments, and to adapt assessment to the information needs of teachers, clarity of purpose has been lost. Among other issues, a key distinction between assessment of learning and assessment to document achievement should be made.

What Is Assessment?

The term *assessment* has been cast about so routinely in recent educational discussions, debates, and deliberations, it would seem that everyone knows what assessment is. Such an assumption is probably incorrect. There is certainly no standard usage of the term: it is used in so many different ways, in so many different contexts, and for so many different purposes, that it can mean almost anything.

At least four definitions of assessment can be seen in current literature dealing with assessment. To some educators, assessment refers to new *for-*

mats for gathering information about students' achievements; for example, "portfolio assessment." To others, assessment refers to a new *attitude* toward gathering information, an attitude that is perhaps kinder and gentler than that represented by standardized testing. The term *assessment* has also come to represent a new *ethos*, one of empowerment, in which assessments are designed and implemented primarily to serve the information needs of students and teachers. Finally, assessment has been used to refer to a new *process*, often with medical or psychological connotations, as in the gathering and synthesizing of information about a person that a physician or counselor would conduct as part of diagnosing and treating the person's condition.

Each of these usages contributes to a definition of assessment. First, any definition of assessment must be applicable to existing, emerging, and future conditions, formats, and contexts. Other things being equal, a more generalizable definition would be preferred over a narrow one. Many researchers and practitioners concur that notions about assessment need to be broadened (cf. Baker & Stites, 1991; Cizek & Rachor, 1994; Ferrara & McTighe, 1992; Stiggins, 1991a).

Examples of what a broadened conceptualization might look like have been presented by Airasian (1994), who suggests that assessment should include "the full range of information teachers gather in their classrooms: information that helps them understand their pupils, monitor their instruction, and establish a viable classroom culture" (p. 5), and by Baker and Stites (1991), who envision formal student assessments of cognitive and noncognitive characteristics, in which "students will need to demonstrate their commitment to tasks over time, their workforce readiness, [and] their social competence in team or group performance contexts" (p. 153).

Second, it would be desirable for a definition of assessment to convey an attitude that enhanced the position of assessment in instruction and would be readily embraced by educators. For example, a colleague of mine recently related that portfolio assessment would never have achieved its current level of acceptance had it been called *individual folder-based measurement*.

Third, a definition that recognizes that assessments should serve, as opposed to drive, instruction would be preferable. Although there are still some proponents of what has been called *measurement-driven instruction* (Popham, 1987), such a view was probably never in the mainstream of psychometric thought, even though this strategy has been used repeatedly—and successfully—to accomplish curricular aims. It is instructive to recall the words E. F. Lindquist (1958), founder of the large-scale Iowa Tests of Basic Skills, uttered nearly 40 years ago:

> I cannot emphasize too strongly, however, that it is definitely not the function of planners of scholarship and college entrance examination programs to determine or to *set* any education goals. Certainly it is not their province to attempt through the test to *bring about changes* in the high school curriculum, no matter how desirable. (p. 10, emphasis in original)

Finally, a definition of assessment should provide a link to educational processes that seek the welfare of each student. It is possible to recognize that assessments have administrative uses as well as instructional value. Nonetheless, it seems proper to weight a definition of assessment more heavily gathering accurate information that is relevant to *students'* needs. Again, quoting Lindquist (this time, 20 years ago), placing ancillary concerns above students' needs has long been an enduring temptation:

> I have been rather disappointed in developments within the educational testing field. Tests seem to me to have gone farther away from higher and higher precision and more accuracy in measurement. There seems to be less of an effort to provide a really faithful, dependable picture of the abilities and aptitude of the individual child, and more concern with group achievement along the lines that are of interest to school administrators, who are out to make a record, more interested in average scores and how they may be used politically, and more interested, perhaps, in getting the information needed for those purposes at a lower price in terms of both time and money. (quoted in Kohn, 1975, p. 20)

Incorporating the preceding facets into a single definition of educational assessment yields the following proposed definition:

> *assessment* \uh ses' mənt\ (1) v.t.: the planned process of gathering and synthesizing information relevant to the purposes of (a) discovering and documenting students' strengths and weaknesses, (b) planning and enhancing instruction, or (c) evaluating progress and making decisions about students. (2) n.: the process, instrument, or method used to gather the information.

The essence of the proposed definition is that assessment is a planned process designed to accomplish a specific educational purpose, with the primary beneficiary of the process being the student. Again, it is recognized that other uses of assessments may be warranted, such as research or accountability. In developing and implementing a definition of *assessment*, it should be remembered that such purposes ought to be secondary uses of educational assessment information.

At the same time, it is important to retain a useful distinction between assessment as an integrated aspect of instruction and assessment as dissociated from instruction for purposes of evaluation. In the former case, the assessment is embedded in instructional events. Such embedding is increasingly common; indeed, not only is it a truism that students learn from exposure to assessments, but there are also situations in which a particular assessment constitutes the entirety of a desired instructional event. In these instances, the instructional value of the assessment experience is inextricably linked to formative information that is acquired by the students simultaneously.

In the latter case, the assessment may be grounded in students' instructional experiences. However, assessments designed primarily for evaluation need not—and often do not—intend to provide incidental instructional value. These instances include those in which the assessment is conducted to arrive at an instructional or placement decision that must be made. In either case, the assessment information is gathered with the intent and result that the student is the primary beneficiary.

RECONCEPTUALIZING ASSESSMENT

A beginning step in promoting implementation of a revised definition of assessment would be to show how current misuse of the term is unacceptable. However, it is not simply a minor alteration in a definition that is at issue, but a radical reconceptualization of classroom measurement. To demonstrate the necessity for the radical reconceptualization, it may be useful to provide an illustration.

The following scenario probably occurs frequently in professors' offices. A graduate student has come to seek advice on a thesis or dissertation. The student may introduce the first part of the dialogue with something like "I want to do a survey," or "I think I'd like to do a MANOVA," or "I want to use LISREL."

The student, possibly wanting to reveal that he or she paid attention in statistics class, offers to utilize a sophisticated statistical software package or to apply an avant garde analytic avenue. The professor, who probably has his or her own ideas about proper sequence in the design and conduct of research, responds instinctively: "Use a survey for what? Why MANOVA? Why not EQS instead of LISREL? And, by the way, what *is* the research question? What are you trying to find out?"

Painfully, the team of scholars tries to retrace the considerations that led to the decisions concerning the data analytic method of choice. Too often, a fascinating methodological possibility cloaks the absence of specific research questions.

Specialists in educational measurement have increasingly been encountering a similar situation. A currently common request of measurement practitioners is for assistance with classroom assessment from those who say, "I want to use portfolios."

One thesis of this chapter is that the burgeoning interest in portfolios, performance assessments, and so on can appropriately be placed in the same category as the statements about surveys, MANOVAs, and LISREL. Of *course*, many educators want to use portfolios; everyone does, lately. Multivariate methods are vital; LISREL is in; portfolios are what's happening in educational measurement.

Nothing is inherently wrong with any of these approaches. The desire to use the most up-to-date methodologies is probably natural. However, this urge reflects the same kind of misconceptualization involving the information gathering (i.e., the assessment) process. The common error is that a data collection procedure or a data analytical technique is often considered *prior* to establishing an understanding of the nature of the research question to be answered.

This fundamental error has lead to the purposes and effects of educational assessment being profoundly misunderstood by many diverse audiences. It is certainly possible that these (mis)behaviors have been conditioned by the strong emphasis on data analytic techniques that occurs during graduate training in education and psychology. As Cone and Foster (1991) have observed:

> Graduate students learn complex, sophisticated statistical procedures to test data obtained in elegant, internally and externally valid experimental designs. But they are rarely exposed to the training needed to evaluate whether the data they obtain so cleverly and analyze so complexly are any good in the first place. (p. 653)

It has also been well-documented that teachers and administrators get little relevant training in educational assessment, either prior to entering the profession or while they are in service (see O'Sullivan & Chalnick, 1991; Plake & Impara, this volume; Schafer & Lissitz, 1987; Ward, 1980; Wise, Lukin, & Roos, 1991). Even when some training is provided, too frequently it can focus only on mechanistic methods for accomplishing tasks that teachers will not ordinarily need to perform in a classroom (Stiggins, 1991b). Almost never are teachers and administrators enculturated into a way of viewing educational assessment as a special case of research design.

Assessment as Research Design

Most producers of educational research and consumers of educational journals are probably familiar with the traditional outline of a scholarly article. Typically, such an article begins with a "Background" or "Introduction" section that introduces the reader to the issues or context that motivated the research. Additionally, this section often provides a review of previous research on the topic. A second section, "Objectives" or "Purpose" or "Statement of the Problem," follows the introduction. This section provides the specific question that the research attempts to answer or the specific problem it addresses. A third section common to many research articles is a "Methods" or "Procedures" section, which outlines the particular strategy that the author will use to address the research question. A fourth section, usually "Results" or "Findings," simply presents the outcome of the procedures applied to the problem. A final section, "Implications" or "Discussion" or "Recommendations," relates the findings to the original research question in a way that goes beyond the findings. This section consists of the author's attempt to make sense of the findings, by showing how the findings refine what is known about the topic under study or by providing a unique interpretation of the findings.

This familiar framework, encountered when *reading* about research, also applies when used as a process for *designing* a research study. The sequence

of the events seems intuitive. In designing a study, a researcher would first assemble a critical mass of background information on a topic, then refine his or her initial curiosity into a specific research question, then design a procedure for answering the question, implement the procedure, observe the results, and speculate regarding what the results might mean.

The reconceptualization of assessment suggested here relies heavily on the metaphor of assessment as research design. In approaching assessment, educators would do well to design the assessment process much as a researcher would set out to seek answers to a research question. A model of the process would contain the familiar steps. First, an educator would acquire background information, then pose specific assessment questions, develop or select methods to gather the information, and so on. Table 1 shows the issues that might be addressed at each stage of the assessment process, if a model of assessment as research design were adopted.

The list of questions to be addressed at each stage of the assessment process is not exhaustive. However, it is suggested that the issues listed in Table 1 form a useful heuristic for designing a single assessment or an assessment program, as well as for evaluating assessments currently being used. Using this model, assessment—like research design—is the purposive configuration of events to acquire information bearing on an important question in a fair, accurate, and efficient manner. Conceiving of assessment in this way has the potential to broaden the universe of valuable educational outcomes that are assessed; reduce redundancy of assessment information; enhance the match between the targets of assessment and the strategies used to gather information about those targets; focus assessments so that they more directly bear on the questions of interest; and promote usefulness, meaningfulness, and interpretability of the information yielded by assessments.

NEW ASSESSMENTS FOR NEW EDUCATIONAL OUTCOMES

As the universe of valuable educational outcomes expands, so too must the array of instruments necessary to assess those outcomes. While traditional assessments have often targeted a student's ability to demonstrate the acquisition of knowledge (i.e., achievement), new methods are needed to assess a student's level of understanding within a content area and the organization of the student's cognitive structures (i.e., learning). This section explores some of the work in these areas.

First, because this mistake occurs with such frequency even in the literature on assessment, it is important to emphasize that an accurate perspective on the place of new assessment methods does not view the new modes

TABLE 1
Assessment as Research Design

Background
    Is the assessment needed? What information about students is desired?
    What benefits and adverse consequences might accrue from the assessment, and for whom?
    Is the information desired already being gathered in some other way? Is the planned
        assessment redundant?

Purpose
    What specific research question(s) will the assessment answer? For example, is the target of
        the assessment to gather information about students' cognitive organization (i.e.,
        learning) or to elicit a performance (i.e., achievement)?
    Will the assessment yield reasonably clear, unambiguous answers to the research questions?
    What will be done with the assessment information? For example, will the information be
        used to enhance students' understandings, to aid in instructional planning, for evaluation,
        or for accountability purposes?

Methods
    What alternative methods or instruments are available to obtain the information desired?
    If appropriate instruments are not available, can they be developed?
    What trade-offs exist in terms of time, cost, utility, and the like of the various options?
    Which method provides the best match with the purpose of the assessment?
    How likely is it that the chosen method will provide adequate, accurate information? How
        will possible sources of contamination to the information be controlled or reduced?

Results
    What is the level of quality of the information gathered? Is it sufficient for making the
        instructional, evaluative, or other decisions desired?
    Is additional, supplementary information available to enhance the credibility and usefulness
        of the assessment?
    How should the results be reported so that they are meaningful to key audiences (e.g.,
        parents, students, teachers, administrators)?

Discussion
    How should the assessment information be interpreted? What are reasonable, cautious
        interpretations of the results? Which interpretations are tentative? Which are
        unwarranted?
    What are some alternative interpretations of the information? How plausible are those
        interpretations?
    Which additional questions about student learning or achievement have been left
        unanswered by the assessment? Why were certain valuable educational outcomes not
        assessed?

---

as replacements for traditional assessments. In essence, the root of the problem is a confusion about the purposes of assessments and the failure to recognize that that assessments can serve different purposes; these purposes require different instruments to accomplish the job. The confusion is amply illustrated in popular and professional literature: One recent article was an attempt by its authors to argue a proposition displayed in the title of the article, "Why We Should Replace Aptitude Tests with Achievement Tests" (Kirst & Rowen, 1993, p. 40).

Even the popularity of the phrase *alternative assessment* is perhaps somewhat unfortunate, in that it connotes some assessment formats (e.g., performances, portfolios, essays, projects) as alternative ways of gathering *the same kind* of information about students. For example, portfolios are sometimes suggested as alternatives to standardized achievement tests. In fact, these two assessment strategies are oriented toward answering two dramatically different assessment questions: the portfolio provides a measure of individual student growth with respect to (usually) individual student goals; the standardized achievement battery provides a measure of a student's relative standing among peers on common educational content. The practice of obtaining *both* kinds of information is not at all a dissonant desire. Instead, these divergent assessment goals simply reflect the long-standing reality that absolute performance is almost never completely understood without the interpretive assistance provided by comparative information.

Therefore, just as learning does not replace achievement, it does not make sense to talk about new forms of assessment replacing traditional forms. Nonetheless, because the number and complexity of the assessment targets we seek information about has expanded, currently available methods of assessment, designed with specific purposes in mind, will be insufficient. New forms of assessment, designed to assess *other* outcomes are necessary. As others have observed, "tests can predict failure without an understanding of what causes success, but intervening to prevent failure and enhance competence requires deeper understanding" (Mislevy et al., 1991, p. 2). Many of the new forms of assessment have been conceived with the intention of acquiring this kind of deeper understanding.

A framework for considering the expanded array of cognitive processes worthy of assessment is provided by Glaser et al. (1987). These authors suggest six dimensions of cognition that lend themselves to assessment: (1) knowledge organization and structure; (2) depth of problem representation; (3) quality of mental models; (4) procedural efficiency; (5) automaticity of performance; and (6) metacognitive skills.

According to Glaser et al. (1987), knowledge organization and structure can be assessed to differentiate between novice and expert skill development: a novice would possess cognitive structures that are loosely organized, unconnected, or poorly related, whereas the expert's organization would be highly interconnected and developed. Similarly, highly skilled individuals are able to present detailed, abstract representations of the task in problem-solving situations, while the less skilled individual may focus only on surface features of the problem.

Highly skilled learners develop sophisticated mental models that allow them to cognitively visualize and utilize systems of operations to guide their performance. Less-skilled learners lack such models or possess models that are not as refined. Less-skilled learners are also often bound to routinized, multistep algorithms in which they follow a sequential program of steps to solve a problem; the more highly skilled learner develops the ability to recognize which of the steps in a sequence may not be necessary for addressing the task and is able to solve problems more efficiently.

Automaticity refers to the ability to attack a problem-solving or performance situation and rely on internalized, automatic procedures. According to cognitive information processing theory, the greater the extent to which aspects of the task can be addressed with automaticity, the more the learner can focus on novel or unusual aspects of the problem. Highly skilled learners possess automaticity to a greater degree than less-skilled learners. Finally, metacognition (Flavell, 1979) refers to the individual's ability to reflect on and monitor his or her own learning and cognition. More highly skilled students possess a greater number of and fluency with metacognitive strategies than novices.

A growing number of researchers and theorists have suggested new approaches for assessing the kinds of cognitive outcomes described by Glaser et al. (1987). Snow and Lohman (1989) have carefully documented the implications of cognitive psychology for educational assessment. They state:

> As cognitive analysis is brought to bear on educational goals, the psychological nature of those goals is better understood. The question is: What constitutes expertise in field X, and how does it develop? The answer, even if provisional, provides a theory for test design. (p. 321)

One framework for measuring varying levels of expertise has been suggested by Royer, Cisero, and Carlo (1993), who examined techniques and procedures for assessing cognitive skills. Their framework of assessment procedures is explicitly organized along the lines of the six cognitive skills enumerated by Glaser et al. (1987) and described previously. In addition to summarizing and evaluating measurement procedures that might be appropriate for each of the six goals, Royer et al. also observe that "cognitive assessments are most useful in situations where a cognitive task analysis has preceded the choice of measurement procedures" (p. 238). If assessment is viewed as a special case of research design, as suggested earlier in this chapter, their admonition provides a reminder that a specific research question is a critical *a priori* foundation for successful assessment.

Mislevy et al. (1991) have proposed a way of looking at cognitive assessments. Their framework is presented as an alternative to the traditional test models of classical test theory or item response theory. Essentially, existing theories model the likely measure of an individual's true score or standing on a latent trait based on observed responses that the examinee makes to test items.

Mislevy et al. (1991) propose an alternative test theory designed to assess student understanding. The distinction between, for example, classical test theory and what Mislevy et al. call *supermodels* is equivalent to the earlier distinction made between achievement and learning, with classical test theory oriented to assessing the extent to which students can demonstrate accomplishment in a subject area and the supermodels oriented to assessing construction and sophistication of cognitive structures. A further distinction between the two kinds of models is that the latter permits more confident exploration and hypotheses about student misunderstandings or inaccurate conceptualizations.

Figures 1–3 show an example, reproduced from Mislevy et al. (1991), of how understanding of forces and balance can be modeled. Balance beam tasks are developed specifically to represent cognitive levels of understanding (in this case, denoted categories from 0 to 5, although these categorical values actually represent detailed descriptions of cognitive states of understanding (see Mislevy et al., 1991, p. 11). Figure 1 shows how the problem types can be coded to represent the varying problem types (e.g, E = "Equal" problems in which there are matching weights and distances on each side of a fulcrum; D = "Dominant" problems in which each side has equal weights, but unequal distances from the fulcrum; S = "Subordinate" problems involving unequal distances from a fulcrum, but equal weights; and so on). Figure 2 shows what an initial state of understanding might look like for a student; the horizontal bars in the Cognitive Level section of the figure graphically illustrate probabilities of the student having a particular level of understanding (categories 0–5). Figure 3 illustrates how the inference about the cognitive level of understanding for the student would change after he or she responded incorrectly to an S type problem; here the most probable inference about the student would be a cognitive level of understanding equal to that described as category 1. Students would attempt problems until a certain level of confidence about their cognitive state were achieved.

Assessments like those suggested by Mislevy et al. have also been called *cognitively diagnostic assessments* (CDA) (Nichols, 1994; Nichols, Chipman, & Brennan, 1995). In addition to providing some history regarding the need for and characteristics of CDA, Nichols also proposes a framework to provide guidance in developing cognitively diagnostic assessments and he suggests which skills CDA developers should possess.

CLASSROOM INFERENCES ABOUT LEARNING AND ACHIEVEMENT

Earlier, it was asserted that, by nature, all assessment is an inferential process. The challenge of conducting high-quality assessment is the challenge of ensuring that *observable* regularities in students' performances reflect accurate, meaningful distinctions in *unobservable* characteristics or standing on

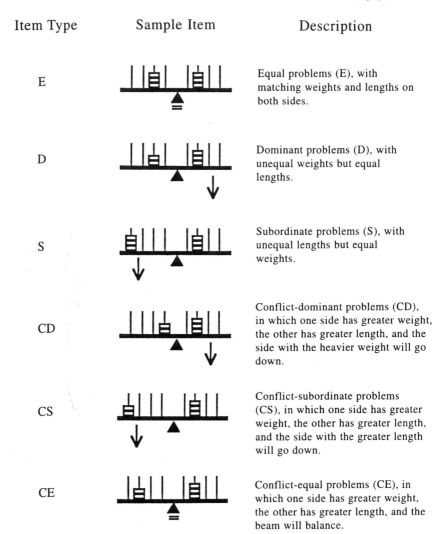

Item Type	Sample Item	Description
E		Equal problems (E), with matching weights and lengths on both sides.
D		Dominant problems (D), with unequal weights but equal lengths.
S		Subordinate problems (S), with unequal lengths but equal weights.
CD		Conflict-dominant problems (CD), in which one side has greater weight, the other has greater length, and the side with the heavier weight will go down.
CS		Conflict-subordinate problems (CS), in which one side has greater weight, the other has greater length, and the side with the greater length will go down.
CE		Conflict-equal problems (CE), in which one side has greater weight, the other has greater length, and the beam will balance.

FIGURE 1

Sample balance beam task types (from Mislevy et al., 1991). Reprinted by permission of Educational Testing Service, the copyright owner.

underlying constructs. Messick (1989) has described this inferential process in his chapter on validity:

> Test behaviors are often viewed as samples of domain behaviors (or as essentially similar to domain behaviors) for which predictions are to be made or inferences drawn. Test behaviors are also viewed as signs of other behaviors that they do not ordinarily resemble and as indicants of underlying processes or traits. (p. 15)

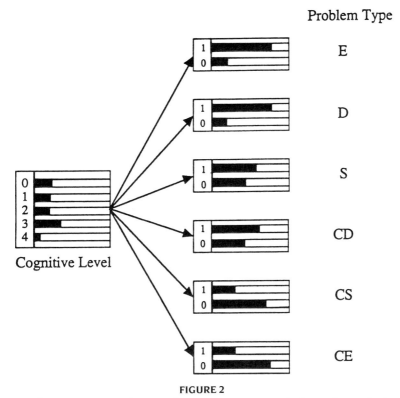

FIGURE 2

Initial inference regarding student competence on balance beam tasks
(from Mislevy et al., 1991). Reprinted by permission of Educational Testing
Service, the copyright owner.

For classroom assessment, then, it is essential to acquire a clarity of purpose with respect to the nature of the inference desired. With a clear assessment purpose in mind, assessments can be designed or selected that match the purpose; such a match is necessary (though not sufficient) for enhancing the confidence one can have in the inferences to be drawn from the assessment results. Again, it is worth remembering that *an inferential leap is always required when generalizing from the data obtained from any student assessment performance to what is usually considered to be information yielded by the assessment or "facts" about that student.* This principle was referred to earlier by T. L. Good and Brophy (1986) who observed that

> [the] relationships between prior learning and subsequent performance are imperfect at best. The absence of a particular behavior does not mean that the person does not know anything about it, and the disappearance of a behavior observed in the past does not mean that it has been forgotten or that the ability to perform has been lost. (p. 134)

Problem Type

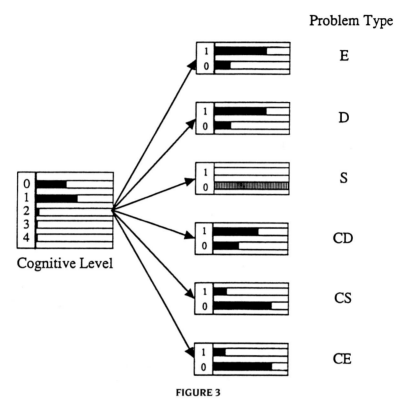

FIGURE 3
Revised inference regarding student competence on balance beam tasks
(from Mislevy et al., 1991). Reprinted by permission of Educational Testing
Service, the copyright owner.

Such a caveat may tempt some to conclude that the challenge of assessment is too great and that the information about students yielded by assessments is too tentative. However, the science of measurement exists solely to ascertain and improve the quality of data generated by assessments. Though never perfect, well-designed and well-conducted assessments can yield information that is necessary, accurate, dependable, and useful for educational decision making. With these caveats in mind, the remainder of this section will present a suggested framework for classroom assessments that makes explicit the match between various assessment formats and desired inferences.

A Framework for Classroom Assessments

In elementary and secondary school classrooms, learning and achievement are both valuable goals. For each individual student, attainment of these goals depends on the complex interrelationships among a number of variables, including student background characteristics, prior learning, motivation, teacher characteristics, instructional quality, classroom environment, parental support, and a host of other factors. These factors cannot be minimized and are the grist of much research in education and the social sciences. However, no matter what other factors are involved in bringing a student to a level of understanding or accomplishment, it is nonetheless a valuable educational endeavor—indeed, a professional obligation—to determine with as much confidence as possible what a student's level of understanding or accomplishment might be.

These kinds of information about student knowledge, skill, and ability can be of interest to many audiences and are used to make a wide variety of educational decisions. For example, Mehrens and Lehmann (1991) list 19 different uses falling into five categories: instructional, guidance, administrative, research, and program evaluation. Regardless of whether the assessments used to gather the information necessary to make these decisions are teacher-made, state-supplied, or commercially produced, it is essential that the instruments match a clear purpose.

A discernable trend has been for more of the "action" in assessment to take place closer to the classroom. One research report recently proclaimed, "Classroom Teachers Move to Center Stage in the Assessment Arena—Ready or Not!" (Jett & Schafer, 1992, p. 1). Classroom teachers are becoming more intimately involved in conceiving, constructing, coordinating, and conducting assessments, especially new forms of assessment such as portfolios (see Maeroff, 1991) or student exhibitions (see Sizer, 1992). Consequently, it is increasingly important for educational professionals to be able to determine the best match between the purpose of an assessment—that is, the desired inference—and the strategy suited to collecting the information.

Table 2 presents a taxonomy of classroom assessment approaches. Four explanatory notes about the table are warranted. First, the taxonomy depicts targets and methods that are associated primarily with cognitive outcomes. Although assessments targeting other areas such as the affective domain are gaining renewed interest (see Popham, 1994), the cognitive domain remains the primary focus in most elementary and secondary educational settings.

Second, Table 2 presents a correspondence between commonly used, well-researched assessment approaches (with which most educators, especially classroom teachers, would have some familiarity) and the underlying learning or achievement targets they might best address. This means, for example, that many of the techniques and procedures for measuring cognitive skill presented by Royer et al. (1993), which are still in a developmental phase, would not yet be suitable for inclusion. As those authors caution:

> There is a gaping research hole that prevents the acceptance of virtually all of the assessment procedures reviewed in this article. In all of the research we read, there was not a single report of a reliability index for an assessment procedure and indexes of validity were available only as [strong] inferences. (p. 235)

TABLE 2
Taxonomy of Assessment Approaches

	Assessment approaches
Achievement targets	
Content acquisition	Select-type formats (e.g., multiple choice, true/false, alternate choice, matching)
	Supply-type formats (e.g., short answer, fill in the blank, label a diagram)
Procedural knowledge	Describe a process (e.g., lab experiment, operate a machine, construct a flowchart, direct observation, "show your work," "tell the steps you followed")
Performance	Demonstrations (e.g., build a birdhouse, repair a car, write an essay, debate an opponent, recite a poem, compose a song, lead a discussion, compete in an event, create a sculpture)
Learning targets	
Content acquisition	Concept mapping
Procedural knowledge	Think-aloud protocols; interviews
Cognitive change	Portfolios

Third, the term *performance* as in "performance assessment" can lead to some confusion. In essence, all student behaviors that could be used for assessment purposes can be called performances, whether that behavior is filling in an oval on the bubble sheet of a norm-referenced test or a carefully rehearsed speech for a public speaking class. For purposes of clarity it might be preferable to refer to behaviors of the latter type as *demonstrations*. The term *responses* could be used to denote activities in which the student responds either by selecting or producing a brief response to a stimulus. A key distinction here is that demonstrations have a substantial component of student choice in configuring the task or problem solution; the student may also have wider latitude regarding interaction with the person responsible for administering the assessment. Response situations ordinarily involve highly structured stimuli or prompts and provide little leeway for students to configure the problem, develop an original solution, or interact with the person conducting the assessment. Nonetheless, to avoid confusion, demonstrations of the sort described will be referred to as "performances." The assessment of these performances will involve active demonstrations of student knowledge, skill, or ability.

Finally, it should be realized that all of the assessment approaches listed in Table 2 can be more or less "authentic." To the extent that items students respond to or tasks they attempt reflect important content or processes that are *useful in contexts outside the classroom*, those assessments become more authentic. When assessments are "purely academic" exercises, to use that phrase precisely, then those assessments are less authentic. Wiggins (1989) has promoted a conception of more authentic tasks as those that have value for student learning in and of themselves and apart from any value the tasks might have for evaluation. All of the assessment approaches listed in Table 2 can, and probably should, be designed to be as authentic as possible to maximize student interest, motivation, and transfer.

As can be inferred from the upper portion of Table 2, test developers and classroom teachers have more experience developing assessments targeted toward the documentation of achievement than toward the exposure of learning. The varieties of select- and supply-type formats listed in Table 2 for measuring content acquisition are used in most elementary and secondary classrooms. Similarly, direct teacher observation of students engaged in a process and the familiar "show your work" directions to students solving mathematics problems have a long history of use in the assessment of procedural knowledge. Because of their familiarity and because nearly all introductory textbooks in educational measurement address the approaches referred to in the upper portion of Table 2 (see, for example, Mehrens & Lehmann, 1991); these approaches will not be described here.

The demonstrations listed as examples of how performance accomplishments are measured represent just a sample of the possibilities. Recently the use of actual demonstrations to document accomplishment of what a student can *do* has supplanted other measures of achievement, combining elements of content acquisition and procedural knowledge. Excellent guides for designing and scoring performances are also available in some educational measurement textbooks, (e.g., Oosterhof, 1994, chap. 15) and elsewhere (e.g., Baker, Aschbacher, Niemi, & Sato, 1992).

On the other hand, many classroom teachers have considerably less experience designing and using assessments that focus on student learning. Three approaches to assessing learning outcomes shown in the table are described briefly in the paragraphs that follow.

Concept Mapping

Concept mapping is a tool for examining a student's self-reported cognitive organization (see Novak, 1977; Novak & Gowin, 1984). Students, who are first trained regarding how to produce a concept map, are usually provided with a list of key concepts in a subject matter and asked to represent those concepts in two-dimensional form. The students are also directed to create the representations in such a way as to graphically illustrate superordinate and subordinate concepts and to include "linking words" or terms that clarify the illustrated relationships between represented concepts. When completed, the representations that contain the graphical and semantic elements are called *concept maps*.

Each map is an important window into an individual student's cognitive organization, as each map contains the key concepts, organized by the student according to what he or she perceives to be the structure of the subject matter (e.g., hierarchical, linear, "weblike"), using the linking words to show relationships such as branching between concepts. Figures 4 and 5 illustrate differing levels of understanding of subject matter in a science class on ocean organisms.

Two concept maps are shown in Figures 4 and 5. The figures are taken from a study by Haney (1993); they were completed by eighth grade students studying a science unit on ocean organisms. Students were provided with training in producing the maps and, at the end of the unit, with a list of 30 key concepts from the unit. Figure 4 shows the concept map produced by a student with identifiable gaps and errors of understanding. For example, *sand channel* is represented in the map as subordinate to *echinoderms* with the linking words "they have." In fact, the sand channel is simply the habitat of echinoderms; it is also not at a similar level as other concepts listed at this level, such as *snails* and *fish*. It can also be recognized that *arthropods* are not *vertebrates*, *fish* are not *mammals*, and so on.

Figure 5 shows the concept map produced by a student with a relatively complete and accurate conceptualization of the unit on ocean organisms. Examination of the map reveals no errors and comparatively sophisticated use of branching and linking words. Of the 30 concepts that were provided to the students for inclusion in their maps, over half of them (17) were incorporated into the map in Figure 5.

It is apparent that concept maps, such as those shown in Figures 4 and 5 can be used by teachers as a pretest measure to gauge students' entering conceptions about a subject. They can also be used to verify conceptions, trace misconceptions, investigate the sophistication of students' cognitive organization, and assist in instructional planning. The evaluation uses of concept maps are uncertain or, at least, are underinvestigated at this time.

Think-Aloud Protocols

Think-aloud protocols are structured exercises in which students reveal their thinking processes orally or in writing. Early studies by Bloom and Broder (1950) compared the self-reported, written problem-solving strategies used by expert and novice students in a college setting. By providing the novices with explicit review of their strategies and comparison with the strategies used by experts, Bloom and Broder were able to demonstrate the value and efficacy of focusing on procedural knowledge. The use of think-aloud procedures has been extended to elementary and secondary education; these

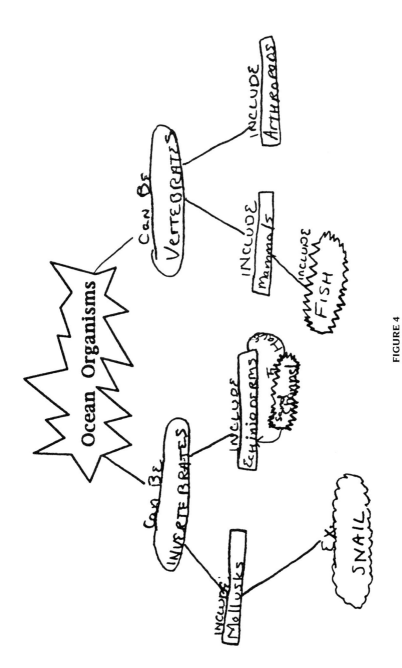

FIGURE 4

Concept map showing errors of conceptualization (from Haney, 1993).

Gregory J. Cizek

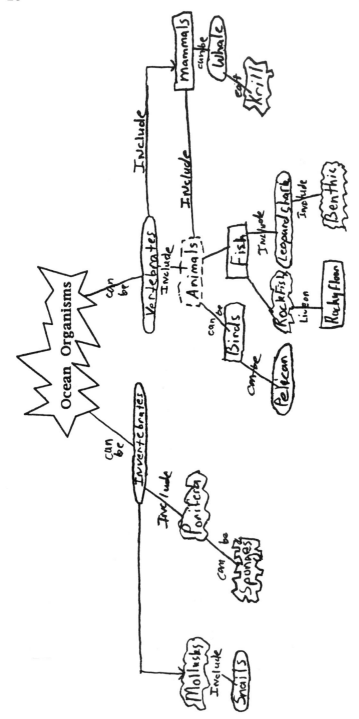

FIGURE 5

Concept map showing comparatively well-organized schema (from Haney, 1993).

procedures have also been suggested for assessment of cognitive as well as social skills (Camp & Bash, 1981). Although oral think-aloud protocols are frequently used, it may be especially beneficial for elementary and secondary students to produce and maintain written documentation of think-aloud exercises for future reference.

Portfolios

Portfolios are purposeful collections of student work; for example, writing samples, audiotapes of speeches, artwork, lab reports, even mathematics worksheets. Portfolios provide an opportunity for students, teachers, parents, and others to glean a more holistic view of changes in students' performance over time. In some applications, portfolios are used simply as a repository for these collections. This use of portfolios can enhance the teacher's ability to explain evaluations at parent–teacher conferences, or provide documentation of achievement. These uses will not be discussed here, although currently they may be the most prevalent implementation.

Portfolios enjoy much recent popularity although this is probably not due to how far the technology for their use has progressed. For example, research into the reliability of individual student portfolio scores has been discouraging (see Koretz, McCaffrey, Klein, Bell, & Stecher, 1993); currently, they rarely achieve the level of accuracy or dependability necessary for making decisions about individual students. However, portfolios are commendable for their ability to convey educationally worthwhile instructional targets and practices. Additionally, one reason why portfolios have achieved broad acceptance by educators is that they represent a way in which teachers can become more closely involved with assessing students and assessment can become more closely intertwined with instruction (see Cizek, 1993a). Maeroff (1991) has described this phenomenon:

> Expense and time may well turn out to be the brakes on the alternative assessment movement, both for the development of the instruments and for their use. But thumbing through a portfolio with a student or watching a student perform a task—whatever the psychometric worth of such assessments—adds a degree of intimacy that can be refreshing in an age of depersonalized appraisal. (p. 281)

Although the benefits described by Maeroff are certainly desirable, the use of portfolios for assessing learning provides perhaps the greatest promise for this assessment approach. To accomplish an assessment of learning, portfolios must be used as purposeful samples, over time, of student performance or products relative to specific educational outcomes. The key distinction in using portfolios is their ability to address the research question, "How have this student's cognitive abilities changed over time?" Many researchers are currently investigating the challenges that arise in structuring the sampling to answer that question more clearly and have proposed solutions to design, implementation, and scoring issues (Arter & Spandel, 1992; Herman, Gearhart, & Aschbacher, 1994; Myford & Mislevy, 1995; Stecher & Herman, this volume).

As with all other assessment information, the answer to questions about how a student's learning has changed over time requires an inferential leap from the data displayed in the portfolio. One frontier in educational measurement is the design and dissemination of information to classroom educators regarding how to implement portfolios in such a way as to enhance the accuracy of the inference. A continuing challenge for curriculum and subject matter experts is to develop models of competence development in ways that are useful for classroom-level portfolio assessment applications.

CONCLUSIONS AND SUGGESTIONS
FOR THE FUTURE

A significant theoretical divide has formed between the constructs of learning, achievement, and assessment. Substantial advances have been made in the cognitive sciences that suggest new models for teaching and learning are necessary (Gallagher, 1994). The advances predict profound changes in the way that instruction is integrated with assessment. These advances have stimulated a heightened awareness of diverse assessment purposes; they have provided the ability to design and implement assessments tailored to the divergent objectives of measuring learning for diagnostic purposes and documenting achievement for accountability and evaluative purposes.

On the other hand, to other audiences these theoretical distinctions may be of little interest. For example, for parents, employers, legislators, and others, achievement is the salient goal. For an employer who seeks to hire someone to work at a corporation office in Brazil, it is a trivial matter that the student has "learned" Portuguese if the person lacks the ability to demonstrate accomplished speaking, reading, or writing in the language.

These differences in perspective for various audiences suggest areas for future development. First, although educators have many decades of experience administering and interpreting assessments that target achievement, we have considerably less experience with newer approaches to assessing learning. As mentioned earlier, further investigation of the ways in which teachers can use assessments targeted at learning to improve individual instruction is essential.

Second, a practical concern is how to communicate the results of cognitive assessments of learning to various interested audiences. The schematic representations of competence illustrated in Figures 2 and 3 do not readily lend themselves to interpretation by parents, students, or others. Speaking in reference to technical developments in testing, Hambleton (1994) has observed that

> In looking back over my 25 years in the educational testing field, I'm struck by the strong technical advances that have been made and the very modest advances that have been made when it comes to reporting criterion-referenced information in ways that users can understand. (p. 1)

For the future, measurement specialists and educational psychologists, collaborating with teachers, parents, and students will need to develop new ways of representing the fuller range of information now available about student learning.

Finally, the nexus of assessment and evaluation is always a nettlesome issue. Teachers' grading practices have been shown to be highly variable, and grades to be somewhat unreliable indicators of student achievement (see Brookhart, 1994; Cizek, Rachor, & Fitzgerald, 1996; Hoge & Coladarci, 1989; Loyd & Loyd, this volume). Further investigation of and improvement in teachers' grading practices is warranted. Also, while it is recognized that not all assessments must serve an evaluative function, it seems reasonable to investigate how new forms of assessment might generate new forms of evaluation. To ask the question in a simplistic manner, What might cognitively diagnostic report cards look like?

In conclusion, the magnitude of changes in the way learning, achievement, and assessment are defined places these constructs at a crossroads. The educational reforms they portend are consequential. For educators who are interested in understanding students' understanding, new approaches such as cognitively diagnostic assessments offer much hope for promoting future learning, applying learning, and instructional planning. Advances in the assessment of learning are proving to be of value in increasing students' abilities to monitor their own understanding and refine the processes they use to learn new knowledge and skills.

Acknowledgment

The author is grateful for the support of this work provided by the University of Toledo College of Education and Allied Professions. Responsibility for errors in conceptualization, analysis, or conclusions rests solely with the author.

References

Airasian, P. W. (1988). Symbolic validation: The case of state-mandated, high-stakes testing. *Educational Evaluation and Policy Analysis, 10*(4), 301–313.

Airasian, P. W. (1994). *Classroom assessment* (2nd ed.). New York: McGraw-Hill.

Anastasi, A. (1967). Psychology, psychologists, and psychological testing. *American Psychologist, 22*(4), 297–306.

Arter, J. A., & Spandel, V. (1992). Using portfolios of student work in instruction and assessment. *Educational Measurement: Issues and Practice, 11*(1), 36–44.

Baker, E. L., Aschbacher, P. R., Niemi, D., & Sato, E. (1992). CRESST *performance assessment models: Assessing content area explanations.* Los Angeles: UCLA Center for Research on Evaluation, Standards, and Student Testing.

Baker, E. L., & Stites, R. (1991). Trends in testing in the USA. In S. H. Fuhrman & B. Malen (Eds.), *The politics of curriculum and testing* (pp. 139–157). London: Falmer.

Bereiter, C. (1990). Aspects of an educational learning theory. *Review of Educational Research*, 60, 603–624.

Bloom, B. S., & Broder, L. J. (1950). *Problem-solving processes of college students*. Chicago: University of Chicago Press.

Brookhart, S. M. (1994). Teachers' grading: Practice and theory. *Applied Measurement in Education*, 7(4), 279–301.

Camp, B., & Bash, M. (1981). *Think aloud: Increasing social and cognitive skills*. Champaign, IL: Research Press.

Chi, M. T. H., Glaser, R., & Rees, E. (1982). Expertise in problem solving. In R. Sternberg (Ed.), *Advances in the psychology of human intelligence* (Vol. 1, pp. 7–75). Hillsdale, NJ: Erlbaum.

Cizek, G. J. (1990). The case against the SAT [Book review]. *Educational and Psychological Measurement*, 50(3), 701–706.

Cizek, G. J. (1993a). Alternative assessment: Yes, but why? *Educational Horizons*, 72(1), 36–40.

Cizek, G. J. (1993b). Rethinking psychometricians' beliefs about learning. *Educational Researcher*, 22(4), 4–9.

Cizek, G. J., & Rachor, R. E. (1994). The real testing bias: The role of values in educational assessment. *NASSP Bulletin*, 78(560), 83–93.

Cizek, G. J., Rachor, R. E., & Fitzgerald, S. M. (1996). Teachers' assessment practices: Preparation, isolation, and the kitchen sink. *Educational Assessment*, 3(2), 159–179.

Collins, A., & Stevens, A. L. (1982). Goals and strategies of inquiry teachers. In R. Glaser (Ed.), *Advances in instructional psychology* (Vol. 2, pp. 65–119). Hillsdale, NJ: Erlbaum.

Cone, J. D., & Foster, S. L. (1991). Training in measurement: Always the bridesmaid. *American Psychologist*, 46(6), 653–654.

Doll, W. E. (1993). *A post-modern perspective on curriculum*. New York: Teachers College Press.

Ferrara, S., & McTighe, J. (1992). A process for planning more thoughtful classroom assessments. In A. Costa, J. Bellanca, & R. Fogarty (Eds.), *If minds matter: A foreword to the future* (pp. 337–347). Palatine, IL: Skylight.

Flavell, J. H. (1979). Metacognition and cognitive monitoring: A new area of cognitive-developmental inquiry. *American Psychologist*, 34, 906–911.

Gallagher, J. J. (1994). Teaching and leaning: New models. *Annual Review of Psychology*, 45, 171–195.

Gagné, R. M. (1970). *The conditions of learning* (2nd ed.). New York: Holt, Rinehart & Winston.

Geiger, K. (1991, December 12). Tests, trivia, and tears: Time to rethink how America tests. *Education Week*, p. 4.

Glaser, R. (1984). Education and thinking: The role of knowledge. *American Psychologist*, 39, 93–104.

Glaser, R., Lesgold, A., & Lajoie, S. (1987). Toward a cognitive theory for the measurement of achievement. In R. Ronning, J. Glover, J. C. Conoley, & J. Witt (Eds.), *The influence of cognitive psychology on testing and measurement* (pp. 96–131). Hillsdale, NJ: Erlbaum.

Glaser, R., & Silver, E. (1994). Assessment, testing, and instruction: Retrospect and prospect. *Review of Research in Education*, 20, 393–419.

Good, C. V. (Ed.). (1973). *Dictionary of education* (3rd ed.). New York: McGraw-Hill.

Good, T. L., & Brophy, G. E. (1986). *Educational psychology* (3rd ed.). New York: Longman.

Hambleton, R. K. (1994, April). *Scales, scores, and reporting forms to enhance the utility of educational testing*. Paper presented at the annual meeting of the National Council on Measurement in Education, New Orleans, LA.

Haney, J. (1993, October). *Concept mapping in the junior high school classroom as it relates to science achievement and the examination of conceptual change*. Paper presented at the annual meeting of the Mid Western Educational Research Association, Chicago.

Herman, J., Gearhart, M., & Aschbacher, P. (1994, April). *Portfolios for classroom assessment: Design and implementation issues*. Paper presented at the annual meeting of the American Educational Research Association, New Orleans, LA.

Heyneman, S. P., & Ransom, A. W. (1990). Using examinations and testing to improve educational quality. *Educational Policy*, 4(3), 177–192.

Hoge, R. D., & Coladarci, T. (1989). Teacher based judgments of academic achievement: A review of literature. *Review of Educational Research*, 59(3), 297–313.

Jett, D. L., & Schafer, W. D. (1992, April). *Classroom teachers move to center stage in the assessment arena—Ready or not!* Paper presented at the annual meeting of the American Educational Research Association, San Francisco.

Kirst, M., & Rowen, H. (1993, September 8). The incentive gap: Why we should replace aptitude tests with achievement tests. *Education Week*, 13(1), 40, 42.

Kohn, S. (1975). The numbers game: How the testing industry operates. *Principal*, 54(6), 11–23.

Koretz, D., McCaffrey, D., Klein, S., Bell, R., & Stecher, B. (1993). *Reliability of scores from the 1992 Vermont portfolio assessment program* (CSE Tech. Rep. No. 355). Los Angeles: RAND Corporation.

Lindquist, E. F. (1958, November). *The nature of the problem of improving scholarship and college entrance examinations.* Paper presented at the Invitational Conference on Testing Problems, Educational Testing Service, Princeton, NJ.

Maeroff, G. I. (1991). Assessing alternative assessment. *Phi Delta Kappan*, 73(4), 272–281.

Mayer, R. E. (1987). *Educational psychology: A cognitive approach.* Boston: Little, Brown.

Mehrens, W. A., & Lehmann, I. J. (1991). *Measurement and evaluation in education and psychology* (4th ed.). Fort Worth, TX: Holt, Rinehart & Winston.

Messick, S. (1989). Validity. In R. L. Linn (Ed.), *Educational measurement* (3rd ed., pp. 13–104). New York: Macmillan.

Mishler, E. G. (1979). Meaning in context: Is there any other kind? *Harvard Educational Review*, 49, 1–19.

Mislevy, R. J., Yamamoto, K., & Anacker, S. (1991). *Toward a test theory for assessing student understanding* (Research Report No. RR-91-32-ONR). Princeton, NJ: Educational Testing Service.

Myford, C. M., & Mislevy, R. J. (1995). *Monitoring and improving a portfolio assessment system* (Research Report No. 94-05). Princeton, NJ: Educational Testing Service.

National Commission on Testing and Public Policy. (1990). *From gatekeeper to gateway: Transforming testing in America.* Chestnut Hill, MA: Author.

Nichols, P. D. (1994). A framework for developing cognitively diagnostic assessments. *Review of Educational Research*, 64, 575–603.

Nichols, P. D., Chipman, S. F., & Brennan, R. L. (Eds.). (1995). Cognitively diagnostic assessment. Hillsdale, NJ: Erlbaum.

Novak, J. D. (1977). *A theory of education.* Ithaca, NY: Cornell University Press.

Novak, J. D., & Gowin, D. B. (1984). *Learning how to learn.* New York: Cambridge University Press.

Oosterhof, A. (1994). *Classroom applications of educational measurement* (2nd ed.). New York: Macmillan.

O'Sullivan, R. G., & Chalnick, M. K. (1991). Measurement-related course work requirements for teacher certification and recertification. *Educational Measurement: Issues and Practice*, 10(1), 17–19, 23.

Palincsar, A. (1986). The role of dialogue in providing scaffolded instruction. *Educational Psychologist*, 21, 73–98.

Palincsar, A., & Brown, A. L. (1984). Reciprocal teaching of comprehension-fostering and comprehension-monitoring activities. *Cognition and Instruction*, 1, 117–175.

Popham, W. J. (1987). The merits of measurement-driven instruction. *Phi Delta Kappan*, 68, 679–682.

Popham, W. J. (1994). Educational assessment's lurking lacuna: The measurement of affect. *Education and Urban Society*, 26(4), 404–416.

Reid, D. K., & Stone, C. A. (1991). Why is cognitive instruction effective? Underlying learning mechanisms. *Remedial and Special Education*, 12(3), 8–19.

Resnick, L. B., & Resnick, D. P. (1992). Assessing the thinking curriculum: New tools for educational reform. In B. R. Gifford & M. C. O'Connor (Eds.), *Changing assessments: Alternative views of aptitude, achievement, and instruction.* (pp. 37–75). Boston: Kluwer.

Rowntree, D. (1982). *A dictionary of education.* Totowa, NJ: Barnes & Noble.

Royer, J. M., Cisero, C. A., & Carlo, M. S. (1993). Techniques and procedures for assessing cognitive skills. *Review of Educational Research, 63*, 201–243.

Schafer, W. D., & Lissitz, R. W. (1987). Measurement training for school personnel: Recommendations and reality. *Journal of Teacher Education*, 38(3), 57–63.

Shepard, L. A. (1991). Psychometricians' beliefs about learning. *Educational Researcher*, 20(6), 2–16.

Sizer, T. R. (1992). *Horace's school: Redesigning the American high school.* New York: Houghton Mifflin.

Snow, R. E., & Lohman, D. F. (1989). Implications of cognitive psychology for educational measurement. In R. L. Linn (Ed.), *Educational measurement* (3rd ed., pp. 263–332). New York: Macmillan.

Stiggins, R. J. (1991a). Assessment literacy. *Phi Delta Kappan*, 72(10), 534–539.

Stiggins, R. J. (1991b). Relevant classroom assessment training for teachers. *Educational Measurement: Issues and Practice*, 10(1), 7–12.

Thorndike, E. L. (1931). *Human learning.* New York: Appleton Century Crofts.

Ward, J. G. (1980). Teachers and testing: A survey of knowledge and attitudes. In L. M. Rudner (Ed.), *Testing in our schools* (pp. 15–24). Washington, DC: National Institute of Education.

Wiggins, G. (1989). A true test: Toward more authentic and equitable assessment. *Phi Delta Kappan, 70*, 703–713.

Wiggins, G. (1992). Creating tests worth taking. *Educational Leadership*, 49(8), 26–33.

Wise, S. L., Lukin, L. E., & Roos, L. L. (1991). Teacher beliefs about training in testing and measurement. *Journal of Teacher Education*, 42(1), 37–42.

Wittrock, M. (Ed.). (1977). *Learning and instruction.* Berkeley, CA: McCutchan.

Wolf, D., Bixby, J., Glenn, J., & Gardner, H. (1991). To use their minds well: New forms of student assessment. *Review of Research in Education, 17*, 31–74.

CHAPTER

2

Classroom Assessment: A
Multidimensional Perspective

GARY D. PHYE
Iowa State University

INTRODUCTION

Classroom assessment is one of the most hotly debated topics in educational circles. These debates appear not only in the professional literature but in the popular press as well. In addition to reading reports about comparisons that involve students from the United States and other nations, we have all seen comparisons in the local press of schools in our own districts. Somewhere between the international comparisons at one extreme and the local scene at the other, the political realities of restructuring educational policy and systems at the national level also have an impact on the teacher in the classroom.

As suggested by the chapter title, the topic of classroom assessment is multidimensional. In addition to national, state, and local goals being defined as learning outcomes, in many cases accountability is also a big part of the picture. This latter point is best reflected in the definition of *effective teaching*. Almost all textbooks used in educational psychology or curriculum and instruction courses define an *effective teacher* as one whose students have demonstrated learning as a result of being in that teacher's classroom. Many of the hotly debated issues are centered here and here is where questions arise. The primary issue facing us as educators is *how* is the demonstration accomplished. This *accountability* issue basically boils down to the bottom line question of, Do you have evidence of classroom learning outcomes for your students?

At this point, all kinds of questions arise. What do you mean by *learning*? Is there not more to classroom learning than simple textbook knowledge? Do not students have to develop socially and emotionally as well as cognitively? Is there not more than one way to measure classroom learning? Is there a difference between learning and achievement? Is there not more than one way of making comparisons? Is there not more than a single way to set standards? The answer to all of these questions is yes. This is why the issue of classroom assessment must be addressed from a multidimensional perspective. Teachers and other professionals in the schools use assessment to answer a multitude of questions every day. The nature of the question being asked dictates the approach one takes to assessment. This essentially means that *no single approach* to classroom assessment is adequate to answer all of the questions arising within the classroom.

In this chapter we make the basic assumption that the primary reason for engaging in classroom assessment is to support and improve student learning. As a result, I will first provide a context for some of the aforementioned questions by considering different instances when classroom teachers use assessment data for making educational decisions. This will be followed by a discussion of teacher competence. What should teachers know about classroom assessment? This discussion constitutes a major section of the chapter. Consideration is given not only to formal and informal assessment of groups and individual students but to whom the results are communicated. This latter ability, communication of results, of course is predicated on the type of questions being asked by different people (e.g., student, parent, school board, state department of education). The second major section of this chapter focuses on issues related to *the type of knowledge* being assessed. This section is devoted to the realization that a *learning outcome* can be defined in a number of different ways. This reflects the truism, *how* you measure learning is *what* you get.

On a typical day, the following comments can be heard in teacher's lounges across the country.

"We need to find another screening instrument for kindergarten roundup next year. Too many of the children in my class this year do not have sufficient prereading readiness skills."

In an *elementary school* lounge, the following comment was heard. "We started the unit on fractions this week. I am going to have to prepare a short seatwork assignment to find out if everyone is making progress. If I start to lose them during the first week, my experience is that it is almost impossible for the students who don't understand to catch up."

At a *middle school*, the following conversation might be heard. "I wonder at times what is being taught in math at the elementary grades. My class this year was not ready for our new math program. I am thinking about developing a pretest for next year so I have some idea where to start my instruction."

"My class seems to be on par with last year's class, but I am still trying to develop individual instruction for three of my inclusion children. I also have one child who just moved in to the district that I suspect may need to be referred for special needs assessment."

"Say, how are your parent–teacher conferences going? I sure am glad we have portfolio materials as well as test scores for parents this year. You know, I really wish we had some information to provide parents about academic self-concept or personal well-being. Parents are always asking me how I see their child. What I really think is important at this age is how children see themselves."

At a *senior high*, the following conversation was taking place between the basketball and volleyball coaches. "Julie came in the other day and was worried about the minimum competency test for graduation. She is being recruited by a number of Division I programs and she didn't do very well on the practice test given during her junior year."

"I am glad to see that she is thinking about academics as well as sports. She checked with me about her GPA in the basic courses and she is OK there. Also, she did get a 21 on her ACT so we know she has the ability to be successful at a number of colleges. I think this reflects the fact that she has really been thinking academics during this last year."

What do these scenarios have in common? All of these situations that teachers commonly encounter involve some form of assessment. All situations reflect instances when teachers need assessment information to effectively deal with everyday classroom problems. This is by no means an exhaustive accounting of situations when assessment data are used by teachers. It has been suggested by Stiggens and Conklin (1992) that teachers spend one-third to one-half of their professional time on assessment-related activities.

If assessment requires so much of a teachers professional time, both inside and outside the classroom, what should a teacher know about classroom assessment? In a general sense, this is the question we will address in the following section. Attention will be given first to a listing of competency standards recommended for all teachers. This will be followed by a consideration of four different types of assessment activities any teacher can expect to encounter. Last, but not least, is a discussion of two different perspectives that can be taken when interpreting the results of any one or all of the previously considered assessment options.

TEACHER COMPETENCE

A teacher's professional role and responsibilities for student assessment can be conceptualized as falling along a time continuum. As comments heard in the lounge would suggest, assessment activities occur prior to instruction, during instruction, and after instruction. Assessment prior to instruction provides a teacher information about individual differences among students as well as an understanding of the background or prior knowledge of the class as a whole. These assessment activities provide the basis for *planning instruction*. Assessment during instruction provides information about the overall progress of the class as well as specific information about individual students. These assessment activities provide the basis for *monitoring progress* during learning. Following the teaching of a specific unit, semester, academic year, or the like, decisions must be made about the achievement of short- and long-term instructional goals. In addition to these activities, communication skills are needed to *interpret and report* performance standards or levels of achievement to students and parents. On a wider scale, these communication skills facilitate a teacher's involvement in the wider community of educators. This might include such professional responsibilities as (1) serving on a state committee involved with the development of learning goals and associated assessment methods, (2) participating in a review of district or state assessment programs, and (3) interpreting the results of state, national, and international assessment programs.

Recently (1990), a cooperative effort by the American Federation of Teachers, the National Council on Measurement in Education, and the National Education Association resulted in the development of a list of standards for teacher competence in educational assessment of students. These standards are intended to guide the preservice and inservice training of educators, the accreditation of preparation programs, and the future certification of all educators. By establishing these standards for teacher competence in student assessment, the associations subscribe to the view that student assessment is an essential part of teaching and that effective teaching cannot exist without appropriate student assessment. The seven standards articulating teacher competence in the educational assessment of students are highlighted in the following paragraphs.

1. Teachers should be skilled in *choosing* assessment options appropriate for instructional decisions. Assessment options are quite diverse and include text-embedded and curriculum-embedded questions and tests, standardized criterion and norm-referenced tests, oral questions, spontaneous and structured performance assessment, portfolios, exhibitions, demonstration, rating scales, writing samples, paper–pencil tests, seatwork and homework, peer and self-assessments, student records, observations, questionnaires, interviews, and projects and products.

2. Teachers should be skilled in *developing* assessment methods appropriate for instructional decisions. Teachers develop the bulk of assessment tools used in the classroom. However, simply developing an assessment tool is not sufficient. Assessment tools may be accurate and fair (valid) or invalid. Unfortunately, teachers lack ready access to assessment specialists. This means that, to be in compliance with this principle, teachers must be able to determine the quality of the assessment tools they develop. This is probably the major deficiency exhibited by teachers in the field (see Chapter 3).

The responsibility for this deficiency has traditionally been the college and university programs vested with the preparation of teachers. Even today, preservice curriculums in many programs do not include a course in the development and evaluation of teacher-made assessment tools.

3. Teachers should be skilled in *administering, scoring, and interpreting* the results of both commercially produced and teacher-produced assessment methods. This standard simply recognizes that good tools can be used inappropriately. Part of the issue is one of ethics. For example, when administering a commercially produced standardized test (e.g., *Iowa Test of Basic Skills*), should a teacher prompt students or extend the time period? An example of the second element (scoring) might involve grading practices when using teacher-produced essay exams. Can a teacher develop and use an analytic scoring template with essay items or only a global impressionistic method? The third element, interpreting results, may be the most difficult skill to acquire. It is not simply a matter of reporting results in a student conference or a parent–teacher conference; explaining what the results mean is the type of information students and parents seek. For example, following the scoring and posting of results from a teacher-produced activity, a common question asked by students is, How did I do? For interpretative purposes, the teacher must implicitly frame the question asked in terms of the question, Compared to what? There are three obvious ways to interpret a students performance: (1) compared to previous efforts by the student, (2) compared to a standard or mastery of the learning outcome being assessed, or (3) compared to other persons who attempted the task (rest of the class). In summary, a well-developed assessment tool can be incorrectly administered, poorly scored, or misinterpreted. If this occurs, the teacher has lost any benefit from the time and effort spent in the development of a valid assessment tool.

4. Teachers should be skilled in using assessment results when *making decisions* about individual students, planning teaching, developing curriculum, and school improvement. This principle recognizes that teachers are in a position to make educational decisions. This decision making involves judgments that directly affect the lives of a number of people. Consequently, these judgments should be as reliable and valid as possible. While personal opinion always plays a role in decision making, the basis for an educational decision should be public record, not privately held beliefs for which their is no public documentation. Of course, well-developed, appropriately administered, and accurately interpreted assessment tools provide this public documentation. I am using the term *public documentation* in the following sense. The basis for a judgment resulting in a educational decision should be open to inspection by others. This in part addresses the "accountability" issue implicit in the standards.

5. Teachers should be skilled in developing valid student *grading* procedures that use pupil assessments. Teachers who meet this standard will have the conceptual and application skills that follow. They will be able to devise,

TABLE I
Matrix for Classifying Assessment Options

	Formal instruments and activities: Options	Informal instruments and activities: Options
Group assessment	1. Text-embedded tests 2. Curriculum-embedded tests 3. Commercial criterion tests 4. Commercial normed tests 5. Rating scales 6. Performance tests 7. Questionnaires	1. Oral questions 2. Writing samples 3. Seatwork 4. Homework 5. Paper–pencil tests 6. Rating scales 7. Exihibitions 8. Portfolios 9. Demonstration 10. Peer assessment 11. Interviews
Individual assessment	1. Performance assessment 2. Standardized norm-referenced tests 3. Standardized criterion-referenced tests 4. Curriculum-embedded tests	1. Observation 2. Oral questioning 3. Writing sample 4. Homework 5. Seatwork 6. Paper–pencil tests 7. Portfolios 8. Interviews 9. Self-assessment 10. IEP monitoring 11. Error analysis

implement, and explain a procedure for developing grades composed of marks from various assignments, projects, in-class activities, quizzes, tests, and or other assessments. Teachers will understand and be able to articulate why the grades they assign are rational, justified, and fair, acknowledging that such grades reflect their preferences and judgment. Teachers will be able to recognize and avoid faulty grading procedures such as using grades as punishment. They will be able to evaluate and modify their grading procedures to improve the validity of the interpretations made from them about students' attainments [American Federation of Teachers, National Council on Measurement in Education, & National Education Association (AFT, NCME, NEA), 1990]. In reality, this standard is an articulated special case of the immediately preceding standard.

6. Teachers should be skilled in *communicating* assessment results to students, parents, other lay audiences, and other educators. While this standard overlaps with previous standards, when considered within the context of a parent–teacher conference, additional concerns arise. As expressed by the

committee that developed the standards document (AFT, NCME, NEA, 1990), teachers will understand and be able to give appropriate explanations of how the interpretation of student assessments must be moderated by the student's socioeconomic, cultural, language, and other background factors. Teachers will be able to explain that assessment results do not imply such background factors limit a student's ultimate educational development. They will be able to communicate to students and their parents or guardians how they may assess the student's educational progress. Teachers will understand and be able to explain the importance of taking measurement errors into account when using assessments to make decisions about individual students. Teachers will be able to explain the limitations of different informal and formal assessment methods. They will be able to explain printed reports of the results of pupil assessments at the classroom, school district, state, and national levels.

7. Teachers should be skilled in *recognizing* unethical, illegal, and otherwise inappropriate assessment methods and uses of assessment information. Teachers who meet this standard will have the conceptual and application skills that follow. They will know those laws and case decisions that affect their classroom, school district, and state assessment practices. Teachers will be aware that various assessment procedures can be misused or overused, resulting in harmful consequences such as embarrassing students, violating a student's right to confidentiality, and *inappropriately using student's standardized achievement test scores to measure teaching effectiveness* (AFT, NCME, NEA, 1990).

Rarely have we seen such organizations as the American Federation of Teachers, National Education Association, and the National Council on Measurement in Education endorse a common view. This common vision, attests to the significance of these standards for classroom teachers. The standards articulated in the Standards for Teacher Competence in Educational Assessment of Students (AFT, NCME, NEA, 1990) have played a major role in planning the format for this handbook. Further, this material is not copyrighted, and reproduction and dissemination is encouraged. Consequently, I want to acknowledge that I have in some cases reproduced sections of material from each standard verbatim. I did this to convey directly the voice of the committee responsible for development of the standards.

While the standards are couched in terms of teacher competencies, the issues considered also can be approached from a functional perspective. Given the many student assessment methods addressed, how can we conceptualize *how* teachers might use these methods? One approach I have used with preservice teachers is to organize student assessment methods using the 2 by 2 matrix shown in Table 1. This matrix basically acknowledges that classroom assessment always involves (1) groups or individuals, or both, and (2) may be formal or informal. This provides one way of organizing assessment options identified in the first standard. It is a consideration of assessment options to which we now turn.

ASSESSMENT OPTIONS

Assessment requires a significant portion of a teachers professional time and energy. This fact is a reflection of the importance of classroom assessment. We must, however, never lose sight of the principle that assessment of any type is conducted in order to answer specific educational questions about individuals within the class or the class as a whole. Further, the primary purpose of assessment is to support and improve student learning.

The matrix presented in Table 1 is only one way of organizing a discussion of assessment options. Also, the terminology used in Table 1 requires explanation. While the two headings, group assessment options and individual assessment options are well defined, formal and informal are not. I am using the adjective *formal* to identify commercially prepared instruments and activities that are standardized in terms of content and assessment procedure. These instruments and activities may be either norm referenced or criterion referenced. In either case, the critical factor is the inclusion of technical information that provides insight for interpreting results and making decisions. These instruments and activities are ones teachers would *select* to use in the classroom. The instruments and activities may have been developed commercially, by a state board of education, or by a school district. I am using the adjective *informal* to identify instruments and activities *developed* by the classroom teacher. Typically, these activities and instruments are not standardized. Rather, they are developed to address a specific instructional questions relative to a specific child or the class as a whole. Such instruments and activities are not accompanied by technical information and are frequently used as elements of a grading plan.

It is readily apparent that the individual cells are not mutually exclusive. An assessment option could be employed for answering questions about the class as a whole as well as particular individuals that make up the class. The multidimensional nature of classroom assessment precludes the development of simple "assessment checklists" that would specify an exact relationship between instructional questions and assessment options. This is a reaffirmation that the classroom teacher is the key element in the selection and development assessment options.

Formal Group Assessment

The two assessment options most easily recognized are standardized *norm-referenced* and *criterion-referenced* tests. The standardized norm-referenced achievement test is one of the most frequently used assessment options.

While obtained results have little to offer the classroom teacher in terms of instructional decisions, results are of value when questions arise at the school district, state, or national level. For example, at the school district level, information about grade performance (group) has implications for curriculum development or modification. In Iowa, criterion-referenced achievement tests have been developed by many school districts in specific content areas. These instruments have been standardized in the sense that "local norming" has been carried out and in many instances minimal standards developed that define mastery of basic instructional goals and achievement targets. Also, student performance on these locally standardized instruments are frequently reviewed annually, with reference to grade-level performance on standardized norm-referenced tests having state and national norms. This is done with the idea that the norm-referenced data serve for cross-validation on the locally defined achievement targets.

Teachers frequently find that information from criterion-referenced instruments can be used more easily for modifying classroom goals and achievement targets. Also, minimum competency testing required in some schools at points of transition (e.g., graduation), usually take the form of standardized criterion-referenced tests.

Textbook publishing companies also provide classroom teachers with assessment materials that accompany the textbook. These materials invariably include unit tests and assorted performance assessment activities. Such assessment options can be used by classroom teachers in a variety of ways. As *text-embedded* tests developed to determine learning progress, they provide us with valuable information on which to base group instructional decisions. *Curriculum-embedded* tests may take the form of beginning-of-the-year pretests or end-of-the-year post-tests. In either case, the instruments are subject-matter specific. Pretests would be used to assess group preparedness in terms of prior grade achievement. Post-tests would be used to determine the maintenance and durability of achievement targets defined in terms of grade-level competency. Pretests and post-tests used in this manner might be considered examples of curriculum-embedded tests employed on a districtwide basis.

Including *questionnaires* within this category of assessment options may strike many teachers as unusual. However, information about students' academic self-concepts (Chapter 6) or personal well-being (Chapter 7) can facilitate instructional planning. In both cases, the assessment instrument takes the form of a questionnaire that asks students' to report their attitudes and feelings relative to the school setting. In terms of academic self-concept, a standardized instrument (Self Description Questionnaire; Marsh, 1992) is commercially available. This instrument is designed for middle school and secondary school students. This is a well-designed instrument, has good psychometric properties, and provides information about "how" students view their own academic strengths and weaknesses. The assessment of personal well-being is still in the research stages of development. Although several assessment instruments are reviewed in Chapter 7, availability is limited. In most cases, one must go to the research literature or personally contact instrument developers to obtain questionnaires. The assessment instruments and activities that have been developed focus on the elementary and middle school populations. This discussion of academic self-concept and personal well-being is a reminder that factors other than cognitive skills influence classroom learning and achievement.

Formal Individual Assessment

The assessment options considered under this category typically are employed when making educational decisions for special needs children. The inclusion movement requires that the regular classroom teacher and the special education teacher collaborate in meeting an eligible child's educational needs. The dimension that distinguishes this category of options from the formal group assessment category is one of focus. Rather than trying to obtain information to aid in making group instructional decisions, the focus in on a single child. The child under consideration requires something other than the basic group instructional method being employed. This child may be gifted or developmentally delayed. In either case, information is required on which instructional decisions can be based. Initially, the educational decision of concern is one of placement or eligibility. These types of educational decisions are made based on information obtained from standardized norm-referenced instruments. These instruments typically measure aptitude (intelligence) or academic achievement. In addition to the use of norm-referenced instruments, some school districts have developed criterion-referenced instruments reflecting the district's curriculum. In this case, a curriculum-embedded assessment system could be used to initiate referrals for further testing with norm-referenced instruments.

This is possible because many of these curriculum-embedded assessment systems reflect the district's achievement targets ranked within and between grades. Thus, if a third grade child is demonstrating achievement in reading that correspond to first grade achievement, a referral for formal staffing may be initiated. Formal staffing would involve the classroom teacher, educational specialists, the parents, and an administrative representative and rely heavily on standardized norm-referenced assessment options. However, once eligibility and placement decisions are made, the classroom teacher must know how to use the obtained information in making initial decisions about instructional level and instructional activities.

In summary, a common reason for using *formal* assessment options is that we are typically trying to determine the *status* of what has been previously learned or, more specifically, what has been achieved. This is the case whether assessment options are norm referenced or criterion referenced. When determining the status of a student's knowledge, we are assessing prior knowledge. This is the case whether we use a pretest to determine entry instructional level or a post-test at the end of an instructional unit to determine what was learned (achieved).

The *informal* assessment options to be considered next are typically conducted *during* instruction. Obtained information takes the form of feedback (progress report) for both teacher and student(s). In a real sense, informal assessment options provide information about a *work in progress*. As teachers, an important point to remember is that informal assessment options must also be reliable and valid (accurate and fair).

Informal Group Assessment

This category of assessment options contain the activities that consume most of a teachers professional time. Also, these activities are an integral part of instructional techniques in classrooms where teachers are monitoring the learning process. These activities, for the most part, are teacher prepared and informal in nature. In many cases, the assessment option produces a permanent record (e.g., seatwork, writing samples homework, rating scales, and structured interviews), although this is not always the case (oral questions during class and peer assessments). These assessment options typically are used within a teaching unit to determine class progress. Information from these assessment activities may well identify individuals who will require special attention. In such cases, individual assessment options must then be considered.

I have included exhibitions, demonstration, and portfolios because they are teacher prepared and everyone in the class typically is involved. However, these assessment options typically are thought of as achievement measures rather than measures of learning process (work in progress). Exhibitions and demonstration are typically capstone exercises based on knowledge acquired earlier in the academic year. As such, they reflect a level of achievement that has been attained through learning that was guided by instruction. These assessment options are not to be employed in lieu of options used to measure learning. Rather, they are assessment options reflecting durability and synthesis of prior learning. These assessment activities also can be designed to take advantage of authenticity. That is, the capstone exercises may be simulations of activities encountered outside the classroom.

Portfolio assessment can be used in a number of different ways with the main function being a system for establishing a permanent record of achievement.

Informal Individual Assessment

In any individual classroom, the distinction between informal group options and informal individual options is fuzzy. With the exception of special needs students, most informal individual assessment and informal group assessment options are the same. A teacher approaches the interpretation of group assessment data from a collective frame of reference in making group instructional decisions. If, however, follow up of an individual student is warranted, that child's record is evaluated singly. In such cases, the use of error analysis is a option infrequently employed on a group basis.

Inclusion students working below grade placement require special consideration. Assessment options for these students typically would be developed on an individual basis. While the previously mentioned options could be employed with these students, the content being taught and assessed would differ. Also, the context for assessment would differ in that many of these students would be working on individualized educational programs (IEPs). The impact of mandated procedures involved with the implementation and evaluation of IEPs would also have to be considered when assessing the learning outcomes of these children.

COMMUNICATING ASSESSMENT RESULTS

Every school day in this country, a common question being asked by fellow students or parent(s) following an assessment activity is, How did you do? There are basically three ways to respond to such a question. On the one hand, a comparison could be made with a student's previous efforts on the same type of learning activity. In this case, past efforts are the basis for making an evaluative judgment. On the other hand, performance could be compared with an achievement target. For example, if proficiency on the algebra test is defined as 70% correct and our student correctly solved 8 out of 10 problems, the criterion or standard has been met. In this instance, the basis for making an evaluative judgment is a teacher-defined expectation. The third basis for comparison is one where a student is compared to other students rather than a standard or past achievement. Now, an evaluate judgment is make about achievement compared to other comparable students in (1) the class, (2) the school district, (3) the state, or (4) the nation.

As we all know, the question, Which approach is best? is hotly contested in educational circles. Actually, this is a nonissue. A competent classroom teacher should be able to articulate group and individual student performance in all three ways. The reason why the question of which approach is best is a nonissue is because we cannot adequately address educational questions that arise using only one or two of the three possible comparisons. For example, in a parent–teacher conference the following questions might arise. "Has Gary's Algebra homework improved from last quarter?" "Gary has been having some trouble with the current unit on quadratic equations. Is he meeting minimal standards for acceptable progress?" "Gary wants to go to State University when he graduates. However he must be in the top half of his class to be admitted. Does attending State U seem to be a reasonable goal?"

This exercise simply reveals the third dimension of our multidimensional perspective. Not only are different types of activities and instruments (commercial or teacher prepared) used when assessing learning and achievement (group or individuals) but three frames of reference in which to communicate the results of instruction.

It must also be recognized that persons other than teachers, students, and parents have need for assessment result. In addition to questions pertaining to student learning and achievement, issues of curriculum and standards must be addressed. Two sixth grade teachers at the same school, teaching vastly different content and maintaining vastly different standards for performance, create havoc in the system. By analogy, this situation could exist at the school district level, the state level, and the national level. Issues such as these will be addressed in Chapters 15–17 of the handbook. General issues and current efforts involved with developing standards at the building level, the state level, and the national level will be the topics under consideration.

FRAMEWORKS FOR ASSESSMENT

The aforementioned assessment options are "tools of the trade" for teachers. To carry the metaphor a bit further, tools serve a particular function. The primary function to be served by assessment is to improve student learning. While the assessment options are listed in Table 1, "knowing how" to use the options in promoting learning implies pedagogical knowledge on the part of the teacher. The critical feature in an assessment system in a teacher's knowledge of *how* to use an assessment option to address questions pertaining to academic learning. Consequently, the questions about student learning and achievement drive the selection and development of assessment options listed in Table 1.

However, the academic learning demonstrated by students is not of a single type. Classroom learning can run the gamut from rote memorization of vocabulary, facts, and concepts, to critical thinking, reasoning, and problem solving. To help teachers identify and assess different kinds of academic learning, several frameworks for assessment have been developed. The two most frequently used frames of reference are Bloom's taxonomy of the cognitive domain (Bloom, Englehart, Furst, Hill, & Krathwohl, 1956) and Quellmalz's framework for evaluating the reasoning process (Quallmalz, 1987). Both approaches are used extensively by commercial producers of assessment materials as well as classroom teachers engaged in developing informal assessment options. While there are similarities, the two frameworks also have some basic differences. One obvious difference is the "spirit of the times" in which the respective frameworks were developed.

Bloom's taxonomy reflects the influence of behaviorism that characterized both educational and psychological theory in the 1950s. Learning was viewed as behavior and no inferences were make about what went on inside a student's head. Thinking and reasoning were topics addressed directly by philosophers but only indirectly by teachers. Consequently, thinking activities within the cognitive domain were couched in terms of instructional objectives and learning outcomes.

Quellmalz's approach reflects the contemporary influence of cognitive theory and provides a basis for assessing the constructive process of learning. Further, the cognitive influence is reflected in the emphasis placed on the reconstruction of knowledge. For an extensive discussion of assessing reasoning strategies in the classroom, see Chapter 5.

Bloom's Taxonomy

Every educational textbook I have used over the past 25 years has included Bloom's taxonomy of the cognitive domain. One of the strengths of Bloom's taxonomy is that it lends itself to the development of instructional objectives as well as assessment targets. One problem with Bloom's taxonomy is that it is becoming dated. According to Bloom's framework, thinking can be subdivided into six levels: (1) knowledge, (2) comprehension, (3) analysis, (4) application, (5) synthesis, and (6) evaluation. As the term *levels* would imply, the framework is assumed to be a hierarchy with knowledge being the simplest level of thinking and the most complex being evaluation.

Since the 1950s, a great deal of educational research has been conducted to investigate the various levels of learning proposed by Bloom. Today, most teachers and researchers would agree that knowledge defined simply as memory for words, facts, and concepts reflects the simplest form of academic learning. At the higher levels, two issues arise. The first pertains to the distinction between application and comprehension. In the research literature, a student's ability to apply what has been learned defines *comprehension*. In other words, the student's ability to apply knowledge is our best evidence as teachers that our instructional efforts are understood by the child. Consequently, the common view today is that *comprehension* and *application* are synonyms. The second issue is raised by Richard Stiggens (1994), who questions the assumption that the taxonomy levels are necessarily hierarchical in nature. This assumption means that each successive level (from knowledge to evaluation) represents a more complex cognitive challenge for the learner. Stiggens (1994) expresses his concern in the following way:

> I find that I cannot accept this part of this particular vision of the reasoning process. I think that we can pose very complex knowledge and comprehension exercises that far outstrip analysis and synthesis tasks in terms of their level of cognitive challenge. (p. 239)

Based on a large number of consultations with classroom teachers, I share the concern expressed by Stiggens. For example, asking a child to provide an opinion about something read or discussed may be based on the cognitive strategies of analysis and synthesis. On the other hand, this is not a requirement to express an opinion. If the rational for the opinion includes evidence of analytical thinking and synthesis, then we have evidence of higher order thinking. If however, the rationale for the opinion is "this one is best because I like it," no evidence of analytical thinking or synthesis exists. Yes, the child has offered an opinion of an evaluative nature, but opinions do not always require the use of higher order thinking skills. As Stiggens has suggested, the *manner* in which the question is posed and the *requirements imposed* on the response identify the complexity of thinking skills being assessed.

Quellmalz's Framework

Following an extensive review of the professional literature featuring the teaching of reasoning and thinking, Quellmalz (1987) identified five components basic to most programs. These five components are (1) recall, (2) analysis, (3) comparison, (4) inference, and (5) evaluation. These components are not hierarchically organized. However, basic to Quellmalz's framework is the proposition that thinking and reasoning are not content free. Thinking and problem solving are always carried out within a context and arise out of a knowledge base. In other words, thinking and problem solving are cognitive procedures used to construct an answer, solution, or idea within a content area (knowledge base). In this regard, the terms *recall* and *knowledge* are used synonymously. All four kinds of reasoning beyond recall require the application of a thinking or reasoning component to construct a solution to the assessment probe (option). At this point, I simply mention that a excellent explanation of the Quellmalz approach to assessing classroom reasoning strategies awaits in Chapter 5.

Student Motivation

An interesting observation based on a comparison of the two frameworks is the absence of the application and comprehension levels or components in Quallmalz's classification scheme. This reflects a change over the last 40 years in the way educators and psychologists view higher order thinking skills. The comprehension and application of reasoning components in a content area are viewed as the means by which students' construct or re-structure knowledge. Further, there is growing sentiment that the construction or restructuring of knowledge requires an *active* learner. This is simply an acknowledgment that student motivation of a self-regulated nature is an integral part of any constructive or reconstructive effort on the part of the child being assessed. This dimension (self-regulation) is becoming an interesting issue as performance (authentic) assessment comes into increasing use in the classroom.

The issue of motivation or self-direction as it affects classroom assessment frequently is ignored. However, with the increased use of demonstrations, projects, and the like as performance assessment options, we can no longer ignore the issue. One way in which this issue can be addressed is by determining the amount of support or direction being provided by the teacher. The question of self-direction on the part of students is critical when evaluating the significance of a student's performance. Who did the planning, was the time schedule teacher dominated or the result of student time-management skills, and so forth? In other words, what is the student's responsibility?

Reasoning and problem solving as examples of higher order thinking skills are more than just thinking activities. Both types of activities are assumed to be *initiated* and *carried out* by the student. This suggests that the classroom assessment of reasoning and problem solving must be conducted in a manner consistent with the assumption that performance is owned by the student not the teacher. The inclusion of the assumption that a product created by students should be self-directed suggests a third procedural framework when considering performance assessment in the classroom.

A Functional Framework

Here we introduce a functional knowledge framework that extends the cognitive content (Bloom) and reasoning components (Quallmalz) frameworks we have been discussing. We see the three frameworks as complementary.

From a functional frame of reference that emphasizes personal knowledge construction, various kinds of knowledge can be identified. This functional perspective has been identified as *knowing what*, *knowing how*, and *knowing when*. In the research literature, this gets translated into (1) declarative knowledge, (2) procedural knowledge, and (3) strategic knowledge (Phye, 1992). Basically, *declarative knowledge* involves knowledge in the form of vocabulary, facts, concepts, and other bits of information that student's has stored in long-term memory. Consequently, there is agreement among the three frameworks on this point. Declarative knowledge (Phye), knowledge (Bloom), and recall (Quallmalz) are viewed in basically the same way. *Procedural knowledge* is demonstrated when a student can combine, reconstruct, group, or assimilate declarative knowledge so that it can be used procedurally (a course of action). Procedural knowledge would include analysis, synthesis, and evaluation within Bloom's framework plus analysis, comparison, inference, and evaluation from Quallmalz's framework. The point to consider is that these cognitive activities identified by Bloom and Quallmalz can be thought of as cognitive procedures. In terms of academic learning, this involves the proceduralization of information into organized plans, strategies, ideas, and the like. When assessing procedural knowledge, we have evidence that a student "knows how to use knowledge." *Strategic knowledge* involves knowing *when* as

TABLE 2
Assessing Declarative, Procedural, and Strategic Knowledge in the Classroom

Type of learner	Memory retention performance	Transfer performance	Kind of knowledge
Nonlearner	Poor	Poor	None
Nonunderstander	Good	Poor	Declarative
Guided understander	Good	Good	Procedural
Self-directed understander	Good	Good	Strategic

well as *how* to use declarative and procedural knowledge to construct a learning outcome.

The inclusion of procedural and strategic knowledge in an assessment framework is acknowledgment of the *inert knowledge* problem in the classroom (Whitehead, 1929). When provided an opportunity to use declarative and procedural knowledge they have learned, many students still expect to be told "how and when." However, this knowing "how and when" characterizes self-regulated learners. Consequently, unless strategic knowledge is also included in our assessment framework, classroom assessment is incomplete. How this is to be accomplished is the question. Mayer (1987) has suggested the assessment of both memory retention and transfer to identify nonlearners, nonunderstanders, and understanders (Mayer, 1987, pp. 12–13). The use of transfer performance as an assessment option is the focus for the remainder of the chapter.

TRANSFER AS AN ASSESSMENT TOOL

Earlier, when discussing Quallmalz's framework, it was noted that Bloom's levels of comprehension and application had been dropped. I mentioned that this reflects an attitude among cognitive researchers that application is the means by which comprehension is assessed. Phrased differently, the assessment of academic understanding requires evidence of procedural and strategic knowledge in terms of knowing "how and when." Reference back to Table 1 reveals that our assessment tools are typically used to measure "what" students know (declarative knowledge). In many cases (particularly authentic performance tasks), we must also assess procedural and strategic knowledge. This essentially involves evidence that students can use strategic transfer as a reasoning and problem-solving tool (Phye, 1992). The manner in which assessment results differ is provided in Table 2. Evidence of declarative knowledge is obtained when a student produces good evidence of memory retention but demonstrates poor transfer performance. Evidence of procedural knowledge is obtained when a student produces good evidence of memory retention and good evidence of transfer performance under guided instruction. Evidence of strategic knowledge is obtained when a student provides good evidence of memory retention and good transfer performance in the absence of teacher support.

Learning and transfer are not separate mental operations. Transfer performance is simply a way educators can assess student learning that involves reasoning and problem solving. In most classrooms, memory retention (what a student remembers) is all that is assessed. This *initial phase* in the assessment cycle provides evidence of declarative knowledge. The *second assessment phase* in the assessment cycle involves guided transfer. In this case, as teachers, we help students understand "how" to construct strategies and plans—a course of action. Here, a teacher is teaching for transfer by showing students how to transfer prior knowledge and adapt it procedurally to the task at hand. Successful completion of the performance assessment task during the second cycle provides evidence of procedural knowledge. The assessment of strategic knowledge is simple the *third phase* in the assessment cycle. Strategic transfer is the means by which we assess strategic knowledge (for an extended discussion see Phye, 1992). Strategic transfer is defined as the *volitional* use (knowing how and when) of prior academic knowledge by a student to reason and solve academic problems (Phye, 1996). Stated simply, given a second domain task requiring highly similar declarative and procedural knowledge for task completion, students are on their own.

This three-phased assessment cycle would not be employed extensively. There are many occasions when declarative knowledge is the achievement target of an instructional unit. However, at some point in the instructional unit, when students are asked to restructure or construct a strategy or plan based on what they know, procedural knowledge would be assessed informally as the teacher teaches for transfer. There are times during an academic year, however, when authentic performance assessment should reflect strategic knowledge. This might be at the end of a semester or academic year. These capstone assessments should be structured to provide evidence that a child has learned to use strategic transfer as a problem-solving tool (Phye, 1992). The ability to use strategic transfer as a problem-solving tool is simply one element in the development of a self-regulated learner.

SUMMARY

Classroom assessment is truly multidimensional. A single approach to assessment will not effectively provide evidence of both student learning and achievement. Also, in addition to using commercially available assessment instruments and techniques, teachers must be prepared to develop their own assessment options to facilitate student learning and demonstrate student achievement. Further, these assessment options can be employed with both groups and individuals. Chapters 10–14 of this handbook provides insight into the development of assessment options within various content domains (mathematics, social studies, foreign languages, and art).

Even when attention is restricted to the assessment of classroom learning, the assessment process is not simple. The major conclusion that could be derived from our discussion of assessment frameworks might go something like this. In the classroom, it is not only the assessment option that determines what we get as evidence of learning or achievement. How we use the assessment instruments or techniques also determine the nature of the knowledge a student is demonstrating. *How* we assess determines *what* we get (declarative, procedural, or strategic knowledge). The view that classroom learning and classroom assessment go hand in hand is the theme of this chapter. Without classroom learning, there is no need for assessment. Without assessment, there is no evidence of classroom learning.

References

American Federation of Teachers, National Council on Measurement in Education, & National Education Association (AFT, NCME, NEA). (1990). *Standards for teacher competence in educational assessment of students*. Washington, DC: Author.

Bloom, B. S., Englehart, M. D., Furst, E. J., Hill, W. H., & Krathwohl, D. R. (Eds.). (1956). *Taxonomy of educational objectives: Handbook 1. Cognitive domain*. New York: McKay.

Marsh, H. W. (1992). *Self Description Questionnaire: A theoretical and empirical basis for the measurement of multiple dimensions of preadolescent self-concept: A test manual and a research monograph*. Macarthur, Australia: University of Western Sydney, Publication Unit, Faculty of Education.

Mayer, R. E. (1987). *Educational psychology: A cognitive approach*. Boston: Little, Brown.

Phye, G. D. (1992). Strategic transfer: A tool for academic problem solving. *Educational Psychology Review, 4*, 393–420.

Phye, G. D. (1996). Academic learning and remembering. In G. D. Phye (Ed.), *Handbook of academic learning: The construction of knowledge*. San Diego, CA: Academic Press.

Quellmalz, E. (1987). Developing reasoning skills. In J. B. Baron & R. J. Sternberg (Eds.), *Teaching thinking skills: Theory and practice* (pp. 86–105). New York: Freeman.

Stiggens, R. J. (1994). *Student-centered classroom assessment*. Englewood Cliffs, NJ: Prentice-Hall.

Stiggens, R. J., & Conklin, N. F. (1992). *In teacher's hands: Investigating the practices of classroom assessment*. Albany: State University of New York Press.

Whitehead, A. N. (1929). *The aims of education*. New York: Macmillan.

CHAPTER 3

Teacher Assessment Literacy: What Do Teachers Know about Assessment?

BARBARA S. PLAKE
JAMES C. IMPARA
University of Nebraska—Lincoln

In their role in the classroom, it is estimated that teachers spend up to 50% of their instructional time in assessment-related activities (Stiggins, 1991). For an activity that commands such a high proportion of their professional practice, teachers receive little or no formal assessment training in the preparatory programs (Schaffer, 1993; Schaffer & Lissitz, 1987; Wise, Lukin, & Roos, 1991). Further, teachers frequently report feeling ill-prepared to undertake assessment-related activities (Ward, 1980).

Current instructional practices emphasize the integration of assessment and instruction, with the goal of "seamless" educational practices that combine teaching with an on-going analysis of student progress toward instructional goals (Airasian, 1991). Further, with the introduction of "authentic" assessment strategies, teachers need to be more skilled in assessment because they often are involved directly in the administration and scoring of these assessments.

Some studies have attempted to quantify the level of teacher preparation in educational assessment of students. Schaffer (1993) reports that at least 50% of the teacher certification programs in the United States require no measurement course. Those programs that do require educational measurement course work often do not include adequate coverage of the assessment

strategies most useful to teachers. O'Sullivan and Chalnick (1991) surveyed
state departments of education and found that very few required an assessment course for initial certification. These studies have addressed the issue
of teacher preparation either indirectly, by ascertaining curriculum requirements for teacher preparation programs, or through teacher self-report of
competency or confidence levels in assessment. Although these studies
provide useful information that permit inferences about levels of teacher
assessment literacy, they do not focus directly on the actual knowledge
levels of practicing teachers in the area of educational assessment of their
students.

In 1990, through a collaborative effort between the American Federation
of Teachers (AFT), the National Education Association (NEA), and the National Council on Measurement in Education (NCME), a set of "Standards
for Teacher Competence in the Educational Assessment of Students" was
developed and published (AFT, NCME, NEA, 1990). These standards specify
seven competency areas for teachers in the area of assessment. These competency areas are

1. Choosing assessment methods appropriate for instructional decisions.
2. Developing assessment methods appropriate for instructional decisions.
3. Administering, scoring, and interpreting the results of both externally
   produced and teacher-produced assessment methods.
4. Using assessment results when making decisions about individual students, planning instruction, developing curriculum, and improving
   schools.
5. Developing valid pupil grading procedures.
6. Communicating assessment results to students, parents, other lay audiences, and other educators.
7. Recognizing unethical, illegal, and other inappropriate methods and
   uses of assessment information.

Under a grant to NCME by the W. K. Kellogg Foundation, a national survey
was undertaken to measure the competency levels of teachers in these seven
competency areas. Although directed by NCME, members of the advisory
committee for the project included representatives from NEA and AFT. The
project consisted of two developmental phases: first, an instrument was
developed to measure teacher knowledge in the seven competency areas;
and second, a national administration of the instrument was undertaken.[1]
An overview of the development efforts and the results of the national administration are published elsewhere (Plake, Impara, & Fager, 1993; Impara,
Plake, & Fager, 1993). In this chapter, highlights of the study are pre-

sented along with a more detailed analysis of teacher performance on the instrument.

NATIONAL SURVEY OF TEACHER ASSESSMENT LITERACY

As stated previously, the AFT, NCME, NEA (1990) "Standards for Teacher Competence in the Educational Assessment of Students" served as the framework for developing a measure of teacher assessment literacy. For each of the 7 competency areas, 5 multiple-choice test questions were developed, yielding an instrument with 35 multiple-choice items designed to assess teacher assessment literacy.

Validation of the Instrument

To provide evidence that the items in the instrument are valid indicators of the competency standard they were designed to measure, two panels of measurement experts were asked to evaluate the items in light of the competency standards. These experts represented measurement specialists in academic and practitioner settings. One panel of 10 measurement specialists was given information about the competency standard the items were designed to measure and asked to rate, on a low–high scale (1 = low; 5 = high), the degree to which they felt the item-to-competency standard alignment was appropriate. The second panel, independent of the first, also consisted of 10 measurement specialists. These panelists were given the items and the competency standards and asked to make an independent judgment of the competency standard(s) best measured by each item. The results of these judgments indicated a high level of alignment of items to competency standards.

In addition to the item review by these two panels of measurement specialists, the AFT, NCME, and NEA members of the advisory committee also reviewed the items for clarity, validity, and appropriateness.

Testing directors or persons in similar positions were contacted in each of the 50 state education agencies and asked to identify a person we could contact in each of four randomly selected school districts for participation in the national survey of teacher assessment literacy. Endorsement of the project by NEA, AFT, and the Assessment Task Force subcommittee of the Education Information and Assessment Committee (EIAC; a consortium of state agency personnel who monitor surveys and other data collection efforts by the federal government) provided motivation for the states to participate in the study. Once the contact person in each school district was identified by the state testing director, he or she was contacted and asked to participate in this national effort. Participation involved randomly identifying 12 teachers across elementary, middle, and high school levels. Materials were sent directly to the district contact person with instructions to deliver the materials to the selected teachers. These teachers were provided a packet that contained an introductory letter, test directions, the test, a machine scorable answer sheet, and a stamped, addressed envelope to return their test answer sheet to the project leaders.

The national survey was undertaken in the Fall of 1992. A total of 555 teachers returned usable answer sheets, representing 45 of the 50 states. Table 1 shows the participation rate of the 50 states.

Results

Of the 555 teachers who participated in the national survey, the majority of the teachers reported between 6 and 12 years of teaching experience. Table 2 shows the identification of these teachers by tenure in teaching. These demographics are consistent with the overall years of experience of teachers nationally (J. Schneider, personal communication, February 5, 1992), adding credence to the inference that these teachers are representative of teachers nationally.

Overall, the mean performance on the 35-item instrument was 23.20 (standard deviation [SD] = 3.30) or near 66% correct. Given that many teachers set 70% as the passing score on their classroom tests, most teachers participating in the national survey would receive a failing grade based on their demonstrated knowledge of educational assessment of students. Across the seven competency areas, teachers showed the highest level of competency in the area of Administering Assessment (average performance on the five item subset was 3.96 [SD = 0.90] and the lowest level of competency in the area of Communicating Assessment Results (mean = 2.70, standard deviation = 1.21). Teacher performance across the seven competency areas is summarized in Table 3. We found it interesting that the area with the lowest performance levels by teachers, Communicating Assessment Results, also showed the highest variability. Therefore, although generally an area of weakness for teachers, it is, for some teachers, an area of strength.

To better understand the performance of teachers across these seven competency standards, Table 4 presents the proportion of teachers correctly answering each of the items, within each competency area. In addition, the point biserial correlation between item and total test performance is also shown (indicating the item's sensitivity to overall ability differences of the teachers in the study).

An examination of Table 4 reveals several items that were either very difficult for these teachers (items with the proportion correct less than .30) or ones that were very easy for them (those items with p values of .90 or greater). There were a total of four very difficult items, two each from

TABLE I
Participation Rate of the 50 States in the National Survey of Teacher Assessment Literacy

State	Number of districts	Number of teachers
Alabama	4	20
Alaska	1	7
Arizona	1	4
Arkansas	0	0
California	2	13
Colorado	2	8
Connecticut	1	7
Delaware	1	9
Florida	0	0
Georgia	3	19
Idaho	0	0
Illinois	1	5
Indiana	1	11
Iowa	3	28
Kansas	4	25
Kentucky	2	12
Louisiana	1	6
Maine	1	9
Maryland	1	5
Massachusetts	0	0
Michigan	2	14
Minnesota	2	14
Mississippi	0	0
Missouri	0	0
Montana	1	5
Nevada	2	18
Nebraska	4	25
New Hampshire	0	0
New Jersey	2	7
New Mexico	2	17
New York	1	8
North Carolina	2	18
North Dakota	3	17
Ohio	2	13
Oklahoma	1	8
Oregon	1	8
Pennsylvania	2	16
Rhode Island	2	11
South Carolina	3	14
South Dakota	2	17
Tennessee	2	11
Texas	2	16
Utah	3	23
Vermont	2	10
Virginia	1	11
Washington	3	17
West Virginia	2	10
Wisconsin	2	12
Wyoming	2	14

Barbara S. Plake and James C. Impara

TABLE 2
Number of Years in Teaching of the Teachers Who
Participated in the National Survey of Teacher
Assessment Literacy

Number of years teaching	Number of teachers
Less than 5	59
6–12	156
13–18	129
19–24	116
25 or more	82

competency area 5 (Using Assessments for Grading) and area 7 (Recognizing Unethical Practices). These items are presented in Table 5. The items that were easy for these teachers are shown in Table 6. Five of the seven competency areas had at least one item that turned out to be quite easy for these teachers: competency areas 1 (Choosing Assessment Methods: two items); 2 (Developing Assessment Methods: two items); 3 (Administering, Scoring, and Interpreting Assessments: two items); 5 (Using Assessments for Grading: two items); and 7 (Recognizing Unethical Practices: two items). It is interesting to note that the two competency categories that revealed the most difficult items (competency areas 5 and 7) also contained items that were among the easiest for these teachers. This suggests some spotty knowledge in these areas—some aspects were very strong and some very weak.

In addition to measuring teachers' levels of knowledge in these seven competency areas, the instrument also asked teachers about their background in assessment training and some of their perceptions about assessment. In particular, teachers were asked their perceptions about the utility of teacher-made and standardized achievement tests for making instructional decisions, how comfortable they feel in interpreting standardized test results, if they had taken a measurement class previously and, if so, how re-

TABLE 3
Average Performance by Teachers across the Seven Competency Areas

Competency area	Mean	SD	Total possible
Choosing an Assessment	3.26	0.93	5
Developing Assessments	3.22	0.80	5
Administering Assessments	3.96	0.90	5
Using Results—Decisions	3.40	1.11	5
Using Results—Grading	3.19	0.78	5
Communicating Results	2.70	1.21	5
Recognizing Ethical Issues	3.26	0.78	5

TABLE 4
Item Performance by Competency Area

Competency area	Item	Proportion correct	Point biseral discrimination
Choosing Assessment Methods	1	.973	0.04
	2	.540	0.41
	3	.933	0.11
	4	.556	0.37
	5	.468	0.16
Developing Assessment Methods	6	.939	0.06
	7	.127	0.11
	8	.778	0.09
	9	.955	0.11
	10	.430	0.22
Administering, Scoring, and	11	.899	0.22
Interpreting Assessments	12	.937	0.11
	13	.658	0.22
	14	.490	0.33
	15	.987	0.02
Using Assessments for Decision Making	16	.823	0.18
	17	.742	0.36
	18	.570	0.41
	19	.457	0.27
	20	.825	0.20
Using Assessments for Grading	21	.239	0.17
	22	.260	0.01
	23	.968	0.07
	24	.819	0.27
	25	.919	0.06
Communicating Assessment Results	26	.446	0.27
	27	.571	0.21
	28	.414	0.31
	29	.684	0.37
	30	.614	0.47
Recognizing Unethical Practices	31	.201	0.14
	32	.869	0.17
	33	.929	0.16
	34	.987	0.02
	35	.291	0.07

cently. They were also asked if they were interested in learning more about educational assessment for students and what would be their preference for instructional methods in assessment. Summary information for these questions is presented in Table 7.

An analysis was undertaken to investigate if teacher performance on the test measuring their knowledge in the seven competency areas differed as a function of the teacher's background or perceptions. No significant

TABLE 5
Test Items with Proportion Correct Less than .30

Item 7. Developing Assessment Methods
Which of the following actions would most likely increase the reliability of Mrs. Lockwood's multiple-choice end-of-unit examination in physics?
 a. Use a blueprint to develop the test questions.
 b. Change the test format to true–false questions.
 c. Add more items like those already in the test.
 d. Add an essay component.

Item 21. Using Assessment—Grading
Of the following, which choice typically provides the most reliable student-performance information a teacher might consider when assigning a unit grade?
 a. Scores from a teacher-made test containing two or three essay questions related directly to instructional objectives of the unit.
 b. Scores from a teacher-made 20 item multiple-choice test designed to measure the specific instructional objectives of the unit.
 c. Oral responses to questions asked in class of each student over the course of the unit.
 d. Daily grades designed to indicate the quality of in-class participation during regular instruction.

Item 22. Using Assessments—Grading
A teacher gave three tests during a grading period and she wants to weight them all equally when assigning grades. The goal of the grading program is to rank order students on achievement. In order to achieve this goal, which of the following should be closest to equal?
 a. Number of items
 b. Number of students taking each test.
 c. Average scores.
 d. Variation (range) of scores.

Item 31. Recognizing Unethical Practices
In some states testing companies are required to release items from prior versions of a test to anyone who requests them. Such requirements are known as:
 a. Open-testing mandates.
 b. Gag rules.
 c. Freedom-of-information acts.
 d. Truth-in-testing laws.

Item 35. Recognizing Unethical Practices
Mrs. Overton was concerned that her students would not do well on the State Assessment Program to be administered in the Spring. She got a copy of the standardized test form that was going to be used. She did each of the following activities to help increase scores. Which activity was unethical?
 a. Instructed students in strategies on taking multiple-choice tests, including how to use answer sheets.
 b. Gave students the items from an alternative form of the test.
 c. Planned instruction to focus on the concepts covered in the test.
 d. None of these actions are unethical.

performance differences were found for questions pertaining to the perception of the utility of either teacher-made or standardized test results for instructional purposes. There was a significant performance difference (F

TABLE 6
Test Items with Proportion Correct Greater than .90

Item 1. *Choosing Assessment Methods*
What is the most important consideration in choosing a method for assessing student achievement?
  a. Ease of scoring the assessment.
  b. Ease of preparing the method of assessment.
  c. Accuracy of assessing attainment of instructional objectives.
  d. Acceptance by the school administration.

Item 3. *Choosing Assessment Methods*
Mrs. Bruce wished to assess her students' understanding of the method of problem solving she had been teaching. Which assessment strategy below would be most valid?
  a. Select a textbook that has a "teacher's guide" with a test developed by the authors.
  b. Develop an assessment consistent with an outline of what she has actually taught in the class.
  c. Select a standard test that provides a score on problem solving skills.
  d. Select an instrument that measures students' attitudes about problem solving strategies.

Item 6. *Developing Assessment Methods*
A teacher wants to document the validity of the scores from a classroom assessment strategy she plans to use for assigning grades on a class unit. What kinds of information would provide the best evidence for this purpose?
  a. Have other teachers judge whether the assessment strategy covers what was taught.
  b. Match an outline of the instructional content to the content of the assessment strategy.
  c. Let students in the class indicate if they thought the assessment was valid.
  d. Ask parents if the assessment reflects important learning outcomes.

Item 9. *Developing Assessment Methods*
Mr. Woodruff wanted his students to appreciate the literary works of Edgar Allen Poe. Which of his test items shown below will best measure his instructional objective?
  a. "Spoke the raven, nevermore" comes from which of Poe's works?
  b. True or False: Poe was an orphan and never knew his biological parents.
  c. Edgar Allen Poe wrote:
      1. Novels
      2. Short stories
      3. Poems
      4. All of the above
  d. Discuss briefly your view of Poe's contribution to American literature.

Item 12. *Administering, Scoring, and Interpreting Results*
Students in Mr. Jakman's science class are required to develop a model of the solar system as part of the end of unit grade. Which scoring procedure below will maximize the objectivity of these student projects?
  a. When the models are turned in, Mr. Jakman identified the most attractive models and gives them the highest grades, the next most attractive gets a lower grade, and so on.
  b. Mr. Jakman asks other teachers in the building to rate each project on a 5-point scale based on their quality.
  c. Before the projects are turned in, Mr. Jakman constructs a scoring key based on the critical features of the projects as identified by the highest performing students in the class.
  d. Before the projects are turned in, Mr. Jakman prepares a blueprint or blueprints of the critical features of the product and assigns scoring weights to these features. The models with the highest scores receive the highest grades.

continues

TABLE 6
(continued)

Item 15. *Administering, Scoring, and Interpreting Results*
When the directions indicate each section of a standardized test is timed separately, which of the following is acceptable test-taking behavior?
  a. John finishes the vocabulary section early; he then rechecks many of his answers in that section.
  b. Mary finishes the vocabulary section early; she checks her answers in the previous test section.
  c. Jane finishes the vocabulary section early; she looks ahead at the next test section but does not mark her answer sheet for any of these items.
  d. Bob did not finish the vocabulary section; he continues to work on that section when the testing time is up.

Item 23. *Using Assessments—Grading*
When a parent asks a teacher to explain the basis for his or her child's grade, the teacher should:
  a. explain that the grades are assigned fairly, based on the student's performance and other related factors.
  b. ask the parents what they think should be the basis for the child's grade.
  c. explain exactly how the grade was determined and show the parent samples of the student's work.
  d. indicate that the grading scale is imposed by the school board and the teachers have no control over grades.

Item 25. *Using Assessments—Grading*
During the most recent grading period Ms. Johnson graded no homework and gave only one end-of-unit test. Grades were assigned only on the basis of the test. Which of the following is the major criticism of how she assigned the grades?
  a. The grades probably reflect a bias against minority students that exist in most tests.
  b. Decisions like grade assignment should be based on more than one piece of information.
  c. The test was too narrow in curriculum focus.
  d. There is no significant criticism of this method providing the test covered the unit's content.

Item 33. *Recognizing Unethical Practices*
A state uses its statewide testing program as a basis for distributing resources to school systems. To establish an equitable distribution plan, the criterion set by the State Board of Education provides additional resources to every school system with student achievement test scores above the state average. Which cliche best describes the likely outcome of this regulation?
  a. Every cloud has its silver lining.
  b. Into each life some rain must fall.
  c. The rich get rich and the poor get poorer.
  d. A bird in the hand is worth two in the bush.

Item 34. *Recognizing Unethical Practices*
In a school where teacher evaluations are based in part on their students' scores on a standardized test, several teachers noted that one of their students did not reach some vocabulary items on a standardized test. Which teacher's actions is considered ethical?
  a. Mr. Jackson darkened circles on the answer sheet at random. He assumed Fred, who was not a good student, would just guess at the answers, so this would be a fair way to obtain Fred's score on the test.

continues

TABLE 6
(continued)

___

b. Mr. Hoover filled in the answer sheet the way he thought Joan, who was not feeling well, would have answered based on Joan's typical in-class performance.
c. Mr. Stover turned in the answer sheet as it was, even though he thought George, an average student, might have gotten a higher score had he finished the test.
d. Mr. Lund read each question and darkened in the bubbles on the answer sheet that represented what he believed Felicia, a slightly below average student, would select as correct answers.

___

(3,547) = 3.54, $p < .02$) though, depending on how comfortable the teachers reported feeling about interpreting standardized achievement tests. Significant performance differences were found between categories of teachers reporting themselves to be very comfortable interpreting standardized assessment results (mean for these 85 teachers was 23.92, SD = 3.74) and those reporting feeling very uncomfortable interpreting standardized test results (mean for these 67 teachers was 22.34, SD = 3.10). An additional follow-up looked at the differential performance of teachers across the seven competency areas as a function of their self-reported level of comfort in interpreting standardized test results. A significant MANOVA was found (Rao's F (21,1554) = 1.68, $p < .03$). There were significant performance differences for competency area 6 (Communicating Assessment Results; F(3,547) = 4.99, $p < .002$) and competency area 7 (Recognizing Unethical Practices, F (3,547) = 3.51, $p < .02$). Again, those teachers reporting higher levels of comfort in interpreting standardized test results showed higher performance on these two subscales. Means and standard deviations for teacher performance, as a function of their responses to the question pertaining to their comfort in interpreting standardized test results, are presented in Table 8.

Significant performance differences were also found when comparing overall test performance for those teachers who reported having taken a measurement class and those who reported not having previous course work or experience in measurement (F (1,548) = 4.94, $p < .03$). The 162 teachers who reported no previous course work in measurement had an average overall test score of 22.72 (SD = 3.32) while those teachers, 388 in all, who reported having previous course work in measurement had an average overall test score of 23.41 (SD = 3.36).

In terms of total scores, no other significant overall performance differences were found. However, when the scores from the seven competency areas were analyzed individually, differences were found among the teachers who preferred receiving measurement instruction from a college course ($n = 51$) and the 36 teachers who did not care for any of the means listed for receiving measurement information (neither in-service, professional brochure, college course, or self-instructional video). This difference was

TABLE 7
Summary of Teacher Responses to Background and Perception Questions

Question: Teacher-developed assessment information should be used extensively to enhance instruction

Response options	Number selecting	Percent
Disagree	27	4.9
Tend to disagree	43	7.7
Tend to agree	227	40.9
Agree	251	45.2
Missing	7	1.3

Question: Standardized test information should be used extensively to enhance instruction

Response options	Number selecting	Percent
Disagree	154	27.7
Tend to disagree	206	37.1
Tend to agree	145	26.1
Agree	44	7.9
Missing	6	1.1

Question: I am very comfortable in interpreting information from standardized tests.

Response options	Number selecting	Percent
Disagree	67	12.1
Tend to disagree	186	33.5
Tend to agree	213	38.4
Agree	85	15.3
Missing	4	0.7

Question: Have you ever taken a class, either in-service or in college, that had tests and measurements as the major emphasis?

Response options	Number selecting	Percent
No	162	29.2
Yes	338	69.9
Missing	5	0.9

Question: About how long ago was your most recent tests and measurements class?

Response options	Number selecting	Percent
Less than a year ago	17	3.1
1–5 years ago	79	14.2
6–10 years ago	75	13.5
More than 10 years ago	223	40.2
I don't remember	6	1.1

continues

TABLE 7
(*continued*)

Question: What would be the best way for you to become more proficient in interpreting test scores?

Response options	Number selecting	Percent
In-service	328	59.1
A pamphlet provided by a professional organization	65	11.7
A college course in testing	51	9.2
A self-instructional video	67	12.1
Some other method of communication	36	6.5
Missing	8	1.4

Question: Which statement best indicates your interest in becoming more proficient in interpreting test scores and in student assessment in general?

Response options	Number selecting	Percent
I am very interested	192	34.6
I am somewhat interested	278	50.1
I am not really interested	54	9.7
My level of proficiency is high; I don't need any more proficiency in student assessment	26	4.7

Question: How many years experience as a classroom teacher do you have?

Response options	Number selecting	Percent
Less than 5 years	59	10.6
6–12 years	156	28.1
13–18 years	129	23.2
19–24 years	116	20.9
25 years or more	82	14.8
Missing	13	2.3

revealed on competency area 5 (Using Assessments for Grading). Average performance on this five-item subscale was 3.41 (SD = 0.80) for those teachers expressing preference for a college course and 2.86 (SD = 0.76) for the teachers who did not elect any of the listed options.

A significant performance difference on competency area 2 (Developing Assessment Methods) was found for teachers with differing levels of teaching experience (Rao's $F [28,1915] = 1.55, p < .04$). Average performance by teachers across years of experience is displayed in Table 9. Teachers with 19–24 years of teaching experience had the highest mean score (mean = 3.40). Teachers with five or fewer years of teaching experience had the next higher mean score on this competency area (3.34). Teachers with the longest tenure

TABLE 8
Performance on Assessment Literacy Instrument as a Function of Self-Reported Comfort in Interpreting Standardized Test Results

Response choice	n	Overall test performance		Competency area performance[a]	
		Mean	SD	6	7
Disagree	67	22.34	3.10	2.46	3.01
Tend to disagree	186	22.92	3.26	2.56	3.36
Tend to agree	218	23.48	3.32	2.75	3.27
Agree	85	23.92	3.74	3.09	3.22

[a]Competency Area 6: Communicating Assessment Results; Competency Area 7: Recognizing Unethical Practices.

in the classroom, those with 25 or more years of teaching, had the lowest mean score (3.08).

The teachers who indicated that they felt their level of proficiency in educational assessment was already high and that they did not feel the need for additional exposure to educational assessment information did not perform significantly better than those teachers who were very interested in becoming more proficient in interpreting test scores and in student assessment in general. Nonsignificant differences in test performance were also found regardless of the recency of the teacher's exposure to assessment information. The most prevalent answer to the question of recency of measurement information in a class or in-service was more than 10 years ago. Therefore, many teachers are in the educational system whose measurement skills are not only not current (and the results of this survey would suggest

TABLE 9
Performance on Competency Area 2 (Developing Teacher-made Tests) by Years of Teaching Experience

Years of teaching experience	Performance on competency 2	
	Mean	SD
Less than 5 years	3.14	0.88
6–12 years	3.14	0.79
13–18 years	3.23	0.70
19–24 years	3.40	0.82
25 years or more	3.08	0.80
Missing		

are rusty at best), they have most likely not been exposed to the current assessment movement involving performance assessment approaches.

DISCUSSION AND CONCLUSIONS

The results of the national survey of teacher assessment literacy give empirical evidence of the anticipated woefully low levels of assessment competency for teachers. On the average, teachers earned failing marks on the overall assessment, with an average correct of 66%. More experienced teachers tended to show performance superior to their less experienced counterparts on administering, scoring, and interpreting assessment results and those teachers who have had measurement course work (with a college class or in-service with a major emphasis in tests and measurement) showed higher overall knowledge than did teachers who lack this background. Even so, the performance of teachers with exposure to measurement content is still not impressive; their overall average was less than a point higher than that of their untrained counterparts.

The evidence gathered from this study and the literature documenting the opportunity for teachers to obtain preservice exposure to assessment information suggests that it is time for the education community to recognize that teachers are ill-equipped to successfully undertake one of the most prevalent activities of their instructional program: student assessment. This is especially salient due to the current trend in student assessment, involving an increase in assessment strategies such as performance, portfolio, and other types of "authentic assessments." These strategies require even more knowledge about assessment as they more directly involve the teacher in the administration and scoring or the results than do multiple-choice assessments.

References

Airasian, P. W. (1991). Perspectives on measurement instruction. *Educational Measurement: Issues and Practice*, 10(1), 13–16, 20.
American Federation of Teachers, National Council on Measurement in Education, National Education Association (AFT, NCME, NEA). (1990). Standards for teacher competence in the educational assessment of students. *Educational Measurement: Issues and Practice*, 9(4), 30–32.
Impara, J. C., Plake, B. S., & Fager, J. J. (1993) Teachers' assessment background and attitudes toward testing. *Theory in Practice*, 32(2), 113–117.
O'Sullivan, R. G., & Chalnick, M. K. (1991). Measurement related course work requirements for teacher certification and recertification. *Educational Measurement: Issues and Practice*, 10(1), 17–19, 23.
Plake, B. S., Impara, J. C., & Fager, J. J. (1993). Assessment competencies of teachers: A national survey. *Educational Measurement: Issues and Practice*, 12(1), 10–12.
Schaffer, W. D. (1993). Assessment literacy for teachers. *Theory in Practice*, 32(2), 118–126.

Schaffer, W. D., & Lissitz, R. W. (1987). Measurement training for school personnel: Recommendations and reality. *Journal of Teacher Education*, 38(3), 57–63.

Schneider, J. (February 5, 1992). Personal communication.

Stiggins, R. J. (1991). Relevant classroom assessment training for teachers. *Educational Measurement: Issues and Practice*, 10(1), 7–12.

Ward, J. G. (1980). Teachers and testing: A survey of knowledge and attitudes. In L. M. Rudner (Ed.), *Testing in our schools* (pp. 15–24). Washington, DC: National Institute of Education.

Wise, S. L., Lukin, L. E., & Roos, L. L. (1991). Teacher beliefs about training in testing and measurement. *Journal of Teacher Education*, 42(1), 37–42.

CHAPTER 4

Classroom Assessment as Inquiry

ROBERT C. CALFEE
Stanford University

WALTER V. MASUDA
University of California, Berkeley

What should the classroom teacher know and be able to do in assessing student achievement? This question is at the core of this part of the handbook, each chapter taking slightly different form depending on the author's lens. Teacher's roles in this task range from technician to researcher, engineer to artist. While each role bears on effective classroom assessment, we will emphasize the "design engineer" metaphor—somewhere between designer and applied researcher—as the most appropriate fit for today's educational climate.

A handbook chapter promises both context and depth on a topic. Accordingly, we begin with a brief review of assessment practices and policies over the past half-century as they bear on the classroom teacher's role in judging student achievement. Next we propose several criteria for gauging the adequacy of classroom assessment practices at the local school site. Then comes a framework for the process of classroom assessment as inquiry or applied research. The final section attempts to reconcile an issue raised at the outset—the tension between the demands of external and internal mandates for assessing student achievement.

Assessment takes different shapes depending on subject matter (including the formal and informal curricula) and developmental level. At the risk of limiting our review, but at the gain of speaking to specific issues, we illustrate our points along the way with examples from reading and writing in the elementary and middle years of schooling. By limiting our attention to academic attainments, we neglect affective and social outcomes. These elements appear in the background, but the reality is that the motivational and social consequences of instruction are poorly represented in today's assessment practices; they appear not to be valued by the society as direct consequences of schooling and hence are seldom "tested."

By exploring language and literacy, we restrict ourselves to the nontechnical domains; math and science may pose quite different tasks for assessment. On the other hand, language and literacy are among the most significant academic outcomes of schooling during early years of formal education. By concentrating on the early years of schooling, we avoid daunting problems in high school education: disconnected curricula, large student–teacher ratios (not class sizes, but number of contacts), an emphasis on subject matter more than students, and the shift from standards of relative progress toward standards of absolute accomplishment.

This handbook encompasses a broad audience, and our concluding thoughts offer an agenda for researchers, practitioners, and policy makers. Classroom assessment is clearly in the midst of a paradigm shift. Not too many decades ago, the teacher ruled the roost when it came to gauging student achievement. Beginning in the 1950s, standardized tests have not only dominated large-scale accountability; they have also infiltrated the classroom, replacing and undermining the teacher's professional judgment. Since the late 1980s, the United States has begun to rethink its reliance on standardized-test technology as a vehicle for accountability and a lever for influencing instructional practice. If "what you test is what you get," then we seem not to have "gotten" what we want and hence this time of reflection, of paradigm shift, of uncertainty and anxiety (Darling-Hammond, Ancess, & Falk, 1995; Farr & Tone, 1994; Harp, 1991; Herman, Aschbacher, & Winters, 1992; Kane & Mitchell, in press; Mitchell, 1992; Tierney, Carter, & Desai, 1991; Valencia, Hiebert, & Afflerbach, 1994; Winograd, 1994). Our review of this complex situation leads to a simple but challenging conclusion (also see Cizek, this volume): *the capacity of classroom teachers, as members of a professional community, to assess student achievement by means of less than fully standardized methods and to connect these assessments to the ongoing improvement of the instructional program is critical for meeting the national agenda of ensuring high-quality education for all students.*

Given the current upheaval in assessment generally and classroom assessment in particular, deciding what to include and what to exclude has been difficult. This chapter offers a conceptual and practical analysis of classroom assessment more than a listing of sources and citations. We have relied for background on several recent works. Stiggins (1994) offers a comprehensive and eminently practical account of tools and techniques for the teacher (see also Popham, 1995, and Airaisan, 1994, who emphasize testing somewhat more than assessment). Wiggins (1993) presents a quite different account: he discusses the conceptual and philosophical underpinnings for assessment linked to curriculum and instruction (also see Glaser & Silver, 1994; Tittle, 1994), and that places greater weight on "growing" than "grading." Hambleton (in press) provides a broad review of the research on assessment methods, as do the papers in Baron and Wolf (1996) and Martin-Kneip, Thornburg, and Cookson (1994). Finally, we have drawn from a collection of papers written over the past two decades by the first author on the theme of assessment as a professional activity (Calfee, 1987; Calfee, 1995; Calfee & Drum, 1979; Calfee & Hiebert, 1991; Calfee & Perfumo, 1996; Calfee & Venezky, 1969; Hiebert & Calfee, 1992).

TEACHER AS ASSESSOR: WHERE HAVE WE BEEN AND WHERE ARE WE HEADED?

In his chapter on assessment for the 1984 *Handbook of Reading Research*, Johnston pointed out the hazards of relying on any one method to the neglect of others. Concerned about wholesale reliance on mandated multiple-choice tests, he ended his chapter with a question: "What if . . . history had predisposed us toward an individualized, descriptive, process-oriented assessment model instead of the standardized group, silent reading model?" (p. 168). Since Johnston's chapter, educators have moved toward teacher-based classroom assessment of student achievement, especially in reading and writing. This shift and the underlying tension between external mandates for public accountability and internal methods appropriate to classrooms and local audiences, will be a significant theme in this chapter.

Before World War II, assessment depended almost entirely on the classroom teacher. Except for a few large urban districts, standardized tests were unknown. Teachers administered tests of their own devising, evaluated the results, and assigned grades. They determined when students had special needs and defined appropriate actions. Accountability was a local matter between teachers, students, and parents. Reliability meant consistency; if a student's grades varied a great deal from one test to another, there was a problem. Validity depended on instruction; a valid test covered what had been taught.

By the mid-1950s, standardized tests had become a substantial force in the assessment of student achievement (Office of Technology Assessment, 1992). Districts and then states turned to objectively scored multiple-choice tests as primary indicators for judging student achievement and school effectiveness. The teacher's role in assessment diminished sharply, especially in the elementary grades. "Learning disability" emerged as a largely test-dependent syndrome that today afflicts more than 1 in 20 students. In areas like reading and mathematics, textbook series included analogues to standardized tests. Supporting the movement was the machinery of psychometrics—alpha coefficients, point-biserials, predictive validity, and a host of other methods and concepts that even today are mysterious to most practitioners. Assessment became increasingly an external decree (Cole, 1988).

Beginning in the 1980s, rumbles were felt: alternative assessment, portfolios, performances and exhibitions. One force behind the movement was the inadequacy of recognition tests for gauging "high-level" curriculum outcomes (Resnick, 1987). A second force was the call by teachers and policy makers for greater professionalism (Darling-Hammond & Godwin, 1993).

These developments, while they return attention to the teacher's role, are by no means a retreat to the past. Social–cognitive perspectives of learning transcend both the "learn the facts and skills" of earlier decades *and* the behavioral objectives of the 1950s. Yesterday's factory-model society has given way to an information age. In the United States, the goal of equal education has moved from an ideal to a necessity, from opportunity to reality. At a time of greater expectations, the raw materials—children and the families from which they come—are at increased risk of poverty, broken homes, and distressed communities. These tensions center attention on several basic questions: what should be taught, how should it be taught, how should achievement be gauged? And they are marked by fundamental transformations in how educators think about the outcomes of schooling.

Production matters more than *recognition*: students must demonstrate that they can actually do something, not just pick the "one right" answer.

Projects matter more than *items*: a choice of depth over breadth, of validity over reliability.

Informed judgment matters more than *mechanized scoring*: the Scantron cannot replace the teacher in the assessment process.

A final ingredient in the mix is the effort to better balance internal and external assessment. Administrative pressures for accountability by principals, school boards, state superintendents and governors, and federal agencies have instituted assessment systems that address certain problems in certain ways:

- *Origins*: development and validation of assessment methods by a central agency responsible to a top-level policy maker.
- *Methods*: adherence to standardized procedures and routinized administration; professional judgment is neither needed nor permitted.
- *Outcomes*: cost-effective methods yielding simple numbers that either pass or fail a set criterion.

Advocates of internally mandated assessment have challenged each of these policy facets:

- *Origins*: development and validation of methods by a professional community of teachers directly responsible to themselves and their clientele.
- *Methods*: reliance on procedures springing from a shared understanding of curriculum and instruction, procedures adapted to situational context.
- *Outcomes*: case-effective (i.e., expensive) methods requiring informed judgment and yielding complex "portraits."

Internal assessment is more compatible with cognitive schooling, while external assessment fits the behavioral model.

To be sure, some recent innovations have an "anything goes" quality (e.g., Harp, 1991; Tierney et al., 1991; but also see Belanoff & Dickson, 1991) and easily become occasions for reinventing and rebuilding the wheel. Schools and teachers, with limited time and resources, are unlikely to succeed in their pursuit of new projects unless they have clear purpose, practice, and audience. But alternative assessments also support reform practices in curriculum and instruction and support emerging calls for professionalization. The key to realizing this potential is the creation of a clear and practical conceptual framework for classroom assessment and the development of working models that demonstrate the value of alternative approaches. The following sections address these two issues, but first a brief digression.

TEACHER-BASED ASSESSMENT OF STUDENT ACHIEVEMENT: A SCENARIO

The following scenario illustrates professional assessment of student learning. While we have a specific teacher in mind, the amalgam includes several instances of best practice. Ms. K's 32 third and fourth graders span a range of backgrounds, interests, and ability levels. Several youngsters have been labeled learning disabled, others are on free lunch (the family is poor), and eight fourth graders were on the retention list until Ms. K took them in.

In September and early October, Ms. K conducted "little lessons" on short texts and familiar topics. Small groups of students read, analyzed, and presented their assignments. By mid-October, Ms. K recorded brief entries about each student in her journal: proficiencies, predilections, and problems. Students also compiled their own personal journals: free writing (a Monday task) and assigned topics (Wednesday or Thursday). Samples of student work (individual and group) appeared on the walls. Each student assembled a folder of reading–writing papers.

For post-Halloween parent conferences, Ms. K prepared a one-page summary for each student listing areas of particular competence and particular needs. Each summary mentioned literature, science, social studies,

citizenship, art/music, and physical education. What about reading and writing? Ms. K responds: "We work on reading and writing all day long; we don't
study them separately."

In late March, the teacher gathers the class: "We've only a month of school
left, and it's time for our big project. This spring the project will be *Roots*—
your family history. When you finish the project, you'll have a *book* of your
own to keep." The Roots project is Ms. K's culminating assignment for the
school year. It yields a genuine product, but also provides a context for
summative assessment of individual students.

The project proceeds in three phases. First is the viewing of excerpts from
the television series. Students discuss the story and prepare book reports as
prologues to their own texts. For Ms. K, the reports assess student proficiency in the narrative concepts of character, plot, setting, and theme.

The second phase covers several biographical pieces, from *Little House on
the Prairie* to a newspaper article about Colin Powell. The aim is to construct
a shopping list of informational categories and sources to guide students'
research into their family's past. A wall chart constructed by the students
lists interviews, bibles and genealogies, letters and photo albums as sources
of background information. Much of the work is collaborative; the teacher
notes the contributions of specific students, along with their effectiveness as
group participants.

The third and final phase is the completion of each student's "Roots book"
for presentation at back-to-school night. The reports are extensive, a hun-
dred pages or more. Each includes a title page, table of contents, dedication
("To my parents, without whom this report would not be possible"), thematic
overview (the Roots story), research on *My Family*, and a "Forward to the
Future" piece where students describe their lives in the year 2000 after high
school graduation. The books represent substantial writing, artwork, graphics, and artifacts; behind the scenes is extensive redrafting, peer review, final
polishing, and preparation for the back-to-school night.

How does assessment fit into this picture? The link among student learning, curriculum, and instruction may appear seamless and difficult to sort
out. A conversation with Ms. K, however, offers insights into the process,
which takes even clearer shape when viewed through the lens of the following *design framework*:

What? How does the assessment connect with what is taught and how it
   is taught?
Why and for whom? What are the purposes and goals of the assessment?
   Who are the audiences?
How, when, and by whom? What are the methods and what is the schedule?
Bottom line? How is the assessment interpreted and reported?

Winograd (1994) describes "six problems worth solving" that cover comparable ground: *goals, audiences, tasks, standards, methods, linkage to instruction*. Like-

wise, Educational Testing Service (1995), the bulwark of standardized testing, has proclaimed that

> Subject matter experts are struggling to develop a national consensus about *what* students should know and be able to do, while advances in cognitive science continue to improve our understanding of *how* they learn [and how they know]. Teachers are moving away from a teacher-centered delivery of discrete bits and pieces of knowledge toward an approach that stresses the integration of knowledge through student participation in active and reflective learning. . . . Assessment is also being seen in an entirely new light. . . . Good assessment should emulate today's understanding of good teaching practices and reinforce new instructional goals. (pp. 4–5)

The tract also lists problematic aspects of performance assessment:

- The purpose is often unclear.
- Tasks are difficult to develop.
- Teacher involvement and training are inadequate.
- Dependable scoring is hard to do, given standards of validity, reliability, and fairness.
- Authentic assessment is costly and time consuming.

While slight differences appear in these agendas, the commonalities are substantial. And so let us review Ms. K's scenario through these lenses.

What?

This facet of the framework is a special strength in Ms. K's scenario. Exploring the dimensions of the design reveals several significant features that, although often implicit and intuitive, emerge during discussions with her.

The assessment is *integrative*. The Roots project yields a wealth of information about reading and writing, along with research skills. The portrait extends across a broad reach of the elementary curriculum, formal (literacy, literature, social studies, art) and informal (initiative, cooperation, persistence). The casual observer may see a collage, but Ms. K has a design in mind and weaves the distinctive elements into her final narrative for each student.

The assessment emphasizes *top-level* competence. From Ms. K's perspective, the critical achievements are "big picture and top-down": the capacity to wrestle with the overall structure of a discourse, an awareness of audience, a sense of thematic coherence. To be sure, the final products are polished, and Ms. K's evaluations touch on the micro-skills of spelling, grammar, neatness, and "nice touches." Her chief goal for the students, however, is not a neat paper, but a compelling and comprehensible work.

The assessment emphasizes *meta-language*, the students' capacity to explain their performance. When you were young, you had to "show your work" in math problems; the right answer with the wrong reasoning did not count. Ms. K adheres to the same principle. Small group activities in planning, reviewing, and presenting all encourage student discourse that reveals students' thinking. Ms. K expects her students to employ *technical language*, to use the labels and concepts that promote transferrable strategies. She resorts to direct instruction only rarely, mostly at the beginning of the year, and to ensure that all students know the technical language and can use it.

Finally, an important part of "what" encompasses students' capacity to work both independently and with support. She notes in her journal the amount of guidance each student needs to complete the job, and the fluency with which they approach revision, important information for students, parents, and next year's teacher.

Why and for Whom?

The purposes and goals of the Roots project—indeed, of the entire school year for Ms. K—are grounded in a sense of professional responsibility. The primary goal in this classroom is to inform Ms. K about students' growth in curriculum domains that she can clearly explicate. For her, assessment is not a technical activity, not a response to mandates, not a matter of assigning end-of-unit tasks. She has a vision for her students, and the entire program—curriculum, instruction, and assessment—centers around this vision.

Ms. K's primary audience is herself. Secondarily, she has students and parents in mind. She is less interested in administrators, policy makers, and researchers. In fact, if asked about the audience for assessment, she is likely to wonder about the question.

How, When, and by Whom?

This facet is another strength of the scenario. First, Ms. K's assessments are not casual. She relies on intuition but, when pressed, reveals an awareness of design and method. She depends on anecdote more than numbers, qualitative more than quantitative evidence. She is familiar with the concepts of consistency and predictive validity but focuses on what academics refer to as *construct validity* and *generalizability*.

Her assessments are *situated*. As noted previously, students vary in the amount of support and encouragement they need during the project, in their approach to the task, in their ability to sustain the effort, in their willingness to assist and to seek out assistance. The social dimension is especially significant for Ms. K. She encourages students to serve as peer reviewers and to learn to monitor and criticize their own work. She not only records data about these features of student achievement, she also varies conditions so that students sometimes work with teacher support, sometimes as part of a group, sometimes on their own.

Her assessments are *continuous*. Ms. K varies her methods throughout the school year, focusing on the basics in the early months, looking at broader and deeper competencies as the year progresses. Asked about "growth," she can offer evidence about student progress over the year; to be sure, her analysis again is more likely to take shape as qualitative descriptions rather than "reading rate."

Finally, the assessments are *multifaceted*. Ms. K relies on a wide variety of data—her notes, student writing, observations across a variety of group settings, conversations with individual students, and a close reading of students' approach to the Roots project. These sources are woven throughout her summary.

As for the "whom," Ms. K is responsible for the entire matter. She designs, implements, schedules, analyzes, interprets, and reports. To be sure, she draws upon an impressive depth of experience and breadth of resources. She knows the literature, consults with colleagues, and seeks critical reactions from clients.

The Bottom Line?

Ms. K analyzes and interprets the evidence in various ways. Her chief aim is a school year that is memorable for students and their families. Asked about accountability, she points to the collection of Roots books displayed around the classroom at year's end. The display may lack the precision of percentile scores, but it holds respect from students eager to describe and discuss their work.

Ms. K is principled about analyzing and reporting her assessments. She relies on developmental standards. Her journal notes are synoptic, readable only by other professionals, but her mileposts are as clear as a scope-and-sequence chart. Her assessments are not numeric, but they refer to growth and to the relative strengths and weaknesses of individual students. For example, here is a portion of her summary for one student:

> Sam is immature for a fourth grader, and he will need help if he is to do well in fifth grade. His oral language skills are great, and he works hard on topics that interest him: science, computers, and games. He has progressed in writing and spelling, but needs to improve before he enters middle school. He is better at writing reports than stories. He lacks the empathy that I expect in an 11-year-old, and this shows up in his group work. He likes cooperative tasks, but can be overbearing and strong willed. He does not listen well and is impatient with boring tasks like documenting or summarizing.

Ms. K prepares a summary for each student, which she attaches to the district's report card. She finds that most parents value these comments more than the official grades. Negative comments are sometimes tough to take, but Ms. K reports that most parents are willing to hear about problems when the report also includes suggestions about solutions. Parents are pleased about the Roots project, which they view as a sound indicator of their student's achievement during the school year. The fifth grade teachers find Ms. K's comments interesting but are not quite sure how to use the information. They have grown accustomed to her idiosyncrasies, but would prefer to know the student's level in the basal reading series. They are also uneasy because Ms. K. gives most students As in reading and writing. She points to the projects as justification; most students did excellent work.

One Story

The preceding scenario raises both questions and answers. It contrasts with one extreme in which the teacher relies on computer reports of student performance on specific objectives that have been mastered or that require further worksheet practice and another extreme in which the teacher asks clients to trust impressions supported by little or no evidence.

Imagine the enormous collection of scenarios that encompass the activities of other teachers throughout the United States, along with the work of conceptualizers, researchers, administrators, policy makers, and the broad community of clients interested in improving classroom assessment of student achievement—and improving support for these achievements. Comprehending this collection is a daunting task and requires conceptual lenses of the greatest clarity. We turn next to the elaboration of the framework sketched at the beginning of the scenario.

UNDERSTANDING THE EXAMPLE: A CONCEPTUAL FRAMEWORK

A *design framework* constitutes a set of lenses for looking at a problem. In this section we examine more carefully the four lenses just laid out, which highlight the contrast between classroom assessment and externally mandated standardized tests.

What Should Be Assessed?

This question is at root a curriculum matter. As Murphy and Smith (1990) put it, "Coming up with a portfolio . . . is choosing what to teach" (p. 1). Curriculum choices are social and political matters and can arouse considerable passion. The "politics of literacy" has a particularly divisive history. Basic skills versus reading for meaning, phonics versus whole language, basal readers versus integrated reading–writing—the catalogue of battlegrounds is impressive. Given the aspiration toward a fully educated citizenry, the national commitment to equal educational opportunity, and the emergence of an information society, *functional literacy* is inadequate for today's students. The alternative goal is *critical literacy*, the capacity to use language in all forms to think, to solve problems, and to communicate (Calfee, 1994).

The classroom teacher is frequently in the middle of the battle, especially when it comes to assessment. Policy makers and administrators with a penchant for management and accountability prefer assessments that are efficient, objective, and cheap; hence, a preference for curriculum outcomes that meet these same criteria. A basic-skills curriculum is relatively easy to describe. The outcomes are divided into objectives, each of which is presented for study, repeated for practice, and tested for mastery. The process is mechanistic and can be readily computerized. A critical-literacy curriculum is more subtle, more interactive, more holistic. In this curriculum, the first grader's reading of Lionni's *Swimmy* can be judged in part by reading rate and errors but also requires an ear attuned to stress and style, to the child's sense of audience reaction and engagement. The interplay between parts and wholes is ongoing; analysis and synthesis are part of every lesson. The teacher needs X-ray vision (and audition) to detect skills and strategies embedded in complex activities. The teacher must also be capable of explicating the curriculum to various audiences—parents, colleagues, administrators, and (of course) students.

Why and for Whom?

An analysis of why suggests several possibilities, which vary in the degree of authenticity. One "why" is to *guide instruction* for the class and for individual students. If September's activities suggest a lack of writing capabilities and a disinterest in writing, the teacher may decide to emphasize small-scale writing activities during the holiday months. If three students enter in midyear, all newly arrived from Cambodia with limited English, no need to administer a diagnostic test; direct observation offers more valid data. In general, classroom-based assessment is the most authentic source of information when the primary purpose is to guide instruction.

A second "why" is *feedback* to students, to parents, and to other teachers. Students are accustomed to tests: worksheets with smiley faces, spelling tests marked 15/20, paragraphs with red checks showing spelling and punctuation errors. They are less aware of the larger purposes of the process, even when they ask, "Will this be on the test?" They expect standardized tests in the spring and have interesting opinions about this machinery (Paris, Turner, & Lawton, 1990). But their meta-knowledge of assessment is scanty. As for parents and colleagues, while assessment has the potential to evoke serious discussions of student learning, the routines of grades, conferences, and casual remarks are more commonplace.

A third "why" is *accountability* to the principal and to district officials. This purpose/audience category marks the shift from internal to external. To be sure, the principal in a small school or district may serve as a head teacher and the superintendent may be a frequent classroom visitor. In most situations, however, administrators' responsibilities do not connect directly with curriculum and instruction. They may support the idea of writing portfolios and a student play may be a delightful digression, but their bottom line is typically standardized, numerical, and aggregable.

Accountability becomes especially complex and remote when the stage shifts to large urban districts, and to the state and national levels. In general, tests are mandated by external authorities, and the classroom teacher's professional judgment is largely overlooked. Efficiency, standardization, objectivity, aggregability, and concerns about technical reliability and validity are the primary criteria. While some efforts are being initiated to introduce more authentic methods and to listen to teachers' voices, such efforts are under attack for a variety of reasons. These events are not the focus of this chapter, but those interested in classroom assessment should examine the efforts of California, Vermont, Kentucky, Maryland, and several other states to implement assessments that capture the flavor of the classroom but that serve for large-scale accountability (e.g., Koretz, Stecher, Klein, & McCaffrey, 1994). A parallel set of stories informing these issues springs from the National Assessment of Educational Progress—the "nation's report card"—and the New Standards project (Resnick & Resnick, 1992). We will return to this theme later in the chapter.

How, When, and by Whom?

The short answer to these questions is that assessment is best embedded within regular classroom activities, ongoing throughout the school year, with the teacher acting as the designer, manager, and interpreter. This approach to assessment places the teacher in the role of an applied researcher, whose "experiments" are a vital part of ongoing professional responsibility and growth (Calfee & Hiebert, 1991).

As noted at the outset, the current proliferation of articles, volumes, and newsletters on alternative assessment offers a rich array of practical approaches, many of which appear promising and engaging. The advice generally assumes that the teacher is free to select activities, and that assessment is ongoing. To be sure, some states and districts now mandate alternative assessments, and textbook and test publishers are producing prepackaged portfolio systems.

By and large, the movement reflects genuine engagement by classroom teachers in assessment of student achievement. These aspirations often rest on a thin conceptual base: a file cabinet filled with student folders for display to interested parties but lacking commentary, context, or evaluation. Individual teachers gain notoriety as "portfolio persons," and alternative assessment springing from decisions by local teachers and schools is most likely to engender enthusiasm (Calfee & Perfumo, 1993).

On another front, the decisions in this section are "managed." States or districts mandate ("encourage") alternative assessment, as an activity valuable in its own right, as a complement to state-level testing or as a replacement for standardized tests (Pelavin, 1995). While teachers may be involved in the design of these programs, the response to external mandates nevertheless tends often to be "anxiety, fear, and resentment" (Calfee & Perfumo, 1996).

Standards for Classroom Assessment

How can one determine the adequacy of an assessment system, as reflected in its design and implementation, in the answers to the questions just listed? From one perspective, adequacy might be gauged by existing standards. For the classroom teacher, standards have been laid out by the major associations and the National Council on Measurement in Education (American Federation of Teachers, National Council on Measurement in Education, & National Education Association, 1990) covering the *skills* required for proficient assessment: choosing, developing, administering, interpreting, instructional decision making, grading, and communicating the results. We emphasize *skills* because the standards use the term and because of the practical how-to-do character of the standards, which have less to say about conceptual matters.

Another set of standards from research communities [American Educational Research Association, American Psychological Association, & National Council of Measurement in Education, (AERA, APA, & NCME), 1985] focus on testing, but cover other assessment activities as well. These standards speak repeatedly of the importance of shared responsibility among all parties—developer, user, and reporter—in establishing the validity of test results. The tone throughout the manual, however, aims more toward research and development, with little or no practical advice for users like classroom teachers.

Finally, national organizations concerned with ethics in testing and assessment have issued standards that, while aimed at test publishers and policy makers, also have implications for practitioners (e.g., National Council for Measurement in Education, 1995; National Forum on Assessment, 1995). The impact of these documents remains to be seen.

The tension between testing and assessment, between instruction and accountability, between internal and external perspectives appears in the standards arena and elsewhere. The standards for classroom assessment center around the teacher's knowledge of principles and methods that are more directly linked to testing than to assessment. Research on teachers' capacities to gauge student growth and accomplishment (e.g., Stiggins & Conklin, 1992) typically uses psychometric standards as the criterion. These standards, most clearly reflected in the AERA/APA/NCME manual, can serve as important guides for measuring student accomplishments, especially in the later grades and especially when the appraisal must cover a broad span of skills and knowledge. But, when the task is to gauge student progress, especially in the early years of schooling and especially when depth of understanding matters more than breadth of scope, standards of a different character are needed (Calfee, in press; Paratore, 1995).

What might more appropriate and comprehensive standards look like? An adequate answer to this question would go beyond the scope of this chapter. Let us suggest, however, that a major task for the future—given that teacher assessment of student achievement receives the emphasis that we think it merits—is to build standards addressing this question.

ASSESSMENT AS INQUIRY

The most significant feature in the recent emergence of alternative strategies for classroom assessment centers around the teacher's professional role. In this section we explore the concept of *classroom assessment as applied social science research* (Calfee & Hiebert, 1991; Cronbach, 1988; Shuell, 1988). The foundations for this proposition are longstanding. For example, Cronbach (1960) identified three principal features of assessment: careful observations, a variety of methods and measures, and integration of information. His list meshes with elements commonly found in textbooks on research methods: *planning, implementation, interpretation*, and *decision making*. A research study begins with a question and a hypothesis (one or more) that lead to the creation of a design, a plan for varying factors that influence performance. Then come the pragmatics of collecting and analyzing data, of compiling evidence. The next task is interpretation: what do the findings mean, what about the alternative interpretations, how might the original hypotheses be reformulated to reflect the results? Finally comes the job of deciding what to do with the interpreted findings, the bottom line. The process is not linear but interactive and cyclic, not a sequence of stages but a set of distinctive processes, a roller coaster more than an elevator.

These four elements parallel the design framework presented earlier (what, why and for whom, when and how, interpretation and reporting), but from a different perspective. Assessment, as commonly practiced today, is more akin to appraisal than inquiry, driven by neither curiosity nor the aim of improving conditions. In the inquiry model, the "what," may begin with curriculum elements, but these are viewed not as fixed objectives but as hypotheses. The answer to "why and for whom" is illustrated in Ms. K's scenario: as an inquiring teacher, Ms. K was driven by a professional impulse to understand and shape student learning, and she was the primary audience for the results. The "when, how, and bottom line" issues connect most directly to the elements of the inquiry model. In essence, the teacher who operates in the inquiry mode takes full responsibility for assessment, and switches from an activity-driven model ("assessment is something that you do") to a conceptual model ("assessment is a way of thinking about teaching").

What does the inquiring teacher need to know? In this section we sketch an answer to this question, focusing on pragmatic issues. As noted earlier, this proposal must be understood within the context of current developments in literacy instruction. The tacit and piecemeal collage that constitutes today's literacy curriculum is being replaced by a more coherent and integrated set of objectives, not only in state frameworks and scope-and-sequence charts but in the teacher's intellectual armamentarium (Tuman, 1987). The concept of instruction as experimentation is being cultivated, shifting emphasis from activities and content coverage toward participative and engaging classroom experiences (Calfee & Patrick, 1995).

Planning Assessment: Hypotheses and Designs

In developing a research plan, a person needs to keep two questions in mind: what needs to be known and what evidence will illuminate the issues? "What needs to be known" takes shape as a *research hypothesis*. "What kind of evidence" requires a *research design*. The toughest hurdle in becoming a researcher is learning to think about a problem, and design probably comes next on the list. The preparation and work situations of teachers offer few opportunities or incentives for either of these tasks.

We can illustrate the planning task by a classroom situation in which vocabulary skills are the focus of the assessment. Vocabulary is an important outcome of literacy instruction. If students are to comprehend complex texts and compose readable compositions, they need to be proficient in vocabulary—not a simple accumulation of words but a mastery of concepts, of interrelated collections of ideas, where words serve as labels for communicating ideas.

A *hypothesis* is a tentative explanation forwarded as a basis for investigation. The inquiry method begins by posing alternative hypotheses and then sets up a range of situations to explore these alternatives. A more traditional assessment method begins with a conclusion and then seeks supporting data. In the example, Sam, a newcomer in a fourth grade class, is rumored to have a poor vocabulary. The rumor, whatever the source, is a hypothesis. The teacher assesses his vocabulary with a standardized instrument. Discovering his grade level on the Nelson–Denny vocabulary test to be 2.4, two grades below expectation, the teacher places him in the low-ability reading group for remedial instruction. The assessment is complete. The hypothesis, "Sam is not very smart," is confirmed. The (tacit) explanation is simple; some children learn words easily and others take more practice.

A different frame of mind emerges if the teacher assumes that Sam possesses a substantial vocabulary (most nine-year-olds do). The new hypothesis, an alternative to the notion that Sam lacks words, is that Sam's vocabulary storehouse has not been adequately tapped by previous assessments. The *design* task is to create situations that explore Sam's mental storehouse. This exploration does not beg the question; it may well be that Sam lacks the range and depth of concepts expected of a fourth grader.

What might a design for this problem look like? Suppose the teacher considers the following questions:

Under what conditions can Sam use and explain commonplace words?
Under what conditions does he have trouble with such words?
How does he handle less familiar words, including technical terms important in reading instruction (e.g., *define, mean the same, main idea, character*)?
What does he think it means to explain a word?
What does he say during and after a test about his strategies for handling vocabulary?
How does he respond with various kinds of support from peers? From the teacher? From different kinds of text clues (e.g., words defined in a passage, in a glossary)?

The questions suggest how a hypothesis can point toward the initial stages of a design, toward controlled variation in conditions for observing performance. If Sam fails *petroleum* under some conditions but succeeds under others, then he understands the word, and testing conditions affect his performance. Both the teacher's understanding of his problem and the choice of a course of action (an instructional experiment) can be guided by the findings.

Several practical decisions confront the teacher in designing an assessment. One critical choice is whether to work with *groups* or *individuals*. Group testing often brings to mind paper-and-pencil tasks but alternatives exist. Individual assessment provides greater latitude but is costly and raises issues of class management. A second consideration is whether the assessment is *oral* or *written*. For a reading teacher, the answer might seem obvious. But if one views literacy as the effective use of language in all its forms, then mastery of the printed word is only one curriculum outcome. A third factor is the selection of a *production* or *recognition* task. A test may require the student to write a sentence with *petroleum* or to pick the correct answer (oil) from a set of choices. The first option takes more time to prepare and evaluate but is potentially more informative than the second. Finally comes the question of whether the information is needed for immediate *short-term* purposes or summative *long-term* decisions. A quickie quiz can be what is needed, but a student's ability-group placement should not depend on a brief multiple-choice test simply because time is limited.

The time dimension is particularly important in assessment design. Publishers, in constructing tests and correlated textbook series, cannot adapt assessment practices to local situations. The basic practice is to administer tests at the end of units or chapters, with a "final" at year's end, often in the form of a standardized test. The teacher has other options. For instance, rather than opening to the first textbook page on the first day of school, the teacher may spend a week or so in informal assessment to determine the range of student abilities and interests. The "lost time" can pay returns when instruction is modified to fit the findings. Throughout the year, "on-the-fly" assessment assures that learning and transfer have taken place. The concept of *dynamic assessment* (Brown, Campione, & Day, 1981; Lidz, 1987) captures the spirit of ongoing and curriculum-linked appraisals. At the end of the year, large-scale student projects and exhibitions offer a contextualized opportunity for gauging student growth and accomplishments. Interestingly (and distressingly), discussions of yearlong planning of assessment do not appear in any of the sources reviewed for this chapter.

Collecting Data

Once hypotheses and design are in place, attention turns to the development of appropriate methods. At least, such is the classical image of the research process. In fact, the process is actually more iterative. As noted in the vocabulary example, design factors may define methods, and thinking about appropriate methods can lead to a rethinking of hypotheses and design.

The typical menu of assessment methods includes standardized tests, along with social science techniques like ethnography, think alouds, and experiments (Creswell, 1994; Jaeger, 1988). The methods fall on a continuum from informal tasks that give students considerable freedom of expression to formal techniques that significantly constrain performance.

For assessment as inquiry, the middle ground probably offers the classroom teacher the most valuable strategies for collecting data. Here, rather than relying on social science disciplines for guidance, a better answer may lie in the refinement of best instructional practice: observation and interviewing, discussion and questioning, sampling student work including writing, informal inventories, as well as various testing approaches.

Observation and Interviewing

The most fundamental source for direct assessment of student learning achievement is what the teacher gains from looking and listening. To be sure, it is hard to pat your head and rub your tummy at the same time, to attend simultaneously to both instruction and observation.

The classroom, to the casual observer, is a blooming buzzing confusion. How to make sense of it? What to look for? The following six facets are foundational for systematic observation (Calfee & Calfee, 1976):

1. *Who are the students*? How many are in the classroom? How are they organized into groups? Who are the target students and where are they located?

2. *Who are the adults?* How many are there? What is each one's status and role? Who are they working with?
3. *What is going on?* For each of the definable groups, what is the activity (reading, writing, talking, worksheets, whatever)?
4. *Who is instructing, and how?* Teacher, aide, tutor? Is the instructor lecturing, asking questions, managing, facilitating, observing?
5. *What is the content of instruction?* What subject matter? What skills and activities seem to be the focus? Is the focus clear? What materials and supports?
6. *How are the students responding?* Are they attentive? Productive? Interested and engaged? What seems to be the level of performance? Of interaction?

In approaching observation as an assessment method, the teacher confronts two hurdles. First, it is probably impossible to monitor all six facets for all students while simultaneously managing instruction. The solution is focus—select the facets and students critical for a given purpose, and put everything else into the background. If the teacher has a clearly defined question in mind, then focus should reflect the needs of the question.

Second, it is difficult to see very much when fully engaged with instruction. This problem can be solved in two ways. Learning to observe requires occasions when the teacher is free to observe students while they are under the tutelage of another person (a colleague, a student teacher, maybe even the principal!). Even brief opportunities give the teacher a new perspective on students, to focus on individuals and track their response to the ebb and flow of classroom events. "David seems never to join the discussion. I put him in front of the group on the reading rug so I could keep track of him. Now I see that he is totally distracted by the posters that I tacked underneath the chalkboard! I should move either David or the posters." Classroom observation is typical in preservice programs but is seldom part of continuing professional development.

The other way to find time for observation is to spend less time on direct instruction. Small group activities and individual assignments offer occasions for students to demonstrate their learning while the teacher checks on progress. All too often, however, the teacher's attention remains fixed on instructional activities; the teacher uses the time to work with a small group of students with special needs or roams the classroom looking for chances to correct errors or tell students what to do. Given the emphasis in U.S. schools on time on task and direct instruction, it requires discipline to concentrate on looking rather than doing.

Interviewing may seem complicated and time consuming, and it can be if taken to extremes. We have in mind a simpler notion, one that can sometimes be captured in a 30-second exchange with a student about an assignment or by special attention to student responses during classroom discussion. On rare occasions, the teacher may need to have a longer talk with a youngster; consider this situation as the ideal starting point, a model for planning how to collect information during more sporadic exchanges.

Given time to plan and interact with an individual student, then the *funnel approach* to interviewing offers a strategy for efficiently obtaining both broad and focused information from a student (Calfee, 1985, pp. 84ff). The method starts with general queries and moves toward more specific requests, ending with a multiple-choice task. In this example the teacher's queries Martha, who is having problems with story comprehension:

"Martha, tell me what you remember about Emma's story. What did you like the most?"

"You said that Emma's horse was a character in the story. What are some reasons why the horse is a character?"

"You said that Emma is also a character. Tell me about how Emma and her horse are the same and different as characters?"

"What do you think are Emma's feelings when they ride up to the angry crowd? How do you think her horse feels? Why? Do you think they are both angry? Scared? Proud?"

This brief exchange can tell the teacher about Martha's understanding of personification. In addition, the teacher has the opportunity to couple assessment with instruction. The point is *not* to lead the student to say "The horse didn't feel anything." For all we know, the horse did. Rather, the purpose is to discover whether the student can distinguish the author's purpose in communicating Emma's feelings. This objective is subtle and takes skill and patience to assess. "Why" questions are especially important in delving into underlying reasons, but they require scaffolding and support. Young children are great at asking "why" questions, but we know as adults that answering these can be difficult. One of the most important outcomes of schooling is the capacity to reflect, to explore internal thoughts and reasons.

Discussion and Questioning

Our focus in this section is assessment in group settings, because instructional decisions often entails the collective rather than individuals. The key to effective discussion is strategic questioning, hence the linking of these two topics.

As Bean (1985; also Alvermann, Dillon, & O'Brien, 1987; Cazden, 1988) notes, classroom discussion is "a problem that remains difficult to explore" (Bean, 1985, p. 336). The Socratic ideal is seldom realized; more common is the pseudo-Socratic method, where the teacher's actual goal is to elicit the correct answer. Bean suggests teacher-guided and student-generated questioning strategies as alternatives: leading the group through a variation on the funnel approach to explore a problem, and guiding students to adopt a similar approach for themselves. He notes that fostering student-generated questioning is especially effective for low-achieving students, which fits with other findings on meta-cognitive instruction. Bean assumes that questioning and discussion aims toward a predetermined response. The group is discussing a text, and the goal is the correct interpretation of a particular issue. A different view of discussion, both for instruction and assessment, relaxes this restriction to open a broader vista of questioning and discussion.

Graesser, Lang, and Horgan (1988) suggest leads for improving discussion. Their analysis of questions from television talk shows and newspaper columns (e.g., Dr. Ruth and Ann Landers) led them to propose three dimensions: *why* is the questioner asking the question, *what kind* of question is being asked, and *how* is the questioner handling the situation.

Why is the question asked? School questions aim for a right answer. The teacher knows what it is, students understand this and realize that their job is to come up with the prize. Outside of school, a question is more often a genuine effort by one person to gain knowledge from someone else. Students may be startled when classroom discussion takes this turn and reluctant to respond. With guidance and reassurance, however, students can engage in lively and informative exchanges.

The "why" may be the most significant barrier to effective classroom discussion. Reflecting on how a question sounds to the other person can lead to the realization that the purpose appears other than intended. "Johnny, will you help Sue with that word?" is not a question but a command. "What was happening in the story at the end of yesterday's lesson?" asks for information but also lays a foundation for moving onward. "Don't you think that the character of Emma is different than we first thought?" invites a yes-or-no answer, probably yes, and is unlikely to generate much of a response. The tensions in setting purpose for classroom discussions are real; the teacher's responsibility is to establish learning goals, and so discussion should not be aimless. On the other hand, students' skills in framing problems and solving them are important outcomes, which are difficult to achieve when the frames and the solutions are completely predetermined.

What kind of question? Graesser et al. (1988) offer a long list under this category, many of which can be categorized under *wh*-headings (who, what, where, and so on—an excellent list for classroom reference). These questions cover a range that extends from literal details through inference and on to opinion.

The "how" of questioning is real but subtle. It includes such matters as the questioner's assumptions about the other person, the scope of the question, and the support and genuineness of the exchange. It encompasses the many "extras" that contribute to an engaging discussion. For example, Nystrand and Gamoran (1991) have demonstrated the importance of "uptakes" in supporting active classroom discussion; the teacher who responds genuinely with, "Gee, that sounds interesting—say more" is likely to promote richer responses from all students. The teacher who sets a broad purpose for the discussion and then loosens the reins allowing students to conduct the discussion opens the door for occasional chaos, but also sets the stage for interactions that inform him or her about student understandings (Calfee, Dunlap & Wat, 1994).

Sampling Student Work: Portfolios

During a typical school day, students create a variety of relatively permanent artifacts. In many classrooms, the worksheet exercise still predominates: activities designed for practice, the work of a few moments, exacting little more than recognition or copying information, with little clear purpose for the student. With the arrival of higher standards, an emphasis on demonstrated performance, and the requirement to "show your work," classrooms increasingly include a more informative collection of student work. These are often assembled as *portfolios*, which span the range from writing to mathematics, from science to social studies. To be sure, portfolios may be little more than collections, but in the best instances they take shape as major projects requiring significant amounts of time, engaging the creative impulse, and reflecting meaningful personal investment.

Methods for analyzing ongoing student work for assessment purposes is a topic for a complete volume, and we must limit our comments to a few critical matters. First, work samples can inform both *product* and *process*. At the micro-level, this combination comes down to the correct answer arrived at in the correct manner. The student solving a word problem lays out the details of his or her analysis ("show your work"), but must also come up with the appropriate analysis. At a macro-level, a writing portfolio shows the student's progression from early ruminations about a writing assignment through the design of a composition (an outline) to the first draft, then through the stages of review, revision, and final polishing and publication. The final result merits judgment as a product, but understanding the entire process grounds the teacher's assessment for instructional purposes.

A second issue centers around the *medium of expression* employed for the assessment. School tasks often rely on formal academic media—verbal media, most often writing. Springing from the concept of multiple intelligences, a practical strategy is to encourage students to demonstrate their understanding and skills in a variety of ways. We are not suggesting that "anything goes;" learning the academic game is important for success in many areas of the real world. But the student who can draw informative and compelling portraits of the solar system shows an understanding of the concept, even if he or she cannot prepare a credible written report. The assessment confirms the knowledge base and leaves the job of teaching the student to write—and probably to discuss—what he or she knows about various topics.

The third matter is *explication*, confirming that a student can apply present accomplishments to new situations, checking out performance in other settings, and asking the student to explain how he or she has approached the task. These tasks are tough for the assessor, but are important for understanding student learning.

Tests

The strengths and limits of group-administered, multiple-choice methods are a source of vexatious debate (Mehrens & Kaminski, 1989). A skillfully developed recognition test provides considerable information about achievement, in a group setting, at little cost in time, effort, scoring, and analysis. Unsurprisingly, teachers, students, administrators, and psychometricians all favor this approach for some purposes. The advantages sometimes outweigh the limitations, sometimes not. A recognition task offers students a chance to show what they know at minimal cost, but those who haven't learned to play the testing game can be misled by plausible alternatives. Recognition tasks put a premium on covering the material, but the ability to digest and organize has the higher payoff for long-term learning. Life is not a multiple-choice test, and hence the continuing concern about the influence about the impact of recognition tasks in shaping the goals of schooling.

Standardized tests respond in part to the needs for large-scale accountability, but recent developments in less than fully standardized (Calfee, Kapinus, & Pearson, 1996) methods for large-scale assessment offer promising models for the classroom teacher. A variety of models have been explored during the past 10 years; the now defunct California Learning Assessment System (CLAS; California Assessment Program Staff, 1989) illustrates the potential of the LTFS paradigm as a model for summative classroom assessment. To assess literacy achievement, CLAS incorporated three elements: (1) individual student analysis of an extended piece of writing, (2) work as a part of a group sharing these analyses and planning a composition on a related topic, and (3) individual composition of a finished work. From a design perspective, CLAS was a masterpiece, combining major ingredients of authentic literacy within a structure that was partly standardized but also provided flexibility. Classroom teachers looking for an integrated instructional model that supports progress in reading and writing can certainly benefit from studying this system. The demise of CLAS was due to problems in implementation (California teachers learned about the assessment far too late and with far too little in the way of supportive professional development), to a mismatch of costs and benefits (the assessment was costly in time and money, and the holistic scoring offered few benefits for instructional feedback), and to political brawls.

The point is that externally mandated tests need not undermine the concept of assessment as inquiry. To the contrary, an appropriately designed state or national assessment system may serve as the skeleton for certain aspects of inquiry-based assessment at the local level. The challenge is to

design a system that models effective assessment practices, to provide opportunities for professional development that connect practitioners with the
model, and to incorporate local assessments with those externally mandated. Several states are providing leadership along these lines, but their
experiences also demonstrate the political challenges of this effort.

Interpreting the Evidence: What Do the Data Mean?

Interpretation is the task of giving meaning to observations and shaping
generalizations for decision making. Interpretation entails going beyond the
information given to broader meanings. Inquiry is not linear; instead, interpretation must be embedded in the questions that guide data collection and
the evaluation of the evidence. It must connect with the questions that motivated the assessment.

Interpretation demands of the teacher both reflection and expression,
both time and occasion to ponder the evidence. Pondering often means
talking with colleagues. As several observers have noted, the conditions of
schooling allow few opportunities to reflect (Fraatz, 1987; Rosenholz, 1989).
A person is more likely to reflect, write, and report when there is purpose
and audience. Testing practices that emphasize quantitative reporting evoke
bookkeeping more than professional assessment. While one finds frequent
exhortations for teachers to become researchers (Cochran-Smith & Lytle,
1993), there is little opportunity for professional expression (Bridge & Hiebert, 1985).

Interpretation builds on two criteria: consistency of the evidence and
strength of the argument. Psychometricians refer to these criteria as *reliability*
and *validity*. While other standards exist, we focus on these two because they
link testing practice and the inquiry model of classroom assessment. Validity
and reliability are often equated with statistics and hence impracticality. Yet
each can be phrased in pragmatic form: reliability asks "Does the evidence
appear dependable?" and validity asks "Does the evidence appear to address
the questions of primary concern?"

Defining *validity* for less than fully standardized assessments at the classroom level poses a challenge (Calfee, in press). Problems and possibilities
can be illustrated by a concrete example. Consider a fourth grade teacher
newly assigned to a school in a low-income urban neighborhood. It is mid-
year, the previous teacher is on health leave, and her notes and the principal's remarks suggest that the class lacks both background experience and
language development. Starting with the lesson plan left by the former
teacher, the teacher opens a discussion of the Constitution:

"Today we're going to study the U. S. Constitution. Who can tell me something about the Constitution?" [Silence.]

"What about the federal government? The government in Washington?"
[Again, silence; clearly a problem.] [The teacher writes on the board: *President,
Congress*, and *Supreme Court*.]

"Who can tell me about these words? [Still no response. The teacher then begins a lecture on the Constitution: "We have just celebrated the 200th anniversary . . ."]

What does this episode tell us about the students? The teacher appears to have reached the tacit conclusion that the youngsters lack knowledge about the Constitution. Given the evidence (nonresponsiveness), what other hypotheses might be entertained and what is the appropriateness of each?

For example, consider the following interpretations: the principal is right—the students lack basic knowledge; the previous teacher is right—the students' language ability is much below the fourth-grade level of comprehension.

The evidence is consistent with either or both of these interpretations, but can also be explained in other ways. The students are not accustomed to open-ended questions and have not been taught strategies for brainstorming. They feel uneasy with a new teacher and reluctant to give foolish answers. They know a fair amount about how government works, but not under the official labels.

The reason for considering alternative interpretations is that they call for alternative courses of action. In fact, establishing the validity of an interpretation almost always calls for experimentation—for changing conditions and collecting additional evidence.

For instance, the teacher might entertain the hypothesis that students lack discussion strategies, that they have not been taught to handle open-ended questions. To evaluate this idea, the teacher plans a discussion for the following day around the topic of weather. The students may be unfamiliar with the Constitution, but they surely know about weather. "Today's lesson is about *weather*. What words come to mind when you think about this topic?" Suppose the response is once more silence. The teacher now has evidence to support the notion that something is at work other than a lack of knowledge. A strategic move at this point is to scaffold the discussion by offering "starters." Directing students' attention to the window, the teacher asks "What is today like?" "Cloudy?" "Right! What was it like yesterday?" "Cold." "OK—those are weather words! What other weather words do you know?" By lesson's end, the teacher is likely to have more trustworthy evidence about the conditions under which students can be engaged in a discussion. The teacher can then more validly assess content knowledge about abstract topics like the U.S. government.

Moss (1995) has proposed the concept of *hermeneutic validity*, which depends on multiple sources of evidence that employ qualitative analysis to address various hypotheses. The approach differs from the statistical methods typically found in testing textbooks. An important feature of this approach is the reliance on interaction among professionals to support the validity of an argument. In Great Britain, teachers employ *moderation* as a foundational principle for assessing achievement; teacher teams routinely review samples of student work, which they evaluate according to rubric systems and must then defend, both agreements and disagreements (Drummond & Pollard, 1988; Harlen, 1994). Bringing the underlying reasoning to the surface is the primary goal of moderation not just interrater reliability.

Unreliability of teacher judgments has been the center of controversy in the United States. Several studies, mostly of large-scale assessment projects, have explored the conditions under which teachers succeed or fail to yield similar ratings of student work samples (e.g., Koretz et al., 1994). Less research is available on consistency within classroom settings. *Consistent, stable*, and *dependable* are all synonyms for the concept of reliability. Validity and reliability are actually different sides of the same coin. Validity asks about external consistency: is the interpretation stable over variations that might matter? Reliability asks about internal consistency: is evidence stable over conditions that should not matter? In the preceding illustration, for instance, the teacher might find that conditions supporting student discussion early in the week fall apart on Friday or that strategies effective in a teacher-led setting do not work when students are assigned to cooperative groups. Validity emphasizes consistency around a concept, whereas reliability emphasizes consistency around the individual. Standardizing the task and context increases reliability but at the risk of decreasing validity.

Messick (1995) describes the central issue of assessment as *the degree to which the evidence supports the inferences that are made from the scores*. The question is, has the rater really measured what it is about which conclusions are being drawn? Designing, collecting, and organizing information about students are seldom high on the list of priorities laid out for teachers; setting activities and covering the content receive more emphasis. Assessment tends to be mechanized through testing instruments. The observant and thoughtful teacher, combining the skills of instructor, experimenter, and clinician, is in a far better position to create a data base for sound instructional decisions.

Planfulness is a critical ingredient for realizing this ideal. The teacher is in a unique position to collect and weigh evidence from a wide array of alternative sources to identify the student's areas of strength and need. However, significant barriers stand in the way of realizing this goal; as one teacher expressed it:

> Often there is not time to focus sufficiently on the individual student to really determine what they need, because with the clerical work we have to do, the record-keeping, the accountability stuff that we have to do, it just does not allow time . . . (Fraatz, 1987, p. 29; also Stephens et al., 1995).

Decision Making

Assume that the teacher has gathered evidence about some aspect of student achievement and is satisfied with its meaning and consistency. What is to be done with the information? Again, the inquiry is seldom linear, but assessment serves little purpose unless it leads to decisions and actions. Assessment decisions may serve for gauging student progress and accomplishment, and they can also serve to refine curriculum and instruction, both short term and long term. At this point the cycle comes full circle.

Decisions do entail alternatives and choices. For instance, in the previous example, the teacher may conclude that there is value in taking the time to establish methods and standards for classroom discussion using commonplace topics *before* settling down to a focus on content. But given the enormous content to be covered in most textbooks, the decision must be balanced against the time investment.

A related issue is the investment in individual students. The teacher's use of concept mapping techniques increases the flow of discussion, but a handful of students still hold back. One decision is to search for topics of interest and relevance to this group, but at the cost of covering the assigned topics. At some point the teacher must move from adapting the curriculum and place more responsibility on individuals. Student self-assessment offers an option seldom explored as an adjunct to teacher assessment. Advocates of alternative assessment methods have urged that students learn to monitor and evaluate their performance, but have less to say about purposes and methods to support this process. The teacher–parent–student conference (Klimenkoff & LaPick, 1996; Stiggins, 1994) offers a concrete proposal toward this end. The student has the responsibility to establish goals for each quarter, to collect information and evaluate progress toward the goals, and finally to report this assessment to the teacher and parents. At one level, this strategy would seem to relieve the teacher of the assessment burden, but in fact it entails an even greater challenge—it is easier for the teacher to do the assessment than to teach young children (or distractable adolescents) to reflect on their own accomplishments.

A task of particular difficulty at this stage is the establishment of standards. Much has been said at the national level about the importance of world-class standards for U.S. students (Eisner, 1995; McLaughlin & Shepard, 1995; Pashley & Phillips, 1993; Resnick & Resnick, 1992). The substance behind the rhetoric remains fairly thin. Most systems come down to impressionistic scales that range from "poorest" to "best"; recall the earlier example from the National Assessment of Educational Progress.

The classroom teacher faces a similar challenge in assigning grades (Brookhart, 1994). The testing model handles the standards issue mechanically, either by emphasizing competitive rating (grading on the curve) or establishing arbitrary standards (above 90 means an A). The inquiry model of assessment calls on the teacher, as part of a professional team, to set standards of performance grounded in complex student performance. At some points in the school year and throughout students' path through the grades, standards should emphasize growth and progress. Given differences among entering kindergartners, it makes little sense to set up fixed hurdles for year's end—the critical judgment here focuses on development in a range of curriculum domains, both academic (language and preparation for reading) and social (capacity to work with a group and to take appropriate responsibility for individual actions). For the student leaving third grade, the demands of the fourth grade curriculum provide a foundation for establishing standards of accomplishment that should be explicit for all involved—student, teacher, and parents. More is involved than assigning a grade. Here the standards question is clear-cut: what must entering fourth graders be able to do, and how well should they be able to do it to ensure success in the later elementary grades?

BACK TO THE FUTURE—AND AHEAD

Assessment as inquiry is rare in today's U.S. schools. Where it appears, it is often associated with other innovative programs like whole language, portfolios, and teacher as researcher, among others. It is usually an effort by one or two teachers and seldom emerges in schoolwide restructuring activities, which tend to emphasize organizational reforms over curriculum and instruction. Individual implementation of alternative assessment at the classroom level is often an add-on to routine testing procedures.

As noted at the beginning of the chapter, professional assessment by the classroom teacher is an essential concomitant to fundamental changes in the nation's curriculum (Educational Testing Service, 1995). To take full advantage of advances in our understanding of social–cognitive learning (e.g., Bruer, 1993), the teacher as inquirer will have to move from theory to practice, from isolated individuals to schoolwide teams. Two tasks will determine whether the inquiry model actually becomes part of professional practice: (1) bridging the chasm between externally mandated testing and locally determined assessment, and (2) designing general methods to support the inquiry model in a practical manner.

Externally mandated tests capture the headlines. A school's image—and local property values—depend on its relative ranking as reported by the state or local district test scores. The pressure is interminable to sustain high scores and raise low ones by the most direct means possible: aligning instruction to match the surface features of the test, eliminating from the test pool those students who are likely to do poorly, and preparing students for the specifics of the mandated instrument. The usual advice is to design tests worth teaching to, but the reality is that virtually any instrument can be subverted.

Two strategies offer promise in dealing with such issues. The first is to ensure that the instrument is indeed worth teaching to; that is, to design tests that are sensitive to the most appropriate instruction (Shepard, 1995). In California, for instance, CLAS was ideally suited to assess the outcomes of an integrated reading–writing curriculum. The state's decision in 1995 to terminate CLAS and replace it with multiple-choice tests provides teachers with little incentive to move away from worksheets and practice tests.

The second strategy is to incorporate teacher judgment in a systematic and public way in reports of externally mandated assessments. Several states have explored the possibilities of this strategy, with varied success. In Vermont, for instance, the classroom teacher plays a major role in assisting students in the development of achievement portfolios, which teacher teams then rate for quality. But the classroom teacher's judgment of his or her own students are not included in the process; observations, interviews, knowledge of the process of portfolio development and other forms of classroom performance play no role in judging the student's performance. In Kentucky, an array of assessments is included in the statewide assessment, including on-demand tests and portfolios. The latter are rated at the local level, often by the classroom teacher. Again, the teacher's professional judgment is weighed less heavily than decontextualized data sources.

State efforts to incorporate teacher judgment as part of the overall accountability picture face serious obstacles (Freedman, 1993; LeMahieu, Gitomer, & Eresh, 1995). Teaching has become a semi-profession in recent decades, and the public is understandably uneasy about trusting teacher judgment at a policy level (Cizek, Rachor, & Fitzgerald, in press). When psychometric criteria are applied to teacher ratings, they seldom attain the levels of interrater consistency typical of interitem reliability for standardized tests. We question the appropriateness of applying psychometric criteria in this instance, arguing that the inconsistencies are not "errors" but reflect the sensitivity of human judges to a range of achievement dimensions that are important for improving instruction but not captured by standardized tests. To be sure, it is possible to standardize the rating process so that teachers behave like "scoring machines," but this approach misses the point.

In fact, the primary benefits of bringing teacher judgment into the policy arena is the potential for a broader and more informative array of assessment outcomes than is possible with unidimensional tests. These benefits come at some cost. The major expense is professional development. Neither in preservice preparation nor in ongoing professional development do teachers receive the background knowledge and opportunity for refining skills essential for assessment as inquiry. In virtually every state that has employed teacher judgment, the main response by teachers has been plaudits for the opportunity for professional development and interaction with other teachers. They also report that the preparation and time for exchanges are far from adequate.

A second cost is trust. Policy makers and administrators are more comfortable when teachers are assembled in an auditorium, given a day or two of extensive preparation on a strictly defined task, and then set to supervised work. The level of control may reassure those in power, but it misses the point. The most appropriate location for assessment of student achievement is the classroom context. The challenge, of course, is for practitioners to overcome the tension between their roles as advocates (their primary task to support student learning) and as assessors. For some purposes (e.g., completion of the high school degree), decontextualized appraisal may make sense as one element in the overall assessment. But to gauge the learning accomplishments of younger students, the classroom teacher is in a unique position to make informed and trustworthy judgments, which should be included as part of the accountability record. For this move to happen, the public must be assured that the judgment is trustworthy, it must then make its trust explicit, and it must include this information in the public record.

Developing an appropriate methodology is a demanding task. Collecting student work is fairly straightforward; difficulties arise in deciding how to select work samples and how to assess the samples in an informative, consistent, and reportable manner. The concept of the *Teacher Logbook* addresses these issues (Calfee & Perfumo, 1993; Figure 1). The logbook is designed around three tasks: *documentation* of evidence bearing on student performances; *summary judgment* of student achievement; and a *curriculum record*.

A critical precursor to the logbook is the establishment of a developmental curriculum, a small set of critical strands for a given subject matter, including mileposts that serve as targets for growth. In story comprehension, for example, four outcomes are generally recognized as critical: character, plot, setting, and theme. For kindergartners, appreciating the moral of simple fables may be a reasonable goal. By third grade, students may be expected to identify thematic issues implicit in a work such as *Charlotte's Web* and express the meaning of the work in personal terms. Sixth graders should be fully capable of employing thematic elements in their own compositions and identifying multiple themes in collections of related texts.

As shown in the figure, student summaries appear at the beginning of the logbook, because these are critical in reporting student achievement. Imagine a procedure in which, on a regular basis, perhaps once a quarter, the teacher conducts a formal rating of each student's achievement level in the summary section of the logbook. The entries reflect the teacher's judgment about each student's location on the developmental curriculum scale. For instance, a teacher might judge a third grade student as handling theme like a first grader, still at the level of mundane morals.

The journal in the middle of the logbook provides space for the teacher to record ongoing information relevant to student performance: observations, informal assessments of student activities and projects, and questions requiring further thought and action. The notes are a natural place for comments about student portfolio entries, along with more formal assessments. Curriculum planning ends the logbook. These entries, unlike routinized "lesson plans," reflect long-term working plans organized by curriculum goals, with room for commentary and revision.

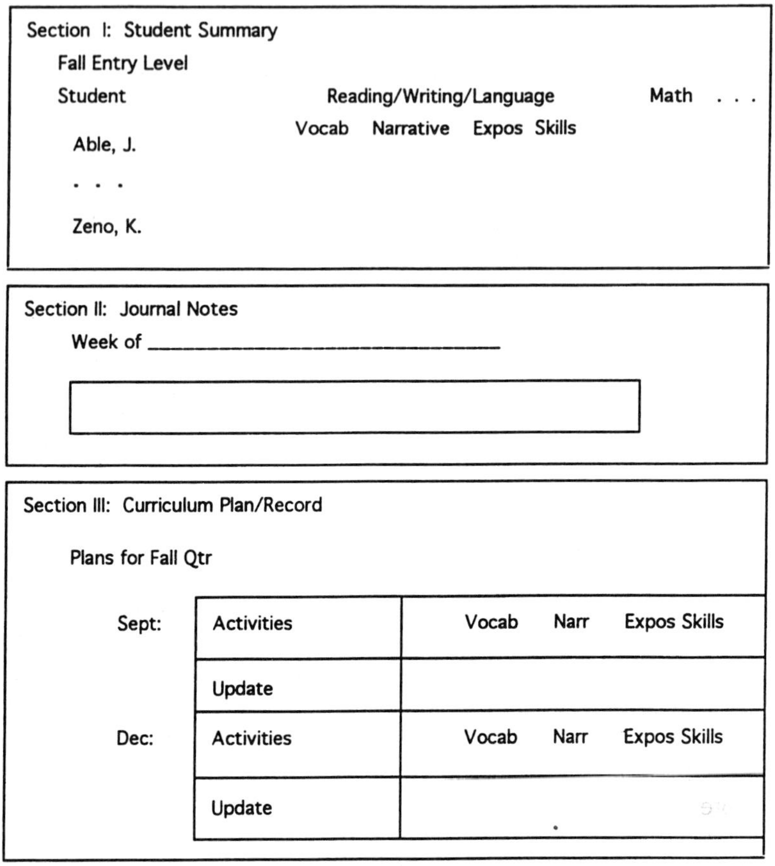

Section I: Student Summary
Fall Entry Level

Student	Reading/Writing/Language				Math ...
	Vocab	Narrative	Expos	Skills	
Able, J.					
. . .					
Zeno, K.					

Section II: Journal Notes
Week of _____

Section III: Curriculum Plan/Record

Plans for Fall Qtr

Sept:	Activities	Vocab	Narr	Expos Skills
	Update			
Dec:	Activities	Vocab	Narr	Expos Skills
	Update			

FIGURE I
The teacher logbook.

The logbook concept builds on the notion that the teacher, with a developmental curriculum in mind, regularly records brief notes about individual students in the "profile" section. The comments provide a concrete record for reflection and action. An empty profile sheet is a reminder that the student has slipped from sight. A sheet showing a long list of "books read" but with no evidence of written work is a prod to encourage the student to put his or her thoughts on paper. Teachers often keep mental records of this sort; the logbook acts as a "memory jogger," a basis for reflection and assessment.

The logbook also offers a basis to address issues of validity and reliability through *panel judgment*. Much like Olympic judges, classroom teachers can validate their evaluations through cross-checks (another application of "moderation"). Technically, the panel judgment process is a special instance of generalizability theory (Shavelson & Webb, 1991).

The logbook means a change in teaching practice. As noted earlier, alternative classroom assessment often appears in combination with other elements: whole language rather than basal readers, cooperative instruction rather than didactic teacher talk, school-based decision making rather than top-down direction, the teacher as professional rather than as civil servant. Such strategies offer the opportunity for fundamental reform in U.S. schooling. Present-day reform efforts are piecemeal and incoherent, overwhelming teachers with multiple demands. Teacher enthusiasm and commitment in these programs can be impressive, but the high costs and limited benefits are often discouraging. The authentic assessment movement seems likely to falter and fail unless connected to the other elements in a manner that continues to meet internal classroom needs (valid data for instructional decisions) while satisfying external policy demands (reliable information for accountability purposes). The teacher's logbook is a bridge for spanning this chasm. For the logbook to become a reality will require establishment of a serious audience for this activity and provision of adequate professional development.

Absent such support, the movement may eventually fall of its own weight. Selected teachers will continue to rely on their professional judgment for deciding what to teach and how to teach it and for rendering assessments to interested audiences. External authorities may entertain the idea of portfolios, performances, and exhibitions, but cost effectiveness will eventually carry the day, and another chance to improve the quality of schooling in the United States will have slipped through our fingers. There is some reason for optimism. The convergence over the past 50 years of cognitive theory and research, more far-reaching psychometrics, and a renewed understanding of practical professionalism—this convergence should leave us hopeful about the promise of classroom assessment as inquiry.

References

Airaisan, P. (1994). *Classroom assessment*. New York: McGraw-Hill.

Alvermann, D. E., Dillon, D. R., & O'Brien, D. G. (1987). *Using discussion to promote reading comprehension*. Newark, DE: International Reading Association.

American Educational Research Association, American Psychological Association, & National Council of Measurement in Education. (1985). *Standards for educational and psychological testing*. Washington, DC: Author.

American Federation of Teachers, National Council on Measurement in Education, & National Education Association. (1990). Standards for teacher competence in educational assessment of students. *Educational Measurement: Issues and Practice*, 9(4), 30 32.

Baron, J. B., & Wolf, D. P. (Eds.). (1996). *Performance-based student assessment: Toward access, capacity, and coherence*. Chicago: National Society for the Study of Education.

Bean, T. W. (1985). Classroom questioning strategies: Directions for applied research. In A. C. Graesser & J. B. Black (Eds.), *The psychology of questions* (pp. 42–65). Hillsdale, NJ: Erlbaum.

100

Robert C. Calfee and Walter V. Masuda

Belanoff, P., & Dickson, M. (Eds.). (1991). Portfolios: Process and product. Portsmouth, NH: Boynton/ Cook Publishers.

Bridge, C. A., & Hiebert, E. H. (1985). A comparison of classroom writing practices, teachers' perceptions of their writing instruction, and textbook recommendations on writing practices. Elementary School Journal, 86, 155–172.

Brookhart S. M. (1994). Teachers' grading: Practice and theory. Applied Measurement in Education, 7, 279–301.

Brown, A. L., Campione, J. C., & Day, J. D. (1981). Learning to learn: On training students to learn from text. Educational Researcher, 10, 14–21.

Bruer, J. T. (1993). Schools for thought. Cambridge, MA: MIT Press.

Calfee, R. C. (1985). Experimental methods in psychology. New York: Holt, Rinehart, & Winston.

Calfee, R. C. (1987). The school as a context for assessment of literacy. The Reading Teacher, 40, 738–743.

Calfee, R. C. (1994). Critical literacy: Reading and writing for a new millennium. In N. J. Ellsworth, C. N. Hedley, & A. N. Baratta (Eds.), Literacy: A redefinition (pp. 19–38). Hillsdale, NJ: Erlbaum.

Calfee, R. C. (1995). Implications of cognitive psychology for authentic assessment and instruction. In T. Oakland & R. Hambleton (Eds.), International perspectives on academic assessment (pp. 25–48). Boston: Kluwer Academic Publishers.

Calfee, R. C. (in press). Assessing the development and learning of literacy over time. In J. Flood, D. Lapp, & S. B. Heath (Eds.), Handbook for literacy educators; Research on teaching the communicative and visual arts. New York: Macmillan.

Calfee, R. C., & Calfee, K. H. (1976). Reading and mathematics observation system: Description and measurement of time usage in the classroom. Journal of Teacher Education, 27.

Calfee, R. C., & Drum, P. (1979). How the researcher can help the reading teacher with classroom assessment. In L. B. Resnick & P. A. Weaver (Eds.), Theory and practice of early reading (pp. 173–205). Hillsdale, NJ: Erlbaum.

Calfee, R. C., Dunlap, K. L., & Wat, A. Y. (1994). Authentic discussion of texts in middle grade schooling: An analytic-narrative approach. Journal of Reading, 37, 1–14.

Calfee, R. C., & Hiebert, E. H. (1991). Classroom assessment of reading. In R. Barr, M. Kamil, P. Mosenthal, & P. D. Pearson (Eds.), Handbook of research on reading (2nd ed , pp. 281–309). New York: Longman.

Calfee, R. C., Kapinus, B., & Pearson, P. D. (1996). Validation practice and policy in the use of less-than-fully-standardized methods for large-scale assessment. Washington, DC: Council of Chief State School Officers.

Calfee, R. C., & Patrick, C. P. (1995). Teach our children well. Stanford, CA: The Portable Stanford Book Series.

Calfee, R. C., & Perfumo, P. (1993). Student portfolios: Opportunities for a revolution in assessment. Journal of Reading, 36, 532–537.

Calfee, R. C., & Perfumo, P. (Eds.). (1996). Writing portfolios: Policy and practice. Hillsdale, NJ: Erlbaum.

Calfee, R. C., & Venezky, R. L. (1969). Component skills in beginning reading. In K. S. Goodman & J. T. Fleming (Eds.), Psycholinguistics and the teaching of reading. (pp. 91–110). Newark, DE: International Reading Association.

California Assessment Program Staff. (1989). Authentic assessment in California. Educational Leadership, 46(7), 6.

Cazden, C. (1988). Classroom discourse. Portsmouth, NH: Heinemann.

Cizek, G. J., Rachor, R. E., & Fitzgerald, S. M. (in press). Teachers' assessment practices: Preparation, isolation, and the kitchen sink. Educational Assessment.

Cochran-Smith, M., & Lytle, S. L. (1993). Inside outside: Teacher research and knowledge. New York: Teacher's College Press.

Cole, N. (1988). A realist's appraisal of the prospects for unifying instruction and assessment. In C. V. Bunderson (Ed.), Assessment in the service of learning (pp. 103–117). Princeton, NJ: Educational Testing Service.

Creswell, J. W. (1994). Research design: Qualitative and quantitative approaches. Thousand Oaks, CA: Sage Pub.

Cronbach, L. J. (1960). *Essentials of psychological testing.* New York: Harper Collins.
Cronbach, L. J. (1988). Five perspectives on the validity argument. In H. Wainer & H. Braun (Eds.), *Test validity* (pp. 3–17). Hillsdale, NJ: Erlbaum.
Darling-Hammond, L., Ancess, J., & Falk, B. (1995). *Authentic assessment in action.* New York: Teachers College Press.
Darling-Hammond, L., & Godwin, A. L. (1993). Progress toward professionalism in teaching. In G. Cawelti (Ed.), *Challenges and achievements in American education* (pp. 19–52). Alexandria, VA: Association for Supervision and Curriculum Development.
Drummond, M. J., & Pollard, A. (1988). *Assessing children's learning.* London: David Fulton.
Educational Testing Service. (1995). *Performance assessment: Difficult needs, difficult answers.* Princeton, NJ: Author.
Eisner, E. W. (1995). Standards for American schools. *Phi Delta Kappan, 76,* 758–764.
Farr, R., & Tone, B. (1994). *Portfolios and performance assessment.* San Antonio, TX: Harcourt Brace.
Fraatz, J. M. B. (1987). *The politics of reading.* New York: Teachers College Press.
Freedman, S. W. (1993). Linking large-scale testing and classroom portfolio assessments of student writing. *Educational Assessment, 1,* 27–52.
Glaser, R., & Silver, E. (1994). Assessment, testing, and instruction: Retrospect and prospect. *Review of Research in Education, 20,* 393–419.
Graesser, A. C., Lang, K., & Horgan, D. (1988). A taxonomy for question generation. *Questioning Exchange, 2,* 3–16.
Hambleton, R. K. (in press). Advances in assessment models, methods, and practices. In D. A. Berliner & R. C. Calfee (Eds.), *The handbook of educational psychology.* New York: Macmillan.
Harlen, W. (Ed.). (1994). *Enhancing quality in assessment.* London: Paul Chapman Publishing.
Harp, B. (1991). *Assessment and evaluation in whole language programs.* Norwood, MA: Christopher-Gordon Publishers.
Herman, J. L., Aschbacher, P. R., & Winters, L. (1992). *A practical guide to alternative assessment.* Alexandria, VA: Association for Supervision and Curriculum Development.
Hiebert, E. H., & Calfee, R. C. (1992). Assessment of literacy: From standardized tests to performances and portfolios. In A. E. Farstrup and S. J. Samuels (Eds.), *What research says about reading instruction* (pp. 70–100). Newark, DE: International Reading Association.
Jaeger, R. M. (1988). *Complementary methods for research in education.* Washington, DC: American Educational Research Association.
Johnston, P. H. (1984). Assessment in reading. In P. D. Pearson (Ed.), *Handbook of reading research* (pp. 147–182). New York: Longman.
Kane, M. B., & Mitchell, R. (Eds.). (in press). *Implementing performance assessment: Promises, problems, and challenges.* Hillsdale, NJ: Erlbaum.
Klimenkoff, M., & Lapick, N. (1996). Promoting student self-assessment through portfolios, student-facilitated conferences, and cross-age interaction. In R. C. Calfee, & P. Perfumo (Eds.), *Writing portfolios: Policy and practice.* Hillsdale, NJ: Erlbaum.
Koretz, D., Stecher, B., Klein, S., & McCaffrey, D. (1994). The Vermont portfolio assessment program: Findings and implications. *Educational Measurement: Issues and Practice,* 13(2), 3–16.
LeMahieu, P. G., Gitomer, D. H., & Eresh, J. T. (1995). Portfolios in large-scale assessment: Difficult but not impossible. *Educational Measurement: Issues and Practice,* 14(3), 11–16, 25–28.
Lidz, C. (Ed.). (1987). *Dynamic assessment: An interactional approach to evaluating learning potential.* New York: Guilford Press.
Martin-Kneip, G. O., Thornburg, D. G., & Cookson, P. W., Jr. (1994). The politics of assessment: Local, state, and national perspectives [Special issue]. *Educational Policy,* 8.
McLaughlin, M. W., & Shepard, L. A. (1995). *Improving education through standards-based reform.* Stanford, CA: National Academy of Education.
Mehrens, W. A., & Kaminski, J. (1989). Methods for improving standardized achievement tests: Fruitful, fruitless, or fraudulent. *Educational Measurement: Issues and Practice,* 8, 14–22.
Messick, S. (1995). Validity of psychological assessment: Validation of inferences from persons' responses and performances as scientific inquiry into score meaning. *American Psychologist,* 50, 741–749.

Mitchell, R. (1992). *Testing for learning: How new approaches to evaluation can improve American Schools.* New York: Free Press.

Moss, P. A. (1995). Themes and variations in validity theory. *Educational Measurement: Issues and Practice,* 14(2), 5–13.

Murphy, S., & Smith, M. A. (1990). Talking about portfolios. *Quarterly of the National Writing Project and the Center for the Study of Writing,* 12(1), 1–3, 24–27.

National Council for Measurement in Education. (1995). *Code of professional responsibilities in educational measurement.* Washington, DC: Author.

National Forum on Assessment. (1995). *Principles and indicators for student assessment systems.* Cambridge, MA: National Center for Fair and Open Testing (FairTest).

Nystrand, M., & Gamoran, A. (1991). Instructional discourse, student engagement, and literature achievement. *Research in the Teaching of English,* 25, 261–290.

Office of Technology Assessment. (1992). *Testing in American schools: Asking the right questions* (OTA–SET–519). Washington, DC: U.S. Government Printing Office.

Paratore, J. R. (1995). Assessing literacy: Establishing common standards in portfolio assessment. *Topics in Language Disorders,* 16(1), 67–82.

Paris, S. G., Turner, J. C., & Lawton, T. A. (1991). A developmental perspective on standardized achievement testing. *Educational Researcher,* 20(5), 12–20.

Pashley, P., & Phillips, G. W. (1993). *Toward world-class standards: Linking international and national assessments.* Princeton, NJ: Educational Testing Service.

Pelavin, S. (1995). *Performance assessments in the states.* Washington, DC: Pelavin Associates.

Popham, J. (1995). *Classroom assessment: What teachers need to know.* Boston: Allyn & Bacon.

Resnick, L. B. (1987). *Education and learning to think.* Washington, DC: Academy Press.

Resnick, L. B., & Resnick, D. P. (1992). Assessing the thinking curriculum: New tools for educational reform. In B. R. Gifford & M. C. O'Connor (Eds.), *Changing assessments: Alternative views of aptitude, achievement, and instruction* (pp. 37–75). Boston: Kluwer Academic.

Rosenholz, S. J. (1989). *Teachers' workplace.* White Plains, NY: Longman.

Shavelson, R. J., & Webb, N. M. (1991). *Generalizability theory: A primer.* Newbury Park, CA: Sage.

Shepard, L. A. (1995). Using assessment to improve learning. *Educational Leadership,* 52(5), 38–43.

Shuell, T. J. (1988). The role of the student in learning from instruction. *Contemporary Educational Psychology,* 13, 276–295.

Stephens, D., Pearson, P. D., Gilrane, C., Roe, M., Stallman, A. C., Shelton, J., Weinzierl, J., Rodriguez, A., & Commeyras, M. (1995). Assessment and decision making in schools: A cross-site analysis. *Reading Research Quarterly,* 30(3), 478–499.

Stiggins, R. J. (1994). *Student-centered classroom assessment.* New York: Merrill.

Stiggins, R. J., & Conklin, N. F. (1992). *In teachers' hands: Investigating the practices of classroom assessment.* Albany: State University of New York Press.

Tierney R. J., Carter, M. A., & Desai, L. E. (1991). *Portfolio assessment in the reading-writing classroom.* Norwood, MA: Christopher-Gordon Publishers.

Tittle, C. K. (1994). Toward an educational psychology of assessment for teaching and learning: Theories, contexts, and validation arguments. *Educational Psychologist,* 29, 149–162.

Tuman, M. (1987). *A preface to literacy: An inquiry into pedagogy, practice, and progress.* University: University of Alabama Press.

Valencia, S. W., Hiebert, E. H., & Afflerbach, P. P. (Eds.). (1994). *Authentic reading assessment: Practices and possibilities.* Newark, DE: International Reading Association.

Wiggins, G. P. (1993). *Assessing student performance.* San Francisco: Jossey-Bass.

Winograd, P. (1994). Developing alternative assessments: Six problems worth solving. *Reading Teacher,* 47, 420–423.

CHAPTER

5

Classroom Assessment of Reasoning Strategies

EDYS QUELLMALZ
SRI *International*

JANITA HOSKYN
University of Arkansas, Little Rock

INTRODUCTION

Classroom teachers face the daunting, yet challenging task of guiding their students' growth in an ever-increasing array of domains. At the heart of most educational reform efforts in curriculum, instruction, and assessment are the principles of constructivist, meaning-centered learning; that is, authentic contexts for learning, student-centered and project-based curricula, and in-depth study of challenging content. Effective classroom practices place the teacher in the role of coach, facilitator, and guide, rather than director, lecturer, and fount of all knowledge. With the paradigm shift to constructivist principles, coupled with the widespread recognition of the exponential explosion of knowledge, it is no wonder that the focus of schooling has shifted from the acquisition of knowledge to the command of strategic reasoning. Indeed, Goal 3 of the National Education Goals proposes that American schools will ensure that all students learn to use their minds well and demonstrate competency in challenging subject matter (National Education Goals Panel, 1993). Only by being able to identify, access, and apply information in ever-expanding and changing domains will the students of today be equipped to function as the citizens of tomorrow.

Handbook of Classroom Assessment
Copyright © 1997 by Academic Press, Inc. All rights of reproduction in any form reserved.

In this chapter, we address a key challenge confronting classroom teachers: how to employ systematic, sound methods to monitor and assess the growth of their students' reasoning strategies. We draw upon the experience we have had over the past 10 years with programs designed to promote higher-order thinking. Many of our examples come from the Multicultural Reading and Thinking Program (McRAT), a statewide program supported by the Arkansas Department of Education (Quellmalz & Hoskyn, 1988). We have organized the chapter into seven sections: (1) a brief overview of some frameworks proposed for characterizing strategic reasoning, (2) applications of a framework we have used, (3) general guidelines for sound measurement of reasoning strategies, (4) classroom examples of assessments of student reasoning, (5) guidelines for providing professional development and support to schools, (6) approaches for evaluating thinking curricula, and (7) a look ahead at ways in which technology can support the assessment of reasoning strategies.

SOME COMMON CONCEPTUALIZATIONS OF PROBLEM SOLVING AND CRITICAL THINKING

The disciplines of psychology and philosophy have contributed the basic paradigms of problem solving and critical thinking. Psychologists have studied the underlying cognitive operations individuals employ as they engage in the *process* of implementing reasoning strategies to address academic, practical, or novel problems. Philosophers have focused on the features and the *products* of critical thinking. Although the literature within these fields uses different terminology, careful comparison of the concepts of critical thinking, inquiry, and problem solving reveals substantial overlap.

Psychological research on problem solving has revealed that the cognitive processes of analysis, comparison, induction, and deduction are called on as individuals identify the nature of a problem, access appropriate information, connect and use information to solve the problem, and evaluate their success. This problem solving model seems to hold for generalized problem solving as well as for domain-specific tasks (Bransford & Stein, 1984; Chi, Glaser, & Rees, 1982; Newell & Simon, 1976).

In the field of philosophy, John Dewey defined the reflective thinker as one who carefully and persistently examines an action, proposal, or belief and uses knowledge to test consequences and possible solutions (Dewey, 1933). Robert Ennis has classified critical thinking into skill clusters that involve clarifying issues and terms, identifying components of arguments, judging the credibility of evidence, using inductive and deductive reasoning, handling argument fallacies, and making value judgments. Ennis defines critical thinking as reasonable and reflective thinking focused on deciding what to believe and do (Ennis, 1987).

These fundamental views of reasoning have been applied in educational practice. For example, Bloom's taxonomy was developed to place educational test items and objectives into a hierarchy (Bloom, 1971). Polya has advanced a conceptual model of problem solving in mathematics that is widely used in mathematics curricula. He proposed four stages in which problem solvers begin by understanding the problem, then move to devising a plan, carrying out the plan, and finally, looking back and extending the problem to other contexts (Polya, 1957). Resnick and Klopfer (1989) have proposed "the thinking curriculum" where concepts are continually at work in the contexts of reasoning and problem solving. Both philosophy and psychology, regardless of the terminology used, seem to reference a basic set of underlying cognitive and meta-cognitive operations that students must use to apply reasoning to build new knowledge structures.

A FRAMEWORK OF REASONING STRATEGIES

If we hope to teach students to develop generalized and specialized reasoning strategies, we must provide a coherent framework that will help them understand how these general and specific strategies relate to each other and how they can be brought to bear on academic and practical tasks. A framework for assessing reasoning in classrooms should meet the following criteria:

- The strategies are common to numerous conceptualizations of problem solving and critical thinking proposed by eminent psychologists, philosophers, and educators.
- The strategies have clear applications to academic, practical, and novel situations.
- There are a manageable number of strategies.
- The strategies are referred to by terms that can be clearly understood by students and the lay public.
- The strategies can be placed in a coherent framework (Quellmalz, 1985).

In this chapter we present a reasoning strategies framework that has been employed over the past decade in a series of curriculum and assessment programs (Quellmalz, 1987; 1991). The framework serves as a heuristic for planning and implementing such programs. Figure 1 presents a definition of reasoning that merges the research-based problem-solving cognitive and meta-cognitive processes identified in psychological research with the conceptual analyses of formal and informal logical reasoning proposed in critical thinking paradigms by philosophers. Research from cognitive psychology emphasizes goal-directed problem solving and sustained reasoning in significant complex, authentic tasks. Philosophers' models contribute criteria for judging if reasoning is valid and well done.

Strategic reasoning involves the deliberate deployment of fundamental cognitive and meta-cognitive/self-monitoring strategies to solve a problem or accomplish a task. Strategic reasoning occurs when students engage in purposeful, extended lines of thought during which they

- Analyze the problem's or task's essential components and terms.
- Compare the task or assignment to problem types or schema they have addressed previously.
- Gather and connect relevant information and attempt solutions.
- Monitor and evaluate the adequacy of information and procedures for drawing conclusions and/or solving the problem.

The most commonly identified, fundamental cognitive operations and meta-cognitive strategies are

Cognitive Strategies	Meta-cognitive Strategies
Analyze	Plan
Compare	Draft and tryout
Infer, interpret, apply	Monitor and revise
Evaluate	Evaluate and reflect

FIGURE I

Definition of strategic reasoning.

Each of the *cognitive strategies* represent basic ways that we process and use information:

1. *Analysis* involves dividing a whole into its distinctive elements and understanding the relationship of the parts to the whole.
2. *Comparison* involves identifying similarities and differences and understanding their overall significance.
3. *Inference and interpretation* involve use of various forms of inductive and deductive reasoning, including applications of rules or heuristics to reach a conclusion or solve a problem.
4. *Evaluation* involves making judgments about what to believe or do based on explicit criteria and supporting evidence.

Meta-cognitive strategies are defined as self-conscious, deliberate ways that skilled individuals deploy and monitor their reasoning strategies as problems are initiated, attempted, solved, and reflected on. Meta-cognitive strategies are not used in a lockstep, linear sequence, they are used recursively as strategies for meeting goals or solving problems are attempted. Typically, effective problem solvers are aware of and can explain what they intend to do, what they are doing, how the strategies seem to be working, if the strategies accomplished the goal, and if the approach would be an effective way to address similar problems in the future.

1. *Planning* involves analysis of a problem, comparison of its elements to previously encountered problems and identification of potentially suitable strategies for addressing the problem.
2. *Drafting and trying out* typically involve a series of attempts to apply strategies to solve a problem or fulfill an assignment.
3. *Monitoring and revising* are interim checks and adjustments to see if sub-goals are being met and if attempted strategies are approaching a solution.
4. *Evaluation and reflection* involve looking back at the adequacy of a solution to a particular problem or task as well as self-appraisal of the efficiency and effectiveness of the strategies or approaches used.

These cognitive and meta-cognitive strategies are fundamental, recurring forms of reasoning used to address significant, authentic, complex problems in academic disciplines and practical situations. The strategies have been identified in studies of the performance of skilled individuals and experts in various domains. Unskilled individuals, on the other hand, often do not employ strategic reasoning. Moreover, they may not be aware of how to monitor their own progress, identify difficulties, or activate alternative strategies. The framework is not meant to denote a hierarchy since the nature of the problem to which the strategies are applied will dictate the difficulty level of the task.

EXAMPLES OF REASONING STRATEGIES IN CONTENT DOMAINS AND IN PRACTICAL SITUATIONS

The four categories of reasoning strategies are fundamental "ways of knowing" in academic subject domains and also in our daily lives. Table 1 presents some examples of familiar, significant reasoning activities in such domains.

For example, analysis of the major elements of any story—its plot, characters, setting, and theme—is a major factor in understanding and appreciating narratives portrayed in novels, on television, or in movies. In social science, many discussions of current or historical events begin with analyses of key political, economic, and social elements of those events. In practical situations, analysis of the important features of a product is a key component of shopping and purchasing.

Comparison is a fundamental activity in appreciating different cultures or historical periods or in tracing changes in climate or fossil records. Comparison shopping is a key activity in most contemporary cultures. Interpretations of literature, applications of problem solving strategies, predictions of trends, or tests of hypotheses are central forms of inquiry. Evaluation, that

TABLE 1

Examples of Reasoning Strategies in Four Content Domains and Practical Application

Reasoning strategy	Domain				
	Literacy	Social Science	Science	Mathematics	Practical application
Analyze	Narrative Story elements Plot events Character traits Setting Style Persuasive issue Position Reasons Evidence Conclusion Expository Main idea Support and elaboration Organization and coherence Style	Narrative Elements of an event Features of a culture Features of a historical period	Components of a process Features of animate and inanimate objects Evolution of species	Problem components Solution steps and strategies	Elements of television programs Elements of current event Features of consumer products Ingredients of food products
Compare	Narrative elements Themes Points of view Evidence Accuracy Organization	Leaders Cultures Political systems Ideologies Time periods Accounts of an event	Regions Climates Scientific processes Energy sources Habitats Ecosystems	Problem types Operations Strategies Estimates Results	TV programs Political candidates Athletic teams Job offers Health plans Restaurants
Infer and interpret	Themes Motivation Mood Bias Predict cause and effect	Causes and influences Predict future effects Infer consequences	Test hypotheses Draw conclusions Infer consequences Link cause and effect Interdependencies	Apply procedures and strategies Plan strategies Trial and error Estimate Interpret data	Infer movie themes Balance personal budget Predict people's behavior
Evaluate	Significance Coherence Clarity Style Believability	Significance of contributions Practicality Credibility of arguments Alternative interpretations	Soundness of scientific procedures Credibility of conclusions Significance of findings Feasibility Impact	Adequacy of solution Effectiveness of strategies Efficiency of "elegant" solution	Quality of a book TV program or movie Choose a job Vote for a candidate or proposal Choose a diet plan Choose the best product to purchase Evaluate environmental impact

is, determining worth and quality, employs criteria and standards to judge excellence and inform decisions about what to believe and do.

Meta-cognitive strategies are also becoming goals in academic instruction. Research on skilled writers, for example, has illuminated the effectiveness of writing processes such as planning, drafting, and revising. Reading research has revealed differences in the meta-cognitive strategies used by mature and immature readers before, during, and after reading. Before reading, mature readers understand the task and set a purpose, activate prior knowledge, and choose appropriate strategies. In contrast, poor readers start reading without knowing why, without preparation, and without considering how to approach the material. During reading, good readers focus their attention, monitor their comprehension, use fix-up strategies when lack of understanding occurs, and use text structure to assist comprehension. Unskilled readers, on the other hand, are easily distracted, do not know they do not understand, read to get done, and add on rather than integrate new information (Wisconsin Department of Public Instruction, 1988).

Meta-cognitive strategies are also the key features of Polya's conceptual model for problem solving (Polya, 1957). Polya proposed four stages: (1) understanding the problem, when students analyze the problem elements, the information needed and given, and venture guesses about the solution; (2) devising a plan, when students consider if the problem is similar to one solved before (comparison) and consider what problem solving strategies such as diagrams, manipulatives, or looking for patterns might help; (3) carrying out the plan, when students implement the plan and try alternative strategies; (4) looking back and extending, when students evaluate whether their answer is reasonable, close to an estimate, or could have been solved in other ways.

IMPLICATIONS FOR ASSESSMENT

Once a reasoning framework with a manageable number of strategies to teach and assess has been identified, teachers need to specify the types of curricular activities and related assessment tasks that will require use of the strategies. We make the following recommendations for the design of assessments of reasoning strategies:

1. *Present problems or tasks that represent important, recurring issues or activities.* In the subject domains, these would be items and assessment tasks that would ask for understanding and interpreting literature, historical and contemporary events, life and physical science, and uses of mathematics and problem solving. The examples in Table 1 and the content standards proposed for academic subject areas offer some possibilities. Such tasks should be both significant and authentic.

2. *Emphasize purposeful, sustained, reasoning that requires integration of reasoning strategies rather than demonstration of discrete, isolated skills.* Complex questions might ask for analysis and evaluation of a text rather than identification of one idea or element. Mathematical tasks could ask for problem solving rather than strings of unrelated computations.

3. *Develop assessment tasks that permit multiple interpretations or solutions, rather than one right answer.* In mathematics, nonroutine problems would permit multiple approaches and solutions. Social science issues should permit alternative points of view and conclusions.

4. *Present formats that elicit explanation and demonstrations of inquiry processes, not just the answer.* When students show their work and explain their reasoning, teachers can assess strengths and weaknesses.

5. *Present assessment tasks and problems that represent a range of generalization and transfer.* The goal is to build capacity, so assessments must measure applications to previously unencountered problems.

6. *Assess reasoning strategies directly, not as undifferentiated components of a more complex solution.* To rate performance on a task as "acceptable" will not identify strengths and weaknesses of reasoning or content knowledge.

7. *Assess meta-cognitive strategies for planning, revision, and self-evaluation.* If being strategic means being effective, teachers should deliberately promote and assess these strategies.

General Assessment Approaches

Classroom assessments may be designed to serve quite different purposes, from accountability to ongoing monitoring. Assessments may be formal paper–pencil tests and performance assessment tasks or informal progress checks that rely on teacher questioning, observation, running records, or assessment of portfolio entries and work in progress. Distinctions have been made among assessment approaches that are on-demand, curriculum embedded, portfolio based, or exhibitions. *On-demand assessments* tend to be formal and less frequent, as summative evaluations of a year of study. Often, on-demand assessments are for accountability purposes and may not have been developed within the school. Writing assessments administered each year by the state are examples of on-demand assessment. In the McRAT program, students write pre- and postunit essays requiring analysis, comparison, inference, or evaluation. Recently, the McRAT program has administered an *integrated assessment* at the beginning and end of the school year. In these assessments, students read a story, analyze its elements, compare a specified element (e.g., characters), develop an inference or interpretation (e.g., character trait, theme), and evaluate an issue.

Curriculum-embedded assessments tend to occur during or at the end of units of study. They are intended to link up closely with instruction and are often devised by teachers in the school. For example, throughout a unit on the industrial revolution, students in a high school history class were asked to record evidence and reasons to support whether the Carnegies and Rockefellers were captains of industry or robber-barons. The students' final assignment was to write an essay supporting their position. In a sixth grade McRAT class, students were asked to write an essay evaluating the benefits and hardships of being an immigrant in the United States.

Portfolio assessments appraise samples of student work produced in the course of a project or unit or for an entire school year. Assessments of portfolios are often devised by teachers and students in whose classrooms the portfolios are used. In a fourth grade unit on the California Gold Rush, for instance, one student portfolio entry assessed was a chart analyzing the physical, economic, social, and psychological conditions experienced by the Forty-Niners. Another entry assessed was a chart comparing these conditions before and after the Forty-Niners came to California. The culminating portfolio entry was an essay evaluating whether the hardships the Forty-Niners endured were worth the gains. In Alaska, the Juneau School District has developed a first grade language arts portfolio that collects reading samples (one per quarter) accompanied by a "reading record sheet," a reading attitude survey, two writing samples per quarter, a speaking–listening skills checklist (one per quarter), teacher anecdotal observations, oral language cassette tapes, developmental spelling lists, reading logs, and drawings and illustrations (one per quarter) selected by the student.

Exhibitions are typically designed as culminating, summative demonstrations of accomplishment. For example, seniors in the Sullivan High School in Chicago, a member of the Coalition of Essential Schools, are required to demonstrate their ability to engage thoughtfully with difficult texts by participating successfully in a 90-minute seminar on several such texts, then writing an acceptable essay on the ideas embedded in the texts (McDonald, 1992).

Assessment Formats

Classroom teachers may draw on a number of assessment formats to measure student progress. Teachers may use *selected-response formats* such as multiple choice, true–false, and matching. Selected-response formats tend to pose questions or problems of limited scope and have one right answer. Their advantage is that they can efficiently assess a large body of factual knowledge such as the stages of photosynthesis and respiration or the names of internal organs. Selected response formats can also assess reasoning if questions reference a finite body of information that supports clearly determined answers. A multiple-choice question could ask for identification of one way in which photosynthesis and respiration are similar. Developers of selected-response items intended to measure reasoning must confirm that the answer sought must be figured out by the student and does not simply require recall of information provided in material studied. Thus, a question asking how human rights compare to legal rights will not require comparative reasoning if the comparison was explained in a textbook so that students need only recall someone else's thinking.

Open-ended formats ask students to construct answers of varying lengths, from short answers to full essays. Open-ended formats allow for multiple correct responses or interpretations. Open-ended formats can also ask for explanations of reasoning. Since answers will vary, criteria for acceptable responses must be specified and applied consistently by judges (teachers, students, and others). In the McRAT program, students frequently infer character traits. Short answer, open-ended questions might ask for one or two actions of the character that would indicate he was persistent. More extended open-ended questions might ask for identification of a character's action and an explanation of why it indicated that she was brave. In one McRAT class, students were asked to infer character traits that helped Karana in *The Island of the Blue Dolphins* to survive.

Performance assessment tasks tend to pose complex problems, projects, or investigations that require students to engage in sustained reasoning in which they construct solutions and explanations. Typically, alternative solutions or interpretations are accepted and expected. Performance assessments may elicit student responses in the forms of written essays, graphic or visual displays, oral presentations, or multimedia demonstrations and performances. Teachers may assess student behaviors and products as students work on a task or project. Planned observations, oral questions, and running records have been used to record student behavior systematically. Both student behavior and work need to be assessed by applying specific criteria or guidelines that reference the features and quality levels of desired responses. In a mathematics class, McRAT students were asked to infer the characteristics of a "typical seventh grade student" by developing, analyzing and interpreting a survey conducted with all seventh graders in the school. Students worked in small groups to collect and analyze the data, draw conclusions, and report their findings. This was followed by an evaluation of the effectiveness of the survey. Throughout the project, the teacher assessed assignments and involved students in evaluations of their own work. As another example, the integrated assessments used in the McRAT program are formal performance assessment tasks of reading, thinking, and writing. In some literacy programs, running records are used by teachers to document periodically students' development along a continuum from "emergent" to "independent" in the areas of talking and listening, reading, and writing.

In accord with the movement toward stressing depth of understanding over breadth of coverage, open-ended and performance-based assessments tend to be favored for assessing reasoning strategies, especially for classroom-level monitoring and feedback. Multiple methods are likely to provide a range of evidence for judging students' progress in developing reasoning strategies as well as the basic skills that support them.

DEVELOPING CLASSROOM ASSESSMENTS OF REASONING STRATEGIES

Planning Classroom Assessments

Reasoning strategies should be enfolded into the year-long goals of instructional programs. Resnick and Klopfer (1989) assert that, in a thinking curriculum, "there is no choice between a content emphasis and a thinking skill emphasis. No depth in either is possible without the other" (Resnick & Klopfer, 1989, p. 10). To assess students' progress, teachers should work together to develop plans for assessing curricular goals. Teams of teachers can both provide common standards for their grade levels and collaborate on the design and development of the assessments they will use in their classrooms. Teacher teams can also work together to judge with consistency the quality of samples of students work, analyze assessment results, and consider their implications for instruction.

An approach many teachers have found useful is to develop an assessment planning chart for a unit like the one in Table 2 (Stiggins, Rubel, & Quellmalz, 1986). We recommend that a teacher team begin by developing a chart for a familiar unit taught each year. It might be on stories, skeletal structures, or the Westward movement. The sample chart includes recall in addition to each of the four reasoning strategies: analyze, compare, infer and interpret, and evaluate. The assessment formats are selected response, open-ended, teacher questions and observations, and performance assessment. The teacher team may begin by listing the key content addressed in the unit. Key content in a unit on stories, for example, might be the story elements—plot, character, setting, and theme. Key content of the skeletal structures unit might be the structures of bones and the movements or functions they permit. Key content of the Westward movement might be economic, social, and geographical conditions in the East and in the West.

Once the key content of the unit has been specified, teachers can begin the finding or creating assessment questions and tasks that would measure reasoning about key concepts. We recommend that teacher teams begin by searching existing assessment resources in texts, project materials, and published tests for promising questions and tasks designed to measure the unit content. By classifying these assessment questions and tasks into the categories of reasoning strategies, the teacher team can determine what additional questions and tasks still need to be developed. Sets of selected-response and open-ended questions, teacher oral questions and observations can assess component strategies and content. More sustained,

TABLE 2

Assessment Planning Chart for Grade Level 9 Social Studies Unit on Tools and Technology

	Selected response	Open-Ended	Teacher questions observations	Performance task
Recall	Match the name of the tool to its use.	How did they preserve meat?	How did they prepare food?	The shipwreck problem
Analysis	Which tool was needed to make clothing?	What tools are necessary for hunting?	What food sources did not require tools?	You can't take them all. Which tools and supplies do you need most? Why?
Comparison	What is one way their heating methods are like ours?	How did their ways to store food compare to ours?	Compare their building methods to ours.	
Inference	What would happen if . . .	Why do you use more tools than Gahno?	What are the advantages of modern tools?	
Evaluation	Which tool would be best for making arrows?	Which invention was most important? Why?	Which food preparation is healthiest?	

complex performance assessment tasks and projects can assess integration of components. Development of an assessment planning chart will stimulate teachers on the team to agree on how the reasoning strategies about key content will be measured.

Sample Assessments of Reasoning and Meta-cognitive Strategies

To implement the assessment plan, the teacher team can proceed to develop assessment questions and formats not found in available sources. In this section, we present examples of assessments that programs have used to assess directly reasoning and meta-cognitive strategies.

Analysis

Questions asking students to identify distinctive features may be as simple as "What are the parts of a plant?" to "What political, economic, religious, and cultural factors were afoot in France prior to the Revolution?" Assessments of reasoning should be asking students to apply the strategies to previously unencountered situations and problems. A particular danger with analysis questions is that students will be asked to identify the features or parts of something (e.g., a butterfly, Cubism, osmosis, a car engine) that they have already been taught, thereby turning the question into one of recall. Assessments of students' ability to *use* any of the reasoning strategies must require that students perform the cognitive operation *themselves*, rather than regurgitate previously presented material. A common misconception is that analysis questions are easy. In fact, the complexity and scope of the phenomena to be analyzed will determine the difficulty level of the question. Analysis of the use of symbolism in a Shakespeare play presents quite a challenge.

Visual mapping techniques are formats particularly well-suited for classroom assessments of analytical reasoning. Outlines, timelines, genealogical charts, diagrams, graphs, pie charts, and flowcharts are tools used in various domains to distill and communicate key ideas, features, and processes. Concept maps are being used to assess the breadth and depth of subject matter knowledge. Mapping formats can be used to assess both analytical reasoning and meta-cognitive planning strategies. A compelling benefit of mapping formats is that they tend to rely less on language and writing fluency, thereby allowing students with a variety of learning styles or limited English proficiency to show what they know.

In literacy curricula, story maps are frequently used to assess children's understanding of story elements. In the world of work, storyboards are used by professionals to plan the key messages of presentations and multimedia products. Figure 2 presents an example of a story map developed by a McRAT

FIGURE 2
Analysis story map (from Quellmalz & Hoskyn, 1988).

student for the story, "Sing Down the Moon." The story map describes the
title of the story, setting, main characters, goal, problem, important epi-
sodes, and the resolution. The use of arrows to signal the progression of
story elements, along with the drawings of clouds, quivers, knives, and ho-
gans provide additional detail about the student's "story comprehension"
and, more important, the student's engagement in the task. Students quickly
adapt and personalize formal story map boxes to "picture" the story. In "The
Sign of the Beaver," for example, a student drew beaver footprints to signal
the progression from one event and story element to the next.

Essays and presentations are assessment formats that can tap an often
neglected dimension of analytical reasoning, the relationship of the parts to
the whole. Simply identifying the parts of something does not provide evi-

Student Version

  Did I name and define what I analyzed?
  Did I name important parts or groups of information about it?
  Did I describe enough information and examples for each group or part?
  Did I explain how the parts relate to the whole and why they are important? So what?

Teacher Version
Evaluative Criteria For Student Responses

Responses	1	2	3	4
1. Names/identifies defines object, idea, event being analyzed	No	Implies	Names	Defines
2. Identifies important and distinctive categories are the categories important? is there a sufficient number of categories?	None	Few	Enough	Sufficient important
3. Describes and explains the attributes within categories how much description and explanation? of how many categories?	None or inaccurate	Few partial	Some enough	Fully developed
4. Explains why and how the categories are significant to the reader or entity being analyzed for how many categories? how clearly, thoroughly?	Not at all	A few somewhat	Some	Well
(Optional)				
5. Organizes categories and descriptions logically	Not at all			For entire paper

FIGURE 3
Rating guides: Analyze.

dence that the interrelationships of form, function, and significance are understood. Studies of literature or ecologies, for example, stress understanding the integration and interdependencies of elements. McRAT students learn to address the question, "so what?" when they perform analyses.

Open-ended questions, essays, mapping formats, and other performance tasks must be assessed by explicit criteria that clearly define the features of desired responses and the range of quality presented in student work. In the McRAT program, we have developed rating criteria for assessing the quality of student's analytical, comparative, inferential, and evaluative reasoning. Figure 3 presents two versions of the rating guides for analytical reasoning—one for use by teachers, the other by the students themselves. The student version engages students in the meta-cognitive activities of self-monitoring and evaluation. In the McRAT program, students may use the rating guides in peer evaluation groups or independently. Teachers can observe student discussions or collect students' written answers to the rating guide questions to assess the students' development of self-evaluation strategies.

Comparison

Educators often also consider comparison a simple task. It depends. The complexity of the entities being compared and the number of features along which they are compared will determine the difficulty of a comparison task. Selected-response formats often ask about only one feature and whether the entities are similar or different on that feature or dimension. However, classroom assessments can use matching, multiple-response formats to allow students to check off a number of features on which two entities are the same or different. For example, the question, "How do the senses of bats and cats differ?" could be a multiple choice question or a checklist of possibilities. We have found that younger students learn comparison strategies most readily when they begin with comparisons of simple phenomena along one or two dimensions. Open-ended formats allow both identification of similar or different features and explanation of reasons for the differences and a response to "So what?" To avoid comparison deteriorating into a laundry list of similarities and differences, the "So what?" question moves students into an explanation of the significance of the comparison. Comparison questions might ask, "How are a news article and an editorial different?" "How did the views of Hamilton and Jefferson differ?" "How do the styles of Surat and Monet differ?" For each comparison, the answer to "So what?" leads the student to explain the importance or consequences.

Mapping formats can be useful for assessing students' identification of similarities and differences. Figure 4 presents a format that has been used in a number of curricular areas. The comparison of two characters was developed by a fourth grade student. The comparison diagrams help students to identify differences and similarities and organize them for inclusion in an essay. This particular format could be used as a standard portfolio entry to assess students' ability to identify similarities and differences between other characters, leaders, countries, animals, or political systems. Classroom assessment of comparison strategies should also gather explanations of the reasons and significance.

Infer

Inference and interpretation strategies require students to gather information or evidence and explain how the body of evidence supports a conclusion. Applications of rules or problem solving approaches also fall in this reasoning category. Selected-response inference questions with one right

Directions: Write the category for comparison in each box.
List differences in outside circles. List likenesses in overlapping circles.

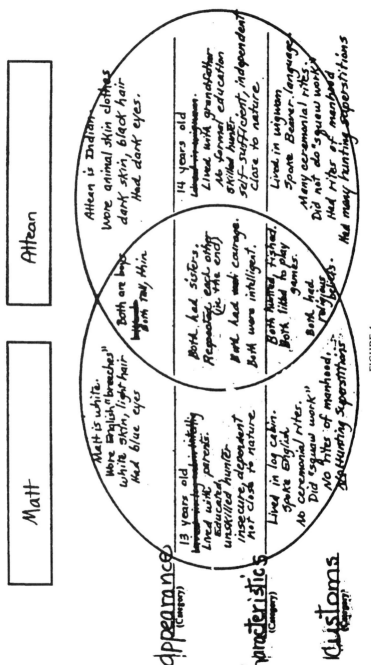

FIGURE 4
Comparison map.

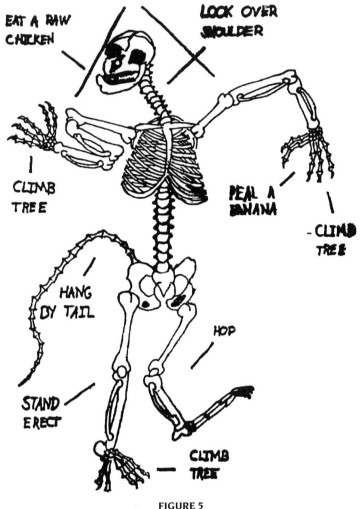

FIGURE 5
Infer: Skeletal structures.

answer need to be carefully constructed. Open-ended formats can be used to collect information about students' progress through the process of developing interpretations and drawing conclusions. For example, students could be asked to prepare a list of citations from a story that would support an interpretation that the mood created was a happy or scary one. In mathematical investigations, students might be presented with a series of questions where they enter data, organize and present them in a graph or chart, and state a conclusion or solution. In science investigations, students might

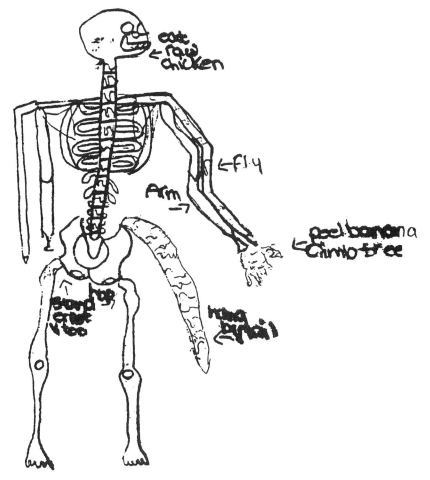

FIGURE 5 (*Continued*)

be asked to develop an hypothesis, collect and enter data, organize and interpret them, and state and defend a conclusion.

Figure 5 presents two drawings of creatures prepared as part of a culminating presentation for a sixth grade science unit on skeletal structures. Students had studied the shapes and functions of bones for several weeks. Their presentation was to draw a picture of the skeleton of a creature who could do certain things. The students named their creatures and made presentations to the class explaining the skeletal formations and movements permitted. At first glance, the two drawings seem vastly different in quality. A closer inspection focusing on the criteria for making appropriate inferences, however, reveals that the student producing the less "well-drawn" picture did, indeed, draw accurate renditions of many of the skeletal structures that would permit the specified movements. Some of the skeletal structures (for climbing a tree and hopping) were not drawn, but those that were, were the correct applications, suggesting a stronger command of inferential reasoning strategies than first seemed apparent.

Figure 6 presents an essay written by a McRAT student in which she proposes a trait that characterizes Karana, the main character in *The Island of the Blue Dolphins*. The student states the trait, provides descriptions of Karana's actions in the story as evidence of the trait, and considers other possible interpretations.

Evaluate

Evaluation incorporates the other reasoning strategies as students analyze evidence, compare competing claims, apply criteria, and arrive at a decision. It is extremely difficult to develop selected-response questions for evaluative judgment. A variety of open-ended formats can provide teachers with evidence of students' command of components of the decision-making process as well as their defense of their final conclusion. Even very young students, with some scaffolding, can bring evidence to bear in support of a position. Figure 7 presents a format used to structure second grade students' planning for a persuasive essay addressing the question of whether all the TV sets in America should be unplugged so that children would be better educated. The planning sheet asked students to select a position (I agree, I disagree). As we can see, this student held a strong position and vehemently eradicated any trace of the other stated position. The planning sheet provided structure, or scaffolding, for the information that should be provided as support; that is, names of specific programs and reasons why they were beneficial or harmful. Students then referred to the planning sheets to write their persuasive essays. By assessing such planning activities, the teacher can determine if students understood how to formulate strong support based on specific evidence and reasons relating it to the position. Similar planning sheets could be used by students evaluating other issues.

Figure 8 presents an essay written by a fifth grade student about the Westward movement. The students were asked to take the role of a pioneer and to evaluate the issue, "Was it worth it?" This question has been used as a "template question" for evaluating the benefits and hardships of pioneers, Olympic athletes, great leaders, the Forty-Niners, lottery winners, immigrants, and the struggle against odds by main characters in numerous novels. In this essay, the student clearly fulfills the criteria of stating a position, citing evidence, presenting reasons to support the position, and acknowledging, if not refuting, another possibility ("It's your choice."). The essay is also an example how such open-ended formats can permit assessment of depth and breadth of content knowledge as well as reasoning strategies. Teachers could decide to record a separate rating, for example, for the accuracy and breadth of historical content.

PROFESSIONAL DEVELOPMENT AND SUPPORT

The development of classroom assessments of reasoning strategies needs to be part of an ongoing professional development effort that integrates instruction and assessment. Research on successful reform efforts indicates that effective professional development must be focused, sustained, ongoing, and collaborative. The McRAT program uses findings from a body of research (e.g., Guskey, 1986; Osterman & Kottkamp, 1993; Sparks and Simmons, 1989) as the basis for its professional development component. The findings indicate that to change classroom practices, teachers need extensive training that includes modeling the desired practices. Moreover, teachers need continuous support from administration, competent and easily used technical assistance, and clear evidence that their changes are benefiting students. Offered on a volunteer basis, thousands of teachers nationwide are involved in the McRAT program.

Changing Classroom Practices

The infusion of new strategies for reasoning and assessment within the classroom curriculum can be exciting for both teachers and students. As teachers in the McRAT program learn the reasoning strategies, they focus on ways to apply them in the classroom using curriculum materials and resources already available and ones with which they are familiar. For example, a fifth grade teacher may teach the concept of immigration each year because it is part of the school curriculum at that grade level. An infusion of reasoning strategies might result in a unit of study including an analysis of the process of becoming a U.S. citizen, comparison of the plight of an immigrant in the 1800s and an immigrant today, inferring what everyday life is like in a strange country, and evaluation of the benefits and hardships of being an immigrant in the United States. The teacher encourages students to assess their own work individually, in pairs, or in small groups and make revisions necessary for improvement. The "did I?" criteria for each reasoning strategy described earlier in this chapter provide guidance for student self-assessment throughout the process.

As students become engaged and assume increasingly more responsibility for their own learning and assessment, the teacher's role evolves from classroom director to that of facilitator. For most teachers, this change occurs slowly over time with occasional frustration as they implement new practices in the classroom. Given the time and support needed, most teachers embrace the changes in classroom practice and feel empowered to meet the

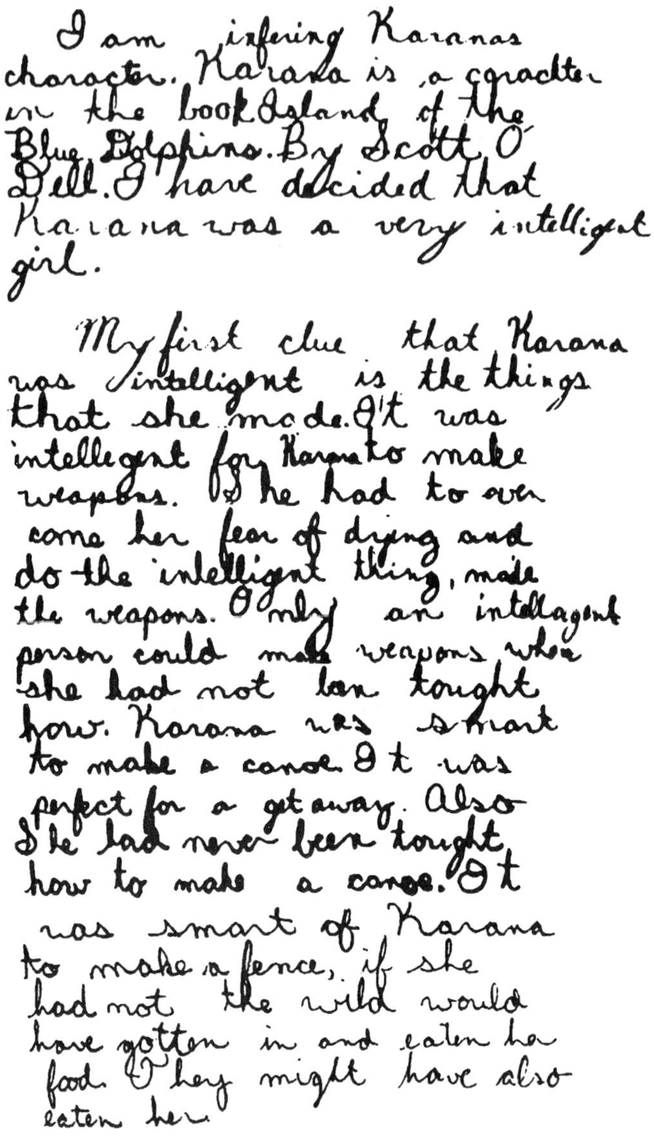

I am infering Karanas
character. Karana is a caracter
in the book Island of the
Blue Dolphins. By Scott O
Dell. I have decided that
Karana was a very intelligent
girl.

My first clue that Karana
was intelligent is the things
that she made. It was
intelligent for Karana to make
weapons. She had to over
come her fear of dying and
do the intelligent thing, made
the weapons. Only an intellagent
person could make weapons when
she had not ben tought
how. Karana was smart
to make a canoe. It was
perfect for a get away. Also
She had never been tought
how to make a canoe. It
was smart of Karana
to make a fence, if she
had not the wild would
have gotten in and eaten her
food. They might have also
eaten her

FIGURE 6
Infer: Character trait essay.

My second clue was that she made friends with the wild dogs. The dogs can help her get food and they can help her keep the food away from the gulls. They would be good company.

My third clue that Karana was intelligent was that she went with the white men. If she did not go with the white men they would think she was dead. Then they would think she was so they would not come back again. Then she would die of old age.

Other people could say Karana was brave or determined. Brave because she always risked her life. Determined because she always went at it. But I have weighed the facts and decided she was intelligent.

FIGURE 6 (Continued)

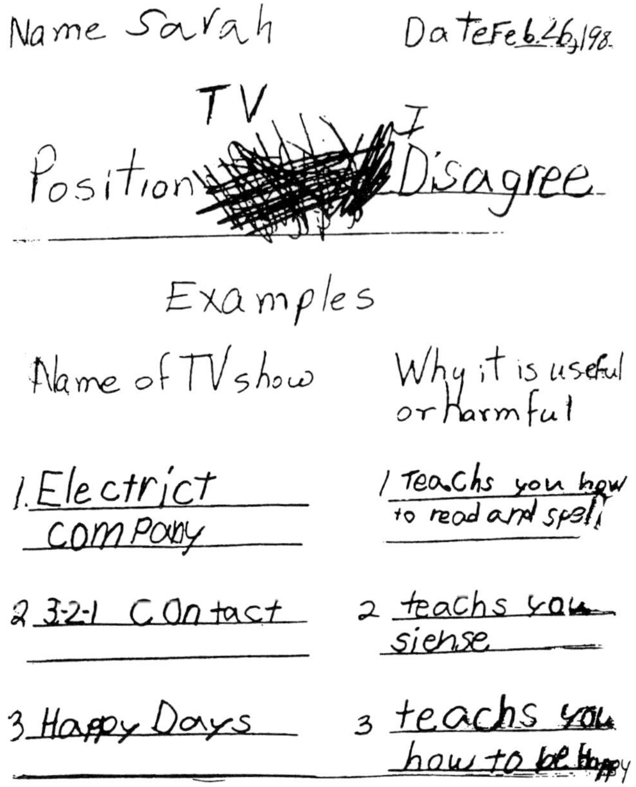

Name Sarah   Date Feb 26, 198.

TV

Position ~~~~~~~~~ Disagree

Examples

Name of TV show   Why it is useful
                          or harmful

1. Electrict   1 Teachs you how
   company   to read and spell

2 3-2-1 Contact   2 teachs you
                          siense

3 Happy Days   3 teachs you
                          how to be happy

FIGURE 7
Evaluate: Planning sheet.

challenge. The McRAT professional development program provides the long-term support needed to make this transition. First, each group of approximately 25 teachers becomes a critical mass. They support and "peer coach" each other as they simultaneously receive training and implement the program with students. Second, the professional development schedule allows time for teachers to meet with the trainer for reinforcement and feedback, for classroom visits, for modeling strategies in the classroom, and for training and working sessions. The administrators are involved and supportive of the program.

Preparing Teachers for Classroom Assessment of Reasoning Strategies

Ongoing assessment is built into each McRAT lesson. Students plan, monitor, review, and revise throughout the lesson. During the training sessions,

26 June, 1864

Jo my very best friend Jessi

I know it was my division to come out here but I
don't think you should. I mean here homesteaders can buy 160 ocr
of land for just $26.°° I know you think that okay, except for one
things, women do not have that advantage.
    Here you could live on land but if you didn't live on it for
five years and improve it they would take it away from you.
    Survival here is very hard especially with the terrible storms
and various amounts of rain or should I say falling grasshoppers
all lumber is expensive and railroad shipping is too expensive all
    You can't keep animals off of crops and when it rains mud
oozes through or from the houses and gets on food. Snakes and gophers
come through with the mud. Normally the snakes are poisonous.
    Well dear friend its still your choice but I'm coming back
East because I can't take it any longer.

your truthful and trustworthy
friend,
Christina

FIGURE 8
Evaluate: Essay.

McRAT teachers become proficient in using criteria from the rating guides to assess student reasoning. A significant part of each training session is given to modeling scoring by the trainer and practicing scoring by the teachers to reach agreement. Teachers also practice using essay evaluations for instructional decision making where a reason is given for an essay score followed by a recommendation for instruction.

McRAT teachers receive further assessment training as they prepare to participate in regional or state pre- or postscoring sessions. A random sample of essays that have been scored by classroom teachers are rescored in these centralized scoring sessions to provide data for program evaluation and feedback to schools on student progress. The development and refinement of assessment instruments is ongoing. Teachers collaborate on such activities as the development of new writing prompts or locating appropriate literature and developing questions for the integrated assessment.

Scheduling Professional Development

Sustained, high-quality staff development is needed to ensure lasting changes in classroom practices. Some estimate reform efforts require at least three to five years. The McRAT program involves teachers in a two-year professional development process. The first year includes approximately nine days scheduled throughout the school year with an initial three-day session, usually in August, followed by three additional full days and a series of half-day sessions. Administrators are strongly encouraged to participate in at least the initial three days of training. The focus of the training is on instructional strategies, lesson design, and assessment procedures. Half-day sessions provide time for collaboration, curriculum evaluation, lesson development, portfolio and recordkeeping, and practice with application of the rating criteria.

A three-day summer institute is held each summer for all teachers who have completed the first year or more in the program. It involves outstanding speakers, small- and large-group sessions for teachers and administrators, and many opportunities for networking across the program. Teachers demonstrate lessons, exhibit examples of student work, and receive new information and training on assessment materials and procedures for the following year.

The second year focuses on more advanced techniques, including team teaching and thematic curriculum development. The second year also continues peer coaching. A total of four days are scheduled throughout the school year.

Developing and Maintaining Leadership

Teachers who have successfully completed the two-year staff development program are eligible to become a McRAT leader by completing an additional six-day leadership program. McRAT leaders become teacher mentors, coordinators of the program in their school districts, and key personnel in the implementation of schoolwide projects. After one year in this apprenticeship role, a McRAT leader can become a certified McRAT trainer.

Building Support for Change

Administrative leadership and support are essential. Principals are involved in every aspect of the McRAT program. Planning for implementation is collaborative. While the principles and content of the staff development remain constant, flexibility is maintained in areas such as scheduling and implementation.

The collaborative efforts among Arkansas Department of Education personnel and teachers and administrators in local schools was important to gaining funds from the Winthrop Rockefeller Foundation, Chapter II, and the Arkansas Department of Education. Since 1987, the funding from the Arkansas Department of Education has supported the development and dissemination of materials to teachers, all training costs, research and evaluation, grants to local schools for teacher release, and employment of part-time regional trainers in each of 15 educational cooperatives. The University of Arkansas at Little Rock assists with research and evaluation and offers two graduate courses each year, Multicultural Reading and Thinking I and II. In 1992, McRAT received validation from the National Diffusion Network, U.S. Department of Education, and became a national program. As such, the program's materials and procedures, including its assessment approaches, have been recognized as valid and replicable.

EVALUATION OF THE THINKING CURRICULUM

The information that teachers gather as they assess their students' reasoning strategies can be important evidence about the effectiveness of efforts to implement a thinking curriculum. In the McRAT project, the integrated assessments administered at the beginning and end of the school year are combined with a collection of student work in the McRAT portfolio. A sample of essays and their accompanying planning sheets, mapping activities, and student self-evaluations are combined with student reflections on what they have learned, an overall summary of the students' reasoning strategy development by the teacher, pre- and post-assessments for each of the reasoning strategies, records of conferences with students, teachers, and parents, and relevant samples of student work in other subjects. Classroom observations and videotapes of student presentations can also add to the database. The goal is to improve students' reasoning strategies, so an array of systematically gathered, sound classroom assessments is essential for continuous progress toward that goal.

LOOKING AHEAD

Technology is becoming increasingly available in our schools. As it opens avenues for student access to resources and experts, the need for students to be able to use strategic reasoning will become even more essential. Teachers will be able to track what resources students try to access and how well they use resources in projects and problem solving tasks. Students will keep on-line, electronic portfolios that will enable teachers to assess work in progress and finished products. Students will be able to receive feedback from distant peers and experts.

Teachers will be able to draw on assessment resources stored in on-line resource banks. Teachers will be able to collaborate with teachers in geographically distributed sites on the development, evaluation, and interpretation of assessments of reasoning. For both students and teachers, the classroom will have no bounds, and the demands and opportunities for thoughtful, lifelong learning will be available to all. We must be sure that we have equipped our students to use their minds well.

References

Bloom, B. S. (Ed.). (1971). *Taxonomy of educational objectives handbook: Cognitive domain*. New York: McGraw-Hill.

Bransford, J. D., & Stein, B. S. (1984). *The IDEAL problem solver*. New York: Freeman.

Chi, M. T. H., Glaser, R., & Rees, E. (1982). Expertise in problem solving. In R. J. Sternberg (Ed.), *Advances in the psychology of human intelligence*, (Vol. 10). Hillsdale, NJ: Erlbaum.

Dewey, J. (1933). *How we think*. Boston: Heath.

Ennis, R. H. (1987). A taxonomy of critical thinking dispositions and abilities. In J. B. Baron & R. J. Sternberg (Eds.), *Teaching thinking skills: Theory and practice*. New York: Freeman.

Guskey, T. R. (1986). Staff development and the process of educational change. *Educational Researcher*. 15(5).

McDonald, J. P. (1992). Exhibitions: Facing outward, pointing Inward. *Studies on exhibitions* (No. 4). Providence, RI: Brown University.

National Education Goals Panel. (1993). *The national education goals report. Building a nation of learners: Vol. 1. The national report*. Washington, DC: Author.

Newell, A., & Simon, H. A. (1976). Computer science as empirical inquiry. *Communications of the ACM*, 19, 113–126.

Osterman, K. F., & Kottkamp, R. B. (1993). *Reflective practice for educators: Improving schooling through professional development*. Newbury Park, CA: Corwin Press.

Polya, G. (1957). *How to solve it: A new aspect of mathematical method* (2nd ed.). Garden City, NY: Doubleday.

Quellmalz, E. S. (1985, October). Needed: Better methods for testing higher order skills. *Educational Leadership*, 43(2), 29–35.

Quellmalz, E. S. (1987). Developing reasoning skills. In J. R. Baron & R. J. Sternberg (Eds.), *Teaching thinking skills: Theory and practice*. New York: Freeman.

Quellmalz, E. S. (1991). Developing criteria for performance assessments: The missing link. *Applied Measurement in Education*, 4(4), 319–332.

Quellmalz, E. S., & Hoskyn, J. (1988, April). Making a difference in Arkansas. The multicultural reading and thinking project. *Educational Leadership*, 45, 51–55.

Resnick, L. B., & Klopfer, L. E. (1989). *Toward the thinking curriculum. Overview*. Arlington, VA: Association for Supervision and Curriculum Development.

Sparks, G. M., & Simmons, J. M. (1989). Inquiry-oriented staff development: Using research as a source of tools, not rules. In S. Caldwell (Ed.), *Staff development: A handbook of effective practices*. Oxford, OH: National Staff Development Council.

Stiggins, R., Rubel, E., & Quellmalz, E. (1986). *Measuring thinking skills in the classroom*. Washington, DC: National Education Association.

Wisconsin Department of Public Instruction. (1988). *Metacognitive strategies of good and poor readers*. Madison, WI: Author.

CHAPTER

6

Academic Self-Concept: Beyond the Dustbowl

HERBERT W. MARSH
University of Western Sydney—Macarthur, Campbelltown, Australia

RHONDA CRAVEN
University of New South Wales, St. George, Australia

INTRODUCTION

In the United States and many other countries there is a growing tendency for classroom teachers, school counseling staff, school administrators, and parents to assume that schools are responsible for students' personal and social development. For this reason, there is considerable interest in assessing and maximizing students' self-esteem and self-concept. Implicit in this focus is the usually unstated assumption that improvements in general self-esteem or specific components of self-concept will lead to improved academic achievement and other desirable academic outcomes. Based in part on this assumption, self-concept enhancement activities are included as a component of the school curriculum in some school districts and teachers are sometimes called on to make judgments about the self-concepts of their students as part of normal classroom assessment and school reporting practices.

A positive self-concept is also valued as a desirable outcome in itself, especially in educational settings but also in many other disciplines such as social, counseling, developmental, and sports psychology. Brookover and Lezotte (1979), in their model of effective schools suggested that maximizing academic self-concept, self-reliance, and academic achievement should be major goals of schooling. In fact, most educational policy statements list the development of a positive self-concept as one of the most important goals of education. For example, "The Common and Agreed National Goals of Schooling" (Australian Education Council, 1989), the first agreement on the aims of Australian education at a national level, identified the need "to enable all students to achieve high standards of learning and to develop self-confidence, optimism, high self-esteem, respect for others, and achievement of personal excellence."

This importance placed on the enhancement of self-concept is usually based on the premise that high self-concept will lead to feelings of self-worth and self-acceptance. In addition, enhancing self-concept is considered to be a desirable educational goal in itself. Research to be summarized here suggests that the attainment of a positive academic self-concept affects academic behavior, academic choices, educational aspirations, and subsequent academic achievement. Furthermore, educational interventions that successfully produce short-term changes in skills, aptitudes, or academic achievement are unlikely to have longlasting effects unless corresponding changes are made in related areas of self-concept. However, little direction is given to teachers on the structure of self-concept as a construct, its relationship to other variables, and techniques for enhancing self-concept. Rather it is assumed that teachers can readily enhance self-concept in the classroom. In contrast Hattie's (1992) meta-analysis of self-concept enhancement studies found that teachers were less effective at enhancing self-concept than many other change agents. It seems that the importance of theoretical and empirical findings needs to be investigated further prior to developing self-concept enhancement interventions that have significant practical implications for the classroom. That is, it is not possible for teachers to enhance self-concept if its structure and relationship to other variables is not understood.

For these reasons, the purpose of this chapter is to summarize research on the structure, assessment, measurement and enhancement of academic self-concept in educational settings. In pursuing this aim, we will provide an overview of: the theoretical structure of self-concept; the nature of valid and reliable self-concept measurement instruments; the relationship of self-concept to other constructs; and self-concept enhancement interventions. Discussion will focus on a model of self-concept originally developed by Richard Shavelson and his colleagues (Shavelson, Hubner, & Stanton, 1976) and subsequently revised by Marsh in collaboration with Shavelson and other colleagues (e.g., Marsh, 1990c, 1993a; Marsh, Byrne, & Shavelson, 1988; Marsh, Craven, & Debus, 1991; Marsh & Hattie, 1996; Marsh & Shavelson, 1985; Shavelson & Marsh, 1986) and on the set of Self-Description Questionnaire (SDQ) instruments that are based on the Shavelson et al. model and its subsequent revision. Throughout the chapter we will discuss the classroom implications of recent advances in self-concept theory and research.

THE STRUCTURE AND MEASUREMENT
OF SELF-CONCEPT

Background

Psychological terms like *self-concept* and *self-esteem* are encountered so widely in everyday usage that there is an implicit assumption that "everybody knows what it is." Some researchers reserve the term *self-esteem* for the evaluative component of self-description and use the term *self-concept* for descriptive components of self-description. However, Shavelson et al. (1976; also see Marsh, 1993a) argued that self-concept is both descriptive and evaluative. Thus, for example, statements such as "I am good at mathematics," "I can run a long way without stopping," and "I look forward to English class" all have both evaluative and descriptive components. Furthermore, typical application of the construct of self-esteem in research based on measures derived from the Rosenberg instrument (Rosenberg, 1965, 1979) emphasizes a hierarchical, overarching, general, or global construct that at least implicitly incorporates many (or all) specific components. Hence, for purposes of this chapter and in our research, we use the term *self-esteem* to mean general (or global) self-concept and distinguish between this and specific components of self-concept (e.g., physical, social, academic).

The widespread usage of terms like *self-esteem* and *self-concept* may account for much of the popularity of the self-concept construct, but it also introduces potential problems in that many researchers have not felt compelled to provide any theoretical definition of what they are measuring nor a systematic evaluation of their self-concept measures. For example, reviews of self-concept research written prior to the 1980s (e.g., Burns, 1979; Shavelson et al., 1976; Wells & Marwell, 1976; Wylie, 1974, 1979) often noted the lack of theoretical basis in most studies, the poor quality of self-concept measurement instruments, methodological problems, and a general inconsistency in reported findings. Similar observations led Hattie (1992) to describe this period as one of "dustbowl empiricism" in which the predominant research design in self-concept studies was "throw it in and see what happens." Weak theory and research leads to poor-quality classroom practice. Many teachers also experience difficulty measuring, assessing, and enhancing students' self-concepts. Like some researchers, they assume that they understand the structure of the construct and, perhaps, strategies of how to enhance it.

Self-concept is a hypothetical construct and so its usefulness must be established by investigations of its construct validity. Ideally, construct validation is an ongoing process in which theory and classroom practice are used to develop a measure; empirical research is used to test the theory and the measure; both the theory and the measure are revised in relation to research; and theory and research are used to inform practice. Practice in isolation of advances in research and theory would be static. Thus, theory,

Herbert W. Marsh and Rhonda Craven

measurement, empirical research, and classroom practice are inexorably intertwined so that the neglect of one will undermine the others. Reality seldom matches this ideal. Particularly in the past, self-concept assessment has been based on ad hoc or "one-shot" endeavors that were not soundly based on theory, not systematically evaluated, and not refined on the basis of subsequent theoretical or substantive developments. Weak measures substantially undermine research and theory evaluation, thereby limiting their contribution to improvements in classroom practice.

Following Shavelson et al. (1976), studies of the construct validity of self-concept can be broadly classified as within-construct (internal or structural) studies and between-construct (external) studies (also see Messick, 1989, for more general discussion). Within-construct studies explore the internal structure of self-concept, attempting to define what self-concept actually is. They test, for example, the dimensionality of self-concept and may seek to show that the construct has consistent, distinct multidimensional components (e.g., physical, social, academic self-concept) or that a specific domain like academic self-concept has multiple dimensions (e.g., mathematics, English, history). Implicit in this aspect of construct validity is the possibility that a construct is multidimensional. Even if a construct is hypothesized to be unidimensional, however, it is important to test empirically this within-construct assertion (i.e., to show that it is not multidimensional) as part of the construct validation process. Within-construct studies typically employ empirical techniques such as factor analysis or multitrait–multimethod (MTMM) analysis. Between-construct studies attempt to establish a logical, theoretically consistent pattern of relations between measures of self-concept and other constructs. The resolution of at least some within-construct issues should be a logical prerequisite to conducting between-construct research, but between-construct research has predominated self-concept research until recently. This has been problematic in that self-concept as a construct has been utilized by both teachers and researchers to relate to other variables without first understanding the nature of its structure. Teachers and researchers need to understand the structure of self-concept as a basis for the selection and interpretation of reliable assessment instruments and advances in theory to develop and implement appropriate classroom practices to maintain and enhance self-concept. The development of appropriate theoretical models and tests of the construct validity of measures based on this theory should be the basis for subsequent advances in theory and classroom practice.

The Shavelson et al. Model

Shavelson et al. (1976) noted important deficiencies in self-concept research, concluding that "it appears that self-concept research has addressed itself to substantive problems before problems of definition, measurement, and interpretation have been resolved" (p. 470). However, unlike many other reviews, Shavelson et al. emphasized

> our approach is constructive in that we (a) develop a definition of self-concept from existing definitions, (b) review some steps in validating a construct interpretation of a test score, and (c) apply these steps in examining five popularly used self-concept instruments (p. 470).

In other words Shavelson et al. identified the importance of construct validation and set out to test the construct validity of self-concept based on theory and research current at the time.

Shavelson et al. (1976) began their review by developing a theoretical definition of self-concept. An ideal definition, they emphasized, consists of the nomological network containing within-construct and between-construct components. As discussed previously, the within-construct portion of the network pertains to specific features of the construct—its components, structure, and attributes and theoretical statements relating these features. The between-construct portion of the definition locates the construct in a broader conceptual space, indicating how self-concept is related to other constructs. Thus, for example, dividing self-concept into academic, social, and physical components is a within-construct proposition whereas a related between-construct proposition is that academic self-concept is more strongly related to academic achievement than are physical and social self-concepts.

Shavelson et al. (1976), integrating features from many definitions, defined *self-concept* to be one's self-perceptions that are formed through experience with and interpretations of one's environment. They are influenced especially by evaluations by significant others, reinforcement, and attributions for one's own behavior. Shavelson et al. emphasized that self-concept is not an entity within the person, but a hypothetical construct that is potentially useful in explaining and predicting how a person acts. These self-perceptions influence the way one acts, and these acts in turn influence one's self-perceptions. Consistent with this perspective, Shavelson et al. noted that self-concept is important as both an outcome and a mediating variable that helps to explain other outcomes. Thus, for example, academic self-concept may be an important outcome that is influenced by an experimental intervention. Alternatively, academic self-concept may mediate the influence of an academic intervention that is designed to enhance academic achievement. In this second example, the intervention effect on academic achievement is due at least in part to the effect of the intervention on academic self-concept, which in turn influences academic achievement. In this sense, the effect of the intervention on academic achievement is facilitated by the effect of the intervention on academic self-concept even though the enhancement of academic self-concept may not be the main aim of the study. Shavelson et al. identified seven features critical to their definition of the self-concept construct:

1. It is organized or structured, in that people categorize the vast amount of information they have about themselves and relate these categories to one another.

2. It is multidimensional, and the particular dimensions reflect a self-referent category system adopted by a particular individual or shared by a group or both.

3. It is hierarchical, with perceptions of personal behavior in specific situations at the base of the hierarchy, inferences about the self in broader domains (e.g., social, physical, and academic) at the middle of the hierarchy, and a global, general self-concept at the apex (Shavelson et al. likened this structure to a hierarchical representation of intellectual abilities with Spearman's g [see Vernon, 1950] at the apex).

4. The hierarchical general self-concept—the apex of the hierarchy—is stable, but as one descends the hierarchy, self-concept becomes increasingly situation specific and, as a consequence, less stable. There are reciprocal relations between self-concept at each level in that self-perceptions at the base of the hierarchy may be attenuated by conceptualizations at higher levels and changes in general self-concept may require changes in many situation-specific instances.

5. Self-concept becomes increasingly multidimensional as the individual moves from infancy to adulthood.

6. Self-concept has both a descriptive and an evaluative aspect such that individuals may describe themselves ("I am happy") and evaluate themselves ("I do well in mathematics"). Evaluations can be made against some absolute ideal (the five minute mile), a personal, internal standard (a personal best), a relative standard based on comparisons with peers, or the expectations of significant others. Individuals may differentially weight specific dimensions.

7. Self-concept can be differentiated from other constructs. For example, academic and physical self-concepts can be differentiated from academic achievement and physical fitness, respectively.

Shavelson et al. (1976) also presented one possible representation of this hierarchical model in which general self-concept appeared at the apex and was divided into academic and nonacademic self-concepts at the next level. Academic self-concept was further divided into self-concepts in particular subject areas (e.g., mathematics, English). Nonacademic self-concept was divided into three areas: social self-concept, which was subdivided into relations with peers and those with significant others; emotional self-concept; and physical self-concept, which was subdivided into physical ability and physical appearance. Further levels of division were hypothesized for each of these specific self-concepts so that, at the base of the hierarchy, self-concepts were of limited generality, quite specific, and more closely related to actual behavior. This model posits a structure of self-concept that resembles British psychologists' hierarchical model of intellectual abilities (Vernon, 1950), where general ability (like Spearman's g) was at the apex. The model of self-concept produced turned out to be so important, in part, because it provided a blueprint for a new generation of multidimensional self-concept instruments that have had an important influence on both theory and classroom practice.

Shavelson et al. (1976) systematically applied the construct validity approach to self-concept research in a classic review that had a profound influence on the field. They argued that the starting point of a construct validity approach is a definition of the construct to be evaluated that provides a blueprint for constructing self-concept instruments, for designing within-construct studies of the proposed structure of self-concept, for testing between-construct hypotheses about relations with other constructs and, eventually, rejecting and revising the original construct definition. Shavelson et al. demonstrated this approach in the evaluation of five then-popular self-concept instruments: Brookover's Self-Concept of Ability Scale, Coopersmith's Self-Esteem Inventory, Gordon's How I See Myself Scale, the Piers–Harris Children's Self-Concept Scale, and Sear's Self-Concept Inventory. However, based on this review, there was only modest support for their hypothesized domains and none of these five instruments was able to differentiate among even the broad academic, social, and physical domains. However the basic assumption of this model that asserted that self-concept was a multidimensional construct was important for the development of research and an extension of understandings of within-construct issues and has important classroom practice implications for the assessment, measurement and enhancement of academic self-concept.

Self-Description Questionnaires

More recently researchers have developed instruments that are designed to measure specific facets of self-concept. Based on the Shavelson et al. model, Marsh developed the SDQ instruments for preadolescent primary school students (SDQI), adolescent high school students (SDQII), and late adolescents and young adults (SDQIII) (see Marsh, 1990c). Reviews of subsequent SDQ research (Byrne, 1984; Hattie, 1992; Marsh, 1990c, 1993a; Marsh & Shavelson, 1985; Shavelson & Marsh, 1986) supported the multidimensional structure of self-concept and demonstrated that self-concept cannot be adequately understood if its multidimensionality is ignored. The set of three SDQ instruments have provided particularly strong tests of the Shavelson et al. model and have been evaluated to be among the best multidimensional instruments in terms of psychometric properties and construct validation research (Boyle, 1994; Byrne, 1984; Hattie, 1992; Wylie, 1989). For example, Hattie (1992, pp. 82–83) considers the

> SDQ to be an excellent measure of the various first-order dimensions of self-concept as proposed by Shavelson et al. The estimates of reliability are consistently high, and tests are based on a multifaceted model of self-concept. The set of SDQs are the best set of measures available.

Unlike most earlier research, the initial focus of SDQ research was on within-construct concerns (Marsh, 1990c, 1993a). It was reasoned that the determination of whether theoretically consistent and distinguishable dimensions of self-concept exist and their content and structure should be prerequisite to the study of how these dimensions, or overall self-concept, are related to other variables. In adopting such an approach, atheoretical and purely empirical approaches to developing and refining measurement instruments were rejected. Instead, an explicit theoretical model was taken to be the starting point for instrument construction, and empirical results were used to support, refute, or revise the instrument *and* the theory on which it is based. In applying this approach, the Shavelson et al. (1976) model was judged to be the best available theoretical model of self-concept. Implicit in this approach is the presumption that theory building and instrument construction are inexorably intertwined and that each will suffer if the two are separated. In this sense the SDQ instruments are based on a strong empirical foundation and a good theoretical model. Consistent with this approach, SDQ research provided support for the Shavelson et al. model, but also led to its subsequent revision.

SDQ research began by critically evaluating the within-construct components of the Shavelson et al. model and the psychometric properties of the SDQ instruments. SDQ scales were posited on the basis of the Shavelson et al. model, item pools were constructed for each scale, and factor analyses and item analyses were used to select and refine the items eventually used to represent each scale. For example, the final version of the SDQI instrument assesses three areas of academic self-concept (reading, mathematics, and general school self-concept), four areas of nonacademic self-concept (physical ability, physical appearance, peer relations, and parent relations) and a general self-scale. Preadolescent children are asked to respond to 76 simple declarative sentences (e.g., "I'm good at mathematics") with one of five responses: false, mostly false, sometimes true/sometimes false, mostly true, true. Each of the eight facets of self-concept has a score from 8 to 40, which is based on the total score for eight questions measuring each facet on the SDQI. Each of the eight questions for the self-concept scale can receive a score of 1 to 5. A score of 1 is assigned if a positively worded statement on self-concept is answered as false, indicating the child does not have a high self-concept. An additional 12 of the 76 questions are negatively worded to disrupt response biases; however, as research has revealed that preadolescents do not respond validly to these items, they are not included in the scoring of the SDQI. Therefore the SDQI measures eight facets of self-concept with each scale scored on the basis of eight positively worded questions (see Figure 1).

Evaluation of within-construct issues showed that the internal consistency of the scales from all three SDQ instruments was good, typically in the .80s and .90s. The stability of SDQ responses was also good, particularly for older children. For example, the stability of SDQIII scales measured on four occasions varied from a median of .87 for a 1-month interval to a median of $r = .74$ for intervals of 18 months or longer. Dozens of factor analyses by diverse samples differing in gender, age, country, and language have consistently identified the factors that each SDQ instrument is designed to measure. Marsh (1989) summarized factor analyses of more than 12,000 sets of responses from the normative archives of the three SDQ instruments. In addition to clearly identifying all of the factors that each of the three SDQ instruments is designed to measure, the results indicate that the domains of self-concept are remarkably distinct (median values of r among the SDQ scales vary between .1 and .2 for the three SDQ instruments).

A subset of SDQII items was included on the large, nationally representative National Educational Longitudinal Survey (NELS), the most recent of a series of studies by the U.S. Department of Education's National Center for Educational Statistics. The purpose of this survey is to collect and disseminate statistics and other data related to education in the United States. This data, containing thousands of variables, is widely available to educational researchers and policy makers and is expected to be a basis for thousands of educational research studies. Marsh (1994) compared SDQII responses based on 17,544 responses from U.S. 10th grade students and 1,147 responses from Australian 10th grade students that are part of the SDQII test norms. Confirmatory factor analysis (CFA) demonstrated similar factors underlying responses by students from both countries and provided good support for the equality of factor loadings. Mean differences between responses by U.S. and Australian students were small and the pattern of gender differences was similar for both countries. Structural equation models relating mathematics and English achievement scores, school grades, self-concepts, and school-average abilities replicated and extended results discussed in this chapter. These results support the construct validity of the SDQII responses in the NELS survey. Other research has demonstrated the SDQ factors in responses by English, Canadian, German, Austrian, Spanish, South African, and Chinese respondents. Taken together, this research supports for robustness of the SDQ factor structure and the broad applicability of the SDQ instruments.

The research summarized here demonstrates the importance of understanding that self-concept is a multidimensional structure. In practice this means students can have different self-concepts in different areas. That

SELF-DESCRIPTION QUESTIONNAIRE-I

Your Name:_____   Circle one: Boy   Girl

School:_____   Grade:_____ Age:_____

Teacher: _____   Date:_____

This is a chance to look at yourself. It is not a test. There are no right answers. and everyone will have different answers. Be sure that your answers show how you feel about yourself. PLEASE DO NOT TALK ABOUT YOUR ANSWERS WITH ANYONE ELSE. We will keep your answers private and not show them to anyone.

When you are ready to begin, please read each sentence and choose an answer. (You may read quietly to yourself as I read aloud.) There are five possible answers for each question: "True," "False," and three answers in between. There are five boxes next to each sentence, one for each of the answers. The answers are written at the top of the boxes. Choose your answer to a sentence and make a check mark in the box under the answer you choose. DO NOT say your answer out loud or talk about it with anyone else.

Before you start, there are three examples below. A student, Bob, has already answered two of these sentences to show you how to do it. In the third example you must choose your own answer and put in your own check mark.

		FALSE	MOSTLY FALSE	SOME-TIMES FALSE/ SOME-TIMES TRUE	MOSTLY TRUE	TRUE
EXAMPLES						
1. I like to read comic books 1		☐	☐	☐	☐	☑ 1

Bob checked the box under the answer "True." This means that he really likes to read comic books. If Bob did not like to read comic books very much. he would have answered "FALSE" or "MOSTLY FALSE."

2. In general, I am neat and tidy .... 2 ☐ ☐ ☑ ☐ ☐ 2

Bob answered "SOMETIMES FALSE, SOMETIMES TRUE." because he is not very neat, but he is not very messy either.

3. I like to watch T.V. .... 3 ☐ ☐ ☐ ☐ ☐ 3

For this sentence you have to choose the answer that is best for you. First you must decide if the sentence is "TRUE," or "FALSE," or somewhere in between. If you really like to watch T.V. a lot, you would answer "TRUE" by making a check mark in the last box. If you hate watching T.V., you would answer "FALSE" by making a check mark in the first box. If your answer is somewhere in between, then you would choose one of the other three boxes.

If you want to change an answer you have marked, you should cross out the check mark and put a new check mark in another box on the same line.

For all the sentences be sure that your check mark is on the same line as the sentence you are answering. You should have one answer and only one answer for each sentence. Do not leave out any of the sentences. Once you have started, PLEASE DO NOT TALK. Turn over the page and begin.

FIGURE 1

The instruction page and the first page of the SDQI instrument. (Reprinted with permission of the author.)

	FALSE	MOSTLY FALSE	SOME-TIMES FALSE/ SOME-TIMES TRUE	MOSTLY TRUE	TRUE	
1. I am good looking	1					1
2. I'm good at all **SCHOOL SUBJECTS**	2					2
3. I can run fast	3					3
4. I get good marks in **READING**	4					4
5. My parents understand me	5					5
6. I hate **MATHEMATICS**	6					6
7. I have lots of friends	7					7
8. I like the way I look	8					8
9. I enjoy doing work in all **SCHOOL SUBJECTS**	9					9
10. I like to run and play hard	10					10
11. I like **READING**	11					11
12. My parents are usually unhappy or disappointed with what I do	12					12
13. Work in mathematics is easy for me	13					13

	FALSE	MOSTLY FALSE	SOME-TIMES FALSE/ SOME-TIMES TRUE	MOSTLY TRUE	TRUE	
14. I make friends easily	14					14
15. I have a pleasant looking face	15					15
16. I get good marks in all **SCHOOL SUBJECTS**	16					16
17. I hate sports and games	17					17
18. I'm good at **READING**	18					18
19. I like my parents	19					19
20. I look forward to **MATHEMATICS**	20					20
21. Most kids have more friends than I do	21					21
22. I am a nice looking person	22					22
23. I hate all **SCHOOL SUBJECTS**	23					23
24. I enjoy sports and games	24					24
25. I am interested in **READING**	25					25
26. My parents like me	26					26

FIGURE 1 (*Continued*)

is, a child can have a high self-concept in mathematics but may have a low self-concept in reading. If teachers are assessing self-concept, this multidimensionality cannot be ignored, a single measure of self-esteem or general self-concept will not adequately characterize the diversity of students' self-concepts in specific academic and nonacademic areas. The SDQ results also highlight the need for researchers and teachers to adequately account for within-construct issues prior to assessing self-concepts. Current theory suggests that self-concept assessment instruments need to be selected based on current advances in theory and research, measure multidimensional components of self-concept, and have demonstrated construct validity based on within-construct research. Basically, the quality of assessment practice is only as good as the quality of theory and research on which the development of the measurement instrument is based. To explore this issue further we intend to provide a brief overview of new understandings of the structure, measurement and assessment of young children's self-concepts that emerged with the development of good instrumentation.

The Marsh–Shavelson Model

Whereas SDQ results provide strong support for the Shavelson et al. model and the multidimensionality of self-concept, they also posed some complications. The strong hierarchical structure posited by Shavelson et al. required self-concepts to be substantially correlated, but the small sizes of correlations actually observed implied that any hierarchical structure of the self-concept responses must be much weaker than anticipated. More specifically, in the Shavelson et al. model math and verbal self-concepts were assumed to be correlated substantially so that they could be described in terms of a single higher-order academic self-concept. Factor analyses, however, resulted in correlations between verbal and math self-concepts that were close to 0. Complications such as these led to the Marsh–Shavelson revision (Marsh, 1990c; Marsh et al., 1988; Marsh & Shavelson, 1985; Shavelson & Marsh, 1986) of the original Shavelson et al. model.

The Shavelson et al. model posits that self-concept is hierarchically ordered as well as being multidimensional. Marsh and Hocevar (1985; Marsh & Shavelson, 1985) used confirmatory factor analysis to test first-order and higher-order structures in response to the SDQI by students in grades two to five. In preliminary first-order models the correlations among the SDQI factors were estimated, but no special assumptions about the pattern of correlations were made. However, both the Shavelson et al. model and the design of the SDQI assume that a systematic hierarchical ordering of the domains of self-concept underlies these correlations among first-order factors. For example, the SDQI measures four nonacademic domains and three academic domains of self-concept so that one reasonable hypothesis would be that the seven first-order factors would form two second-order factors (academic and nonacademic), a finding that would be consistent with the Shavelson et al. model.

The hierarchical structure of self-concept was examined by testing and comparing several competing models. In one model, a single, general self-concept factor was proposed to explain the relationships among the first-order factors, but this model was unable to fit the data very well at any year level. In a second model, two second-order factors were proposed: one defined by the four nonacademic factors and one defined by the three academic factors. This model fit the data better than the first model but still was not adequate. The final model took into account previous research showing verbal and math self-concepts to be nearly uncorrelated. Two second-order academic factors—math/academic and verbal/academic self-concepts—and a second-order nonacademic factor were found. This model fit the data significantly better than any other models for each of the four years in school. These results were consistent with Shavelson et al.'s assumption that self-concept is hierarchically ordered, but the particular form of this higher-order structure was more complicated than originally proposed. These findings led to the Marsh–Shavelson revision of the Shavelson et al. model that differs from the original model primarily in that there are two higher-order academic factors, math/academic and verbal/academic, instead of just one (see Figure 2A). A similar model was also supported, particularly the need for two separate higher-order academic factors, by Marsh (1987b) with responses by late-adolescents to the SDQIII.

Marsh et al. (1988) extended tests of the revised Marsh–Shavelson model by evaluating responses to the verbal, math, and general school scales from three different self-concept instruments. Hierarchical CFA was again employed and the critical test was whether correlations among these nine first-order factors could be adequately explained by a single higher-order factor as posited in the original Shavelson et al. model or whether two higher-order factors as posited in the Marsh–Shavelson revision were required. The results showed conclusively that the Marsh–Shavelson revised model was superior. All three verbal self-concept scales were nearly uncorrelated with each of the three math self-concept scales and, in the hierarchical model, the verbal/academic and math/academic higher-order factors were uncorrelated. These results provided strong support for the generality of earlier SDQ research and for the revised model and imply that the structure of self-concept is more complicated than previously thought. There is not just one higher-order factor (i.e., general self-concept or self-esteem), rather there are at least three second-order factors (nonacademic, verbal/academic, and math/academic). Self-concept is not simply a conglomerate of different facets but is hierarchically ordered. As we will discuss later, understanding the hierarchical structure of self-concept has important implications for self-concept enhancement assessment and implementation.

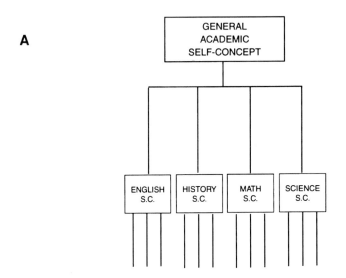

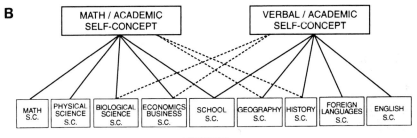

FIGURE 2
(A) The academic portion of Shavelson, Hubner, and Stanton's (1976)
original model and (B) an elaboration of Marsh and Shavelson's (1985)
revision that includes a wider variety of specific academic facets (S. C. =
self-concept). (From Marsh, Byrne, & Shavelson, 1988, pp. 366–380.
Reprinted with permission.)

Academic Self-Description Questionnaires

Marsh, Byrne, and Shavelson critically evaluated the Marsh–Shavelson
model. Support for this revised model was based primarily on demonstrating
apparent problems with the original Shavelson et al. model. Whereas there
was strong evidence that a single higher-order academic component was
insufficient, there was not strong support that just two higher-order academic factors were sufficient. Part of the problem, they argued, was that the

revised model had not been presented in sufficient detail. To remedy this problem, they provided a more detailed development of the academic structure in the revised model (Figure 2B) and how it differs from the academic portion of the original Shavelson et al. model (Figure 2A). The specific academic domains in Figure 2B were selected to broadly reflect core school subjects in a typical academic curriculum, and the subject areas are roughly ordered from relatively pure measures of the math/academic component to relatively pure measures of the verbal/academic component. To evaluate this model it was necessary to design new academic self-concept instruments that included a wider variety of specific academic self-concept domains.

Marsh (1990d) designed the Academic Self Description Questionnaires (ASDQ) I and II for elementary and high school students. In consultation with school administrators, "core" subjects like those in Figure 2B and other "noncore" school subjects taken by all students were determined, and a separate six-item self-concept scale was constructed for each subject. The ASDQI and ASDQII respectively consist of 13 scales (7 core, 5 noncore, 1 general) and 16 (9 core, 6 noncore, 1 general) scales. For each scale, the wording of the six items is parallel except for the particular subject area. For example, one of the six items is "I learn things quickly in science" and students respond to this item on a six-category true–false response scale like that used on the SDQII. In addition, there is a general school scale in which the term "most school subjects" is substituted for the specific academic subjects.

First-Order Factor Analyses

Preliminary exploratory factor analyses were conducted on ASDQI and ASDQII responses. For ASDQI responses, all 13 self-concept scales that the instrument was designed to measure were identified and the reliability estimates for each scale varied from .88 to .94. For ASDQII responses, 16 reasonably well-defined factors were identified, and reliability estimates for the 16 scales varied from .88 to .95. However, the English language and English literature factors were not well differentiated even though all the remaining factors corresponded unambiguously to one of the scales the instrument was designed to measure. A 15-factor solution resulted in a well-defined solution in which variables from the two English scales loaded on the same factor. CFA results also resulted in well-defined solutions that fit the data well. These results demonstrate that students are remarkably effective in distinguishing among a diverse set of academic self-concepts.

Correlations among the 13 ASDQI factors were all positive, varying from .04 (physical education and music) to .91 (science and social studies). The general school factor was correlated substantially more with the core academic factors (.26 to .73; median = .62) than with the other factors (.18 to .34; median = .30). Physical education was correlated substantially with health (.73) but not correlated substantially with any other scales, suggesting that a second-order physical education factor may be necessary. The art, music, and religion factors were not substantially correlated with any other scales, suggesting that they could not be well explained by second-order factors.

The correlations among the 16 ASDQII factors varied from $-.03$ (physical education and music) to .98 (English language and English literature). The extremely high correlation between the two English scales suggests that secondary students did not distinguish between English language and literature. The general school factor was correlated substantially more with the core academic factors (.40 to .75; median $=$ .59) than with the other factors (.21 to .49; median $=$ .29). Physical education was substantially correlated with health (.55) but not correlated substantially with any other factors, suggesting like ASDQI results that a second-order physical education factor may be necessary. Art was substantially correlated with industrial arts and, to a lesser extent, music and religion, but not to other factors, suggesting that a second-order art factor may be necessary.

Higher-Order Factor Analyses

The intent of higher-order factor models is to explain relations among first-order factors with one or more higher-order factors. For both the ASDQI and ASDQII studies, the initial analyses were conducted on the set of core academic factors like those in Figure 2B. A model positing just one (general academic) higher-order factor, as predicted, was not able to fit the data in either study. The fit of the model with two higher-order factors (verbal/academic and math/academic) was reasonably good and clearly better than the one-factor model. Freeing additional parameters improved the fit somewhat, but the parameter estimates still clearly supported the two higher-order factor model. However, in all the models much of the reliable variance in the first-order factors could not be explained in terms of the higher-order factors.

Subsequent analyses were conducted on the entire set of core and non-core ASDQ scales for each instrument. These additional first-order factors were included specifically to test the limits of the generality of the Marsh–Shavelson model. Consistent with expectations, neither one nor two higher-order factor models were able to adequately explain relations among the larger sets of first-order factors. In each case, at least two additional higher-order factors—defined substantially by the physical education and art first-order factors—were required. Even these more complicated four higher-order factor models were only moderately successful in fitting the data, and again, much of the variance in first-order factors could not be explained in terms of the higher-order factors. It was also important to note that in all the different analyses, the first-order general school factor loaded substantially on the second-order math/academic and second-order verbal/academic factors but was nearly unrelated to second-order factors defined by the remaining noncore scales.

Implications of ASDQ Research

ASDQ studies extended previous research by examining a greater diversity of academic self-concepts domains than heretofore considered and provided reasonable support for the Marsh–Shavelson model when consideration was limited to core academic factors like those in Figure 2B. It is important to emphasize, however, that much of the variance in many of the first-order factors was not explained by the higher-order factors (i.e., residual variances of the first-order factors were large). Whereas the two higher-order factors were able to explain correlations among the first-order factors with reasonable accuracy, the actual levels of self-concept on many of the first-order factors cannot be accurately inferred from the two higher-order factors. Thus, support for the theoretical model should not be interpreted to mean that academic self-concept in subjects like computer studies, handwriting, geography, history, foreign languages, and commerce can be well represented by more general components of academic self-concept. The results show quite the opposite.

Because previous research has not considered such a diversity of academic self-concepts, a substantively important question is whether or not students differentiate among self-concept associated with specific school subjects. Perhaps the most remarkable finding is that students can differentiate self-concept in so many different school subjects to a much greater extent than had been previously recognized. If researchers and teachers are specifically interested in self-concept in particular academic subjects, then they should measure self-concept with scales specific to those subjects in addition to, perhaps, more general academic self-concept scales. The design features of the ASDQ instruments provide researchers and teachers with an easy way to measure academic self-concept in different school subjects that is applicable across most educational settings.

Implications of Research Advances

Recent advances in theory, research, and development of instrumentation provide a firm basis for guiding teachers on the structure, assessment and measurement of self-concept. Assessment practices need to take account of the multidimensionality of self-concept and employ measurement instruments with demonstrated construct validity. Specific facets of students' self-concepts need to be assessed to glean an accurate assessment of the diversity of individual's self-concepts in specific areas of interest to teachers.

THE RELATIONSHIP OF SELF-CONCEPT TO
ACADEMIC ACHIEVEMENT

Background

Wylie noted that "many persons, especially educators, have assumed unhesitatingly that achievement and/or ability measures will be related strongly to self-conceptions of achievement and ability and to over-all self-regard as well" (1979, p. 355). Not surprisingly, particularly for studies of school-aged children, some measure of academic achievement is one of the criteria used most frequently to validate self-concept interpretations and has also been the focus of much SDQ research. Many teachers have also assumed that self-concept affects academic achievement. Implicit in this assumption is that feeling good about one's abilities in an academic area fosters academic striving behaviors (e.g., persistence) that can maximize and even change academic achievement.

In the Shavelson et al. model, academic self-concept is one component of overall self-concept, and it is divided into self-concepts in particular content areas such as math and reading. Support for the construct validity of SDQ interpretations and the Shavelson et al. model requires that academic achievement be correlated more positively with academic self-concept than with nonacademic or overall self-concept and that verbal and math achievement indicators be correlated more highly with self-concepts in matching content areas than with other domains of self-concept. In the most extensive meta-analysis of the achievement/self-concept relationship, Hansford and Hattie (1982) found that measures of ability or performance correlated about .20 with measures of general self-concept, but about .40 with measures of academic self-concept. Similarly, Shavelson and Bolus (1982) found that grades in English, mathematics, and science were correlated more highly with matching areas of self-concept than with general self-concept, and Bachman (1970) reported that IQ correlated .46 with academic self-concept but only .14 with general self-concept. In her review of studies relating self-concept to academic achievement, Byrne (1984) also found that nearly all studies report that self-concept is correlated positively to achievement while many find achievement to be correlated more strongly with academic self-concept than with general self-concept. This research supports the separation of academic self-concept from general and nonacademic components of self-concept and that a relation is present between academic self-concept and academic achievement. The purpose of this section is to review briefly research that explores this relationship.

SDQ Research

SDQ research has emphasized the distinctiveness of self-concepts in verbal and mathematical content areas, as well as the separation of academic and nonacademic components of self-concept. In the SDQI test manual Marsh (1988b) reviewed 11 studies relating SDQI responses by preadolescents to verbal, math, and general academic achievement assessed by objective tests and teacher ratings. These showed that, for the 136 correlations between academic achievement indicators and the four *nonacademic* SDQ domains, few were statistically significant, most were negative, and only 1 correlation was significantly positive. The 16 correlations between self-concept in reading and verbal achievement indicators varied from .18 to .57 (median = .39), and every one was statistically significant. The 12 correlations between math achievement and self-concept in math varied from .17 to .66 (median = .33), and all were statistically significant. These results suggest that specific academic facets of self-concept have a relationship with the associated area of academic achievement.

SDQIII responses by high school students reinforce these findings. Marsh and O'Niell (1984) found that math achievement correlated .58, .27, and .11 with math, general academic, and verbal self-concepts whereas English achievement correlated .42, .24 and .19 with verbal, general academic and math self-concepts. The nine nonacademic scales, including general self-concept, were not significantly related to any of the achievement scores. The pattern of results provides stronger support for the content specificity of self-concept/achievement relations than did the SDQI studies. This content specificity is even more dramatic when the two achievement scores are used to predict each of the SDQIII scales; the beta weights relating math achievement to verbal self-concept and English achievement to math self-concept are significantly negative. In the second study (Marsh et al., 1988), responses by Canadian high school students to four SDQIII scales (math, verbal, general academic, and general self) were related to school grades in mathematics and English. Math achievement correlated .55, .34, and .20 with math, general academic, and verbal self-concepts whereas English achievement correlated .24, .47 and .20 with verbal, general academic, and math self-concepts. Again, general self-concept was not significantly related to any of the achievement indicators. Although English achievement correlates more with general academic self-concept than verbal self-concept in this study, the pattern of results still supports the content specificity of self-concept/ achievement relations. As in the first study, this content specificity is even more dramatic when the two achievement scores were used to predict each self-concept score.

ASDQII Responses

Marsh (1992) extended these earlier studies by evaluating relations between more specific components of academic self-concept based on ASDQII responses and school performance in eight core school subjects. Following the logic of construct validation, academic achievement in each school subject should correlate more highly with the corresponding academic self-concept scale than with any other self-concept scale. Thus, for example, grades in English classes should correlate highly with English self-concept and more highly with English self-concept than any other ASDQ scale. Also, consistent with the extreme differentiation among different self-concept facets found earlier, it was hypothesized that academic self-concept scales would be more differentiated—less correlated—than the corresponding academic achievement scores. Consistent with predictions,

1. Correlations between matching areas of achievement and self-concept were large and statistically significant for all eight content areas (values of r vary from .45 to .70; mean $= .57$). Furthermore, each area of achievement was systematically less correlated with other (nonmatching) academic self-concept scales.

2. Correlations among the eight achievement scores (.42 to .72; mean $r = .58$) were substantially larger than correlations among the eight academic self-concept scales (.21 to .53; mean $r = .34$).

These results are consistent across school grades for two different semesters and across students in different year groups. Although not a focus of this research, it is interesting to note that the set of six ASDQII scales for the noncore subjects are substantially less correlated with school grades (values of r of $-.170$ to .281). More sophisticated CFA models showed that academic self-concept in each content area was primarily a function of achievement in the matching school subject, and achievements in other subjects contributed little to its prediction.

Considerable research shows that academic achievement is correlated substantially more with academic self-concept than nonacademic or general self-concept. SDQ research extended these findings by showing that relations between math and verbal self-concepts and math and verbal achievement are very content specific. Most previous research on relations between academic achievement and academic self-concept has been limited to relations between general measures of the two constructs or has used only one or two specific content areas to represent each construct. The ASDQ research is apparently unique in considering relations between academic self-concept and achievement in such a wide variety of content areas. Hence, whereas the content specificity of relations between academic achievement and self-concept found here is consistent with previous research, the findings reflect an extension of previous research. It is also important to note that the *sizes* of these correlations based on ASDQII responses are substantially larger than those typically reported (e.g., Byrne, 1984; Hansford & Hattie, 1982; Marsh, 1986, 1990c). Previous research has found that self-concept/achievement relations are larger if the self-concept measures reflect academic rather than nonacademic or general components of self-concept. Hence, it is not surprising, perhaps, that even higher correlations of self-concept/achievement are found when self-concept and achievement are measured in even more specific content areas.

The Causal Ordering of Academic Self-Concept and Academic Achievement: Multiwave, Longitudinal Panel Analyses

Do changes in academic self-concept lead to changes in subsequent academic achievement? This critical question has important theoretical and practical implications but is not answered by research considered thus far in this chapter. Byrne (1984), for example, noted that much of the interest in the self-concept/achievement relation stems from the belief that academic self-concept has motivational properties such that changes in academic self-concept will lead to changes in subsequent academic achievement. Calsyn and Kenny (1977) contrasted self-enhancement and skill development models of the self-concept/achievement relation. According to the self-enhancement model, self-concept is a primary determinant of academic achievement. Support for this model would provide a strong justification for self-concept enhancement interventions explicit or implicit in many educational programs. In contrast, the skill development model implies that academic self-concept emerges principally as a consequence of academic achievement. According to this model, the best way to enhance academic self-concept is to develop stronger academic skills.

Despite the importance of this issue, well-established paradigms did not exist prior to the 1980s. Because self-concept and academic achievement are not readily amenable to experimental manipulations, most research has relied on longitudinal panel data in which both self-concept and achievement are measured on at least two occasions (i.e., a two-wave two-variable design). Recently there has been important developments in the application of CFA approaches to structural equation modeling using statistical packages such as LISREL (Joreskog & Sorbom, 1988) for the analysis of these longitudinal panel designs.

Previous Research

In her classic review of the academic self-concept research, Byrne (1984) examined studies purporting to test causal predominance between self-concept and academic achievement. Such studies, she noted must satisfy three prerequisites: (1) a statistical relationship must be established, (2) a clearly established time precedence must be established in longitudinal studies, and (3) a causal model must be tested using statistical techniques such as CFA. Byrne (1984) and subsequently Marsh (1990b) reported only three studies satisfying these prerequisites in which academic self-concept and achievement were each measured on at least two occasions and CFA was used to test causal models.

1. In a two-wave study, Byrne (1986) found no effect of prior achievement on subsequent self-concept or of prior self-concept on subsequent

achievement. She questioned the appropriateness of combining school grades and academic achievement into a single construct, however, and one of her two indicators of academic self-concept apparently was weak.

2. Shavelson and Bolus (1982), using CFA, reported that prior academic self-concept affected subsequent performance in each of three school subjects. In their study, the effects of prior achievement on subsequent academic self-concept were not statistically significant, supporting the predominance of academic self-concept over academic achievement. Shavelson and Bolus, however, cautioned that the size and nature of their study (99 seventh grade students from a single school and a T1/T2 interval of only four months) dictated caution in generalizing the results.

3. Newman (1984; also see Marsh, 1988a), using CFA, considered math achievement tests and self-concept in math collected in grades 2, 5, and 10. For both the grade 2/grade 5 and the grade 5/grade 10 intervals, prior achievement had a significant effect on subsequent self-concept in math, but prior self-concept in math had no effect on subsequent math achievement.

Several characteristics and potential limitations of these three studies require further attention. The Byrne and the Shavelson and Bolus studies each involved only two data waves, which were collected in the same academic year, whereas the Newman study included three waves that spanned eight years. By CFA standards, the sample sizes were dubiously small for studies by Shavelson and Bolus (N = 99) and by Newman (N = 84 to 143 for different correlations when pairwise deletion was used to construct the correlation matrix, and N = 75 when casewise deletion for missing data was used). Academic achievement was inferred from school grades by Shavelson and Bolus, from standardized test scores by Newman, and from both school grades and standardized test scores by Byrne.

An important advantage of the CFA approach is that it incorporates reliability estimates into the analysis so long as there are multiple indicators of a construct. If a construct is inferred from a single indicator, its reliability cannot be estimated and this substantially weakens the CFA approach. Byrne had two indicators of both academic self-concept and achievement, but Shavelson and Bolus had only single indicators of achievement (school grades) whereas Newman inferred math self-concept on the basis of a single rating item. Shavelson and Bolus did not explore this limitation in their study, although its implications may not be too serious, since school grades are likely to be fairly reliable. Inferring self-concept on the basis of responses to a single self-response item is apparently a much more serious problem in the Newman study. Therefore, in a subsequent reanalysis of the same data, Marsh (1988a) found that the data were not strong enough to warrant any clear conclusions. His results found support for both self-concept affecting achievement and achievement affecting self-concept, depending on the assumed reliability of the single-indicator constructs.

Despite inconsistent results and apparent methodological limitations in these three studies, it is interesting that the findings vary depending on how academic achievement was inferred. Shavelson and Bolus (1982) inferred academic achievement from school grades and found the causal predominance of academic self-concept over school grades. Newman (1984) inferred academic achievement from standardized test scores and argued for the predominance of academic achievement over academic self-concept (but see Marsh, 1988a). Byrne (1986) inferred academic achievement from a combined construct based on both school grades and standardized test scores and found no support for the causal predominance of either construct. Although interpretations should be made cautiously, this pattern is consistent with Marsh's suggestion (Marsh, 1987a) that the effect of prior academic self-concept on subsequent achievement is more likely if achievement is inferred from school grades that may be more responsive to effort and motivational influences than from standardized test scores.

In summary, it is useful to provide an overview of important design features in this area of research. Ideally, studies will (1) measure academic self-concept and academic achievement (school performance, standardized test scores, or preferably both) at least twice (i.e., a two-wave study) and preferably more frequently; (2) infer all latent constructs on the basis of multiple indicators; (3) consider a sufficiently large and diverse sample to justify the use of CFA and the generality of the findings; and (4) fit the data to a variety of CFA models that incorporate measurement error and test for likely residual covariation among measured variables. If both test scores and school grades are collected in the same study, then they should be considered separate constructs unless there is empirical support for combining them to form a single construct. If any of the latent constructs are measured with a single measured variable, an a priori estimate of reliability should be used and the sensitivity analysis should be conducted on the full model to determine the generality of the conclusions. Based on these criteria, no previous study is fully adequate.

A Longitudinal Panel Study Based on the Youth in Transition Data

Marsh (1990b), incorporating design the features listed previously, tested the causal ordering of academic self-concept and academic achievement with data from the large, nationally representative Youth in Transition study (Bachman & O'Malley, 1986; Marsh, 1987a). He considered data from Times 1 (early 10th grade), 2 (late 11th grade), 3 (late 12th grade), and 4 (one year after normal high school graduation). Three latent constructs were considered: academic ability (T1 only) inferred on the basis of four standardized test scores, academic self-concept (T1, T2, and T4) inferred from responses to two (T4) or three (T1 and T2) self-rating items, and school grades (T1, T2,

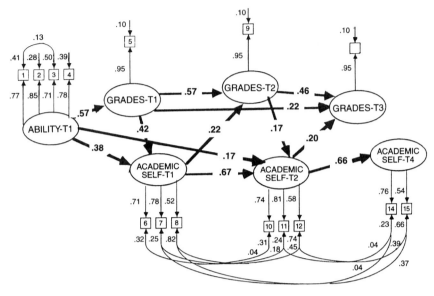

FIGURE 3
A structural equation model of the longitudinal panel design relating
academic achievement and academic self-concept on multiple occasions:
the standardized effects of prior ability, school grades, and academic self-
concept on subsequent school grades and academic self-concept. The
boxes represent measured variables used to infer each latent construct (the
ovals). The straight lines (in bold) connecting the different latent constructs
represent path coefficients. Nonsignificant path coefficients are excluded
for purposes of clarity. The curved lines represent correlated residuals
between measured variables. (From Marsh, 1990.
Reprinted with permission.)

T3). Analyses were conducted on responses from the 1,456 students who had
complete data at T1, T2, and T3. The initial a priori model (Figure 3) was
based primarily on the temporal ordering of the data collection (i.e., T1
variables precede T2 variables). At T1, there were three constructs: academic
ability, school grades, and academic self-concept. Academic ability was posited to precede school grades because students were asked to report their
grades from the previous year. Similarly, at T2, school grades preceded academic self-concept. At T3 and at T4 only one construct was considered and
no casual ordering was necessary.
    Of particular importance are the effects of latent constructs in one wave
on latent constructs in subsequent waves. Parameter estimates for the final

model showed that, at T2, academic self-concept is influenced by academic ability and T1 academic self-concept but not T1 grades. At T2, school grades are influenced by both T1 academic self-concept and T1 school grades. Similarly, school grades at T3 are influenced significantly by both T2 academic self-concept and T2 grades. Academic self-concept at T4 was influenced significantly by academic self-concept at T2 (there was no T3 academic self-concept measure) but not by T3 school grades.

Particularly since the results were replicated across two different intervals, the findings provide strong support for the effect of prior self-concept on subsequent school grades. In neither of the intervals was the effect of prior school grades on subsequent academic self-concept statistically significant. Hence, the effects of academic self-concept are "causally predominant" over those of school grades, and these results provide strong support for the self-concept enhancement model of the self-concept/achievement relation.

The causal ordering of academic self-concept and academic achievement is a particularly important issue for the study of self-concept in educational settings. Given this importance, the lack of good-quality research is surprising. The Marsh (1990b) study is important because it is one of the few studies—along with, perhaps, Shavelson and Bolus (1982)—to provide defensible evidence for the effect of prior academic self-concept on subsequent academic achievement and because it is apparently methodologically stronger than previous research. These results provide a clear answer to the question "Do changes in academic self-concept lead to changes in subsequent academic achievement?" Hence, enhancing a child's academic self-concept is not only a desirable goal but is likely to result in improved academic achievement as well.

THE INFLUENCE OF FRAME-OF-REFERENCE EFFECTS

Background

Students must evaluate their academic accomplishment in relation to some standard or frame of reference. Even if students achieve similar accomplishments, their academic self-concepts will differ if they have different frames of reference. Pertinent self-concept assessment and appropriate classroom practice depend on teachers being able to interpret these differing self-perceptions accurately. Here we describe theoretical models and empirical support for two different frame-of-reference effects. In the internal/external frame of reference (I/E) model, it is proposed that students compare their own ability levels in different academic subjects in addition to the more typical social comparison process (Suls, 1977) of comparing their own ability levels to those of other students. In the big fish, little pond effect (BFLPE), it is proposed that academic self-concept is influenced substantially by the ability levels of other students in the immediate context in addition to one's own ability level.

The Internal/External Frame-of-Reference Model

The I/E model (Marsh, 1986, 1994; Marsh et al., 1988) was designed to explain why verbal and math self-concepts are so distinct. Verbal and mathematics achievements are highly correlated (values of r of .5 to .8). Individuals who are good in one area tend to be good in the other. Verbal and math self-concepts are nearly uncorrelated. People think of themselves as "math" persons or "verbal" persons. According to the I/E model, verbal and math self-concepts are formed in relation to both external and internal comparisons, or frames of reference:

- *External Comparisons.* According to this social comparison process, I compare my self-perception of my own ability in math and in reading with the perceived abilities of other students within my frame of reference (e.g., other students in my classroom or year in school). I use this external, relativistic impression as one basis for my self-concept in each area.
- *Internal Comparisons.* According to this ipsativelike process, I compare my self-perceived ability in math with my self-perceived ability in English. I use this internal, relativistic impression as a second basis for arriving at my self-concept in each area.

External comparison processes should lead to a positive correlation between verbal and math self-concepts (because the achievements are substantially correlated). Internal comparison processes should lead to a negative correlation between verbal and math self-concepts (because the difference between math and verbal skills contributes to a higher self-concept in one area or the other). The joint operation of both processes, depending on their relative strength, should lead to the near-zero correlation between verbal and math self-concept that has been observed in empirical research.

The I/E model also predicts a *negative* direct effect of mathematics achievement on verbal self-concept and of verbal achievement on math self-concept. For example, math self-concept is higher when math skills are good (the external comparison) *and* when math skills are better than reading skills (the internal comparison). High verbal skills detract from a high math self-concept. The I/E model generates a specific and perhaps unexpected pattern of relations among verbal and math self-concept, and verbal and math achievement. According to the model (see Figure 4),

1. Math and verbal skills are highly correlated with each other while math and verbal self-concepts are substantially less correlated. (The I/E model

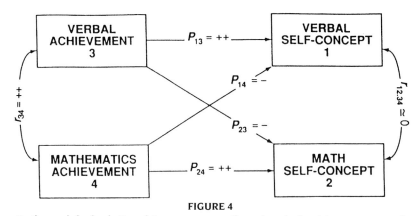

FIGURE 4
Path model of relationships among math and verbal achievements and
math and verbal self-concepts: the internal/external frame-of-reference
model. Coefficients indicated $++$, $-$, and 0 are predicted to be high
positive, low negative, and approximately zero, respectively. (From Marsh,
1986, pp. 129–149. Reprinted with permission.)

does not require that the verbal/math correlation be 0, but only that it be
substantially smaller than the typically large correlation between verbal and
math achievement levels.)

2. Verbal achievement has a strong, positive direct effect on verbal self-
concept, but a small, negative direct effect on math self-concept.

3. Math achievement has a strong positive effect on math self-concept,
but a weaker, negative direct effect on verbal self-concept.

Marsh (1986, 1990c, 1993a; Marsh et al., 1988) consistently found near-
zero correlations between math and verbal SDQ self-concepts: SDQI
responses in 10 studies of students in years 4, 5 and 6, for SDQII responses
in 5 samples of high school students, and for SDQIII responses in 5 samples
of late adolescents and young adults. Canadian high school students completed scales from three self-concept instruments (the SDQIII and two others) and correlations between the three math scales and the three verbal
scales varied from $-.05$ to $+.08$. English and math self-concept scores based
on responses by over 14,000 U.S. students completing the nationally representative High School and Beyond (HSB) survey were uncorrelated ($r =
-.024$). The small correlation between verbal and math self-concepts is
counterintuitive and contrary to the original Shavelson et al. model but is
consistent with the I/E model and the Marsh–Shavelson revised model.

Stronger tests of I/E predictions are possible when there are math and
verbal achievements as well as math and verbal self-concepts. In 13 SDQ

studies, Marsh found

1. Correlations between indicators of verbal and math achievement were substantial (.42 to .94).
2. Correlations between measures of verbal and math self-concepts were much smaller (−.10 to +.19).
3. Path coefficients from verbal achievement to verbal self-concept and from math achievement to math self-concept were all significantly positive.
4. Path coefficients from math achievement to verbal self-concept, and from verbal achievement to math self-concept were significantly *negative*.

This pattern of results was subsequently replicated for responses to each of three different self-concept instruments (Marsh et al., 1988), for very large nationally representative samples of U.S. high school students in the High School and Beyond study (Marsh, 1990c) and in the National Longitudinal study (Marsh, 1994), and in Skaalvik and Rankin's recent 1995 study of responses by Norwegian students. These results provide support for I/E model predictions across age, instruments, nationality, and achievement indicators.

The I/E Model with Self-Concept
and Self-Efficacy Responses

In contrast to the consistent support for the I/E model based on Australian, Canadian, and U.S. studies, the model was not supported in a recent Norwegian study by Skaalvik and Rankin (1990). Based on their findings, Skaalvik and Rankin (1990, p. 550) concluded that "the prediction of a near-zero correlation between math and verbal self-concepts was not supported and the substantial correlation between cognitive and verbal self-concepts by itself calls into question the generality of the I/E model." However, they obtained self-concept responses by asking students to judge their ability to successfully answer specific math and verbal achievement items, a standard operationalization of self-efficacy. This led Marsh, Walker, and Debus (1991) to pursue the distinction between self-efficacy and self-concept responses for the I/E model.

Perceived self-efficacy is defined as the self-perceptions of one's skills and capabilities to execute courses of action required to deal with prospective situations. It is hypothesized to promote appropriate task choice, motivation, sustained effort and persistence in the face of difficulty, future performance, and subsequent self-efficacy. Self-efficacy is typically measured in a specific domain. Bandura (1986) is very critical of global self-concept measures, and of course, we agree with this concern. Self-efficacy responses are typically more domain specific than SDQ responses, but this distinction is not inherent as self-concept could also be assessed in more specific domains.

Both self-efficacy and self-concept responses should predict subsequent choice, motivation, and effort, even after partialing out levels of prior achievement. However, they are likely to differ in the influence of frame-of-reference effects. Such effects are directly implicated in self-concept responses since students use performance by others (external comparisons) and their own performance in other domains (internal comparisons) to establish frames of reference for evaluating their own performance. Self-efficacy judgment focuses on assessment of the individual's capabilities in relation to the specific criterion items, minimizing the influence of frame-of-reference effects. Using CFA models of math and verbal measures of self-concept, self-efficacy, and achievement Marsh, Walker, and Debus (1991) found (1) correlations between math and verbal self-concepts are substantially less positive than correlations between math and verbal self-efficacy responses, and (2) support for the internal comparison component of the I/E model—the negative effects of math achievement on verbal self-concept and of verbal achievement on math self-concept—is stronger for self-concept responses than self-efficacy responses.

Self-efficacy studies do not focus on the standards or frames of reference used to evaluate performance. Such standards may be implicit, but they must exist. Even if frame of reference has little influence on expectations of solving a problem, it may influence evaluations of the performance's worthiness, which may be important in predicting subsequent behavior. For example, consider two students who are equally able at mathematics but who differ in terms of verbal skills. Because they are likely to have similar math self-efficacies, differences in math self-efficacies will not predict differences in subsequent behaviors. According to the I/E model, however, the student with poorer verbal skills will have a better math self-concept, and this will influence subsequent task choice, effort, persistence, course work selection, and future math performance. This prediction assumes that it is not the self-efficacy responses per se that affect subsequent behavior but rather students' cognitive, affective, or motivational mediating processes that the performance expectancies instigate. Skaalvick and Rankin (1995) recently replicated the Marsh, Walker, and Debus (1991) findings and supported their speculations by showing that math and verbal self-concepts influenced corresponding measures of intrinsic motivation, effort, and anxiety whereas math and verbal self-efficacy responses did not.

Broader Implications of the I/E Model

The research summarized here has focused on the surprisingly low correlation between math and verbal self-concepts that is consistent with the internal comparison process, but the implications probably have much broader generality. To illustrate this suggestion, consider two athletes: a weekend sports enthusiast who is reasonably good at golf, tennis, and a variety of other sports, but who is best at golf (with a handicap of 10) and a professional tennis player who is also a good golfer (with a handicap of 2). Asked how good they were at golf, it would be reasonable for the professional tennis player to say "pretty good" (because she is so much better at tennis) whereas the weekend sports enthusiast might say "good" (because golf is her best sport). Objectively, the professional tennis player is a better golfer, but if asked to complete self-concept of golf and tennis scales the weekend sports enthusiast may have as high or even a higher self-concept of golf than the professional athlete. We also suspect that the internal comparison process explains in part why correlations among all scales on each of the SDQ instruments are so low and why correlations among ASDQII scales are so much lower than correlations among achievement scores in the same subjects.

These results also have a number of interesting implications for classroom teachers. Research and common sense suggest that positive feedback that lacks credibility is likely to be ineffective. Hence, teachers must judiciously seek to provide positive reinforcement that is credible. To achieve this goal, however, teachers must be able to gauge accurately student self-concepts in different academic areas. Whereas SDQ research has found that teachers are able to infer students' academic self-concepts with moderate accuracy, their responses reflect primarily student ability and do not incorporate the internal comparison process. Hence, when teachers were asked to infer the self-concepts of low-ability students in different academic areas, they inferred their self-concepts to be uniformly low. In contrast to teacher inferences, the internal comparison process implies that even the least able students may have an average or even above average academic self-concept in their best academic subjects even if their skills are below average in that particular subject. Conversely, when asked to infer the self-concepts of academically gifted students, teachers judged them to be high in all academic areas. In contrast, actual student self-concepts were much more differentiated. Even academically gifted students will be relatively poorer in some school subjects and, consistent with the internal comparison process, may have academic self-concepts that are average or below average in these subjects even if their academic skills are above average. Thus, according to the internal comparison process, everyone feels more positively about himself or herself in some areas and everyone feels less positively in some other areas. In addition to these internal frames of reference, the context of other students also provides an important external frame of reference by which we judge ourselves.

The Big Fish, Little Pond Effect

Marsh (1984b, 1984c; Marsh & Parker, 1984) proposed a frame of reference model called the big fish, little pond effect to encapsulate external frame of reference effects. In this model, it is hypothesized that students compare their own academic ability with the academic abilities of their peers and use this social comparison impression as one basis for forming their own academic self-concept. The BFLPE occurs when equally able students have lower academic self-concepts when they compare themselves to more able students, and higher academic self-concepts when they compare themselves with less able students. For example, if average ability students attend a high-ability school then their academic abilities will be below the average of other students in the school and this will lead to academic self-concepts that are below average. Conversely if these students attended a low ability school, then their abilities would be above average in that school and this would lead to academic self-concepts that are above average. Similarly, the academic self-concepts of below average and above average pupils will depend on their academic ability but also will vary with the type of school they attend. According to this model, academic self-concept will be correlated positively with individual achievement (brighter children will have higher academic self-concepts) but negatively related to school-average achievement (the same children will have lower academic self-concepts in a school where the average ability is high).

The BFLPE is an example of external frame-of-reference effects that may have an impact on students attending selective schools. Consider a capable student who has been evaluated as the top student throughout primary school. If accepted into a selective high school, the student may be below average or average relative to other students in this school rather than at the top of the class. This can have detrimental effects on the self-concept of the student, who is no longer a big fish in a small pond (top of the class) but is in a large pond full of even larger fish (average or below average in a high-ability school). Anecdotal support for these contentions comes from in-service programs conducted by one of the authors for Australian teachers from selective schools. Teachers in these programs often reported that new students in year 7 experience difficulties in adjusting to selective schools. One teacher mentioned that she was most concerned because many of her new year 7 students were in tears for the first year they attended a higher-ability school. After hearing information such as presented in this chapter, a school counsellor from a selective school conducted a simple survey in which students in each year group were asked to indicate how bright they were relative to other students in the state. He reported to one of the authors of this chapter that, on average, students' self-perceptions of their academic ability declined about 5 percentage ranks for each year they had been in the selective high school.

Case study evidence also supports the underlying processes of the BFLPE (Marsh, 1991). A student named Ilona was attending an academically selective Australian high school, but she was doing poorly and not attending school regularly. A change in employment forced her parents to move and Ilona changed to a new high school that was not a selective school. Due to her poor progress at the last school Ilona was initially placed in a class with the least able students in the school. It quickly became evident, however, that she was a very able student and she soon worked her way into the most advanced classes in the new school. Her parents found that she was taking school more seriously and spending more time on her homework. Ilona indicated that at the old (selective) school she had to work really hard to get just average marks which was not worth the effort. However, if she worked hard in her new school she could be one of the best which was apparently worth the effort.

Research Support

The operation of the social comparison process underlying the BFLPE has been supported in numerous studies (e.g., Marsh, 1984b, 1984c, 1987a, 1994; Marsh & Parker, 1984). Marsh and Parker (1984) sampled sixth grade classes from high and low socio-economic status (SES) areas in the same geographical area. The two samples differed substantially in terms of reading achievement and IQ scores. In path models of the relations among achievement, school-average ability, and responses to the SDQI, the direct effect of school-average ability on academic self-concept was negative in models that controlled for individual achievement, individual SES, or both.

In an American study based on 87 high schools, Marsh (1987a; also see Bachman & O'Malley, 1986) found that the effects of school-average ability on academic self-concept were negative whereas the effects of school-average SES on academic self-concept were negligible. He also found that African-Americans, particularly those in segregated schools, did not differ substantially from Caucasian students in terms of academic self-concept even though there were substantial differences in terms of standardized achievement test scores. Whereas this pattern might suggest that the academic self-concept responses were "culturally biased," this is exactly the pattern predicted to occur in the BFLPE. African-Americans had academic ability test scores that were below average, but—particularly in the segregated schools—compared themselves to classmates who also had below-average test scores. Therefore, while their academic self-concepts were somewhat below average (due, perhaps to self-perceptions that were independent of the immediate school context), they were not nearly as low as ability tests would suggest.

The results of Marsh's analysis also clarified the distinction between academic ability and grade-point average (GPA), their respective influences on self-concept, and how this influenced frame of reference effects. The 87 schools in the study differed substantially in terms of school-average academic ability, but not school average. Apparently schools "graded on a curve" GPA (i.e., measures of school-based performance were not externally moderated) such that the distribution of grades was similar from one school to the next even though academic ability levels differed substantially. This substantial frame of reference effect influences GPA independent of academic ability; equally able students have lower GPAs in high-ability schools than in low-ability schools. Marsh demonstrated that this frame of reference effect influencing GPA was separate from, but contributed to, the BFLPE on academic self-concept. In further analysis of this same data, Marsh and Rowe (1996) replicated the finding using a multilevel modeling approach and demonstrated that the BFLPE generalized across all levels of initial ability level including the very brightest students.

Research that utilizes a variety of different experimental and analytical approaches also supports the existence of the BFLPE. Sociologists studying school context effects have found that school-average ability and particularly school-average SES are related to educational and occupational aspirations or attainments. In a review of this largely American literature, Alwin and Otto (1977) reported that school-average ability was negatively related to aspirations whereas school-average SES tended to be positively associated with aspirations.

Rogers, Smith, and Coleman (1978) ranked a group of children in terms of academic achievement in their whole classroom and in terms of academic achievement across the sample. They found that the within-classroom rankings were correlated more highly with self-concept than the group ratings. Schwarzer, Jerusalem, and Lange (1983; also see Jerusalem, 1984) examined the self-concepts of West German students who moved from nonselective, heterogeneous primary schools to secondary schools that were streamed on the basis of academic achievement. At the transition point students selected to enter the high-ability schools had substantially higher academic self-concepts than those entering the low-ability schools. However, by the end of the first year in the new schools, no differences in academic self-concepts for the two groups were present. Path analyses indicated that the direct influence of school type on academic self-concept was negative. The most able students in the low-ability schools were less able but had much higher academic self-concepts than the least able children in the high-ability schools.

In a study of academically disadvantaged children, Strang, Smith, and Rogers (1978) tested the self-concepts of children who attended some classes with other disadvantaged children and other classes with nondisadvantaged children. Academically disadvantaged children were assigned randomly to experimental and control groups and children in the experimental group were given a treatment to enhance the saliency of their membership in the regular classrooms. At the conclusion of the treatment these students reported lower self-concepts than those in the control group. In a meta-analysis of the effect of ability grouping on self-concept C. L. Kulik (1985; see also C. L. Kulik & Kulik, 1982; Marsh, 1984b) compared children in streamed and unstreamed classes. They found that high-ability students tended to have lower self-concepts and low-ability students higher self-concepts when placed in streamed classes.

Brookover (1989) examined frame-of-reference effects on academic self-concept from the perspective of the extent to which students in different schools were streamed according to ability. In schools with ability streaming, low-ability students tend to be placed in classes with other low-ability students and high-ability students tend to be placed in classes with other high-ability students. To the extent to which students use other students within their class as a frame of reference, low-ability students in streamed classes should have higher academic self-concepts (because they compare themselves primarily to other low-ability students) than low-ability students in unstreamed classes. High-ability students in streamed classes, however, should have lower academic self-concepts (because they compare themselves primarily to other high-ability students) than high-ability students in unstreamed classes. Thus, streaming should tend to increase the academic self-concepts of low-ability students and decrease the academic self-concepts of high-ability students. Consistent with these predictions, Brookover found that the academic self-concepts were much less variable in schools that streamed their classes.

Reuman (1989) found that between-class ability grouping produced lower academic self-concepts for high-ability children and higher academic self-concepts for low-ability children. Reuman asked students if they would compare their test scores with those of a classmate and whether the selected classmate was perceived to be more or less able than they were. Consistent with the social comparison process, between-class ability grouping was associated with systematic differences in the perceived ability of the comparison classmate; high-ability children were more likely to select classmates with higher abilities than their own and low-ability children were more likely to select classmates with lower abilities than their own. These results support the role of social comparison processes in mediating the effects of ability grouping.

Davis (1966) suggested a model similar to the BFLPE in a study of career decisions of American college men. Davis sought support for a theoretical explanation of why the academic quality of a college had so little effect on career choice. Expanding the educational policy implications of his research, Davis (1966, p. 31) concluded:

> Counselors and parents might well consider the drawbacks as well as the advantages of sending a boy to a "fine" college, if, when doing so, it is fairly certain that he will end up in the bottom ranks of his graduating class. The aphorism "It is better to be a big frog in a small pond than a small frog in a big pond" is not perfect advice but it is not trivial.

Such advice may also be relevant for evaluating the likely impact of attending academically selective high schools.

The social comparison theory underlying the BFLPE also has important implications for the practice of integrating children with learning disabilities

(LD) into regular classrooms (i.e., "mainstreaming"). Marsh and Johnston (1993) reported that moving LD children from special classes with other LD children into regular, mixed-ability classes was likely to result in lower academic self-concepts for LD children. This result is consistent with the social comparison theory in that the average ability level of students in the mixed-ability classes is higher than in the special classes. Thus, LD children are likely to feel less academically able in comparison with non-LD children in regular classrooms than with other LD children in special classes. They noted that these findings are opposite to predictions based on labeling theory which suggests that LD children would feel negatively stigmatized by being placed in a special class with other disadvantaged children. Burns's review of this literature led him to conclude that placement of LD children in special schools resulted in an improvement in self-concept and that self-concept was positively related to the length of time LD students spent in the special schools. He interpreted these results as favoring social comparison theory, but also noted that part of the problem may be that special schools do not prepare students for integration into mainstream society.

Chapman (1988) conducted a meta-analysis of studies of LD children's self-concepts. Of particular relevance to this chapter was his comparison of LD students who were (1) completely segregated in special classes, (2) partially segregated for some work and partially integrated in regular classes with non-LD students, and (3) "unplaced" in completely integrated settings (i.e., LD students in regular classes who were not receiving LD remedial assistance). Whereas LD children in all three settings had poorer self-concepts than non-LD children, the setting did make a difference. For general self-concept students in fully segregated and partially segregated settings did not differ from each other but had better self-concepts than did unplaced LD students in regular classrooms. For academic self-concept fully segregated children had higher self-concepts than partially segregated students and both groups had substantially better self-concepts than unplaced LD students. The decrement associated with being an unplaced LD student in regular classrooms was substantially larger for academic self-concept than for general self-concept. These results support social comparison theory, but are complicated by the potential confounding between the type of setting and the amount of special assistance LD students received in the different settings.

Summary

In summary, a growing body of research from different levels of education and from different countries shows that school-average ability is negatively related to academic self-concept. Equally able students tend to have lower academic self-concepts if they attend academically selective schools than if they attend schools in which the average ability level is lower. These results provide strong support for the social comparison processes underlying the BFLPE and contribute to our understanding of the formation of academic self-concept. For policy makers and parents, however, it may be even more important to know how school-average ability and the BFLPE influence other academic outcomes such as school-based performance, external examinations, course selection, academic aspirations, and subsequent university performance.

The Effect of School-Average Ability on Other Academic Outcomes

The results of the BFLPE are very important for understanding the formation of academic self-concept and testing frame of reference models. However, particularly parents and classroom teachers should also be prompted to ask "So what?" What are the consequences of attending high-ability schools on other academic outcomes and how are these related to academic self-concept?

In response to this question, Marsh (1991) examined the influence of school-average ability on a wide variety of subsequent outcomes. He emphasized the role of academic self-concept and educational aspirations formed early in high school as mediators of the effects of school-average ability on subsequent outcomes. The High School and Beyond (HSB) data was utilized for this study. This large, longitudinal data base contained data for approximately 1000 randomly selected American high schools and 30 randomly selected students from each school. Measures were completed by the students when they were in year 10 (T1), year 12 (T2), and two years after graduation from high school (T3). Marsh, in a series of path analyses that controlled for background variables, related school-average ability to 17 outcome variables collected at T1, T2 or T3: self-concept (academic and global), academic choice behavior (taking advanced courses), academic effort (time on homework and class preparation), school-based academic performance, scores on a battery of standardized tests, aspirations (educational and occupational) at T1 and T2, and subsequent university attendance and aspirations (educational and occupational) at T3.

The results of the complicated path analysis (Marsh, 1991) were easily summarized. The total effects of school-average ability were not significantly positive for any of the 17 outcome variables and were significantly negative for 15 of 17 outcome variables. School-average ability most negatively affected academic self-concept as in the BFLPE studies and educational aspirations as suggested in studies of school-context effects. Controlling for these two T1 variables substantially reduced the negative effects of school-average ability on other outcome variables. This suggests that effects of school-average ability were mediated in part by academic self-concept and educational aspirations. Even after controlling for all T1 outcomes, however, school-average ability still negatively affected 7 of the 11 outcomes at T2 and T3. This implies that school-average ability continued to affect negatively T2 and T3 outcomes beyond its already substantial negative effect at T1.

In summary, equally able students attending higher-ability high schools were likely to select less demanding courses and to have lower academic self-concepts, lower GPAs, lower educational aspirations, and lower occupational aspirations in both years 10 and 12 of high school, and to have lower educational and occupational aspirations two years after the normal graduation from high school. Attending higher-ability schools also negatively affected T2 standardized test scores and subsequent college attendance, though these effects were smaller. For many T2 and T3 outcomes, there were statistically significant negative effects of school-average ability beyond those that could be explained in terms of T1 outcomes. This implies that there are additional negative effects of school-average ability during the last two years of high school beyond the already substantial negative effects found early in high school. Marsh (1991, p. 445) concluded:

> The academic outcomes associated with attending higher-ability schools were not commensurate with the ability levels of students attending these schools, and no academic advantages of such schools were observed for any outcomes. The negative effects of school-average ability were primarily mediated by academic self-concept and educational aspirations.

These findings call into question the supposed advantages of attending higher-ability schools. Even though the disadvantages of attending higher-ability schools may not generalize to all higher-ability schools and to all individual students, the results of this and other BFLPE studies demonstrate that it is unjustified to assume that attending higher ability schools will necessarily result in any academic advantages. On the basis of BFLPE research, it appears that higher-ability schools on average do not provide academic benefits beyond those provided by lower-ability schools and apparently disadvantage at least some students attending these schools.

Classroom Implications

Consider the following plausible interpretation of the BFLPE. When reasonably bright students first attend a selective school, they are confronted with the reality that they are no longer one of the brighter students. In fact, depending on how selective the school is, they may be one of the least bright students. There are many ways of dealing with this ego threatening and stressful situation. One of the most common appears to be readjusting academic self-concept so that it more realistically reflects the standing of these students within this new academic environment. Apparently, educational aspirations also fall so as to be consistent with academic self-concept and the new, academic standing of these students. From these changes in academic self-concept and educational aspirations flow a number of additional changes. These include decisions about how these students will spend their time, what classes they will select, subsequent levels of academic achievement, and subsequent university attendance. The underlying problem, it seems, is that students need to feel good about their academic accomplishments, which reinforces further academic pursuits. Apparently, it is more difficult for students to establish and maintain these positive feelings in academically selective schools than in nonselective schools. Whereas other scenarios could be developed to explain how students cope with attending academically selective schools, the scenario presented here is consistent with research summarized previously.

Competitive Orientations and Frames of Reference

Social comparison theory provides the theoretical rationale for the BFLPE. It may be inevitable that students evaluate themselves in relation to their classmates independent of whatever schools do to reinforce or counter the BFLPE. Appropriately designed programs may counter some of the negative consequences of the BFLPE, but it seems that high-ability schools are typically structured to accentuate the effect. For example, the BFLPE is likely to be larger in highly competitive settings that use standardized, normative assessments that encourage students to compare their performances with other students so that most students know their "class rank." Highly competitive environments in which all students know how their performances compare with those of other students are likely to have a few "winners" and a lot of "losers." We suspect that the BFLPE can be altered by changing the competitive orientation of a school and the nature of feedback provided to students. Whereas we have no direct evidence of these suppositions (but see Marshall & Weinstein, 1984), indirect support comes from a related physical education study of the effects of different aerobics training programmes (Marsh & Peart, 1988).

High school girls were randomly assigned to one of three intervention groups. They completed a physical fitness test and the SDQII prior to and immediately following a six-week intervention. Two experimental groups participated in aerobics training that emphasized either a competitive or a cooperative orientation, whereas a control group participated in an unstructured game of volleyball with little emphasis on competition or strenuous activity. The two experimental groups differed in the nature of motivational cues given by the instructor and the exercises. Cooperative exercises required the cooperation of at least two girls whereas the competitive exercises were performed individually. The competitive feedback emphasized the relative performances of different students and focused on whoever performed best for a particular exercise, whereas the cooperative feedback emphasized individual progress in relation to previous performances of the individual.

For both groups there were a total of 14 35-minute classes during the six-week intervention period.

Both the competitive and cooperative programs significantly enhanced physical fitness relative to pretest scores and in comparison to the control group. The cooperative program also significantly enhanced self-concept of physical ability, but the competitive program produced a significant *decline* in self-concept of physical ability. There was a similar, much weaker pattern of results for self-concept of physical appearance. Differences on other SDQII scales were nonsignificant. The results provide further support for the importance of considering multidimensional self-concepts in the evaluation of specific interventions and environmental characteristics. A potential weakness of the study is the lack of a follow-up. A six-week intervention is unlikely to be sufficiently powerful to have any lasting effect on physical fitness unless the girls continue to participate in physical activities. It seems probable that the competitive group, with their lowered self-concepts of physical ability, would be less likely than the cooperative group to participate further. Hence, the differential advantages of the cooperative group over the competitive group may be even larger if a long-term follow-up had been conducted.

It was not surprising that cooperative programs had a more positive effect on physical ability self-concept. What may seem surprising is that those in the competitive group actually declined in physical ability self-concept despite their increased physical fitness. It seems like the competitive program forced participants to compare their own physical abilities with those of the most physically able participants to a much greater degree than had been the case prior to the intervention or in the other groups. In a setting with a few winners and a lot of losers, the average level of self-concept is likely to decline. Although participants apparently were aware that they were more fit at the end of the competitive program, there was an even greater shift in the standard of comparison that they used to evaluate themselves. This explanation reflects the operation of social comparison processes akin to those used to explain the Big Fish Little Pond Effect in which self-concept reflects both actual accomplishments and the frame of reference used to evaluate the accomplishments.

The Combined Effects of the Big Fish, Little Pond Effect and the Internal/External Frame-of-Reference Model

We have focused on a general or total measure in testing the BFLPE, but it is possible that a separate ability context is established in different school subjects, as is implied in the I/E model. Marsh (1990a) tested this proposal by combining the BFLPE and I/E models in a single study based on the HSB data. In this study, math and English self-concepts were posited to be a function of individual levels of mathematics and English achievement and of school-average levels of mathematics and English achievement. As in the I/E model the separate effects of mathematics and English achievement on the corresponding areas of self-concept were considered. As in the BFLPE the effects of school-average achievement on academic self-concept was considered. What is new is that the separate effects of school-average mathematics achievement and school-average English achievement were considered simultaneously.

Findings were consistent with predictions from the I/E model. Consistent with the BFLPE, school-average achievement had a negative effect on academic achievement. The important new finding, however, was that these negative effects of school-average achievements in mathematics and English were very content specific. School-average mathematics achievement had a negative effect on math self-concept but a slight positive effect on English self-concept. Conversely, school-average English achievement had a negative effect on English self-concept but a slight positive effect on math self-concept. It is interesting to note that school-average mathematics, despite its negative effect on math self-concept, had a slightly positive effect on English self-concept. That is, if I attend a high school where the other students are mathematical geniuses, my math self-concept will suffer but my English self-concept may be a little higher. The converse set of effects were observed for school-average English achievement. This finding is consistent with the general observation that an influence that positively affects mathematics self-concept is likely to have a negative effect on English self-concept and vice versa. This pattern of counterbalancing effects apparently reflects the internal comparison process embodied in the I/E model.

Special Programs for Gifted and Talented Students: The Big Fish Strikes Again

BFLPE studies described earlier seem to have important implications for the educational strategies used with gifted and talented (GAT) students. However, important limitations in the studies may limit the generalizability of BFLPE results to GAT settings. In particular, BFLPE studies are based primarily on de facto selection processes in which students are not explicitly selected to be in selective schools on the basis of academic achievement and other academic accomplishments. Hence, it is important to evaluate the effects of GAT classes in relation to issues raised in the BFLPE studies.

The purposes of the following two studies described by Marsh, Chessor, Craven, and Roche (1995) were to test predictions based on the BFLPE about the effects of participation in full-time GAT primary school classes over time and in relation to matched students attending mixed-ability classes. A major emphasis is on the differential effects on academic and nonacademic components of self-concept, and also on the effects of initial ability levels. In both studies, GAT students attending a GAT class were matched to students of equal ability who are attending mixed-ability classes.

Research Evidence

In Study 1, students in the GAT program experienced significant declines in three domains of academic self-concept over time and in relation to matched comparison students. There were no significant differences in four nonacademic self-concept domains. In Study 2, students in the GAT program also experienced significant declines in three academic self-concept scales over time and in relation to comparison students. There were no significant differences in nonacademic self-concepts. In both studies this general pattern of results was reasonably consistent across gender, age, and initial ability. Both studies had some other important features that warrant further consideration and may provide information useful to policy and future research.

A critical feature of these studies was the separation of different components of self-concept. Consistent with a priori predictions based on theory and previous research, participation in GAT programs had a negative effect on academic self-concept and no effect on nonacademic self-concept. This prediction is important, because most previous GAT research has relied primarily on agglomerate total self-concept scores that confound differences in academic and nonacademic self-concept. The results demonstrate that in future GAT research it is critical for researchers to use well-developed, multidimensional self-concept scales that at least distinguish between academic and nonacademic components of self-concept.

In Study 2, measures were collected from only two occasions. Whereas there was a decline in the academic self-concepts of the GAT students across these two occasions, there was no way to determine when the decline occurred. In Study 3, however, measures were collected from three occasions. Here the results showed that there were declines between the first two occasions, but there were new, additional declines between the last two occasions.

Anecdotal results from Study 2 may also bear on the issue of acceleration. The nine-year-old GAT participants were accelerated nearly a year ahead of their matched (in terms of age) comparison students prior to entry into the GAT program. Even though acceleration was not encouraged by the schools, it may not be surprising that parents who seek to enroll their children in GAT classes also encouraged the schools to accelerate their children. The nine-year-old GAT students had substantially lower academic and nonacademic self-concepts than matched comparison students, prior to the start of the GAT program. These results may suggest, perhaps, that acceleration may have detrimental effects on self-concept that are also consistent with the BFLPE. Accelerated students are in a context with older students who are physically, socially, emotionally, and academically more mature. Hence, the

BFLPE may generalize to nonacademic self-concepts. This investigation was not designed to evaluate acceleration and the data are not adequate to support any conclusions. We offer these speculations as a direction for further research.

Strategies for Counteracting the BFLPE

Participation in GAT programs is not "bad," but may have unanticipated, negative effects on one important outcome: academic self-concept. Some individual students may be immune to the BFLPE, and there may be strategies to counteract the BFLPE such as

1. Expanding the basis for selecting students to include criteria other than standardized test scores. It appears that students of all ability levels are influenced by the BFLPE. However, it may be that highly independent students who gain self-satisfaction from individual improvement, achieving personal bests, and mastery of new skills are likely to be less negatively affected by the BFLPE than students who gain satisfaction from competing with and "beating" other students and from being the "best" student in their class.

2. Developing assessment tasks that encouraged individual students to pursue projects that are of particular interest to them to reduce social comparison. To the extent that students pursue their own unique projects and feel positive about the results, they should be able to maintain a positive academic self-concept even if other students in the GAT program are "more able" according to traditional IQ tests.

3. Avoiding a highly competitive environment that encourages the social comparison processes underlying the BFLPE. Ironically, it seems that some GAT programs intentionally foster a highly competitive environment that is likely to exacerbate the BFLPE rather than to counteract it.

4. Providing students with feedback in relation to criterion reference standards and personal improvement over time rather than comparisons based on the performances of other GAT students. To the extent that feedback emphasizes how each student compares with other students in the same class, the BFLPE is likely to be exacerbated.

5. Emphasizing to each student that she or he is a very able student and valuing the unique accomplishments of each individual student so that all students can feel good about themselves.

6. Enhancing students' feelings of connection, bonding, or identification with other GAT students in their class and with the GAT group as a whole.

7. Selecting or training teachers who are sensitive to these special needs of GAT students (although we suspect that good GAT teachers are the same teachers who are most effective in non-GAT classrooms).

An important direction of further research is to identify individual student characteristics that predict students who will benefit most from GAT programs and evaluate policies that maximize benefits. Previous research has focused on the definition of talent and the identification of GAT students, but more emphasis is needed on identifying students who will benefit most from particular types of programs such as full-time GAT classes. Such research may facilitate the development of matching optimally effective GAT programs with individual's preferred learning styles.

HIERARCHICAL STRUCTURE OF SELF-CONCEPT IN DIFFERENT DOMAINS

The major focus of this chapter is on academic self-concept and its relation to academic outcomes. In this research we have traced a clear pattern of development in self-concept research. Historically, researchers focused on a broad global component of self-concept that did not differentiate between academic and nonacademic self-concept. Particularly beginning with the Shavelson et al. (1976) model and Byrne's (1984) review, there has been more emphasis on an academic self-concept that is distinguished from non-academic and global components of self-concept. Also consistent with the Shavelson et al. model, there were separate scales for verbal and math self-concepts on each of the SDQ instruments. In continuing this trend, the Marsh–Shavelson model eventually led to the development of the ASDQ, which was based on the assumption of a much more differentiated academic self-concept. Within-construct studies of the structure underlying ASDQ responses and between-construct studies of relations between ASDQ responses and academic achievement in different school subjects supported this assumption. Whereas much of the SDQ research has focused on the academic domain, we briefly review some parallel developments in other domains that are also of interest to classroom teachers.

Physical Self-Concept

Tests of the Generalizability of Findings in Other Domains

Marsh (1993d) related single-item measures of physical and academic self-concept to 14 field and laboratory indicators of physical fitness and to academic achievement for a large (N = 6283), national representative sample of Australian students aged 9–15 years. Correlations between self-concept and the corresponding external criteria increased steadily with age in both the physical and academic domains. These results are consistent with results discussed earlier in that with increasing age, self-concept responses apparently become more consistent with relevant external sources that students used in forming their self-concept responses. This apparently explains why significant others are more accurate in inferring self-concepts of older students than younger students. This trend is also consistent with our explanation of why levels of self-concept decline during preadolescent years. Also consistent with earlier, discussion the correlation between physical and academic self-concepts in this study declined with age (i.e., the self-concept became more differentiated).

Although girls had slightly lower physical fitness self-concepts than boys, correlations with objective indicators were similar for boys and girls. Consistent with predictions from frame-of-reference research reviewed earlier, relations were stronger *after* controlling for gender and particularly age, suggesting that self-concepts are formed relative to other students of a similar age and gender. Thus, for example, performance by a young girl may be poorer in absolute terms than those of older girls and boys but still be good relative to those of other girls who are in the same year in school and thus lead to a positive physical self-concept. Whereas the directions of relations were consistent with a priori predictions for all 14 fitness indicators, the global measure of physical self-concept was more strongly related to some components of fitness (e.g., cardiovascular endurance, power, dynamic strength, and body composition) than others. Consistent with multidimensional perspectives of physical fitness, indicators from a variety of fitness domains contributed to fitness self-concepts. However, because the data base contained only a single-item measure of physical self-concept, it was not possible to test the construct validity of multiple dimensions of physical self-concept.

The Physical Self-Description Questionnaire

Marsh (in press) reviewed the status of physical self-concept measurement and the development of the Physical Self-Description Questionnaire (PSDQ). Early interest focused on global measures of esteem and their relation to body image. More recently, greater emphasis has been placed on multidimensional self-concept instruments that typically contain one or more physical scales (like the physical ability and physical appearance scales on the SDQ instruments) that can be differentiated from other specific domains of self-concept and general self-concept. However, such scales may combine and confound apparently distinguishable physical components such as health, body composition, physical attractiveness, physical fitness, and strength (Fox & Corbin, 1989; Marsh & Richards, 1988b). Inevitably, such concerns led to the development of multidimensional physical self-concept scales such as the PSDQ (Marsh, in press; Marsh, Richards, Johnson, Roche, & Tremayne, 1994).

The PSDQ is designed to measure nine specific components of physical self-concept (strength, body fat, activity, endurance/fitness, sports competence, coordination, health, appearance, flexibility), global physical self-concept, and global esteem. The theoretical rationale for the PSDQ is based on the Marsh–Shavelson self-concept model and previous SDQ research. The PSDQ scales reflect some scales from the SDQ instruments (physical ability, physical appearance, and self-esteem), scales from the earlier version of the PSDQ presented by Marsh and Redmayne (1994) and an attempt to parallel components of physical fitness identified in Marsh's (1993c) hierarchical CFA of physical fitness indicators that resembles classic hierarchical models of intelligence.

As in SDQ research, initially PSDQ research focused on the within-construct concerns, emphasizing in particular tests of the hypothesized factor structure underlying PSDQ responses. Marsh et al. (1994) found support for the a priori PSDQ factor structure in two samples of high school students and the replicability of the PSDQ factor structure in responses by men and women. In a MTMM study of relations between PSDQ responses and responses to two other physical self-concept instruments Marsh et al. (1994) also found support for the convergent and discriminant validity of PSDQ responses. Marsh (in press-c) evaluated the (test–retest) stability of PSDQ responses collected from the same respondents on four occasions. Across the 11 PSDQ scales, the internal consistency at each occasion was good (median alpha = .92) and the stability over time varied from median r = .83 for a 3-month period to median r = .69 for a 14-month period. Application of CFA models of MTMM data (with occasions as the multiple methods) supported the discriminant validity of the PSDQ scales. Marsh, Hey, and Roche (1996; also see Marsh, Perry, Horsely, & Roche, 1995) also demonstrated the usefulness of the PSDQ for elite athlete groups by showing the factor structure underlying PSDQ responses was similar in four samples: some of Australia's most elite athletes in residence at the Australian Institute of Sport, elite-athlete and non-elite-athlete students attending a prestigious sport high school, and students attending a non-sport high school. Marsh (in press-b), however, also noted the need to consider more specific components of physical self-concept that are particularly relevant to elite athletes. Following this suggestion, Marsh, Hey, Johnson, and Perry (1995) described initial development of the elite-athlete SDQ (EASDQ) designed to measure six components (skill, body, aerobic fitness, anaerobic fitness, mental competence, and overall performance) of elite-athlete self-concept. CFAs of responses by elite athletes from a selective sports high school and from the Australian Institute of Sport each identified the six a priori factors and provided good support for the factorial invariance of responses across the two groups. Hierarchical CFA provided good support for a single higher-order factor and the invariance of the hierarchical structure across the two groups.

Marsh and Redmayne (1994) pursued between construct aspects of construct validity by relating responses to an earlier version of the PSDQ to a small battery of physical fitness tests. Marsh (1995a) extended this research by relating PSDQ responses to a set of 25 external criteria, including measures of body composition, physical activity, endurance, strength, and flexibility. Each external validity criterion was predicted a priori to be most highly correlated with one of the PSDQ scales. In support of the convergent and discriminant validity of the PSDQ responses, every predicted correlation was statistically significant and most predicted correlations were larger than other correlations involving the same criterion. Ongoing research is evaluating the usefulness of PSDQ responses in relation to an intervention designed to enhance physical fitness (also see Marsh & Peart, 1988) and models of change positing the central of role physical self-concept in maintaining or enhancing levels of physical activity that lead to health-related physical fitness. Because many of the conceptual issues in physical self-concept research (convergent and discriminant validity, gender differences, frame of reference effects including the big fish, little pond effect, causal models of relations between self-concept and other desirable outcomes) parallel more general concerns, physical self-concept research provides a unique opportunity to test and extend the generalizability of research in other areas of self-concept.

Artistic Self-Concept

Vispoel (1993) argued that the measurement of artistic self-concepts has been largely ignored by educators and self-concept researchers. To remedy this problem, he designed the high school version of the Arts Self-Perception Inventory (ASPI) to parallel the Self-Description Questionnaire II (SDQII; Marsh, 1990c). Year 7 students completed the ASPI, SDQII, and a background survey of interest, grades, and noteworthy accomplishments in the arts and other school-related activities. Factor analysis demonstrated that the ASPI reliably measured the four factors that it was designed to assess (dance, drama, music, and visual art). Each ASPI scale was relatively uncorrelated with other ASPI scales (median $r = .26$) and with the SDQII scales (median $r = .17$) and was most highly correlated with criteria in the same area of the arts.

Vispoel (1995) subsequently developed an adult version of the ASPI to parallel the SDQIII and conducted a similar study with university students. He replicated the hierarchical structure of SDQIII responses and demonstrated that ASPI responses could be explained in terms of four first-order factors consistent with the ASPI design and one second-order artistic factor. The second-order artistic factor was modestly related to global self-concept in his hierarchical CFA and reasonably independent of other self-concept factors. Also, except for a relation between the first-order dance self-concept and the second-order physical self-concept scale, the ASPI first-order factors were reasonably independent of the SDQIII self-concept factors. Noting overall support for his extension of the Marsh–Shavelson model to include a second-order artistic self-concept factor, Vispoel also cautioned that the artistic self-concept hierarchy was not very strong and that correlations among the artistic self-concept factors were only moderate. For this reason, he emphasized that researchers should focus on the first-order factors, a recommendation consistent with SDQ research in general (e.g., Marsh, 1990a, 1993a).

Marsh and Roche (1995) extended Vispoel's research by comparing ASPI and SDQII responses by elite performing arts (dance, music, and drama) students attending a selective performing arts school with non-performing arts students attending the same school. They endorsed Vispoel's emphasis on interpretations of first-order artistic self-concepts instead of the higher-order factor, but also hypothesized that the pattern of relations among ASPI factors and between ASPI and SDQ factors in Vispoel's research may not generalize to responses by elite performing arts students attending a se-lective performing arts high school. More specifically, based on frame-of-reference studies from academic self-concept research, they predicted that the performing arts self-concept factors would be even more distinct (less correlated with each other) and more highly correlated with self-esteem and school self-concept for performing arts students than for non-performing arts students. In an application of the known group difference approach to construct validity, elite dance, music, and drama students had substantially higher dance, music, and drama self-concepts, respectively. CFA demon-strated the 15 (11 SDQII and 4 ASPI) a priori self-concept factors from the two instruments and the complete invariance of factor loadings across per-forming arts and non-performing arts samples. Consistent with a priori pre-dictions based on academic self-concept theory, however, there were group differences in the factor correlations. Whereas dance, music and drama self-concepts were moderately correlated for non-performing arts students, they were uncorrelated for performing arts students. Also, these performing arts self-concepts were more highly correlated with self-esteem and school self-concept for performing arts students than non-performing arts students. Results support the ASPI's usefulness but also suggest added complexities for Vispoel's (1995) proposed extension of the Marsh–Shavelson hierarchical model of self-concept to include performing arts.

SELF-CONCEPT ENHANCEMENT

Introduction

The enhancement of self-concept is considered to be a desirable educational goal. However, self-concept is stable over time and relatively insensitive to many external influences, including intervention studies. Well-controlled in-terventions typically do not lead to statistically significant and substantial changes in self-concept because of the use of weak interventions, the use of potentially powerful interventions with such small sample sizes or weak designs that effects are unlikely to be statistically significant, and a poor fit between the intended goals of the intervention and the specific dimensions of self-concept used to evaluate the interventions. Many intervention studies have been designed to enhance self-concept in a wide variety of settings, but these studies have typically been plagued with these methodological flaws. Therefore, there is no definitive answer as to the most appropriate techniques for enhancing self-concept despite a vast literature on the topic. Meta-analyses are suggestive that self-concept can be enhanced, and enhancement research can capitalize on recent advances in theory, development of multidimensional measuring instruments with demonstrated validity based on theoretical models, and the use of direct and indirect enhancement strategies. In this section we present an overview of intervention studies designed to enhance self-concept based on Hattie's 1992 meta-analysis, summarize the results of some SDQ studies, outline a "construct validity approach" to evaluating the interpretation of self-concept enhancement effects, and discuss the implications of this research for classroom practice.

Hattie's (1992) Meta-Analyses

Given the volume, diversity and contradictory findings from self-concept intervention studies, traditional literature reviews are difficult to undertake and perhaps unduly biased by the preconceptions of the reviewer (i.e., many contradictory claims could be supported by a careful selection of the studies considered). Glass (1976, 1977) proposed meta-analysis as a useful research tool for a more systematic review that could counter possible selectivity biases in a traditional review. Meta-analysis refers to the "statistical analysis of a large collection of analysis results from individual studies for the purpose of integrating the findings" (Glass, 1976, p. 3). Basically it involves analyzing comparable elements from previous studies to ascertain trends in the findings of the research literature. "In simple terms, a meta-analysis enables us to reduce the findings of disparate studies to a common or comparable value, and this common value can then be related to various independent variables identified in the particular research area" (Hansford and Hattie, 1982, p. 123). Meta-analysis involves calculating a standardized estimate of the effect—an effect size—and relating effect size to characteristics of different studies included in the meta-analysis. Hattie (1992) conducted an extensive meta-analysis to investigate the effectiveness of self-concept interventions. From *Psychological Abstracts* and other sources 650 studies were located, but only 89 contained sufficient data for meta-analysis. Hattie (1992) noted "that so many studies had to be rejected is a reflection of the quality of research conducted in the area of self-concept change" (p. 227).

From the 89 articles, 485 effect sizes were calculated with the average size being .37 (SD = .12). Hattie (1992, p. 227) concluded that 10% of those who experienced an intervention increased their self-concept compared with the control group. This conclusion was based on the differences between change scores for experimental and control subjects in that 65% of people in all self-concept programs included in the study enhanced their self-concept compared to 55% of people in the control group. Hattie (1992) also found that effect sizes were higher for adults compared to children, for lower socioeconomic groups compared to middle socioeconomic groups, for groups with previously diagnosed problems compared to groups without problems, and for noneducational settings compared to educational settings. Of concern is the finding that, even though a great majority of the educational programs were conducted by teachers, the effectiveness of teachers as self-concept enhancement agents was below average.

In examining enhancement approaches, Hattie (1992, p. 233) found that cognitively oriented interventions appear to be most effective. The mean effect size of .12 for affective programs suggests that this type of enhancement program is relatively ineffective, with the possible exception of creative self-awareness programs. Hattie, however, noted considerable variation in effect size for different studies within affective categories, which is probably attributable to the quality of the change agent (e.g., therapist). No major differences were noted between studies in which direct self-change was the aim (e.g., therapy), studies where change was brought about by indirect methods (e.g., enhancing academic achievement), studies in which the intervention was direct and indirect (e.g., a reading program combined with a self-concept program such as counseling), and studies in which the intervention was not associated with self-change (e.g., longitudinal studies). Hattie's meta-analysis is an important contribution to the self-concept literature. However, due to the number of poor-quality enhancement studies in general, we are as yet to gain an understanding and assessment of best available practice. As Hattie (1992, p. 236) notes, "there were too many fair and poor studies, too many studies were rejected because they evaluated programs by intuition, too few studies with follow-ups, and too few studies that included control groups." To these concerns, we would add that too few studies have used well-validated, multidimensional self-concept instruments in which at least some of the scales are closely matched to the intended goals of the intervention.

SDQ Intervention Studies

Recent advances in theory and measurement provide a stronger basis for the evaluation of potentially powerful intervention programs that systematically target specific components of self-concept. Well-controlled interventions have typically not systematically affected self-concept, despite many possible biases that would be expected to produce changes in self-concept responses (e.g., placebo effects, acquiescence to the experimenter, post-group euphoria). Marsh, Richards, and Barnes (1986a, 1986b) suggested two reasons for this lack of success. First, much of the research is based on ill-defined measures of self-concept rather than on multidimensional measures where some of the dimensions are specifically relevant to the focus of the intervention. If none of the facets of self-concept used in an evaluation match the intended outcomes of the intervention, then significant effects are unlikely to be found. This is a particularly serious problem in studies that rely solely on global measures of self-concept, using what Hattie (1992) refers to as the "throw it in and see what happens" approach. Second, the size of the effect is typically small relative to probable error because the intervention is weak or because a potentially powerful intervention is administered to only a small number of subjects.

Marsh et al. (1986a, 1986b) presented a construct validity approach to the study of intervention effects and the validity of interpretations based on multiple dimensions of self-concept. They argued that specific dimensions of self-concept most relevant to the intervention should be affected most, while less relevant dimensions should be affected less and serve as a control for response biases. Applications of this approach have demonstrated that changes due to interventions that target nonacademic facets of self-concept (Marsh et al., 1986a, 1986b) or academic facets of self-concept (Craven, 1989; Craven, Marsh, & Debus, 1991; Marsh & Richards, 1988a) are specific to the goals of the intervention. These interventions clearly demonstrate that the multidimensionality of self-concept as defined in the Shavelson et al. model is critical to consider in research designs that aim to enhance self-concept. This advance in methodology in combination with recent developments in theory and measurement instruments has provided the basis for overcoming some limitations of past self-concept enhancement research by ensuring considerations of measurement instruments, interventions, and theory are intertwined.

The Outward Bound Standard Course Study

Outward Bound courses provide a setting for individuals to recognize and understand their own weaknesses, strengths, and resources and thus find within themselves the wherewithall to master the difficult and unfamiliar (Marsh et al., 1986a, 1986b). The Outward Bound standard course is a 26-day residential program for 17–25-year-olds. It comprises physically and mentally demanding outdoor activities. Newman's (1980) theoretical review of self-concept, attributional, and environmental development concluded that "From this framework the ideal Outward Bound process emerges as a therapeutic model" (p. 341). Marsh et al. (1986a, 1986b) found that participation in the standard course ($n = 361$) had a significant effect on the nonacademic (SDQIII) dimensions of self-concept most related to the course goals and produced a more internal locus of control. Adapting the logic of construct validity to interrogate interpretations of the intervention effect, they reported that (1) gains were significantly larger for the SDQIII scales predicted a priori to be most relevant to the goals of the program compared to less relevant SDQIII scales, (2) the effect sizes were consistent across 27 different Outward Bound groups run by different instructors at different times of the year in different locations, and (3) the size and pattern of the gains were maintained over an 18-month follow-up period. The specificity of the effects on different SDQIII scales and their stability over the 18 month follow-up period argued against the operation of short-term response biases such as the post-group euphoria effect, and the consistency of effects across the groups argued for the generalizability of the self-concept enhancement due to the Outward Bound intervention. Hattie's (1992) meta-analysis of self-concept enhancement studies showed this effect to be among the largest and most consistent effects in his meta-analysis.

The Outward Bound Bridging Course

The bridging course was developed to produce significant gains in the cognitive domain, especially in language and mathematics, through an integrated program of remedial teaching, normal schoolwork, and experiences likely to influence personality in general and self-concept and self-esteem in particular (Marsh & Richards, 1988a). The bridging course is a six-week residential experience for underachieving adolescent males that was conducted in an isolated environment away from school. The selection process was designed to create substantial parental involvement and engender a belief in the program's effectiveness. The course design was based on the Outward Bound philosophy and McClelland's (1965) achievement motivation theory. This study was like the standard course study, in that it evaluated the effect of a course run by Outward Bound on multiple dimensions of self-concept as measured by one of the SDQ instruments, a short multiple time series design was used, the generality of effects was examined across different course offerings of the same (or a similar) program, and a construct validity approach was used to assess the validity of the findings. The study differs from the standard course study, in that the primary focus of the bridging course was on educational objectives rather than the nonacademic goals of the standard course, subjects were 13–16-year-old low-achieving males rather than self-selected 17–25-year-old males and females, subjects responded to the SDQI rather than the SDQIII, and the academic nature of the intervention made it possible to assess the intervention with objective achievement tests as well as with multiple dimensions of self-concept. The bridging course resulted in significant effects on SDQI academic scales that were significantly larger than effects for nonacademic SDQ scales and also significant gains in objective measures of academic achievement.

The Juxtaposition of the Two Outward Bound Interventions

The juxtaposition of the two Outward Bound interventions and their contrasting predictions provides a powerful test of the multidimensionality of self-concept. The Outward Bound standard course goals were primarily nonacademic. It was predicted, and found, that the program affected primarily nonacademic self-concept and had much less impact on academic self-concept. The size and pattern of results were maintained in an 18-month follow-up study. The Outward Bound bridging course goals were primarily academic. It was predicted, and found, that the program affected primarily academic self-concepts and had much less effect on nonacademic self-concepts. There were also corresponding effects on reading and math achievement. The contrasting set of results provides particularly strong support for the use of multidimensional self-concept measures in intervention studies. For example, if only a general measure of self-concept or self-esteem had been used in these studies, the interventions would have been concluded to be much weaker and much of the richness of understanding the match between intended goals and outcomes would have been lost.

Marsh and Peart Study

The results of the Marsh and Peart (1988) study previously discussed also demonstrated the domain specificity of intervention effects. This study was specifically designed to enhance physical self-concept and the significant self-concept effects were limited to the SDQ physical self-concept scales. This supports the construct validity of interpretation of the intervention and the self-concept responses. This study, however, also demonstrated another potential problem for intervention studies. Consistent with predictions, both cooperatively and competitively oriented interventions had a positive effect on physical fitness. However, the cooperatively oriented intervention also had a positive effect on physical self-concept whereas the competitively oriented intervention had a negative effect on physical self-concept.

As suggested by the Marsh and Peart study, even if participants recognize that their performances (physical fitness in this case) are improved, their self-concepts may actually be lowered if the performance gains are more than offset by changes in the standards that participants use to evaluate themselves. If the goal of the intervention is to enhance performance, affective domains, and motivation levels, then this situation may undermine seriously the value of the intervention. If the model of reciprocal effects of performance and self-concept is correct, the failure to enhance self-concept implies that improved performance levels may deteriorate. Particularly if maintenance of the improved performance is likely to depend on motivational levels after the intervention (as with physical fitness maintenance), then a better strategy is to construct interventions designed to enhance both performance or skills and self-concept. Enhancing both is more likely to have lasting effects than enhancing either one or the other. The Marsh and Peart study established that performance enhancement does not lead necessarily to improved self-concept. Some interventions that make limitations in participants more salient in relation to the performances of others (social comparison effects) or objective standards may inadvertently undermine self-concept, particularly if participants are not already aware of these limitations. Because of this apparent role of self-concept in studies designed to improve performance, it is recommended that appropriately constructed multidimensional measures of self-concept be used even if self-concept improvement is not an explicit goal of the intervention. These results have important implications for teaching strategies to improve achievement and self-concept and suggest that simultaneously enhancing associated facets of self-concept and achievement may help to maintain short-term gains.

Craven, Marsh, and Debus Study

Craven et al. (1991; Craven, 1989) implemented a new enhancement intervention in a primary school setting based on both direct and indirect enhancement approaches. The major purpose of the study was to enhance reading and mathematics self-concept, and secondary effects were predicted to occur in self-attributions and academic achievement. Participants were primary school students who had low academic self-concepts. The intervention was a combination of internally focused performance feedback and attributional retraining. The intervention emphasized both reading and math. Two potentially powerful change programs based on performance feedback and attributional feedback were combined. To enable students to generate appropriate systems of self-reinforcement that would assist to enhance academic self-concept by a direct means, ability attributional statements (Schunk, 1981, 1983, 1985) were coupled with performance feedback. This type of feedback, which the researchers labeled *internally focused feedback*, was devised to train students to directly change low self-concept attributions to high self-concept attributions. Brophy's (1981) guidelines for effective praise were incorporated in this strategy by ensuring internally focused feedback was delivered contingently, infrequently, and for appropriate gains in performance to ensure the feedback was credible while avoiding random praise and global positive reactions. Attributional feedback was also used as a component of the treatment to enhance self-concept by an indirect means. The underlying assumption was that the relationship of academic self-concept and self-attribution is reciprocal so that change in attributions should be associated with change in academic self-concept (see Marsh, 1984a). The treatment was applied in educational settings including both the regular classroom (by the classroom teacher) and withdrawn assistance groups (by the researchers).

The results demonstrated that the researcher-administered treatment was successful in enhancing targeted facets of self-concept and some logically related self-attributions. The intervention resulted in statistically significant effects for the targeted areas of self-concept (reading and math) and smaller effects in related areas (school and general). No significant effects were found in areas of self-concept unrelated to the intervention. The intervention also led to an increase in students' attributions to effort in success situations (e.g., I succeeded because I tried hard.) The findings support (1) the effectiveness of the intervention as a means to enhance self-concept, (2) the importance of including multiple dimensions of self-concept in intervention studies, and perhaps, (3) the combination of direct and indirect self-concept enhancement strategies.

Despite its similarities to the successful researcher-administered treatment, the intervention administered by teachers in the regular classroom context did not result in significant changes in self-concept. The effectiveness of the treatment when administered by external researchers indicates the capacity of the treatment principles to instigate processes of self-concept change. Craven et al. (1991; Craven, 1989) suggested that teacher-generated effects would be more positive if (1) the frequency of reinforcement schedules could be more consistently maintained by teachers, (2) the intervention was introduced at the beginning of the school year to ensure students perceived feedback as salient and credible, and (3) the treatment implementation period was extended. The authors also suggested a time lag after the completion of an intervention may be needed to allow changes in self-concept to increase desirable academic striving behavior and subsequent achievement. The features of this suggested research design have been incorporated in a large-scale self-concept enhancement in progress study.

Craven, Marsh, and Debus In-Progress Study

To expand on the findings of the Craven et al. study (1991) Craven, Marsh, and Debus implemented a large-scale enhancement study utilizing the intervention techniques in the former study. The study incorporated a teacher-administered and researcher-administered interventions. The intervention again comprised attributional feedback and internally focused feedback. Praise as reinforcement feedback was the primary basis of the intervention, and teachers were encouraged to consider Brophy's (1981) guidelines for effective praise when administering the treatment. Effective strategies utilized in the Craven et al. (1991) scale self-concept enhancement study were refined and implemented in order to investigate the effectiveness of a potentially strong intervention. Preliminary analyses of this in-progress study suggest that aspects of both the researcher-administered and teacher-administered interventions were successful in effecting self-concept enhancement relevant to the goals of the intervention, but that the teacher-administered intervention was much weaker than the researcher-administered intervention. There were also significant aptitude treatment interactions in which the intervention was most effective for students who initially had the lowest academic self-concepts.

This "in-progress" study also identified a potentially important methodological problem in this type of study referred to here as *diffusion effects* and an apparent solution to this problem. Previous research has demonstrated that teacher-mediated interventions can diffuse to nontarget students (Cooper, 1977; Good and Brophy, 1974; Withall, 1956). This research suggests that changes in teacher behavior to target students is likely to be associated with changes in teacher behavior toward nontarget students. Good and Brophy (1974) suggest that predicting and controlling for diffusion effects is critical in studies designed to change teacher behavior. Particularly for studies that involve teacher-administered interventions and within-classroom designs (i.e., experimental and control group students are in the same classroom), controls for diffusion effects should be included. In the present investigation, two control groups were incorporated into the research design: a within-class control group (randomly assigned control students within experimental classes in which the experimental intervention was administered) and an external-diffusion control group (students in a different class in which the experimental intervention was not administered to any students and the teacher was not trained to administer the intervention). Preliminary results indicated a significant diffusion effect in that within-class control participants experienced greater gains in academic self-concept than students in the external diffusion control group. Consistent with the main component of the study, the diffusion effects were larger for academic components of self-concept and the diffusion effects were larger for students with initially lower academic self-concepts. In further support of this interpretation, teacher self-assessment of performance in isolating the intervention to target students and written anecdotal evidence from teachers also identified a diffusion effect.

Summary

Previous research typically has been unable to show much effect of interventions designed to enhance general self-concept. In contrast, recent studies have found significant changes in the specific area of self-concept most logically related to the goals of the intervention. Typically, in these studies, a potentially powerful intervention was evaluated with a strong experimental design and a multidimensional self-concept instrument in which some of the scales were directly relevant to the intended goals of the intervention whereas other scales were less relevant. The importance of this match between outcome measures and program goals was demonstrated. In each study, self-concept scales most relevant to the intervention were affected most; other self-concept scales were affected less or not at all. The inclusion of less relevant areas of self-concept also provides a control for placebolike effects and, perhaps, may also be relevant for detecting unintended effects. These studies provide compelling support for the claim that self-concept cannot be understood adequately if its multidimensionality is ignored.

The critical evaluation of the SDQ intervention studies also demonstrates the relevance of a construct validity approach to evaluating intervention effects by adapting strategies from more traditional approaches to construct validation, quasi- and nonexperimental research, and qualitative research techniques. In this approach we begin with the premise that, if intervention effects are consistent with a priori predictions, then there is support for the construct validity of interpretations of the intervention and the measures of the outcome variables (e.g., a multidimensional self-concept instrument). However, construct validity interpretations must be critically evaluated in relation to alternative interpretations, because reliance on "face validity" as the sole or primary basis of support is generally unacceptable (e.g., Messick, 1989). Whereas the introduction of strong experimental designs based on, for example, random assignment is helpful in countering some alternative explanations, many threats to the validity of interpretations of intervention effects are not resolved by random assignment. Although these concerns are applicable to all intervention studies, they are of particular relevance to self-concept intervention studies in which the primary outcome measures must ultimately be some sort of self-report measure. As used here, the "construct validity approach" actually refers to a wide range of potential strategies used to evaluate the validity of interpretations from intervention studies. Particularly in the SDQ studies reviewed here we have highlighted several such strategies: (1) the specificity of effects to components of self-concept most relevant to the intervention compared to less relevant "control" self-concept scales; (2) the stability of short-term effects over time; (3) the consistency of effects over multiple administrations of the intervention; (4) the effects of the intervention on related constructs, some of which do not involve self-report measures; and (5) the effects based on alternative forms of the intervention that are designed to test interpretations of how the intervention works (e.g., the competitive vs. cooperative interventions in the Marsh and Peart, 1988, study). This list of suggestions clearly is not exhaustive. Furthermore, the most appropriate strategies must depend in part on the specific study, and so this list is not meant to be prescriptive. We do prescribe, however, authors of all self-concept enhancement studies should be obligated to critically evaluate the construct validity of their interpretation against viable alternative explanations. In pursuing this ideal, researchers need to more critically evaluate the theoretical basis of their intervention, the quality and appropriateness of measurement, the methodological adequacy of their research, and the relevance for practice. Adherence to such a prescription should greatly improve the quality of research in this area compared to, for example, the set of studies reviewed in the Hattie (1992) meta-analysis.

Promising Strategies for Enhancing Self-Concept
in Classroom Settings

Self-concept enhancement studies can contribute to (1) identifying strategies to assist educators to enhance student self-concept in specific facets, (2) identifying techniques to enhance self-concept and related constructs, (3) helping students feel good about themselves and their abilities, and (4) assisting children with low self-concept to regard themselves as worthwhile. Self-concept enhancement studies are typically designed to change self-concept *directly*, by utilizing praise and performance feedback, or *indirectly*, by targeting a related construct that is posited to affect self-concept. Both approaches are potentially effective.

Direct Intervention Studies

Hattie (1987) in a synthesis of 7827 studies relating to the achievement outcomes from schooling found that feedback was the most important moderator variable for enhancing achievement. He found relatively large effect sizes for different types of feedback. For example the effect size for reinforcement was 1.13, remediation and feedback was .65, and mastery learning based on feedback was .50. Homework with feedback that provided students with information about how and why they understand or misunderstand and strategies for future improvement was much more effective than homework without feedback. J. A. Kulik and Kulik (1988) found that feedback is effective when it is positive and immediate; and Brockner, Derr, and Laing (1987) found low self-concept individuals performed worse following negative feedback. As Hattie (1992, p. 251) notes "feedback is probably among the most powerful modifiers of one's self-concepts, and critical when changing others' self-concepts".

　　Interventions designed to enhance self-concept directly typically employ performance feedback as a component of the treatment. Schunk (1985) considers that performance feedback can influence self-efficacy by providing information to students that they are mastering skills. "Feedback that students are making progress (e.g. 'That's correct' and, 'You're doing much better') informs them that they are acquiring skills and knowledge, which can sustain motivation and enhance learning efficacy" (Schunk, 1985, p. 216). Feedback on actual performance is also deemed a desirable educational goal in classroom settings. The underlying assumption in this approach is that the provision of performance feedback will encourage children to generate feelings of competency, which should directly enhance self-concept. Praise is widely used to convey performance feedback. It is often used, however, without considering appropriate strategies to maximize its effectiveness. Praise enhances performance more than tangible feedback (e.g., Barringer & Gholson, 1979). Praise is recommended as a desirable form of reinforcement because it is thought to build self-esteem and encourage pupil effort. However, as Brophy (1981) noted, praise is not always reinforcing and is often determined by teachers' perceptions of student needs rather than by the quality of their performance. He suggested 12 guidelines for praising effectively to overcome the problems of ineffective praising strategies, which include (1) specifying the accomplishment, (2) ensuring praise is credible, (3) providing information to students about their competence, (4) attributing success to effort and ability, and (5) ensuring praise is delivered contingently and infrequently. By praising sparingly and meeting the criteria of contingency, specificity, and credibility, teachers can teach children to attribute outcomes to their own efforts or ability and thus assist them to gain a sense of personal control. Hence, effectively presented praise that is credible may be an important component for an intervention designed to enhance academic self-concept.

The utilization of performance feedback based on effective praise strategies will enhance self-concept only if the feedback is internalized by the child. Feedback that informs a child he or she has done well on a specific mathematics task does not mean the child will think he or she in general is good at mathematics. An internal mediating process is involved in transfering the feedback to a self-concept internalization whereby the child receives performance feedback ("You have done that mathematics task well"), perceives their efforts as competent ("I did well on that task"), generalizes the feedback to a subject area ("I'm good at mathematics"), and internalizes this feedback as a positive feeling or a self-concept internalization ("I feel good about my abilities in mathematics"). Typically, self-concept researchers have not defined specific components of internally mediating processes that directly affect self-concept, simply assuming that performance feedback will generate positive outcomes. By not focusing interventions to target directly the internal mediating process involved in enhancing self-concept, the effectiveness of interventions based on performance feedback is limited. Consistent with this view, previous research suggests that techniques focusing on internal mediating processes would be an effective manipulation to directly enhance self-concept. For example, Ames (1978; Ames & Felker, 1979) found that children with a high self-concept reinforce themselves more than children with a low self-concept. Andrews and Debus (1978) suggested that a necessary development "in future programs would be the shift from the use of arbitrary external reinforcement systems in the acquisition stage to the generating of systems of self-reinforcement that would operate to support attributional change" (p. 165). Training children with a low self-concept to utilize systems of self-reinforcement to generate desirable internal mediating processes would ensure performance feedback is internalized. An additional advantage of such an intervention design is the emulation of an ecologically natural internal mediating process for self-concept enhancement. Directly targeting self-concept via the internal mediating process of self-reinforcement would seem a desirable inclusion in an enhancement intervention.

Indirect Intervention Studies

Self-concept is postulated (e.g., Marsh, 1984a) to be linked into a network of relationships with other variables (e.g., achievement, self-attributions). Adaptive behavioral tendencies, characteristic of children with a high self-concept, are often identified as mediating processes that positively affect constructs related to self-concept. By examining mediating processes that enhance effects on constructs related to self-concept, intervention strategies can be identified to indirectly enhance self-concept via the enhancement of a related construct. Marsh (1988b) demonstrated a consistent pattern of relations between multidimensional self-concepts and multidimensional self-attributions for the causes of success and failure. Results from the Marsh, Cairns, Relich, Barnes, and Debus (1984) study suggest that high self-concept is correlated substantially with attributions for success attributed to ability ($r = .59$) or effort ($r = .55$). Differences in the way children attribute outcomes to causes are shown to be related to school performance, self-concept, self-efficacy, and academic behavior (e.g. Covington, 1984; Marsh et al., 1984; Relich, Debus, & Walker, 1986; Schunk, 1985; Weiner, 1986).

Indirect self-concept enhancement treatments that incorporate attributional feedback might be expected to contribute to the enhancement of self-concept via an emphasis on internal (effort, ability) attributions. Successful outcomes that are ascribed to the self are thought to result in greater self-esteem than success that is externally attributed (e.g. Marsh, Relich, & Smith, 1983; Marsh, Smith, & Barnes, 1983). Research (Brown & Weiner, 1984; Covington & Omelich, 1979c; Nicholls, 1976) emphasizes competency as the dominant source of self-concept because results suggest that praise for ability is most valued. Thus praise for effort alone may not be sufficiently rewarding for the student. However, research (Schunk, 1982, 1983, 1985, 1986) has demonstrated that praise for effort is also critical because this promotes perceptions of self-efficacy and contributes to enhancing skills. These results suggest that in interventions there is a need to balance an image of both competency and diligence as sources of self-concept.

Self-worth theorists suggest that students use self-serving strategies to preserve public and private impressions of competency when risking failure (Covington, 1985; Covington & Omelich, 1979a, 1979b, 1984; Nicholls, 1979, 1983). Marsh et al. (1984, p. 5) noted that "a substantial body of literature has demonstrated that subjects are more likely to attribute their own success to internal causes such as ability and effort, while attributing failure to external causes." This pattern of attributions has been termed the *self-serving bias*, and it is interpreted as an attempt to protect self-esteem. By taking credit for success and denying blame for failure individuals may be able to protect their self-concept. Alternatively, Marsh (1986) used the term *self-serving effect* instead of *self-serving bias*. He noted that denial of responsibility for failure was a reasonable response for children who had a high academic self-concept, were academically able, and were seen as academically able by their teachers. Encouraging children with a low self-concept to increase self-reinforcement by emulating naturally occurring self-reinforcing processes utilized by children with a high self-concept would seem a useful component of an intervention to enhance self-concept indirectly via changes in patterns of self-attributions.

Implications for Developing Interventions to Enhance Self-Concept

Many self-concept interventions are administered in special settings removed from the classroom by individuals who do not interact with the participants in naturalistic settings. The extent of control by the researcher over the administration of the intervention probably explains in part why this procedure has been effective. As yet, the value of intervention embedded in ecologically undisturbed settings (e.g., classrooms) and mediated by ecologically natural agents (e.g., teachers) has not been shown to be as effective. Given that researcher control over the administration, timing, and delivery of interventions in naturalistic settings may be limited by external circumstances, this procedure may be difficult to incorporate in well-controlled research designs. However, designing interventions to be administered in naturalistic settings is a desirable goal since this is the target setting where interventions have most direct practical significance. Given that Hattie (1992) has found that teachers are not particularly effective at enhancing self-concept, thorough training methods may need to be instigated to ensure teachers comprehend how to implement a self-concept intervention and recognize the value in doing so.

Training administrators of treatments to use praise effectively and training pupils to generate functional systems of self-reinforcement to enhance self-concept reinforcing strategies and self-attributional styles are posited to be effective strategies for incorporation in academic self-concept enhancement treatments. Training children to emulate ecologically natural internal mediating processes (e.g., the self-serving effect, success attributions to ability and effort) utilized by children with a high self-concept seems worthwhile. Applying these strategies to ecologically undisturbed settings and ensuring components of interventions are mediated by ecologically natural agents would extend the application of previous and new research findings. Examination of current research and theory points to the possibility of strengthening the development of current interventions by utilizing both direct and indirect approaches.

SUMMARY

Self-concept cannot be adequately understood if its multidimensional, domain-specific nature is ignored. The same person can have a high self-concept in some domains (e.g., physical and social) and a poor self-concept in other domains (e.g., mathematics and English). Of particular relevance to this chapter, academic specific measures of self-concept are more useful to the study of academic behaviors and accomplishments than global and nonacademic measures of self-concept. Similarly, self-concept cannot be adequately understood and assessment interpreted by teachers if the role of frames of reference are ignored. The same objective indicators can lead to disparate self-concepts depending on the appropriate frame of reference. Social comparison theory that provides the theoretical underpinning for the BFLPE is one approach for studying frame of reference effects that has a long history in social psychology. The internal comparison process in the I/E model suggests a very different but complementary approach. Renewed interest in the impact of discrepancies between how I am and the standards I use to evaluate myself, although fraught with methodological problems and complications, offers a potential unification of various frames of reference effects.

Our research has increasingly led to the conclusion that general self-concept—no matter how it is inferred—may not be a particularly useful construct. Shavelson et al. (1976) initially hypothesized that general self-concept should be the most stable facet in their hierarchy. The general self-concept scale on the SDQIII, however, has the lowest long-term stability even though its internal consistency is among the highest of the scales. Similarly, the general school scale is less stable than more specific domains of academic self-concept, even though its internal consistency is high. The findings suggest that these more general domains—at least, as they are reflected in global scales typically used to measure general self-concept—are affected more by short-term response biases, short-term mood fluctuations, or some other short-term time-specific influences.

General self-concept apparently cannot adequately reflect the diversity of specific self-concept domains. If the role of self-concept research is to better understand the complexity of self in different contexts, to predict a wide variety of behavior, to provide outcome measures for diverse interventions, and to relate self-concept to other constructs, then the specific domains of self-concept are more useful than a general domain. Particularly in educational settings, the separation of academic from nonacademic and general domains of self-concept provides important support for this contention. Interestingly, work leading to the Marsh–Shavelson revision suggests that these criticisms of an overreliance on general self-concept also apply to the usefulness of a general academic self-concept. Because math and verbal self-concept are nearly uncorrelated, they cannot be adequately explained by a general academic self-concept. We am not arguing that researchers should abandon measures of general self-concept and general academic self-concept, but rather that more emphasis needs to be placed on content-specific dimensions of self-concept. Researchers should be encouraged to consider multiple dimensions of self-concept particularly relevant to the concerns of their research, supplemented, perhaps, by more general measures. Likewise, teachers need to be encouraged to utilize multidimensional assessment instruments rather than unidimensional assessment instruments that solely measure global measures of self-concept. Self-concept enhancement should target specific facets of self-concept rather than the common practice of targeting general self-concept. For example, if a child has a low reading self-concept the most direct means of enhancing this facet of self-concept is by directly targeting it rather than general self-concept. Further support for these recommendations comes from the evaluation of studies that relate general and content-specific dimensions of self-concept to other constructs (see Marsh, 1990c) and relations involving educationally relevant outcomes that are the focus of the research summarized here.

We have focused on academic self-concept in this chapter, but many of the issues and implications for classroom practice are relevant for other domains of self-concept. We briefly reviewed some of our recent research in the areas of physical and artistic self-concept in support of this claim. Because many of the conceptual issues in physical and artistic self-concept research (convergent and discriminant validity, hierarchical structures, gender differences, frame-of-reference effects including the big fish, little pond effect, causal models of relations between self-concept and other desirable outcomes) parallel more general concerns in self-concept research, this new research provides a unique opportunity to test and extend the generalizability of our interpretations from other areas self-concept research.

The design and implementation of good-quality self-concept enhancement studies is providing promising directions for future research and classroom practice. These studies suggest that self-concept enhancement has potentially the most potent effects when interventions are focused on specific facets of self-concept. It is time for the days of giving "feel good" reinforcement and "throw it in and see what happens" to be replaced with sophisticated systematic measurement, assessment and enhancement strategies that take into account the multidimensionality of self-concept. We have attempted to point out that theory, instrument development, and classroom practice are all inextricably intertwined. Current advances suggest the time is now ripe for both self-concept researchers and teachers to forge new understanding beyond the dustbowl of previous research and, in the process, help more students maximize their full potentials.

Acknowledgments

We thank Barbara Byrne, Raymond Debus, John Hattie, Dennis Hocevar, Lawrence Roche, Richard Shavelson, Ian Smith, and other colleagues who have contributed to research that is summarized in this chapter.

References

Alwin, D. F., & Otto, L. B. (1977). High school context effects on aspirations. *Sociology of Education*, 50, 259–273.

Ames, C. (1978). Children's achievement attributions and self-reinforcement: Effects of self-concept and competitive reward structure. *Journal of Educational Psychology*, 70, 345–355.

Ames, C., & Felker, D. W. (1979). Effects of self-concept on children's causal attributions and self-reinforcement. *Journal of Educational Psychology*, 71, 613–619.

Andrews, G. R., & Debus, R. L. (1978). Persistence and the causal perception of failure: Modifying cognitive attributions. *Journal of Educational Psychology*, 69, 1–8.

Australian Education Council. (1989). *The common and agreed national goals of schooling*. Canberra: AGPS.

Bachman, J. G. (1970). *Youth in transition: Vol. 2. The impact of family background and intelligence on tenth-grade boys*. Ann Arbor, MI: Institute for Social Research.

Bachman, J. G., & O'Malley, P. M. (1986). Self-concepts, self-esteem, and educational experiences: The frogpond revisited (again). *Journal of Personality and Social Psychology*, 50, 33–46.

Bandura, A. (1986). *Social foundations of thought and action: A social cognitive theory*. Englewood Cliffs, NJ: Prentice-Hall.

Barringer, C., & Gholson, B. (1979). Effects of type and combination of feedback upon conceptual learning by children: Implications for research in academic learning. *Review of Educational Research*, 49, 439–478.

Boyle, G. J. (1994). Self-Description Questionnaire II: A review. *Test Critiques*, 10, 632–643.

Brockner, J., Derr, W. R., & Laing, W. N. (1987). Self-esteem and reactions to negative feedback: Towards greater generalizability. *Journal of Research in Personality*, 21, 318–334.

Brookover, W. B. (1989). *Self-concept of ability scale—A review and further analysis*. Paper presented at the annual meeting of the American Educational Research Association.

Brookover, W. B., & Lezotte, L. W. (1979). *Changes in schools characteristics coincident with changes in student achievement*. East Lansing: Michigan State University. (ERIC Document Reproduction Service No. ED 181 005)

Brophy, J. (1981). Teacher praise: A functional analysis. *Review of Educational Research*, 51, 5–32.

Brown, J., & Weiner, B. (1984). Affective consequences of ability versus effort ascriptions: Controversies, resolutions, and quandaries. *Journal of Educational Psychology*, 76, 146–158.

Burns, R. B. (1982). *Self-concept development and education*. London: Holt, Rinehart & Winston.

Byrne, B. M. (1984). The general/academic self-concept nomological network: A review of construct validation research. *Review of Educational Research*, 54, 427–456.

Byrne, B. M. (1986). Self-concept/academic achievement relations: An investigation of dimensionality, stability, and causality. *Canadian Journal of Behavioural Science*, 18, 173–186.

Calsyn, R., & Kenny, D. (1977). Self-concept of ability and perceived evaluations by others: Cause or effect of academic achievement? *Journal of Educational Psychology*, 69, 136–145.

Chapman, J. W. (1988). Learning disabled children's self-concepts. *Review of Educational Research*, 58, 347–371.

Cooper, H. M. (1977). Controlling personal rewards: Professional teachers' differential use of feedback and the effects of feedback on the student's motivation to perform. *Journal of Educational Psychology*, 69, 419–427.

Covington, M. V. (1984). The motive for self-worth. In R. L. Ames & L. Ames (Eds.), *Research on motivation in education* (pp. 78–114). London: Academic Press.

Covington, M. V. (1985). Ability and effort valuation among failure-avoiding and failure-accepting students. *Journal of Educational Psychology*, 77, 446–459.

Covington, M. V., & Omelich, C. L. (1979a). Are causal attributions causal? A path analysis of the cognitive model of achievement motivation. *Journal of Personality and Social Psychology*, 37, 1487–1504.

Covington, M. V., & Omelich, C. L. (1979b). Effort: The double-edged sword in school achievement. *Journal of Educational Psychology*, 71, 169–182.

Covington, M. V., & Omelich, C. L. (1979c). It's best to be able and virtuous too: Student and teacher evaluative responses to successful effort. *Journal of Educational Psychology*, 71, 688–700.

Covington, M. V., & Omelich, C. L. (1984). An empirical examination of Weiner's critique of attributional research. *Journal of Educational Psychology*, 76, 1214–1225.

Craven, R. G. (1989). *An examination of self-concept: The interrelationship of teachers', parents and children's perceptions of self-concept, and their influence in enhancing self-concept.* Unpublished B.A. Honours thesis, University of Sydney, Australia.

Craven, R. G., Marsh, H. W., & Debus, R. (1991). Effects of internally focused feedback and attributional feedback on the enhancement of academic self-concept. *Journal of Educational Psychology*, 83, 17–26.

Davis, J. A. (1966). The campus as a frog pond: An application of theory of relative deprivation to career decisions for college men. *American Journal of Sociology*, 72, 17–31.

Fox, K. R., & Corbin, C. B. (1989). The Physical Self-Perception Profile: Development and preliminary validation. *Journal of Sports and Exercise Psychology*, 11, 408–430.

Glass, G. V. (1976). Primary, secondary, and meta-analysis research. *Educational Researcher*, 5, 3–8.

Glass, G. V. (1977). Integrating findings: The meta-analysis of research. *Review of Research in Education*, 5, 351–379.

Good, T. L., & Brophy, J. E. (1974). Changing teacher and student behavior: An empirical investigation. *Journal of Educational Psychology*, 66, 390–405.

Hansford, B. C., & Hattie, J. A. (1982). The relationship between self and achievement/performance measures. *Review of Educational Research*, 52, 123–142.

Hattie, J. (1987). *Enhancing self-concept.* Unpublished Master of Education thesis, University of New England, NSW, Australia.

Hattie, J. (1992). *Self-concept.* Hillsdale, NJ: Erlbaum.

Jerusalem, M. (1984). Reference group, learning environment and self-evaluations: A dynamic multi-level analysis with latent variables. In R. Schwarzer (Ed.), *The self in anxiety, stress and depression* (pp. 61–73). Amsterdam: North-Holland/Elsevier.

Joreskog, K. G., & Sorbom, D. (1988). *LISREL 7: A guide to the program and applications.* Chicago: SPSS, Inc.

Kulik, C. L. (1985). *Effects of inter-class ability grouping on achievement and self-esteem.* Paper presented at the 1985 annual meeting of the American Psychological Association, Los Angeles.

Kulik, C. L., & Kulik, J. A. (1982). Effects of ability grouping on secondary school students: A meta-analysis of evaluation findings. *American Educational Research Journal*, 21, 799–806.

Kulik, J. A., & Kulik, C. C. (1988). Timing of feedback and verbal learning. *Review of Educational Research*, 58, 79–97.

Marsh, H. W. (1984a). Relationships among dimensions of self-attribution, dimensions of self-concept, and academic achievements. *Journal of Educational Psychology*, 76, 1291–1380.

Marsh, H. W. (1984b). Self-concept: The application of a frame of reference model to explain paradoxical results. *Australian Journal of Education*, 28, 165–181.

Marsh, H. W. (1984c). Self-concept, social comparison and ability grouping: A reply to Kulik and Kulik. *American Educational Research Journal*, 21, 799–806.

Marsh, H. W. (1986). Verbal and math self-concepts: An internal/external frame of reference model. *American Educational Research Journal*, 23, 129–149.

Marsh, H. W. (1987a). The big-fish-little-pond effect on academic self-concept. *Journal of Educational Psychology*, 79, 280–295.

Marsh, H. W. (1987b). The hierarchical structure of self-concept and the application of hierarchical confirmatory factor analysis. *Journal of Educational Measurement*, 24, 17–19.

Marsh, H. W. (1988a). Causal effects of academic self-concept on academic achievement: A reanalysis of Newman (1984). *Journal of Experimental Education*, 56, 100–104.

Marsh, H. W. (1988b). *Self Description Questionnaire: A theoretical and empirical basis for the Measurement of multiple dimensions of preadolescent self-concept: A test manual and a research monograph.* San Antonio, TX: The Psychological Corporation. (Republished in 1992, Publication Unit, Faculty of Education, University of Western Sydney, Macarthur.)

Marsh, H. W. (1989). Age and sex effects in multiple dimensions of self-concept: Preadolescence to adulthood. *Journal of Educational Psychology*, 81, 417–430.

Marsh, H. W. (1990a). The influence of internal and external frames of reference on the formation of math and English self-concepts. *Journal of Educational Psychology*, 82, 107–116.

Marsh, H. W. (1990b). The causal ordering of academic self-concept and academic achievement: A multiwave, longitudinal path analysis. *Journal of Educational Psychology*, 82, 646–656.

Marsh, H. W. (1990c). A multidimensional, hierarchical self-concept: Theoretical and empirical justification. *Educational Psychology Review*, 2, 77–172.

Marsh, H. W. (1990d). The structure of academic self-concept: The Marsh/Shavelson model. *Journal of Educational Psychology*, 82, 623–636.

Marsh, H. W. (1991). The failure of high ability high schools to deliver academic benefits: The importance of academic self-concept and educational aspirations. *American Educational Research Journal*, 28, 445–480.

Marsh, H. W. (1992). The content specificity of relations between academic achievement and academic self-concept. *Journal of Educational Psychology*, 84, 43–50.

Marsh, H. W. (1993a). Academic self-concept: Theory measurement and research. In J. Suls, (Ed.), *Psychological perspectives on the self* (Vol. 4, pp. 59–98). Hillsdale, NJ: Erlbaum.

Marsh, H. W. (1993b). The effects of participation in sports during the last two years of high school. *Sociology of Sport Journal*, 10, 18–43.

Marsh, H. W. (1993c). The multidimensional structure of physical fitness: Invariance over gender and age. *Research Quarterly for Exercise and Sport*, 64, 256–273.

Marsh, H. W. (1993d). Physical fitness self-concept: Relations to field and technical indicators of physical fitness for boys and girls aged 9–15. *Sport and Exercise Psychology*, 15, 184–206.

Marsh, H. W. (1994). Using the National Longitudinal Study of 1988 to evaluate theoretical models of self-concept: The Self-Description Questionnaire. *Journal of Educational Psychology*, 80, 439–456.

Marsh, H. W. (in press-a). Construct validity. Physical Self Description Questionnaire responses: Relations to external criteria. *Journal of Sport and Exercise Psychology*.

Marsh, H. W. (in press-b). The measurement of physical self-concept: A construct validation approach. In K. R. Fox (Ed.), *The physical self: From motivation to well-being*. Champaign, IL: Human Kinetics.

Marsh, H. W. (in press-c). Physical Self Description Questionnaire: Stability and discriminant validity. *Research Quarterly for Exercise and Sport*.

Marsh, H. W., Byrne, B. M., & Shavelson, R. (1988). A multifaceted academic self-concept: Its hierarchical structure and its relation to academic achievement. *Journal of Educational Psychology*, 80, 366–380.

Marsh, H. W., Cairns, L., Relich, J., Barnes, J., & Debus, R. L. (1984). The relationship between dimensions of self-attribution and dimensions of self-concept. *Journal of Educational Psychology*, 76, 3–32.

Marsh, H. W., Chessor, D., Craven, R. G., & Roche, L. (1995). The effects of gifted and talented programs on academic self-concept: The big fish strikes again. *American Educational Research Journal*, 32, 285–319.

Marsh, H. W., Craven, R. G., & Debus, R. (1991). Self-concepts of young children aged 5 to 8: Their measurement and multidimensional structure. *Journal of Educational Psychology*, 83, 377–392.

Marsh, H. W., & Hattie, J. (1996). Theoretical perspectives on the structure of self-concept. In B. A. Bracken (Ed.), *Handbook of self-concept*. (pp. 38–90) New York: Wiley.

Marsh, H. W., Hey, J., Johnson, S., & Perry, C. (1995). Elite Athlete Self Description Questionnaire: Hierarchical confirmatory factor analysis of responses by two distinct groups of elite athletes (in review).

Marsh, H. W., Hey, J., & Roche, L. A. (1996). *The structure of physical self concept: Elite athletes and physical education students*. (in review).

Marsh, H. W., & Hocevar, D. (1985). The application of confirmatory factor analysis to the study of self-concept: First and higher order factor structures and their invariance across age groups. *Psychological Bulletin*, 97, 562–582.

Marsh, H. W., & Johnston, C. F. (1993). Multidimensional self-concepts and frames of reference: Relevance to the exceptional learner. In F. E. Obiakor & S. Stile (Eds.), *Self-concept of exceptional learners: Current perspectives for educators* (pp. 72–112). Dubuque, IA: Kendall/Hunt.

Marsh, H. W., & O'Niell, R. (1984). Self Description Questionnaire III (SDQ III): The construct validity of multidimensional self-concept ratings by late-adolescents. *Journal of Educational Measurement*, 21, 153–174.

Marsh, H. W., & Parker, J. W. (1984). Determinants of student self-concept: Is it better to be a relatively large fish in a small pond even if you don't learn to swim as well? *Journal of Personality and Social Psychology*, 47, 213–231.

Marsh, H. W., & Peart, N. (1988). Competitive and cooperative physical fitness training programs for girls: Effects on physical fitness and on multidimensional self-concepts. *Journal of Sport and Exercise Psychology*, 10, 390–407.

Marsh, H. W., Perry, C., Horsely, C., & Roche, L. A. (1995). Multidimensional self-concepts of elite athletes: How do they differ from the general population? *Sport and Exercise Psychology*, 17, 70–83.

Marsh, H. W., & Redmayne, R. S. (1994). A multidimensional physical self-concept and its relation to multiple components of physical fitness. *Journal of Sport and Exercise Psychology*, 16, 45–55.

Marsh, H. W., Relich, J., & Smith, I. (1983). Self-concept: The construct validity of interpretations based upon the SDQ. *Journal of Personality and Social Psychology*, 45, 173–187.

Marsh, H. W., & Richards, G. (1988a). The Outward Bound Bridging Course for low achieving high-school males: Effect on academic achievement and multidimensional self-concepts. *Australian Journal of Psychology*, 40, 281–298.

Marsh, H. W., & Richards, G. E. (1988b). The Tennessee Self Concept Scales: Reliability, internal structure, and construct validity. *Journal of Personality and Social Psychology*, 55, 612–624.

Marsh, H. W., Richards, G., & Barnes, J. (1986a). Multidimensional self-concepts: The effect of participation in an Outward Bound program. *Journal of Personality and Social Psychology*, 45, 173–187.

Marsh, H. W., Richards, G., & Barnes, J. (1986b). Multidimensional self-concepts: A longterm followup of the effect of participation in an Outward Bound program. *Personality and Social Psychology Bulletin*, 12, 475–492.

Marsh, H. W., Richards, G. E., Johnson, S., Roche, L., & Tremayne, P. (1994). Physical Self Description Questionnaire: Psychometric properties and a multitrait-multimethod analysis of relations to existing instruments. *Sport and Exercise Psychology, 16,* 270–305.

Marsh, H. W., & Roche, L. A. (in press). The structure of artistic self-concepts for performing arts and non-performing arts students in a performing arts high school: "Setting the stage" with multigroup confirmatory factor analysis. *Journal of Educational Psychology.*

Marsh, H. W., & Rowe, K. J. (1996). The negative effects of school-average on academic self concept: An application of multilevel modeling. *Australian Journal of Education, 40,* 65–87.

Marsh, H. W., & Shavelson, R. J. (1985). Self-concept: Its multifaceted, hierarchical structure. *Educational Psychologist, 20,* 107–125.

Marsh, H. W., Smith, I. D., & Barnes, J. (1983). Multitrait and multimethod analyses of the Self Description questionnaires: Student-teacher agreement on multidimensional ratings of student self-concept. *American Educational Research Journal, 20,* 333–357.

Marsh, H. W., Walker, R., & Debus, R. (1991). Subject-specific components of academic self-concept and self-efficacy. *Contemporary Educational Psychology, 16,* 331–345.

Marshall, H. H., & Weinstein, R. S. (1984). Classroom factors affecting students' self-evaluations. *Review of Educational Research, 54,* 301–326.

McClelland, D. C. (1965). Towards a theory of motive acquisition. *American Psychologist, 20,* 321–333.

Messick, S. (1989). Validity. In R. L. Linn (Ed.), *Educational measurement* (3rd ed., pp. 13–104). New York: Macmillan.

Newman, R. S. (1980). Alleviating learned helplessness in a wilderness setting: An application of attribution theory to Outward Bound. In L. J. Fyans (Ed.), *Achievement motivation: Recent trends in theory and research* (pp. 312–345). New York: Plenum.

Newman, R. S. (1984). Achievement and self-evaluations in mathematics. *Journal of Educational Psychology, 76,* 857–873.

Nicholls, J. G. (1976). Effort is virtuous, but it's better to have ability: Evaluative responses to perceptions of effort and ability. *Journal of Research in Personality, 19,* 306–315.

Nicholls, J. G. (1979). Quality and equality in intellectual development: The role of motivation in education. *American Psychologist, 34,* 1071–1084.

Nicholls, J. G. (1983). Conceptions of ability and achievement motivation: A theory and its implications for education. In S. G. Paris, G. M. Olson, & C. H. Patterson (Eds.), *Theories of counseling and psychotherapy* (pp. 37–73). New York: Harper & Row.

Relich, J. D., Debus, R. L., & Walker, R. (1986). The mediating role of attribution and self-efficacy variables for treatment effects on achievement outcomes. *Contemporary Educational Psychology, 11,* 195–216.

Reuman, D. A. (1989). How social comparison mediates the relation between ability-grouping practices and students' achievement expectancies in mathematics. *Journal of Educational Psychology, 81,* 178–189.

Rogers, C. M., Smith, M. D., & Coleman, J. M. (1978). Social comparison in the classroom: The relationship between academic achievement and self-concept. *Journal of Educational Psychology, 70,* 50–57.

Rosenberg, M. (1965). *Society and the adolescent child.* Princeton, NJ: Princeton University Press.

Rosenberg, M. (1979). *Conceiving the self.* New York: Basic Books.

Schunk, D. H. (1981). Modeling and attributional effects on children's achievement: A self-efficacy analysis. *Journal of Educational Psychology, 73,* 93–105.

Schunk, D. H. (1982). Effects of effort attributional feedback on children's perceived self-efficacy and achievement. *Journal of Educational Psychology, 74,* 548–556.

Schunk, D. H. (1983). Ability versus effort attributional feedback on children's perceived efficacy and achievement. *Journal of Educational Psychology, 75,* 848–856.

Schunk, D. H. (1985). Self-efficacy and classroom learning. *Psychology in the Schools, 22,* 208–223.

Schunk, D. H. (1986). Extended attributional feedback: Sequence effects during remedial reading instruction. *Journal of Early Adolescence*, 6, 55–66.

Schwarzer, R., Jerusalem, J., & Lange, B. (1983). *The change of self-concept with respect to reference groups in school*. Paper presented at the 1983 annual meeting of the American Educational Research Association, Montreal.

Shavelson, R. J., & Bolus, R. (1982). Self-concept: The interplay of theory and methods. *Journal of Educational Psychology*, 74, 3–17.

Shavelson, R. J., Hubner, J. J., & Stanton, G. C. (1976). Self-concept: Validation of construct interpretations. *Review of Educational Research*, 46, 407–441.

Shavelson, R. J., & Marsh, H. W. (1986). On the structure of self-concept. In R. Schwazer (Ed.), *Anxiety and cognitions* (pp. 305–330). Hillsdale, NJ: Erlbaum.

Skaalvik, E. M., & Rankin, R. J. (1990). Math, verbal, and general academic self-concept: The internal/external frame of reference model and gender differences in self-concept structure. *Journal of Educational Psychology*, 82, 546–554.

Skaalvik, E. M., & Rankin, R. J. (1995). A test of the internal/external frame of reference model at different levels of math and verbal self-perception. *American Educational Research Journal*, 35, 161–184.

Strang, L., Smith, M. D., & Rogers, C. M. (1978). Social comparison, multiple reference groups and the self-concepts of academically handicapped children before and after mainstreaming. *Journal of Educational Psychology*, 70, 487–497.

Suls, J. M. (1977). Social comparison theory and research: An overview from 1954. In J. M. Suls & R. L. Miller (Eds.), *Social comparison processes: Theoretical and empirical perspectives* (pp. 1–20). Washington, DC: Hemisphere Publishing.

Vernon, P. E. (1950). *The structure of human abilities*. London: Methuen.

Vispoel, W. P. (1993). The development and validation of the Arts Self-Perception Inventory for Adolescents. *Educational and Psychological Measurement*, 53, 1023–1033.

Vispoel, W. P. (1995). Self-concept in the arts: An extension of the Shavelson model. *Journal of Educational Psychology*, 87, 134–145.

Weiner, B. (1986). *An attributional theory of motivation and emotion*. New York: Springer-Verlag.

Wells, L. E., & Marwell, G. (1976). *Self-esteem: Its conceptualization and measurement*. Beverly Hills, CA: Sage Publ.

Withall, J. (1956). An objective measurement of a teacher's classroom interactions. *Journal of Educational Psychology*, 47, 203–212.

Wylie, R. C. (1974). *The self-concept* (Rev. ed., Vol. 1). Lincoln: University of Nebraska Press.

Wylie, R. C. (1979). *The self-concept* (Vol. 2). Lincoln: University of Nebraska Press.

Wylie, R. C. (1989). *Measures of self-concept*. Lincoln: University of Nebraska Press.

Assessment of Subjective Well-Being during Childhood and Adolescence

TIMOTHY A. BENDER

Psychology Department, Southwest Missouri State University, Springfield

INTRODUCTION

The subjective well-being of adults has been a popular research topic during the last three decades. Much of this research includes studies of subjective well-being in elderly populations and national studies of the quality of life. As part of these research efforts, several self-report measures of subjective well-being were designed and models of subjective well-being were proposed. Most of the models define subjective well-being in terms of affective and cognitive or judgmental components (Andrews & Withey, 1976; Diener, 1984, 1994; Schwarz & Strack, 1991). Detailed reviews of research on the subjective well-being of adults are found in Andrews and Robinson (1991), Chamberlain (1988), Diener (1984, 1994), and Strack, Argyle, and Schwarz (1991). Unfortunately, little information regarding the subjective well-being of students is found in the literature.

A great amount of research has been published regarding students' self-concepts and self-esteem. However, these constructs are not the same as subjective well-being. All three reflect something about students' self-perception, but each construct has a different focus. Self-concept refers to a student's perceptions of his or her identifying characteristics. Self-esteem, or self-worth, reflects the student's evaluative response to those characteristics.

Subjective well-being refers to a student's affective and cognitive assessment of life in general (Andrews & Withey, 1976; Diener, 1984, 1994). Although a great amount of research, model building, and instrument design has occurred in the areas of students' self-concepts and self-esteem, the same cannot be said for subjective well-being.

The primary goal of writing this chapter was to provide the reader with information regarding the assessment of subjective well-being in students from kindergarten through 12th-grade. Attaining this goal was made difficult by the fact that I could find no model of students' subjective well-being in the literature. Instead, researchers have applied adult models to assessment of students. Therefore, I have chosen first to review some of the research related to one popular model of adults' subjective well-being (Diener, 1984, 1994). A complete review of Diener's model would require more than one chapter. Readers who desire a more detailed discussion of the subtleties of this model should refer to the original sources. In the process of reviewing this model, I build a framework for a model of subjective well-being in students. My choice of Diener's model was a matter of expediency. A large amount of research has been devoted to testing and refining Diener's model, making it one of the more comprehensive models available. Also, Diener's model has influenced the development of the assessment of subjective well-being in students. My second goal is to use research regarding children's self-concept and self-worth to discuss developmental issues that may affect the assessment of students' subjective well-being. Third, I discuss the assessment of subjective well-being in students, as well as three self-report instruments designed to reflect that well-being.

SUBJECTIVE WELL-BEING

According to Andrews and Withey (1976) and Diener (1984, 1994), subjective well-being refers to a person's subjective assessment of the quality of his or her life. This assessment consists of affective and cognitive–judgmental components. The affective component is frequently referred to as *happiness* (Strack et al., 1991), but it includes both positive and negative affect. A strong feeling of happiness involves the perception of both a relatively large amount of positive affect and a relatively small amount of negative affect. In terms of assessment, this implies that it is inappropriate to evaluate the affective component of subjective well-being solely in terms of a lack of negative affect (Diener, 1994). For example, a person who is no longer depressed is not necessarily happy. The cognitive–judgmental component of subjective well-being is called *life satisfaction*. Life satisfaction is a person's evaluation of the quality of his or her life as a whole (Diener, 1984, 1994; Veenhoven, 1991).

Positive and Negative Affect

The relationship between positive and negative affect depends on a variety of factors, including the duration of the time span being rated and how affect is measured (Diener, 1994; Diener, Larsen, Levine, & Emmons, 1985). For short durations, that is, those under a few weeks, positive affect and negative affect will have an inverse relationship. However, if respondents are asked to rate the happiness they experienced during the previous months or more, positive and negative affect will be more independent. This relationship is partially clarified when the frequency of affect is considered separately from the intensity of affect (Diener et al., 1985). An inverse relationship exists between the frequency of positive and the frequency of negative affect. The more often a person experiences positive affect, the less often that person experiences negative affect. However, a positive relationship exists between the intensity of positive and the intensity of negative affect. A person who experiences positive affect intensely also experiences negative affect intensely. If a person rates his or her average affect for a period of several weeks or more, the positive relationship for intensity mediates the inverse relationship for frequency. As a result, ratings of positive and negative affect appear to be relatively independent (Diener, 1984; Diener et al., 1985).

Unfortunately, separating affect frequency from intensity only partially explains the data regarding the relationship between positive and negative affect. Diener (1994) discusses other complicating factors, such as the particular emotions that are measured and whether the measures are verbal or nonverbal. Diener (1994) suggests that positive and negative affect should be assessed separately. However, complete independence should not be expected.

The distinction between affect intensity and frequency is important when assessing subjective well-being. Chamberlain (1988) and Diener, Sandvik, and Pavot (1991) recommend that affect intensity should not be assessed in the study of subjective well-being. Support for this recommendation is found in the research literature. First, differences in affect intensity have not been found to be related to differences in overall happiness or life satisfaction (Larsen & Diener, 1987). Second, affect intensity cannot be measured as accurately as affect frequency (Diener, Sandvik, & Pavot, 1991). Third, affect intensity is not necessary for respondents to report a feeling of happiness. As long as the perceived frequency of positive affect is sufficiently great, people report feelings of happiness (Diener, Sandvik, & Pavot, 1991). Fourth, intense emotional responses, including positive emotional responses, can have undesirable effects. This is not a characteristic that logically would be associated with subjective well-being.

Life Satisfaction

Diener (1984, 1994) defines *life satisfaction* as a global assessment of the quality of one's life. The distinction between global life satisfaction and life satisfaction as the aggregate of satisfaction in specific life domains is a tenuous one, but one that is important to the assessment process. As a global construct, life satisfaction is assumed to be a unidimensional factor that is fairly consistent over time and context but sensitive to changes in the quality of life. It is assumed to exist apart from satisfaction in specific domains such as family, friends, and income. Moderate positive correlations among satisfaction in various specific domains provides some support for the existence of global life satisfaction (Lewinsohn, Redner, & Seeley, 1991).

Instruments based on a global model often provide a single score representing life satisfaction. Satisfaction in specific domains is not assessed. Instead, items refer to satisfaction with life in general. This type of instrument is preferred when the goal is to examine and compare life satisfaction between different groups. A global index allows a meaningful comparison between groups because the same construct is assessed in all groups. The global index of life satisfaction also is preferred for examining changes in general life satisfaction over time.

The multidimensional approach to the study of life satisfaction focuses on satisfaction in specific life domains. Instruments based on a multidimensional model should provide several scales reflecting satisfaction with various life domains, such as family, friends, and income. If a global life satisfaction score is determined, it is often a summation of the individual domain satisfaction scores. A multidimensional instrument is preferred when the goal is to obtain detailed information about the life satisfaction of an individual or when satisfaction in specific domains is of greater interest than general life satisfaction. Counselors and therapists may prefer to assess a client's life satisfaction as a multidimensional construct. A profile of satisfaction in specific domains may be more meaningful than a global rating of life satisfaction.

The multidimensional approach to life satisfaction introduces several additional issues. The first concerns determining which of many domains to include in the assessment. Andrews and Robinson (1991) report that an aggregate of 5 to 15 domain satisfaction scores can account for 40 to 60% of the variance in global life satisfaction. Domains may include family, friends, income, sex life, health, education, attractiveness, and many other areas. Determining which domains to include in an assessment depends on the goals of the researcher. Obviously, if researchers are interested in specific domains, they should be included. However, if the goal is to attain a detailed analysis of the life satisfaction of individuals, satisfaction in those domains that are of importance to the respondents must be assessed.

The second issue concerns the appropriate determination and use of an aggregate estimate of global life satisfaction. Frequently, aggregate estimates are a simple summation of the separate domain satisfaction scores. This procedure ignores the relative importance of the domains to the respondents' overall life satisfaction. Those domains that have the greatest impact on a person's life satisfaction are those that are the most important to that person (Andrews & Withey, 1976; Diener, 1984). A weighted aggregate may provide a more accurate estimate of an individual's overall or global life satisfaction than a summed aggregate. However, Andrews and Robinson (1991) report that a simple additive model is as predictive of global life satisfaction as are more complex models. Furthermore, a weighted combination does not allow meaningful comparisons to be made between persons or groups, because each person may use different weights.

Students' Life Satisfaction

Our understanding of students' life satisfaction will benefit from both the global and multidimensional approaches to its assessment. The global approach is useful for comparisons of the life satisfaction of different populations of students. Examples include students with and without problem behavior, learning-disabled and nondisabled students, high-achieving and low-achieving students, or students from single-parent families and those from dual-parent families. The global approach also should be used for studies of the longitudinal change in subjective well-being. The multidimensional approach provides a more detailed description of the life satisfaction of individual students or groups of students. It should be used in the longitudinal study of satisfaction with specific contexts, such as changes over time in satisfaction with parental relations vs. peer relations.

Developmental Issues in Self-Perception

Because an interest in students' subjective well-being has been pursued only recently, very little research related to its development is available. However, research regarding students' self-concept and social cognition provides direction for research concerning the development of students' subjective well-being. Unfortunately, much of the research regarding students' self-perceptions is cross-sectional. Many of the reported age-related differences in students' self-concept may be cohort differences rather than true developmental differences. The separation of cohort differences from developmental trends depends on the use of longitudinal or cross-sequential research paradigms.

Perceptions of Global Self-Worth

Susan Harter and her coworkers developed several multidimensional instruments for assessing the self-concept of students. The Self-Perception Profile for Children (SPPC) provides a profile of scores reflecting a student's self-concept in academic competence, social acceptance, athletic competence, physical appearance, and behavioral conduct (Harter, 1985). The Self-

Perception Profile for Adolescents (SPPA) also includes subscales reflecting the student's self-perception of job competence, romantic appeal, and the ability to make close friends (Harter, 1988). One additional subscale found in both profiles is global self-worth. This subscale reflects a student's global judgment of happiness and liking of oneself (Harter, 1985).

Similarities exist between Harter's construct of global self-worth and subjective well-being. The content of the items in the global self-worth subscale are similar to the content of the items in the Student's Life Satisfaction Scale (Huebner, 1991c). Table 1 presents the items from the global self-worth subscale of the SPPC (Harter, 1985). Also, Harter's unique item format taps both positive and negative affect in some items. On items that tap happiness, the children first decide if they are most like the happy or the unhappy description. Then they decide to what extent the description fits.

Another similarity between global self-worth and life satisfaction lies in the multidimensional model Harter (1986, 1990a) uses to describe the relationship between global self-worth and the various self-concept domains of her instruments. Global self-worth is influenced by, but separate from, students' self-perceptions in specific self-concept domains. This is similar to the assumption that global life satisfaction is influenced by, but separate from, satisfaction in specific life domains. Harter (1986, 1990a) reported comparisons between students' global self-worth and a weighted aggregate measure of self-worth. The weightings were based on the respondents' ratings of the importance of the various domains. The aggregate measure ac-

TABLE 1
Items from the Global Self-Worth Subscale of the Self-Perception Profile for Children[a]

Some kids are often unhappy with themselves	but	Other kids are pretty pleased with themselves.
Some kids don't like the way they are leading their life	but	Other kids do like the way they are leading their life.
Some kids are happy with themselves as a person	but	Other kids are often not happy with themselves.
Some kids like the kind of person they are	but	Other kids often wish they were someone else.
Some kids are happy being the way they are	but	Other kids wish they were different.
Some kids are not very happy with the way they do alot [sic] of things	but	Other kids think the way they do things is fine.

Note. Respondents first choose that side which best describes them, then choose between "sort of true" and "really true" (p. 11).
[a]Adapted from Harter (1985).

counted for approximately 25 to 55% of the variance in global self-worth (Harter, 1986, 1990a).

Harter (1987, 1990a) reported age-related differences in the relative contribution of the various self-concept domain scores to global self-worth. The main contributors to elementary and middle school students' global self-worth were physical appearance and social acceptance. For middle school students the role of social acceptance was stronger than it was for the elementary school students. Also, academic competence, athletic competence, and behavioral conduct were less important to middle school students' global self-worth than they were for the younger students (Harter, 1987, 1990a).

Based on Harter's work with global self-worth, I predict that developmental trends will be found in the factors that contribute to students' subjective well-being. As children develop both socially and cognitively, different life domains will become important to them. Domains that had been important will fade. For example, students' satisfaction with friends is expected to become a stronger contributor to their subjective well-being as they approach adolescence and will fade as they progress through later adolescence. I also expect that aggregate measures of life satisfaction will be found to be moderately and positively related to global measures of life satisfaction, especially if the relative importance of the various domains are taken into account when the aggregate is determined.

Differentiation of Self-Concept

Research evidence suggests that, as students develop, their self-concepts become more differentiated. Marsh, Barnes, Cairns, and Tidman (1984) and Marsh, Parker, and Barnes (1985) present evidence that older children perceive themselves in terms of a greater number of fairly independent dimensions than do younger children. Marsh et al. (1984) administered the Self-Description Questionnaire to children in grades 2 through 5. A separate factor analysis was produced for each grade. The older children displayed a more differentiated self-concept, as illustrated by weaker correlations among several of the factors for the older children than for the younger ones. However, Marsh et al. (1985) found no evidence of continued differentiation during adolescence.

Harter (1990a, 1990b) also suggests that self-concept differentiates into increasing numbers of domains as children develop. Children under seven years were found to combine the self-perception of scholastic and athletic competence into a single factor (Harter, 1990a, 1990b). Students older than seven years separated these factors. However, as Harter (1990b) indicates, some evidence of the differentiation of self-concept may be due to the use of different instruments for students in different age ranges. For example, Harter used different instruments to assess the self-concepts of children and adolescents. Factor analyses of these instruments revealed five self-concept factors for children and eight for adolescents (Harter, 1990a, 1990b). However, the scale that was designed for adolescents (Harter, 1988) had several new items that did not appear in the children's scale (Harter, 1985). Most of these new items loaded on the three new factors. Therefore, the existence of the new factors may simply reflect the difference in the item content of the two instruments.

Differentiation of the self-concept may be related to cognitive development. In a study that was briefly discussed by Harter (1986), educably retarded children in grades 3 through 6 demonstrated the same factor structure as younger nonretarded children in the four- to seven-year age range. The global self-worth subscale did not appear in the factor analysis of the responses of either group, nor were the global self-worth items related to any other factor. Based on these results, Harter (1986) assumed that the differentiation of the self-concept was more strongly related to mental age, that is, cognitive development, than to chronological age.

Evidence of the importance of cognitive development to life satisfaction also was found by Fabes (1987). Tenth-grade students were assigned to either a higher or lower cognitive development group based on a test of reasoning ability. The students were asked to evaluate their perceived quality of life by identifying one area of life that was the most satisfying and one that was the most unsatisfying. Students with higher cognitive development tended to identify more social and interpersonal issues and fewer self-related issues than the lower-scoring students.

Two problems exist in much of the research on the differentiation of students' self-perceptions. The first is that, as discussed previously, almost all of the research is cross-sectional. The reported differences in self-perception may reflect only cohort differences. The second problem involves the use of factor analyses. It is not appropriate to use different instruments for different age groups, then to use resulting differences in the factor structures as evidence in support of the differentiation of self-concept. The different instruments may have different factor structures by virtue of the items in the instruments rather than due to the age of the respondents.

To establish the existence of a developmental differentiation of self-perception, researchers should use a cross-sequential paradigm. The self-perception of students in each cohort should be assessed longitudinally with the same instrument. If a change in the factor structure consistently appears for the same age range in each cohort, differentiation may be supported. This change could appear as an increase in factors or a change in factor loadings. If the factor structure does not change, differentiation still could be supported if the correlations between the cluster scores are significantly and consistently lower for the older ages. Once the appropriate research design is employed, evidence of a differentiation of subjective well-being likely will be found. However, it is too early to predict the form of that differentiation or what domains will be involved.

Other Age-Related Differences

Age-related differences in self-perception may be related to social development. The development of the self-concept parallels the development of
social cognition. A stable self-concept does not appear in children until they
can reliably distinguish between themselves and others. Selman (1980) indicates that around eight years of age children begin to understand that
others have separate beliefs and attitudes. This is also the age at which
Harter (1990a) suggests children start to verbally express a somewhat stable
self-worth.

As students develop, new social skills and different social concerns become important to them. Students evaluate themselves in terms of their
self-perceived competence in these new skills and concerns. This may lead
to developmental differences in which domains are important to students'
self-concepts. For example, close friendship is not differentiated from peer
acceptance until early adolescence (Harter, 1990b). Research on the development of friendships indicates this is also the approximate age at which
the perception of friends shifts from an activity-oriented approach to a concern about mutual trust and security (Selman, 1980).

Based on cross-sectional research, Marsh et al. (1984) reported a decline
in self-concept from the second-grade sample to the fifth-grade sample. Self-
concept regarding students' relationships with peers dropped from the
second- through the fourth-grade sample, then increased in the fifth-grade
sample. Self-concept scores for physical abilities, physical appearance, reading, math, and all school subjects declined from the second-grade sample
through the fifth-grade sample. This decline also was evident in the total
academic self-concept, nonacademic self-concept, and general self-concept
scores. Marsh et al. (1984) tentatively interpreted this decrease in scores to
be the result of a combination of the tendency for children to use more
normative comparison information as they age and the tendency for younger
children to exhibit a positive bias in their self-perception. In other words, the
high self-concept scores of the younger children declined as they engaged in
a more realistic comparison.

Marsh et al. (1985) also found grade-related differences in the self-
concepts of students in grades 7 through 12. Students in the upper grades
scored increasingly higher on the self-concept regarding relationships with
the opposite sex but lower for relationships with parents. For 8 of the 11 self-
concept scores, as well as the total academic and total self scores, scores
were highest in seventh-, eleventh-, and twelfth-grade samples. The lowest scores were usually in the ninth-grade sample. Harter (1986) suggested
that ninth-grade students experience more conflict regarding the self than
do younger or older students. This conflict within the self was interpreted
as a possible explanation for lower scores on self-concept scales (Harter,
1986).

Children under Eight Years

Special attention needs to be given to research regarding the self-perception of children under eight years of age. Several limitations in the ability of these young children to engage in and report self-perception make it difficult to reliably and accurately assess their self-concept (Harter, 1990a, 1993). These limitations make it inappropriate to use self-report techniques to assess the global self-worth of children under eight years (Harter, 1986, 1990a). According to Harter and Pike (1984) and Harter (1990a), children under eight years do not have a generalized sense of self-worth that can be assessed accurately through self-report techniques. Although children from ages four to seven years can communicate their self-perception, they do so in concrete terms, using preferences and possessions. Harter (1990a) also reports that these younger children cannot determine the relative importance of different domains. According to Harter (1993), the younger children treat personal characteristics as if they are univalent. For example, younger children would perceive a person as being either all good or all bad, but not both relatively good and relatively bad. Younger children rely on the use of basic emotions in their affective descriptions (Harter, 1993). It is not until approximately age eight years that children start to use self-related affective descriptions, such as pride. Finally, both Harter (1990a, 1993) and Marsh (1986) suggest that younger children are more likely than older children to express their self-perception in overly positive terms.

Behavioral indexes of self-concept and self-worth may be more appropriate than self-report items with children under age eight years (Harter, 1990a). Behaviors that express confidence, curiosity, initiative, and independence and those that indicate an ability to adapt to change or stress may characterize younger children with higher levels of self-worth (Harter, 1990a). Harter (1990a) has been working with these types of indicators in the development of a scale to assess self-worth in young children.

A student's ability to judge his or her life satisfaction and assess his or her happiness also requires the ability to express self-evaluations. Therefore, it also will be difficult to assess the subjective well-being of students under eight years of age. Non-self-report indicators of subjective well-being should be devised. Such indicators may include behavioral assessments (Harter, 1990a; Huebner, 1994) or ratings by teachers or parents.

Developmentally Appropriate Instruments

Harter (1990b) presents a strong case for the use of developmentally appropriate instruments when assessing students' self-perceptions. Assessment must be sensitive to changes in both the structure and content of students' self-perceptions. As Harter (1990b) also indicates, developmental change may require changes in the instruments used at different developmental levels. These changes are likely to include alterations in content, item format, and language. However, the use of developmentally appropriate instruments poses serious problems for researchers (Harter, 1990b). If researchers are interested in longitudinal change in self-perception and different instruments are used for the different developmental levels, it will be impossible to determine if differences in the performance are due to developmental change or the use of different instruments. A similar problem exists if different instruments are required for special populations, such as mentally retarded students or students with learning disabilities.

ASSESSING SUBJECTIVE WELL-BEING IN ADULTS

A brief review of the assessment of subjective well-being in adults provides a standard against which instruments for use with students can be compared. Traditionally, subjective well-being in adults has been assessed through the use of forced-choice, self-report measures. The use of self-report instruments assumes that the respondents can assess and accurately report their affect and life satisfaction. As suggested previously, this becomes problematic when assessing the self-perceptions of children. The self-reports of adults may also be suspect if they are influenced by current mood, social desirability, and other contextual factors. Regardless of the potential weakness of self-report measures, traditional scales have provided useful information regarding the subjective well-being of adults.

The use of alternative methods has been strongly encouraged (Diener, 1994; Sandvik, Diener, & Seidlitz, 1993). Examples of alternative methods include ratings from others, memory for positive and negative events, open-ended questionnaires, and daily logs (Sandvik et al., 1993). The psychometric properties of many alternative methods have been found to be similar to those of traditional self-report measures of subjective well-being (Diener, Sandvik, Pavot, & Gallagher, 1991; Sandvik et al., 1993). A variety of non-self-report measures also have been found to correlate well with self-report measures (Myers & Diener, 1995; Pavot & Diener, 1993; Sandvik et al., 1993).

Most of the measures of subjective well-being in adults are research instruments, rather than clinical instruments. That is, the instruments were designed primarily to assess the subjective well-being of different samples of respondents. They were not designed to be used in the diagnosis of abnormal behavior. Because the instruments are research instruments, they often lack norms. Although norms may be extrapolated from research results, they are not useful for clinical diagnoses.

Evidence of the reliability of measures of subjective well-being is extensive. Because measures of subjective well-being must be sensitive to changes in well-being, a high temporal stability is not expected nor desirable. Okun and Stock (1987) reported a mean test–retest reliability of .74 for multiple-item instruments and .69 for single-item instruments. Pavot and Diener (1993) reported test–retest coefficients ranging from .49 to .71, with time spans ranging from six months to six years. The lower coefficients were usually associated with the longer intervals. Somewhat lower test–retest reliabilities were reported by Horley and Lavery (1991), who found temporal stabilities in the range of .01 to .45 for various instruments over a period of seven years.

Estimates of the internal consistency of various measures of subjective well-being also are positive. Alpha coefficients ranging from .53 to .96 have been reported (Okun & Stock, 1987; Pavot & Diener, 1993; Sandvik et al., 1993). Okun and Stock (1987) reported a mean internal consistency of .81. Scales with greater numbers of items usually have the greater alpha values (Andrews & Robinson, 1991).

Measures of subjective well-being in adults have moderate convergent and divergent validity. Okun and Stock (1987) found a mean intercorrelation of .69 for measures of life satisfaction and .45 for measures of happiness. However, the mean of correlations between measures of life satisfaction and happiness was .49. Thus, the convergent and divergent validity of measures of life satisfaction received the greater support. When measures of subjective well-being are compared with related measures, the most positive relationship often is found to be with measures of self-esteem. Subjective well-being also is positively correlated with successful striving toward goals, extraversion, and measures of satisfaction in specific domains, such as the standard of living, family, work, health, and community (Diener, 1994).

Social desirability influences adults' responses on instruments that assess subjective well-being (Diener, Sandvik, Pavot, & Gallagher, 1991; Kozma & Stones, 1988). It often is interpreted as a personality characteristic that inflates or enhances scores on subjective well-being measures. However, social desirability does not invalidate measures of subjective well-being (Diener, Sandvik, Pavot, & Gallagher, 1991; Kozma & Stones, 1988). Therefore, controlling for social desirability often is not necessary (Diener, Sandvik, Pavot, & Gallagher, 1991).

The effect of current mood on the assessment of subjective well-being is less clear. Schwarz and Strack (1991) present a model of subjective well-being in which current mood is the basis for respondents' evaluation of their subjective well-being. However, if other information is more salient or if the current mood is attributed to other events, respondents engage in a cognitive comparison process to judge their subjective well-being. Therefore, the effect of current mood on subjective well-being depends on what other information is available at the time of the assessment (Schwarz & Strack, 1991). Diener, Sandvik, Pavot, and Gallagher (1991) suggest that repeated assessment of subjective well-being at different times should balance mood effects.

Finally, subjective well-being is not strongly related to differences in demographic variables (Andrews & Robinson, 1991; Diener, 1984). In Diener's

(1984) review, data indicate that people who are married, have adequate income, gained higher levels of education, and live in wealthier countries have slightly higher levels of subjective well-being. African-Americans may have lower levels of subjective well-being than whites, but this is confounded with other variables (Diener, 1984). The relationship of subjective well-being with gender and age is often weak and inconsistent (Diener, 1984).

ASSESSING SUBJECTIVE WELL-BEING IN STUDENTS

In the educational literature, *well-being* has been defined so broadly as to become meaningless. Page and Page (1993) included the ability to relate to others, self-acceptance, coping, problem solving, and decision making in their definition of *emotional well-being*. Adams, Gullotta, and Markstrom-Adams (1994) defined *psychological well-being* as including self-worth, self-confidence, self-efficacy, psychological comfort, and satisfaction with oneself. Therefore, two criteria guided my search for instruments designed to measure the subjective well-being of students. The first criterion was that the instrument must have been designed specifically to assess life satisfaction or affect or both. The second criterion was that any instruments designed to assess students' affect must have included both positive and negative affect.

Only three instruments meet my selection criteria. The instruments include the Perceived Life Satisfaction Scale (PLSS: Adelman, Taylor, & Nelson, 1989), the Student's Life Satisfaction Scale (SLSS: Huebner, 1991c), and the Multidimensional Student's Life Satisfaction Scale (MSLSS: Huebner, 1994). All three research instruments assess only the life satisfaction component of subjective well-being. According to their authors, both the PLSS and the SLSS were designed to assess life satisfaction from a global or unidimensional perspective. The MSLSS was designed to assess life satisfaction from a multidimensional approach.

Perceived Life Satisfaction Scale

The PLSS was developed to assess students' dissatisfaction with their material and physical well-being, relationships with friends and family, home and school environments, personal development, and recreation or entertainment (Adelman et al., 1989). It consists of 19 items that are rated on a six-point Likert scale. In scoring the PLSS, ratings of 1 or 2 are given two points, ratings of 3 or 4 are given one point, and ratings of 5 or 6 are given zero points. Scores range from 0 to 38, with the higher scores reflecting greater dissatisfaction (Adelman et al., 1989). Huebner and Dew (1993c) used a different scoring system, in which the ratings were summed, yielding scores ranging from 19 for the lowest level of satisfaction to 114 for the highest level. All of the items are positively worded, so there is no reverse scoring. It is recommended that the directions and questions be read to the students. A card on which the response choices are printed in large letters is provided to the students during the testing to help them remember the meaning of the response ratings. Table 2 lists the items in the PLSS (Adelman et al., 1989).

Samples

Four databases were used in the development of the PLSS. All four samples were composed of students attending schools in the Los Angeles area. The use of multiple samples is desirable, but the generalizability of the samples may be questioned. The number of students per grade was not reported. The ethnic mix was inconsistently reported.

TABLE 2
Items from the Perceived Life Satisfaction Scale[a]

How satisfied do you usually feel when you think about . . .

the amount of spending money you usually have?

the amount of time you can spend doing anything you want?

the amount of control you have over your life?

going to school?

the opportunities you have to learn new things and improve your skills?

your physical appearance, such as your height, weight, hairstyle?

your progress at school compared to others in your classroom?

the way you get along with your mother?

the way you get along with your father?

how physical [sic] fit and energetic you are?

the amount of time you can spend watching TV?

the type of clothes you wear?

nonschool activities such as hobbies, sports?

the type of neighborhood where you live?

the type of place (home, apartment, etc.) where you live?

the way you get along with your friends?

the goals you have set for your future?

the number of friends you have?

the type of job you'll get when you stop school?

Note. Items are rated on a six-point Likert scale.
[a]Adapted from Adelman et al. (1989).

The first sample consisted of 110 males and 111 females, from families with low to moderate income. Ages ranged from 9 to 19 years (mean = 14.5, SD = 2.8). The ethnic mix included 32% African-Americans, 22% Hispanics, and 16% unspecified minorities. Sample 2 consisted of 97 males and 82 females from middle income families. Ages ranged from 11 to 16 years (mean = 13.2, SD = 1.0). The ethnic mix included 7% Asian-Americans, 7% Hispanics, and 2% unspecified minorities. Sample 3 consisted of 24 males and 44 females from moderate to high income families. Ages ranged from 8 to 18 years (mean = 12.9, SD = 2.9). The ethnic mix included 12% Asian-Americans and 1% unspecified minorities. Sample 4 consisted of 34 males and 13 females who were referred to a mental health center. Ages ranged from 7 to 16 years (mean = 11.1, SD = 2.5). The ethnic mix included 24% unspecified minorities.

Reliability

The internal consistency of the PLSS is similar to that of adult instruments. Alpha coefficients ranging from .74 to .89 have been reported (Huebner & Dew, 1993b; Smith, Adelman, Nelson, Taylor, & Phares, 1987). The test–retest reliability is unclear because no time spans were reported. Adelman et al. (1989) reported a Pearson's coefficient of .85 from a sample of 37 students. Smith et al. (1987) reported test–retest reliabilities of .63 for special education students and .72 for regular education students.

Validity

No factor analysis was reported in Adelman et al. (1989), but Huebner and Dew (1993b) conducted a principal components factor analysis with a promax oblique rotation. Although the scoring of the PLSS provides only a single life satisfaction score, the results of the factor analysis indicate it provides a multidimensional assessment. A four-factor solution was determined to be the most appropriate. All item loadings over .35 were reported. Four items loaded above .35 on two factors, but only two items had dual loadings within .05 of each other. The factor analysis accounted for approximately 57% of the total variance. Their sample include 107 males and 115 females, with a mean age of 15.5 years (SD = 1.5). Sixty-nine students were in the eighth grade, 2 in the ninth, 106 in the tenth, 4 in the eleventh, and 41 in the twelfth grade. The ethnic mix included 115 African-Americans and 1 Native American.

Scores on the PLSS and other instruments reveal a moderate convergent and discriminant validity. In Adelman et al. (1989), scores on the PLSS were negatively correlated (−.29) with students' perceptions of the degree of control at school. Students with a low sense of personal control tended to be more dissatisfied. For the responses of the children in the mental health centers, the scores on the PLSS were positively correlated (.55) with scores on a measure of children's depression and negatively correlated (−.54) with expectations for improvement in problems at home and in school (Adelman et al., 1989). Students who were more dissatisfied were also more depressed and did not expect improvement of their problems at home or in school.

Huebner and Dew (1993c) reported positive correlations between their scoring of the PLSS and subscales of the Self-Description Questionnaire II (Marsh, 1988). Life satisfaction was positively correlated with respondents' perceptions of their relationships with their parents (.47), relationships with members of the opposite sex (.36), relationships with members of the same sex (.33), emotional stability (.33), general school self-concept (.32), honesty (.22), physical appearance (.22), math self-concept (.16), and verbal self-concept (.10). Huebner and Dew (1993c) also reported that parents' ratings of their children's satisfaction were positively related to their children's scores on the PLSS (.42). Dew and Huebner (1994) found scores on the PLSS to be positively correlated with scores on the SLSS (Huebner, 1991c).

The PLSS is moderately effective in its ability to distinguish between different populations of students, who would logically be expected to differ in life satisfaction. Adelman et al. (1989) found students in mental health centers to be more dissatisfied than students in regular education programs. They also found that, within the mental health center sample, the depressed students were less satisfied than the nondepressed students. However, Smith et al. (1987) found no differences in life satisfaction between students in regular and special education classes.

Demographics

As with scores on adult instruments, scores on the PLSS are not strongly related to demographic variables. Adelman et al. (1989) reported no differences in the mean PLSS scores between the three public school samples,

TABLE 3
Items Similar to Items in the Student's Life Satisfaction Scale

I like the way my life is going.
I feel good about my life.
I would change my life, if I could.
I have the things I want.
My life is not as good as other kids' lives.

Note. Items are rated on a five-point Likert scale. Because permission to reproduce the items was not granted, these items are not those that appear on the SLSS (Huebner, 1991c).

males and females, or students from different ethnic backgrounds. There was some indication that, in the lowest income school, the older students were less satisfied than younger students. However, this result was confounded by the existence of a large minority population in the lowest income school. In the sample from the mental health centers, females were less satisfied than males, and older students were less satisfied than younger students (Adelman et al., 1989).

Huebner and Dew (1993c) found no differences related to age, grade, or gender. Students in lower socioeconomic status (SES) levels were less satisfied than students in higher SES levels. However, this relationship was confounded by the higher proportion of students from minority populations in the lower SES levels.

Source

The items composing the PLSS can be found in Table 2 and in Adelman et al. (1989).

Student's Life Satisfaction Scale

The initial development of the Student's Life Satisfaction Scale was reported in Huebner (1991a, 1991b, 1991c) as an attempt to develop a global, unidimensional test of the life satisfaction appropriate for use with children and adolescents. Initially containing nine items, the SLSS was reduced to seven. Analyses involving both versions are reported in the literature. All items require the respondents to provide global ratings of their life satisfaction without reference to specific content areas, such as family, school, or friends. The time span for this judgment is the "past several weeks" (Huebner, 1991c, p. 233). Table 3 presents items similar to those found in the SLSS. Ratings are recorded on a four-point scale, ranging from 1 = never to 4 = always. Two of the items are negatively worded and require reverse scoring. Scoring the SLSS results in a single score, ranging from 7 to 28 for the seven-item version, with higher scores indicating greater satisfaction. The reading level was determined to be appropriate for as low as the third grade (Huebner, 1991c). Administration of the SLSS includes reading the instructions and the test items to the children.

Samples

Several samples of children and adolescents served as respondents in the development of the SLSS. Most of these samples were from rural and urban school districts in the Midwest or the Southeast. The number of students per grade level is usually reported. However, the ethnic mix of the samples is often limited, that is, predominantly white, or is not well reported.

Huebner (1991a) used 50 males and 29 females, ranging in age from 10 to 13 years (mean = 11.54). No minority students were in the sample. Huebner (1991b) used 128 males and 125 females, ranging in age from 7 to 14 years (mean = 10.54). Sixty-one students were from the third grade, 49 from the fourth, 57 from the fifth, 59 from the sixth, 17 from the seventh, and 10 from the eighth grade. The sample was predominantly white. The number of students from ethnic minorities was not reported. Two studies were included in Huebner (1991c). In the first study, the same database as found in Huebner (1991b) was reported. Subjects in the second study were from four samples. Overall, there were 165 males and 165 females from grades four through six and eight. Ages ranged from 8 through 14 years. The number of students from ethnic minorities was not reported.

Reliability

The internal consistency is similar to those found for adult instruments. Alpha coefficients ranging from .82 to .85 have been reported (Huebner, 1991a, 1991c). Huebner (1991c) reported a test–retest reliability of .74 over a period of one to two weeks. Although the data are limited, the reliability of the SLSS is similar to the reliability of adult instruments.

Validity

Huebner (1991c) conducted a principal components factor analysis on separate samples of respondents and found one factor that accounted for approximately 46–47% of the variance in scores in each analysis. Huebner (1991b) combined the SLSS items with items that were written to assess positive and negative affect. A principal components analysis with a varimax rotation resulted in seven factors. The first factor consisted primarily of the nine items from the SLSS. The second factor was mostly positive affect, with some cross-loading from life satisfaction items. Factors 3 and 4 were primarily negative affect, with some cross-loading from life satisfaction items in factor 3 and both life satisfaction and positive affect in factor 4. The remaining factors included too few items to be meaningful. Huebner and Dew (1993a) conducted separate principal components analyses for the African-American subjects and the white subjects. Both resulted in single factors with similar loadings. Dew and Huebner (1994) reported a principal components analysis of the combined data from Huebner and Dew (1993a) and found a single factor.

The factor analyses should be interpreted with caution. Huebner (1991c) and Huebner and Dew (1993a) used a principal components analysis, with no rotation. This procedure increases the likelihood of finding a single general factor. Therefore, the claim that the SLSS provides a global assessment of life satisfaction may be inflated. However, Huebner (1991b) included a varimax rotation and the life satisfaction items mostly fell into a single factor, with some cross-loading with affect factors. This supports the assertion that the SLSS measures life satisfaction as a unidimensional construct.

The convergent validity of the SLSS is well supported. Scores on the SLSS correlated with other measures of subjective well-being in a range of .34 to .62 (Huebner, 1991c). These other measures included four measures of affect, one scale that contained both affect and life satisfaction items, and one single-item life satisfaction question. Dew and Huebner (1994) found the SLSS to be positively correlated (.58) with scores on the PLSS (Adelman et al., 1989).

Scores on the SLSS also were found to correlate with related measures. Huebner (1991a) reported correlations of .65 with a measure of self-esteem, .23 with a measure of extraversion, −.51 with a measure of anxiety, −.48 with a measure of the external locus of control, and −.46 with a measure of neuroticism. Huebner (1991a) also compared scores on the SLSS with responses to single-item satisfaction ratings of various specific domains. The SLSS scores correlated positively with satisfaction with family (.65), self (.57), neighborhood (.49), opportunities for fun (.40), school life (.31), city (.28), and friends (.18).

Huebner and Alderman (1993) found scores on the SLSS to be positively correlated with scores on measures of self-esteem (.65) and negatively correlated with scores on measures of child depression (−.61) and loneliness (−.56) for a combined sample of normally achieving and lower-achieving students. Huebner and Alderman also reported a positive correlation (.42) with normally achieving students' judgment of the quality of life in school.

Dew and Huebner (1994) reported scores on the SLSS to be positively correlated with parents' ratings of their childrens' life satisfaction (.48) and various subscales on a multidimensional measure of self-concept (.15 to .62). Dew and Huebner also found a negative correlation (−.52) between the SLSS and a measure of the external locus of control.

Discriminant validity was supported by results that indicated no significant relationship between scores on the SLSS and social desirability (Huebner, 1991c), grade point (Huebner, 1991a; Huebner & Alderman, 1993), or IQ (Huebner & Alderman, 1993).

Evidence that the SLSS can distinguish between populations of students who logically may be expected to differ in life satisfaction is limited but positive. Huebner and Alderman (1993) reported that emotionally handicapped students scored lower than non-emotionally handicapped students. Huebner and Dew (1993a) found that African-American students scored lower than white students. Further analysis indicated that this difference was not due to any instrument bias against African-American students.

Demographics

Scores on the SLSS were not related to age (Dew & Huebner, 1994; Huebner, 1991a, 1991c), gender (Huebner, 1991a, 1991c), grade level (Huebner, 1991a),

TABLE 4
Items Similar to Items in the Multidimensional Students'
Life Satisfaction Scale

Members of my family get along with each other very well.

I like the way my parents treat me.

I enjoy spending time with my friends.

My friends pick on me.

I enjoy learning in school.

School makes me feel bad about myself.

I wish I lived in a better neighborhood.

The people in my town are friendly.

I am a fun person.

People think I am attractive.

Note. Items are rated on a four-point Likert scale. Because permission to reproduce the items was not granted, these items are not those that appear on the MSLSS (Huebner, 1994).

parents' occupational status (Huebner, 1991a), or parents' marital status (Huebner, 1991a). However, Huebner and Alderman (1993) and Dew and Huebner (1994) reported that scores on the SLSS were positively related to SES.

Source

The content of the seven-item scale can be found in Huebner (1991a).

Multidimensional Student's Life Satisfaction Scale

The MSLSS is designed to assess life satisfaction as a multidimensional construct. Designed for use with children in grades 3 through 8, the MSLSS assesses children's satisfaction in five areas, including family, friends, school, living environment, and self (Huebner, 1994). Respondents are asked to rate how often they experience satisfaction with specific events in these areas. The MSLSS consists of 40 items that are rated on a four-point scale, in which 1 = never, 2 = sometimes, 3 = often, and 4 = always. Some of the items are negatively worded and require reverse scoring. Scoring the MSLSS results in separate scale scores for each of the five domains. These scores are determined by summing the ratings and dividing by the number of items in that domain. In the initial testing of the MSLSS, the items from the SLSS (Huebner, 1991c) were included. Because these did not form a separate factor and were correlated with the total MSLSS score, they were assumed to be redundant and dropped. Administration involves reading the directions, then allowing the respondents to continue at their own pace. Table 4 contains items similar to those used in the MSLSS.

Samples

Because this test was developed only recently, only two samples are reported. School districts from rural, suburban, and urban areas are represented. A wide variety of socioeconomic levels is also represented. The number of students in each grade level is reported. The number of African-American students is reported for each sample.

The initial development was completed with a sample of 144 males and 168 females from three school districts from a Southeastern state. The sample consisted of 63 third-, 63 fourth-, 78 fifth-, 39 sixth-, and 69 eighth-grade students. The mean age was 10.9 years (SD = 2.0). The ethnic mix included 69 African-American students and 12 students in unspecified minorities. The second study involved 212 male and 201 female students from four schools in three districts near or in a metropolitan area in the Southeast. The sample included 155 third-, 145 fourth-, and 111 fifth-grade students. Grade level data were missing for two children. The mean age was 8.97 years (SD = .91). The ethnic mix included 85 African-American students and 33 students in unspecified minorities (Huebner, 1994).

Reliability

The internal consistency is in the high end of the range found with adult scales. Alpha coefficients of .92 for the full scale score, .79 and .82 for the family subscale, .81 and .85 for the friends subscale, .83 and .85 for the school subscale, .82 and .83 for the living environment subscale, and .78 and .82 for the self subscale were reported (Huebner, 1994). No measures of test–retest reliability were reported.

Validity

The factor structure was consistent across the two samples. The factor analysis supports the interpretation of the MSLSS as a multidimensional measure of life satisfaction. In Study 1, Huebner (1994) employed a principal components analysis with an oblique rotation. A five-factor solution was determined to be the most appropriate and accounted for 49.5% of the variance. The five factors matched the domains the MSLSS was designed to tap. Little cross-factor loading was evident. One item did not load the highest on its intended domain. In Study 2, the five-factor solution was tested with a different sample of students. Four items did not load the highest on their intended domain, three items loaded highest in their intended domain, but showed some cross-loading, and one item did not load on any factor. The five-factor solution accounted for 47.3% of the variance and showed very high congruence with the first factor structure (Huebner, 1994).

The convergent and discriminant validity of the MSLSS is moderately strong. With the exception of the friends subscale, the five domain scores correlated positively with all of the subscales of the Self-Description Questionnaire I (SDQI: Marsh, 1990). The friends subscale was not significantly related to self-concept scores regarding physical appearance. All five domain scores also were positively correlated with scores on instruments that assessed satisfaction with friendships and school life.

Each subscale of the MSLSS was most strongly correlated with a logically related measure. The strongest correlation for the family subscale was with Marsh's (1990) subscale for parental relations (.54). The school subscale correlated the most strongly with scores on an instrument designed to measure the perceived quality of school life (.68). The self subscale correlated most strongly with the general self-concept subscale of the SDQI. The living environment subscale correlated most strongly with Marsh's (1990) subscale for parental relations (.40). The strongest correlation for the friends subscale was with an instrument that was designed to measure satisfaction with friendships (.56). The discriminant validity is supported by the fact that the weaker correlations were with conceptually less similar measures (Huebner, 1994).

Demographics

Huebner (1994) found that African-American children had a lower overall satisfaction score and were less satisfied about friends and their living environment than white children. In Study 2 (Huebner, 1994), fourth graders were more satisfied with friends than were the third graders. No differences for gender were reported.

Source

The items in the MSLSS can be found in Huebner (1994).

Summary

Of the three instruments, those developed by Huebner appear to have the most promise. The PLSS (Adelman et al., 1989) is a multidimensional tool that provides only a unidimensional score. The SLSS (Huebner, 1991c) and the MSLSS (Huebner, 1994) measure students' life satisfaction as they were designed. The internal consistency of the three instruments is very good. Evidence of temporal stability is inconsistently and incompletely reported.

All three instruments have acceptable convergent and discriminant validity for research instruments. All three scales can be criticized for the lack of norms. The mean global life satisfactions and domain satisfactions at each grade level would be useful information in exploring the development of life satisfaction in students.

Several limitations apply to the assessment of subjective well-being in students. The first is that no assessment has included both positive and negative affect. Only life satisfaction has been measured. The second limitation is that the instruments are only self-report measures. Non-self-report measures of students' subjective well-being are needed. This should facilitate the assessment of happiness and life satisfaction, or at least domain satisfaction, in children under age eight years. More instruments need to be designed to assess subjective well-being in students of ages other than between 8 and 14 years. Finally, norms for subjective well-being need to be established for students at various ages or grade levels.

Alternative Approaches: Good and Bad

One alternative approach to the study of subjective well-being in students is to assess social and psychological constructs that are assumed to contribute to students' subjective well-being (Andrews & Robinson, 1991). To fully explore the effects of social and psychological factors on students' subjective well-being, the factors and subjective well-being must be assessed. Unfortunately, the assumption that these factors actually affect students' subjective well-being often is not tested. One construct that has been studied as a potential determinant of subjective well-being is students' perceptions of control (Adelman, Smith, Nelson, Taylor, & Phares, 1986; Connell, 1985). Two instruments that were designed to assess students' perceptions of control include the Perceived Control at School Scale (Adelman et al., 1986) and the Multidimensional Measure of Children's Perceptions of Control (Connell, 1985).

A poor, but often attempted alternative to the direct study of subjective well-being is to study related concepts such as self-concept and self-esteem, then to assume that the results apply to subjective well-being. This is not a recommended procedure. Although the assumption that students' self-concepts and self-esteem are related to subjective well-being is likely to be a safe assumption, the assumption that data about self-concept and self-esteem directly apply to subjective well-being is not. Treating subjective well-being as if it were identical to self-concept or self-esteem has led to the meaningless and broad definitions of *well-being* that often are found in the education literature. It is recommended that research on self-concept and self-esteem be used only to guide research on subjective well-being.

Do not use existing scales or subscales that have face validity as measures of subjective well-being unless data indicate that these scales actually do assess subjective well-being. Subscales like the global self-worth subscale of the SPPC (Harter, 1985) or the SPPA (Harter, 1990b), and the happiness and satisfaction subscale of the Piers–Harris Children's Self-Concept Scale (Piers, 1984) are examples. On the surface, these subscales appear to assess subjective well-being. However, these scales were not designed to assess subjective well-being nor has their validity as measures of subjective well-being been determined.

Directions for Research

The most immediate goal for continued research is the development of instruments to measure students' happiness and life satisfaction. The three instruments discussed in this chapter were designed to measure only life satisfaction. No instruments were found that assessed the affective component of students' subjective well-being. Although instruments do exist that measure students' affect, none assess both positive and negative affect in a manner consistent with the model of subjective well-being. Finally, no instruments exist that assess both life satisfaction and happiness.

The components of subjective well-being should be assessed from both the unidimensional and multidimensional perspectives. The unidimensional approach facilitates the study of subjective well-being as a global construct that exists independent of various life domains. This approach allows the comparison of global subjective well-being between groups of students. Multidimensional instruments provide detailed information about students' satisfaction with specific domains. A combination of approaches allows researchers to determine the contributions of subjective well-being in specific domains to the global subjective well-being.

Alternative assessment procedures also should be explored. The use of only self-report techniques limits the type of information available. The addition of procedures other than self-report provides a more complete understanding of subjective well-being in students (Diener, 1994). Diener urged researchers to consider such varied indexes as records of nonverbal behaviors, ratings from others, physiological measures, cognitive processing, online mood sampling, sampling of cognitive content, in-depth interviews, mood-sensitive tasks, and choice of tasks. With both self-report and non-self-report measures, alternatives to the traditional Likert scale item format should be designed. For example, younger children may be more responsive to a pictorial rating scale than to a verbal format.

The measurement of subjective well-being may be influenced by potential confounds like social desirability, current mood, and positivity bias. Although social desirability has been determined to have little impact on the assessment of subjective well-being in adults, the impact on students' responses still must be explored. Schwarz and Strack (1991) suggest that current mood is often the basis for self-reports of subjective well-being. Because current mood is more dynamic in children and adolescents than in adults, it is important to determine its effect on the validity of students' self-reports of subjective well-being. Finally, some confounds, such as positivity bias, may show developmental trends. Therefore, the effects of these confounds may influence the type of instruments that are designed to assess the subjective well-being of students of various ages.

As researchers design instruments to measure students' subjective well-being they must be aware of developmental changes in students' self-perceptions. For example, children under age eight years may not be able to articulate their subjective well-being on a self-report instrument. Also, the specific life domains that contribute to students' subjective well-being may change as the students develop socially and cognitively. Therefore, instruments that are appropriate for younger children may not be appropriate for preadolescents or adolescents.

Finally, along with the construction of new and better instruments to assess students' subjective well-being, researchers need to generate truly developmental research programs. Ideally, these programs should use a cross-sequential design to separate cohort effects from actual developmental trends in students' subjective well-being. Although such research is expensive and time consuming, it is necessary for an accurate understanding of the development of students' subjective well-being.

References

Adams, G. R., Gullotta, T. P., & Markstrom-Adams, C. (1994). *Adolescent life experiences* (3rd ed.). Pacific Grove, CA: Brooks/Cole.

Adelman, H. S., Smith, D. C., Nelson, P., Taylor, L., & Phares, V. (1986). An instrument to assess students' perceived control at school. *Educational and Psychological Measurement, 46,* 1005–1017.

Adelman, H. S., Taylor, L., & Nelson, P. (1989). Minors' dissatisfaction with their life circumstances. *Child Psychiatry and Human Development, 20,* 135–147.

Andrews, F. M., & Robinson, J. P. (1991). Measures of subjective well-being. In J. P. Robinson, P. R. Shaver, & L. S. Wrightsman (Eds.), *Measures of personality and social psychological attitudes* (pp. 61–114). San Diego, CA: Academic Press.

Andrews, F. M., & Withey, S. B. (1976). *Social indicators of well-being: Americans' perceptions of life quality.* New York: Plenum.

Chamberlain, K. (1988). On the structure of subjective well-being. *Social Indicators Research, 20,* 581–604.

Connell, J. P. (1985). A new multidimensional measure of children's perceptions of control. *Child Development, 56,* 1018–1041.

Dew, T., & Huebner, E. S. (1994). Adolescents' perceived quality of life: An exploratory investigation. *Journal of School Psychology, 32,* 185–199.

Diener, E. (1984). Subjective well-being. *Psychological Bulletin, 95,* 542–575.

Diener, E. (1994). Assessing subjective well-being: Progress and opportunities. *Social Indicators Research, 31,* 103–157.

Diener, E., Larsen, R., Levine, S., & Emmons, R. (1985). Intensity and frequency: Dimensions underlying positive and negative affect. *Journal of Personality and Social Psychology, 48,* 1253–1265.

Diener, E., Sandvik, E., & Pavot, W. (1991). Happiness is the frequency, not the intensity, of positive versus negative affect. In F. Strack, M. Argyle, & N. Schwarz (Eds.), *Subjective well-being: An interdisciplinary perspective* (pp. 119–139). Oxford: Pergamon.

Diener, E., Sandvik, E., Pavot, W., & Gallagher, D. (1991). Response artifacts in the measurement of subjective well-being. *Social Indicators Research, 24,* 35–56.

Fabes, R. A. (1987). Contextual judgments of quality of life and adolescent cognitive development. *Adolescence, 22,* 841–848.

Harter, S. (1985). *Manual for the Self-Perception Profile for Children.* Denver, CO: University of Denver.

Harter, S. (1986). Processes underlying the construction, maintenance, and enhancement of the self-concept in children. In J. Suls & A. G. Greenwald (Eds.), *Psychological perspectives on the self* (Vol. 3, pp. 137–181). Hillsdale, NJ: Erlbaum.

Harter, S. (1987). The determinants and mediational role of global self-worth in children. In N. Eisenberg (Ed.), *Contemporary topics in developmental psychology* (pp. 219–242). New York: Wiley.

Harter, S. (1988). *Manual for the Self-Perception Profile for Adolescents.* Denver, CO: University of Denver.

Harter, S. (1990a). Causes, correlates, and the functional role of global self-worth: A life-span perspective. In J. Kolligan & R. Sternberg (Eds.), *Perceptions of competence and incompetence across the life-span* (pp. 67–98). New Haven, CT: Yale University Press.

Harter, S. (1990b). Issues in the assessment of the self-concept of children and adolescents. In A. H. La Greca (Ed.), *Through the eyes of the child: Obtaining self reports from children and adolescents* (pp. 292–325). Boston: Allyn & Bacon.

Harter, S. (1993). Developmental changes in self-understanding across the 5 to 7 shift. In A. Sameroff & M. Haith (Eds.), *Reason and responsibility: The passage through childhood* (pp. 1–28). Chicago: University of Chicago Press.

Harter, S., & Pike, R. (1984). The Pictorial Perceived Competence Scale for young children. *Child Development, 55,* 1969–1982.

Horley, J., & Lavery, J. J. (1991). The stability and sensitivity of subjective well-being measures. *Social Indicators Research, 24,* 113–122.

Huebner, E. S. (1991a). Correlates of life satisfaction in children. *School Psychology Quarterly, 6,* 103–111.

Huebner, E. S. (1991b). Further validation of the Students' Life Satisfaction Scale: The independence of satisfaction and affect ratings. *Journal of Psychoeducational Assessment, 9,* 363–368.

Huebner, E. S. (1991c). Initial development of the Student's Life Satisfaction Scale. *School Psychology International, 12,* 231–240.

Huebner, E. S. (1994). Preliminary development and validation of a multidimensional life satisfaction scale for children. *Psychological Assessment, 6,* 149–158.

Huebner, E. S., & Alderman, G. L. (1993). Convergent and discriminant validation of a children's life satisfaction scale: Its relationship to self- and teacher-reported psychological problems and school functioning. *Social Indicators Research, 30,* 71–82.

Huebner, E. S., & Dew, T. (1993a). An evaluation of racial bias in a life satisfaction scale. *Psychology in the Schools, 30,* 305–309.

Huebner, E. S., & Dew, T. (1993b). Is life satisfaction multidimensional?: The factor structure of the Perceived Life Satisfaction Scale. *Journal of Psychoeducational Assessment, 11,* 345–350.

Huebner, E. S., & Dew, T. (1993c). Validity of the Perceived Life Satisfaction Scale. *School Psychology International, 14,* 355–360.

Kozma, A., & Stones, M. J. (1988). Social desirability in measures of subjective well-being: Age comparisons. *Social Indicators Research, 20,* 1–14.

Larsen, R. J., & Diener, E. (1987). Affect intensity as an individual difference characteristic: A review. *Journal of Research in Personality, 21,* 1–39.

Lewinsohn, P. M., Redner, J. E., & Seeley, J. R. (1991). The relationship between life satisfaction and psychosocial variables: New perspectives. In F. Strack, M. Argyle, & N. Schwarz (Eds.), *Subjective well-being: An interdisciplinary perspective* (pp. 141–169). Oxford: Pergamon.

Marsh, H. W. (1986). Self-serving effect (bias?) in academic attributions: Its relation to academic achievement and self-concept. *Journal of Educational Psychology, 78,* 190–200.

Marsh, H. W. (1988). *The Self-Description Questionnaire-II*. San Antonio, TX: Psychological Corporation.

Marsh, H. W. (1990). *The Self-Description Questionnaire-I. Manual*. Campbelltown NSW Australia: University of Western Sydney.

Marsh, H. W., Barnes, J., Cairns, L., & Tidman, M. (1984). Self-description questionnaire: Age and sex effects in the structure and level of self-concept for preadolescent children. *Journal of Educational Psychology, 76*, 940–956.

Marsh, H. W., Parker, J., & Barnes, J. (1985). Multidimensional adolescent self-concepts: Their relationship to age, sex, and academic measures. *American Educational Research Journal, 22*, 422–444.

Myers, D. G., & Diener, E. (1995). Who is happy? *Psychological Science, 6*, 10–19.

Okun, M. A., & Stock, W. A. (1987). The construct validity of subjective well-being measures: An assessment via quantitative research syntheses. *Journal of Community Psychology, 15*, 481–492.

Page, R. M., & Page, T. S. (1993). *Fostering emotional well-being in the classroom*. Boston: Jones & Bartlett.

Pavot, W., & Diener, E. (1993). The affective and cognitive context of self-reported measures of subjective well-being. *Social Indicators Research, 28*, 1–20.

Piers, E. V. (1984). *Revised manual for the Piers-Harris Children's Self-Concept Scale*. Los Angeles: Western Psychological Services.

Sandvik, E., Diener, E., & Seidlitz, L. (1993). Subjective well-being: The convergence and stability of self-report and non-self-report measures. *Journal of Personality, 61*, 317–342.

Schwarz, N., & Strack, F. (1991). Evaluating one's life: A judgment model of subjective well-being. In F. Strack, M. Argyle, & N. Schwarz (Eds.), *Subjective well-being: An interdisciplinary perspective* (pp. 27–47). Oxford: Pergamon.

Selman, R. L. (1980). *The growth of interpersonal understanding*. New York: Academic Press.

Smith, D. C., Adelman, H. S., Nelson, P., Taylor, L., & Phares, V. (1987). Students' perception of control at school and problem behavior and attitudes. *Journal of School Psychology, 25*, 167–176.

Strack, F., Argyle, M., & Schwarz, N. (Eds.). (1991). *Subjective well-being: An interdisciplinary perspective*. Oxford: Pergamon.

Veenhoven, R. (1991). Questions on happiness: Classical topics, modern answers, blind spots. In F. Strack, M. Argyle, & N. Schwarz (Eds.), *Subjective well-being: An interdisciplinary perspective* (pp. 7–26). Oxford: Pergamon.

PART II

Standardized Assessment

Assessment during the Preschool Years

CHERYL E. SANDERS

Metropolitan State College of Denver

INTRODUCTION

Early childhood education is a topic that has received considerable attention recently (D. L. Johnson, Howie, Owen, Baldwin, & Luttman, 1993). This focus has led to an increased interest in the psychoeducational assessment of preschool children. According to Miller and Sprong (1986), a vast amount of public and private funding is used for cognitive assessment of young children. In addition, due to the passage of Public Law 99–457, significantly more preschoolers will undergo psychoeducational assessment (Bracken, 1987; Faust & Hollingsworth, 1991). In turn, stronger demands are being made for psychometrically sound and clinically useful methods for testing preschool children (Faust & Hollingsworth, 1991).

The approaches most often utilized for the psychoeducational testing of preschoolers include standardized intelligence tests and screening tests (Flanagan & Alfonso, 1995). A recent survey conducted by the Preschool Special Interest Group of the National Association for School Psychologists revealed that psychologists use traditional intelligence tests 33–64% of the time even though 42% of them indicated that traditional assessments were inadequate for at-risk preschoolers and preschoolers with handicaps [National Association of School Psychologists/American Psychological Association (NASP/APA) Preschool Interest Group, 1987]. Flanagan and Alfonso (1995) have identified two positions regarding the use of intelligence tests.

The first position stresses utilizing intelligence tests for aiding decision making in the diagnosis and classification process as long as the test's limitations are considered carefully (Bracken, 1987; Flanagan & Alfonso, 1995; Flanagan, Sainato, & Genshaft, 1993). The opposing side strongly states that traditional intelligence tests are "inherently flawed" and under no circumstance should be used for the identification process (Neisworth & Bagnato, 1992).

A great deal of literature provides support for the opposing view. Bracken (1987) argued that most preschool instruments are not sufficiently sound by any standard. For instance, some assessments are not accompanied by a manual. Moreover, a number of technical inadequacies have been identified, such as severe limitations in floor gradients, item gradients, and reliability (Barnett & Macmann, 1992; Barnett & Paget, 1988; Bracken, 1981, 1987; Flanagan et al., 1993). According to the National Association for the Education of Young Children (1989), early testing may negatively affect children's self-esteem, with a disproportionate impact on low-income and minority children.

Neisworth and Bagnato (1992) argued that the use of standardized intelligence tests for preschoolers with special needs is extremely unfair and faulty. Standardized procedures seriously penalize young children with developmental delays and disabilities because the tests assess the child's disabilities rather than abilities (Fuchs, Fuchs, Benowitz, & Barringer, 1987). Thus, the use of intelligence tests for this population must be abandoned (Neisworth & Bagnato, 1992). "For whom are intelligence test publishers designing these tests if they cannot be used with nearly ½ the kids who need to be assessed?" (Neisworth & Bagnato, 1992).

Despite the vast criticism, the use of standardized intelligence assessments is widespread. Bagnato and Neisworth (1994) reported that the majority of school psychologists use intelligence tests to determine program eligibility for preschoolers. In addition, Bracken (1987) noted an increasing trend to view the preschool period as the beginning of the time in which valid assessment of cognitive functioning can be made. Moreover, research findings supporting the predictive validity of standardized intelligence instruments [i.e., Rose and Wallace (1985) and Siegel (1979) reported that scores obtained on developmental assessments for children 18–30 months of age are reasonably good predictors of later IQ] fuel the view that standardized intelligence tests should be used to assess young children

Bracken (1987) pointed out that insufficient attention has been focused on the quality of existing instruments used in preschool assessment. Hence, it is vital that information regarding the instruments most commonly used for psychoeducational assessment of preschoolers is readily available. Therefore, the purpose of this chapter involves describing information pertaining to five standardized intelligence tests and three screening instruments that are commonly used with the aforementioned population. The *traditional intelligence tests* to be discussed include the Wechsler Preschool and Primary Scale of Intelligence—Revised (WPPSI-R; Wechsler, 1989), McCarthy Scales of Children's Abilities (MSCA; McCarthy, 1972), Stanford–Binet, fourth edition (S-B IV; Thorndike, Hagen, & Sattler, 1986b), Kaufman Assessment Battery for Children (K-ABC; Kaufman & Kaufman, 1983), and Woodcock–Johnson Psycho-Educational Battery—Revised: Tests of Cognitive Ability (WJ-R COG; Woodcock & Johnson, 1990) as they have been identified as instruments frequently used with preschoolers (Molfese, Helwig, & Holcomb, 1993; Neisworth & Bagnato, 1992). The *screening instruments* to be described include the Miller Assessment for Preschoolers (MAP; Miller, 1982), Denver II Screening Inventory (Denver II; Frankenburg et al., 1990), and Comprehensive Identification Process (CIP; Zehrbach, 1985). The following information will be provided about each instrument: title, author, date of publication, characteristic or variable measured, age of child, examiner qualifications, administration time, number of items or subscales, nature of responding, nature of scoring, interpretation of scores, reliability, validity, critiques or comments. Unless indicated otherwise, the presented information was obtained from the individual assessment's manual, as Miller and Sprong (1986) indicated that the underlying psychometric construction of each test is most accurately represented in the test manual. Some information regarding reliability, validity, and general comments was obtained from posthoc research.

Prior to describing the individual assessments, the following definitions are provided to clarify subsequent discussion.

Item gradient is a reliability index that does not get much attention in the literature but, according to Bracken (1987), is extremely important in preschool assessment. It refers to how rapidly standardized scores increase as a function of a child's success or failure on a single test item. The larger the resulting standardized score difference in relation to changes in a single raw score, the less effective the instrument is in assessing the ability. Therefore, item gradient information allows one to determine the extent that the test effectively differentiates among various ability levels.

A *test floors* index has been identified as the most frequently cited problem with preschool assessment instruments (Bracken, 1987; Bagnato, Neisworth, & Butler, 1991, as cited in Neisworth & Bagnato, 1992; Flanagan & Alfonso, 1995). Test floors are representative of whether there are sufficient numbers of easy items to distinguish between children of average abilities. On many preschool instruments children frequently answer few, if any, questions correctly (Bracken, 1987). Flanagan and Alfonso (1995) argued that test floors of standardized intelligence tests are poor, especially for children at the lower end of the preschool age range.

STANDARDIZED INTELLIGENCE TESTS

Wechsler Preschool and Primary Scale of Intelligence—Revised

The author is David Wechsler (1989).

Characteristic or Variable Measured

Global intelligence and multidimensional intelligence.
Age of child: three years–seven years three months.
Examiner qualifications: A trained person can administer and score the assessment under supervision. Interpretation of the scores should be handled by an individual with graduate school and professional training.
Administration time: 1 hour 15 minutes.

Number of Items or Scales

The instrument contains two groups of subtests denoted as the performance scale and the verbal scale. The subtests included in the performance scale are object assembly, geometric design, block design, mazes, picture completion, and animal pegs. The verbal scale is composed of the following subtests: information, comprehension, arithmetic, vocabulary, similarities, and sentences. The subtests animal pegs and sentences are denoted as optional.

Nature of Responding

Performance Scale.   Object assembly involves fitting together pieces of puzzles to form meaningful wholes. This task is to be completed within a specified time limit. Geometric design is made up of two different tasks. During the first task, the child looks at a simple design and with the stimulus still in view, points to one exactly like it from a variety of four designs. The second task involves having the child draw a geometric figure from a printed model. The block design subtest requires the child to analyze and reproduce patterns made from flat, two-colored blocks. This is a timed test. The maze exercise is also a timed test, where the child is asked to complete pencil–paper mazes of increasing difficulty. Picture completion involves having the child identify what is missing from pictures of common objects or events. Last, animal pegs assesses the speed and accuracy to which the child can place pegs of correct colors in holes below a series of pictured animals.

Verbal Scale. The information subtest requires the child to demonstrate his or her knowledge about events and objects in the environment by having the child either point to a picture or provide a verbal response to various questions. The comprehension subtest involves asking the child to respond verbally to questions pertaining to reasons for actions and consequences of events. Arithmetic tests include picture items (i.e., which rabbit is the biggest?), simple counting tasks, and more difficult word problems. During the vocabulary subtest the child is asked to name pictured objects and provide verbal definitions for orally presented words. The similarities subtest is composed of two types of tasks. The first task requires the child to point to which of several pictured objects is most similar to a group of pictured objects that share a common feature. The second task requires the child to complete a verbally presented sentence that reflects a similarity or analogy between two things. Last, the sentences subtest involves having the examiner read out loud sentences followed by having the child repeat the sentences verbatim.

Nature of Scoring

For most of the subtests, points ranging from zero to two are earned for the responses. Scoring is subjective for the comprehension, vocabulary, similarities, and mazes subtests with a guide provided in the manual. For the animal pegs and sentences subtests scoring is based on completion time and number of errors and omissions. A new feature, bonus points, allows the child to earn extra points for fast and accurate performance on the object assembly and block design subtests. It should be noted that the examiner will discontinue administering a particular subtest after a specified number of incorrect responses are given. A child will earn a performance IQ score, verbal IQ score, and a full scale IQ (sum of performance IQ and verbal IQ scores).

Interpretation of Scores

After obtaining raw scores for each individual subtest, the raw scores are converted to scaled scores. For each subtest, distributions of raw scores at each age level are converted to a scale with a mean of 10 and a standard deviation of 3. (It should be noted that raw scores of zero have been assigned scaled scores of at least one and as high as six. Discussion of this will take place in the general comments section.) Scales are interpreted by IQ equivalents of the scaled scores. These equivalents are provided in the manual. In addition, qualitative interpretation of IQ scores can be found in the test manual. The following interpretations of IQ scores are provided: 130 and above—very superior; 120–129—superior; 110–119—high average; 90–109—average; 80–89—low average; 70–79—borderline; and below 70—deficient.

Reliability

Reliability coefficients for subtests, performance scale, verbal scale, and full scale for all ages are reported in the test manual based on the split-half method with the exception of the animal pegs subtest because it is a speeded test. The average correlation coefficients for the subtests ranged from .63 to .86. The correlation coefficients for the performance IQ, verbal IQ, and full scale IQ were .92, .95, and .96, respectively.

Due to the subjective nature of scoring for some of the subtests, inter-scorer agreement was reported. These correlation coefficients were .96 for comprehension, .94 for vocabulary, .96 for similarities, .94 for mazes, and .88 for geometric designs.

Test–retest stability was reported for the performance IQ, verbal IQ, and full scale IQ. The coefficients were .88, .90, .91, respectively.

Validity

Results from factor analytic studies support a two-factor structure (verbal and performance) of the WPPSI in the normal population (Hollenbeck & Kaufman, 1973; Silverstein, 1986) Thus, there is strong empirical evidence for interpreting the performance IQ and verbal IQ as distinct dimensions. However, slight variations have been found for some socioeconomic groups and low-ability children (Heil, Barclay, & Endres, 1978; Maxwell, 1972). These findings also pertain to the WPPSI-R.

Intercorrelations of the 12 WPPSI-R subtests for nine age groups are reported in the manual as well. There tends to be a high degree of inter-relatedness among the subtests within the performance and verbal scales as well as relative independence among subtests within the performance and verbal scales. In addition, a relative independence of subtests across the two dimensions is apparent. The median intercorrelations within the perform-ance and verbal scales were .40 and .57, respectively. A median correlation of .33 was reported for the subtests across the two scales. The median cor-relation of the performance subtests with the performance scale was .55, while the median correlation of the verbal subtests with the verbal scale was .65.

Concurrent validity was also reported in the test manual. Table 1 provides data reported in the test manual as well as other posthoc research. As indi-cated by the table, adequate evidence supporting the concurrent validity of the WPPSI-R is apparent. For instance, McCrowell (1994) noted that school psychologists can use the WPPSI-R and S-B IV interchangeably among pre-school children. The only caution involved the verbal test differences be-tween the two instruments. These differences may be because the WPPSI-R verbal score includes five subtests while the S-B IV only has three at the preschool level. In addition, the nature of the tests differ, with the WPPSI-R

TABLE I
Concurrent Validity of WPPSI-R

		WPPSI-R		
		PIQ	VIQ	FSIQ
WPPSI	PIQ	.82		
	VIQ		.85	
	FSIQ			.87
WISC-R	PIQ	.75		
	VIQ		.76	
	FSIQ			.85
S-B IV	Comp.	.56	.73	.74
S-B LM	Comp.	.85[a]	.75[a]	.82[a]
MSCA	GCI	(.73)[b]	.77 (.70)[b]	.81 (.81)[b]
	Verbal index		.75	
	Perf. index	.71		
K-ABC	Simult. proc.	.37	.31	.41
	Seq. proc.	.31	.41	.43
	Mental proc.	.41	.42	.49
WJ-R	BCA			.66[c]
PPVT-R[d]		.30[e]	.31[e]	.34[e]

[a]Gerken and Hodapp (1992)
[b]Karr, Carvajal, and Elser (1993)
[c]Flanagan and Alfonso (1995)
[d]Dunn and Dunn (1981)
[e]Faust and Hollingsworth (1991)

being more colorful and entertaining to the children while the S-B is more pictorial. Other possibilities include the scoring and item difficulty of these subtests (McCrowell, 1994).

General Comments and Critiques

The WPPSI-R is a revision of the Wechsler Preschool and Primary Scales of Intelligence. Alterations that were made through the revision process included restandardization to update the WPPSI 20-year old norms, extension of the age range, revision of test items and materials, and an increase in appeal to the test takers (Faust & Hollingsworth, 1991). According to Sattler (1988), the WPPSI-R has been reviewed as a significant improvement over the original WPPSI because of the improved standardization and overall psychometric properties.

Criticism of the instrument, however, still exists. Some of the administration and scoring procedures tend to be complex, particularly with the geometric designs subtest because the examiner must determine whether or not a response meets as many as 12 different criteria on a single design (Slate & Saddler, 1990). Whitten, Slate, Shine, and Raggio (1994) investigated 57 WPPSI-R protocols completed by seven different examiners. Results revealed many errors (i.e., failing to record examinee response, assigning incorrect point values to examinee responses, and determining incorrect basal and/or ceilings). When these errors were corrected, full scale IQs changed on 53% of the protocols including one potential diagnostic error. Reschly and Wilson (1990) argued that these errors, in part, stem from complex administration and scoring procedures. These errors are of great concern, since scores often play an important role in diagnosing and classifying children, especially those involving special education decisions.

Other weaknesses of the WPPSI-R include the amount of time it takes to administer the test. Sattler (1988) pointed out that the 75-minute administration time is too long for children three to four years of age. The abbreviated form, consisting of the block design, vocabulary, arithmetic, and comprehension subtests, can be a helpful substitute but lacks the strong psychometric properties of the long form (Tsushima, 1994).

In terms of the WPPSI-R's predictive validity, Flanagan and Alfonso (1995) argued that little is known. However, Kaplan (1993) reported that WPPSI-R scores were obtained three to eight months prior to enrolling 50 middle and upper-middle class children into kindergarten. These scores were correlated with such abilities as listening, reading, math, and word analysis two years later (as the children were completing first grade). Highly significant correlations were found between achievement and verbal IQ and full scale IQ scores. A nonsignificant correlation was computed between achievement in the aforementioned areas and performance IQ. A simple multiple regression analysis revealed that no additional variance in any of the achievement areas studied was accounted for by performance IQ, once verbal IQ was taken out of the equation. Thus, Kaplan (1993) cautioned examiners not to recommend a preschooler for placement in accelerated curriculum on the basis of nonverbal strengths when verbal scores are weak.

Other psychometric problems were discovered by Flanagan and Alfonso (1995). Their critical review of the technical characteristics of the WPPSI-R revealed that 3 of the 12 subtests have item gradient violations, all the subtests for ages 2 years 6 months and 2 years 11 months have inadequate subtest floors with the exception of the object assembly subtest, and the verbal scale has inadequate floors until age 3 years 3 months. In addition, the test–retest stability was rated "inadequate" because the test–retest studies described in the test manual were conducted on samples that spanned an age range of 3 years 0 months to 7 years 3 months and included persons who were not preschoolers.

On the positive side, the standardization for the WPPSI-R is considered "good," recency of the normative data rated as "adequate," representativeness of the U.S. population was considered "good," and the overall rating was "adequate," according to Flanagan and Alfonso (1995). In addition, there is strong support for the division of subtests into the verbal and performance scales (Gyurke, Stone, & Beyer, 1990; Wechsler, 1989). The WPPSI-R can distinguish borderline and mild mental retardation (IQ range 50–70) at the lowest end of the preschool age range. Hence, Flanagan and Alfonso (1995) claimed that the WPPSI-R can assess functioning across various levels of ability and that the total test score provides a better estimate of ability than most other standardized intelligence tests.

McCarthy Scales of Children's Abilities

The author is Dorothy McCarthy (1972).

Characteristic or Variable Measured

General intelligence level as well as strengths and weaknesses in abilities. Age of child: 2 years 4 months–8 years 7 months.

Examiner qualifications: The test manual indicates that the instrument should be administered by an individual who has received professional training.

Administration time: 45–50 minutes for children under five years of age; 1 hour for children five years and older.

Number of Items or Scales

The MSCA consists of the following subscales: verbal, perceptual–performance, quantitative, memory, and motor. The verbal subscale (composed of five subtests), the perceptual–performance subscale (composed of seven subtests), and the quantitative subscale (involving three subtests) make up a composite of overall cognitive ability. The memory subscale consists of four subtests from the composite cognitive scale, while the motor subscale is made up of five subtests, two of which are subtests from the composite cognitive scale.

Nature of Responding

Verbal Subscale. Pictorial memory involves having the child recall visually and verbally an object previously presented by the examiner. Word knowledge allows the child to identify (by pointing and naming) and define common objects. Verbal memory requires the examinee to repeat word series and sentences as well as retell stories read by the examiner. During verbal fluency, the child is asked to think quickly of words falling into various categories. This is a timed test whereby the examiner records all the words provided by the child in the first 20 seconds. Opposite analogies involves having the child provide opposites of key words in statements spoken by the examiner.

Perceptual–Performance Subscale. Block building requires the examinee to build four structures (copying the examiner) out of one-inch cubes. The child is asked to assemble a series of six puzzles that form pictures of common animals and foods during the puzzle solving subtest. This is a timed test. During the tapping sequence subtest the child is required to imitate eight sequences of notes tapped by the examiner on a four-key xylophone. Right–left orientation involves having the child demonstrate knowledge of right and left by using his or her own body parts to answer questions provided by the examiner. Some of the items refer to a picture of a boy or a girl. Draw a design requires the child to copy geometric shapes drawn by the examiner or provided in a model already drawn. Draw a child involves having the examinee draw a child of the same sex. Finally, the child is asked to classify 12 blocks in various ways during the conceptual grouping subtest.

Quantitative Subscale. Orally presented questions involving numbers or basic arithmetical computation are presented to the child during the number questions subtest. The child is asked to answer verbally. Numerical memory involves having the child repeat a series of digits in the same order and reversed order as presented by the examiner. Counting and sorting involves asking the child to count and sort blocks into equal groups.

Memory Subscale. The memory subscale consists of the pictorial memory, tapping sequence, verbal memory, and numerical memory subtests previously described.

Motor Subscale. Leg coordination involves six items exploring the maturity of motor coordination in the lower extremities. One example activity is asking the child to walk backward. Arm coordination involves the same exploration only examining the upper extremities. Imitative action requires the child to copy the simple motor movements of the examiner. The other two subtests include draw a design and draw a child previously described.

Nature of Scoring

Scale indices for each of the five subscales are derived from the results. These indexes have a mean of 50 and a standard deviation of 10. The general cognitive index (GCI) is a score representing the child's overall cognitive ability. This score is computed by the sum of the verbal, perceptual–performance, and quantitative subscales and has a mean of 100 and a standard deviation of 16.

Interpretation of Scores

The scale indices and the GCI can be transformed into percentile ranks by using the tables provided in the test manual. In addition, these scores can be explained in terms of estimated mental age.

Reliability

Internal consistency correlation coefficients for all the subscales ranged from .79 to .93. In addition, Shellenberger (1977) used a Spanish-speaking sample and reported an average internal consistency correlation coefficient of .93. Split-half correlations were computed for all the subtests except the memory tests, right–left orientation, and draw a child. Test–retest statistics were computed for these subscales. The average standard error of measurement for the general cognitive scale was 4.1 points with a standard deviation of 16, while the standard error of measurement (SEM) for the subscales ranged from 3.4 to 4.7 with a standard deviation of 10. Test–retest stability coefficients for the general cognitive scale was .90 and for the individual subscales ranged from .75 to .89. Consistent with these findings, Bryant and Roffe (1978) and Davis and Slettledahl (1976) reported stability coefficients of .85 and .84, respectively, for the GCI and stability coefficients ranging from .62 to .76 for the individual subscales. Thus, the six subscales appear to be internally consistent and stable. The indexes derived from the test, especially the GCI, are quite accurate indicators of ability on tasks of the MSCA.

Validity

Concurrent validity of the MSCA is illustrated in Table 2. These statistics provide evidence that the MSCA is assessing abilities similar to those being tapped into with other standardized tests.

One study focusing on the predictive validity was included in the manual. Predictive validity with the Metropolitan Achievement Tests (1970) was substantiated with high correlations for the perceptual–performance and quantitative subscales. The correlation was mediocre for the GCI and very poor for the verbal, memory, and motor subscales (Salvia & Ysseldyke, 1985).

General Comments and Critiques

According to Kaufman and Kaufman (1977), the MSCA has many strengths placing it among the best of available instruments used to preschool assessment. The strengths include a detailed technical manual, which provides a clear framework for examiners; a gamelike and nonthreatening nature of materials, making it an attractive activity for young children; and ordering of tests conducive to the examiner establishing a good rapport with the exam-

TABLE 2
Concurrent Validity of MSCA

	MSCA Verbal	P–P	Q	GCI	Memory	Motor
WPPSI-R PIQ	.24[a]	.49[a]	.49[a]	.50[a] (.73)[b]	.32[a]	.24[a]
VIQ	.65[a]	.27[a]	.36[a]	.63[a] (.70)[b]	.52[a]	.16[a]
FSIQ	.52[a]	.45[a]	.50[a]	.67[a] (.81)[b]	.50[a]	.23[a]
S-B IV V	.55[c]			.65		
Abst–vis				.56		
Q				.29		
STM				.66		
Comp				.67		
PPVT[d]	.50[c]					
WJ-R BCA					.62[e]	
Columbia Mental Maturity Scale[f]	.15[g]	.74[g]	.53[g]	.54[g]	.14[g]	.51[g]

[a]Faust and Hollingsworth (1991)
[b]Karr, Carvajal, and Elser (1993)
[c]Molfese, Helwig, and Holcomb (1993)
[d]Dunn (1965)
[e]Woodcock and Johnson (1990)
[f]Burgemeister, Blum, and Lorge (1972)
[g]Gomez-Benito and Forns-Santacana (1993)

inee. The technical limitations of the MSCA involve a lack of social intelligence items, problems with testing older children, difficulty pertaining to the scale interpretation, and lack of verbal reasoning and puzzle solving for older children. These limitations apply mainly to very young and older children. Therefore, Kaufman and Kaufman (1977) suggested that the MSCA should not be used as a primary assessment tool for older gifted children and younger retarded children. For three- to six-year-olds, the technical contributions far outweigh the limitations.

In terms of psychometric properties, most of the critiques are negative. Bracken (1987) noted that the test manual presents "meager evidence of validity." Most of the studies that are presented in the manual were conducted on a small sample size and conclusions need to be made with "caution." Evidence of inadequate test floors is apparent. Bracken (1987) pointed out that the typical 2½-year-old fails to answer a single item correctly on 11 of the 18 subtests. Kaufman (1982) found that some learning disabled children earned GCI scores in the mental retardation range. The MSCA may overidentify low abilities and specifically mental retardation. In addition, Salvia and Ysseldyke (1985) pointed out that the MSCA's usefulness with

exceptional children is unsubstantiated since this population was not included in the standardization process, and no evidence for validity of the
scales with this specific group are mentioned. As Bracken (1981) indicated,
the MSCA should not be used for classification purposes, but it is a useful
diagnostic tool.

On the other hand, some critics argue that the MSCA is an accurate estimation of general school functioning (Kaufman & Kaufman, 1977). In addition, Kaufman (1982) found a higher correlation between the GCI and IQ;
thus, it is acceptable to use the GCI as an index of mental functioning.
Moreover, Kaufman (1982) reported that research with black children en-
dorses the validity of the MSCA with this population. He contended that the
MSCA is nondiscriminatory in regards to race.

Stanford–Binet Intelligence Scale, Fourth Edition

The authors are R. L. Thorndike, E. P. Hagen, and J. M. Sattler (1986a).

Characteristic or Variable Measured

Cognitive abilities that provide an analysis of pattern as well as the overall
level of an individual's cognitive development.

Age of child: two years–adult.

Examiner qualifications: No specific guidelines are provided in the test
manual. It is stated that the examiner needs to be familiar with the
standard procedures and sensitive to the needs of the examinee.

Administration time: 1 hour to 1 hour 30 minutes.

Number of Items or Scales

The S-B IV consists of four separate scales: verbal reasoning, abstract–visual
reasoning, quantitative reasoning, and short-term memory. The verbal reasoning, abstract–visual reasoning, and short-term memory scales are made
up of four subtests each. The quantitative reasoning scale consists of three
individual subtests. Therefore, the entire assessment includes 15 different
tests; however, no one examinee will ever be administered all of these tests.

Nature of Responding

Verbal Reasoning. The vocabulary subtest involves having the child provide a definition for common words or objects presented pictorially as well
as orally. The comprehension subtest requires the examinee to identify various objects or body parts by pointing to a provided picture of a child and
providing a verbal response. During the absurdities subtests, the child is
presented with an extraordinary situation and asked to provide an explana-

tion from multiple choice answers or from his or her own verbal response. Verbal relations involves having the examiner present four objects verbally to the child. The child is asked to describe a similarity among the first three things that is not true for the fourth item.

Abstract–Visual Reasoning.   The pattern analysis subtest requires the examinee to construct models made out of blocks. The child is asked to duplicate a model constructed by the examiner and use cubes to copy a picture of a cube pattern within a specified amount of time. The copying subtest involves having the child duplicate in a paper and pencil drawing the examiner's design (written or made with blocks). During the matrices subtests, the examinee is asked to fill in the matrices provided in the record booklet. The paper folding and cutting subtest involves having the child fold and cut papers similar to how the examiner folded and cut.

Quantitative Reasoning.   The quantitative subtest requires the child to provide an answer or choose from multiple choice answers to questions involving numbers. The number series subtest requires the examinee to fill in the missing components of a series. Equation building involves having the child solve problems presented in a numerical equation.

Short-Term Memory.   Bead memory involves asking the examinee to reproduce a bead layout presented in either a pictorial form or with actual beads on a bead stick. Memory for sentences requires the child to reproduce the sentences first presented by the examiner. Similarly, memory for digits requires the same response except that the stimuli are digits and reversal is also a component. Memory for objects involving showing a number of stimulus cards to the child at the rate of one card per second. The child is then asked to identify the pictures in the same order.

Note that the S-B IV is based on an adaptive-testing format to alleviate administration time wasted on tests items that are too easy or too difficult for the examinee. The pattern of adaptive testing is called *multistage testing*. In the first stage, the child is given the vocabulary test. The outcome of this test serves as an indicator of the entry level at which testing should begin on the remaining 14 tests. In the second stage, the examiner determines basal and ceiling levels of each test for each individual examinee. Individual test items are arranged in levels of incremental difficulty; thus, facilitating the adaptive testing format.

Nature of Scoring

A total raw score for each subtest and subscale can be calculated. In addition, an overall composite score is obtained. The subtest raw scores can be converted into normalized standard scores with a mean of 50 and a standard deviation of 8 using conversion tables provided in the test manual, while the subscale and composite raw scores can be converted into normalized standard scores with a mean of 100 and standard deviation of 6.

Interpretation of Scores

The standard scores for individual subtests, scales, and the composite can be interpreted in terms of percentile rank.

Reliability

Internal consistency coefficients for each scale ranged from .95 to .97 for all age levels (Bracken, 1987; Flanagan & Alfonso, 1995). In addition, the total test reliability coefficient was .90 (Bracken, 1987). In terms of test–retest stability, Bracken (1987) reported that this reliability coefficient was at or above .90. Flanagan and Alfonso (1995), however, argued that this statistic is "inadequate," because the sample size was too small and the representativeness of the sample was not acceptable. Moreover, all subtests on the S-B IV recommended for children two to three years of age have inadequate floors. It is not until age 5 that all recommended preschool subtests have adequate floors (Flanagan & Alfonso, 1995). In terms of total test floors, most of the preschool tests are unacceptable. For example, Flanagan and Alfonso (1995) pointed out that a child two years six months old who earns a raw score of 1 on all of the recommended subtests for this age level will earn a total test score of 88, placing him or her at the upper end of the low-average range of ability. Thus, the S-B IV does not distinguish very effectively between children who possess average and low-average abilities at the lower end of the preschool age range (Bracken, 1987). Item gradients also appear to be a problem. Six of the eight subtests recommended for preschoolers have "inadequate" item gradients throughout most of the preschool range, making the S-B IV largely insensitive to small variations in ability (Bracken, 1987; Flanagan & Alfonso, 1995).

Validity

Evidence of concurrent validity is provided in Table 3. According to Laurent, Swerdlik, and Ryburn (1992) and Flanagan and Alfonso (1995), results from a number of validity studies suggest that the S-B IV is as valid of a measure of general mental ability as other tests.

Questions pertaining to construct validity are apparent. There is virtually no support for the division of subscales into verbal reasoning, abstract–visual reasoning, quantitative reasoning, and short-term memory for preschoolers (Kline, 1989; Molfese, Yaple, Helwig, Harris, & Connell, 1992;

TABLE 3
Concurrent Validity of S-B IV

		S-B IV V	Abst–ivs	Q	STM	Comp
WPPSI-R	PIQ					.56[a]
	VIQ					.73[a]
	FSIQ					.74[a]
MSCA	GCI	.65[b]	.56[b]	.29[b]	.66[b]	.67[b]
WJ-R	BCA					.69[c] (.77)[d]
K-ABC	Simult proc.					.58[e]
	Seq. proc.					.58[e]
	Mental proc.					.65[e]
	Achiev.					.74[e]
	Nonverbal					.31[e]
S-B LM	Comp					.78[f]
PPVT-R		.71[g]				.54[h]
DAS[i] GCA						.77[d]

[a]Wechsler (1989)
[b]McCarthy (1972)
[c]Woodcock and Johnson (1990)
[d]Flanagan and Alfonso (1995)
[e]Kaufman and Kaufman (1983)
[f]Bower and Hayes (1995)
[g]Johnson, Howie, Owen, Baldwin and Luttman (1993)
[h]Hodapp (1993)
[i]Differential Abilities Scale (GCA, General Conceptual Ability) (Elliot, 1990)

Sattler, 1992). Moreover, Flanagan and Alfonso (1995) argued that this instrument should be used as a measure of global functioning at the preschool age range as opposed to focusing on specific aspects of abilities.

In terms of predictive validity, evidence appears strong. Laurent *et al.* (1992) revealed that scores earned on the S-B IV correlated highly with scores earned on achievement tests. Flanagan and Alfonso (1995) also agreed that the predictive validity of the composite score is strong.

General Comments and Critiques

The S-B intelligence test in its various revisions has been very popular since 1916. As time has passed other assessments such as the Wechsler tests and the K-ABC (Aiken, 1987; Lubin, Larsen, & Matarazzo, 1984) became more popular and replaced the S-B.

The S-B IV was based on a variant of the Cattell–Horn model of fluid and crystallized intelligence (McCallum, 1990). The instrument under discussion, the S-B IV, is a revision of the S-B LM, although Keith, Cool, Novak, White, and Pottebaum (1988) and Thorndike (1990) argued that the S-B IV is not a revision but a new test. Changes occurring from the S-B LM to the S-B IV included an increase in the number of items per task, six new types of items, items grouped in 15 tests, administration and scoring changes, a well-defined theoretical orientation, a change from age to point scale, updated norms, and suggestions for abbreviated batteries. Silverman and Kearney (1992) argued that each instrument, S-B LM and S-B IV, is useful for different populations. The S-B LM should be used as a supplemental test to obtain further information about the highly gifted population while the S-B IV should be utilized with other populations.

In addition to questioning the population to be assessed with the S-B IV, other concerns have been expressed. D. L. Johnson et al. (1993) conducted a study involving a group of three-year-olds being assessed via the S-B IV. Results revealed that several of the subtests were not comprehensible to three-year-olds. In addition, they pointed out a problem with scoring. For instance, when a child fails on any item of a subtest, that particular subtest is not included in the scoring. However, if a child provides one correct answer during the subtest, the subtest score is included; thus, the child who gets one item correct receives a low score.

On the other hand, D. L. Johnson et al. (1993) reported that the three-years-olds did find the S-B IV to be interesting and testing materials to be attractive. Other strengths include "good" standardization, "good" representativeness of the U.S. population in the norms, and "adequate" updating of the norms (Flanagan & Alfonso, 1995). In comparison with the PPVT-R (Dunn & Dunn, 1981), Sattler (1988) pointed out that the S-B IV offers different types of problems while the PPVT-R deals with one type of response set. Moreover, the S-B IV is preferable over the PPVT-R if a wide range of intellectual abilities are to be assessed (D. L. Johnson et al., 1993).

Kaufman Assessment Battery for Children

The authors are Alan S. Kaufman and Nadeen L. Kaufman (1983).

Characteristic or Variable Measured

Intelligence in terms of an individual's style of solving problems and processing information; there is an emphasis on individual level of skill.

Age of child: 2½–12½ years.

Examiner qualifications: Psychologists and professionals with other titles who have considerable training and experience in individual psychological or psychoeducational assessment.

Administration time: 45 minutes for preschoolers; 1 hour 15 minutes for elementary aged children.

Number of Items or Scales

The K-ABC consists of three separate scales: the sequential scale, the simultaneous processing scale, and the achievement scale. The sequential scale is made up of three subtests. The simultaneous processing scale consists of seven subtests, while the achievement scale involves six subtests.

Nature of Responding

Sequential Scale. Hand movements involves having the child repeat hand motions previously modeled by the examiner. Number recall requires the examinee to repeat a series of digits in the same order as the examiner. Word order is a subtest administered to 4–12-year-olds. This subtest involves having the child touch a series of silhouettes of common objects in the same sequence as the examiner orally presented them.

Simultaneous Processing Scale. The magic window subtest requires the child to identify objects through a partially closed window. Face recognition involves having the examinee select from photographs one or two faces that he or she was exposed to previously. Gestalt closures requires the child to name objects or scenes in a partial or complete "inkblot" drawing. During the triangles subtest, the examinee is asked to assemble triangles to match a presented model. Matrix analogies requires the child to select pictures or designs that accurately complete a visual analogy. Spatial memory involves recollection of picture placement on a page to which the child was previously exposed. During the photo series subtest, the child is asked to place photographs of events in chronological order.

Achievement Scale. Expressive vocabulary requires the examinee to identify objects presented in photographs. During faces and places, the child is asked to name well-known people, fictitious characters, or places presented in photographs or drawings. The arithmetic subtest involves having the child demonstrate knowledge of numbers, counting, and computational skills. The riddles require the examinee to infer names of concrete or abstract concepts when given a list of characteristics. Reading–decoding involves having the child identify letters and read words. During the reading–understanding subtest, the child is asked to demonstrate reading comprehension by following commands presented in sentences.

Nonverbal Scale. This scale is composed of selected subtests previously described that can be used for hearing-impaired, speech and language disordered, and non-English speaking children.

Nature of Scoring

Raw scores for the sequential processing, simultaneous processing, and achievement processing scales are obtained from the K-ABC. In addition, a mental processing composite score can be obtained from the sum of the sequential and simultaneous processing scales. These four scores can be converted into standard scores with a mean of 100 and a standard deviation of 15. The mental processing composite score for the nonverbal scale can be converted into a standard score with a mean of 10 and a standard deviation of 3.

Interpretation of Scores

Tables provided in the manual can be used to convert the standard scores into age equivalents, grade equivalents, national percentile ranks, and sociocultural percentile ranks. Verbal descriptors for these conversions are also provided in the test manual.

Reliability

Internal consistency coefficients for the subtests ranged from .70 to .93. Therefore, the test manual provides strong evidence of internal consistency with no coefficients below .70 and very few below .75. The global scales ranged from .86 to .93.

Evidence for test–retest reliability was also adequate. Test–retest reliability coefficients ranged from .77 to .95. The practice effect was most pronounced for the simultaneous processing scale. Stability coefficients for the individual subtests were shown to be adequate for nearly all of the subtests. Achievement subtests were considered "excellent," while the face recognition subtest at the preschool level reported a coefficient of .62, revealing that this subtest may not yield consistent results over time. The mean SEM for the global scales in the preschool ages ranged from 3.9 to 5.7. Mean SEMs for the subtests in the preschool ages ranged from 1.0 to 7.2.

Intercorrelations between the global scales ranged from .41 to .66. These correlations were high enough to justify the combination of the scales into a global measure of intelligence. In addition, the correlations were moderate enough to confirm the separate existence of each scale. The average intercorrelations among subtests with the mental processing composite ranged from .21 to .50 with a median of .33. The achievement scale ranged from .55 to .69 with a median of .60.

Validity

Construct validity is discussed in the test manual in terms of five different areas. First of all, the manual points out that the instrument taps into developmental change. That is, there is a significant differentiation between ages of examinees. The means show steady increases across age ranges. Second, evidence of internal consistency is strong (see the discussion in the Reliability section). Third, results from factor analyses provide evidence of construct validity. A principal components analysis of all 11 subtests identified two clearcut factors (sequential and simultaneous–achievement) for 2½- to 3-year olds and three clearcut factors for ages 4–12. A confirmatory analysis (used to confirm the already identified factors) was successful at confirming three factors at all age levels (Willson, Reynolds, Chatman, & Kaufman, 1983, as cited in Kaufman & Kaufman, 1983). A fourth area discussed in terms of construct validity involved strong evidence of convergent and discriminant validation. Evidence is provided, showing that the K-ABC correlates with relevant variables and does not correlate with irrelevant variables. Last, evidence of construct validity is provided by showing strong correlations between the K-ABC and other tests purporting to measure the same concept. Table 4 illustrates the concurrent validity of the K-ABC. According to Anastasi (1982), construct validity should be "moderately high but not too high to an already available test" because a new test assessing the same exact concept would be needless replication.

Evidence of predictive validity was shown when correlating K-ABC standard scores with scores on the PPVT-R (Dunn & Dunn, 1981). Correlations between the two instruments ranged from .67 to .82 for normal school-aged, culturally different, and educably mentally retarded.

General Comments and Critiques

According to Moran (1989), standardized tests should be modified to better reflect language abilities of severely handicapped children. Children may be intelligent enough to comprehend the test items but cannot respond. The K-ABC is the answer to this request. This instrument is also valuable as a second measure of cognitive ability for children where English is a second language. Since standardized assessments like the Wechsler scales understand cognitive abilities yet penalize the child because of difficulty processing English, the K-ABC can be a useful tool (Teale, 1988).

In terms of psychometric properties, there appear to be some "unacceptable" areas. Bracken (1987) pointed out that the subtest internal consistency coefficients fail to achieve "acceptable" levels of .80. In addition, he argued that the instrument contains weak subtest floors at age 4 years 6 months and up and total test floors at ages 2 years 6 months and 3 years. Item gradients are not adequate, failing to meeting his criterion through age 4 and barely meeting the criterion after age 4 years.

On the other hand, Bracken (1987) argued that the K-ABC is the one instrument with the most documentation of validity. The test manual presents more than 40 studies validating it's validity. "The large number of K-

TABLE 4
Concurrent Validity of K-ABC

		K-ABC Simult. proc.	Seq. proc.	Mental proc.	Achiev.	Nonverbal
WPPSI	PIQ	.50	.41	.55	.47	.44[a]
	VIQ	.28	.37	.37	.64	.17[a]
	FSIQ	.47	.46	.55	.66	.36[a]
WPPSI-R	PIQ	.31	.41	.42		
	VIQ	.37	.31	.41		
	FSIQ	.41	.43	.49		
S-B: IV	Comp. (normal pop.)	.58	.58	.65	.74	.31
	Normal preschl. pop.	.15	.39	.36	.57	.44
	High-risk preschl. pop.	.54	.56	.66	.52	.62
PPVT-R				.58–.75		

[a]Wechsler (1989)

ABC validity studies . . . is truly remarkable" (Bracken, 1987, p. 324).
Moreover, the test–retest reliability is strong.

Woodcock–Johnson Psycho-educational Battery—Revised

The authors are Richard W. Woodcock and M. Bonner Johnson (1990).

Characteristic or Variable Measured

Cognitive abilities, scholastic aptitudes, and achievement.
Age of child: 2–90 years.
Examiner qualifications: Background and training in test administration.
Administration time: 30–40 minutes for the seven tests in the WJ-R cognitive standard battery; 20–30 minutes for the early development scale.

Number of Items or Scales

The K-ABC consists of 21 separate tests. The early development scale (an early development measure) is composed of seven of these tests.

Nature of Responding

Memory for names (creatures) and memory for sentences involve having the child identify or repeat the object or words presented previously. Visual matching requires the examinee to locate and circle two identical numbers

TABLE 5
Concurrent Validity of WJ-R COG

		WJR BCA
WPPSI-R	FSIQ	.66[a]
S-B IV	Comp.	.69 (.77)[a]
K-ABC	Mental proc.	.69 (.74)[a]
	Achiev.	.53
MSCA	GCI	.62 (.71)[a]

[a]Flanagan and Alfonso (1995)

in a row of six numbers during a specified amount of time. Incomplete words is a tape recorded test where the child listens to a recorded word that is missing one or more phonemes. The child is required to identify the complete word. Visual closure involves having the child identify drawings that are altered in some way. Picture vocabulary requires the examinee to recognize or name unfamiliar pictured objects. During analysis synthesis, the examinee is asked to determine the missing component of an incomplete logic puzzle. Feedback is provided by the examiner. Visual–auditory learning involves having the child associate new visual symbols with familiar words orally and translate a series of symbols into verbal sentences. During memory for words, the child is asked to repeat a list of unrelated words in the correct sequence as the examiner presented them. Cross-out requires the examinee to identify 5 drawings in a row of 20 that are identical to the first drawing in the row. An audiotape presents word parts in proper order during the sound blending test. The child is asked to say the whole word after hearing the parts. Picture recognition involves having the examinee recognize a subset of previously presented pictures within a field of distracting pictures. During oral vocabulary, the child is asked to state a synonym and an antonym of a word presented orally by the examiner. Concept formation requires the child to derive a rule from a complete stimulus set. Feedback is provided by the examiner. Delayed recall memory for names and Delayed recall visual–auditory learning involve having the child recall names of creatures and symbols presented in the previous tests, memory for names, and memory for sentences. Numbers reversed requires the examinee to orally present (in reverse order) items previously presented from an audio tape. Sound patterns involves having the child determine if complex sound patterns presented from an audiotape are same or different. Spatial relations requires the examinee to select, from a series of shapes component parts needed to make a given whole shape. During listening comprehension the child is asked to listen to a short tape-recorded passage and then supply single words that are missing at the end of the passage. Last, verbal analogies involves having the examinee complete phrases with words that indicate appropriate analogies.

Nature of Scoring

All items on the WJ-R are scored 1 or 0, with the exception of memory for sentences (this tests uses 2, 1, or 0 points). The broad cognitive ability (BCA) index is a composite score. Raw test and composite scores can be converted to standard scores by utilizing the tables provided in the test manual. The standard scores have a mean of 100 and a standard deviation of 15.

Interpretation of Scores

Scoring on the WJ-R is interpreted on the following four levels: (1) qualitative, the child is observed during the test, analysis of the child's errors; (2) level of development, the sum of the item scores; (3) degree of mastery, the quality of performance on tasks; (4) comparison with peers, the deviation from a reference point in a group. The standard scores resulting from the WJ-R can be interpreted in terms of age equivalents, grade equivalents, extended age scores, extended grade scores, relative mastery index (RMI), and percentile ranks. Extended age and grade scores use superscript numbers to delineate percentile ranks falling above and below the average median for age and grade. RMIs allow statements to be generated about the child's predicted (expected) level of mastery on tasks similar to ones included in the WJ-R.

Reliability

Internal consistency coefficients and SEMs for all the tests are in the high .80s and low .90s.

Validity

The test manual indicates that evidence for content validity can be obtained by examining the types of items and nature of tasks in each test. No quantitative evidence was presented. Evidence of concurrent validity is presented in Table 5. In terms of construct validity, a pattern of relatively low intercorrelations among factors indicates that these factors are measuring different aspects of cognitive ability.

General Comments and Critiques

According to the critical review conducted by Flanagan and Alfonso (1995), the WJ-R is among the better instruments to be used with very young children because it was rated technically adequate across most of the criteria. This review compared the WJ-R with other standardized instruments, including the S-B IV, WPPSI-R, DAS, and BSID II (Bayley Scales of Infant Development Bayley, 1993). The WJ-R and BSID II were considered the most adequate.

The characteristics receiving "good" ratings by Flanagan and Alfonso (1995) included standardization sample size, recency of normative data, representation of the U.S. population in the sample, item gradients, and internal consistency. In fact, the WJ-R was found to have the better item gradients across the preschool age range than any other instrument included in the review. In addition, test floors received an "adequate" rating with the exception of the incomplete words subtest, which did not appear adequate until age 4 years 4 months. The overall rating for evidence of validity was "adequate" as well.

It appears that the WJ-R is a technically sound instrument with the capability of detecting small differences in ability for 48–50% of the individuals in the normal population who earn standard scores at or below the mean. This instrument can also make distinctions within borderline and mild mental retardation in the middle and upper preschool age ranges. Overall, Flanagan and Alfonso (1995) argued that the WJ-R is best conceived as a general ability measure for individuals in the preschool range.

In terms of weaknesses of the instrument, test–retest stability was one area of concern because the test–retest studies cited in the test manual were conducted on samples ranging in age from 5 years to 80 years. Hence, these samples included nonpreschoolers. In addition, this instrument has a limited use for intervention or remedial programs since the overall information obtained from the assessment cannot tell the practitioner what the child can do but what he or she cannot do (Flanagan & Alfonso, 1995).

SCREENING INSTRUMENTS

Miller Assessment for Preschoolers

The author is Lucy Jane Miller (1982).

Characteristic or Variable Measured

The purpose is to identify children in need of further evaluation; it helps define children's strengths, weaknesses, and possible avenues of remediation; the test score indicates how a child's performance compares to other children of his or her age.

Age of child: 2 years 9 months–5 years 8 months.

Examiner qualifications: No specialized training is necessary; educational or clinical personnel should administer and score the instrument.

Administration time: 20–30 minutes.

Number of Items or Scales

The instrument consists of 27 individual items. These items are grouped into the following three scales: sensory and motor abilities, cognitive abilities, and combined abilities. The foundation and coordination indexes are derived from the sensory and motor abilities scale. The verbal and nonverbal indexes are derived from the cognitive abilities scale. The complex task index is computed from the combined abilities scale.

Nature of Responding

Sensory and Motor Abilities. The foundations index involves assessment of basic motor tasks and awareness of sensations. Many of these items are items found in standard neurological examinations. Examples include awareness of body parts in relation to others, movement patterns, and finger location. The coordination index consists of items testing complex gross, fine, and oral motor tasks. For instance, the examinee is asked to build a tower from blocks and copy the walking behavior of the examiner.

Cognitive Abilities Scale. The verbal index includes language items assessing memory, sequencing, and comprehension. Example items include word and digit repetition and answering questions such as "What do you do with your ears?" The nonverbal index consists of memory, sequencing, visualization, and performance of mental manipulations not requiring spoken language. Tasks include such things as putting blocks away in a container in a sequence started by the examiner.

Combined Abilities Scale. The complex tasks index involves items that tap into a combination of abilities. Example items include having the child draw a person and asking the child to imitate the posture of the examiner.

Nature of Scoring

Each item earns a green, yellow, or red score. The green score indicates that the item was performed within normal limits. The yellow or caution zone delineates that the examinee is scoring within the 6–25 percentile range among children of that particular age range. The red or stop zone indicates that the examinee is score within the 0–5 percentile range among children of that particular age group. The scorer then tallies the total number of greens, yellows, and reds.

Interpretation of Scores

Using a table provided in the test manual, final percentile ranks can be determined based on the number of red and yellow scores the child earned.

The final performance of the child is classified as the follows: red indicates that the child's overall functioning falls within the 0–5 percentile range; yellow indicates the child's overall functioning falls within the 6–25 percentile range; and green denotes that the child's overall functioning is at the 25 percentile or better indicating function within the normal limits. Other optional supplemental scores can be obtained for use to those who want only to screen. These scores include percentile score by performance index, percentile score by item, and change over time.

Reliability

An internal reliability coefficient for all items on the instrument of .79 was reported. The amount of variation between observed and true scores (SEM) was reported as 0.5%. Therefore, examiners can feel confident that the obtained scores from the MAP are fairly accurate indicators of a child's abilities.

Test–retest reliability was reported as relatively stable based on a study where subjects were administered the MAP two times within a four week time period. In addition, interrate reliability coefficients were .98 for the total MAP and .84–.99 for individual subtests.

Validity

Evidence of concurrent validity of the MAP includes a significant positive relationship between the MAP total score and the Illinois Test of Psycholinguistic Ability (ITPA). Approaching significance were correlations between the MAP complex and verbal scores with the WPPSI verbal and performance scales. No significant correlations were obtained when comparing the MAP total score with the WPPSI-Full Scale IQ Score (FSIQ) ($r = .27$) or MAP total score with the Southern California Sensory Integration Test (SCSIT).

According to the test manual, the MAP is difficult to compare with other screening instruments such as the Denver Developmental Screening Test (DDST) because of the various scoring techniques. However, the MAP accurately detected 24% more children as needing further evaluation than the DDST. In addition, the MAP placed 75% of all preacademic problem children in red or yellow scoring zones. Of these individuals 50% fell into the red zone.

In terms of content validity, the manual addresses this issue in four areas. First, a test specification table provided in the manual provides a systematic examination of the content of the MAP with respect to representativeness of the behavior assessed. A second table identifies items that clearly differentiate performance of the basis of age. A varimax rotated factor matrix was computed, and six primary factors emerged. Items from the foundation index did not cluster. Last, a correlation analysis of each item and each index with the examinee's total score revealed that all items were found to be contributing significantly to the total MAP score. Five indexes correlated at high levels with the total MAP score, ranging from .65 to .78.

General Comments and Critiques

A critical review of preschool screening instruments revealed that the MAP is one of the most technically sound ones available (Miller & Sprong, 1986). Miller and Sprong (1986) revealed that the MAP met the following criteria: significant interexaminer reliability, clear description of the administration procedures, description of the special qualifications necessary to administer and score the instrument, clear description of the normative sample, adequate normative sample size, promotion of test reliability and validity through the use of systematic item analysis during item construction and selection, and evidence of concurrent validity. On the other hand, Miller and Sprong (1986) found a few areas of concern, including no information in the test manual regarding measures of central tendency and variability of test scores reported, unacceptable evidence of concurrent validity, and unacceptable estimates of test–retest reliability. In addition, the divisions of red, yellow, and green scoring zones appear to be arbitrary.

Comprehensive Identification Process

The author is R. Reid Zehrbach (1985).

Characteristic or Variable Measured

Identify handicapped children who are not yet participating in an organized school or preschool program who are eligible for specialized programming.

Age of child: 2½–5½ years.

Examiner qualifications: The administration involves a station approach with a screening team typically composed to a team leader, three to five child interviewers, one parent interviewer, two hearing and vision screeners. The parent and child interviewers may be paraprofessionals. It is recommended that the other team members be professionals.

Administration time: 25–35 minutes.

Number of Items or Scales

The CIP consists of the following seven screening areas: fine motor, cognitive–verbal, gross motor, speech and expressive language, social–affective, hearing and vision, and medical history. The subtests are organized in six-month age intervals. For each age interval, five tasks are included under each scale. The test items are adapted from other assessments, particularly the Stanford–Binet intelligence tests.

Nature of Responding

Fine motor subtests tap into fine motor skills. Example items include having the child turn a doorknob or remove a jar lid. Older examinees may be asked to cut paper with scissors and copy symbols from a provided symbol booklet.

Cognitive–verbal subtests focus on the child exhibiting an understanding of verbal commands. For instance, the examinee is required to repeat single words such as *ball* or *kite*. An older child is asked to responds to requests such as "Give me the longer stick."

Gross motor subtests tap into gross motor abilities. Example items include having the child balance on one foot or stand on tiptoe. Older children are asked to hop forward on one foot for two hops or walk forward heel-to-toe for five steps.

Speech and expressive language subtests consist of an articulation screening and an assessment of expressive language. The articulation screening involves asking the child to repeat words initially verbalized by the examiner. The expressive language assessment requires the child to respond to statements such as "Tell me about this toy" or "I wonder what's happening in this picture."

Hearing and vision screening is an assessment of basic auditory and visual abilities. The test manual recommends that this portion of the assessment be conducted by professionals in the field.

Medical history information is obtained via the parent interview.

Nature of Scoring

The CIP is not designed to yield a numerical score. A classification of P (pass), R (refer to rescreen), or E (evaluate) is assigned to a child's behavior in each of the developmental areas assessed. This assessment is based on the "minimal-acceptable" behavior (MAB) philosophy. This means that if the child fails one to three of the five tasks in each area, tasks at the next lower level will be administered. If the child passes items at a higher level, the passes are credited against failures at a lower level.

Interpretation of Scores

The pattern of the ratings (P, R, and E) is reviewed and a decision to pass, refer child to an agency to gather additional data through screening, or refer child to an agency for a complete evaluation is made. A child passes the assessment if the number of failures earned is zero or one. An R is earned if the examinee fails two or three times; and an E is earned if the child exhibits failure more than three times.

Reliability

No data regarding the reliability of the instrument were provided in the manual.

Validity

The only validity information provided in the test manual referred to two-year follow-up studies conducted in Iowa, Rhode Island, Minnesota, Kentucky, Illinois, and Georgia. The number of children from these areas who passed the CIP and later were eligible for a special service is very low. In addition, a significant number of these children who were identified by the CIP as needing further evaluation were provided with special attention before kindergarten and required no special services while in kindergarten. Therefore, the number of false positives and false negatives diagnosed from the CIP is small.

General Comments and Critiques

A critical review of preschool screening instruments by Miller and Sprong (1986) identified a handful of strengths of the CIP. These strengths included clear definition of the normative sample, description of special qualities of the examiner and scorer, and clear description of the administration procedures. Moreover, Lichtenstein and Ireton (1984) indicated that the CIP manual provides a clear framework for the process of screening. In addition, they applauded the inclusion of parent involvement in the screening process.

On the other hand, many weaknesses have been identified. According to Lichtenstein and Ireton (1984), the major weaknesses of the CIP are the psychometric qualities. For instance, Miller and Sprong (1986) pointed out the following problems: inadequate normative sample size, inadequate promotion of reliability and validity through the use of systematic item analysis during item construction and selection, no mention of the measures of central tendency and variability of test scores reported, inadequate evidence of concurrent and predictive validity, failure to provide a significant test–retest reliability coefficient, and inadequate interexaminer reliability coefficient. In addition, the logic of the MAB for each age level appears sound but no specific rationale is provided regarding the assignment of items to age levels and no data regarding how this approach words in practice are provided (Lichtenstein & Ireton, 1984). Moreover, the method used to establish cutoff points for categories P, R, and E are not clarified (Miller & Sprong, 1986).

Denver II

The authors are W. K. Frankenburg, J. Dodds, P. Archer, B. Bresnick, P. Maschka, N. Edelman, H. Shapiro (1990).

Characteristic or Variable Measured

Screen for developmental delays; compare a child's performance on a variety of tasks to the performance of other children of the same age.
Age of child: Birth to six years.
Examiner qualifications: Professional, paraprofessional, or someone highly trained in psychoeducational assessment.
Administration time: 20–25 minutes.

Number of Items or Scales

The Denver II is composed of 125 tasks or items. These items are arranged into the following four sectors: personal–social, fine motor–adaptive, language, and gross motor. In addition, the examiner completes five "test behavior" items.

Nature of Responding

The personal–social sector focuses on the child's ability to take care of himself or herself as well as social intelligence. Example items for very young children include placing a toy that the child seems to enjoy on a table slightly out of the child's reach. The child passes this item if he or she tries to get the toy. Items for older children include asking parents if the child can put on a T-shirt without assistance or prepare a bowl of cereal without assistance.

The fine motor–adaptive sector involves tasks related to fine motor abilities. For instance, a very young examinee may prompted to grasp a rattle. An older examinee is required to draw a person or copy symbols provided by the examiner.

The language sector focuses on communicative abilities. Example items for young children include seeing if the child responds to a bell that he or she cannot see or if the child laughs out loud. Example items for older children involve having the child define words like *banana* or *lake* or asking the child to put five of eight blocks on a specified surface.

The gross motor sector taps into gross motor skills. For instance, examiners will assess a young child's leg and arm activity while the child is lying on his or her back. Older children are required to hop on one foot or walk in a straight line for four or more steps placing the heel no more than one inch in front of the toe without holding on to any support.

Nature of Scoring

Each item can earn one of the following four scores: P for pass, F for fail, N.O. for no opportunity, or R for when the child refuses to attempt the task. The examinee is administered at least three items nearest to and totally falling before his or her age line. "Normal" items are those subtests that fall to the right of the age line. Failure of these items is considered normal. Scores earned on these items are not considered for interpretation. "Caution" items are those that fall on or between the 75–90th percentile of the age line and the child refuses to attempt or earns an F. "Delayed" items are those falling completely to the left of the age line (past the 90th percentile) on which the child receives an F or R. "No opportunity" items are those items that do not fall within the age line and are not considered for interpretation. "Advanced" items involve tasks that fall completely to the right of the age line and the examinee passes successfully. These are tasks that most children can perform at a later age.

Interpretation of Scores

Three types of classifications result from completion of the Denver II. The first classification is "normal." This means that the child earned no "delayed" scores and, at the maximum, one "caution" score. The second classification is "suspect." This means that the examinee may need special programming yet the examiner would like to rescreen the child one to two weeks after the initial screening to rule out such factors as fatigue or illness. The child must earn two or more "caution" scores and/or one or more "delayed" scores to receive this classification. The last type of classification is "untestable." This means that the examinee either earned "refusal" scores on one or more items falling completely to the left of the age line or on more than one item intersected by the age line in the 75–90th percentile area. If a child receives this classification a rescreening is recommended.

Reliability

Evidence of the Denver II's reliability is discussed in the manual in terms of a study involving four trained screeners examining and observing 38 children from 10 age groups. The concurrent examiner–observer reliability ranged from .95–1.00 with the mean reported as .99 and a standard deviation of .16. A 7–10 day test–retest stability coefficient ranged from .50 to 1.00 with a mean of .90 and a standard deviation of .12.

Validity

No specific data were provided to show evidence of the Denver II's validity. In terms of content validity, the authors of the manual argued that the test's acceptance all over the world provides sufficient evidence. In addition, new items included on this assessment were selected by professionals in child development and pediatrics.

General Comments and Critiques

The Denver II is a revision of the Denver Developmental Screening Inventory (Frankenburg & Dodds, 1967). The changes occurring through the revision include more language items, updated norms, and easier administration and scoring (the Denver II includes a videotape for training examiners).

The Denver II appears to have achieved the purpose for which it was intended; namely, the early identification of children who are not developing normally. It should be noted that a sparse amount of literature focusing on this instrument's psychometric qualities is available. Based on the information provided in the test manual, it is easy to say that psychometrically, the Denver II has areas of concern.

CONCLUSION

As indicated by Bracken (1987), there still is considerable need to focus attention on the quality of assessment of preschool children. Standardized intelligence tests and screening instruments are heavily utilized by most psychologists (Bagnato & Neisworth, 1994; NASP/APA Preschool Interest Group, 1987). Thorough attention to this review of instruments reveals that no one assessment is flawless. Moreover, each assessment carries its individual strengths; while one test may be useful with a particular population, another may not. Therefore, it can be concluded that any and all information pertaining to these instruments is useful to the practitioner who needs to decide which test would be best for each individual preschooler needing evaluation.

Intelligence Tests

Bracken (1987) argued that one area needing more focus pertains to more and better formal training for examiners. A study conducted by Whitten, et al. (1994) investigated administration and scoring errors on 57 WPPSI-R protocols completed by seven examiners. Results revealed that examiners made frequent errors, including failing to record examinee responses, assigning incorrect point values to examinee responses, and determining incorrect basals or ceilings. When examiner errors were corrected, the total scores were changed on 57% of the protocols, which could have lead to one potential diagnostic error. The authors concluded that the errors may be due to inadequate training. Hodapp (1993) also pointed out that diagnostic skills including test administration, test interpretation, and knowledge of validities and reliabilities of selected tests is critical in the assessment process, particularly when assessing toddlers and preschoolers because of their unique developmental characteristics, such as short attention spans.

Another problem area identified by Bracken (1987) is the psychometric qualities of preschool assessments. It seems that, even with recent revision of many intelligence tests, not much has changed with regard to technical adequacy of these measures (Flanagan & Alfonso, 1995). There appears to be a lack of standardized criteria for these tests, which contributes to the continued use of inadequate assessments. When reviewing and comparing various assessments, it is difficult to do so due to the lack of standardized criteria to be used as a guide. Some psychometric characteristics, however, have been identified as critical to the diagnostic procedure. These include total test floors, predictive validity, construct validity, and concurrent validity.

The total test floor of any intelligence test is more important than subtest floors because placement decisions are based largely on the child's overall level of intelligence or total test score. According to Flanagan and Alfonso (1995), at the very least, intelligence tests must differentiate children of average, low average, borderline, and mild mental retardation ranges. Many assessments do not. Bracken (1987) argued that any instrument that does not produce a total test score of 70 or below should not be used to assess mildly retarded let alone more severely retarded children.

Validity is an issue largely due to the inconsistencies in the definition of intelligence. Neisworth and Bagnato (1992) claimed that there are as many definitions of intelligence as there are tests for intelligence. Since there is little or no agreement on the definition of this construct, attempts to validate its validity may be futile (Flanagan & Alfonso, 1995).

Lack of predictive validity of intelligence tests for preschoolers is clearly evident (Goodman, 1990). Early intelligence testing cannot make useful predictions of a child's future status (Neisworth & Bagnato, 1992). Flanagan and Alfonso (1995) claimed that this is true because of the assumption that what is being measured is stable; therefore, an individual's relative standing in a group, for the most part, is static. Moreover, most practitioners who work with preschoolers are interested in functional skills and adaptive behaviors rather than IQ or academic achievement. It is unlikely that information about predictive validity will be very useful to practitioners, especially those planning instructional programs and intervention.

Evidence of intelligence tests' concurrent validity is also being questioned. According to Flanagan and Alfonso (1995), information obtained from correlating two assessments of intelligence may add little to support construct validity or diagnostic utility of either instrument. Moreover, criterion measures most frequently used to demonstrate concurrent validity of intelligence tests are other intelligence tests. The extent to which these other intelligence measures are reliable and free from bias varies and may not be known.

Screening Instruments

Problems and areas of concern about screening instruments are also prominent. Conclusions drawn from the review of assessments included in this chapter reveal that screening instruments in general possess very weak psychometric qualities. In fact, most instruments provide no basic rationale for why a particular scoring method or criteria is being used. In addition, Teale (1988) pointed out that the two most prominent negative consequences resulting from using screening instruments are (1) not recognizing a disorder and (2) assigning an "at-risk" label to a nonhandicapped child.

Additional Information

For the most part, using a global IQ score as the only basis for making diagnostic and classification decisions about preschoolers is dangerous. A recent survey completed by 83% of the membership of the NASP/APA Preschool Special Interest Group revealed that 40% of young at-risk preschoolers and preschoolers with handicaps who were tested for first-time program eligibility would have been declared "untestable" if their eligibility for enrollment in an early intervention program were to have been based on the results from the traditional tests of intelligence (e.g., WPPSI-R, MSCA, S-B, K-ABC, DAS, WJ-R). Conclusions from this study revealed that it was rare that any of the traditional intelligence tests provided sufficient data alone to determine either child status or program eligibility (Neisworth & Bagnato, 1992). Most will argue that multiple sources of data should be used in the evaluation process.

So, what should these "other" sources of data include? Nearly all school psychologists involved in the study just discussed indicated wanting information on alternative measures (Neisworth & Bagnato, 1992). L. J. Johnson and Beauchamp (1987) indicated that many early childhood practitioners are using criterion-referenced or curriculum-based assessments of multimeasure batteries to assess infants and preschool children for program eligibility, program goal planning, and progress evaluation. Moreover, Stiggins (1985) argued that the information teachers utilize the most to teach students does not come from standardized tests but from tests they themselves develop. Although limitations of alternate approaches to assessment have not been carefully examined (Barnett & Macmann, 1992; Bracken, 1994), it appears that their inclusion in the assessment process is vital.

Overall, it is evident that there are many options for preschool assessment. Standardized instruments including the traditional intelligence tests, screening instruments, and alternative measures should be carefully considered by practitioners. Strengths and weaknesses will be apparent in every measure. Early childhood practitioners should decide which assessments to use based on the intended purpose of the assessment.

References

Aiken, L. R. (1987). *Assessment of intellectual functioning*. Boston: Allyn & Bacon.

Anastasi, A. (1982). *Psychological testing* (5th ed.). New York: Macmillan.

Bagnato, S. J., & Neisworth, J. T. (1994). A national study of the social and treatment "invalidity" of intelligence testing for early intervention. *School Psychology Quarterly, 9*, 81–101.

Barnett, D. W., & Macmann, G. M. (1992). Decision reliability and validity: Contribution and limitations of alternative assessment strategies. *Journal of Special Education, 25*, 431–452.

Barnett, D. W., & Paget, K. D. (1988). Implementing alternative service delivery in preschool settings: Concepts and procedures. In J. Graden, J. E. Zins, & M. J. Curtis (Eds.), Alternative educational delivery systems: Enhancing instructional options for all students (pp 291–308). Washington: National Association of School Psychology.

Bayley, N. 91993). *Bayley Scales of Infant Development—II*. San Antonio, TX: Psychological Corporation

Bower, A., & Hayes, A. (1995). Relations of scores on the Stanford-Binet Fourth Edition and Form L-M: Concurrent validation study with children who have mental retardation. *American Journal on Mental Retardation, 99*(5), 555–563.

Bracken, B. A. (1981). McCarthy Scales as a learning disabilities diagnostic aid: A closer look. *Journal of Learning Disabilities, 14*, 128–130.

Bracken, B. A. (1987). Limitations of preschool instruments and standards for minimal levels of technical adequacy. *Journal of Psychoeducational Assessment, 4*, 313–326.

Bracken, B. A. (1994). Advocating for effective preschool assessment practices: A comment on Bagnato and Neisworth. *School Psychology Quarterly, 9*, 103–108.

Bryant, C. K., & Roffe, M. W. (1978). A reliability study of the McCarthy Scales of Children's Abilities. *Journal of Clinical Psychology, 34*, 401–406.

Burgemeister, B. B., Blum, L. H., & Lorge, I. (1972). *Columbia Mental Maturity Scale*. New York: Harcourt Brace Jovanovich.

Davis, E. E., & Slettedahl, R. W. (1976). Stability of the McCarthy Scales over a one-year period. *Journal of Clinical Psychology, 32*, 798–800.

Dunn, L. M. (1965). *Peabody Picture Vocabulary Test*. Circle Pines, MN: American Guidance Service.

Dunn, L. M., & Dunn, L. M. (1981). *Peabody Picture Vocabulary Test—Revised*. Circle Pines, MN: American Guidance Service.

Elliot, C. D. (1990). *Differential Ability Scales: Introductory and technical handbook*. San Antonio, TX: Psychological Corporation.

Faust, D. S., & Hollingsworth, J. O. (1991). Concurrent validity of the Wechsler Preschool and Primary Scales of Intelligence—Revised (WPPSI-R) with two criteria of cognitive abilities. *Journal of Psychoeducational Assessment, 9*, 224–229.

Flanagan, D. P., & Alfonso, V. C. (1995). A critical review of the technical characteristics of new and recently revised intelligence tests for preschool children. *Journal of Psychoeducational Assessment, 13*, 66–90.

Flanagan, D. P., Sainato, D., & Genshaft, J. L. (1993). Emerging issues in the assessment of young children with disabilities: The expanding role of school psychology. *Canadian Journal of School Psychology, 9*, 192–203.

Frankenburg, W. K., & Dodds, J. B. (1967). The Denver Developmental Screening Test. *Journal of Pediatrics*, 71, 181–191.

Frankenburg, W. K., Dodds, J., Archer, P., Bresnick, B., Maschka, P., Edelman, N., & Shapiro, H. (1990). *Denver II; Reference manual*. Denver, CO: Ladoca.

Fuchs, D., Fuchs, L. S., Benowitz, S., & Barringer, K. (1987). Norm-referenced tests: Are they valid for use with handicapped students? *Exceptional Children*, 54, 263–271.

Gerken, K. C., & Hodapp, A. F. (1992). Assessment of preschoolers at-risk with the WPPSI-R & the Stanford-Binet L-M. *Psychological Reports*, 71, 659–664.

Gomez-Benito, J., & Forns-Santacana, M. (1993). Concurrent validity between the Columbia Mental Maturity Scale and the McCarthy Scales. *Perceptual and Motor Skills*, 76, 1177–1178.

Goodman, J. F. (1990). Infant intelligence: Do we, can we, should we assess it? In C. Reynolds & R. Kamphaus (Eds.), *Handbook of psychological and educational measurement of children* (pp. 183–208). New York: Guilford Press.

Gyurke, J. S., Stone, B., & Beyer, M. (1990). A confirmatory factor analysis of the WPPSI-R. *Journal of Psychoeducational Assessment*, 8, 15–21.

Heil, J., Barclay, A., & Endres, J. M. (1978). A factor analytic study of WPPSI scores of educationally deprived and normal children. *Psychological Reports*, 42, 727–730.

Hodapp, A. F. (1993). Correlation between S-B:IV and PPVT-R scores for young children. *Psychological Reports*, 73, 1152–1154.

Hollenbeck, G. R., & Kaufman, A. S. (1973). Factor analysis of the Wechsler Preschool and Primary Scales of Intelligence (WPPSI). *Journal of Clinical Psychology*, 29, 41–45.

Johnson, D. L., Howie, V. M., Owen, M., Baldwin, C. D., & Luttman, D. (1993). Assessment of three-year olds with the Stanford-Binet Fourth Edition. *Psychological Reports*, 73, 51–57.

Johnson, L. J., & Beauchamp, K. D. (1987). Preschool assessment measures: What are teachers using? *Journal of the Division for Early Childhood*, 12, 70–76.

Kaplan, C. (1993). Predicting first-grade achievement from pre-kindergarten WPPSI-R scores. *Journal of Psychoeducational Assessment*, 11, 133–138.

Karr, S. K., Carvajal, H., & Elser, D. (1993). Concurrent validity of the WPPSI-R and the McCarthy Scales of Children's Abilities. *Psychological Reports*, 72, 940–942.

Kaufman, A. S. (1982). An integrated review of almost a decade of research on the McCarthy Scales. In T. Kratochwill (Ed.), *Advances in school psychology* (Vol. 2) (pp. 119–169). Hillsdale, NJ: Erlbaum.

Kaufman, A. S., & Kaufman, N. L. (1977). *Clinical evaluation of young children with the McCarthy Scales*. New York: Grune & Stratton.

Kaufman, A. S., & Kaufman, N. L. (1983). *Kaufman Assessment Battery for Children—Revised; Test manual* Circle Pines, MN: American Guidance Service.

Keith, T. Z., Cool, V. A., Novak, C. G., White, L. J., & Pottebaum, S. M. (1988). Confirmatory factor analysis of the S-B:IV: Testing the theory-test match. *Journal of School Psychology*, 26, 253–274.

Kline, R. B. (1989). Is the Fourth Edition Stanford-Binet a four-factor test? Confirmatory factor analyses of alternative models for ages 2 through 23. *Journal of Psychoeducational Assessment*, 7, 4–13.

Laurent, J., Swerdlik, M., & Ryburn, M. (1992). Review of validity research on the S-B intelligence scale: Fourth Edition. *Journal of Psychoeducational Assessment*, 4(1), 102–112.

Lichtenstein, R., & Ireton, H. (1984). *Preschool screening*. Orlando, FL: Grune & Stratton.

Lubin, B., Larsen, R. M., & Matarazzo, J. D. (1984). Patterns of psychological test usage in the United States: 1935–1982. *American Psychologist*, 39, 451–454.

Maxwell, A. E. (1972). The WPPSI: A marked discrepancy in the correlation of the subtests for good and poor readers. *British Journal of Mathematical Statistical Psychology*, 25, 283–291.

McCallum, R. S. (1990). Determining the factor structure of the Stanford-Binet: Fourth Edition—The right choice. *Journal of Psychoeducational Assessment*, 8, 436–442.

McCarthy, D. (1972). *McCarthy Scales of Children's Abilities*. New York: The Psychological Corporation.

McCrowell, K. L. (1994). Comparability of the WPPSI-R and the S-B:IV among preschool children. *Journal of Psychoeducational Assessment*, 12, 126–134.

Miller, L. J. (1982). *Miller assessment for preschoolers*. Littleton, CO: Foundation for Knowledge in Development.

Miller, L. J., & Sprong, T. A. (1986). Psychometric and qualitative comparison of four preschool screening instruments. *Journal of Learning Disabilities*, 19, 480–484.

Molfese, V. J., Helwig, S., & Holcomb, L. (1993). Standardized assessments of verbal intelligence in 3-year-old children: A comparison of biomedical and psychoeducational data in a longitudinal sample. *Journal of Psychoeducational Assessment*, 11, 56–66.

Molfese, V. J., Yaple, K., Helwig, S., Harris, L., & Connell, S. (1992). Stanford-Binet Intelligence Scale (Fourth Edition): Factor structure and verbal subscale scores for three-year-olds. *Journal of Psychoeducational Assessment*, 10, 47–58.

Moran, B. M. (1989). Removing community barriers from language tests. *Language, Speech, and Hearing Services in Schools*, 20(4), 431–432.

National Association for the Education of Young Children. (1989). NAEYC position statement on standardized testing of young children 3 through 8 years of age. *Young Children*, 43(3), 42–52.

National Association of School Psychologists/American Psychological Association (NASP/APA) Preschool Interest Group. (1987). Preschool practices, problems, and issues. *Preschool Interests*, 2(3), 1–11.

Neisworth, J. T., & Bagnato, S. J. (1992). The case against intelligence testing in early intervention. *Topics in Early Childhood Special Education*, 12, 1–20.

Reschly, D., & Wilson, M. (1990). Cognitive processing versus traditional intelligence: Diagnostic utility, intervention implications, and treatment validity. *School Psychology Review*, 19, 443–458.

Rose, S. A., & Wallace, I. F. (1985). Cross-modal and intramodal transfer as predictors of mental development in fullterm and preterm infants. *Developmental Psychology*, 17, 90–98.

Salvia, J., & Ysseldyke, J. E. (1985). *Assessment in special and remedial education* (3rd ed.). Boston: Houghton Mifflin.

Sattler, J. M. (1988). *Assessment of children* (3rd ed.). San Diego, CA: Jerome M. Sattler.

Sattler, J. M. (1992). *Assessment of children* (4th ed.). San Diego, CA: Jerome M. Sattler.

Shellenberger, S. A. (1977). *A cross-cultural investigation of the validity of the Spanish version of the McCarthy Scales of Children's Abilities for Puerto Rican children*. Unpublished doctoral dissertation, University of Georgia, Athens.

Siegel, L. (1979). Infant perceptual, cognitive, and motor behaviors as predictors of subsequent cognitive and language development. *Canadian Journal of Psychology*, 33, 382–395.

Silverman, L. K., & Kearney, K. (1992). The case for the S-B L-M as a supplemental test. *Roeper Review*, 15(1), 34–37.

Silverstein, A. B. (1986). Cluster analysis of the Wechsler Preschool and Primary Scales of Intelligence. *Journal of Psychoeducational Assessment*, 4, 83–86.

Slate, J. R., & Saddler, C. D. (1990). Improved but not perfect. *NASP Communique*, p. 20.

Stiggins, R. J. (1985). Improving assessment where it means the most: In the classroom. *Educational Leadership*, 43, 69–74.

Teale, W. H. (1988). Developmentally appropriate assessment of reading and writing in the early childhood classroom. *Elementary School Journal*, 89(2), 173–183.

Thorndike, R. L. (1990). Would the real factors of the Stanford-Binet Fourth Edition please come forward? *Journal of Psychoeducational Assessment*, 8, 412–415.

Thorndike, R. L., Hagen, E. P., & Sattler, J. M. (1986a). *Guide for administration and scoring the Stanford-Binet Intelligence Scale* (4th ed.). Chicago: Riverside Publishing.

Thorndike, R. L., Hagen, E. P., & Sattler, J. M. (1986b). *The Stanford-Binet Intelligence Scale 4th ed. Technical Manual*. Chicago: Riverside Publishing.

Tsushima, W. T. (1994). Short form of the WPPSI and WPPSI-R. *Journal of Clinical Psychology*, 50, 877–880.

264

Cheryl E. Sanders

Wechsler, D. (1989). *Manual for the Wechsler Preschool and Primary Scale of Intelligence—Revised.* San Antonio, TX: Psychological Corporation.

Whitten, J., Slate, J. R., Shine, A. E., & Raggio, D. (1994). Examiner errors in administering and scoring the WPPSI-R. *Journal of Psychoeducational Assessment, 12,* 49–54.

Woodcock, R. W., & Johnson, M. B. (1990). *Woodcock-Johnson Psycho-Educational Battery—Revised. Tests of Cognitive Ability.* Allen, TX: DLM Teaching Resources.

Zehrbach, R. R. (1985). *Manual for the comprehensive identification process.* Bensenville, IL: Scholastic Testing Service.

CHAPTER 9

The Role of Standardized Achievement Tests in Grades K–12

TIM ANSLEY
University of Iowa

INTRODUCTION

Few topics in education have been surrounded by controversy to the extent standardized achievement tests have. For years these tests have been the focus of a great deal of criticism. For example, these tests have been accused of narrowing the curriculum in each of the areas tested. Some argue that this has taken place because teachers have been forced to teach to the objectives measured by these tests at the expense of other important objectives. They have been accused of measuring no higher level objectives because the predominant item type is multiple choice. These tests clearly have generated a great deal of discussion. Considering that these batteries typically take up approximately four hours of time, the amount of focus given these tests is truly remarkable.

In this chapter, these controversial aspects of standardized tests are addressed. The focus of the chapter is the appropriate use and interpretation of standardized test scores. The discussion is centered on achievement tests in grades K–12. One controversial area that will not be discussed is the use of these instruments at the primary level (grades K–2). The appropriateness of standardized norm-referenced tests for the youngest students is currently an area of great disagreement. Such appropriateness issues are beyond the scope of this chapter. However, it should be noted that, these issues aside,

Handbook of Classroom Assessment

the discussion here of issues in test interpretation and use in grades 3–12 generalizes quite nicely to the early grades. This discussion begins with a consideration of the differences in the testing situations in elementary versus secondary schools. Once these differences have been discussed, the interpretation and use of standardized test scores are explored. In general, there are more similarities than differences here across all grade levels.

THE UNIQUE CHALLENGES OF SECONDARY SCHOOL TESTING

While most of the criticism of standardized testing is not at all specific to particular grade levels, clearly external testing at the secondary level presents a series of unique problems, particularly when compared to testing at the elementary level. At the elementary level, there are generally far fewer problems with all aspects of external testing. Virtually all aspects of external testing, from test administration to interpretation of results, run more smoothly at the elementary level. These differences usually cause secondary teachers to find less relevance in external testing programs. Most of the difficulties at the secondary level are related to the structure of the schools and curricula. Whereas most elementary schools are structured with largely self-contained classrooms, where one teacher has primary responsibility for a class of 25 to 30 students, secondary schools are generally structured in a more diverse manner. Teachers at this level usually have responsibility for four to six different classes in a particular academic discipline. A secondary teacher might see as many as 150 students each day, but be responsible for only one part of their school day.

Teacher–Student Attitudes

Such a difference in school structure has obvious implications for teachers' roles in and attitudes about external testing programs. For example, suppose a school district annually administers a standardized achievement battery in grades 3, 5, 8, and 10. It is likely that the students in grades 3 and 5 spend most of their school days with a single teacher or, at least, a single teacher has primary responsibility for one group of students. If this is the case, then that same teacher will most likely be involved in the administration of the standardized battery as well as its interpretation with both students and parents. At this level teachers are the key link in the evaluation process. In addition, at the elementary level, teachers are more aware of the academic development of students across disciplines. Simply put, elementary teachers are generally much more involved with the whole child than secondary teachers.

In contrast, in grades 8 and 10 teachers might have contact with each student as few as 40 minutes each day. And, their exposure to a student's development in disciplines other than their own is often limited to conversations in the faculty lounge or before and after school. These teachers also will most likely be involved in the administration of the test battery. But their outlook and the outlook of their students are often very different from that of elementary teachers and students. For elementary teachers and students the testing activities are much more consistent with their daily routine. Staying in a single room with a single teacher for an extended period of time is typical for elementary students. It is not at all typical for students at the secondary level. Such an activity is often a huge departure from their routine. Furthermore, elementary students are accustomed to interacting with their teacher, the test administrator. At the secondary level, it is possible, particularly in larger schools, that the students have never been directly taught by the test administrator. Often, the test administrator at the secondary level is a "homeroom" teacher who may have minimal contact with this particular group of students, and this contact is often limited to an occasional 10–15 minute period of school housekeeping activities. Therefore, it should not be surprising that elementary students and teachers feel more invested in the testing process.

The movement away from traditional junior high schools to the concept of a middle school with a more integrated curriculum will probably enable the students and teachers in those intermediate grades to enjoy the benefits typically found in testing at the elementary level. However, this will only make the climate of external testing at the high school level seem even more strained and unusual than is presently the case. Special steps must be taken at the upper grade levels to ensure the relevance of test results to teachers and students.

Because of the uniqueness of this activity at the secondary level, both students and teachers may be fairly uncomfortable during the testing period. The implications of this discomfort are potentially far-reaching. Given an unusual situation and potentially a different authority figure with whom to interact, there is obviously a clear possibility for apprehension or at least distraction among secondary students. This apprehension can be manifested in a variety of ways. Most such manifestations do not facilitate the collection of valid test scores. Students at the secondary level are much more likely to act out or misbehave in the face of an unusual situation. In addition, in the presence of an untested authority figure, the possibility of the "substitute teacher syndrome" can come into play. Clearly, there are potentially damaging possibilities of lack of motivation among secondary students as they take the standardized battery.

Closely related to students' attitudes and reactions are the attitudes of teachers toward external testing results. As is true of most aspects of the academic climate, students' attitudes often mirror teachers' attitudes. Generally, teachers' attitudes toward standardized testing are better at the elementary level. The reasons for this discrepancy are largely the same as those cited previously. At the elementary level, teachers are much more an integral part of the testing process, including everything from the preparation for and administration of testing to the dissemination and interpretation of the results. At the elementary level, teachers typically run or are involved in the entire testing process. Schools often have parent–teacher conferences at the elementary level for the purpose of discussing the results of an external testing program.

At the secondary level, teachers who administer the tests may not know the students under their charge. And, worse yet, the teachers may never see the results for the students in their classes. Hence, teachers at the secondary level often do not see the relevance of the testing program and view the process as a needless intrusion on their working environment. If teachers demonstrate these feelings to the students prior to or during the testing process, student motivation will likely suffer. Consider the situation in which a teacher is administering a standardized test battery. Suppose the teacher begins the administration of the tests by saying something like the following to the students, "Today you will be taking test x. Don't ask me why you're doing this; it's been mandated by the school administration. I remember taking tests like these as a student, and I didn't like them anymore than you do. Fortunately, they aren't very important; nobody even looks at these scores. So let's just try to get through this time as easily as possible. Remember, I don't want to be here anymore than you do." Perhaps no teacher would actually be so openly cynical, but such an attitude, even if not so strongly shared, would have a great influence on students' attitudes.

Curriculum Fit

Another factor related to the perceptions of students and teachers to external testing at the secondary level is the nature of the secondary curriculum. At the elementary level, the curricula in most subjects are fairly clearly defined. This makes matching those curricula a reasonable task for most types of external achievement tests. However, at the secondary level, curriculum match is a major difficulty for external achievement tests. While it may be clear what fourth grade math entails, it is very difficult to describe, let alone measure, what ninth grade math entails. In secondary schools, students enroll in various levels or branches of a particular curriculum area according to their interests or their aptitudes. Therefore, a high school achievement battery cannot possibly claim to match well with a secondary school's mathematics curriculum.

The same is true for science and most other academic areas. For example, the grade 11 science test in a standardized achievement battery cannot typically measure objectives relevant to student course work in chemistry. This test is intended to be taken by all students, and as such, it cannot measure concepts to which some of the examinees have not been exposed. This is a source of consternation to many school personnel on reviewing such a test. Tests of this nature are generally designed to measure the ability to interpret scientific writings and the outcomes of scientific experiments. While this test will not be able to assist in evaluating how well students have mastered the principles of chemistry or physics, it can monitor the growth of students in using and interpreting scientific information. While this may not bear directly on specific science curriculum concerns, it is still worthwhile information. After all, students who have had chemistry or physics should surely be stronger at interpreting scientific information, even information from a fairly general context. For teachers to approach such tests with a favorable attitude requires that steps be taken to ensure that teachers understand that the intent of these tests is not to assist in the evaluation of specific courses in the secondary science curriculum. Rather the intent is to monitor the progress of students in using the science they have learned in school in interpreting scientific information.

Add to these difficulties the fact that secondary school personnel and students often feel inundated with external measurements, and it is clear why many secondary school personnel are skeptical about testing. Students are asked to take the PSAT, the SAT, the ACT, a norm-referenced achievement test, perhaps an alternative assessment measure, and several interest or vocational measures. Even if teachers never get involved in some of these tests, they are still keenly aware of the prevalence of testing at the secondary level. Of course, the problem is only exacerbated by the school boards, parent groups, and media who often overinterpret test scores or use them inadvisably as a tool for assessing the effectiveness of specific teachers.

USEFULNESS OF STANDARDIZED ACHIEVEMENT TESTS

The purposes of many of the tests taken by secondary students are self-evident. For example, the SAT and ACT have unmistakable uses that are obvious to everyone. Likewise the PSAT serves as a gatekeeper for National Merit scholarships. Aptitude or interest inventories also play clearly defined roles. Any student can easily understand the usefulness of an instrument such as the Differential Aptitude Tests (Bennett, Seashore, & Wesman, 1992). However, the purposes of standardized achievement batteries such as the Iowa Tests of Educational Development (Feldt & Forsyth, 1993a) or the Metropolitan Achievement Tests (Psychological Corporation, 1993) are often unclear to students and secondary school educators. Students often view such tests as irrelevant to their own goals or needs. In many cases, their teachers probably share this lack of certainty as to the usefulness or importance of such instruments. Of course, in some cases, this uncertainty on the parts of students and faculty is expressed as outright skepticism. So why are these achievement batteries used?

Any norm-referenced achievement battery (elementary and secondary) has the same general purposes: (1) to evaluate students' growth, (2) to evaluate students' relative strengths and weaknesses in academic areas, and (3) to indicate the status of students or groups of students within a relevant normative group. While most people would identify the third purpose as the primary role for standardized tests, most of the authors of these batteries hold the first two purposes as more important. Clearly, the availability of normative data enables status-type comparisons of students or groups of students. It is also clear that such information is of considerable interest to students, parents, educators, and the general public.

Status Statements

Many of the problems associated with norm-referenced achievement tests can probably be traced to this interest or, more specifically, to the overemphasis and misinterpretations of such information. There is a certain seductiveness in the percentile ranks associated with standardized test scores. Curiosity and competitiveness drive humans to be tantalized with the notion of where they rank. Most, perhaps all, parents are curious about how their child compares with other children of the same age. Clearly, such information, kept in perspective, is a useful piece of the puzzle in evaluating students' academic progress. Unfortunately, this perspective is often lost. Instead of viewing test scores as one piece of evaluative data that must be interpreted in light of other available academic indicators, often parents view these scores in isolation, leading to a troublesome overemphasis of the usefulness of these scores. Perhaps even more troubling for educators is when school boards, the public, or the media try to consider standardized test scores in the absence of other assessment data. The result is almost always unfortunate for schools. School personnel often find themselves in the uncomfortable position of being on the defensive, trying to justify their roles and the progress of their students to groups of people who have already decided, based on a very small piece of evaluation evidence, that the schools are not performing adequately. This represents a gross misuse of test scores and clearly leads to negative attitudes toward the instrument that brought on the distress. Some might argue that this is tantamount to killing the messenger, but the fact remains that educators' professional lives are often not enhanced by standardized test results.

This problem is exacerbated at the secondary level because of the lack of communication between schools and parents regarding test results. Most secondary students' standardized test scores are sent home in a small brochure, containing little detailed information regarding the appropriate interpretation of the results. At the secondary level, if students fail to see the relevance of an activity, many will likely respond with a halfhearted effort. This is true whether the setting is academic or extracurricular. This is in clear contrast with the behavior of students at the elementary level, who are much more apt to be accepting of activities in school without questioning or grumbling and still produce their best effort.

An even more troubling problem is that secondary teachers themselves often never see the results for their students on the standardized battery. It is no wonder that teachers might not see the value in such a measurement endeavor and that parents misinterpret the test scores. The problem of secondary teacher access to standardized test results is a serious one that must be resolved if a school hopes to have a successful norm-referenced testing program. Like nearly everything that goes on in schools, the ultimate success or failure of a testing program depends on the involvement and endorsement of the school's faculty.

At the elementary level, particularly in a self-contained classroom, the list report of test results is returned to the classroom teacher, who can then consider the results for each student in light of the other information available regarding each student's academic progress. These integrated interpretations are often shared directly with the parents and sometimes even the students. However, at the secondary level, this simple reporting procedure becomes considerably more difficult. Teachers here typically see students for only one period each day, and they typically have five or six different classes of students each day. List reports for standardized test scores are usually separated by grade, a distinction that is not conducive to easy interpretation or even easy perusal for classroom teachers. Instead of being delivered a list of the students in their classes, teachers are required to go to the main office or a counselor's office to be able to view their students' test scores. Of course, to do this, teachers must sift through the entire list for a given class that will often contain a large number of students they do not have in class. Thus, most secondary teachers never see their students' test results, and therefore, they have little reason to see any value in this testing process. This perception is likely to be passed on to the students, and the result is a test viewed as strictly an external evaluation tool, with no relevance to the teachers or students. Motivation problems are an obvious byproduct of such a system.

Test publishers have begun to take steps to alleviate part of this problem. Some tests make available, through special coding of the answer sheets, a class list of the test results of the students in each class a teacher instructs. Thus, Ms. Brown can receive a list of the students' test results for her fifth period American literature class. This would be one step schools could take to improve their standardized testing environment.

This discussion has focused on the last of the three purposes of a standardized norm-referenced testing program. As noted already, this status interpretation is not what most measurement experts would identify as the primary role of such a testing program. Instead, most would argue that these tests serve most importantly to monitor students' growth and relative strengths and weaknesses. Such information should be particularly useful to teachers and students. This, after all, should be the essence of measurement. If the results of a test do not directly benefit the student, the teachers, and the academic program, the wisdom of implementing the measure should be questioned.

Monitoring Growth

Monitoring the growth or progress of students is a primary objective in all academic areas. Teachers routinely do this with each of their students during the course of a year or semester. The process of monitoring growth from year to year, however, transcends the purview of individual teachers. To make evaluations of growth requires the presence of some sort of frame of reference. Teachers can certainly discuss the progress of students from year to year, but such discussions are necessarily imprecise because two teachers will no doubt use somewhat different criteria for evaluating student progress. One of the primary purposes of norms is to provide a frame of reference for monitoring growth. When compiled over years, the results of a norm-referenced standardized achievement battery can provide a longitudinal data base suitable for evaluating the growth of students in the academic areas assessed by the battery. Such a longitudinal look at students' growth is of interest at the student level and at the group level. For example, consider the set of hypothetical standard scores for a science test in an achievement battery:

Grade	3	4	5	6	7	8	9	10	11	12
Score	185	200	214	227	239	250	260	268	275	280.

Suppose it is known, based on the normative information available, that a typical student at that level improves by 10 points on this test's standard score scale from grade 9 to grade 10. This particular student improved by only 8 points during this year. Hence, this student's progress in science is slightly below average relative to the norm group in question. Whether this performance merits concern obviously depends on several factors. For a clear evaluation, a student's growth must be judged in light of the growth of the entire class. If the class has improved on average by 12 points on this science test, the student in question has shown considerably less growth than might have been expected. In addition, other factors that may have influenced this student's performance must be considered. Was the student ill on the day of the test? Did something occur that may have distracted the student and thus contributed to poorer performance? Clearly, the scores from standardized tests must be viewed in the larger context of all evaluation information available. Given these caveats, it is difficult to dispute that standardized tests provide a unique piece of the educational evaluation puzzle. It is also difficult to argue that this information is not important or interesting. Obviously, this does assume the tests being used measure important objectives.

A topic related to the evaluation of growth using a standardized achievement battery is the choice of the metric to be used. All multilevel standardized tests provide a developmental score scale. However, this score scale often seems arbitrary and it lacks obvious interpretability. For example, in the situation just presented, this standard score scale has little intuitive appeal. The typical amount of growth of 10 points from grade 9 to grade 10 is simply an attribute of this scale for a particular norm group. Teachers and students will not have a clear sense of the meaning of a score of 268 without a fair amount of other information provided. This lack of clarity detracts considerably from the practical usefulness of these scores for any persons except measurement experts or counselors.

At the elementary level, standardized tests have an extremely helpful scale available. The grade equivalent (GE) scale provides a very useful frame of reference for interpreting students' test scores and progress across years. A student's scores of 5.2 (fifth grade, second month) in grade 5 and 6.2 (sixth grade, second month) in grade 6 clearly indicate a typical year's growth in a particular area. Other standard score scales lack this clarity. Unfortunately, grade equivalents are not very meaningful at the secondary level.

Consider, for example a grade equivalent of 11.3 for an 11th grade student on a science test. How would such a score be interpreted? A GE of 11.3 implies this student's performance is consistent with that of the typical 11th grade student in the 3rd month of the school year. But how can we describe this typical student? At the elementary level, given the fairly fixed nature of the curriculum, a GE of say 5.3 can be clearly understood. Most elementary teachers could accurately describe the abilities of a typical student at a given point in a school year. However, this is typically not possible at the secondary level. For the science GE just given, consider the nature of the secondary science curriculum. Students in grade 11 vary widely in the science courses taken and enrolled in. Many students might be enrolled in chemistry. Others may be taking biology or advanced biology. Some students might be taking two science courses during their junior year, while others may be taking none. Thus, envisioning the typical 11th grade student is not possible in most secondary areas because of the diverse nature of the curriculum and the many different paths students follow as they work toward graduation.

Given the lack of relevance of GEs and the lack of intuitive appeal of developmental standard scores, a convenient scale for monitoring growth at the secondary level is needed. Fortunately, such a scale is readily available. Percentile ranks can be quite useful as a metric for interpreting students' growth. Percentile ranks have the clear advantage of being easily understood and interpreted by virtually all audiences. The main limitation in using percentile ranks for describing growth is that average growth is indicated when a percentile rank remains fairly constant in value over time. For example, if in grade 9 a student's national percentile rank in mathematics problem solving is 72 and in grade 10 that student's percentile rank is also 72, this implies that this student grew at an average rate for students of that achievement level. This is somewhat disconcerting because we typically link the notion of growth with an increase in scores. However, an increase in percentile rank actually signifies above average growth at a particular achievement level. And, of course, a decrease in percentile rank does not indicate a lack of growth; instead, it implies slower than typical growth among students at that level of achievement. If the audiences for test results can be instructed in the interpretation of percentile ranks used for evaluating growth, these values provide a very convenient scale for monitoring student achievement longitudinally.

A final note regarding the use of percentile ranks for assessing growth should be made. In carrying out such interpretations on this metric, it is important to understand that the significance of magnitudes of differences differs according to the students' relative levels of achievement. That is, a difference from year to year of 10 points on the percentile rank scale may be extraordinary for students at some ability levels and rather typical for students at other levels. Consider the nature of most distributions of scores on measures of academic achievement. It is reasonable to assume that most such distributions resemble the classic bell-shaped curve for general populations of students. In such a distribution, there is a heavy concentration of scores near the median. Given this concentration, a small change in an actual score value in the middle of the distribution can lead to a relatively large change in percentile rank. With so many scores clustered in close proximity, any change will involve surpassing or falling behind large numbers of other scores. Thus, for students of average levels of achievement, a difference in percentile rank of 10 from one year to the next is probably not atypical. On the other hand, if a student at the fifth percentile increased by 10 points on the percentile rank scale, this would be very impressive. Given the scarcity of data in the extremes of most score distributions, a change of this magnitude in percentile rank would most likely be considered substantial (see Table 1).

Individual Profiles

Another important use for standardized achievement test scores is in the evaluation of areas of relative strengths and weaknesses. This is the classic idea of a profile. This represents another unique contribution norm-referenced tests can provide school personnel, students, and parents. For many students, it is clear where their main area of strength lies. For others, however, this may not be at all clear. To be able to judge relative strengths and weaknesses requires that the performance of students on different measures be compared against common benchmarks. Teachers can discuss stu-

TABLE I
General Benchmarks for Evaluating
Relatively Important Changes in Achievement
from Year to Year

Original PR Level	PR Change
85–99	8
65–84	11
35–64	15
15–34	11
1–14	8

dents' work across disciplines, but it is typically not possible to specify areas of strength and weakness with great confidence because the students are in different classes, being compared with different students. The norms for a standardized test are compiled on a common group across all areas, thus enabling statements of relative strength and weakness within individual students or groups of students. As is often the case in examining and interpreting standardized test scores, these scores most typically reinforce the judgments of teachers. For some students, however, a profile on a standardized test battery may reveal heretofore unobserved areas of promise or concern.

Summary

The three main uses of standardized norm-referenced achievement tests—observing the status of a student's or group's performance, monitoring growth over time, and identifying areas of strength and weakness—should be carefully considered in evaluating or interpreting scores from these tests. It is also important to recall that the first of these purposes (status statements) is considered the least important role for standardized tests. If a school is not using the results from its standardized testing program for the second and third purposes, it should probably reconsider its allocation of time and money to the testing endeavor or its commitment to obtain useful evaluative information that will assist teachers, students, and parents make the most informed decisions possible to enhance the learning–teaching process.

INTERPRETING STANDARDIZED ACHIEVEMENT TEST SCORES

Any discussion of the usefulness of norm-referenced standardized achievement tests in today's educational climate would be incomplete without some

consideration of the prevailing sentiment and thought regarding such assessment. It is fair to say that standardized tests have been the target of
increasing criticism over the past 10 years. Much of this criticism is clearly
tied to the unprecedented widespread use of these tests in the 1980s. Standardized tests were mandated by state legislatures and used for a large
number of evaluative purposes. Most would say that these test were overused or at least overinterpreted. Tests were often used for purposes for which
they had not been validated. Test scores often became the primary basis for
evaluating students and academic programs in spite of the clearly stated
warnings against such practices in the manuals of these tests. Consider the
following taken from the Iowa Tests of Basic Skills Manual for School Administrators
(Hieronymus & Hoover, 1986).

> When intelligently used in combination with other important types of information,
> the results obtained from these tests should prove very valuable in the appraisal of
> the *total program* of instruction. Unless they are used in conjunction with other in-
> formation, however, they may do serious injustice to teachers and to many well-
> conceived instructional programs. (p. 59)

Test Content

Because such warnings were sometimes ignored, too much emphasis was
placed on test scores, leading to a predictable backlash against standardized
achievement tests. The aspect of these tests that has most often been sin-
gled out for ridicule or criticism has been the nature of the test questions.
Multiple-choice questions have been seriously maligned in recent years.
While some of the criticism of the overemphasis on the results of standardized tests is justified, most of the criticisms of multiple-choice items are
unreasonable. The most often heard criticism of this item type holds that
multiple-choice items can be used only to measure low-level, rote memory-
type objectives. This is clearly incorrect. A good item writer can create
questions of any type to measure higher-order thinking skills. Essay or constructed response items have no inherent advantage over multiple-choice
questions in this regard. Now, clearly, multiple-choice questions are inadequate for some areas, such as evaluating how well a student can produce an
original piece of writing or perform a solo or paint a picture or fix a carbure-
tor. For virtually any other type of objective, multiple-choice tests can be
constructed to provide valid information. For example, the complex area of
mathematics problem solving is one in which multiple choice items can
serve very well to evaluate student progress. This is not to imply that these
questions should provide the only information related to student performance in any area.

One might reasonably speculate about the origin of the notion that
multiple-choice questions are limited to the evaluation of factual recall. It is

probably born out of the experiences of most people with such questions. Most of our experiences with tests and multiple choice items come from school. Most of our exposure has been to teacher-made instruments. It is probably fair to say that most teacher-made multiple-choice tests measure only factual information. This does not reflect a limitation of the item type. Instead, this reflects a limitation of the item writer. It is fairly easy to write a multiple choice item requiring recall of factual detail. Consider the following item.

Which of the following came from Poland to help the United States in the Revolutionary War?
A. Robert Fulton
B. Patrick Henry
C. John Paul Jones
D. Casimir Pulaski

This item is unfortunately typical of teacher-made tests. It reduces the learning process to an endeavor to be proficient at the game show *Jeopardy*. Aside from the factual recall required by the item, an obvious flaw also is in the wording of the item. Many students with no knowledge of Pulaski's contributions will be able to answer this question correctly. Given their busy schedules, it is difficult for classroom teachers to produce high-quality multiple-choice items.

This social studies item is often what most people associate with multiple-choice questions. However, it is possible, although time consuming and difficult, to construct meaningful and challenging multiple choice items. Examples of such items can be found in most standardized achievement tests or in tests such as the ACT or SAT.

It seems clear that the limitation with multiple choice items rests in the item's author rather than in the nature of the item itself. Standardized tests are developed and edited by professional item writers. The items can be tried out and revised. These are luxuries the classroom teacher does not enjoy. It is unreasonable to reject standardized tests because they contain multiple-choice items. Such tests clearly do not provide a complete evaluation of a student or group of students, but they do provide unique information that spans a broad cross-section of the curriculum at all levels of processing, even the highest cognitive levels.

Regardless of the type of test questions used, the test scores must eventually be evaluated and interpreted. A key ingredient in the interpretation of test scores of any type involves knowledge of the content of the tests. When teachers examine the results for their students on a classroom test, interpretation is typically straightforward. The teacher has personally constructed this instrument and is thoroughly familiar with the demands placed on the students by it. The teacher can also readily interpret the mistakes of students because these were likely anticipated in the construction of the test. Meaningful interpretation of test scores requires such familiarity with the test content. Standardized tests therefore, can present some severe difficulties. This can be true at the elementary as well as the secondary level. Every teacher will surely have easy access to a manual accompanying a standardized test that describes the purposes and content of the tests in the battery. Often sample items are available in these manuals. However, this alone is not adequate for proper interpretation of students' test scores. To provide reasonable interpretations of students' performances on standardized tests, the teachers must be very familiar with the actual test being administered. Teachers should be encouraged to obtain a copy of the test battery and carefully review the items. Only when the teachers know exactly what is asked of students can they possibly offer reasonable interpretations of test scores.

Curriculum Evaluation

Teachers' prior knowledge of specific test content raises some interesting issues. Some would say that teachers scrutinizing the content of a standardized test battery will lead to teaching to the test. This is not necessarily a reasonable conclusion. A teacher would surely only be tempted to teach to the test or, worse yet, blatantly cheat if the stakes associated with the test are very high. Given only the three purposes for achievement tests cited previously, there is no reason for a teacher to worry about helping students look especially good on a standardized test. However, it is certainly true that in today's educational environment where accountability is on the minds of so many, the stakes associated with these tests are often quite high indeed. The vast majority of states currently have some sort of mandated testing system. A common part of these mandates is a standardized achievement test. These tests, like many other aspects of education, have become pawns in a political chess game. In most such states, these tests are transformed from evaluation devices to high stakes accountability tools. In many such situations the focus for these tests has shifted completely away from test score interpretations at the student level to interpretations at the school or city level. This is a large departure from the purposes for which these tests are constructed. Given very overt external pressures to "look good," teachers and administrators often feel their curriculum is being dictated to conform to the content of a test battery. This is obviously not a healthy educational environment. In such systems, teachers are not encouraged to examine test content. On the contrary, they are often forbidden to examine the tests. This precludes any interpretation of test scores at the student level or even at the grade group level. It is no wonder that teachers and students question the usefulness of such tests. There are no benefits at the classroom level. Test scores are returned in a vacuum. Teachers can speak only in grossly general terms of the content of the tests, and students see no reinforcement what-soever attached to their efforts.

This is not to imply that standardized tests cannot be reasonably used to assist in the evaluation of school curriculum. A school board, for example, should be interested in its district's performance on a standardized test bat-tery. It is a unique piece of evaluative information. It is, however, just a single piece of a fairly large and complex puzzle of educational achievement. Too often, the importance of such test results is overemphasized by a school board or a local newspaper or community. Given the scope and content of standardized achievement tests, it is unwise to believe that they could serve in isolation as the main piece of a school's evaluation effort.

At the most, these tests can highlight areas that might need to be exam-ined more closely. For example, if a high school typically has scores at the 75th percentile nationally across the tests in a standardized battery but in science the scores have fallen to the 50th percentile for the past several years, there is some reason to investigate the cause of this area of relative weakness. Note that this should be the result of a trend observed over the period of several years and never based on the results of a single test administration.

The ultimate course of action to be taken should not be based solely on the results of the tests. Instead, once the tests have raised a flag of concern, school personnel need to investigate the area in question. Part of this inves-tigation must surely focus on the objectives and content of the standardized tests. If the faculty and administration decide that the test's content is not consistent with their curricular goals, the science test scores should be dis-missed as not relevant. This would obviously call into question why the test was being given at all. Perhaps on review, it is decided that the science curriculum needs revision, new texts, or new laboratory materials. Any such decisions must be based on the judgment of faculty and administration and not on the test scores. The scores must serve only as an indicator. Note again that such interpretations require that teachers be very familiar with the con-tent of the test. This familiarity cannot be gained by an examination of the table of specifications in a test manual. The actual items on the tests must be scrutinized by the teachers.

Teacher Accountability

It should also be noted that, nowhere in the preceding discussion, was mention made of evaluating the performance of individual teachers based on the results of standardized tests. This clearly represents a gross misuse of test scores. The manuals of most achievement batteries offer strong warn-ings against such practice. Consider the following statement from the *Iowa Tests of Educational Development Interpretive Guide for School Administrators* (Feldt & Forsyth, 1993b).

It is not uncommon for teachers to believe they are being judged, personally or as a group, on the basis of test results. It is undeniably true that the quality of teaching influences student achievement, but as noted above, countless other factors also exert an influence. Separating the effects of teaching from all others is virtually impossible. Administrators and others should always remember that the major purpose of the tests is to provide specific information about the needs and abilities of individual students and the student body as a whole. *To use test results to evaluate staff may quickly destroy their value for all purposes.* (p. 96, italics in the original)

It should be obvious from the preceding discussion that the more politicized standardized tests are, the less useful their results will be. One possible method that might be used to relieve some of the accountability pressures often associated with standardized tests is to administer these tests in the fall of the school year. Tests given in the spring clearly have few immediate instructional benefits. The results for these tests are not available until near the end of the school year. Few steps can be taken by teachers to help the current group of students based on their test results. Spring testing carries with it a necessary "backward look" at achievement that invites accountability as a main use for the test scores.

On the other hand, if the test battery is administered in the fall (or mid-year), teachers can typically view the results while they still have a good amount of instructional time remaining with a group of students. Then the focus truly can be student centered.

Standards

Another common and related problem in the interpretation of the results of standardized norm-referenced tests is the confusion between norms and standards. It must be kept in mind that norms represent just a description of average achievement. Norms should not be considered standards or indicators of what constitutes satisfactory achievement. The average achievement in a school typically varies quite a bit from subject to subject. For example, it is conceivable that a school has decided to give much more attention to its science curriculum while at the same time the emphasis placed on skills in using sources of information is minimal. If this school's test scores in subsequent years indicate below average performance in science and above average achievement in using sources of information, the need for improved instruction may still be more serious in using sources than in science.

In evaluating the academic performance of students or groups of students, it is important to consider many factors and not rely solely on test scores of any type. These other factors include the level of aptitude of the students, the nature of the learning environment outside of school, and the scope and sequence of the school's curriculum. Such factors can clearly help explain large differences among students or groups of students. Therefore these factors most likely affect the rank of students or groups of students in comparison to general norms. The quality of instruction is just one determining factor.

The definition of satisfactory performance or an acceptable standard is a subjective decision and must be determined on a student-by-student or school-by-school basis. Each school must decide in terms of its own circumstances and curriculum what should be expected of students. Below average achievement is obviously not necessarily indicative of poor instruction. Many examples of excellent instruction can be found in schools with below average levels of achievement. Of course, it is also true that above average performance is not necessarily cause to celebrate excellence. In most high-achieving schools, there is considerable room for improvement. Once again this discussion reflects one of the dangers associated with standardized norm-referenced tests, the compelling nature of the scores on such tests and the resulting overinterpretation and overemphasis.

Related to this discussion of norms versus standards, many achievement tests are linked to an aptitude test. Indeed an achievement test and an aptitude test are often standardized together for their joint use to enhance the interpretation of pupil performance. Given this scenario, schools can administer both an achievement test and an aptitude test and obtain additional information about their students. Because aptitude is typically viewed as a more stable construct than achievement, schools usually administer an aptitude test far less frequently than an achievement test. For example, many schools administer achievement tests annually but an aptitude test only once or twice to students. The results of aptitude tests from previous years can still be used in conjunction with achievement test scores from the current year to increase the meaningfulness of the achievement test scores.

By considering the scores from these two tests simultaneously, it is possible for schools to interpret achievement test scores more clearly, avoiding some of the pitfalls of confusing norms and standards. If students take both tests, it is possible to identify areas in which achievement might be considered above or below expectation. Given a score on the norm-referenced achievement test, a predicted aptitude test score can be produced, based on the relationship established between these two tests in the standardization sample. Most achievement tests offering this reporting possibility provide information about students, regarding whether performance significantly exceeds or falls short of expectation based on the aptitude test scores.

This can be a powerful interpretive tool, but vigilance against overinterpretation must still be maintained. A discrepancy between performance and predicted performance should not be used to assign stereotypical labels such as underachiever. Nor should such discrepancies be used to evaluate the quality of teaching. Again, this represents just another piece of evaluation information that must be integrated into the total data base used in the assessment of student performance.

Summary

A recurring theme in the preceding discussions has been the warning against using standardized test results as a mechanism for evaluating the quality of instruction. It must be noted, however, that the results of these tests can be used as a partial basis for evaluating instruction. The word *partial* must be heavily emphasized. Clearly, a number of very relevant factors must be considered in the use of standardized tests in the evaluation of instruction. First, these tests are founded on the premise that, within any academic area in a school, certain objectives are held for all students. While these core objectives are crucial parts of the curriculum area, they clearly do not represent its entirety. That is, it must always be kept in mind that standardized tests do not measure the total achievement in any subject or grade. While the objectives measured by these tests usually appear to be essential, they represent only a portion of the desired outcomes of instruction. Thus the results of standardized tests represent necessary but not sufficient information for the evaluation of instructional programs. It is conceivable, although perhaps unlikely, that some schools or classes may perform very well on a standardized achievement battery but still be weak in curriculum areas not included in the battery, such as vocational education, health, music, art, or foreign languages. Standardized tests deal with curriculum areas that are measurable in an objective manner. A number of curriculum areas such as those just listed are not readily measured objectively. These areas cannot be ignored in the evaluation of a school's instructional programs.

It is also necessary to consider that even in those areas measured by standardized tests, local performance is a function of many factors, just one of which is the quality of instruction. The ability of the students, as discussed, is clearly a salient factor. Also important are the quality of the instructional materials and the physical equipment in the school as well as the overall morale in the school.

Perhaps it is most reasonable to summarize these thoughts by noting that *standardized achievement tests must be considered a means to an end and not an end in themselves.* These tests function best and most appropriately to "raise flags." They serve best to draw the attention of faculty to areas of need within a student or group of students. This may involve noting areas in need of remediation within individual students or identifying parts of the entire instructional program most in need of attention. At the student level, these tests can serve as useful guidance tools. Given appropriate emphasis, these tests can enhance teaching and learning. The value of any test not serving this function must be seriously questioned.

USING TEST SCORES

To appropriately integrate the information provided by standardized test scores, a number of questions must be answered. Consider the following very inclusive list adapted from the *Iowa Tests of Basic Skills Manual for School Administrators* (Hieronymus & Hoover, 1986).[1]

Factors to consider in the evaluation of achievement test results include the following.
1. The school's philosophy regarding the development of the skills measured by the tests in the battery.

    a. What relative emphasis is given to the areas assessed in the entire school program?

    b. Is the proportion of time devoted in a school to the areas tested typical of that in the group in which the test was standardized? This is typically a question of how consistent a school's curriculum is with those of most schools nationally as the standardization sample is usually representative of the entire nation.

    c. Is it possible that the achievement profiles of the students in a school be mainly attributable to time allotment or sequence rather than quality of instruction? This brings to mind an experience with a group of elementary teachers. A testing expert was discussing a standardized testing program with a group of elementary teachers in a school system. The testing expert had carefully reviewed the school's achievement test scores over the past several years and had noted a clear and consistent area of weakness among the fourth grade students in the area of map reading. The scores in this area were markedly lower than the other scores for this school. In discussing the results with the teachers, the testing person noted this weakness and asked if there were any obvious reasons for it known to the faculty. The fourth grade teachers informed the testing expert that the low scores were not a matter of concern at all. The achievement test was administered in the fall of the year and most of the map reading skills measured were not taught until the middle of the school year. Note that this judgment depended on the teachers' familiarity with the content of the test. Without this frame of reference, false conclusions would almost certainly be reached relative to quality of the curriculum and instruction. The teachers in this school correctly pointed out that the map reading scores in subsequent years were very consistent with the rest of their students' profiles.

    d. Is a school willing or does a school deem it appropriate to make sacrifices in other areas in the school's program to enhance the areas assessed on the test? Or should the school view their results as satisfactory in light of an enriched curriculum in areas not assessed?

    e. Is the development of the skills measured by the tests in the battery only a function of formal instruction, or has a school effectively developed a coordinated instructional program in all subjects that maintains and nurtures these objectives?

    f. Are students given opportunities to work on real problems requiring the application of the measured skills in settings that are meaningful to each student?
2. Certain administrative factors must also be considered.

[1]It should be noted that similar information can be found in the manuals accompanying most major standardized achievement batteries.

    a. Do teachers deal with such large groups of students that little attention can be given to the individual needs of students?

    b. Are grades and competition overemphasized (at the expense of growth) so that the student who progresses more slowly is continually discouraged.

    c. Are arbitrary standards of achievement established that sacrifice understanding for the sake of short term recall of factual information?

3. Materials available to the students should be considered.

    a. Are adequate materials (books, maps, calculators, special reference materials) readily available for classroom use?

    b. Are students provided with materials appropriate to their levels of understanding and development?

    c. Are students encouraged to read widely, and are a variety of reading materials readily available?

    d. Are teachers provided with adequate materials to offer meaningful remediation and/or enrichment?

4. The outcomes of other evaluation efforts in a school must also be considered.

    a. Are teachers encouraged to follow up the results from an achievement battery with less formal means of more closely examining the areas of weakness in the achievement profile.

    b. Do the achievement test results reinforce the evaluation efforts of teachers? Are the students' results as expected?

    c. What is being done to evaluate the parts of the curriculum not measured by the achievement battery?

    d Are there important objectives measured by the achievement battery that are not emphasized in the school's curriculum?

5. Other factors merit attention in the full evaluation of students' test scores.

    a. Do faculty members understand how responsibilities for achieving the objectives measured by the tests are distributed?

    b. Is there adequate communication within the school to insure continuity and smooth transition of the development of the measured objectives?

    c. What provisions are available for the maintenance of measured objectives?

    d. How are individual differences among students provided for?

    e. Are there particular areas of unexpected strength or weakness?

    f. Do the test scores reflect an overemphasis in certain areas at the expense of others?

    g. Do the test scores suggest a need for revisions in the scope and sequence of the curriculum. Of course, it must be recalled that such decisions would not be based on a single testing. Only a consistent trend in test scores over time could indicate the investigation of such a revision.

    h. Is the motivation or attitudes of students a contributing factor to poorer than expected test performance?

    i. Is the level of familiarity with the particular testing techniques a factor that may be contributing to student performance?

    j. Are the attitudes of teachers, counselors, or administrators an issue in the performance of students?

    k. Are the language characteristics (English as second language) of students a factor to be considered in the evaluation of student achievement?

    l. Is the mobility of the student population a factor to be considered in the evaluation of students' scores?

    m. Is the stability of the school's personnel a contributing factor?

    n. Is community support a factor to be considered in the evaluation of students' level of achievement?

CONCLUSION

This chapter examined the appropriate use and interpretation of standardized norm-referenced achievement tests in the evaluation of educational progress of students in elementary and secondary school. It was argued that such tests can indeed provide unique and valuable bits of evaluative information when kept in the context of the overall set of indicators of academic achievement. These tests provide a means to evaluate the progress of all students in a school, not just the college bound or those in a particular program. Such information is vital to the complete evaluation of a school's academic program. Average ACT or SAT scores certainly provide schools with useful information, but it is information on just a subset of the student body. Evaluation of programs cannot rely on such information alone.

One of the main points in this discussion was the emphasis on the role of the classroom teacher in the testing process. Unless teachers are completely convinced of the usefulness of the tests, the test battery will not yield the information intended. It was also argued that high-stakes testing environments or overuse or overemphasis of test scores will almost certainly harm the evaluation process. An achievement test whose results are of more use to policy makers and administrators than to teachers and students is one whose use should be re-evaluated.

References

Bennett, G. K., Seashore, H. G., & Wesman, A. G. (1992). *Differential aptitude tests*. San Antonio, TX: Psychological Corporation.

Feldt, L. S., & Forsyth, R. A. (1993a). *Iowa tests of educational development*. Iowa City: University of Iowa.

Feldt, L. S., & Forsyth, R. A. (1993b). *Iowa tests of educational development interpretive guide for school administrators*. Iowa City: University of Iowa.

Hieronymus, A. N., & Hoover, H. D. (1986). *Iowa tests of basic skills manual for school administrators*. Iowa City: University of Iowa.

Psychological Corporation. (1993). *Metropolitan achievement tests*. San Antonio, TX: Author.

Assessment of
Classroom Learning

CHAPTER

10

A New Vision of the Nature and Purposes of Assessment in the Mathematics Classroom

FRANK K. LESTER, JR. and DIANA V. LAMBDIN
Indiana University, Bloomington

RONALD V. PRESTON
East Carolina University, Greenville, North Carolina

INTRODUCTION

In a fascinating book about the growth of numeracy in early American society, Cohen (1982) suggests that the mathematics curriculum in early American schools was restricted largely to the study of numbers and the ability to manipulate them according to prespecified rules, which were typically acquired by rote procedures. The view of mathematics suggested by this emphasis was of a static collection of discrete, decontextualized facts, skills, and procedures to be mastered by citizens who would work in an industrial and agricultural economy [National Research Council (NRC), 1989, p. 11]. Moreover, a long history, dating back at least as far as the beginning of the testing movement in America, regards mathematics as a gatekeeper for colleges, businesses, and government agencies—those who cannot attain some predetermined cutoff score on a mathematics aptitude or achievement test are often deemed unfit, thereby effectively closing doors rather than opening them (Haney, Madaus, & Lyons, 1993).

As our view of the nature and purpose of school mathematics has changed, so too has our view of the nature and purpose of assessment. The

Alternative Assessment 51

(i)   How many cubes are needed to build
      this tower?

(ii) How many cubes are needed to build
      a tower like this, but 12 cubes high?

(iii) Explain how you worked out your
      answer to part (ii).

(iv) How would you calculate the num-
      ber of cubes needed for a tower
      n cubes high?

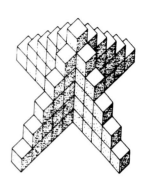

FIGURE 1

Alternative assessment task 1: The skeleton tower problem (reprinted with
permission from Swan, 1984).

following "alternative" assessment tasks, which have appeared in recent
mathematics assessment documents, illustrate just how radically different
contemporary mathematics assessments have become.

The first task, the skeleton tower problem (Figure 1), developed at the
Shell Centre of the University of Nottingham (England), is an example of a
nonroutine task used to assess a wide range of important problem-solving
strategies and thinking processes, among them the ability to attempt simple
cases, organize problem-solving efforts in a systematic manner, spot patterns, find general rules, and explain or justify one's solution. Furthermore,
the task is designed to be easily understood and allow students with a wide
range of abilities and experiences to make progress. Part i can typically be
solved by most students, whereas part iv challenges all but the most capable.
Scoring schemes used for this task focus on understanding the problem,
organizing a systematic attack on it, explaining the results obtained, and
generalizing in words or algebraically (Swan, 1993).

The walkabout stereos activity (Figure 2) was designed by the Educational
Testing Service (ETS) as a part of its effort to develop a "program for inte-

Alternative Assessment 52

The students in Ms. Lee's class are making a consumer guide for products that are important

to young people, like video games, running shoes, and walkabout stereos (portable

radio/cassette players with headsets). The first item the students want to rate is walkabout

stereos. They need your help to develop a rating system.

FIGURE 2

Alternative assessment task 2: The walkabout stereos activity (reprinted
with permission from Educational Testing Service, 1994, p. 10).

grating learning and performance assessment for [middle school] mathematics" (ETS, 1994, inside front cover). The intent of this activity—and all other tasks in the "Packets" program—is to engage students in an extended project of about a week's duration in a manner that links assessment closely with teaching and learning. For the walkabout stereos activity, students are first asked to read a (simulated) newspaper article about how teenagers spend their money. This article serves as a stimulus for introducing the students to the "focus project," that is, the walkabout stereos activity, in which students are to design a consumer rating scale for evaluating and ranking walkabout stereo devices. Students work in small groups to decide how to plan their work on the project, what additional information they need (e.g., various data sources, such as *Consumer Reports*, are available), and how they intend to get the information. Then they carry out their plan, and often on a different day, they prepare written drafts of their solutions. On still another day, all of the groups in the class discuss their solution approaches. This discussion typically leads to each group revising its draft. Once revisions are completed, students are then encouraged to work on an exploratory activity and an application activity. The exploratory activity is related to determining how the total score for a rating system will change when the weight given to an individual part of the total score changes. The application is closely related to the focus project but can typically be completed in a single class session. Teachers are provided various "assessment tools to help [them] capture information about both the process and the products of . . . students' performance, highlighting students' strengths and weaknesses to help guide instruction" (ETS, 1994, p. 6).

The newspaper polls activity (Figure 3) illustrates two important features of mathematics assessment: (1) it should be an integral part of the learning

---

Alternative Assessment 53

The *Evening Star* is interested in a proposal for a new city tax. The story shown below is about a poll the *Star* conducted using a random sample of 100 voters on each of two successive Mondays.

(The story says that the first week the newspaper found 57% in favor of the tax, while in the second week it found 59% in favor. The headline for its story read: "Support Grows for Tax Hike.")

Write a letter to the editor about this story.

FIGURE 3

Alternative assessment task 3: The newspaper polls activity (adapted from National Research Council, 1989, p. 11).

process [Lesh & Lamon, 1992b; National Council of Teachers of Mathematics (NCTM), 1995], and (2) it should provide opportunities for students to "express mathematical ideas by speaking, writing, demonstrating, and depicting them visually" (NCTM, 1989, p. 214).

Just what sort of task is the newspaper polls activity? Is it an assessment task or an instructional task? The NCTM's (1995) second assessment standard, "learning" (discussed later), asserts that any worthwhile assessment task should be designed in a way that promotes students' mathematics learning. A conclusion that can be drawn from this notion is that little, if any, distinction should be made between activities designed for instructional purposes and those designed for assessment purposes. Lesh and Lamon (1992b) concur with this position by pointing out that all classroom activities should "contribute to both learning and assessment" (p. 18). By engaging in writing a letter to the editor about this newspaper story, students are demonstrating not only the extent to which they are able to communicate their knowledge of certain mathematical concepts—in this case random sampling and standard error—but also consolidating their understanding of these concepts and connecting their knowledge of these concepts to a real-world situation. Thus, in light of the new vision of school mathematics assessment, the newspaper polls activity can, and should, be regarded as both an assessment task and an instructional task.

The newspaper polls activity satisfies the second important feature of good assessment tasks in two ways. First, it requires students to evaluate written information containing important mathematical ideas—students must make sense of the newspaper story, identify the relevant and important information, and decide on the position they want to take concerning the story. Second, they must prepare a coherent, convincing letter in which they demonstrate their understanding of the mathematical ideas contained in the story.

Finally, the newspaper polls activity highlights an important different between traditional and contemporary mathematics assessment practices: instead of direct, decontextualized questions about mathematical concepts, students are given tasks that are contextually rich, thereby requiring them to connect their mathematical understandings to real-world situations.

The fourth task, the biking to school problem (Figure 4), like the second and third tasks, shows how assessment tasks can challenge students to demonstrate their understanding of important mathematical ideas—in this case, reading and interpreting graphs—when the mathematics is embedded in a realistic setting. Furthermore, and unlike the preceding tasks, it requires students to express their understanding in two directions: matching graphical representations to verbal descriptions of realistic actions and creating a realistic story to match a graph. This task, perhaps more directly than any of the others, demonstrates the emphasis being placed in today's vision of the school mathematics curriculum on students being able to connect their mathematical knowledge to the everyday world.

Alternative Assessment 54

Match each student's story with the graph that most closely represents it. Also, for the graph at the left, write a story for Jose that matches that graph.

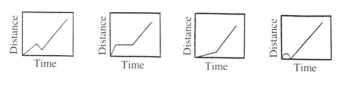

HANK SAID:

I had only just left home when I realized that I had forgotten my gym clothes. So I went back home and then I had to hurry so I wouldn't be late for school.

MINA SAID:

As always I began to ride pretty slowly, but after a while I had to speed up to keep from being late.

RUTH SAID:

I went on my motorbike this morning -- real fast! But, I ran out of gas and had to run the rest of the way. I got to school just in time.

JOSE SAID:

FIGURE 4

Alternative assessment task 4: The biking to school problem (adapted from Terwel, 1990, p. 234).

The foregoing assessment tasks illustrate that school mathematics assessment has changed to ensure consistency with the goals of school mathematics curricula and instruction. This chapter is intended as an introduction to the nature and extent of the changes that have taken place over the past 10 years or so and is organized around six themes: the changing nature of school mathematics and mathematics assessment, forces driving the changes in assessment, promising classroom assessment techniques, building a theory of mathematics assessment, research findings, and ideas for debate.

THE CHANGING NATURE OF SCHOOL MATHEMATICS AND MATHEMATICS ASSESSMENT[1]

School mathematics has witnessed wide-ranging changes recently in both curricula and teaching methods. At the same time, these changes have been accompanied by calls for changes in both classroom and high-stakes assess-

[1]The material in this section is adapted, with permission of the publisher, from Lambdin (in press).

ment. In fact, it is safe to say that, with respect to assessment, mathematics education has experienced a "complete paradigm shift that involves new decision makers, new decision-making issues, new sources of assessment information and new understandings about the nature of mathematics, mathematics instruction, and mathematics learning and problem solving" (Lesh, Lamon, Lester, & Behr, 1992, p. 380). This shift has centered around four issues: (1) changing assumptions about the nature of mathematics, how it is learned, and what it means to teach it; (2) adapting to technology and innovation; (3) clarifying the purposes of assessment; and (4) establishing standards for judging the quality of assessment.

Changing Assumptions about Mathematics, Learning, and Teaching

Mathematics educators are moving from a view of mathematics as a fixed and unchanging collection of facts and skills to an emphasis on the importance in mathematics learning of conjecturing, communicating, problem solving, and logical reasoning. These changes are related to a trend away from viewing learning as human information processing and toward a complex process of model building. Concomitantly, mathematics teaching is moving away from lecture, explanation, and practice of decontextualized procedures toward helping students construct their own knowledge through investigation of realistic mathematical problems. These three key shifts in

TABLE I

Shifts in Thinking about the Nature of Mathematics, Mathematics Learning, and Mathematics Teaching

Assumptions about	Shift from the view that	To the view that
The nature of mathematics	Mathematics is nothing more than a list of mechanistic condition/action rules	Mathematics is a science of patterns
The nature of mathematics learning	Mathematics learning is a cumulative process of gradually adding, deleting, and debugging facts, rules, and skills	Humans are model builders, theory builders, and system builders; they construct their knowledge to describe, explain, create, modify, adapt, predict, and control complex systems in the world (real or possible)
The nature of mathematics teaching	Teaching involves demonstrating, monitoring student activity, and correcting errors	Teaching is an act of enabling students to construct and explore complex systems

thinking (summarized in Table 1) have prompted recent changes in mathematics assessment (cf. Lesh *et al.*, 1992, pp. 381–383).

Adapting to Technology and Innovation

New technologies have resulted in significant changes in the real-world problem-solving situations for which mathematics is useful and in the types of knowledge and abilities that are important today. As a result, technology is exerting a major influence on assessment as well. For example, the availability of handheld calculators and notebook computers with graphing and symbol manipulation capabilities enables students to think differently, not just faster. Teachers must first determine what types of skills and understandings prepare students for using technology optimally and then identify ways to assess the new types of problem solving made possible by technology.

Clarifying the Purposes of Assessment

Related to changing views of mathematics, learning, and teaching are changing views about the purposes of assessment. In general, "the aim of educational assessment is to produce information to assist in educational decision making, where the decision makers include administrators, policy makers, the public, parents, teachers, and students themselves" (Lesh & Lamon, 1992b, p. 4).

Traditionally, for many mathematics teachers, debates about student assessment have been restricted to discussions of grading practices. However, the NCTM has attempted to expand this view by listing grading (or, as they term it *evaluating students' achievement*) as just one of four purposes of assessment (NCTM, 1995). The other purposes they identify include monitoring students' progress, making instructional decisions, and evaluating programs.

Lester and Lambdin Kroll (1991) identified a somewhat different list of purposes. In addition to monitoring student progress and making instructional decisions, they included making decisions about the classroom climate (i.e., an atmosphere that is conducive to active involvement by students and that fosters the development of positive attitudes and beliefs) and communicating to students what is important.

Proponents of changes in assessment use qualitative as well as quantitative data, and focus more on describing student progress than on categorizing individuals or predicting future success. There is a move away from short-answer or multiple-choice tests to increased use of alternatives such as performance assessments, open-ended questions, group projects, portfolios, journal writing, oral reports, and observations. High-stakes assessment is also undergoing significant changes.

Historically, because tests were designed to compare students, efforts were made to standardize testing conditions by placing strict constraints on the time, resources, and tools students could use. By contrast, the newest trend is elimination of as many artificial constraints as possible to create "authentic" assessments or "performance" assessments, although considerable debate continues over how to identify authentic tasks, how to characterize high-quality performance, and how to ensure valid uses of assessment findings.

Establishing Standards for Judging the Quality of Assessment

Along with new assessments comes the need for explicit criteria by which to judge their appropriateness and effectiveness. Thus, the NCTM published *Assessment Standards for School Mathematics* (1995), a document that offers six "standards" (i.e., statements of what should be valued in mathematics assessments) for judging assessments: mathematics, learning, equity, openness, inferences, and coherence. Each of these standards raises important assessment issues.

Standard 1. Mathematics

Few would argue with the assertion that useful mathematics assessments must focus on important mathematics. Yet the trend toward broader conceptions of mathematics and mathematical abilities raises serious questions about the appropriateness of the mathematics reflected in most traditional tests since that mathematics is generally far removed from the mathematics actually used in real-world problem solving. Nevertheless, there is still much debate over how to define important mathematics and who should be responsible for doing so.

Standard 2. Learning

New views of assessment call for tasks that are embedded in the curriculum, the notion being that assessment should be an integral part of the learning process rather than an interruption of it. This raises the issue of who should be responsible for the development, implementation, and interpretation of student assessments. Traditionally, both standardized and classroom tests were designed, using a psychometric model, to be as objective as possible. By contrast, the alternative assessment movement affords teachers much more responsibility and subjectivity in the assessment process. It assumes that teachers know their students best because teachers have multiple, diverse opportunities for examining student work performed under various conditions and presented in a variety of modes. When teachers have more responsibility for assessment, assessment can truly become almost seamless with instruction (Lesh & Lamon, 1992a, 1992b).

Standard 3. Equity and Opportunity

Ideally, assessments should give every student optimal opportunity to demonstrate mathematical power. In practice, however, traditional standardized tests have sometimes been biased against students of particular backgrounds, socioeconomic classes, ethnic groups, or gender (Pullin, 1993). Equity becomes even more of an issue when assessment results are used to label students or deny them access to courses, programs, or jobs. More teacher responsibility means more pressure on teachers to be evenhanded and unbiased in their judgment. Ironically, the trend toward more complex and realistic assessment tasks and more elaborated written responses can raise serious equity concerns, since reading comprehension, writing ability, and familiarity with contexts may confound results for certain groups (Lane, 1993). Similarly, efforts to establish national or state performance goals are often met with resistance because of fears that their use in high-stakes assessment cannot help but result in inequities. Therefore, it is unclear whether recent trends will actually result in increased or decreased equity in mathematics assessment.

Standard 4. Openness

Testing has traditionally been quite a secretive process, in that test questions and answers were carefully guarded and criteria for judging performance were generally set behind the scenes by unidentified authorities. By contrast, many today believe that students are best served by open and dynamic assessment—assessment where expectations and scoring procedures are openly discussed and jointly negotiated. Traditionally, mathematics courses and tests have often been used as filters, to screen students for entry into programs, courses, and jobs; this helps to explain why test questions were kept secret. However, many argue that assessments today should be designed more to describe student proficiencies and deficiencies, to help in making instructional decisions, or to gauge the overall status of the educational system than to categorize individual students. For such purposes, it is argued, criteria can certainly be made more open.

Standard 5. Inferences

Changes in assessment have resulted in new ways of thinking about reliability and validity as they apply to mathematics assessment. For example, when assessment is embedded within instruction, it becomes unreasonable to expect a standard notion of reliability to apply (that a student's achievement on similar tasks at different points in time should be similar), since it is actually expected that students will learn throughout the assessment. Similarly, new forms of assessment prompt a re-examination of traditional notions of validity. Many argue that it is more appropriate to judge validity by examining the inferences made from an assessment than to view it as an inherent characteristic of the assessment itself. Nevertheless, it is difficult to know how new types of assessment (e.g., student projects or portfolios) can be used for decision making without either collapsing them into a single score (thereby losing all their conceptual richness) or leaving them in their raw, unsimplified, difficult-to-interpret form.

Standard 6. Coherence

The coherence standard emphasizes the importance of ensuring that each assessment is appropriate for the purposes for which it is used. As noted earlier, assessment data can be used for monitoring student progress, making instructional decisions, evaluating student achievement, or program evaluation. However, the types of data appropriate for each purpose may be very different. Policy makers and assessment experts often disagree on this issue: the former may have multiple agendas in mind and expect that they can all be accomplished by using a single assessment, while the latter warn against using an assessment for purposes for which it was never intended.

FORCES DRIVING THE CHANGE IN ASSESSMENT PRACTICES

Several forces have contributed to or constrained the assessment reform in school mathematics. These forces include an emphasis on curricula emphasizing problem solving, the school mathematics reform movement, instructional change, pressure imposed by high-stakes assessment, alternative assessment as a means to curricular and instructional reform, the importance of assessment, and reliability and validity issues. Each of these forces is described in the following paragraphs.

Emphasis on Problem Solving

Even before the current mathematics education reform movement began, a focus on problem solving, as the theme of mathematics education in the 1980s, had pointed out deficiencies in the assessment practices being used. Emphasis on the process of solving problems, the thinking that goes into the process, the understanding that some problems have multiple solutions, and the realization that many problems have multiple paths to a solution or even a set of solutions raised the issue of the limitations of assessment practices based only on number of correct answers. By examining key references such as Charles, Lester, and O'Daffer (1987), Charles and Silver (1989),

Kulm (1990a), and Webb (1992), we can gain a sense of the impact that an emphasis on problem solving has on assessment. Each of these references points out that a change in emphasis from relatively low-level knowledge and skill to problem solving and other forms of higher-order thinking requires a concomitant change in assessment practices.

Of particular concern among those who have worked in the area of mathematical problem solving was how to assess student work in a way that gave meaningful information to the teacher and student about the student's learning. Various "holistic" schemes have been proposed for scoring students' problem-solving efforts, each requiring the teacher to do much more than simply score a student's work as right or wrong (Bell, Burkhardt, & Swan, 1992a; Charles et al., 1987; Kulm, 1994; Lester & Lambdin Kroll, 1991; Stenmark, 1991).

Charles et al. (1987) also suggest methods for assessing student progress in problem solving in ways that might not be translated into a score. Included in the techniques they suggest are observation (with comment cards, checklists, or rating scales), informal questioning or structured interviews, and student self-assessment (including attitude inventories). Lester and Lambdin Kroll (1990) have developed a model for mathematical problem solving and assessment that includes the affective domain, performance considerations, and an analysis of the problem that is posed. The affective component of their model considers students' interest in mathematics, willingness to take risks, perseverance, motivation, and tolerance of ambiguity. The performance component is divided into two parts. The first part contains the cognitive processes: understanding the problem, selecting strategies, implementing strategies, stating answers in terms of the data, evaluating the reasonableness of the answers, and monitoring progress. The correct answer is relegated to the second part of this component. The analysis of the problem involves an assessment of the problem type, mathematics content involved, data sources to be used, and so on. Clearly, when compared with an ambitious model of problem solving and the assessment thereof as just outlined, a final answer provides very little information to a teacher who is emphasizing problem solving in the classroom.

Other work in the assessment of mathematical problem solving includes stressing the important information that can be gained from incorrect answers (Marshall, 1989), changing standardized tests so that teachers do not feel pressured to stress lower-level skills (Silver & Kilpatrick, 1989), and allowing students to use manipulatives, calculators, and computers when being assessed (Kulm, 1990b). Collis, Romberg, and Jurdak (1986) point out the difficulty in preparing valid problem-solving items for assessment purposes but also demonstrate how they produced such items using their SOLO (structure of the observed learning outcome) taxonomy. Their superitems consisted of a problem with four questions stemming from it, ranging in difficulty level from the obvious to the use of abstract general principles.

Frederiksen (1984) points out the importance of giving students real-life problems that are "ill-structured" or "fuzzy" (i.e., problems that are not clearly stated or lack sufficient information) in an effort to develop generalized processes for approaching problems. In short, problem-solving research has had a major impact in pointing out the need to reform assessment practices.

The Reform Movement in Mathematics Education

In 1989, two documents were published that have had a profound effect on mathematics education: *Everybody Counts* (NRC, 1989) and *Curriculum and Evaluation Standards for School Mathematics* (NCTM, 1989). Both documents stress mathematics for all students, as well as changes that are needed in curriculum, instruction, and assessment of student learning.

The NRC's document, *Everybody Counts*, had this to say about assessment:

> To assess development of a student's mathematical power, a teacher needs to use a mixture of means: essays, homework, projects, short answers, quizzes, blackboard work, journals, oral interviews, and group projects. . . . We must ensure that tests measure what is of value, not just what is easy to test. If we want students to investigate, explore, and discover, assessment must not measure just mimicry mathematics. (NRC, 1989, p. 70)

The report asserts that current tests too often (1) stress lower-level thinking, (2) become ends in themselves rather than means to promote learning, (3) reinforce a narrow image of mathematics as a subject restricted unique right answers and lockstep procedures for obtaining those answers, and (4) inhibit student learning by relying on unreasonably short time allowances.

The NCTM's *Curriculum and Evaluation Standards for School Mathematics*, commonly referred to as the *Standards*, urges the community of mathematics educators to give decreased attention to assessment that simply counts the number of correct answers, focuses on specific and isolated skills, uses only written tests, and excludes the use of calculators and computers. Instead, focus should be placed on assessment practices that are aligned with the curriculum and instructional methods, use multiple sources of information, and employ appropriate measures for the type of information sought. In addition, these practices should emphasize the extent to which students are growing with respect to their ability to apply and integrate mathematical knowledge, solve problems, communicate mathematically, use mathematical forms of reasoning. Furthermore, the *Standards* stresses the importance of the development of healthy dispositions toward mathematics (e.g., confidence in using mathematics to solve problems and willingness to persevere in mathematical tasks). In sum, the *Standards* insists that, for types of assessment to be aligned with such goals, they will have to be significantly different from traditional tests, quizzes, and homework.

Pressure from High-Stakes Assessment

Two types of pressure could come from the information provided by the various commonly administered district-, state-, and national-level assessments. One type of pressure arises when such assessment points out deficiencies in student achievement that teachers may not be assessing properly in their classrooms. This kind of information includes results from the National Assessment of Educational Progress, which routinely point out difficulties students have with items that stress something other than computation (e.g., see Center for the Study of Testing, Evaluation, and Educational Policy, 1992; Dossey, Mullis, & Jones, 1993; Dossey, Mullis, Lindquist, & Chambers, 1988; Mullis, Dossey, Owen, & Phillips, 1991). Therefore, teachers need assessment tools for skills other than computation and ability to work lower-order exercises. The second kind of pressure that high-stakes assessment places on classroom assessment is that the content and method of high stakes testing often becomes a focal point of the curriculum. As a result of these two pressures, some farsighted educators have seen high-stakes assessment as providing the opportunity to effect change in instruction and assessment at the local level by, for instance, having the state assessment consist of portfolios, as has been done in Vermont (Dietel, 1992). This leads to the next force, where some educators are advocating alternative assessment as a vehicle for curricular and instructional change.

Alternative Assessment as a Driving Force in Curricular Reform

The contention of mathematics educators and those who study testing is that standardized tests influence the instructional practices and emphases of mathematics teachers and not always in a positive way. This phenomenon has been described variously as teaching to the test, "only that which will be tested will be taught" (Kulm, 1990b, p. 72) and, by Bell et al. (1992a), as WYTIWYG (what you test is what you get). This influence would not necessarily be negative if standardized tests reflected the important curricular goals on which mathematics educators agree. However, these tests too often have reflected what is easily tested, which is not necessarily the same as what is considered important (Silver, 1992). In the current reform movement, even some individuals who had previously decried the practice of teaching to the test are seeking to take advantage of WYTIWYG. They want to change the standardized tests and other forms of high-stakes assessment to include open-ended tasks and authentic problem-solving situations in an attempt to force curriculum and instruction to align with these new forms of assessment.

Instructional Change

As actual teacher practices change, alignment requires that the techniques used for assessment change as well (NCTM, 1989). Two examples of such change are the use of technology and cooperative group work, both of which are becoming major parts of some teachers' practices. (Other examples could also be used, but these two have perhaps the most dramatic implications for classroom assessment practices.)

The extent to which technology has changed mathematics instruction and learning is open to debate. On the one hand, evidence indicates that, even though handheld calculators are inexpensive and plentiful, they are still not being widely or effectively used in mathematics classrooms (Kouba & Swafford, 1989). On the other hand, recommendations from the NCTM (1989, 1995) and the NRC (1989) strongly encourage the use of technology in both the teaching and assessing of students. However, only a few recommendations have been made concerning how assessments, particularly tests, should change to reflect the availability of calculators, computers, and other forms of technology.

Harvey (1992) recognizes three types of tests involving the use of calculators: (1) calculator-passive tests, where students are allowed to use calculators on tests designed without calculators in mind; (2) calculator-neutral tests, where students may use calculators, but no items on the test require calculators; and (3) calculator-based tests, where students are allowed to use calculators on a test where at least a portion of it requires calculator use. Of these three approaches, the third is the one that makes good use of the technology and the one that forces educators to change the tests or other assessments used. Calculator-based tests are likely to become more prevalent in the future as more curricula are produced that assume calculators are available to students and integrated into activities (Senk, 1992).

Many teachers are now using cooperative group work for problem solving or extended mathematics projects. Unfortunately, many of these same teachers do not assess the results of students' work on these types of activities because of the difficulties involved (Lambdin Kroll, Masingila, & Mau, 1992). Lambdin Kroll et al. suggest a scheme for grading student group work in solving problems; the scheme includes attention to assessing both group and individual achievement. Other instructional changes, such as emphases on extended projects and performance tasks, also require the use of assessments other than traditional paper–pencil tests.

The Changing View of the Importance of Assessment

A significant force in encouraging the use of alternative assessment techniques is the perception among many mathematics educators that assessment is a natural, indispensable part of the instructional process. This view is captured in NCTM Standard 2 on learning, which calls for assessment tasks to be embedded within the curriculum (NCTM, 1995). Moreover, Stiggins (1988) has found that teachers spend 20–30% of their professional time dealing with issues of assessment. Even with this amount of attention, he has observed significant low-quality assessment being made. Stiggins asserts that low-quality assessment "robs them [students] of an accurate sense of their capabilities and deprives them of a sense of control over their academic well-being" (p. 366). Any aspect of instruction (including assessment) that occupies so much time and carries so much responsibility needs to be examined carefully to see if it is accomplishing the desired goals. The goals of assessment include directing student learning, selecting students, grading students, motivating students, and communicating with students and other concerned parties (Webb & Welsch, 1993). Perhaps at least as important is that assessment influences the instructional decisions that teachers make. Educators should seek to have the best information possible available to them (from the best possible assessment techniques) when making instructional decisions that can have far-reaching consequences.

Reliability and Validity Issues

The reliability and validity of alternative assessment techniques, such as open-ended tasks, are very much a concern, whether they are used in individual classrooms or on standardized tests (Badger, Cooney, & Konold, 1993). Thus, the questionable reliability of tasks associated with alternative assessment could be viewed as a force opposing the reform of assessment. However, Webb (1992) has argued that this problem can be overcome by the aggregation of many different kinds of assessment information. He states that "determining a student's abilities in a variety of situations is more important than obtaining a single score on a highly reliable test" (p. 668). Badger et al. admit that there are validity problems in some forms of alternative assessment but state that "a problem solving test with an open-ended format should have greater validity for real-life problems than a series of multiple-choice items requiring the selection of a single answer" (p. 264). Clearly, reliability and validity are important and controversial issues in alternative assessment at the present. Some experts see these constructs as constraints, but others see use of alternative forms of assessment as a means of increasing reliability and validity. Reliability and validity are further discussed in the constraint section that follows.

Forces Constraining the Use of Alternative Assessment Techniques

The kinds of alternative assessments being recommended at this time are, for the most part, untested by mainstream teachers of mathematics. The effects of such assessment, then, are relatively unknown, although most of the literature assumes them to be beneficial. However, some educators have urged caution in the implementation of these new techniques for a variety of reasons, including time, monetary considerations, knowledge needed to use such assessment, difficulty in creating authentic tasks, validity and reliability concerns, and the potential bias of certain alternative techniques.

Time Constraints

Many of the suggested forms of alternative assessment seem to carry with them the element of increased teacher time. Included in this list are portfolios (Dietel, 1992), journals (Bagley & Gallenberger, 1992), and performance tasks (Wise, 1993). The amount of time involved is viewed variously in the literature. Dietel suggests that portfolios lead to important changes in the classroom (the sacrifice is worth it); Bagley and Gallenberger have found ways of limiting the number of journal entries to a manageable number (compromises can be made); and Wise encourages a weighing of the benefits of performance tasks with the time factor (sometimes the extra time spent may not be worth the additional value received).

Monetary Constraints

Wise (1993) cautions that "alternative measures are expensive to develop and even more expensive to administer and score" (p. 14). In particular, the cost of administrating and scoring large-scale performance tests and portfolios at the state and national level is immense. When the expense of these large-scale assessments comes under attack, the potential benefits of such assessments have to be weighed carefully against the financial outlay.

Knowledge Constraints

A potential problem in using alternative assessment that may not be getting enough attention is the limited knowledge many teachers have concerning assessment techniques in general and, more specifically, alternative techniques. Schafer and Lissitz (1987) conducted a study of teacher education programs and found that most programs (55% for secondary teachers) did not require a course in educational measurement and that many important assessment topics are never mentioned in any course (e.g., general methods or educational psychology) in the undergraduate program. Some of these omissions in mathematics education programs included assessment to guide instruction (not mentioned in 14% of the programs), assessment to determine placement (34%), and assessment to assign grades (13%). In addition, Schafer and Lissitz found that the emphasis in the measurement courses that did exist was on the development of paper–pencil tests and interpreting standardized test scores and statistics. Gullickson (1986) found that most of the teachers (over 90%) in his study do take a measurement course at some time (e.g., graduate work) but almost none of the teachers surveyed reported that the course helped them in the classroom. In particular, teachers disagreed significantly with professors of measurement classes on the priority that should be given to topics such as statistics, nontest evaluation activities, and formative and summative evaluation.

Teachers' knowledge of alternative methods of assessment and how to interpret them may be even more problematic. In the Connected Mathematics Project (CMP), a middle grades mathematics curriculum development project sponsored by the National Science Foundation, some teachers struggle with how to assess student writing and responses to open-ended tasks, apparently getting so caught up in the amount of writing that they do not notice mathematical misunderstanding or errors. There is also the issue of how often to assign certain kinds of activities that are new to mathematics teachers, such as journal writing. As an example of a teacher who probably does not feel completely comfortable with his knowledge of how to assess, consider the following quote:

> If we were doing portfolios . . . you'd just take whatever they did during the quarter and put it in there, and at the end you could kind of go through it with somebody and say, "Well, look, now here's what we did." . . . That's another thing that I've been kind of weak on, and I think is part of assessment, is looking at what kids have produced during math class. (Graue & Smith, 1993, p. 11)

Difficulty in Creating Authentic Tasks

The use of performance assessments has grown in appeal to teachers and researchers in many disciplines. However, the development of good performance tasks has proven a very challenging task. In a recent survey, Perlman (1993) found that very few large school districts are devoting any effort toward developing these tasks. Also, of the few districts that are developing performance assessments, almost all of the emphasis is on creating writing tasks. Perlman is uncertain of the reasons for this lack of development of tasks and whether or not this means that these kinds of assessment are not being used in classrooms.

Reliability and Validity Concerns

As mentioned earlier, some mathematics educators are suggesting that it may be possible to force instruction to change in a positive direction by changing the nature of standardized tests. However, along with the promise of reforming instruction through the use of alternative assessment techniques, some problems must be faced. Silver (1992) points out that, although alternative techniques aligned with curricular goals may be desirable and valid, it is difficult to obtain high reliability scores due to interrater variability, the potential for many different kinds of student responses on open-ended tasks, and that only a small number of tasks can be done by each student. Also, Lesh et al. (1992) suggest that the emphasis placed on assessment tasks having high reliability and validity may be misplaced:

> The alternative assessment movement has often focused on using tests as a leverage point for curriculum reform, and has tended to give relatively little attention to issues such as fairness and reliability in scoring, the usefulness and credibility of results (for decision makers who are not close to the students or instructional settings that are being assessed), and the scope and representativeness of the constructs that are measured (when attention shifts beyond the quality of isolated tasks to the quality of collections of tasks). (p. 380)

Potential for Bias

Clarkson (1992) warns that multiple-choice standardized tests tend to be biased in favor of males, but worries that stressing communication skills in mathematics may not eliminate bias, it may just shift the bias in favor of females. This communication bias appears to be even more problematic, however, with non-native speakers in pseudo-monolingual countries such as the United States, Australia, and England.

PROMISING CLASSROOM ASSESSMENT TECHNIQUES

The literature is replete with articles exhorting mathematics educators to change their assessment techniques. These range from book chapters suggesting a fundamental philosophical shift in teachers' testing practices to articles illustrating how to use journal writing in a middle school classroom or suggesting that assessment change be used to drive curricular change.

Included in the literature are a number of alternative techniques for assessing mathematics learning. Some mentioned most prominently are portfolios, holistic scoring, cooperative group work, informal observations, open-ended tasks, interviews, technology-based assessment, extended projects, concept maps, and journals. Other ideas include allowing students to revise their work and assessing improvement over time. Also receiving considerable attention are methods for scoring these assessments. Three techniques that have received considerable attention are analytic, focused holistic, and general impression scoring. Each of these methods of alternative assessment is discussed briefly in the following paragraphs. At the conclusion of the section, we provide a brief discussion of the merits of developing a theoretical framework for mathematics assessment.

Portfolios

Portfolios are more than simply a diverse body of finished work. They can include "biographies of works, a range of works, and reflections" (Wolf, 1989, p. 37). Dietel (1992), while admitting that portfolios are a major time and resource burden on teachers, writes that the instructional and motivational benefits derived from them can lead to important changes in classrooms. In Vermont, teachers are spending more time on developing problem-solving skills and the understanding of patterns and relationships in mathematics, which were the state goals when the statewide portfolios were instituted there. Knight (1992) reports that, because she used portfolios in her algebra class, she is now using more varied kinds of instruction (e.g., more problem solving and long-term situational problems) so that students have a variety of items to chose from in creating their portfolio. Knight views portfolios as giving insight into students' maturity, self-esteem, writing ability, and their ability to evaluate their own and other students' work. Lambdin and Walker (1994) point out that, although classroom teachers find portfolio assessment difficult and time consuming, the benefits to students can be tremendous. In particular, students often become much more reflective about their own mathematical performance when they assume responsibility for preparing a portfolio of their work.

Assessing Cooperative Group Work

As mentioned earlier, one of the forces driving alternative assessment is that it should be aligned with instruction. As more and more teachers use group work in their instruction, it is important that this form of student work should be assessed (Hiebert, 1992). Lambdin Kroll et al. (1992) have suggested a method for balancing group assessment of problem solving with individual accountability. Their scheme for grading group efforts features a 15-point analytic scoring scale that includes points for understanding the problem, planning a solution, and getting an answer. The 10-point individual portion of the assessment includes a series of follow-up questions designed to ensure that individual students do not simply rely on the efforts of the group.

Leach (1992) has developed a scheme for assessing small-group discussions of problem-solving strategies based on a technique used by some of her social studies colleagues. This approach involves scoring students based on their input toward developing strategies for solving a nonroutine problem in front of the rest of the class. Points are given for determining a strategy, correctly applying a property, moving the discussion along, and so on. Points are deducted for making an incorrect application or monopolizing the discussion. These points are tallied on a checklist that Leach has designed and converted into a grade at the end of the discussion. At the end of the group discussion, the entire class is invited to make comments on alternative strategies for solving the problem. Interest in this discussion is high because the problem is one of the homework problems for the next day and because students seem to enjoy communicating about mathematics. Leach's scheme can be used to assess the quality of cooperative group work, students' mathematical dispositions, their use of alternate strategies in solving problems, and their ability to communicate mathematical ideas.

Teachers' Informal Observations of Students

Observation no doubt has been used by teachers as an assessment tool for as long as there have been teachers. However, many teachers have relegated the important information gained from observation to second-class status behind information that can be gained from a test. Perhaps part of the problem is that observations often are not done in a systematic or disciplined manner, with the idea of gaining information to make instructional decisions or decisions about student progress. Webb (1992) notes that

> Systematic observations of students doing mathematics as they work on a project supported by their responses to probing questions are more authentic indicators of their ability to do mathematics than a test score compiled by totaling the number of correct item responses. (p. 670)

Interviews

Structured interviews are usually conducted with one or two students at a time, with an agenda that might consist of presenting a problem or task, allowing the student(s) to work on it, and then asking probing questions (planned in advance) about the problem (Lester & Lambdin Kroll, 1990). Typical methods of recording data from the interview include use of a rating scale, a checklist, or a brief written report. Burns (1993) has developed a series of videotapes and study guides that provide a particularly useful resource on how to conduct structured student interviews. The popularity of this resource attests to the value of interviews as a source of information about students' mathematical performances.

Open-Ended and Extended Tasks

Tasks that are open-ended allow for assessment of many more facets of doing mathematics than do multiple-choice items. Students are given the opportunity to make numerous conjectures about a situation and explain their thinking or their choice of the model they used to solve the problem

(Silver & Kilpatrick, 1989). Open-ended tasks take more time to complete but reward reflection and communication as opposed to memory and speed.

When students are questioned about the time that it should take to work a math problem, the answer is typically five minutes or less. For Bell et al. (1992a), however, an extended project may last for weeks, making it necessary that the task itself provide a valid learning experience as well as a means of assessment. These authors suggest that some real-world tasks commonly undertaken by the teacher, such as planning a field trip, can be considered by the students in the class as an extended project with multiple paths and solutions. Possible steps for such a project could include (1) looking at trips through simulations, (2) making rough plans, (3) making detailed plans, and (4) going on the trip and evaluating the experience (Bell, Burkhardt, & Swan, 1992b). The walkabout stereos problem discussed at the beginning of this chapter is an example of an extended project suited for use with middle grades students (ETS, 1994).

Concept Maps

White (1992) has suggested that concept mapping can be used with students to show how they see relationships between key concepts or terms within a body of knowledge. He maintains that this activity encourages students to further reflect on the relationships of such terms and to develop a more integrated understanding as opposed to learning isolated facts. Although concept maps have been used as a learning aid and assessment tool in science classrooms for several years (Novak & Gowin, 1984), only recently have they begun to be used in mathematics classrooms. Indications from the few studies that have looked at the usefulness of concept maps suggest that (1) concept maps can assist students in effectively organizing their knowledge of a topic, (2) students come to understand how they learn through the use of concept maps, (3) teachers can gain valuable information about the relationships among concepts that students have already constructed, and (4) concept maps can help teachers identify (mis)conceptions that do not come to the surface when other assessment techniques are used (dos Santos, 1993; Hasemann, 1989; Mansfield & Happs, 1989)

Journals

Journal writing is one of the least used forms of alternative assessment. This may be due, at least in part, to the time-consuming qualities of writing and assessing that writing, the fact that some students say they like mathematics expressly because it has not traditionally required writing, and the very problem of how to assess the students' entries. However, Bagley and Gallenberger (1992) state that "Writing is more than just a means of expressing what we think; it is a means of knowing what we think—a means of shaping, clarifying, and discovering our ideas" (p. 660). These authors use journal writing several times a week. The entries are written during class, they take only about five minutes at a time, and the authors have developed a method of assessing them so that only one-fifth of the journals are graded at any given time. Each entry is made according to a six-question form (e.g., state today's goal; I'm still confused about————) that includes a special topic question that relates to that day's activities. Waywood (1992) uses math journals on a daily basis and offers the following rationale for journal writing: (1) to formulate, clarify, and relate concepts; (2) to appreciate how mathematics speaks about the world; and (3) to think mathematically.

Revision of Student Work

Revision of student work has been suggested in the discussion of more than one type of mathematical activity. Wolf, Bixby, Glenn, and Gardner (1991) see portfolios as collections of student work that is "anything but archival" (p. 58) and that offer students the opportunity to rework and return to earlier work. Not only do students learn to revise their work, they also learn to be critical of it for the purpose of making it better. In the Connected Mathematics Project (mentioned earlier), students have the option of revising their work on partner quizzes after their teacher has given them feedback. Such classroom practices communicate to students not only the idea that chances to improve poor or average work should be given and that even good work can be improved, but also that what students should focus on is not the current product but the improvements being made.

Assessing Improvement over Time

Although averaging students scores over a grading period has long been standard procedure for figuring grades, it actually may not make sense for grades earned early in a course to carry equal weight with those at the end (because later grades may be more reflective of cumulative learning). In response to this notion, Esty and Teppo (1992) have developed a plan for grading based on progressive improvement. In their university course on the language and structure of mathematics offered to non-mathematics majors—a course that seeks to counter the traditional emphasis on "instant mastery" in mathematics (p. 618)—homework, quizzes, and tests in the early stages of the course were scored but not recorded. Feedback was given to students concerning what improvements needed to be made in their early work, but only in the last one-third of the course were grades assigned. In a qualitative study of student interviews about the course, student attitudes about the course were high and there was no significant abuse of the fact that grades were not assigned early in the course.

Scoring Rubrics

Along with use of alternative techniques for assessing student work comes the responsibility of scoring at least some of this work. The California Assessment Program was among the earliest and most ambitious efforts to develop scoring schemes and rubrics for use in high-stakes mathematics assessment (California State Department of Education, 1985; Pandey, 1992). Among the most prominent attempts to develop useful schemes for classroom assessment are those of Charles et al. (1987), Lajoie, Lawless, Lavigne, and Munsie (1993), Lester and Lambdin Kroll (1990), and Stenmark (1991). Lester and Lambdin Kroll (1990) discuss three different schemes—analytic, focused holistic, and general impression scoring—as viable alternatives for assigning scores to students' written work, depending on the type of work and the time factor involved.

Analytic Scoring

This method of scoring is the most time consuming of the three. The processes and result of problem solving can be broken into categories such as understanding the problem, planning a solution, and getting an answer (Lester & Lambdin Kroll, 1990). Each category is assigned a number of points with gradations of that total designated for different strategies employed. For instance two points could be given for a fully workable plan, one point for a partially correct plan, and no points for no plan at all. An even more ambitious scheme is one where a project is assessed on six criteria, ranging from the quality of the question posed to how creative the project was (Lajoie et al., 1993). In the Lajoie et al. rubric, each of six categories receives either "above average" or "average" as its mark. The advantage to the student of analytic scoring is that it provides feedback on what areas in the problem-solving process need attention.

Focused Holistic Scoring

This technique calls for an analysis of the students' whole response as a unit. One approach is to read through the students' papers, separating them into three stacks according to some scheme such as *outstanding, acceptable*, and *missed the point* (Carstens, 1993). From there the papers can be scored more precisely, where the outstanding papers may receive four points; the acceptable ones, three points; and the ones that missed the point no, one, or two points according to some predetermined set of criteria. Arter (1993) argues that, while focused holistic scoring is efficient for large-scale assessment, it is not useful for informing students of areas in need of improvement because students may get the same score for entirely differently reasons.

General Impression Scoring

This method of scoring is the quickest but least informative for the students. The teacher works with no written criteria but simply uses past experience to gauge the quality of the responses. The advantage of this method is that it allows quick feedback to be given to the students on how they performed on a particular problem or task. A teacher would not want to rely entirely on this type of rubric but would use it when time is short and other, more focused scores are available to balance with the results of this assessment (Lester & Lambdin Kroll, 1990).

THEORY OR FRAMEWORK BUILDING

In addition to the many specific ideas being suggested as possible alternatives to traditional mathematics assessment, some researchers and scholars are concerned about developing a theory or framework for mathematics assessment. Webb (1992) maintains that a theory of mathematics assessment separate from general assessment theory needs to be developed, since "the nature of mathematics itself and pedagogical approaches for teaching mathematics warrant consideration of specific assessment techniques in the area of mathematics" (p. 662). As key components to developing such a theory, Webb recommends a critical examination of current assessment practices, the purposes of assessment, the content to be assessed, the issues of validity and reliability, and the problem of how to analyze assessment to gain maximum information.

Goldin (1992) has also argued for a framework for mathematics assessment. Part of his perspective is that he views as faulty the simple strategy of changing the nature of assessment (particularly high-stakes tests) so that curriculum and instruction will fall in line. Instead, he suggests a framework based on a cognitive model. This model would reflect the teacher's prior understanding of what was being assessed and the importance of processes as well as content in the assessment.

Cain and Kenney (1992) take a somewhat different approach. They see parallels between the mathematics assessment reform as outlined by the NCTM *Standards* and the general assessment reform advocated in the "Standards for Teacher Competence in Educational Assessment of Students," which was produced by the American Federation of Teachers, the National Council of Measurement in Education, and the National Education Association. Both sets of standards can be subdivided into three categories: (1) choosing and developing appropriate assessment methods, (2) obtaining and using assessment results, and (3) communicating assessment information. They contend that validity depends on the consistency of the assessment techniques with the course objectives, regardless of the content being assessed.

RESEARCH RESULTS

Unfortunately, woefully few investigations, to date, have examined alternative assessment efforts in mathematics classrooms. However, some research is beginning to be reported, ranging in perspective from studies of assessment techniques in classrooms to attempts to achieve reliability and validity information on alternative assessment tasks. Studies have concentrated on three areas: teacher change, students, and effectiveness of alternative assessment techniques.

Teacher Change

Kulm (1994) has studied the alternative assessment techniques developed and used by teachers in Texas, who were a part of a graduate seminar on alternative assessment that required them to develop assessment tasks for use in their classrooms. The outcomes of these practices were observed and videotaped for analysis. Prior to beginning the research, Kulm developed a model describing the impact that knowledge of alternative assessment techniques has on teacher knowledge and classroom teaching processes. Kulm saw this knowledge and use of alternative assessment methods (problem solving; extended and complex problems; communication via oral, written, and graphic approaches; and work in individual and group situations) as enhancing teachers' knowledge of students' cognition and of effective teaching.

Kulm concluded that, as a result of developing alternative assessment techniques, the teachers also changed their teaching practices. In particular, the use of teaching strategies that have been found to promote higher-order thinking in students increased. Also, the teachers claimed that, as a result of their involvement in the project, they saw improvements in their ability to use questioning techniques that recognize student errors, to develop scoring rubrics, to use open-ended tasks to evaluate problem solving ability, to look for alternative paths to solutions, and to be able to follow the thought processes of students. Kulm concluded that his model appeared to be helpful and that in-service work on alternative assessment can be effective in assisting teachers use methods that enhance higher-order thinking.

Graue and Smith (1993) studied four sixth grade teachers of mathematics from the perspective that classroom assessment should be more like instruction than measurement. These teachers were using a reformed mathematics curriculum and the researchers wanted to examine the interweaving of assessment and instruction in their classrooms. Descriptions of the teachers' thoughts and struggles with assessment are provided in the paper. Graue and Smith concluded that teaching by using a reformed mathematics curriculum can provide the impetus for a change in assessment practice. Each of the four teachers studied took a different path to alter his or her assessment techniques, but change was made in each case. In addition, the teachers

viewed these changes in a positive light, although they often struggled with
how to assess their students.

Student Attitudes and Cognitions

Telese (1993) investigated students' attitudes about mathematics and their
perceptions about mathematics instruction before and after experiencing a
mathematics class where alternative assessment techniques were gradually
introduced over the course of a school year. He found significant improvement in attitudes across grade levels (grades 4 through 11), gender, and
ethnicity. Students noticed a significant change in the number of nontraditional teaching activities in their classrooms from the beginning to the end
of the year, which suggested that their teachers had worked to align their
instruction with the alternative assessments. Interestingly, males scored
higher on attitude toward mathematics than females, but females were more
perceptive of the increase in nontraditional teaching activities employed by
the teachers using alternative types of assessment. Another interesting finding was that high school students showed a greater increase in positive
attitudes toward mathematics than students at any other grade level (elementary or middle school). This ran counter to an assumption Telese had
made going into the study. He had hypothesized that high school students,
having received more traditional instruction in their educational careers,
would be more resistant to change. He concluded from his research that "an
implication of the findings may be that the use of alternative assessment
techniques creates a non-threatening atmosphere which may encourage all
students to participate and to use higher-order thinking skills in mathematical discourse" (Telese, 1993, p. 22).

Finally, in a study of how students responded to the open-ended mathematics question on the California Assessment Program Test, students who
had experienced instruction from teachers with a high level of commitment
to alternative assessment techniques scored significantly higher ($p < .01$)
than other students (Williams, 1991). The other major finding in her study,
however, was that most of the teachers studied evidenced only moderate
commitment to alternative assessment.

Assessment Techniques

For alternative assessment techniques to be worthwhile they must help inform teachers of what students know and what kinds of instructional decisions to make. McMullen (1993) researched the effects that studying and
working with alternative assessment had on the use of these strategies in
the classroom and the use of teaching approaches that enhance higher-order
mathematics learning. From her analysis of quantitative observation data of
teachers involved in a seminar on alternative assessment she determined

that the teachers improved significantly in (1) emphasis on meaning and understanding, (2) encouragement of student autonomy and persistence, and (3) direct teaching of higher-order cognitive strategies. However, her results were not entirely encouraging. In particular, McMullen found that, in using alternative assessment and trying to use higher-order thinking skills in teaching, the teachers discovered a lack of their own understanding of concepts ("I spent all of my time in college learning how to make formulas work" [p. 20]). Also, there was an actual decrease on the item *mathematics is useful and makes sense* over the course of the year. Teachers did not provide many opportunities for students to plan, invent, design mathematical ideas, or work on projects. These negative findings do not appear to be related to the assessment techniques being employed but rather to the educational background and experience of the teachers and the conditions (e.g., large class size) under which they must teach.

ISSUES FOR DEBATE

What is driving the current reform movement in mathematics assessment? Lesh et al. (1992) cogently argue that calls for change are fundamentally intertwined with a whole constellation of new conceptions about the nature of mathematics, problem solving, teaching, and learning. To make their point, they quote Mislevy, concerning the psychological foundations of traditional test theory:

> The view of human learning that underlies standard test theory is not compatible with the view rapidly emerging from cognitive and educational psychology. (Mislevy, Yamamoto, & Anacker, 1992, p. 293)
> The test theory that dominates educational measurement today might be described as the application of 20th century statistics to 19th century psychology. (Mislevy, 1991, p. 234)

Recent reports from organizations such as the National Council of Teachers of Mathematics, the Mathematics Association of America, the American Association for the Advancement of Science, the National Research Council, the National Academy of Sciences, and the Mathematical Sciences Education Board reflect similar views—that traditional mathematics tests are generally inappropriate for our new information age and that new forms of assessment are required to support and interact with the curriculum reforms required by new visions of mathematics, teaching, and learning (Romberg, Zarinnia, & Williams, 1989).

   On the other hand, it can also be argued that many of today's apparently very innovative changes in mathematics curriculum and assessment actually are not really new at all. Lambdin (1993) illustrates this point with a look at assessment recommendations over the past half-century. Many of the assessment ideas being highly touted today have actually been recommended for decades. Yet, for the most part, education has continued to rely on traditional tests as a prominent source of assessment data. Why? Several reasons seem plausible: (1) data from nontraditional assessments (such as observations, interviews, written essays) are often more difficult to collect than conventional test scores; (2) once collected, nontest data are generally more difficult to organize, summarize, and report than test scores; (3) work with nontest data is generally more time consuming, particularly when many students are involved; and (4) familiarity with traditional forms of assessment tends to color expectations of students, parents, supervisors, and the public at large, retarding or even impeding the adoption of innovative methods.

An important question arises. If ideas similar to those discussed in this chapter have been recommended for decades, yet rarely implemented, what hope is there for widespread change in the foreseeable future? Actually, there are several reasons for optimism.

First, there is the well-recognized national furor over the inability of students to think for themselves, to solve problems, to demonstrate number sense, and to reason creatively (NRC, 1989), a furor that is bringing many long-ignored goals of mathematics education to the attention of the public and education authorities. As skills such as estimation, open-ended problem solving, and written expression have begun to be more widely valued by those in authority, they have also begun to receive greater emphasis in external assessment and, as a result, in curriculum, instruction, and classroom assessment.

A second reason for optimism is that the same technology changing the face of mathematics instruction may also help make alternative assessment more feasible. Computers, graphing calculators, videocassettes, videodiscs, and camcorders can be used in innovative ways for both instruction and assessment. Data management and word-processing programs make it almost as efficient to organize notes about students as it used to be to enter numeric grades into a grade book. Certainly, it is much easier to have students work with realistic mathematical situations when computers can provide simulations or when every student can be provided ready access to a powerful calculator.

Yet another reason for optimism is that the mathematics education reform movement has enjoyed broad-based support in recent years. For example, the committees that drafted the NCTM standards documents included a carefully chosen mix of mathematicians, educators, administrators, policy analysts, and classroom teachers. Those documents have been widely cited and exerted much more influence on the educational community than recommendations published in decades past in journal articles or book chapters.

Finally, and perhaps most important, change may actually take hold this time because so many *teachers* have ownership in the reform movement. History shows that changes ordained from above are almost always doomed to failure, whereas grassroots efforts can be successful if there is a large enough groundswell to support them. There is a new sense of interest in and commitment to changes in assessment. At the national level, standardized tests are being modified to include attention to higher-order thinking. At the state level, new assessment instruments are being adopted and new priorities endorsed. Perhaps most important, classroom teachers are involved in many of these changes—in drafting and critiquing policy recommendations; in organizing workshops to explain new ideas to parents, administrators, and peers; and in experimenting with using new methods with their own students. As we approach the new millennium, the mathematics education community is formulating a new vision of mathematics education. Changes in assessment are an integral part of this new vision.

References

Arter, J. (1993, April). *Designing scoring rubrics for performance assessments: The heart of the matter.* Paper presented at the annual meeting of the American Educational Research Association, Atlanta, GA.

Badger, E., Cooney, T. J., & Konold, T. (1993). Evaluation issues. In P. S. Wilson (Ed.), *Research ideas for the classroom: High school mathematics* (pp. 260–276). New York: Macmillan.

Bagley, T., & Gallenberger, C. (1992). Assessing students' dispositions: Using journals to improve students' performance. *Mathematics Teacher, 85,* 660–663.

Bell, A., Burkhardt, H., & Swan, M. (1992a). Balanced assessment of mathematical performance. In R. Lesh & S. J. Lamon (Eds.), *Assessment of authentic performance in school mathematics* (pp. 119–144). Washington, DC: American Association for the Advancement of Science.

Bell, A., Burkhardt, H., & Swan, M. (1992b). Assessment of extended tasks. In R. Lesh & S. J. Lamon (Eds.), *Assessment of authentic performance in school mathematics* (pp. 145–193). Washington, DC: American Association for the Advancement of Science.

Burns, M. (1993). *Mathematics: Assessing understanding* (Series of three videotapes and accompanying teacher discussion guides for grades 2/3, 5 and 7). White Plains, NY: Cuisenaire Co. of America.

Cain, R. W., & Kenney, P. A., (1992). A joint vision for classroom assessment. *Mathematics Teacher, 85,* 612–615.

California State Department of Education (1985). *Mathematics framework for California public schools: Kindergarten through grade 12.* Sacramento: Author.

Carstens, L. J. (1993, April). *From the bottom up: A sourcebook of scoring rubrics designed by teachers.* Paper presented at the annual meeting of the American Educational Research Association, Atlanta, GA.

Center for the Study of Testing, Evaluation, and Educational Policy. (1992, October). *The influence of testing on teaching math and science in grades 4–12.* Chestnut Hill, MA: Boston College.

Charles, R., Lester, F., & O'Daffer, P. (1987). *How to evaluate progress in problem solving.* Reston, VA: National Council of Teachers of Mathematics.

Charles, R. I., & Silver, E. A. (Eds.). (1989). *The teaching and assessing of mathematical problem solving.* Hillsdale, NJ: Erlbaum.

Clarkson, P. C. (1992). Evaluation—Some other perspectives. In T. A. Romberg (Ed.), *Mathematics assessment and evaluation* (pp. 285–300). Albany: State University of New York Press.

Cohen, P. C. (1982). *A calculating people: The spread of numeracy in early America.* Chicago: University of Chicago Press.

Collis, K. F., Romberg, T. A., & Jurdak, M. E. (1986). A technique for assessing mathematical problem-solving ability. *Journal for Research in Mathematics Education*, 17, 206–221.

Dietel, R. (1992 Fall). Portfolios as worthwhile burdens? *The CRESST Line*, pp. 3–5.

dos Santos, V. M. P. (1993). *Metacognitive awareness of prospective elementary teachers in a mathematics content course and a look at their knowledge, beliefs, and metacognitive awareness about fractions.* Unpublished doctoral dissertation, Indiana University, Bloomington.

Dossey, J. A., Mullis, I. V. S., & Jones, C. O. (1993). *Can students do mathematical problem solving?: Results for constructed-response questions in NAEP's 1992 mathematics assessment.* Washington, DC: U.S. Department of Education, Office of Educational Research and Improvement.

Dossey, J. A., Mullis, I. V. S., Lindquist, M. M., & Chambers, D. L. (1988). *The mathematics report card. Are we measuring up?* Princeton, NJ: Educational Testing Service.

Educational Testing Service (ETS). (1994). *The "Packets" program for middle school mathematics.* Princeton, NJ: Author.

Esty, W. W., & Teppo, A. R. (1992). Grade assignment based on progressive improvement. *Mathematics Teacher*, 85, 616–618.

Frederiksen, N. (1984). Implications of cognitive theory for instruction in problem solving. *Review of Educational Research*, 54, 363–407.

Goldin, G. A. (1992). Toward an assessment framework for school mathematics. In R. Lesh & S. Lamon (Eds.), *Assessment of authentic performance in school mathematics* (pp. 63–88). Washington, DC: American Association for the Advancement of Science.

Graue, M. E., & Smith, S. Z. (1993, April). *Conceptualizing assessment from an instructional perspective.* Paper presented at the annual meeting of the American Educational Research Association, Atlanta, GA.

Gullickson, A. R. (1986). Teacher education and teacher-perceived needs in educational measurement and evaluation. *Journal of Educational Measurement*, 23, 347–354.

Haney, W. M., Madaus, G. F., & Lyons, R. (1993). *The fractured marketplace for standardized testing.* Boston: Kluwer Academic Publishers.

Harvey, J. G. (1992). Mathematics testing with calculators: Ransoming the hostages. In T. Romberg (Ed.), *Mathematics assessment and evaluation* (pp. 139–168). Albany: State University of New York Press.

Hasemann, K. (1989). Children's individuality in solving fraction problems. In G. Vergnaud, J. Rogalski, & M. Artique (Eds.), *Proceedings of the 13th International Conference for the Psychology of Mathematics Education: Vol. 2. Individual contributions* (pp. 67–74). Paris, France: G. R. Didactique CNRS–Paris V, Laboratoire, Psydee Paris.

Hiebert, J. (1992). Reflection and communication: Cognitive considerations in school mathematics reform. *International Journal of Educational Research*, 17, 439–456.

Knight, P. (1992). How I use portfolios in mathematics. *Educational Leadership*, 49(8), 71–72.

Kouba, V. L., & Swafford, J. O. (1989). Calculators. In M. M. Lindquist, (Ed.), *Results from the fourth mathematics assessment of the National Assessment of Educational Progress* (pp. 94–105). Reston, VA: National Council of Teachers of Mathematics.

Kulm, G. (Ed.). (1990a). *Assessing higher order thinking in mathematics.* Washington, DC: American Association for the Advancement of Science.

Kulm, G. (1990b). New directions for mathematics assessment. In G. Kulm (Ed.), *Assessing higher order thinking in mathematics* (pp. 71–78). Washington, DC: American Association for the Advancement of Science.

Kulm, G. (1994). *Mathematics assessment: What works in the classroom.* San Francisco: Jossey-Bass.

Lajoie, S. P., Lawless, J., Lavigne, N. C., & Munsie, S. (1993, April). *New ways to measure skills of problem solving, reasoning, connectedness and communication.* Paper presented at the annual meeting of the American Educational Research Association, Atlanta, GA.

Lambdin, D. V. (1993). The NCTM's evaluation standards: Recycled ideas whose time has come? In N. L. Webb (Ed.), *Assessment in the mathematics classroom* (1993 yearbook of the National

Council of Teachers of Mathematics, pp. 7–16). Reston, VA: National Council of Teachers of Mathematics.

Lambdin, D. V. (in press). Trends and issues in the assessment of student achievement. In L. S. Grinstein & S. I. Lipsey (Eds.), *Mathematics education: An encyclopedia*. New York: Garland Publishing.

Lambdin, D. V. & Walker, V. L. (1994). Planning for classroom portfolio assessment. *Arithmetic Teacher, 41*, 318–324.

Lambdin Kroll, D. L., Masingila, J. O., & Mau, S. T. (1992). Grading cooperative problem solving. *Mathematics Teacher, 85*, 619–627.

Lane, S. (1993). The conceptual framework for the development of a mathematics performance assessment instrument. *Educational Measurement: Issues and Practice, 12*(2), 16–23.

Leach, E. L. (1992). An alternative form of evaluation that complies with NCTM's Standards. *Mathematics Teacher, 85*, 628–632.

Lesh, R., & Lamon, S. J. (1992a). Preface. In R. Lesh & S. J. Lamon (Eds.), *Assessment of authentic performance in school mathematics* (pp. v–vi). Washington, DC: American Association for the Advancement of Science.

Lesh, R., & Lamon, S. J. (1992b). Trends, goals, and priorities in mathematics assessment. In R. Lesh & S. J. Lamon (Eds.), *Assessment of authentic performance in school mathematics* (pp. 3–15). Washington, DC: American Association for the Advancement of Science.

Lesh, R., Lamon, S. J., Lester, F., & Behr, M. (1992). Future directions for mathematics assessment. In R. Lesh & S. J. Lamon (Eds.), *Assessment of authentic performance in school mathematics* (pp. 379–425). Washington, DC: American Association for the Advancement of Science.

Lester, F. K., & Lambdin Kroll, D. (1990). Assessing student growth in mathematical problem solving. In G. Kulm (Ed.), *Assessing higher order thinking in mathematics* (pp. 53–70). Washington, DC: American Association for the Advancement of Science.

Lester, F. K., & Lambdin Kroll, D. (1991). Assessment in the classroom: A new vision. *Mathematics Teacher, 84*(4), 276–284.

Mansfield, H., & Happs, J. (1989). Using concept maps to explore students' understanding in geometry. In G. Vergnaud, J. Rogalski, & M. Artique (Eds.), *Proceedings of the 13th International Conference for the Psychology of Mathematics Education: Vol. 2. Individual contributions* (pp. 250–257). Paris, France: G. R. Didactique CNRS–Paris V, Laboratoire, Psydee Paris.

Marshall, S. P. (1989). Assessing problem solving: A short-term remedy and a long-term solution. In R. Charles & E. Silver (Eds.), *The teaching and assessing of mathematical problem solving* (pp. 159–177). Hillsdale, NJ: Erlbaum.

McMullen, B. G. (1993, April). *Quantitative analysis of effects in the classrooms.* Paper presented at the annual meeting of the American Educational Research Association, Atlanta, GA (ED358116).

Mislevy, R. J. (1991). A framework for studying differences between multiple choice and free-response test items. In R. E. Bennett & W. C. Ward (Eds.), *Construction vs. choice in cognitive measurement: Issues in constructed response, performance testing, and portfolio assessment* (pp. 228–247). Hillsdale, NJ: Erlbaum.

Mislevy, R. J., Yamamoto, K., & Anacker, S. (1992). Toward a test theory for assessing student understanding. In R. Lesh & S. J. Lamon (Eds.), *Assessment of authentic performance in school mathematics* (pp. 293–318). Washington, DC: American Association for the Advancement of Science.

Mullis, I. V. S., Dossey, J. A., Owen, E. H., & Phillips, G. W. (1991). *The state of mathematics achievement: NAEP's 1990 assessment of the nation and the trial assessment of the states.* Washington, DC: U.S. Department of Education, Office of Educational Research and Improvement.

National Council of Teachers of Mathematics (NCTM) (1989). *Curriculum and evaluation standards for school mathematics.* Reston, VA: The Council.

National Council of Teachers of Mathematics (NCTM). (1995). *Assessment standards for school mathematics.* Reston, VA: The Council.

National Research Council (NRC) (1989). *Everybody counts: A report to the nation on the future of mathematics education.* Washington, DC: National Academy Press.

Novak, J. D., & Gowin, D. B. (1984). *Learning how to learn.* New York: Cambridge University Press.

Pandey, T. (1992). Test development profile of a state-mandated large-scale assessment instrument in mathematics. In T. A. Romberg (Ed.), *Mathematics assessment and evaluation: Imperatives for mathematics educators* (pp. 100–127). Buffalo: State University of New York Press.

Perlman, C. (1993, April). *Quantifying quality: Results of the* NATD *performance assessment survey.* Paper presented at the annual meeting of the American Educational Research Association, Atlanta, GA.

Pullin, D. C. (1993). Legal and ethical issues in mathematics assessment. In Mathematical Sciences Education Board (Ed.), *Measuring what counts* (pp. 201–223). Washington, DC: National Academy Press.

Romberg, T. A., Zarinnia, E. A., & Williams, S. R. (1989). *The influence of mandated testing on mathematics instruction: Grade 8 teachers' perceptions.* Madison, WI: National Center for Research in Mathematical Science Education, University of Wisconsin.

Schafer, W. D., & Lissitz, R. W. (1987). Measurement training for school personnel: Recommendations and reality. *Journal of Teacher Education, 23*(3), 57–63.

Senk, S. L. (1992). Assessing students' learning in courses using graphics tools: A preliminary research agenda. In T. Romberg (Ed.), *Mathematics assessment and evaluation* (pp. 128–138). Albany: State University of New York Press.

Silver, E. A. (1992). Assessment and mathematics education reform in the United States. *International Journal of Educational Research, 17,* 489–502.

Silver, E. A., & Kilpatrick, J. (1989). Testing mathematical problem solving. In R. Charles & E. Silver (Eds.), *Teaching and assessing mathematical problem solving* (pp. 178–186). Hillsdale, NJ: Erlbaum.

Stenmark, J. K. (Ed.). (1991). *Mathematics assessment: Myths, models, good questions, and practical suggestions.* Reston, VA: National Council of Teachers of Mathematics.

Stiggins, R. J. (1988). Revitalizing classroom assessment: The highest instructional priority. *Phi Delta Kappan, 69,* 363–368.

Swan, M. (Ed.). (1984). *Problems with patterns and numbers: An examination module for secondary schools.* Manchester, England: University of Nottingham, and Joint Matriculation Board, Shell Centre for Mathematical Education.

Swan, M. (1993). Assessing a wider range of students' abilities. In N. L. Webb (Ed.), *Assessment in the mathematics classroom* (1993 yearbook of the National Council of Teachers of Mathematics, pp. 26–39). Reston, VA: National Council of Teachers of Mathematics.

Telese, J. A. (1993, April). *Effects of alternative assessment from the student's view.* Paper presented at the annual meeting of the American Educational Research Association, Atlanta, GA.

Terwel, J. (1990). Real maths in cooperative groups in secondary education. In N. Davidson (Ed.), *Cooperative learning in mathematics: A handbook for teachers* (pp. 228–264). Menlo Park, CA: Addison-Wesley.

Waywood, A. (1992). History and rationale for student mathematics journals: A school perspective. In T. Romberg (Ed.), *Mathematics assessment and evaluation* (pp. 312–316). Albany: State University of New York Press.

Webb, N. (1992). Assessment of students' knowledge of mathematics: Steps toward a theory. In D. Grouws (Ed.), *Handbook of research on mathematics teaching and learning* (pp. 661–683). New York: Macmillan.

Webb, N., & Welsch, C. (1993). Assessment and evaluation for middle grades. In D. T. Owens (Ed.), *Research ideas for the classroom: Middle grades mathematics* (pp. 299–316). New York: Macmillan.

White, R. T. (1992). Implications of recent research on learning for curriculum and assessment. *Journal of Curriculum Studies, 24,* 153–164.

Williams, S. S. (1991). The relationship of commitment to assessment of teachers to student performance on the alternative assessment open-response mathematics question from the California Assessment Program (CAP) Test. *Dissertation Abstracts International, 52,* AAC0571274.

Wise, L. L. (1993, April). *Scoring rubrics for performance tests: Lessons learned from job performance assessment in the military.* Paper presented at the annual meeting of the American Educational Research Association, Atlanta, GA.

Wolf, D. P. (1989). Portfolio assessment: Sampling student work. *Educational Leadership, 46*(7), 35–39.

Wolf, D., Bixby, J., Glenn, J., & Gardner, H. (1991). To use their minds well: Investigating new forms of student assessment. In G. Grant (Ed.), *Review of research in education,* (Vol. 17, pp. 31–74). Washington, DC: American Educational Research Association.

CHAPTER

11

Elementary Social Studies: Instruments, Activities, and Standards

JANET ALLEMAN and JERE BROPHY
Michigan State University

INTRODUCTION

This chapter focuses on assessment of social studies in the elementary class-room. It includes sections on a brief history of assessment in social studies, the present, a broader view of assessment and evaluation; context for social studies assessment; principles for planning and implementing activities with an eye toward assessment; authentic assessment; portfolios; and social studies standards, links to classroom assessment. Before concluding, it of-fers a set of guiding principles.

The authors will briefly summarize the history of assessment and its pos-ture in the classroom, highlight instruments that have been designed to measure elements of the social studies curriculum, and trace the shift from a rather relaxed approach to current efforts to make assessment an integral part of the social studies program. The authors' position is that assessment should become so well integrated that it becomes a part of instruction. To illustrate what this means in practice, we draw upon our previous research that established a theoretical position regarding instructional activities and a set of guiding principles for planning and implementing them.

According to proponents of authentic measures, the planning and imple-mentation of activities designated for assessment should incorporate tasks that extend beyond students' certifying levels of competence. These tasks,

Handbook of Classroom Assessment

labeled *authentic* or *performance based*, are designed to assess students' achievement on the basis of life applications. A section of the chapter will address this form of assessment, using goals-driven examples to illustrate it. Authentic assessment is not new to those who regularly ask students to perform tasks that apply outside the classroom setting. However, formalizing these well-established practices will enhance a teacher's assessment plan.

Another section of the chapter addresses the multifaceted assignment that subsumes more than one type of activity and production and that extends over a period of time. A set of questions is offered for teachers to consider in using portfolios as a part of the social studies curriculum. Venues for students to use in explaining the work represented in their portfolios also are described, along with a set of guidelines for implementation.

The final section addresses social studies standards and their potential influence at the classroom level. Standards can serve as another filter for judging social studies curricula and as a beacon to guide local planning. The chapter concludes with a set of guiding principles developed by the authors for creating, monitoring, and implementing powerful social studies assessment practices.

The authors' intentions are that, as a result of reviewing this chapter, the reader will (1) appreciate the current status of assessment in elementary social studies, (2) realize its importance in creating a solid social studies program, (3) acquire a set of guiding principles for designing assessment activities, (4) consider social studies standards as a tool for guiding the development of an assessment plan or judging the current one to ensure an integrated social science, behavioral science, and humanities approach for achieving academic and civic competence in the classroom; and (5) embrace assessment as a viable part of the curriculum and instruction process.

BRIEF HISTORY OF ASSESSMENT IN SOCIAL STUDIES

While assessment is now considered to go far beyond testing, testing has always had a place in social studies teaching, because evaluation is considered an integral part of curriculum and instruction and because students must be graded for report card purposes. There has also been a mind set that, if an area of learning is important, it must be tested, although traditionally this has been applied mostly to the basic skills subjects. Until fairly recently, social studies tests were not seen as especially important or controversial.

After summarizing what was then known about evaluation in social studies, Dana Kurfman (1982) concluded that teacher-made tests predominated over norm-referenced tests and over tests that came with curriculum materials; that objective tests were used more commonly than essay tests (especially with low-ability students); and that items concentrated on knowledge and skills, with only slight consideration given to affective outcomes. Kurfman also claimed that teachers were not very sophisticated about evaluation, did not engage in it very much, and were not very inventive in their approaches when they did.

One of the most comprehensive sources for helping teachers, evaluation specialists, district coordinators, and social studies supervisors in locating and selecting instruments to evaluate various aspects of K–12 social studies programs is the *Social Studies Evaluation Sourcebook*, which was published almost 20 years ago by the Social Science Education Consortium (Superka, 1978). Instruments described in the sourcebook include general social studies achievement tests, specific knowledge tests in the social science disciplines, and critical thinking skills tests. Instrument analyses are also provided in areas of student attitudes, interpersonal skills, self-concept, personality, values clarification, moral development, and classroom climate.

More recent publications that identify and describe social studies specialty area tests include the 10th and 11th mental measurement yearbooks and supplement (Conoley & Impara, 1994; Conoley & Kramer, 1989; Kramer & Conoley, 1994). Among the tests included are Basic Economics Test; Dimensions of Self-Concept; and Children's Inventory of Self-Esteem.

The 291 evaluation instruments described in the sourcebook and the more recent collections found in yearbooks represent a range of measurement devices that social studies educators can use. These instruments often are incorporated into research initiatives but are rarely used at the classroom level because they are costly in time, trouble, and money. Usually they are not comprehensive enough to reflect the values underlying schools' social studies programs, and districts often are not prepared to use the results to make big changes in their social studies curricula. The individual instruments represent narrow pieces of those curricula and are most helpful when a particular element of social studies needs attention.

Social studies is also a part of a number of national testing programs. The National Assessments of Educational Progress (NAEP) included an assessment of history and literature in 1986. Its findings were described by Ravitch and Finn (1987). The College Entrance Examination Board (CEEB) includes achievement tests dealing with American history and social studies and with European history and world cultures. CEEB (1988) also offers a battery of tests that includes social studies. For high schoolers, especially advanced placement students, numerous state testing programs include a social studies component. This pattern seems to be expanding and is being implemented in earlier grades. Currently, social studies educators are pushing for inclusion in state initiatives because they fear that, if social studies is not substantially represented beginning at the elementary level, it will lose its place as a core subject. In the *Handbook of Research on Social Studies Teaching and*

Learning, Kurfman (1991) reaffirmed that testing has begun to receive serious attention from social studies educators.

A common criticism of social studies tests in the past has been their failure to measure student attainment of major social studies understandings, life applications, appreciations, and higher-order thinking. Koretz (1988), Madaus (1988), and Airasian (1988) all concluded that the prevalent multiple-choice format focuses on low-level knowledge objectives. This form of testing may be valid for a narrow range of social studies phenomena, but it has obvious limitations. On the other hand, forms of testing that require large blocks of time are also questioned, due to the already limited time allocated for social studies instruction.

Other heavily debated issues center around the effects of testing on achievement and the validity of test scores as evidence of actual accomplishment (which we take to mean knowledge, understanding, appreciation, and life application of powerful social studies ideas). The influence of testing on curriculum and instruction can be positive if teachers and administrators take steps to ensure that test results are valid indicators of what students are learning. The first step is to see that the test measures what the school system values.

If it does, the next step is to make sure that the curriculum and the instructional practices are aligned to address the test's goals, objectives, and test-taking skills. If the school values something quite different, then measures congruent with its values must be sought. Finally, if the school's goals and values extend beyond what is measured on tests, the school needs to find other assessment tools that can be added to provide a more complete profile of the social studies learning and to judge the quality of its program. We believe that any robust social studies curriculum, beginning in kindergarten, would need to expand its set of measures beyond conventional tests. Later in the chapter we will address what this range of measures might include.

Assessment that produces feedback with potential implications for adjustments in curriculum and instruction is a desirable feature of a well-planned social studies program. Tests and other assessment measures are woven throughout a goals-driven program. The program as a whole is viewed as a means for moving students toward accomplishment of major goals; namely, the knowledge, skills, attitudes, values, and dispositions to action that are developed in students. All of the program's elements are aligned with the goals—its content, its instructional methods, its activities and assignments, and its assessment measures.

This ideal relationship among program components breaks down, however, if the components begin to be treated as ends in themselves rather than as means to accomplish larger goals. This is what happens to the assessment components when high-stakes testing practices take hold. Theoretically, it is never a good idea to have assessment measures (rather than goals) driving the curriculum.

Currently, several states are developing curriculum frameworks to guide K–12 social studies instruction. In Michigan, the social studies framework task force has insisted that the proposed assessment test for social studies cascade from the curriculum framework. It remains to be seen if the proposed battery of tests will adequately represent the scope of the curriculum and will elicit responses that give evidence of understanding without requiring inordinate amounts of time for testing. Additional assessment measures will need to be woven throughout the program to monitor implementation by teachers and achievement by students. If these challenges can be met and if the assessment package is well aligned with the goals expressed in the framework, these high-stakes tests and results from other, less standardized measures will serve as valid indicators of the health of social studies. On the other hand, if they fail to align with the goals, if they are narrow in scope, or if they fail to incorporate other measures, there is good reason for concern about high-stakes tests distorting the curriculum in undesirable ways.

THE PRESENT: A BROADER VIEW OF ASSESSMENT AND EVALUATION

Recognizing the need for accountability but concerned about the narrowing effect on the curriculum that current versions of high-stakes testing might have, the National Council for the Social Studies (NCSS) and leading scholars who have focused on assessment methods have been arguing for social studies assessment that is well aligned with major social studies goals, more complete in the range of objectives addressed, and more authentic in the kinds of tasks included. NCSS guidelines call for systematic and rigorous evaluation of social studies instruction that (1) bases the criteria for effectiveness primarily on the school's own statement of objectives; (2) includes assessment of progress not only in knowledge but in thinking skills, valuing, and social participation; (3) includes data from many sources, not just paper–pencil tests; and (4) is used for assessing students' progress in learning and for planning curriculum improvements, not just for grading (NCSS, 1990).

In a position statement on testing and evaluation in social studies, the NCSS (1991) emphasized that assessment practices should support school restructuring efforts that favor shared decision making and local leadership at the school level rather than a uniform curriculum or accountability defined only by scores on standardized tests. The statement warned against overreliance on machine-scored tests and favored approaches that balanced such measures with alternatives such as performance or authentic assessments. The latter assessments include tasks such as speaking effectively about or taking a reasoned position on a controversial social issue. They look at the processes that students use, not merely the answers they choose.

According to NCSS (1991), a comprehensive and balanced plan for social studies assessment would include standardized achievement tests that match the values espoused in the school's social studies curriculum, teacher-made tests, and a range of authentic assessment instruments and instructional activities assessed in nontesting situations that reflect curricular goals. Whether adopted test items are from standardized norm-referenced tests, publisher-supplied criterion-referenced tests, or instructional activities created by a textbook company or designed by the teacher or curriculum committee, teachers should ensure that they are closely matched to the goals and objectives of the local social studies curriculum. The evaluation component of the social studies curriculum should be viewed as much broader than testing. Tests can be augmented with performance evaluations of carefully designed instructional activities, laboratory tasks, checklists, portfolios of students' work, or projects done in conjunction with student interviews.

The NCSS Advisory Committee on Testing and Evaluation (NCSS, 1991) recommended the following guidelines:

• *Evaluation instruments* should focus on the curriculum goals and objectives; be used to improve curriculum and instruction; measure both content and process; be chosen for instructional, diagnostic, and prescriptive purposes; and reflect a high degree of fairness to all people and groups.

• *Evaluation of student achievement* should be used solely to improve teaching and learning; involve a variety of instruments and approaches to measure knowledge, skills, and attitudes; be congruent with the objectives and the classroom experiences of the students examined; and be sequential and cumulative.

• *State and local agencies* should secure appropriate funding to implement and support evaluation programs; support the education of teachers in selecting, developing, and using assessment instruments; involve teachers and other social studies professionals in formulating objectives, planning instruction and evaluation, and designing and selecting evaluation instruments; and measure long-term effects of social studies instruction.

THE CONTEXT FOR DEVELOPING A COMPREHENSIVE SOCIAL STUDIES ASSESSMENT PLAN

In planning social studies curriculum and instruction, it is important to emphasize the goals of understanding, appreciation, and life application. Understanding means that students learn both the individual elements in a network of related content and connections among them, so they can explain the content in their own words. Appreciation means that students value the learning because they understand that there are good reasons for learning it. Life application goals are accomplished to the extent that students retain their learning in a form that makes it usable when it is needed in other contexts. As the result of these goals, social studies should inform one's personal, social, and civic thinking and decision making. To address a broader range of goals and objectives and promote life applications, assessment must be expanded beyond the traditional paper–pencil test. Newmann (1990), Newmann, Secada, and Wehlage (1995), Wiggins (1989a, 1989b), and other scholars refer to these attempts as *authentic assessment*.

Since assessment is considered to be ongoing—frequently cast as preliminary, formative, and summative—many instructional activities also can be used as assessment tools. All too frequently, assessment has been defined as the test at the end of the unit; in other words, a summative measure. We believe that assessment must become an integral part of ongoing teaching and learning. Different forms and times for assessment will be determined by the purpose of the learning situation, the kind of information acquired, and how it will be used to accomplish social studies goals. Learning activities play an important role—they are both curriculum components that need to be assessed as such and mechanisms for eliciting indicators of student learning. We use the term *activities* to refer to the full range of classroom tasks, activities, and assignments—anything that students are expected to do, beyond getting input through reading or listening, to learn, apply, practice, evaluate, or in any other way respond to curricular content.

Therefore, activities may call for speech (recitation, discussion, debate, role playing), writing (short answers, larger compositions), or other kinds of goal-directed action (conduct inquiry, solve problems, construct models or displays). They may be done in whole-class, small-group, or individual settings; and teachers need to be mindful of the setting when interpreting students' responses. For example, in a small group, is a student merely imitating peers or has the group stimulated her thinking and enabled her to produce something more sophisticated than she would have if working alone? Conversely, might an independent assessment activity be unexpectedly difficult for some students because all of the learning opportunities that led up to it were done in group settings?

Activities usually lead to some kind of *product*. When used for assessment, products are graded. For most students and parents, attaching a grade gives the activity (and the goal from which it was derived) more value. All "good" activities are intended as means of enabling students to accomplish curricular goals, and students are expected to engage in them for that purpose.

Our position on learning activities has been influenced by recent theory and research on teaching for understanding. Another major influence has been the work of John Dewey, Hilda Taba, Ralph Tyler, and other major curriculum theorists as represented both in their own writings and in the work of more recent authors who have been influenced by them. These include Zais (1976), Fraenkel (1980), and Raths (1971), who have developed lists of desirable features of good activities. We have built on their lists and other writings about activities in four ways. We have (1) expanded them to include additional principles, (2) grouped the principles according to priority levels, (3) distinguished principles that apply to each individual activity from principles that apply only to groups of activities considered as sets, and (4) identified principles describing how teachers might structure and scaffold activities for their students in addition to principles describing features of the activities themselves.

To do so, we have moved back and forth between top-down and bottom-up analyses. The *top-down analyses* involved applying theoretical and logical tests to principles drawn from the scholarly literature. We assessed the validity, breadth of applicability, and level of importance of each of the principles, both by discussing them as abstract generalities and by applying them to particular social studies activities to see if what they implied about the value of the activities matched the judgments we or others had formulated by considering the activities themselves.

For the *bottom-up analyses*, we identified activities suggested in textbook manuals or by teachers that we agreed were particularly useful as well as others that were flawed in various ways. We then analyzed these activities to articulate what made the good activities good and the other activities undesirable or ineffective. As a result of this process, we have developed a theoretical position and a set of principles for planning and implementing learning activities (Brophy & Alleman, 1991).

To appreciate their full implications, it is important to see how the principles fit within our larger theoretical position, which emphasizes teaching social studies for understanding, appreciation, and application. We make the following assumptions about the key features of ideal social studies curricula.

1. Curriculum development should be driven by major long-term goals, not just content coverage lists. Everything in the curriculum, including all forms of assessment, should be included because it is viewed as a means for helping students acquire important dispositions and capabilities, not just cultural literacy construed in a narrow "trivial pursuit" sense.

2. Content should be organized into networks structured around important ideas. These ideas should be taught and assessed for understanding (not just memorization) and application to life outside of school.

3. The knowledge and skills components of the curriculum should be integrated in ways that are consistent with major long-term social education goals. Skills should not be taught or assessed in isolation but used as strategies for applying knowledge in authentic ways.

4. Curriculum units should include activities that, both individually and as a set, complement the other curriculum components and, whether used as preliminary, formative, or summative assessment, constitute a coherent plan for accomplishing major goals.

5. All activities should be assessed with an eye toward their costs as well as their benefits. The limited instructional time for social studies should be spent on essential activities.

6. Students construct knowledge through active information processing and sense making, and they undergo conceptual change and restructuring of their ideas as they do so. Consequently, the key to the effectiveness of an activity is its cognitive engagement potential—the degree to which it gets students thinking actively about and applying the content, preferably with meta-cognitive awareness of their goals and meta-cognitive control of their strategies. This assumption links closely to our belief about the value of ongoing assessment and the importance of documenting students' responses in an effort to track conceptual change.

Summarizing our assumptions and the parallel links between activities and assessment, we think of activities not as ends in themselves, but as means for accomplishing larger curricular goals. Their potential value needs to be judged in reference to these goals, considering their costs as well as their benefits. Activities play key roles throughout an instructional unit. They can be used to preassess, stimulate interest in a new topic, build conceptual understanding, or assess the level of understanding and life application at any juncture in the learning process. Traditionally, assessment has been viewed as evaluation done at the end of a unit or series of lessons. However, monitoring of learning and adjustment of instruction can be carried out at any time. Ongoing assessment can be done by observing the learning process, checking for understanding, introducing a new activity, or assessing students' products using a set of predetermined criteria. We strongly advocate this more comprehensive approach. Within this context, we draw from our activity research to select principles for creating, monitoring, and implementing activities so as to make them effective as both instructional devices and assessment practices. In doing so, we have used the curriculum standards published by the NCSS (1994) as the basis for the instructional goals included in our examples.

PRINCIPLES FOR PLANNING AND IMPLEMENTING ACTIVITIES WITH AN EYE TOWARD ASSESSMENT

We have included all of our principles for designing, selecting, and implementing activities in the appendix to this chapter. In this section, we will highlight the primary principles and a few others that we view as particularly relevant to preparing a comprehensive assessment plan for social studies. We will discuss each principle from an assessment perspective and use examples to demonstrate how well-selected activities can be used for evaluation. Other operating assumptions we are making in this section are that (1) the principles apply whether activities are labeled *assessment* or *instructional*; (2) assessment practices should reflect what is valued instructionally; (3) assessment extends from preinstruction through application; (4) assessment can occur at any time and often is labeled *preliminary, formative,* or *summative*; (5) assessment should lead to self-regulated learners; (6) assessment should inform teaching practices; and (7) the results should be documented to "track" responses and develop learner profiles.

Primary Principles That Apply to Each Activity

There are four primary principles. The first and absolutely essential principle is goal relevance.

Goal Relevance

The content base for activities used as a part of assessment should have enduring value and life application, not just cultural literacy status as a collection of terms that students might encounter in their general reading or social discourse. The assessment activities must reflect what is valued instructionally. This seemingly obvious principle is violated frequently, perhaps because the instruction was not goal driven or the assessment was added as an afterthought rather than planned as a carefully integrated component of curriculum and instruction.

For example, an appropriate activity for exploring ways that the earth's physical features have changed over time in the local region would be to locate these features, ideally by visiting sites and using a range of references, and determine whether the changes resulted from natural causes or human activities (explaining reasons for one's decisions). The entire process as well as the product could serve assessment purposes. If a summative activity were added at the end of a unit, students might be asked to select the one local physical feature that had changed the most and explain why and how, then speculate how it might appear in 20 years. If the goal were to provide for the study of people, places, and environments by interpreting and using various representations of the earth such as maps, globes, and photographs (NCSS, 1994), the summative activity might be to provide students with actual maps, globes, and photos, and ask them to explain which data source would be most appropriate for locating or determining (1) city market areas, (2) local truck routes, (3) air routes between the United States and Asia, (4) the distance between their locale and India, and the like.

The key ideas that provide the content base for the activities need to be represented clearly and accurately. Otherwise, they may create misconceptions. Also, it is best to avoid exotic instructional and assessment examples when possible. The use of local examples is a good idea because it suggests natural ways of illustrating immediate life applications.

Appropriate Level of Difficulty

Each activity must be pitched within the optimal range of difficulty (i.e., the students' zones of proximal development). It must be difficult enough to provide some challenge and extend learning, but not so difficult as to leave many students confused or frustrated. Difficulty levels may be adjusted by adjusting either the complexity of activities themselves or the degree to which the activities are structured and scaffolded for students.

An activity must be structured sufficiently to ensure that students can achieve the goal if they invest reasonable effort in attempting to do so. Also, if the activity is to function as a vehicle for assisting students in accomplishing the goal, the students must undergo certain experiences in the process of engagement. If assessment reveals that students can meet the activity's requirements without engaging in the desired processes (e.g., guess answers without thinking), the activity's value is nullified.

Ordinarily, activities should not combine difficult new procedures with difficult new content. Instead, challenging new processes should be introduced within a context of easy or familiar content. When the main purpose is to get the students to process and apply new content, assessment activities should employ easy or familiar formats and processes. For example, if the goal were for students to understand and use the concepts of supply and demand, using role play to express the relationship of price to supply and demand would be an appropriate process, if the students had role played several times previously. Writing essays about the relationship would be appropriate only if the students were experienced enough at essay composition to be comfortable with that form of expression. Violations of this principle can cause students to become so concerned about the procedural requirements of activities that they fail to attend sufficiently to their content-related purposes (Blumenfeld, Mergendoller, & Swarthout, 1987).

Feasibility

Each assessment activity must be feasible within the constraints under which the teacher must work. The teacher also needs to consider the feasibility of the tasks themselves. For example, if the goal is to determine the students' levels of understanding and sensitivity about hunger, asking students to express in writing how they personally feel when they are hungry would be much more appropriate than having them draw their feelings about it.

Cost Effectiveness

The educational benefits expected to be derived from an activity must justify its anticipated costs in time and trouble (for both teacher and students). Some activities are not worth the time and trouble it would take to implement them. For example, if the goal is for students to develop an understanding and appreciation for global connections and interdependence, class time could be used to discuss how the United States or the local area is interdependent with various places in the world as evidenced by products, ideas, transportation, communication, and so on. Constructing floats, mobiles, or dioramas at home (not during social studies instruction time) could enhance summative evaluation. Each student might present his or her findings using the artifacts as visual examples.

Activities should not be complicated in counterproductive ways, such as by converting them into games that place more emphasis on speed of response than on thoughtful understanding or that focus student attention on winning a competition rather than on learning or applying the content. For example, in a unit focusing on the study of people, places, and environments using the students' homeland and Australia, we would recommend that students write essays comparing the two places or write letters from one site to friends who live in the other but not that they engage in a Trivial Pursuit contest.

Secondary Principles That Apply to Each Activity

Secondary principles are features that are desirable but not strictly necessary (see the appendix). Here we feature those we think are compelling for a solid assessment plan. We have cited a wide variety of assessment activities in our examples, including some that will appear robust and overly ambitious for a particular classroom. We have done this intentionally to illustrate the range of possibilities that can be considered in developing a powerful assessment plan.

Multiple Goals

An assessment activity that simultaneously accomplishes many goals is preferable to one that accomplishes fewer goals (so long as it is just as effective in accomplishing the primary goal). This principle is particularly useful in planning for summative evaluation. Time for this type of assessment is limited, so accomplishing multiple goals through an essay question, a short scenario with an accompanying set of questions that includes an array of charts or maps, a laboratory situation, or a task that calls for analysis and interpretation of a series of pictures representing the big ideas of the unit would be more powerful and cost effective. The best activities are always built around powerful ideas, involve the use of key skills (critical thinking, value analysis, decision making) to process these ideas, and allow students to do so in ways that engage them personally with the content.

Assessment activities that incorporate content and skills from other subjects can also result in desirable integration if the social studies goals remain the focus. For example, the use of math skills would be appropriate and necessary if the activity calls for students to generate, manipulate, and interpret information from atlases, data bases, grid systems, charts, graphs, and maps (NCSS, 1994, p. 85). Most successful integration will occur as natural by-products of goal-oriented attempts to provide opportunities for authentic applications of the content the students are learning. This implies that potential assessment activities should be considered first in reference to major social education goals. For example, the goal might be for students to understand and appreciate how people create places that reflect cultural values and ideas as they build neighborhoods, parks, shopping centers, and the like (NCSS, 1994, p. 85). Recognizing that the students have learned how to write essays in language arts, an appropriate assessment activity might be for them to select a local setting such as their neighborhood and write essays describing how the local people represent their cultural values and ideals. If they have learned about photography in science and have experience in being novice photographers, they might prepare photo journals with narratives that express the reflection of cultural values and ideals of the place.

Motivational Value

Other things being equal, assessment activities that students enjoy (or at least find meaningful and worthwhile) are preferable to activities that they do not enjoy. Like integration, however, enjoyment is important but should not be the focus. Too often, curriculum developers or teachers treat it as primary by planning "fun-testing" activities that lack goal relevance and deal with content at a very superficial level (i.e., Trivial Pursuit, Quiz Bowl, etc.).

Higher-Order Thinking

The best assessment activities challenge students not just to locate and reproduce information but to interpret, analyze, or manipulate information in response to a question or problem that cannot be resolved through routine application of previously learned knowledge. This principle incorporates Newmann's ideas about thoughtfulness in academic activities. For example, if the goal were to develop an understanding of and appreciation for culture and cultural diversity, students might be asked to investigate their own cultural backgrounds—to find examples of language, literature, arts, architecture, traditions, beliefs, values, and behaviors that reflect their heritage and prepare papers or oral presentations explaining how these cultural elements serve to transmit their roots, inform others, and raise new questions for their culture's future. A culminating assessment activity could be to examine similarities and uniqueness across cultures such as by responding to the following questions. (1) How are the generally similar cultures of the United States and Canada different in some respects? (2) How are the generally different cultures of the United States and Japan similar in some respects?

If the goal is to develop an understanding and appreciation of citizenship as it applies to life in the community and the activity called for students to collect live examples, pictures, newspaper clippings, and so on to identify rights and responsibilities of local citizens (NCSS, 1994, p. 73), the accompanying narratives explaining the reasoning behind the selections would serve as powerful indicators of the students' levels of understanding. Sharing responses with peers can provide a venue for individual students to observe and check their interpretations with one another. Guided discourse stimulated by the teacher can further enhance the range of expectation levels. Anecdotal records can serve as documentation and as a means of evaluating growth over time.

Adaptability

Assessment activities that can be adapted to accommodate students' individual differences in interest or ability are preferable to activities that cannot. Other things being equal, assessment activities that offer students some opportunity for choice in deciding what to do or autonomy in deciding how to do it are preferable to those that do not. For example, if the goal is to develop an understanding of and appreciation for the relationship between science, technology, and society and the assessment called for students to collect pictures, "life stories," newspaper and magazine articles, data from interviews, personal experiences documented in anecdotal records, and so on, each student could select his or her data sources as well as decide if the sample should be drawn from a range of technological topics or if it should focus on a specific theme such as transportation, communication, medicine, or warfare. The evaluation criteria would be set in advance. For example, specifications concerning the minimum number of data sources and the manner in which interpretations are to be documented (for example, each with an attached paragraph explaining how science and technology are changing transportation and its impact on humans) would guide the students' work, establish expectations, and serve as the vehicle for analyzing the level of performance.

If the goal is for the students to come to grips with the tensions between wants and needs of individuals and groups through the study of the concepts of fairness, equity, and justice, students could be given the choice of how to find and document examples of these concepts in their community and how to demonstrate their interpretations. For example, they might elect to audiotape their interpretations, write reflective papers about them, prepare photo essays with narrative captions, or create dialogues that focus on them. Providing a range of options to address the same goal allows students to draw on their preferred learning modalities and accommodates developmental differences.

Principles That Apply to Sets of Activities

Whereas the principles in the previous sections apply to each individual assessment activity, the principles in this section apply to sets of assessment activities established to accomplish unit goals. As teachers begin to build comprehensive assessment plans and weave evaluation throughout the instructional process, these principles can prove to be very helpful. A range of examples is provided as a means of illustrating the unlimited possibilities that can be incorporated into the ongoing assessment process.

Variety

The set should contain a variety of assessment activity formats and student response modes. Variety serves as a motivator and a way to accommodate individual differences in student learning styles and activity preferences. For example, during a given unit or marking period, there might be both individual and cooperative activities as well as a range of communication modes (reading, writing, speaking, listening), information-processing requirements, and task forms (communicating, understanding, responding critically, conducting inquiry, solving problems, and making decisions). As part of a preliminary assessment, students could be asked to respond verbally; during formative assessment they might engage in cooperative learning to solve a problem; and as part of summative evaluation, they might be asked to write short response papers (individually) explaining their reasoning behind the proposed solution.

   If the goal were to develop understanding about how people create and change structures of power, authority, and governance (NCSS, 1994, p. 60), carefully scaffolded powerful activities would include field trips, videos, simulations, viewing CD-ROMs with guided discourse, essays, role play, research papers, or surveys. The products derived from these experiences could serve as assessments of learning.

Progressive Levels of Difficulty or Complexity

Assessment activities should progressively increase in levels of challenge as student expertise develops. For example, the goal might be for the students to acquire an understanding of interdependence by examining the relationships and tensions between personal wants and needs and various global concerns such as oil importation, land use, and environmental protection (NCSS, 1994, p. 70). As a preliminary assessment activity students might be asked to list their own wants and needs, differentiate among them, and explain why they were so labeled. As the unit unfolds, they would examine global issues through reading and discourse. Toward the end, they would participate in an activity such as a simulation that put personal and global needs and wants into perspective (i.e., world hunger simulation). The accompanying discourse could be used to measure students' understanding. Anecdotal records or data collected from student interviews might serve as sources of documentation.

As the school year progresses and students acquire more independence, engage in more collaborative efforts, acquire higher-order thinking skills, and become more adept at communication, assessment activities should reflect these cognitive advances. Designing assessment activities that reflect student growth and development obviously should align with what is valued.

Life Application

As teachers' assessment plans become more comprehensive, numerous opportunities for students to apply what they are learning to their lives outside of school become apparent. While life application should be a major strand of every social studies unit, it is not possible to include it in every lesson or instructional activity. However, when planning sets of assessment activities, teachers should seek natural places to incorporate it. For example, for the interdependence goal described earlier, students might be asked to write an editorial as a summative evaluation activity. While this would not necessarily ask students to propose action, it would give them an opportunity to express a position and perspective, after considering not only themselves but others. The activity could begin to build understanding and appreciation for how ideas currently studied in school call for personal and civic decision making.

Full Range of Goals Addressed

An assessment plan should reflect what is valued. As a set, the assessment activities should reflect the full range of goals identified in the unit. If the unit includes values or citizen action goals, assessments that reflect these must be present. For example, goals that call for actual doing should be represented by doing, not merely reading and discussing.

Concrete Experiences

Where students lack sufficient experiential knowledge to support understanding, sets of assessment activities throughout the year should include opportunities for them to view demonstrations, inspect artifacts or photos, visit sites, or in other ways experience concrete examples of the content. For example, if the goal focuses on the ways that human beings view themselves in and over time and students are expected to identify and use various sources for reconstructing the past such as documents, letters, diaries, maps, textbooks, photos, and so on (NCSS, 1994, p 51), concrete experiences for children can be especially valuable. Learning about the conditions of life in past times can be greatly enhanced by handling artifacts, viewing photos or films, or reading or listening to fact-based children's literature in addition to reading textbooks. Teacher-led mini-conferences with individuals or small groups of students can generate data related to knowing, understanding, feeling, and applying.

"Natural" Applications

Activities that are "naturals" for developing understanding of a unit's content should be included in the set for the unit. For example, if the goal is to foster individual development and identity and students are asked to describe the ways in which family, gender, ethnicity, nationality, and institutional affiliations relate to personal identity (NCSS, 1994, p. 88), a class matrix might be created as a tool for analysis and use in writing an essay describing oneself within the context of the class.

If the goal focuses on cultures and the ways in which groups meet their human needs and concerns (NCSS, 1994, p. 79) and students are asked to compare similarities and differences among them, a data retrieval chart should be used. The visual learning tool will sharpen points of comparison and serve as a springboard for structured discourse. Follow-up assessment activities might include an individual essay focusing on patterns that emerge regarding human needs or a cooperative activity that calls for groups to decide which culture is the most technologically advanced and why, which is the least technologically advanced and why, and what group will probably be the next to be influenced by technology and why.

In summary, activities are designed for instruction or assessment. Frequently, they serve a dual purpose. If new or different activities are selected for assessment, they must match the instructional goals. Assessment should be woven throughout instructional units—beginning prior to presenting new content and occurring at suitable junctures thereafter—to monitor, adjust, revise, and expand what is taught. The four primary principles (goal relevance, level, feasibility, effectiveness) must always be adhered to when planning assessment activities. Other principles can be helpful in creating a robust yearlong assessment blueprint (see the appendix).

AUTHENTIC ASSESSMENT

Authentic assessment is the current response to the belief that national norm-referenced tests are incomplete measures by which to judge the achievement of our students. What students do and how their tasks are accomplished are major aspects of authentic assessment. Students become active participants in the entire learning process and become responsible for creating and constructing their responses (Fischer & King, 1995).

We believe that movement in this direction is needed to promote evaluation activities that support the goal of teaching social studies for life application. Additionally, all of the primary principles for assessment activities described previously must be in place. Wiggins (1989a, 1989b) identified authentic assessment with performance of exemplary tasks that replicate the challenges and standards typically confronted by writers, businesspeople, or community leaders in activities such as making presentations before a school board or city council, writing a column for a local newspaper, or critiquing a report. In the social studies classroom, a task (instructional activity used in the assessment mode) might be considered authentic if students' presentations to the school board focusing on recommended changes, their written reports investigating the need to change the school's street crossing, or their posters prepared for heightening ecological awareness in the community were assessed for the quality of their arguments and supportive evidence.

The best evaluation activities make an impact on students beyond certifying their levels of competence. For example, the social studies goal might call for students to develop a position regarding a current social issue, grounding it in knowledge, diverse opinions, and research data gathered from a range of sources. Here, writing an editorial for the local newspaper would be more authentic than writing only to illustrate to the teacher that the students were able to do research and write coherent papers.

Authentic assessment displaces outmoded myths such as the ideas that evaluation must be accomplished using objective tests exclusively, that evaluation must follow instruction, that the "test" must be completed in a single seating, and that it should yield a distribution of scores resembling a bell-shaped curve. It also pushes our thinking toward the use of activities that call for multiple modalities that clearly reflect the range of social education goals that were identified during unit planning.

Walter Parker (1991) recommended the following attributes of authentic assessments:

1. Tasks go to the heart of essential learnings by asking for exhibitions of understandings and abilities that matter.
2. Tasks resemble interdisciplinary real-life challenges, not schoolish busywork that is artificially fragmented and easy to grade.
3. Tasks set standards: they point students toward higher, richer levels of knowing.
4. Tasks are worth striving and practicing for.
5. Tasks are known to students well in advance.

6. Tasks are few in number but representative of the goals addressed.
7. Tasks strike the teacher as worth the trouble.
8. Tasks generally involve a higher-order challenge for which students have to go beyond routine use of previously learned information.
9. All tasks are attempted by all students.

Parker went on to recommend that authentic assessment be incorporated in benchmarks that occur at major academic transitions. For example, in social studies, the students just completing fourth grade might write the fifth grade teacher letters describing what they had learned about regions, how they thought their understanding might relate to the upcoming study of the United States, what they wanted to learn about the United States, and how they thought their learning about regions and states might be useful in their lives. Such a comprehensive activity would serve as a benchmark for launching fifth grade social studies instruction.

PERFORMANCE ASSESSMENT

The literature is fuzzy regarding the distinctions, if any, between authentic and performance assessment. We use these terms interchangeably, along with alternate and expanded assessment. We acknowledge that all school settings are somewhat contrived (as opposed to real-life situations) and we shy away from the debate centered around the corollary of "authentic" assessments that suggests that all other measures are faulty. Instead, in this section, we suggest the laboratory approach as a useful model for assessing student performance regarding a limited set of goals-driven tasks. Due to time limitations and the nature of tasks, the "items" tend to be skill-based although embedded in social studies understandings.

The laboratory model is most often used in high school or college science classes, although we have used it in grade 3 and above. On "test day," stations are located at desks, at bulletin boards, whiteboards, wall charts, computer screens, or other appropriate places displaying social studies content. The displays might include a chart, a graph, a collection of artifacts, a student mural created as a part of the unit, or an open social studies book with a marked passage. Students visit the stations with clipboards, answer sheets, and pencils in hand. Usually each is instructed to begin at an individually specified site and answer the questions related to the display, then move on to the next station when instructed to do so. When all students have visited all of the stations, their responses are checked and on-site demonstrations for clarification and explanation are provided. Incorporating students' work into the material displayed at some of the stations can increase interest and peer respect. Of course, all stations must reflect knowledge and skills inherent in the unit's goals.

For example, if one of the goals of a unit on community is to develop understanding related to the available modes of transportation, students might read about, observe, and experience the various types then discuss the trade-offs in using each. Later, during a laboratory assessment exercise, they might be asked to solve a scenario built around a local trip. They would have access to a city map as well as artifacts such as a taxi receipt, a bus ticket, carpooling data, and connecting schedules. They would decide which mode is most cost effective in terms of time, trouble, money, and so on. At another station, they might be asked to study a map that showed bike paths and then respond to related questions. At a third station, with a specific destination described, they might be asked to write down the directions they would give to a taxi driver.

Given the goals for the community unit, it is likely that manipulations using charts, graphs, schedules, maps, pictures, local newspaper articles, local artifacts, student projects, and so on could be used to promote major understandings as both an instructional lead-up to the assessment and a performance assessment. The emphasis must center on the goals. In designing any form of assessment, the teacher must decide which items to include. Can they be designed to reflect multiple goals? If not, which are clearly represented? If some unit goals are not reflected in the measurement tool, how else might they be assessed?

Helpful hints to consider (Brophy & Alleman, 1996) when planning laboratory-type assessments are as follows:

- Try to make the exercises similar in length.
- Begin each sequence with an easy question and build toward the most challenging one.
- Consider providing optional questions at some of the stations.
- For younger students, arrange for adults or older students to help with reading items or manipulating materials.
- If you are concerned about having a station for each student, divide the number in half. You can have half of the class take the "test" while the other half works on a project in the library, then switch roles. Students can later work in pairs to correct their responses.
- Plan a dry run of the model before you use it.
- After administering several lab "tests" in social studies successfully, gradually add student projects at stations. More advanced students can design questions around their individual and group projects based on the goals of the unit. Provide them with whatever guidelines needed to ensure that they include questions that address higher-order thinking.
- Be open. There are no hard and fast rules for this model, except that the items must be based on your goals and matched to your teaching modalities.

It should be underscored that when designing performance assessment, the primary principles for planning activities need to be in place.

PORTFOLIOS

Fischer and King (1995) define the portfolio as a

> multifaceted assignment that expects more than one type of activity and production for completion and that extends over a period of time. Frequently, it requires a thematic approach to a concept. It can be a learning tool and a form of authentic assessment. The product is reviewed according to established criteria, sometimes known as a rubric, to determine the level of student performance and progress. (p. 5)

Portfolios are visual presentations of students' accomplishments, capabilities, strengths, weaknesses, and progress over time (Fischer & King, 1995). As presentations that reflect learning, they should exhibit a range of modalities and formats, not be mere collections of worksheets and inventories. Portfolios should not drive instruction but serve as by-products of ongoing planning of goals-driven instruction. Their entries should reflect activities that match the goals, are pitched at the appropriate level of difficulty, and are feasible and cost effective. Portfolios can enhance student reflection and self-assessment. They potentially offer a concrete forum for students to use in learning to value their own work. When students are responsible, at least in part, for deciding what to include, they are forced to examine their work from new perspectives.

There are several types of portfolios that teachers can consider (Fischer & King, 1995). The most common include the working portfolio, the showcase portfolio, and the record-keeping portfolio. The working portfolio is the one that the student and teacher assess and evaluate together. Work samples are entered as evidence of learning and growth. Students and teachers select and add samples and records. Parents are encouraged to add comments. The intent is that the working portfolio will serve as a living document of the student's ongoing progress.

The showcase portfolio is parallel to an artist's portfolio and thus represents the student's best work. In this portfolio, the student usually has sole ownership of selections to be included. The showcase portfolio is less useful for assessment purposes because it does not illustrate day-to-day performance.

A third type of portfolio is known as the record-keeping portfolio and usually is used along with the showcase portfolio. Its purpose is to provide a record of the completed assessment and evaluation samples not included in the showcase portfolio. The record-keeping portfolio provides documentation for all completed assignments.

Usually, a student's portfolio would include entries from a range of school subjects. We recommend that, in an elementary student's portfolio, one section (as in one chapter in a text) be designated for social studies exclusively. There might also be a section that is reflective of integrated activities that cut across subjects. Contents of the typical working portfolio would include work in progress such as notes leading up to a class debate discussing the question Should Fifth Graders Assume Total Responsibility for the Safety Patrol?, research notes for an essay on the topic Lessons to be Learned from the Civil War, and data for a mapping project that will ultimately illustrate a student's proposed tourist route for gaining deeper understanding and appreciation regarding the Civil War.

Other items in the social studies section would likely include some product samples—finished, revised, or edited works that illustrate a student's current developmental level and achievement. A completed position paper addressing neighborhood crime, an audiotape of an interview with the mayor, or a collection of snapshots (accompanied by a short narrative) depicting the recent sixth grade community ecological project are examples of the types of entries that a portfolio might contain. Teacher observation and assessment data and parental comments could also be added.

Portfolio entries should mirror the range of social studies goals; namely, knowledge, understanding, appreciation, and life application. All entries should reflect the guiding principles for activity selection and include valuable representations of students' accomplishments as well as where they are developmentally. The complete portfolio section should reflect the "story" of social studies instruction.

The exhibits of student accomplishments found in the portfolio provide ideal stimulants for conferencing. The underlying goal should be to help participants gain insights into the motives, learning processes, and standards surrounding one's performance (Paris & Ayres, 1994). Conferences serve as vehicles to help students assess their progress and make plans for future initiatives. Graves (1983) observed that "Children don't know what they know. When we speak or when someone elicits information from us, it is as informative to the speaker as it is to the listener" (p. 138). Although conferences vary in purpose, they share the intent of raising students' interest in their own learning, in helping them to be more reflective about their learning, and as a result, take more responsibility for it.

Student–teacher conferences built around portfolios provide opportunities for students to explain their work and what has been learned. Meanwhile, the teacher has an opportunity to listen, give feedback, and become informed in an effort to adjust future instruction accordingly. During portfolio conferences, the students and teacher review the portfolio entries, students reflect in words what they have learned and set goals for the immediate future. Teachers provide scaffolding to support students' independence, yet at the same time guide students according to what they need to be doing on their own.

Portfolio planning guides need to be developed jointly by the teacher and students so that expectations are clear. Sample planning guide questions include these:

- How would you describe your social studies entries?

- What piece presented the most challenge to you? Explain.
- Which entry are you least pleased with at this time? Why? What do you plan to do on it next? What kind of assistance do you need?
- Given our current social studies unit and the goals we have established, what type of activity would make it meaningful to you?

Other participants in student conferences might include peers, high school student mentors, school volunteers, and parents. In each instance, the focus should be on the students learning and gaining personal satisfaction from developing understanding and realizing for themselves where revisions or clarity are needed, where more in-depth inquiry is warranted, and so on.

Conferences need to be planned and orchestrated so that each participant clearly understands his or her role and expectations are met with an eye toward the social studies goals. Conferences should underscore the authenticity of students' work. They should provide teachers with valuable insight about the strengths, needs, and perceptions of students (Paris & Ayres, 1994). Peers, mentors, school volunteers, and parents likewise can gain insight. Besides serving as an audience and giving feedback, peers can learn from the dialogue, gain new ideas, and get a pulse on what others are learning.

Parents have the rare opportunity to spend focused time on a school subject with some context surrounding what their children are learning. Conferences give them opportunities to listen to their children as they talk about social studies and the projects they are working on as represented in their portfolios. In the process, they can pick up clues regarding how they can support their children's social studies education. For example, they can be alert to resources that might be helpful on a particular project (magazine or newspaper clippings, an upcoming television documentary, a future lecture at the library, a television news item, a resource person they know, etc.).

Sharing portfolios during student-led conferences strengthens home–school bonds and helps parents to realize that their input is valued. They become a vital part of their children's schooling and soon realize that learning is a lifelong process and not merely the responsibility of the teacher; rather it is the responsibility of the parents, students, and community as well.

We concur with Roe and Vukelich (1994) that portfolio assessment is implemented most effectively in the classroom setting. However, teachers often feel burdened by the imposition of school district and state perspectives that are not in harmony with the goals guiding their portfolio assessment. For the ideal to become practice, the wider environment including the parents, school district, and community at large must endorse the philosophical underpinnings of portfolios and authentic assessment in general.

SOCIAL STUDIES STANDARDS:
LINKS TO CLASSROOM ASSESSMENT

Teachers often feel burdened by academic standards and view them as an inconvenience and distraction from good classroom practice. We would like to encourage social studies educators to consider them a tool for planning and a means of raising the visibility of the subject. Policy makers, educators, parents, and citizens of all kinds will want to know what students should be taught, how they will be taught, and how student achievement will be evaluated. To help teachers address these questions, the NCSS (1994) is circulating a manual entitled *Curriculum Standards for the Social Studies: Expectations of Excellence.* It was created to serve three purposes: to serve as a framework for program design, to function as a guide for curriculum decisions by providing student performance expectations, and to provide examples of classroom activities that will guide teachers as they design instruction. The standards do not represent a set of mandated outcomes or establish a national curriculum for the social studies. Rather, they are intended as guides and criteria to consult as local planning teams seek to integrate state, district, school, department, and classroom curriculum plans for social studies instruction, learning, and assessment.

It is not known whether national standards and assessments will improve social studies. We believe that school districts should undertake their own hard work on standard setting as a point of departure in planning curriculum and developing a comprehensive assessment package that reflects their practice. If schools first develop consensus around locally adopted goals that are congruent with national standards (and state standards if they are available) and then use the goals to guide social studies assessment, they will be recognized for creating powerful social studies programs. In turn, this should enable them to maintain the curriculum time assigned to social studies and sustain local autonomy.

GUIDING PRINCIPLES FOR CREATING,
MONITORING, AND IMPLEMENTING APPROPRIATE
SOCIAL STUDIES ASSESSMENT PRACTICES

The following key ideas have been emphasized throughout this chapter. We offer them as a set of principles for creating, monitoring, and implementing assessment in elementary social studies.

• Assessment practices must be goals driven, appropriate in level of difficulty, feasible, and cost effective.
• Assessment should be considered as an integral part of the curriculum and instruction process.
• A comprehensive assessment plan should represent what is valued in-

structionally. Local initiatives should draw on state and national standards and any other sources that can enhance local developments and practices.

• Assessment should be viewed as a thread that is woven into the curriculum, beginning before instruction and occurring at junctures throughout in an effort to monitor, assess, revise, and expand what is being taught and learned. It is often described as preliminary, formative, summative, ongoing, or focused.

• Assessment should benefit the learner (self-reflection and self-regulation) and inform teaching practices.

• Assessment results should be documented to "track" responses and develop learner profiles.

CONCLUSION

Currently, teachers are faced with many obligations, responsibilities, and frustrations regarding assessment. The professional literature and national conference agendas extol the use of national and state standards, benchmarks, and testing, as well as the potential benefits of classroom assessment with particular attention to the types that are authentic. However, issues of technical quality, equity, and feasibility for large-scale assessment purposes remain unsolved (Herman & Winters, 1994). While these issues are beyond the scope of this chapter, we encourage classroom teachers to move responsibly forward by adopting, adapting, and refining classroom practices, including assessment, that will improve teaching and learning.

APPENDIX

TABLE I
Principles for the Design, Selection, and Evaluation of Activities

Principles	Comments and examples
A. *Primary Principles. These are necessary criteria that must be applied to each individual activity.*	
A1. *Goal relevance.* Activities must be useful means of accomplishing worthwhile curricular goals (phrased in terms of target capabilities or dispositions to be developed in the students). Each activity's primary goal must be an important one, worth stressing and spending time on, and there must be at least logical (preferably empirical) reasons for believing that the activity will be effective as a means of accomplishing that goal.	A1. Many activities included in contemporary social studies series lack an important primary goal and are mostly busywork: word searches, cutting and pasting, coloring, connecting dots, learning to recognize states from their outlines, memorizing state capitals and state symbols. Others are unlikely to accomplish their stated purposes (e.g., offer concrete rewards for performance of good deeds as a way to bring a sense of social responsibility in students).

continues

TABLE 1 (*continued*)

Principles	Comments and examples
A1a. The activity must be built around powerful ideas that are basic to accomplishment of the overall goals of the curriculum. In social studies, these are key concepts and generalizations drawn from the social science disciplines and basic understandings about how and why the social world functions as it does and where and how one fits within it.	A1a. Many activities are built around definitions or facts that are peripheral to the main ideas in the unit and have minimal application potential (e.g., find pictures of products that are made but not used by people—used by animals, automobiles, etc.; identify clothes that would be worn to a birthday party).
A1b. These powerful ideas must be represented accurately. This means not only valid phrasing of concepts and generalizations but also appropriate selection and accurate representation of examples. Otherwise, activities will induce or reinforce misconceptions instead of accurate understandings.	A1b. Social studies activities often violate this principle because they are built around exotic or otherwise unrepresentative content instead of prototypical illustrations of important generalizations (e.g., activities built around igloos, stilt houses, or camping tents instead of activities that develop basic understandings about key features of more typical houses), or because they are built around forced categorizations (e.g., exercises in distinguishing things done at home from things done at school or foods eaten today from foods eaten long ago; classifying foods as for breakfast, lunch, or dinner). The latter problem is often compounded by ambiguous examples that could be placed into either category (reading, turkey).
A1c. Format specifications should promote efficient accomplishment of the primary goal. Response demands made on students should be naturally suited to accomplishment of the primary goal and uncontaminated by artificial complications or unnecessary restrictions.	A1c. Response format specifications often are unnecessarily complicated in ways that may confuse students or distract them from the key ideas (e.g., concept discrimination exercises that require students to color depicted examples in specified ways or to cut and paste labels under them instead of just checking or writing in the proper label under the example). Ill-considered attempts to integrate across subjects often result in activities that violate this principle (see B1a).
A2. *Appropriate level of difficulty.* As implemented (i.e., taking into account not only the activity itself but also the degree of scaffolding provided by the teacher), each activity must be pitched within the optimal range of difficulty (i.e., the students' zones of proximal development). It must be difficult	A2. To the extent that classes are heterogeneous, this principle identifies a dilemma that teachers can only manage as best they can rather than a problem that they can eliminate. Still, too many activities are unnecessary because students already know what they are intended to teach (e.g., use

continues

TABLE I (*continued*)

Principles	Comments and examples
enough to provide some challenge and extend learning but not so difficult as to leave many students confused or frustrated.	clothing and play money to stimulate clothing purchases to teach students that money is exchanged for goods in stores). Many other activities (especially those built around skills that are reviewed year after year, typically at the beginning of the year) are unnecessarily repetitive or otherwise too easy for students. Even more activities embody prior knowledge assumptions or procedural complexities that make them too difficult for students to understand and negotiate successfully (unless the teacher is willing to invest considerable time in advance preparation).
A2*a*. Implicit assumptions about students' ability to access and bring to bear relevant prior knowledge or skills must be justified. Mere exposure to needed knowledge or skills is not sufficient; this prior learning must have been retained and stored in ways that make it accessible, as well as organized or transformed in ways that make it applicable to the activity's response demands.	A2*a*. Activity suggestions often call for students to display or use knowledge that has not been taught in the curriculum and is not likely to have been acquired elsewhere (e.g., have first graders role play scenes from Mexico when all they have learned yet about Mexico is its location on a map).
A2*b*. Structuring and scaffolding of the activity must be sufficient to enable students to accomplish the primary goal if they invest reasonable effort in attempting to do so, yet not be so extensive as to nullify the activity's value as a means of accomplishing that goal. Ordinarily, this will require a degree of individualization in the degree and nature of structuring and scaffolding provided to different students.	A2*b*. To accomplish a given primary goal, the students must undergo certain affective, cognitive, and metacognitive experiences in the process of performing certain tasks. If they are unable to perform those tasks, or if the tasks are (in effect) performed for them by the teacher or by the structure built into the activity's instructions or materials, they will not undergo the desired experiences and the activity will not fulfill its intended function.
A2*c*. Activities ordinarily should not combine difficult new processes with difficult new content. Difficult new processes should be introduced in the context of applying to easy or familiar content. Where the main purpose is to get the students to process and apply new content, the activities should employ easy or familiar formats and processes.	A2*c*. Given limitations in cognitive capacity and working memory, it is wise to avoid complexities that may induce confusion or frustration. One way to do this is to make sure that either the knowledge on which an activity is based or the procedural skills needed to negotiate response demands are familiar and easily accessible to students (thus freeing most of their cognitive capacity for concentration on the less familiar aspects).

continues

TABLE I (*continued*)

Principles	Comments and examples
A3. *Feasibility.* Each activity must be feasible for implementation within the constraints under which the teacher must work (space and equipment, time, types of students, etc.).	A3. Suggested activities are unlikely to be implemented if they call for consumption of expensive or hard-to-find materials, use of specialized equipment, noisy construction work, risk to physical safety or emotional security, and so on.
A3*a.* Activities also must be feasible in the sense that it is possible for students to carry out the instructions unambiguously and complete the activity with a sense of closure and accomplishment.	A3*a.* Some activities are impossible to accomplish unambiguously (e.g., draw a "safe" home or a "hungry" face, tell what a character in an illustration is doing or holding when this is not shown clearly and cannot be inferred from the context). Others could go on indefinitely, without closure, if the instructions were taken literally (list all the products that can be found in the classroom).
A4. *Cost effectiveness.* The social education benefits expected to be derived from an activity must justify its anticipated costs (for both teacher and students) in time and trouble.	A4. Even when feasible for implementation under typical classroom conditions, many suggested activities require more time or trouble than they are worth (time-consuming work on murals or other construction projects, pageantlike "culminating" activities, overly ambitious or complicated simulations and games). Collage and scrapbook activities that call for a lot of cutting and pasting of pictures but not much thinking or writing about ideas linked to major goals also present cost-effectiveness problems. Some activities present problems in both feasibility and cost effectiveness (e.g., to teach the cardinal directions, have students march around the room as you call out "March north," March east," etc.; go outside, use chairs and blankets to construct simulated tents, then have students dramatize activities of desert nomads as they move from place to place).
A4*a.* The version of the activity that will accomplish the goal(s) most directly and with the least time and trouble is preferable to alternative versions that contain needless complications that do not add social education value to the activity and may distract students from its primary goal.	A4*a.* Frequently an activity can be operationalized in different formats (as an ordinary assignment versus as a game; within individual, small-group, or whole-class settings; in connection with individual, competitive, or cooperative reward structures) or with different response demands (oral versus written; respond to close-ended questions by choosing from pro-

continues

TABLE I (*continued*)

Principles	Comments and examples
	vided alternatives versus supplying one's own response; respond to open-ended questions by following a prescribed sequence of steps versus deciding for oneself how to frame and organize a response). Some of these versions might be too structured (e.g., calling for choice from provided responses when genuine accomplishment of the goal would require having students supply their own response), whereas others might introduce unproductive or even counterproductive complications (e.g., converting the activity into a competitive game).
A4*b*. Any assumed prior knowledge or skill that is not already in place (so that it can be made available merely by cueing) must be taught explicitly as part of the introduction to or the initial scaffolding of an activity, and the time and trouble of doing so must be taken into consideration in assessing its cost effectiveness.	A4*b*. The teacher's role in introducing and scaffolding activities for students is elaborated in Section D. The issue is introduced here, however, to underscore the point that the time and trouble required to prepare students for an activity must be included in assessing its costs.
A4*c*. The time spent in activities that cut across subject matter lines should be assessed against the time quotas allocated for those subjects in ways that reflect the cost effectiveness of the activities as means of accomplishing each subject's major goals. If activities are worthwhile at all, it is because they fulfill important curricular purposes, not simply because they cut across subject matter lines. Typically, these curricular purposes can be linked to school subjects and used as rationale for embedding activities within instruction in particular subjects. Where this is not seen as appropriate, curricular planning should include attention to generic goals that transcend particular subjects, as well as allocation of time for accomplishing those goals.	A4*c*. Classroom time allocated for social studies should not be diverted to activities that lack significant social education value. Thus, mural construction that relates to a social studies topic but is not implemented in ways that foster progress toward major social education goals (i.e., that is not structured around major social education understandings) might be justified if planned primarily as an art project and assessed against art time but not if treated as a social studies project and assessed against social studies time. Similarly, a writing or public speaking activity that connects with social studies content but is implemented primarily as a language arts skills exercise should be assessed against language arts time, not social education time.

B. *Secondary principles. These principles identify features of activities that are desirable but not strictly necessary. Each individual activity should embody all of the primary principles listed in Section A and as many of these secondary principles as can be incorporated in ways that are consistent with the primary principles.*

continues

TABLE I (*continued*)

Principles	Comments and examples
B1. *Multiple goals.* An activity that simultaneously accomplishes many goals is preferable to one that accomplishes fewer goals (so long as it is just as effective in accomplishing the primary goal).	B1. This principle is probably the most useful one for distinguishing the best activities from other activities that also meet minimally necessary conditions represented by the primary principles listed in Section A. The best activities are affectively engaging as well as cognitively instructive; provide students with opportunities to use critical and creative thinking, inquiry, problem solving, and decision making in the process of applying knowledge; and call for natural and realistic applications rather than just for isolated practice or artificial forms of application that do not connect to students' lives outside of school.
B1a. Activities that allow for integration across subjects or for inclusion of special topics (e.g., career education) may be desirable, so long as such integration does not interfere with accomplishment of the primary social education goal.	B1a. Some such activities would appear to accomplish multiple goals (e.g., assigning students to combine critical thinking skills and language arts knowledge with historical knowledge to write advertisements that might have been used to lure Europeans to immigrate to colonial Pennsylvania; asking them to compare historical accounts of Paul Revere's ride with the romanticized version in Longfellow's poem and discuss differences between historians and poets in goals, processes, and products). Others, however, seem forced or pointless (e.g., alphabetizing the state capitals, matching cities whose names begin with the same letter, writing a job resume for Thomas Jefferson, looking up the geographical coordinates for Revolutionary War battle sites).
B2. *Motivational value.* Other things being equal, activities that students are likely to enjoy (or at least find meaningful and worthwhile) are preferable to activities that students are not likely to enjoy.	B2. This is an important but nevertheless secondary principle. Unfortunately, curriculum writers often treat it as primary and end up recommending "fun" activities that lack goal relevance, feasibility, or cost effectiveness. Another point worth noting here is that following our other recommended principles will have the effect of addressing most motivation concerns (because this will eliminate tedious, pointless, and otherwise boring activities and because the teacher will introduce and scaffold activities in ways that encourage students to engage in them with motivation to learn).

continues

TABLE I (*continued*)

Principles	Comments and examples
B3. *Topic currency.* Activities built around currently or recently taught powerful ideas are preferable to "orphan" activities built around isolated content.	B3. Current curricula often lack coherence because they address too much content in not enough depth and because continuity is frequently interrupted by insertions (profiles of individuals or brief treatments of special topics not included in the regular text). Unfortunately, activities often focus on briefly mentioned minor details or inserted content rather than on the key ideas that are (or should be) developed in the unit.
B3a. Skills should be developed at places in the curriculum where they can be used naturally as strategies for authentically applying currently taught knowledge rather than being developed through isolated skills exercises that constitute (in effect) a skills curriculum taught separately from the knowledge curriculum.	B3a. Skills curricula often are intrusively superimposed on knowledge curricula in ways that use isolated bits of knowledge as bases for skills exercises, with the result that neither the knowledge nor the skills get applied in natural or useful ways (e.g., charting or graphing unimportant information that is never used, counting how many states' names begin with the letter c, classifying American-made products according to whether they are described as made in the "United States," the "U.S.," or the "U.S.A.").
B4. *Whole-task completion.* Opportunities to complete whole tasks are preferable to isolated practice of part skills, matching of words to definitions, or other work that does not cohere and result in closure as completion of a meaningful task.	B4. This principle is important for both affective and cognitive reasons. Students are likely to be more motivated and to make more significant progress toward major long-term goals when working on whole-task activities than on worksheets limited to vocabulary reinforcement or isolated practice of part skills.
B5. *Higher-order thinking.* The best activities challenge students not just to locate and reproduce information but to interpret, analyze, or manipulate information in response to a question or problem that cannot be resolved through routine application of previously learned knowledge.	B5. Such activities engage students in sustained and thoughtful discourse or writing about content in ways that cause them to think critically and creatively about it as they attempt to conduct inquiry, solve problems, or make decisions.
B5a. Discourse should go beyond recitation to include discussion or debate in which students articulate and defend positions on problematic issues, assess the merits of alternative policy decisions or suggested solutions to problems, develop and test explanations or predictions, and so on.	B5a. Many of the best opportunities for critical thinking, decision making, and other forms of higher-order application occur during teacher–student and student–student discourse (done in pairs, small groups, or whole-class activities). Yet, descriptive research suggests that most dis-

continues

TABLE I *(continued)*

Principles	Comments and examples
	course that occurs in classrooms is recitation, not reflective dialogue.
B5*b*. Writing assignments should call for sustained writing, not just filling in blanks or doing other brief writing.	B5*b*. In particular, such assignments should call for composition of coherent explanations or arguments, not just copying from the textbook or some other information source.
B6. *Adaptability.* Activities that can be adapted to accommodate students' individual differences in interests or abilities are preferable to activities that cannot.	B6. Adaptability is greatest for open-ended divergent activities: performance and cooperative projects that offer a variety of roles for students, inquiry activities in which students can pursue different questions and consult a variety of input sources, and information synthesis or argument development in which students can compose statements of varying length and sophistication and can use a variety of communication modes to report their ideas.

C. *Principles that apply to sets of activities. The principles in Sections A and B apply to each activity considered individually. In contrast, the principles in Section C apply to sets of activities developed as part of the plan for accomplishing the goals of a unit or curriculum strand. Each principle might not apply to each separate activity in the set, but the set as a whole should reflect these principles (insofar as it is possible to do so while still meeting the primary goals).*

C1. *Variety.* The set should contain a variety of activity formats and student response modes.	C1. Such variety accommodates individual differences in students' learning styles and activity preferences (within the constraints imposed by the responsibility to accomplish major goals).
C2. *Progressive levels of difficulty or complexity.* Activities should progressively increase in level of challenge as student expertise develops.	C2. As students become more accomplished in meeting the demands of various activity formats, they can take on more complex assignments, assume greater autonomy in deciding how to organize their responses, gather data from a broader range of sources, and so on.
C3. *Life applications.* Students should get to apply what they are learning to current events or other aspects of their lives outside of school (in ways that make sense given their levels of development).	C3. Many so-called applications are confined to decontextualized "academic" examples or cases that do not allow students to apply concepts or generalizations to their lives outside of school (e.g., making predictions about a fictional country based on supplied information about its geographical features). If students are to develop appreciation for the value of geographic principles, they will need opportunities to

continues

TABLE I (*continued*)

Principles	Comments and examples
	apply them to their lives outside of school (e.g., opportunities to see how these principles help them to understand historical and current developments in their own country).
C4. *Full range of goals addressed.* As a set, the activities should reflect the full range of goals identified for the unit or strand. In particular, to the extent that values or citizen action goals are included along with knowledge and skills goals, the set should include activities designed to develop values or citizen action dispositions. Where the goal implies doing, activities should include actual doing, not just reading or talking about it.	C4. Publishers often claim that their curricula address a full range of goals, but the activities included in these curricula often are confined to knowledge and skill exercises, with little opportunity for application or attention to values or citizen action dispositions.
C5. *Concrete experiences.* Where students lack sufficient experiential knowledge to support understanding, sets of activities should include opportunities for them to view demonstrations, inspect realia or photos, visit sites, or in other ways experience concrete examples of the content.	C5. These concrete experiences are especially important in connection with knowledge that children get little opportunity to develop through their everyday experiences (e.g., conditions of life in past times or in different societies and cultures).
C6. *Connecting declarative knowledge with procedural knowledge.* To the extent that doing so is important as part of developing basic understanding of a topic, students should learn relevant processes and procedural knowledge, not just declarative or factual knowledge.	C6. For example, sets of activities in government and civics units should go beyond teaching facts about government (capitals, names of office holders) to include activities designed to develop understanding of governmental processes (what different levels of government do and how they do it) and citizen participation dispositions and skills (voting, lobbying).
C7. *"Natural" applications.* Activities that are "naturals" for developing understanding of certain content (e.g., charting to compare and contrast different Indian tribes) should be included in the set for the unit.	C7. Retrieval charts and related comparison–contrast methods should be used whenever the content has focused on different examples or cases of concepts (Indian tribes, geographic regions, governmental forms) or generalizations (population development tended to follow water transportation routes prior to the invention of motorized vehicles). Activities built around developing understanding of sequences of causes, effects, and subsequent implications are "naturals" in history teaching. So are activities built around comparison of historical events with contemporary events that appear to be following similar patterns.

continues

TABLE I *(continued)*

Principles	Comments and examples

D. *Implementation principles. The principles in Sections A through C refer to the features of activities themselves. The principles in Section D refer to the ways that activities are implemented and, in particular, the ways that teachers structure and scaffold the activities for their students.*

D1. *Completeness.* A complete activity ordinarily would include the following stages: (*a*) introduction (teacher communicates goals and purposes and cues relevant prior knowledge and response strategies), (*b*) initial scaffolding (teacher explains and demonstrates if necessary, then asks questions or has students work on sample items to make sure that they understand what to do before releasing them to work mostly on their own), (*c*) independent work (students work mostly on their own but with teacher monitoring and intervention as needed), and (*d*) debriefing–reflection–assessment (teacher and students revisit the activity's primary purposes and assess the degree to which they have been accomplished).

D1. This principle operationalizes the point that the key to the effectiveness of an activity is not just physical action or time on task but cognitive engagement with important ideas and that this in turn depends in part on the teacher structuring and teacher–student discourse that occur before, during, and after the students' responses to the activity's demands. Even for an inductive or discovery learning activity, an optimal type and amount of teacher structuring and teacher–student discourse will be needed to maximize the activity's impact.

D2. *Introduction.* If students are to get the intended learning benefits from engaging in an activity, they will need to understand its intended purposes and what these imply about how they should respond to the activity. Such understanding is not self-evident, so teachers will need to develop it in the process of introducing the activity to the students.

D2. Good introductions to activities fulfill at least four purposes or functions: (1) motivating students' interest in or recognition of the value of the activity, (2) communicating its purposes and goals, (3) cueing relevant prior knowledge and response strategies, and (4) establishing a learning set by helping students to understand what they will be doing, what they will have accomplished when they are finished, and how their accomplishments will be communicated or evaluated.

D2*a*. The best way to ensure that students find an activity meaningful and worthwhile is to select or design it with this in mind in the first place. Students are most likely to appreciate the value of activities that involve life applications—that require them to think critically and creatively about content and apply it while trying to solve problems or make decisions on policy or value issues.

D2*a*. Even when activities do not lend themselves well to direct life applications, teachers can stimulate student appreciation of the value of these activities by using strategies for motivating students to learn—stimulating students' curiosity or interest, asking questions designed to get them into a problem-solving mode, building anticipation of the knowledge or skills that the activity will develop, and so on.

D2*b*. Teachers should introduce activities in ways that make their goals and purposes clear to students.

D2*b*. Students should understand that the activity calls for cognitive and affective engagement with important ideas undertaken

continues

TABLE I (*continued*)

Principles	Comments and examples
	to accomplish curricular goals, not just completion of a series of steps to fulfill requirements.
D2c. In introducing activities teachers also should cue any relevant prior knowledge.	D2c. This might include comparison or contrast with previous activities, asking students to use relevant prior knowledge to make predictions about the upcoming activity, explaining where the upcoming activity fits within a sequence or bigger picture, or helping students to make connections between the subject matter content of the activity and their personal knowledge or experiences.
D3. *Initial scaffolding*. Before releasing students to work mostly on their own, teachers should provide whatever explicit explanation and modeling that the students may need to understand what to do, how to do it, and why it is important. To the extent that the activity calls for the use of skills that need to be taught rather than merely cued, such instruction should include explicit explanation and modeling of strategic use of the skills for accomplishing the tasks that are embedded in the activity.	D3. In some cases, teachers may have to work through several examples themselves and then guide students through several more examples using appropriate task simplification, coaching, or other scaffolding strategies before the students will be ready to work mostly on their own. All such instruction should emphasize the use of skills as strategies for accomplishing the activity's goals and should encourage students to retain meta-cognitive awareness of those goals and use them to maintain meta-cognitive control over their subsequent engagement in the activity.
D4. *Independent work*. Once students have been released to work mostly on their own, the teacher should monitor their efforts and provide any additional scaffolding or responsive elaboration on the instructions that may be needed to structure or simplify the task, clear up confusion or misconceptions, or help students to diagnose and develop repair strategies when they have made a mistake or used an inappropriate strategy. This principle implies that activities should be planned so that students will get *feedback* about their performance, not only in the form of information about correctness of responses but also in the form of diagnosis of the reasons for errors and explanation of how these errors may be corrected or general qualitative aspects of performance may be improved.	D4. Such interventions should not involve doing the tasks for students or simplifying them to the point that they no longer can be expected to engage students in the kinds of cognitive processes that are needed to accomplish the activity's goals. Instead, interventions should involve scaffolding within the students' zones of proximal development in ways that allow them to handle as much of the task as they can at the moment and also to progress toward fully independent and successful performance. To the extent possible, teachers should provide *immediate* feedback as they circulate to monitor performance while students are actively engaged in the activity, not just delayed feedback in the form of grades or comments provided at some future time.

continues

TABLE I (*continued*)

Principles	Comments and examples
D5. *Debriefing–reflection–assessment.* Activities should be brought to closure in ways that link them back to their intended goals and purposes. For students, this means *opportunities to assess performance* and to correct and learn from mistakes. Ordinarily there also should be teacher-led *postactivity debriefing or reflection* that re-emphasizes the purposes and goals of the activity, reflects on how (and how well) these have been accomplished, and reminds the students of where the activity fits within the big picture defined by the larger unit or curriculum strand. For teachers, postactivity assessment and reflection includes evaluating the effectiveness of the activity for enabling students to accomplish the goals.	D5. Too often, students work through activities without reflecting thoughtfully on the key ideas that they are supposed to develop and apply, and when they finish the activities, they put them aside without another thought. To minimize this problem, teachers should include a debriefing–reflection–assessment phase following each activity. In addition, as they complete units or curriculum strands, they should lead the students through a review of how the entire set of activities helped them to develop key ideas and make progress toward major goals. Depending on the relative success of the activity and the ascribed reasons for it, this may require follow through in the form of remedial actions or adjustments of plans for next year.
D6. *Optimal format.* Where alternatives are possible, the activity should be implemented in whatever format will maximize the time that the students spend in active and thoughtful cognitive engagement (and thus minimize the time that they spend being passive, confused, or engaged in busywork).	D6. Many activities involving communicating about or debating content, for example, are better done in pairs or small groups than as whole-class activities that offer active roles to just a few students and require the others only to listen.
D7. *Optimal use of instructional time.* If the independent work phase of an activity calls for forms of work that are time consuming but do not require close teacher monitoring, these aspects of the work can be done outside of the time allocated for social studies instruction (during general study periods or at home).	D7. Ordinarily, students should do activities such as reading and taking notes for a research assignment, editing initial drafts for grammar and spelling, or working on elaborate illustrations or constructions during independent work time or at home (assuming that students have access to whatever resources may be needed).

Adapted from Brophy, J., and Alleman, J. (1991). Activities as instructional tools: A framework for analysis and evaluation. *Educational Researcher, 20,* 9–23.

References

Airasian, P. W. (1988). Measurement driven instruction: A closer look. *Educational Measurement: Issues and Practices, 7,* 6–11.

Blumenfeld, P., Mergendoller, J., & Swarthout, D. (1987). Task as a heuristic for understanding student learning and motivation. *Journal of Curriculum Studies, 19,* 135–148.

Brophy, J., & Alleman, J. (1991). Activities as instructional tools: A framework for analysis and evaluation. *Educational Researcher, 20,* 9–23.

Brophy, J., & Alleman, J. (1996). *Powerful social studies for elementary students.* Fort Worth, TX: Harcourt Brace.

College Entrance Examination Board (CEEB) (1988). *1988 Advanced Placement Program national summary reports.* New York: Author.

Conoley, J. C., & Impara, J. C. (Eds.). (1994). *Supplement to the 11th yearbook of mental measurement.* Lincoln: University of Nebraska.

Conoley, J. C., & Kramer, J. J. (Eds.). (1989). *10th yearbook of mental measurement.* Lincoln: University of Nebraska.

Fischer, C., & King, R. (1995). *Authentic assessment: A guide to implementation.* Thousand Oaks, CA: Corwin Press.

Fraenkel, J. (1980). *Helping students think and value: Strategies for teaching the social studies* (2nd ed.). Englewood Cliffs, NJ: Prentice-Hall.

Graves, D. (1983). *Writing: Teachers and children at work.* Portsmouth, NH: Heinemann.

Herman, J., & Winters, L. (1994). Portfolio research: A slim collection. *Educational Leadership, 52,* 48–55.

Koretz, D. (1988, Summer). Arriving in Lake Wobegon: Are standardized tests exaggerating achievement and distorting instruction? *American Educator, 12*(8–15), 46–52.

Kramer, J. J., & Conoley, J. C. (Eds.). (1994). *11th yearbook of mental measurement.* Lincoln: University of Nebraska.

Kurfman, D. (1982). Evaluation in social studies. In Project Span Staff and Consultants (Eds.), *Working papers from Project Span* (pp. 3–27). Boulder, CO: Social Science Education Consortium.

Kurfman, D. (1991). Testing as context for social education. In J. Shaver (Ed.), *Handbook of research on social studies teaching and learning* (pp. 310–320). New York: Macmillan.

Madaus, G. F. (1988). The influence of testing on the curriculum. In L. N. Tanner (Ed.), *Critical issues in curriculum. 87th yearbook of the National Society for the Study of Education* (pp. 83–121). Chicago: University of Chicago Press.

National Council for the Social Studies (NCSS). (1990). *Social studies curriculum planning resources.* Dubuque, IA: Kendall/Hunt.

National Council for the Social Studies (NCSS). (1991). Testing and evaluation of social studies students. *Social Education, 55,* 284–286.

National Council for the Social Studies (NCSS). (1994). *Expectations of excellence: Curriculum standards for social studies.* Washington, DC: Author.

Newmann, F. (1990). Higher order thinking in teaching social studies: A rationale for the assessment of classroom thoughtfulness. *Journal of Curriculum Studies, 22,* 41–56.

Newmann, F., Secada, W., & Wehlage, G. (1995). *A guide to authentic instruction and assessment: Vision, standards, and scoring.* Madison: Wisconsin Center for Education Research.

Paris, S., & Ayres, L. (1994). *Becoming reflective students and teachers: With portfolios and authentic assessment.* Washington, DC: American Psychological Association.

Parker, W. (1991). *Reviewing the social studies curriculum.* Alexandria, VA: Association for Supervision and Curriculum Development.

Raths, J. (1971). Teaching without specific objectives. *Educational Leadership, 28,* 714–720.

Ravitch, D., & Finn, C. E. (1987). *What do our 17-year-olds know?* New York: Harper & Row.

Roe, M., & Vukelich, C. (1994). Portfolio implementation: What about R for realistic? *Journal of Research in Childhood Education, 9*(1), 5–14.

Superka, D. P., Vigliani, A. & Hedstrom, J. (1978). *Social studies evaluation sourcebook.* Boulder, CO: Social Science Education Consortium.

Wiggins, G. (1989a). Teaching to the authentic test. *Educational Leadership, 46,* 41–47.

Wiggins, G. (1989b). A true test: Toward more authentic and equitable assessment. *Phi Delta Kappan, 70,* 203–213.

Zais, R. (1976). *Curriculum: Principles and foundations.* New York: Harper & Row.

CHAPTER 12

Authentic Assessment in Social Studies: Standards and Examples

FRED M. NEWMANN
University of Wisconsin—Madison

This chapter presents standards for authentic assessment in social studies derived from a concept of authentic human achievement. The examples come from teachers and students in schools across the United States who participated in our study of the effects of school restructuring on student learning.[1] The teachers and students who shared their work with researchers were not aware of the specific standards presented here. But by using these standards to describe the intellectual quality of teachers' assessment activities and their students' performance, we were able to examine variability in authentic pedagogy and its effect on student performance in restructured schools.

We found considerable variability in authentic assessment both within and between schools. We also found that authentic assessment practice by teachers contributed significantly to authentic performance by students in elementary, middle, and high schools.[2] The standards were developed initially as a research tool, but after working with and refining them over several

---

[1] The study, known as the School Restructuring Study (SRS), was conducted by the Center on Organization and Restructuring of Schools (CORS), University of Wisconsin—Madison. It is summarized in Newmann and Wehlage (1995), and reported in detail in Newmann and Associates (in press).

[2] For a description of the study and results see Newmann, Marks, and Gamoran (1996) and Newmann and Associates (1996).

years, we think they can help teachers, students and schools define more clearly what constitutes high-quality intellectual work.[3]

PROBLEM: INNOVATIVE TECHNIQUE AND INTELLECTUAL QUALITY

From 1991 to 1994, researchers in our study of school restructuring examined classroom instruction, teachers' assessment tasks, and student performance in more than 130 mathematics and social studies classes in 24 public elementary, middle, and high schools. We found extensive use of innovative techniques: small-group discussions, cooperative learning, role-playing simulations and debates, independent student projects, use of computers for writing and databases, interdisciplinary curriculum, hands-on experiments, written journals, portfolios and exhibitions, student production of visual displays, videos, and pamphlets, and community-based experiences such as volunteer service, internships, and surveys. Most of these techniques seem consistent with notions of constructivist or authentic teaching, because they place students in the more active roles of discussing, writing, producing things, and making decisions about learning, rather than simply listening to the teacher and reproducing what the teacher said.

On the other hand, innovative practice did not necessarily reflect improvements in the intellectual quality of students' experiences. A teacher might replace lecture–recitation with small-group discussion or short answer worksheets with essay questions. But, even with these changes, students might still devote most of their effort to remembering and listing isolated pieces of information rather than thinking critically about how the information helps them understand a powerful idea or solve an important problem. A portfolio that shows a variety of student work over a semester might replace the final examination taken in one sitting, but the portfolio itself could be filled with tasks that failed to demand in-depth understanding of the subject. Conversely, a carefully constructed final exam essay question could lead students to use a few key ideas to develop more complex understanding of an issue.

Assuming the central purpose of teaching is to help students to use their minds well, then education reform must involve more than innovation in teaching technique, method, or procedure. The merit of any technique, whether conventional or innovative, must be judged on its capacity to improve the intellectual quality of student performance.

On what grounds should we judge intellectual quality? Recent debates over standards for curriculum and student outcomes illustrate that the cri-

---

[3]Much of the material in this chapter is taken or adapted from Newmann, Secada, and Wehlage (1995) and Newmann and Wehlage (1995).

teria for quality are highly contested. Judgment of intellectual quality applied to a lesson, assessment activity, or sample of student performance usually implies one or both of the following criteria:

1. *The legitimacy of the content.* That is, whether the subject matter, skill, or disposition is considered appropriate and significant for teaching and learning according to norms of a discipline or the political–legal communities that have authority over education. Debates over Western versus non-Western history, basic skills versus higher-level skills, or what values to teach illustrate widespread public concern about selection of the "proper" content.

2. *Accuracy.* Once agreement is reached on the proper content to teach, the next criterion for intellectual quality is the accuracy of the statements made by teachers, texts, and students. Accuracy usually refers to the extent to which the content and style of the statements is consistent with authoritative knowledge or competence in the relevant discipline or area of expertise. The importance of accuracy as a criterion of quality is illustrated in criticism of curriculum as containing disproven, outdated, or biased material and of student performance containing substantial errors.

Legitimacy of content and accuracy are both important, but we think a third criterion for intellectual quality must be added; namely,

3. *Authenticity.* This is the extent to which a lesson, assessment task, or sample of student performance represents construction of knowledge through the use of disciplined inquiry that has some value or meaning beyond success in school.

This chapter proposes authenticity as a key facet of intellectual quality that is largely independent of assessment technique. It also describes how specific standards for authenticity can be applied to teachers' assessment tasks and to student performance on the tasks.[4]

AUTHENTIC ACHIEVEMENT: FOUNDATION FOR STANDARDS

Why should we be concerned about "authenticity" in education? Are there not already enough ideas—such as higher-level thinking, creativity, basic

[4]The chapter focuses only on assessment tasks and student performance, but we used the vision of authenticity to guide development of standards for instruction as well. The same standards were used to assess the intellectual quality of instruction, assessment tasks, and student performance in both mathematics and social studies. But the scoring of student performance required slight differences in scoring rules between the two disciplines. This chapter presents only the standards for assessment tasks and student performance in social studies. Specific scoring rules for all standards for instruction, assessment tasks and student performance are presented in Newmann, Secada, and Wehlage (1995, Appendix B).

and cultural literacy, disciplinary mastery, career skills, and responsible citizenship—that can serve as standards for intellectual quality?

The aim of authentic standards for intellectual quality is not to replace these goals but to address a serious problem that is neglected even as these goals are ardently pursued. The problem is that the kind of mastery required for students to earn school credits, grades, and high scores on tests is often considered trivial, contrived, and meaningless, by both students and adults. This absence of meaning breeds low engagement in schoolwork and inhibits transfer of school learning to issues and problems faced outside of school.

If conventional school achievement is fraught with these problems, what kind of mastery would be more meaningful? Our definition of *authentic* student achievement is derived from a more general conception of significant human accomplishments through activities that involve skilled intellectual work. Consider the task of designing a bridge. Successful completion of this task illustrates some of the essential intellectual qualities of authenticity. Typically, the work requires using both new and well-established knowledge in the fields of design and construction. New knowledge is produced as special conditions are addressed involving the bridge's particular length, height, peak points of stress and load, and also the impact of possible environmental conditions involving weather extremes of temperature, wind, ice, snow, and floods as well as the possibility of earthquakes. Disciplines of engineering, architecture, science, and mathematics have accumulated bodies of reliable knowledge and procedures for solving the more routine problems of bridge design, but unique problems will require new conceptions of design and construction. When completed, the bridge will be safe and useful to travelers. It may also make a significant aesthetic statement for viewers, and it will likely be considered a personally satisfying accomplishment to those who designed it.

Significant adult accomplishments such as designing a bridge reflect three criteria that can be used to assess the intellectual quality of student achievement as well: *construction of knowledge, disciplined inquiry,* and *value beyond school.*[5] Adults in diverse fields face the primary challenge of constructing or producing, rather than reproducing, meaning or knowledge. They construct knowledge through disciplined inquiry that usege, skills, and technology. They express the results of this disciplined inquiry in written, symbolic, and oral discourse; by making things (products such as furniture, bridges, videos, sculpture), and in performance for an audience (musical, dramatic, athletic). These expressions and products have value beyond success in school; that is, aesthetic, utilitarian, or personal value, to the persons constructing them and to others in the society. We do not expect children to attain levels of competence comparable to skilled adults, but we do want students to de-

---

[5] The conception achievement proposed here is based on the work of Archbald and Newmann (1988), Berlak et al. (1992), Raven (1992), Resnick (1987), and Wiggins (1993).

velop in that direction. To progress on this journey, they should set their sights on accomplished expressions of adult knowledge. That is, they should hone their skills through guided practice in producing original conversation and writing, through repairing and building physical objects, or through artistic and musical performance.

Construction of Knowledge

Persons in the diverse fields just named face the primary challenge of constructing or producing, rather than reproducing, meaning or knowledge. In contrast, the conventional curriculum asks students only to identify the discourse, things, and performances that others have produced (for example, by recognizing the difference between verbs and nouns, between socialism and capitalism; by matching authors with their works; by correctly labeling rocks and body parts). As we emphasize here, student construction of knowledge must be based on understanding of prior knowledge. That is, students must assimilate a great deal of knowledge that others have produced. But the mere reproduction of that knowledge does not constitute authentic academic achievement, because it does not involve interpretation, evaluation, analysis, synthesis, or organization of information that characterizes authentic adult accomplishment.

Disciplined Inquiry

A second defining feature of authentic academic achievement is its reliance on a particular type of cognitive work: disciplined inquiry. Disciplined inquiry consists of three main features: (1) use of a prior knowledge base, (2) striving for in-depth understanding rather than superficial awareness, and (3) expressing conclusions through elaborated communication. In highlighting these features we are not suggesting that young students can be expected to make seminal contributions to the academic disciplines, professions, and arts, but that they are quite capable of engaging in these forms of cognitive work when the work is adapted to students' levels of development.

A broad definition of authentic human accomplishment might not always illustrate disciplined inquiry as suggested by academic study (Gardner, 1983, 1993). For example, feats of wilderness survival that depend largely on ingenuity and courage, forms of athletic prowess, or selfless acts of caring, devotion, and personal sacrifice might all be considered authentic, but they may not illustrate much disciplined inquiry. Since schooling, at a minimum, should promote *academic* study, this conception of human accomplishment is admittedly limited to achievements that depend on the use of formal knowledge. Formal knowledge itself, of course, encompasses an enormous diversity in the liberal arts, applied professions, crafts, along with fields of literature, discourse, and practice that may not be recognized as "disciplines" in schools or universities.

From our point of view, a field of expertise that has accumulated a formal knowledge base and that functions as a community of discourse to advance that knowledge can be considered a discipline, even though it may not have been institutionally established (e.g., through awarding advanced degrees). Examples might include stamp collecting, model railroads, specialized computer user groups, or skydiving.

Prior Knowledge Base

Impressive accomplishments build on prior knowledge that has been accumulated in a field. The knowledge base includes facts, vocabularies, concepts, theories, algorithms, and conventions for the conduct and expression of inquiry itself. The ultimate point of disciplined inquiry is to move beyond former knowledge, through criticism and development of new paradigms. But these advances are themselves stimulated by the foundations of prior knowledge. Most of the cognitive work of school, however, consists of transmitting prior knowledge to students and asking them to accept it as authoritative and reproduce it in fragmented statements.

In-depth Understanding

Disciplined inquiry tries to develop in-depth understanding of a problem rather than only passing familiarity with or exposure to pieces of knowledge. Prior knowledge is mastered, therefore, not primarily to become literate about a broad survey of topics but to facilitate complex understanding on discrete problems. In-depth understanding requires more than knowing a lot of details about a topic. Understanding occurs as one looks for, tests, and creates relationships among pieces of knowledge that can illuminate a given problem or issue. In short, in-depth understanding involves construction of knowledge around a reasonably focused topic. In contrast, many of the cognitive tasks of school ask students to show only superficial awareness of a vast number of topics.[6]

Elaborated Communication

Scientists, jurists, artists, journalists, designers, engineers, and other accomplished adults working within disciplines rely on complex forms of communication to both conduct their work and express their conclusions. The

---

[6]Commitment to depth over coverage entails no necessary narrowing of the curriculum to any particular fields. Diverse fields in the sciences, humanities, and arts can still be pursued over the course of a student's education. Regardless of the field or topics studied, the objective here is to concentrate on depth rather than superficial exposure.

language they use—verbal, symbolic, and visual—includes qualifications, nuances, elaborations, details, and analogies woven into extended exposi- tions, narratives, explanations, justifications, and dialogue. In contrast, much of the communication demanded in school asks only for brief re- sponses: choosing true or false, selecting from multiple choices, filling in blanks, or writing short sentences (e.g., "Prices increase when demand ex- ceeds supply").

Value Beyond School

The third distinction between authentic human achievement and conven- tional school achievement is that authentic achievement has *aesthetic, utilitar- ian*, or *personal value* apart from documenting the competence of the learner. When adults write letters, news articles, insurance claims, or poems; when they speak a foreign language; when they develop blueprints; when they create a painting or a piece of music or build a stereo cabinet; they try to communicate ideas, to produce a product, or to have impact on others be- yond the simple demonstration that they are competent. Achievements of this sort have special value, which is missing in tasks contrived only to assess knowledge (such as spelling quizzes, laboratory exercises, or typical final exams). The cry for "relevant," "student-centered" curriculum, in many cases, simply is a less precise expression of this desire that student accomplish- ment should have value beyond being an indicator of success in school.

Implications

These three criteria—construction of knowledge through disciplined inquiry, to produce discourse, products, and performance that have meaning beyond success in school—can serve as standards of intellectual quality for assess- ing the authenticity of student performance. All three criteria are important. A student may write a letter to the editor, saying he opposes a newly pro- posed welfare plan. This activity may meet the criteria of constructing knowl- edge to produce discourse with value beyond school, but if it shows only shallow understanding of the issues or significant errors, it would be less authentic because of shortcomings in disciplined inquiry.

The conception of authentic achievement is demanding in its insistence on all three standards. In most cases, it would be inappropriate to judge an achievement simply as authentic or inauthentic. Judgment on each criterion is more likely to fall somewhere on a continuum from high to low rather than at either extreme, and a given achievement could be high on some criteria, low on others. The ideal to strive for is high fulfillment of all three.

But, even if authenticity were accepted as a key indicator of intellectual quality, one would not expect all instruction and assessment activities to meet all three standards all of the time. For example, repetitive practice, retrieving straightforward information, and memory drills may be necessary to build knowledge and skill as foundations for authentic performance or to prepare for inauthentic tests required for advancement in the current educational system. The point is not to abandon all forms of "inauthentic" work in school but to keep authentic achievement clearly in view as the valued end.

Why should education aim toward authentic achievement? First, participation in authentic tasks is more likely to motivate students and sustain the hard work that learning requires. Because authentic work has value beyond the demonstration of competence in school and because it permits more comprehensive use of the mind, students will have a greater stake in authentic achievement. Students are more engaged in classrooms that promote authentic achievement (Marks, 1995). Second, authentic academic challenges are more likely to cultivate capacities for higher-order thinking and problem solving useful to both individuals and the society. The mastery gained in school on authentic work is likely to transfer more readily to life beyond school, and this increases the efficiency of the investment in schooling.

How can this general vision of authentic achievement be translated into a more practical vision to guide assessment in schools? Assessment has two critical parts: the kinds of tests, tasks, or other activities that teachers assign to elicit the student work that is assessed; and the criteria teachers use to assess the quality of student work. If assessment is to promote authentic achievement, then teachers should assign assessment tasks consistent with the three criteria, and the criteria should also be the basis for evaluation of the quality of student work. We developed more specific standards for judging the authenticity of each part of assessment. The standards, with examples, are presented in the next two sections.

AUTHENTIC ASSESSMENT TASKS

Since "what you test is what you get," we begin with assessment tasks; that is, the assignments teachers use to evaluate student learning. Assessment tasks communicate to students the kind of intellectual work that is valued. For students to attain authentic academic accomplishment, instruction and assessment must aim toward tasks that demand construction of knowledge through disciplined inquiry and that result in discourse, products, and performance that have value or meaning beyond success in school. We asked teachers to send examples of assessment activities that they relied on to judge how well their students were understanding and mastering their subject. Teachers sent a great variety of tasks. They asked students to complete opinion essays, explain solutions to mathematics problems, compile research reports, draw maps and diagrams, and complete short-answer tests.

We considered only tasks that asked for written work, because as a minimum, all students should learn to write well in both mathematics and social studies. Tasks calling for nonwritten performance such as oral discourse, designing or building physical products, and nonverbal visual displays can also provide impressive evidence of construction of knowledge, disciplined inquiry, and performance that has value beyond success in school (Armstrong, 1994; Herman, Aschbacher, & Winters, 1992). Several of the standards that follow might apply with equal force to a broader range of assessment tasks. But our resources and expertise permitted scoring only students' written performance.

Project staff and practicing social studies teachers scored the authenticity of the assessment tasks sent by the teachers. We used seven standards, described and illustrated next. The standards for tasks reflect the three more general standards for authentic human achievement, as follows:

- Construction of meaning
  1. Organization of information.
  2. Consideration of alternatives.
- Disciplined inquiry
  3. Disciplinary content.
  4. Disciplinary process.
  5. Elaborated written communication.
- Value beyond school
  6. Problem connected to the world.
  7. Audience beyond the school.

We present illustrative tasks that scored high on each of these standards.[7]

Standard 1. Organization of Information

The task asks students to organize, synthesize, interpret, explain, or evaluate complex information in addressing a concept, problem, or issue.

Example

Eighth grade students were asked to write a report comparing immigration past and present. Instructions to students included the following:

[7] Five of the standards were scored on scales from 1–3 and two (elaborated written communication and audience beyond the school) on scales from 1–4. Each assessment task was scored in Madison by a CORS researcher and a currently practicing teacher in social studies, trained by a CORS staff member who also had experience teaching the subject. To judge the teachers' demands and expectations for students, the raters also examined the teacher's comments about the task on a questionnaire and on samples of student performance. If the two-person team did not agree on their initial independent ratings, they discussed the matter until consensus was reached. Over the course of the research about 120 social studies assessment tasks from 67 classrooms were scored.

Immigration has occurred throughout American history. Identify major groups of people entering this country and indicate when most of them came. What events or conditions motivated these different groups to immigrate to the U.S.? How has immigration been regulated and controlled? How has regulation changed over time? Why is immigration now a major issue in this country? In what ways is the issue the same or different now?

This task scored high on organization of information because it required students to synthesize information and make distinctions, comparisons, and generalizations about several aspects of immigration in different historical periods: the key groups, causal conditions, regulatory policy, and relevance to contemporary issues in the United States.

Standard 2. Consideration of Alternatives

The task asks students to consider alternative solutions, strategies, perspectives, or points of view in addressing a concept, problem, or issue.

Example

The following task in eighth grade history required students to construct a persuasive argument. The task stated:

You are to play the role of an advisor to President Nixon after his election to office in 1968. As his advisor, you are to make a recommendation about the United States' involvement in Vietnam.

Your paper is to be organized around three main parts: An introduction that shows an understanding of the Vietnam War up to this point by explaining who is involved in the war and what their objectives are; also in the Introduction, you are to state a recommendation in one or two sentences to make the advice clear.

The body of the paper should be written to convince the President to follow your advice by discussing: (a) the pros of the advice, including statistics, dates, examples and general information to be authoritative; (b) the cons of the advice, letting the President know that the advisor is aware of how others might disagree. Anticipate one or two recommendations that others might give, and explain why they are not the best advice.

The conclusion makes a final appeal for the recommendation and sells the President on the advice.

This task scored high on consideration of alternatives because it explicitly called on students to consider alternative recommendations that the president might receive, such as major escalation of U.S. military action, withdrawal, and working toward international negotiation for peace. In analyzing these alternative courses of action, students would have to demonstrate their understanding of the interests and goals of the contending factions.

Standard 3. Disciplinary Content

The task asks students to show understanding of and/or to use ideas, theories, or perspectives considered central to an academic or professional discipline.

Example

In a high school history course, students were asked to

> Compare FDR's "Three Rs" of the 1930s with Clinton's "jumpstart" proposal to stimu-
> late economic recovery in the 1990s. Include in your comparisons the extent to which
> assumptions and "theory" about the economy of FDR's time were similar to, or differ-
> ent from, more recent economic theory.

This task scored high on content because it required students to show an understanding of the connection between political strategies and economic activity embodied in each of the "Three Rs" (relief, recovery, and reform) during the Great Depression. By asking students to compare and contrast these strategies with President Clinton's proposals for economic recovery, the task required students to connect the historical interventions to recent thinking about economic stability and growth. To do this successfully, students would need to understand the effects of government action and market forces on investment, employment, and earnings.

Standard 4. Disciplinary Process

The task asks students to use methods of inquiry, research, or communication characteristic of an academic or prof ssional discipline.

Example

Students in a fourth and fifth grade social studies class were involved in a year-long study of their community that included a unit on urban geography. Working in small groups, students were given the following task:

> First, select one of the neighborhoods marked on the city map. Second, identify its
> current features by doing an inventory of its buildings, businesses, housing, and
> public facilities. Also, identify current transportation patterns and traffic flow. From
> the information made available, identify any special problems this neighborhood has
> such as dilapidated housing, traffic congestion, or a high crime rate. Third, as a group
> consider various plans for changing and improving your neighborhood. If there is a
> special problem, how will you address it? What kinds of businesses, if any, do you
> want to attract? What kind of housing do you want? Will there be parks and other
> recreation facilities? What transportation patterns do you want? Do you want to make
> the block attractive to different groups of people such as senior citizens and young
> people? After deciding on a plan, draw and label it on the overlay provided with your
> map. Based on what you know about urban geography, indicate in your narrative one
> possible plan that you rejected and say why it was rejected. Indicate how your plan
> will promote the neighborhood features you want.

This task scored high on disciplinary process because it required students to think in some of the same ways as urban planners and geographers. They needed to collect data systematically through observation and recording, use these data as the basis for making generalizations about patterns in human behavior, and make choices about preferred uses of resources and space to fulfill different functions within a community.

Standard 5. Elaborated Written Communication

The task asks students to elaborate on their understanding, explanations, or conclusions through extended writing.

Example

A middle school task required students to write a persuasive essay on one of six topics involving the 1992 presidential election. For example, one of the topics was

> Write an editorial persuading eligible voters to vote. Give reasons why voting counts. Use examples from history telling why voting is important. If possible, describe what might happen if we lost the right to vote.

The instructions specified that student essays would be evaluated on criteria such as the following:

> Your paper included facts learned in class.
> You went beyond what was learned or discussed in class by using a number of different sources of information.
> You clearly stated an opinion and supported it with reasons and argument.

This task scored high on elaborated written communication because it called for students to develop their arguments with reasons and examples from history to show the importance of voting.

Standard 6. Problem Connected to the World beyond the Classroom

The task asks students to address a concept, problem, or issue that is similar to one they have encountered or are likely to encounter in life beyond the classroom.

Example

After studying events surrounding the Rodney King case, eighth grade students were given the following task:

> Write a letter to a student living in South Central Los Angeles conveying your feeling about what happened in that area following the acquittal of police officers in the Rodney King case. Discuss the tension between our natural impulse to strike back at social injustice and the principles of nonviolence.

This task scored high on problem connected to the world, because it asked students to address a fundamental dilemma in human relations: responding to injustice with anger and physical force versus more "peaceful" strategies. Students are likely to encounter this problem often through mass media and their direct experiences.

Standard 7. Audience beyond the School

The task asks students to communicate their knowledge, present a product or performance, or take some action for an audience beyond the teacher, classroom, and school.

Example

The following task was given to fourth grade students:

> Write a letter to a state assembly representative or state senator expressing your opinion about what should be done about threatened eagles along the Mississippi River. Your letter should be persuasive, and it should also do the following:
>
> Communicate knowledge about the subject
> Organize ideas into paragraphs
> Begin sentences in different ways
> Use dialogue to communicate ideas
> Use correct letter format
> Use correct punctuation and spelling
>
> Ask a peer to read your letter and offer constructive criticism. When you are satisfied with your letter, send it.

This task scored high on audience beyond school because it required students to write and send letters to an elected state representative to urge legislative action on a public problem.

Summary

The authenticity of tasks teachers use to assess student achievement depended on the extent to which they met seven standards:

- Organization of information.
- Consideration of alternatives.
- Disciplinary content.
- Disciplinary process.
- Elaborated written communication.
- A problem connected to the world.
- An audience beyond the classroom.

None of the social studies examples scored high on all seven standards, but some scored high on several standards. The task asking students to plan the renewal of an urban neighborhood received high scores on almost all of the standards. Students had to organize information using maps and other data; they had to consider at least one alternative plan; they had to use disciplinary knowledge and processes of urban planners; and they had to write an account that explained how their plan addressed problems and goals for their neighborhood. Students who were to write a position paper that advised President Nixon to take a particular course of action in Vietnam met these same standards. Neither of these tasks asked students to address their work to an audience outside the classroom, but the last example did.

STANDARDS FOR STUDENT PERFORMANCE

What standards should be used to assess the quality of student performance? According to the conception of authentic achievement, we would want to see discourse and products or performance that show construction of knowledge through disciplined inquiry and that have some meaning or value beyond certification of success in school. But the issue here is not simply whether students conduct or engage in these three aspects of authentic performance. Now the challenge is to rate the *quality*, *success*, or *proficiency* of the student's performance.

The quality of student performance was assessed according to the following standards:

- Construction of Knowledge *Meaning*
  Analysis.
- Disciplined Inquiry
  Disciplinary concepts.
  Elaborated written communication.

Within the School Restructuring Study, it was not possible to collect valid information on the meaning or value of each student's performance to the student or an audience beyond school. Judging student work on this standard would require interviews, surveys, or other ways of assessing the actual impact of the students' work. We did decide whether the teachers' assessment tasks posed problems significant beyond school and whether they demanded communication with audiences beyond school. But, because of logistical limitations, we judged the quality of student performance only according to the standards of construction of knowledge and disciplined inquiry.

The standards for student performance were applied to students' writing, completed in response to the assessment tasks sent by their teachers. As explained previously, the project did not have the resources to score nonwritten discourse (e.g., debate or small-group discussion), products (e.g., graphic designs or physical models), or performance. High-quality written performance, critical to success in further education, work, and civic participation, is a necessary but probably insufficient indicator of authentic student achievement.

We present illustrative examples of student performance that scored high on each standard.[8]

Standard 1. Analysis

Student performance demonstrates higher-order thinking with social studies content by organizing, synthesizing, interpreting, evaluating, and hypothesizing to produce comparisons, contrasts, arguments, application of information to new contexts, and consideration of different ideas or points of view.

Example

As part of an end-of-unit assessment, eighth graders were asked to write an essay on the underlying causes of the American Revolution. Instructions indicated that students were to provide a chronological account of the major events, to explain why an action occurred, and to offer an interpretation of its contribution toward the eventual break with England. One student wrote the following:

> The Proclamation of 1763 prevented the colonists from further westward movement, because the British were tired of fighting the Indians over further encroachment by settlers. While this seemed like a reasonable thing from the British point of view, it made the colonists angry. The Stamp Act was passed by the British to raise money to support their army in the colonies, but this produced violence because the colonists believed that taxation without representation was illegal. The Townshend Acts produced the same reaction from the colonists. The need by the colonists to organize their resistance against what they saw as illegal acts by Britain led to the Sons of Liberty. The Committees of Correspondence kept the colonists informed about British actions. The idea of resisting the British spread across the colonies. The Tea Act led to the dumping of tea into Boston Harbor to dramatize colonial opposition. The British became even more oppressive (the colonists called them the Intolerable Acts) by restricting colonial meetings and forcing colonists to quarter soldiers in their homes. These events led to further organizing by the colonists in the form of the Continental Congress and in creating local militia. The Redcoats were on the march to Concord to seize guns that could be used by the colonists to resist British authority

[8]Each standard was scored on a scale from 1–4. Each sample of student performance was scored in Madison by a currently practicing teacher in social studies, trained by CORS staff member who also had experience teaching the subject. About 2700 social studies papers were scored. About 26% of the papers were scored independently by a second rater, randomly assigned. In scoring each scale, precise agreement was achieved about 50% of the time, but in about 90% of the cases, raters were off by no more than one point. The overall correlation of total scores on all three standards was .77.

when Paul Revere rode through the countryside with his warning that "the British are coming." This produced the first battle of the American Revolutionary War.

This essay scored high on analysis because it went beyond a mere chronology of events to include an extended explanation of how one event in this period led to another in a causal chain.

Standard 2. Disciplinary Concepts

Student performance demonstrates an understanding of ideas, concepts, theories, and principles from social disciplines and civic life by using them to interpret and explain specific, concrete information or events.

Example

A fifth grade interdisciplinary unit culminated with students writing a paper that described and explained some environmental problem and its relationship to the quality of human life. The following excerpts were taken from one student's paper entitled, "Overpopulation."

> Demography is the study of populations. Demographers study the populations of communities and countries. Demographers tells us about population statistics and the social, economic, and health characteristics of people. These studies can help us decide if we are overpopulated.
>
> Most people don't understand how overpopulated we are. Experts say that you can't have five minutes of silence without hearing some kind of man-made machine. . . . If overpopulation keeps happening, we will begin to run out of clean air and water, our natural resources will get used up, and we will lose our food supply. Right now we have to feed almost six billion mouths and we can barely do it. According to Paul Ehrlich, "Overpopulation and rapid population growth are intimately connected with most aspects of the current human predicament, including rapid depletion of nonrenewable resources, deterioration of the environment (including rapid climate change), and increasing international tensions. . . ."
>
> Although most population experts agree that overpopulation is bad, not all agree we are overpopulated. Most experts think that overpopulation occurs when a country, state, or city cannot support itself with food, water, and the necessities for living. While experts agree that overpopulation occurs when people can no longer support themselves, they disagree about when this happens. Garret Hardin estimated that the world could feed 300 billion people. Right now we have a world population of "only" six billion. To feed 300 billion we would all have to eat like the average Ethiopian today (one bowl of rice and one cup of water a day). Other experts say we could feed 60 billion people if everyone ate like the average Chinese (small amounts of meat, a lot of rice, and 3 cups of water daily). . . . While we may not be overpopulated right now, most experts are worried about the rate of population increase. In the graph below, we see that the rate of population growth between 1884 and 1984 has been increasing, especially since 1930. . . .
>
> Overpopulation has many fatal effects. It can result in people losing their jobs and to homelessness, hunger, and getting a disease. In some places like Ethiopia and Somalia where there is famine, there is so little food that terrorists steal it for themselves. . . . Overpopulation can also lead to underpopulation. Studies of animals

prove this. Wolves hunt hares. If the hare population rises, that means the wolf population rises, because now they have more food . . . , but the wolf doesn't conserve food. He'll just eat away and when the hares die out, the wolf population begins to die out. . . .

There are many possible solutions to overpopulation. If we could have only one baby per mother, then we could stabilize our population. If we send out more birth control devices, we might slow the population growth. If we educate people on over-population hazards, then they might have less children. If we ask men and women to be sterilized after two children, we could stop the population growth. . . .

But no solution has had any big impact on the problem. . . . We have fallen so deep into this problem that I am not sure it can be solved.

This paper scored high on social studies concepts because it showed a deep understanding of an important demographic concept, population density, and its relationship to a number of social and economic conditions. The paper discussed how overpopulation helps to explain social problems such as hunger, homelessness, and disease. The student recognized ambiguity in the definition of *overpopulation*: experts disagreed on the threshold beyond which life could not be sustained. The student discussed the theoretical model showing overpopulation leading to underpopulation as demonstrated by wolves and hares. The observations in the paper also showed an implicit understanding of "quality of life," the central of theme of the instructional unit.

Standard 3. Elaborated Written Communication

Student performance demonstrates an elaborated account that is clear, coherent, and provides richness in details, qualifications, and argument. The standard could be met by elaborated consideration of alternative points of view.

Example

This task called on 12th grade students to develop a "position paper" on a controversial issue. The following excerpts are from one student's somewhat longer paper justifying U.S. intervention in the Persian Gulf.

There have been numerous instances when the world has witnessed what happens when aggressors are not stopped. Let us look back to 1935 when Mussolini decided to invade and annex Ethiopia. Ethiopia's emperor appealed to the League of Nations, but nothing was done.

Soon afterwards, in 1936, Adolf Hitler reoccupied the Rhineland, thereby violating the Treaty of Versailles. Again, the world ignored these blatant displays of hostility and power. . . .

When Emperor Hirohito of Japan attacked Manchuria in 1931, and then China in 1937, he was simply scolded by the League of Nations. . . .

In 1938, Hitler united Austria and Germany. The world protested, but then gave in to Hitler who said he only wanted to unite the German people. Then, Hitler took the

Sudetenland from Czechoslovakia. As before, concessions were made to appease the aggressor. . . .

In all the examples of unchecked aggression, the moral is the same. The school bully who demands lunch money from other children will not stop until someone stands up to him. If the bully is allowed to harass, intimidate, and steal from other children, it is giving him silent permission to use power against the weak. . . .

Those who complain about the United States acting as a "police nation" would do well to remember that Desert Storm has been a United Nations effort, not solely a U.S. effort. The U.N. Security Council condemned Iraq's invasion and annexation of Kuwait, as did the Arab League. The U.N. imposed mandatory sanctions, forbidding all member states from doing business with Iraq. The European Community, the United States and Japan froze Kuwaiti assets. The United States, Britain, France, Canada, Australia, West Germany, the Netherlands, and Belgium positioned naval vessels to enforce a blockade. . . . Clearly, the United States acted in accordance with the United Nations and with the support of its many members.

There is a time for peace and a time for war. War is a horrible situation, but it is imperative that countries learn to recognize when it is necessary. Perhaps someday the world will be able to solve its problems without violence. In the meantime, we would endanger international security to allow people like Saddam Hussein and his terrorist goons to threaten and overpower independent countries such as Kuwait.

The paper scored high on written communication in social studies because two main points were argued and supported in some detail: aggression should be stopped soon or it will lead to a chain of abuses, and the United States acted not alone but with international support in the Persian Gulf war.

Summary

Three standards were used to assess the intellectual quality of student performance: analysis, disciplinary concepts, and elaborated written communication. While each standard suggests a different dimension of intellectual quality, the best performance would be one that scored high on all three standards. The three examples given here scored high on all three standards. Each demonstrated analysis, subject matter concepts, and elaborated written communication. For example, in writing about the Gulf War, the student analyzed the situation in terms of historical similarities, selected historical analogies, related these analogies to the concept of international aggression, and presented a detailed argument justifying the use of force by the United States in the Persian Gulf.

HOW THE STANDARDS CAN HELP TEACHERS, STUDENTS, AND SCHOOLS

We think the standards can help teachers, students, and schools define more clearly what constitutes high-quality intellectual work. But we do not recommend them as a recipe to be literally adopted and implemented.[9] Instead, they should be used to steer the conversation about reform away from the logistics, management, and politics of new techniques and toward the intellectual quality we seek in classrooms. Enhancing the intellectual quality of education will not be achieved by adoption of specific short-term reforms. It will require years of sustained focus on the issue of intellectual quality. In that spirit, these standards should be debated, tried experimentally, and perhaps modified to further clarify high intellectual standards for pedagogy and student performance.

In their present form, the standards can stimulate reflection about issues of intellectual quality in schools. Small groups of teachers, departments, and even whole schools can use them to reflect on their instruction and assessment. One scenario is for teachers to score and discuss each other's assessment tasks to determine the extent to which they are asking students to construct knowledge, engage in disciplined inquiry, and produce work that has value beyond the classroom. Another possibility is for teacher teams, departments, or the whole school to assess the quality of student writing according to the standards for student performance and discuss the advisability of using similar standards as a basis for student evaluation in all classes. While these standards were developed only for mathematics and social studies, teachers in other subjects can discuss their appropriateness for other disciplines and modify them if necessary.

Discourse about standards for intellectual quality should focus on a few central principles. Long lists of goals, standards, and outcomes distract people's attention from the basic qualities of construction of knowledge, disciplined inquiry, and value beyond school. But our three general criteria and the more specific standards raise the issue of priorities or relative importance among different standards.

In planning how to frame assessment tasks and how to evaluate student performance, should all standards be considered equally important or should some be weighted more heavily than others? Some might argue that depth of conceptual understanding may be more important than analysis or construction of knowledge, because analysis itself can sometimes be directed toward trivial issues. Others might see construction of knowledge and disciplined inquiry as more fundamental than connection to experience beyond instruction, because if the latter is pursued without insistence on the first two standards, intellectual quality would suffer.

We acknowledged earlier that it be would be unrealistic to expect even the most committed teachers to demonstrate high levels of authenticity on all standards for assessment all the time. To maximize coherence for both

---

[9]It would be inappropriate to use these standards for high-stakes evaluation of teachers or in large-scale accountability systems for students and schools, because they were not developed or researched for these purposes.

teachers and students, teachers should try to reach agreement about priorities within the scheme of standards.

These standards of intellectual quality are not likely to resolve persistent dilemmas over "traditional" versus "progressive" notions of schooling. We recognize that some academic objectives (e.g., learning spelling, definitions, and facts) may be accomplished by transmitting decontextualized pieces of knowledge through instructional and assessment activity considered "inauthentic" according to these standards. It is usually assumed that less authentic learning will eventually assist students with more authentic analysis and application. A major issue for teacher deliberation is how to arrive at an appropriate balance between less authentic and more authentic forms of school work that minimizes confusion and contradictions for students and parents.[10]

These assessment standards are silent about the specific content students should be expected to learn in any subject or grade level. It remains to be seen whether meaningful content standards can be developed and broadly accepted in the U.S. schools. If this project is to be successful, it will probably be achieved by some combination of professional organizations and national, state, and local authorities. We think worthwhile content can and ought to be specified for various subjects and grade levels. But there is far too much worthwhile knowledge for all children to learn. Selecting some knowledge as more important than other knowledge, for all children in a democratic nation, is a difficult problem, because even the "knowledge experts" disagree. Ultimately the people have a right to help decide this issue. Thus, what may seem to be a "professional" issue becomes in practice largely a matter of individual taste or group politics.

Whether specific content standards originate primarily from local schools, districts, states, or professional organizations, we think the kinds of standards advanced here can help content standards promote intellectual quality. Without standards of the type we suggest, there is a strong possibility that content standards will continue to encourage mindless coverage of superficial isolated bits of knowledge.

Our standards for authenticity place a major emphasis on disciplinary content, but an *exclusive* focus on specific content standards has the potential to balkanize schools. If standard setting means only that each subject develops a unique set of content to be taught, teachers of different subjects will have little or nothing in common. The lack of a common language for standards across grade levels, subjects, and departments impedes the develop-

---

[10]Concerns have been raised, for example, that students educated through more authentic assessment will not be adequately prepared for conventional standardized tests. Others have suggested that students from educationally disadvantaged homes will be further disadvantaged through application of authentic standards. Newmann, Secada, and Wehlage (1995) and Newmann and Wehlage (1995) offer argument and evidence to show that neither of these concerns seems well founded.

ment of a schoolwide vision, which is important for promoting intellectual quality. The standards of intellectual quality presented here provide educators, parents, and the general public with a common language for talking to one another about teaching and learning, regardless of subject or grade level.

Finally, because they focus on intellectual quality as largely independent of technique, these standards support diversity in teaching style. The standards leave decisions about content to local discretion, and they also dictate no particular teaching style or technique. Authentic instruction can occur in both "teacher-centered" and "student-centered" classrooms. Techniques such as small-group discussions and cooperative learning might rate high or low on intellectual quality. Similarly, classes that were highly structured might rate high or low on the standards. No particular vision of classroom structure, such as the "open classroom," is implied by the standards. Educators can use standards such as these to assess progress toward intellectual quality within a variety of teaching techniques and classroom structures.

Acknowledgment

This chapter was prepared at the Center on Organization and Restructuring of Schools, supported by the U.S. Department of Education, Office of Educational Research and Improvement (Grant No. R117Q00005-95) and by the Wisconsin Center for Education Research, School of Education, University of Wisconsin—Madison. The opinions expressed in this publication are those of the author and do not necessarily reflect the views of the supporting agencies. The conceptual framework, examples, and empirical results were developed in collaboration with Gary G. Wehlage, Walter G. Secada, Helen M. Marks, and Adam Gamoran. This work depended upon the efforts of more than 60 staff members at the Center and the cooperation of teachers, administrators, and students in twenty-four public schools across the United States.

References

Archbald, D., & Newmann, F. M. (1988). *Beyond standardized tests: Assessing authentic academic achievement in the secondary school.* Reston, VA: National Association of Secondary School Principals.
Armstrong, T. (1994). *Multiple intelligences in the classroom.* Alexandria, VA: Association for Supervision and Curriculum Development.
Berlak, H., Newmann, F. M., Adams, E., Archbald, D. A., Burgess, T., Raven, J., & Romberg, T. (1992). *Toward a new science of educational testing and assessment.* Albany: State University of New York Press.
Gardner, H. (1983). *Frames of mind: The theory of multiple intelligences.* New York: Basic Books.
Gardner, H. (1993). *Multiple intelligences: The theory in practice.* New York: Basic Books.
Herman, J. L., Aschbacher, P. R., & Winters, L. (1992). *A practical guide to alternative assessment.* Alexandria, VA: Association for Supervision and Curriculum Development.
Marks, H. (1995). *Student engagement in the classrooms of restructuring schools.* Madison: Center on Organization and Restructuring of Schools, Wisconsin Center for Education Research University of Wisconsin—Madison.
Newmann, F. M., & Associates. (1996). *Authentic achievement: restructuring schools for intellectual quality.* San Francisco: Jossey-Bass.

Newmann, F. M., Marks, H. M., & Gamoran, A. (1996). Authentic pedagogy and student performance. *American Journal of Education*, 104(9), 280–312.

Newmann, F. M., Secada, W. G., & Wehlage, G. G. (1995). *A guide to authentic instruction and assessment: Visions, standards and scoring*. Madison: Center on Organization and Restructuring of Schools, Wisconsin Center for Education Research, University of Wisconsin.

Newmann, F. M., & Wehlage, G. G. (1995). *Successful school restructuring: A report to the public and educators*. Madison, WI: Center on Organization and Restructuring of Schools, Wisconsin Center for Education Research, University of Wisconsin.

Raven, J. (1992). A model of competence, motivation, and behavior, and a paradigm for assessment. In H. Berlak et al. (Eds.), *Toward a new science of educational testing and assessment* (pp. 85–116). Albany: State University of New York Press.

Resnick, L. B. (1987). Learning in school and out. *Educational Researcher*, 16(9), 13–20.

Wiggins, G. P. (1993). *Assessing student performance*. San Francisco: Jossey-Bass.

CHAPTER

13

Foreign Languages:
Instruments, Techniques,
and Standards

NANCY C. RHODES
Center for Applied Linguistics

MARCIA H. ROSENBUSCH
Iowa State University

LYNN THOMPSON
Center for Applied Linguistics

The purpose of this chapter is to provide a brief overview of foreign language assessment in elementary and secondary schools, discuss a variety of current assessment practices, and provide samples of alternative and standardized instruments in use in schools today. A final section will discuss the impact of foreign language standards on instruction and assessment and suggest directions for the future.

HISTORICAL OVERVIEW

In the early history of the United States, the learning of second languages, for the most part, was seen as "a natural part of the curriculum" (Curtain & Pesola, 1989, p. 1). The prevalence of such programs, however, has waxed and waned over the years due to both internal and external factors (Thompson, Christian, Stansfield, & Rhodes, 1990). Most commonly, such programs have been at the high school and college levels (Hewitt, Ryan, & Kuhs, 1993), with the number of programs at the elementary school level varying widely over the years (Curtain & Pesola, 1989).

Handbook of Classroom Assessment

The goals of foreign language instruction and the consequent teaching methodologies have reflected historical events and evolutionary stages in the fields of education and linguistics (Thompson et al., 1990). Among the various foreign language approaches have been the grammar–translation method (pre-World War II), the audiolingual method (post-World War II to the 1960s), the proficiency or communicative approach (1970s to present), and most recently, a content-based approach.

Traditionally, five skill areas have been recognized as part of foreign language education: listening, speaking, reading, writing, and culture. The area of culture has been the least well-defined throughout, although in recent years efforts have been renewed to define curricular content for the teaching of culture (Lorenz et al., 1994a, 1994b; Singerman, 1996).

One of the important concerns of teachers throughout the evolution of foreign language instruction has been how to determine what students have learned. Today, that concern is one of the issues receiving the greatest attention in the field. To be effective, assessment should reflect the teacher's methodological orientation as well as the course content and objectives. A grammar–translation test, therefore, would require students to demonstrate their knowledge of grammar and ability to translate a passage. The student would at no point be expected to reproduce or create with the target language. A communicative/proficiency-oriented test, on the other hand, would focus on the student's ability to use the target language to communicate and function within a context broader than the classroom, including the target language culture.

In reality, assessments that are administered to students do not necessarily reflect the methodology, content, or objectives of the language class. This incompatibility between the class and the assessment is due to a number of factors. Teachers often rely on textbook or standardized tests. Such tests may reflect methodologies or purposes that are not the same as the teacher's. Even if teachers design tests for their own classes, their tests may not match their methodologies. For example, despite the communicative orientation of the curriculum, teachers may unconsciously draw on their memory of tests that they took in foreign language classes (i.e., grammar–translation tests) and produce similar tests.

The coexistence of a variety of trends in testing have further contributed to the confusion that foreign language educators feel. Such trends include the dominance of discrete-point tests and reliance on standardized testing, and the growing interest in open-ended, contextualized alternative assessments that have their roots in the proficiency movement.

As a reflection of the behaviorist approach to language teaching in the 1960s, most traditional assessments of language skills tend to be discrete-point tests, with emphasis on linguistic accuracy, such as grammatical structure and vocabulary. Discrete-point tests tend to focus on single skill areas and evaluate the knowledge of details of the language. Items are typically presented in single sentences or phrases that are unrelated and lack context. The skill areas of reading and writing are evaluated with written tests. Listening comprehension is often evaluated by written responses to items the teacher reads or presents on tape. Discrete-point tests are used especially with grammar–translation and audiolingual methodologies.

Standardized tests, which rely largely on discrete-point items, focus on achievement (acquired knowledge). Easy and practical to administer, they gained acceptance within the language field as they had in other disciplines. As Genesee (1994) states, "More than anything else, standardized tests held out the promise of scientific respectability for language assessment" (p. 3). Hence, schools turned to standardized testing as the answer for assessment of foreign language as well as for other disciplines. With such tests, the teacher could serve merely as an administrator and results were produced that could be regarded as "valid and reliable."

Increasing dissatisfaction with standardized testing, however, has emerged in the field in recent years. Despite being efficient and objective, such tests do not assess the application of knowledge and higher-order skills in meaningful, "real-world" situations, nor do they assess learning outcomes such as critical thinking, creativity, oral communication, and social skills (McTighe & Ferrara, 1994). Educators have realized that, while such tests may be effective in assessing mastery of discrete knowledge of a language, they overlook much of what is going on in the classroom. These tests fail to provide the teacher with information about the teaching and learning process. An additional negative impact of such testing is that it has undermined teacher confidence in their own day-to-day classroom assessment, even though standardized tests had little relation to teacher objectives or the needs of the students being tested (Genesee, 1994).

Since the 1980s, there has been considerable interest among all levels of foreign language education in the development of students' foreign language proficiency in the classroom. Two language proficiency initiatives that were carried out in the early 1980s have had particular impact on foreign language assessment practices: (1) the American Council on the Teaching of Foreign Languages (ACTFL) proficiency guidelines, which were developed for adult learners and are based on the functions learners can comprehend or express, the content or topic areas they can deal with, and the accuracy with which they receive or convey a message (Liskin-Gasparro, 1987); and (2) the oral proficiency interview (OPI), which was designed to assess speaking proficiency (see page 392 for details on the oral proficiency interview). Growing out of the interest in proficiency teaching and testing, alternatives to discrete-point testing have become more common. Tests have begun to include more authentic and open-ended contextualized items for which many answers are possible.

As a result of the ACTFL proficiency guidelines, many states developed proficiency-oriented curricula and offered teachers in-service workshops on the topic. Many textbook publishers developed proficiency-oriented materials to accompany textbooks, and teachers changed or adapted their teaching strategies to help their students achieve the goals described by the proficiency-oriented curriculum (Bartz, 1991). This reorientation of methodology has not as yet, however, had a strong impact in classroom assessment, according to Bartz.

Indeed, in 1986, Omaggio noted that most classroom achievement tests tended to be largely of the discrete-point type regardless of the transition in the 1970s and 1980s toward proficiency-based teaching. Specifically, "an important issue is the naive belief that the introduction of the OPI and the guidelines, per se, would create a change while overlooking the most important agent of change—the classroom teacher" (E. Shohamy, 1990, as quoted in Bartz, 1991, p. 70). Despite efforts by many states to familiarize teachers with the guidelines, many teachers have difficulty applying the guideline concepts to their classroom assessment situations.

Most recently, in all fields of education, educators have put increasing emphasis on measuring the processes inherent in learning and teaching as well as the products. New assessments require students to apply and integrate skill areas by emphasizing complex skills (e.g., ability to analyze, generalize, hypothesize) within a relevant, meaningful context. Open-ended, complex problems challenge students and encourage them to draw their own inferences. In addition, alternative methods of assessment are being advocated as more than just tests; they are, rather, an integral part of classroom instruction. Assessments that fit in the category of "alternative assessment" include performance testing, portfolios, exhibits, demonstration, and dialogue journals. These approaches also call for more student involvement in planning assessment, interpreting the results of assessment, and in self-assessment. See Table 1 for a comparison of characteristics of alternative and traditional assessment.

The national interest in alternative assessment prevalent throughout the education community has begun to lead to changes in assessment practices in the field of foreign languages. In 1995, when assessment instruments were solicited from teachers, schools, school districts, state education offices, and educational research organizations for inclusion in a collection of instruments, both traditional and alternative assessment instruments were received (Thompson, 1995). Among the alternative assessment instruments were portfolios, journals, demonstrations, conferences, and observation checklists. These instruments were used to assess learning outcomes and processes as well as instructional objectives and processes, to encourage student involvement and ownership of assessment, to foment collaboration between students and teachers, and to plan effective instruction.

Baker (1994) notes that teachers who embrace alternative assessments are beginning a complex process in which they will need to change their fundamental beliefs and instructional practices. Rosenbusch (1995) verified

TABLE I
Traditional versus Alternative Assessment

Traditional assessment	Alternative assessment
Characteristics	
• Discrete points are assessed. • Student is assigned a score based on number or percentage correct. • Tests are scored easily and quickly. • Items are often multiple-choice, matching, or true/false. • Items test passive knowledge (student is merely required to recognize the correct answer, not to produce it). When these tests are standardized, they • allow comparisons across populations. • are considered statistically valid and reliable.	• Emphasis is on the process of learning as well as the product. • Assessment tasks involve the application and integration of instructional content. Tasks are often open-ended, offer students a great degree of choice and input, and culminate in individual or group performances. • Language is assessed holistically. Scoring requires judgment and use of scoring criteria (e.g., rubrics). • Assessments often involve multi-step production tasks or require multiple observations and thus require extended time to complete. • Tasks require students to demonstrate knowledge actively through problem-solving, inferencing, and other complex cognitive skills. • Tasks are situation-based or based in the real-world context. • Assessments often have not been evaluated for statistical validity or reliability.
Use	
• Main focus is on the assessment of learning outcomes.	To assess • learning outcomes • learning processes • instructional processes • instructional objectives To encourage • student involvement and ownership of assessment and learning • collaboration between students and teachers To plan effective instruction
Common Formats	
• Multiple-choice response • Discrete-point tests	• Portfolios • Journals • Demonstrations • Conferences • Observations

Note. From K–8 *Foreign Language Assessment: A Bibliography* (p. xvi), by L. Thompson, 1995 (Washington, DC: ERIC Clearinghouse on Languages and Linguistics) (as adapted from Baker, 1990; Herman, Aschbacher, & Winters, 1992; and Lewis, 1992). Copyright 1995 by ERIC. Reprinted with permission.

this through a survey on assessment practices of a group of middle and high school foreign language teachers who were participants in a national institute on technology in education. These teachers expressed considerable dissatisfaction with their current assessment practices. The following comments of teachers were typical: "I'm frozen in the |19|60s, |19|70s and |19|80s." "We are too textbook oriented." Teachers noted that they want to make changes but lack the knowledge to do so: "I need more information on ways to assess all aspects of the curriculum and student progress." "|I| would like to use portfolio assessment." "I need better oral proficiency tools."

According to Baker (1994), teachers must determine which forms of alternative assessment are most useful for which educational purposes, distinguish among assessment instruments of differing quality and appropriateness, and learn to design assessment instruments. It is no wonder that growing interest in alternative assessment at the same time that traditional discrete-point tests are still commonly used makes assessment a challenge for foreign language classroom teachers.

SAMPLE ASSESSMENT INSTRUMENTS

Introduction

Language assessment, especially at the high school level, traditionally has been a matter of relatively informal achievement testing on the part of teachers of individual classes. Individual student assessment is carried out via report cards; grades are typically based on a combination of attendance, oral and written performance in class, and scores on teacher- or textbook-generated quizzes and tests.

No national program of language assessment is required either of states, schools, or individual students. As of 1994, a few states had instituted voluntary standardized testing of language. Pennsylvania, for example, is implementing oral proficiency requirements in a foreign language for all graduating seniors. Statewide assessments vary in terms of the types of tests, with some states relying entirely on standardized tests that can be corrected by computer and others relying on "portfolio assessment," the collection of different types of tests, including writing samples, performance assessments, and the like, for each student (Center for Applied Linguistics, 1995).

There are national programs of standardized language tests that are part of the college admission and placement process and, therefore, are entirely voluntary on the part of the student. College-bound high school students, if they desire, may demonstrate their achievement in a foreign language by taking a standardized test in that language, usually during their last year of high school. Their scores are forwarded to the colleges and universities to which they are applying; high scores can enhance the students' chances for acceptance or can have the effect of "excusing" them from one to two years of basic study of the language in college. In addition, language tests sponsored by national language organizations are available in all of the most commonly taught languages.

As previously mentioned, a growing trend in elementary and secondary foreign language classrooms has been the use of alternative assessment. Such assessment varies widely among school districts and even from classroom to classroom. Increasingly, school districts and language teachers are developing innovative forms of assessment based on communicative language teaching and are sharing these instruments with others. All future assessment activities may be influenced by the new foreign language standards for grades K–12.

Therefore, a wide range of tests are available to teachers today, with an increasing focus on classroom-based, authentic assessment. The following four sections include descriptions of these categories of tests: (1) nationally administered foreign language tests, (2) standardized examinations, (3) statewide tests, and (4) district, local, and teacher-made assessment instruments. The first two categories include tests at the high school level, while the last two include elementary, middle, and high school test descriptions. These tests were selected because they are currently being used in schools and are representative of current trends in foreign language assessment at the elementary, middle, and high school level.[1]

Overview of National Tests

Some of the language teachers' associations and language-related organizations (e.g., American Association of Teachers of French [AATF], American Association of Teachers of German [AATG], American Association of Teachers of Spanish and Portuguese [AATSP], American Council on the Teaching of Foreign Languages, Center for Applied Linguistics, and the Japan Foundation) have tests available to teachers as part of a service to the profession. The number of teachers availing themselves of the opportunity to compare their students to others varies from association to association. Six of the most commonly administered tests are described here.

Japanese Language Proficiency Test

Since 1984, the Japan Foundation has offered the Japanese Language Proficiency Test once a year to measure and certify Japanese proficiency of non-native speakers. The test has been administered in the United States since

[1]Many of the descriptions of statewide, district, local, and teacher-made assessments are from Thompson (1995), an annotated listing of over 100 elementary and middle school foreign language assessment instruments, guidelines, and techniques.

the establishment of the Japan Foundation Language Center in Santa Monica, California, in 1993. In 1994, 82,000 people in 63 cities, including Los Angeles, Chicago, and Vancouver, and cities in 30 countries abroad, as well as 54,000 people in Japan, took the exam. There are four levels of the exam and each level has three sections: characters and vocabulary, listening, and reading and grammar. The criteria for each level are as follows:

- Level 4. Mastered elementary level of grammar, about 100 kanji and 800 words and demonstrates the ability to listen to and understand simple conversation and to read short, simple sentences. Requires 150 hours of study.
- Level 3. Mastered basic grammar, about 300 kanji and 1500 words and demonstrates the ability to listen to and understand everyday conversation and to read simple sentences. Requires 300 hours of study.
- Level 2. Mastered grammar at a relatively high level, about 1000 kanji and 6000 words and demonstrates the listening and reading comprehension ability about matters of a general nature. Requires about 600 hours of study.
- Level 1. Mastered grammar at a high level, about 2000 kanji and 10,000 words and has an integrated command of the language sufficient for life in Japanese society and for providing a useful base for study at a Japanese university. Requires about 900 hours of study.

Examinees who pass the exam are sent certificates of proficiency from Japan. Passing scores are 60% for Levels 2, 3, and 4, and 70% for Level 1 (The Japan Foundation Language Center, 1995).

National French Contest

The American Association of Teachers of French sponsors an annual National French Contest (Le Grand Concours) that, in 1995, attracted almost 75,000 students. The purpose of the contest is to encourage interest among students in the French language and provide an assessment of students at seven levels. The secondary school test includes Levels 01–5 (6 levels total) and the elementary school test has one level (versions A and B). All students of French in the United States are encouraged to participate (their teachers do not have to be members of AATF). Students in the United States who come from Francophone countries are encouraged to take the test but are eligible for only local prizes.

The secondary contest includes both written and tape-recorded listening components. Skills include vocabulary, grammar, culture and civilization, and sound discrimination. To illustrate the range of abilities that can be tested, sample components from the lowest (01) and highest levels (5) are provided:

Level 01.
Vocabulary:
Basic greetings.

Expressions to talk about the weather.
How to tell time.
Names of countries bordering France.
Adverbs of time.
Most common colors.
Common prepositions.
Other.
Grammar:
Verb tenses.
Elision.
Definite, indefinite, and partitive articles and contractions.
Demonstrative adjectives.
Subject pronouns.
Negation *ne . . . pas.*
Other.
Culture and Civilization:
Phrases in greeting, introductions, farewells.
Names of the most important French holidays and explanation of how
    they are celebrated.
Sound Discrimination:
Sound of all the letters of the alphabet.
Sound change with accents.
Statement versus question intonation.
Liaison.
Difference between the sounds of all nasals.
Recognition of the sounds of all combinations of letters.
Level 5.
Everything for Levels 01–4, plus
Grammar:
Recognition of all verb tenses, including the imperfect and pluperfect
    subjunctive.
Thorough review of all aspects of French grammar.
Culture and Civilization:
Introduction to the arts and literature of the 16th, 17th, and 18th
    centuries.

National winners are recognized at the top eight ranks. All contest papers
are machine scored by the AATF office (F. Jenkins, personal communication,
August 25, 1995).

The elementary school Test A includes speaking and listening sections;
Test B is the same as Test A with the addition of a reading comprehension
section. There is documentation that the National French Contest has served
as both a motivating and a learning experience for students in elementary
school French programs. One teacher in a Northern California program found

that, although the National French Contest at the elementary level is very demanding for all who participate, the exercise has been positive for the students for a number of reasons:

- The exam focuses on the importance of oral language skills. In a few minutes of reflection, the students have to regroup all of their knowledge of the language and express it in the most intelligible way possible;
- The students, from an early age, learn to master their fear of expressing themselves orally in a foreign language. They feel, furthermore, an extraordinary pleasure in hearing their own voices recorded; and
- The quality of pronunciation and oral expression in general is much improved, over the last few years, for all those students who participate in the competition (Gabet, 1986).

National German Examination

The American Association of Teachers of German offers an annual National German Examination to assess the language skills of high school students studying German. The tests prove helpful to schools and colleges for placing incoming students in the proper courses. On a practical level, the tests play an important role in the selection of students who win the annual study awards to Germany, since scoring in the 90th percentile or higher on the test is the first step toward being a winner in the selection process.

The tests are administered at Levels II, III, and IV and are suitable for students in the middle of their second, third, and fourth years of high school German instruction. There are 100 items on each test, and it takes approximately an hour to administer. The tests are divided into the following sections (the approximate number of items per category is included in parentheses):

- Listening comprehension; brief interchanges (30–35 items) and longer dialogues (5–10 items).
- Situational questions testing reading and conversational skills (20–22 items).
- Applied structure or grammar (15 items) and idioms in context (10 items) (no conscious grammatical knowledge is expected).
- Comprehension of connected passages of approximately 200 words each (10–15 items).
- Comprehension of some authentic materials (e.g., advertisements) on Level II (3–5 items).

In each test, easier and harder items are arranged in a "wave pattern" to encourage students to continue through the entire test rather than abandoning it at a given point because it has become too hard. The tests are designed so that the average score of all nonnative students taking the test is close to 70.

In recent years, the listening parts of the tests were changed to make the tests more "user friendly." The changes were as follows: (1) the time was lengthened by five minutes to give students more time to respond to the listening items; (2) questions about the listening dialogues were printed in the test booklet and students are now encouraged to read the questions before they hear the dialogue, so that they will know what to listen for; and (3) some of the short listening items are now contextualized. The context makes the range of possible question topics more predictable than if there were no context, but the questions can all be answered independently from each other.

The tests are designed so that they yield reliable scores on all levels of achievement; the coefficients of total test reliability for the 1994 tests ranged between .94 and .95 among the various levels and groups (American Association of Teachers of German, 1994).

National Spanish Examinations

The American Association of Teachers of Spanish and Portuguese is in the process of developing a proficiency-based national Spanish exam, which will be ready for schools to administer in 1997. Since 1957 the AATSP has sponsored the National Spanish Examinations (NSE), which were developed as a motivational, extracurricular activity and contest for students of members of AATSP and its chapters. The NSE, a prochievement test of listening and reading comprehension (including both proficiency-based and achievement-based tasks) designed for junior and senior high school students of Spanish, is a widely used test of Spanish in the United States. In 1995, nearly 70,000 students participated in the exam.

The six levels of the exam are aimed at a wide range of students, from those whose first exposure to the language is in the fall of the year to those in the fifth and sixth year of study, which may include advanced placement classes. Students taking the NSE are placed in three categories—regular (classroom experience only), outside experience (specified amount of travel or study in a Spanish-speaking country), and bilingual native speaker. Each year, a new test battery is developed.

The exam consists of two sections: 30 listening comprehension questions and 50 reading questions. The bilingual students have an additional 20 reading comprehension questions. The national office of the AATSP recognizes the top three scores in each level and category and awards plaques to all winners (M. Quiat, personal communication, November 7, 1995).

In the 1997 NSE, revisions will be incorporated to make the test more proficiency based. The following changes are planned: (1) the vocabulary and grammar subsections will be combined into a section entitled "vocabulary and grammar in context," which will provide the examinee with greater context for the questions; and (2) reading and listening passages will be changed so that instead of a single passage with several questions per passage, there will be a single passage followed by one question. According to Campbell (1995), the single-passage, single-response format is more proficiency based because (1) each test question, instead of testing minor details, attempts to test global understanding and (2) more passages are included, which provides a better assessment of the examinee's ability to deal with a wide variety of topics.

Oral Proficiency Interview

ACTFL, in conjunction with the Educational Testing Service (ETS) and the Federal Interagency Language Roundtable (FILR), developed language proficiency guidelines, based on the government's proficiency scale, to be used in secondary schools and colleges. The guidelines define four major levels of language proficiency: novice, intermediate, advanced, and superior. Traditionally, students have been rated on this scale through a face-to-face speaking test known as the oral proficiency interview (OPI). The OPI progresses through four stages. It begins with a warm-up, which is designed to put the test taker at ease and help the interviewer make a very tentative assessment of the speaker's level of proficiency. During the level check in phase two, the interviewer guides the conversation through a number of topics. The purpose of the level check is to verify the tentative estimate arrived at during the warm-up and permit the speaker to demonstrate the level of language that can be handled with confidence and accuracy. During phase three, the probes, the interviewer raises the level of the conversation to determine the limitations in the speaker's proficiency or to ascertain that the speaker can communicate effectively at a higher level of language. The purpose of the final phase, the wind-down, is to put the speaker at ease by returning to a level of conversation that the speaker can handle comfortably (Stansfield, 1992).

Simulated Oral Proficiency Interview

The simulated oral proficiency interview (SOPI) is a type of semi-direct speaking test that models, as closely as is practical, the format of the oral proficiency interview (Stansfield, 1989). It is scored using the ACTFL speaking proficiency guidelines. Clark (1979) defines a semi-direct test as one that elicits speech by means of tape recordings, printed test booklets, or other nonhuman elicitation procedures. The SOPI is a tape-mediated test designed to elicit language that is similar to language that would be elicited through an OPI. The SOPI can be administered to groups of students and requires no trained interviewer. Correlation studies in five languages have indicated that the SOPI can be used with confidence when administering an OPI is not practical or feasible (Stansfield, 1990). The Center for Applied

Linguistics has available SOPIs (for high school and university level) in Arabic, Hausa, Hebrew, Indonesian, and Portuguese, and SOPIs with self-instructional rater training kits in Chinese, French, German, Japanese, and Spanish. SOPIs measure oral proficiency through a series of prompts that include such tasks as giving directions, describing pictures, recounting a story, comparing and contrasting, arguing in favor of a proposal, and considering hypothetical situations. Instructions and time limits are given on a master tape and examinees record their responses on individual response tapes. CAL has designed the SOPIs for institutional use, and a testing packet includes a master tape, a test booklet, administration instructions, and self-instructional rater training materials.

Overview of Standardized Examinations

Historically, in addition to tests just listed, standardized language exams have been used at the high school level for college-bound students. The major achievement testing programs are College Board tests: the SAT II tests for Chinese, French, German, Italian, Japanese, Latin, Modern Hebrew, and Spanish; and the CLEP (the College Level Examination Program) for French, German, and Spanish. Another College Board program, Advanced Placement (AP), is primarily for students who have participated in a college-level advanced placement course at the high school level; the test is available in French, German, Latin, and Spanish. Finally, the International Baccalaureate assessment is for students who have participated in the highly competitive internationally accredited secondary school program. The tests are described next.

SAT II

The SAT II language tests are of two types: reading only, for French, German, Italian, Latin, Modern Hebrew, and Spanish; and reading and listening for Chinese, French, German, Japanese, and Spanish. They are part of a group of tests, all called SAT IIs, that allow a student to demonstrate achievement in a number of subjects. SAT II test scores are sent to the colleges to which a student is applying, and colleges use the scores as the basis for admission or for placement. The reading only tests are administered frequently during the school year, along with other SAT II tests; the reading with listening tests are administered once a year, and currently only at secondary schools that have agreed to participate.

The tests are not based on a particular textbook or teaching method, but are designed to allow for variation in language preparation. The tests are appropriate for students who have studied the language for three or four years in secondary school or the equivalent. Some second year students also take the tests. Components of the reading test include vocabulary in context, grammatical structure, and reading comprehension. However, there are variations among languages. The listening section tests ability to understand the spoken language through questions such as those based on a picture or photograph, general content questions based on short dialogues or monologues, and questions based on longer dialogues or monologues. Test developers suggest that the best preparation for the tests is the gradual development of competence over a period of years (College Board, 1995c).

CLEP Language Tests

The CLEP language tests are 90-minute examinations designed to measure knowledge and ability equivalent to that of students who have completed two to four semesters of college language study. The tests are standard across the three languages offered: French, German, and Spanish. They consist of two parts: reading and listening. The reading section assesses vocabulary mastery, grammatical control, and reading comprehension. The listening section (presented orally on audiotape) assesses phonemic discrimination, listening comprehension, vocabulary mastery, and the ability to understand the language as spoken by native speakers. The two sections are weighted so that they contribute equally to the total score. Most colleges that award credit for the language examinations award either two or four semesters of credit, depending on how high the student scores on the test (College Board, 1986, 1990, 1995a).

Test candidates must demonstrate their ability to comprehend written and spoken language by answering various types of questions. Although there is slight variation in the three language tests, the components in Table 2 represent the general skills tested in the examinations.

Advanced Placement Programs

The advanced placement programs in high schools are recognized by nearly 2,900 U.S. and foreign colleges and universities, which grant credit or appropriate placement, as well as sophomore standing, to students who have performed satisfactorily on AP examinations. The AP exams are the only College Board high school language tests that assess the four skills of reading, writing, speaking, and listening. Exams are available in French (language and literature), German (language only), Latin (Vergil and Latin literature), and Spanish (language and literature). In 1995, over 56,000 students took the exams. The modern language exams are from 2½ to 3 hours in length and contain a section that is a free response (writing and speaking) and another section of multiple-choice questions (listening and reading). These exams contain a performance section that includes recording student responses on audiotape. The Latin exams include writing and reading only.

TABLE 2
Components of CLEP Language Tests

Reading (50–62% of exam)	
Vocabulary mastery	• Comprehend words and idiomatic expressions in context of printed sentences or situations
Grammatical control	• Identify usage that is structurally correct and appropriate
Reading comprehension	• Read passages representative of various styles and levels of difficulty
Listening (38–50% of exam)	
Sound recognition	• Recognize sounds in single sentences by means of picture identification
Vocabulary mastery	• Understand meaning of words in idiomatic expressions in context of spoken sentences or situations
Listening comprehension	• Understand short dialogues based on everyday situations
	• Understand the language as spoken by native speakers in longer dialogues and narratives

Note. Adapted from *The CLEP Test Information Guide, College Spanish, College French, College German,* College Entrance Examinations Board (1986, 1990, 1995). Reprinted by permission of the College Entrance Examination Board and Educational Testing Service, the copyright owners.

The French and Spanish language exams evaluate performance in the use of language, both in understanding written and spoken language and in responding in correct and idiomatic speech. The literature tests measure the ability to understand, analyze, and interpret literary texts and to write competent critical essays in the language. The German language exam evaluates performance in the use of the language, both in understanding written and spoken German and in responding with ease in correct, idiomatic German. The two Latin exams cover the topics in middle-level college Latin classes (Vergil and Latin literature) (College Board, 1995b).

International Baccalaureate Program

The International Baccalaureate (IB) program, a rigorous program becoming more popular in U.S. high schools, derives its curricula from syllabi provided by the IB headquarters in Geneva, Switzerland. Students have to demonstrate excellence in English, a foreign language, social studies, science, mathematics, and one other area of interest. To earn an IB diploma, students must pass an international IB exam in each of six areas, including foreign language. A score of 4 or above out of 7 on the exams indicates good to excellent performance and allows high school students to get advanced standing or credit in college courses. The IB program offers three foreign language assessments: (1) *Language* B, a test for students who have studied a language as a *foreign* language for a minimum of four to five years, (2) A*b*

Initio, an opportunity for students who have studied language for only two years, and (3) the A2 *Test*, a literature-based program for bilingual speakers. The tests are graded by the classroom teacher as well as external examiners (identified and trained by the IB organization) to ensure uniformity in evaluating students worldwide (Montgomery County Public Schools, 1995).

The description here will focus on the "internal" assessment (conducted within the classroom) of the Language B test. Language B is a criterion-referenced test, with listening, writing (which includes text handling—skimming, predicting, and cloze reading—and written production—controlled and guided free writing), and oral components.

A formal internal assessment is an integral ongoing component of the evaluation plan. Students' oral work is continuously assessed in the final year of the IB foreign language course. Assessment activities include an individual oral component with two facets (10 minutes each). First, the student prepares a presentation for the class on a topic of his or her choice, taken from one of the following three themes: exploring change, exploring groups, or exploring leisure. Second, she or he participates in a general discussion on the topic with the teacher. All presentations and discussions are taperecorded and rated by the teacher. Subsamples of the classes' work are sent to an IB examiner for evaluation.

There is also a group oral assessment, where students participate in problem-solving activities, conduct a discussion about one of the pieces they have written, or discuss a topic of interest to them.

As part of the regular classroom assessment, students are rated on their speaking and writing effectiveness in completing a task and communicating the required message. The criteria for assessing the oral component are included in Table 3.

These criteria are given to the students ahead of time so that they know what the task is and on what they will be rated. The focus of the internal evaluation is on students' growth and development over time, as well as on their performance at the end of the course of study (C. Dahlberg, personal communication, November 8, 1995).

Sample Statewide Tests

The following statewide tests at the elementary, middle, and high school levels were selected because they can serve as models for educators who are currently developing assessments appropriate for the range of foreign language programs in their states. Included are two elementary school, two middle school, and one high school test. The first elementary level sample and the first middle school level sample are both from the state of Louisiana. These assessments are particularly interesting, not only because they are situationally based and incorporate authentic material, but also because

TABLE 3
Language B: Internal Assessment Criteria for Oral Component

Criterion A, Message (The effectiveness of the speaker in completing the task and communicating the required message)	Criterion B, Interaction (The effectiveness of the speaker in maintaining the flow of the discussion)	Criterion C, Language (The accuracy, appropriateness, and fluency of the language used)
Task: How well has the required task been carried out?	*Interaction*: How competently does the speaker interact and/or take the initiative in conversation/dialogue?	*Vocabulary*: To what extent are the vocabulary and idiom of a suitable range?
Message: How clear and/or effective is the message? How appropriate are the responses?	*Coherence*: Does the exchange of ideas flow logically?	*Accuracy*: To what extent is the use of grammatical structures accurate and varied?
Ideas: How relevant, interesting, and/or convincing are the ideas?	*Register*: To what extent is the register appropriate to the interaction?	*Pronunciation/Fluency*: To what extent does the pronunciation contribute to the fluency of the communication?

Note. From *Group Two: Language B Guide* (p. 44), 1994, Geneva: International Baccalaureate Organisation. Copyright 1994 by International Baccalaureate. Reprinted with permission.

they are the result of collaborative efforts by American, Canadian, and Belgian foreign language educators. The second elementary level sample is from North Carolina, where there has been a statewide mandate for foreign language instruction. This listening test, which is closely tied to the statewide elementary-level curriculum, is videotape mediated. The other middle school sample and the high school sample are from New York state, which has a long-standing assessment program. Closely linked to a well-articulated statewide curriculum, the New York assessment instruments are frequently updated to ensure that they accurately reflect the curricula on which they are based. These two tests are of interest also because they test cultural knowledge as well as listening, speaking, reading, and writing skills.

Statewide Elementary School Samples

Sample 1. Fifth Grade French Listening Comprehension Test (French)

Availability:	Restricted: on a consultation basis only
Current users:	Louisiana public schools
Type of FL program:	Elementary school foreign language program
Intended grade level:	5

Intended test use:	Placement, proficiency, program evaluation
Skills tested:	Listening
Test authors:	Manon Beaudet-Deer, Richard J. Guidry, and Margaret K. Singer
Publication date:	1991–1994
Test cost:	Contact Margaret Singer
Test length:	53 items; two 30-minute sessions (possibly longer)
Test materials:	Audiotape, teacher's manual, student booklet, teacher and student questionnaires
Test format:	Multiple choice
Scoring method:	Number correct

This theme-based, multiple-choice test evaluates listening comprehension skills of students after two years of French at the elementary level. Students listen to a series of passages on audiotape for specific pieces of information related to the major, culturally significant, test theme—*Le Festival International de Louisiane* (the International Festival of Louisiana). The skills, concepts, and test items were developed and reviewed by curriculum specialists from throughout the state and abroad. Since this test evaluates listening comprehension only, the student must listen to a series of passages set in "an appropriate situation" as stated for each objective in the state curriculum guide. Every effort was made for the context to be culturally significant, hence the theme of the *Festival International de Louisiane*. The festival represents one of the few contexts in which any student could hear French outside the classroom in Louisiana. The conversations in the test reflect natural and authentic language (natural rhythm, intonation, repetition, hesitations, pauses, etc.). Since oral language is automatically redundant, there is often no need to repeat the conversations. An attempt was made to present logical situations in a logical sequence of events, much as they would happen during a class field trip. Students are not expected to understand every word in each conversation. They need to understand only certain words to capture the meaning of the passage and respond correctly. The test exists in two forms and is based on grade-appropriate standards set by an advisory group of Louisiana educators. These standards for grade 5 are discussed in the Louisiana State Department of Education publication, *Bulletin 1734—French as a Second Language Program Curriculum Guide, Grades 4–8* (1989). See also the grade 8 proficiency exam that tests all four skills. The fifth grade exam was piloted during the 1994–1995 school year.

In the first year, the test development team worked with a testing expert from Quebec, Manon Beaudet-Deer. In the second year, a test item bank was developed through assistance from the University of Liege (Belgium). In the third year, two forms of the test were written. Both forms of the test have good reliability ($r = .84$ and $r = .86$).

There is a parallel version in Spanish.

Contact Address:
Ms. Margaret K. Singer

Foreign Language Manager
Louisiana Department of Education
P.O. Box 94064
Baton Rouge, LA 70804
(504) 342-3453

Sample 2. Third Grade Listening Test (French)

Availability:	Restricted
Current users:	North Carolina public schools
Type of FL program:	Elementary school foreign language program
Intended grade level:	3
Intended test use:	Achievement
Skills tested:	Listening
Test author:	North Carolina Department of Public Instruction and foreign language teachers
Publication date:	1991
Test cost:	Not reported
Test length:	40 items; 45 minutes
Test materials:	Answer booklet, videotape of test items
Test format:	Multiple choice
Scoring method:	Number correct

This multiple-choice listening test is for third graders who started foreign language instruction in kindergarten. The test contains 40 items, which are delivered via videotape. The answer booklet is multiple choice, using graphics rather than the written word. On their answer sheets, students fill in the bubble under the graphic that matches the statement or answers the question. This test is available for purchase to school districts throughout the state. This test is used on a voluntary basis.

This test was developed by a representative group of elementary French teachers, who worked in conjunction with the Department of Public Instruction. They identified a common core of vocabulary and structures to be tested and developed the test items. The test was field tested for two years prior to being administered. Reliability and validity information are available on request.

There is a parallel version in Spanish.

Contact Address:
Dr. Fran Hoch
Chief Consultant for Middle School Education
North Carolina Department of Public Instruction
301 N. Wilmington Street
Raleigh, NC 27601-2825
(919) 715-1797
FAX: (919) 715-2229

Statewide Middle School Samples

Sample 1.   Eighth Grade Proficiency Examination (French)

Available to:	Restricted; still under development
Current users:	Louisiana public schools
Type of FL program:	Middle school sequential
Intended grade level:	8
Intended test use:	Placement, proficiency, and program evaluation
Skills tested:	Listening, speaking, reading, and writing
Test authors:	Manon Beaudet-Deer; Richard J. Guidry; Margaret K. Singer, *et al.*
Publication date:	Not published yet
Test cost:	Contact Margaret Singer
Test length:	1 hour (listening, reading, writing); 7 minutes per student for speaking
Test materials:	Teacher manual, student booklet, cassette, oral proficiency packet (interview, situation)
Test format:	Multiple choice and short answer
Scoring method:	Number correct and holistic

This multiple skills assessment instrument is based on the context of "a trip to Epcot," which is an activity many eighth grade students might actually participate in. The listening, reading, and writing components are group administered and the speaking component is administered individually. The assessment is based on county standards and will be adapted to meet the state framework. The student desiring credit for French I must perform a series of tasks set in real-life situations, as is stated for each objective in the state curriculum guide. In the listening component, the students are asked to identify, categorize, and judge. In the reading component, students select from a menu based on their likes and dislikes. They must decide what can be purchased from the menu based on a set amount of money. The test items are designed to assess performance in the four language skills, based on grade-appropriate standards as set by an advisory board of Louisiana educators. These standards for grade 8 are discussed in Louisiana State Department of Education publication *Bulletin 1734—French as a Second Language Program Curriculum Guide, Grades 4–8* (1989).

This test is a prototype under development, and was piloted, revised, and administered in the Louisiana Public Schools. Teachers developed this instrument under the direction of Manon Beaudet-Deer, Chateauguay School Board, Quebec, and Margaret K. Singer, Louisiana Department of Education. This test was developed in response to middle and high school foreign language teachers' requests for a statewide test to guarantee a better articulated program at the middle school and high school levels.

There is a parallel version in Spanish.

Contact Address:
Ms. Margaret K. Singer

Foreign Language Manager
Louisiana Department of Education
P.O. Box 94064
Baton Rouge, LA 70804
(504) 342-3453

Sample 2. New York State Second Language Proficiency Examination
(Spanish)

Available to:	New York State public and nonpublic schools
Current users:	New York State public and nonpublic schools
Type of FL program:	Middle school sequential foreign language program
Intended test level:	Students who have completed two units of study and achieved "Checkpoint A" learning outcomes
Intended grade level:	8
Intended test use:	Achievement
Skills tested:	Speaking, reading, culture, listening, writing
Test authors:	Teacher consultants and State Education Department staff
Publication date:	1988 (new exam published each June)
Test cost:	Not reported
Test length:	Informal speaking assessment, variable. Formal speaking assessment, four tasks. Listening, 20 items. Reading, 10 items. Writing, two notes of at least 12 words each and 8 items. 90 minutes
Test materials:	Test booklet, answer sheets, scoring sheet for formal speaking test, scoring key
Test format:	Listening and reading sections use multiple-choice items. Writing section uses short answers. Speaking section requires informal classroom evaluation and formal evaluation of performance on four tasks
Scoring method:	Scored by teachers; a sample is then scored by State Education Department staff

This examination tests all skill areas and is usually administered at the end of the school year to eighth graders who have completed two units of study. If students pass the examination, they will earn one unit of high school credit in second language instruction. The test measures learning outcomes at "Checkpoint A" (high school Level 1) of the state syllabus. The syllabus defines communication in terms of four components: functions, situations, topics, and proficiencies. The integration of these components constitutes learning outcomes. These outcomes are presented and measured at three instructional intervals, Checkpoints A, B, and C. At Checkpoint A, students who pass the examination (65%) and are below grade 9, earn one unit of high school credit. This examination is usually taken by eighth grade students who have completed two units of foreign language in the middle school.

Test development and technical information has not been reported.
There are parallel versions in French, Italian, German, and Latin.

Contact Address:
Ms. Mary W. Pillsworth

ESC Specialist
Room 671 EBA
New York State Department of Education
Albany, NY 12234

Statewide High School Sample

New York State Regents Comprehensive Proficiency Examination (Spanish)

Available to:	New York State public and nonpublic schools
Current users:	New York State public and nonpublic schools
Type of FL program:	High school sequential foreign language program
Intended test level:	Students who have completed three units of study and achieved "Checkpoint B" learning outcomes
Intended grade level:	10 and 11
Intended test use:	Achievement
Skills tested:	Speaking, reading, culture, listening, writing
Test authors:	Teacher consultants and New York State Education Department staff
Publication date:	Revised 1990 (new exam published each June)
Test cost:	Not reported
Test length:	3 hours
Test materials:	Test booklet, answer sheet, teacher dictation copy, scoring sheet, scoring key
Test format:	Multiple-choice items for listening and reading portions; short paragraphs for writing portion; speaking section requires formal evaluation on two tasks
Scoring method:	Scored by teachers; samples are sent to the State Education Department for review

This examination tests all skill areas and is usually administered at the end of grades 10 and 11. There is a foreign language requirement for all students seeking a Regents diploma. The examination is given to students who have attained the equivalent of three years of high school level study. It measures learning outcomes at the "Checkpoint B" level of proficiency of the state syllabus. The syllabus defines communication in terms of four components: functions, situations, topics, and proficiencies. The integration of these components constitutes learning outcomes. These outcomes are presented and measured at three instructional intervals, Checkpoints A, B, and C. Students who pass the comprehensive exam with 65% will be awarded three units of second language credit to be applied toward a Regents diploma.

Test development and technical information has not been reported.

There are parallel versions in French, Italian, German, and Latin.

Contact Address:
Ms. Mary W. Pillsworth
ESC Specialist

New York State Department of Education
Room 671 EBA
Albany, NY 12234

Sample District, Local, and Teacher-Made
Assessment Instruments

The samples in this section reflect the range of approaches used in grades K–12 as well as the range of programs. Included are three elementary school tests, the first one an elementary and middle school combination; two middle school tests; and two high school tests. The first assessment bridges both elementary and middle school grades (3, 5, 8) and approaches the assessment of writing as a process. This assessment is also notable because it is one of the few that assesses proficiency in the foreign language separately from content skills. Most immersion programs have not yet identified or created instruments to assess skill in the foreign language that they feel are appropriate for their needs. Since subject content is taught in the foreign language, good performance on standardized content examinations (in English) is seen as an indicator of proficiency in the foreign language. The second assessment, also for immersion programs, also assesses foreign language proficiency, but in speaking and listening. However, it is linked to content in that students respond to situations that are content based, as well as situations that reflect typical social or organizational structures within an elementary school. The third assessment for elementary school is for fifth grade nonimmersion students. The "Teddy Bear Test" is considered to be a prototype because it is thematically based, incorporates authentic text, and allows students to "personalize" their responses.

The two middle school samples are both from middle school sequential foreign language programs. The first offers the teacher an innovative, practical, and flexible method for assessing speaking skills in groups. The second assessment, which requires students to assess their own skills, is representative of a growing tendency to involve students more directly and actively in all aspects of the learning process. The first high school sample was chosen because it represents important trends in assessment. It was inspired by a tape-mediated oral proficiency test (the Simulated Oral Proficiency Interview),[2] which in turn was inspired by the Oral Proficiency Interview, as described earlier. It consists of topics that are related to proficiency in real-life situations and is scored globally using a rubric. The second high school

---

[2] The Simulated Oral Proficiency Interview (SOPI) was developed at the Center for Applied Linguistics (1118 22nd St. NW, Washington, DC 20037). See Stansfield (1989). This tape-mediated test is available in numerous languages. For more information, contact Laurel Winston at CAL (tel. 202-429-9292; fax 202-659-5641; e-mail laurel@cal.org).

assessment is a classroom-based task that allows students to demonstrate their ability to give and follow directions in a foreign language.

Elementary School Samples

Sample 1.　Immersion Second Language Writing Assessment (German)

Availability:	Unrestricted
Current users:	Milwaukee (Wisconsin) Immersion Schools
Type of FL program:	Immersion
Intended grade level:	3, 5, and 8
Intended test use:	Proficiency
Skills tested:	Writing
Test authors:	Milwaukee foreign language immersion teachers
Publication date:	1992 (updated yearly)
Test cost:	Not reported
Test length:	Two 45-minute segments over a two-day period
Test materials:	Test booklet containing target language prompt and space to write final draft
Test format:	Essay question (grade-appropriate prompt)
Scoring method:	Holistic rating (grade-appropriate prompt)

This writing sample is administered to groups of students over a two-day period. On the first day, students see a prompt and work on a rough draft. On the second day, students must write their final draft in the test booklet. They are allowed to use a dictionary. These writing samples are taken at grades 3, 5, and 8 and allow teachers to keep a longitudinal record for each student. Samples are rated by teachers on a five-point, holistic scale. Focus is on what students can actually do, and thus follows current trends in assessment.

Test development and technical information has not been reported. There are parallel versions in Spanish and French.

Contact Address:
Ms. Virginia McFadden
Program Implementor
Milwaukee French Immersion School
3575 South 88th Street
Milwaukee, WI 53228
(414) 327-7052

Sample 2.　CAL Oral Proficiency Exam (COPE) (Japanese)

Availability:	All schools, if they agree to provide test results to CAL for research purposes
Current users:	Various total and partial immersion programs
Type of FL program:	Immersion (total, partial, and two-way)
Intended grade levels:	5 and 6

Intended test use:	Proficiency
Skills tested:	Listening, speaking
Test authors:	Shelley Gutstein, Sarah Goodwin, Nancy Rhodes, Gina Richardson, Lynn Thompson, and Lih-Shing Wang
Publication date:	1988
Test cost:	None
Test length:	15–20 minutes per pair of students
Test materials:	COPE rating scale (one per student), COPE cue cards (Dialogs 1–17), instructions for using the COPE, tape recorder, blank cassette tapes
Test format:	Oral interview or role play
Scoring method:	Holistic, using the COPE rating scale

Using an oral interview or role play technique with two students at a time, the COPE measures a student's ability to understand, speak, and be understood by others in Japanese. The test measures primarily cognitive–academic language skills (the ability to discuss subject matter effectively, e.g., social studies, geography, and science) as well as social language (the ability to discuss family, recreational activities, etc.). The rater evaluates each student's proficiency in terms of comprehension, fluency, vocabulary, and grammar using a simplified holistic scale based on the ACTFL Proficiency Guidelines. Role play or discussion topics include greetings, program of studies, the cafeteria, timelines, using the library, fire drills, social studies trips, school buses, the movies, social life, a party, a science project, future careers, an accident, a fight, unfair rules, and science equipment.

The COPE was developed by the Center for Applied Linguistics (CAL) through federally funded research that identified the need for oral proficiency tests of Spanish for fifth to seventh grades. Steps in the test development process included a review of the literature on oral proficiency testing and existing oral proficiency measures, observations of immersion classes, interviews with sixth grade students and teachers, development and piloting of a trial COPE, and revisions of the COPE based on feedback from the pilot sites. The final COPE was then translated from Spanish into Japanese. The COPE has a concurrent validity index of .62 when compared to the IDEA Proficiency Test (IPT). Test developers suggest that this provides a fair degree of assurance that the COPE validly measures oral proficiency as intended.

See the following:

Gutstein, S., & Goodwin, S. H. (1987). *The CAL Oral Proficiency Exam* (COPE) (Project report). Washington, DC: Center for Applied Linguistics. (ERIC Document Reproduction Service No. ED 331 296)

Rhodes, N., Richardson, G., & Wang, L. S. (1988). *The CAL Oral Proficiency Exam* (COPE) (Project report addendum: Clinical testing and validity and dimensionality studies). Washington, DC: Center for Applied Linguistics. (ERIC Document Reproduction Service No. ED 331 296)

Rhodes, N., & Thompson, L. (1990). An oral assessment instrument for immersion students: COPE. In A. M. Padilla, H. H. Fairchild, & C. Valadez

(Eds.), *Foreign language education: Issues and strategies* (pp. 75–94). Newbury Park, CA: Sage Publ.

Rhodes, N., Thompson, L., & Snow, M. A. (1989). *A comparison of FLES and immersion programs. Final report to the U.S. Department of Education.* Washington, DC: Center for Applied Linguistics. (ERIC Document Reproduction Service No. ED 317 031)

There are parallel versions in Arabic, Chinese, French, German, Russian, and Spanish.

Contact Address:
Ms. Nancy Rhodes
Codirector, FLET Division
Center for Applied Linguistics
1118 22nd Street NW
Washington, DC 20037
(202) 429-9292

Sample 3. Teddy Bear Test—Fifth Grade Level (Spanish)

Availability:	Restricted until test has been finalized
Current users:	Putnam City Schools, Oklahoma City, Oklahoma
Type of FL program:	FLES
Intended grade level:	5
Intended test use:	Proficiency, program evaluation
Skills tested:	Listening, speaking, reading, writing
Test author:	Peggy Boyles
Publication date:	1994
Test cost:	Not reported
Test length:	10 pages
Test materials:	Test, pictures, answer sheet
Test format:	Short answer, matching
Scoring method:	Not reported

This test is based on the ACTFL guidelines (novice level) and draws on a proficiency-based curriculum. The test uses authentic materials and solicits student responses for all skill areas to assess what students can do with their second language. Students see several different pictures of teddy bears at work and at play and are asked to answer questions about the pictures. The purpose of the test is to provide a thematic context for synthesizing novice-level vocabulary in a proficiency-oriented test and to provide an opportunity for students to personalize answers in a testing format.

This is the second draft of the Teddy Bear Test. The first draft was field tested in 1993 with 300 students. The second draft, after revision, was administered to 1572 students in May 1994. For a discussion of the high school level Teddy Bear Test, see P. Boyles (1994). Assessing the speaking skill in the classroom: New solutions to an ongoing problem. In C. Hancock (Ed.),

Teaching, testing, and assessment: Making the connection. Northeast Conference Reports (pp. 87–110). Lincolnwood, IL: National Textbook.
There are no parallel versions in other languages.

Contact Address:
Ms. Peggy Boyles
Foreign Language Coordinator
Putnam City Schools
5401 NW 40
Oklahoma City, OK 73122
(405) 495-5200

Middle School Samples

Sample 1. Columbus Public Schools Level 1 Foreign Language Oral Assessment Kit (All Languages)

Availability:	Contact Robert Robison
Current users:	Columbus Public Schools, Ohio
Type of FL program:	Middle school and high school sequential foreign language
Intended grade level:	8–12
Intended test use:	Proficiency, achievement
Skills tested:	Speaking
Test authors:	Robert Robison et al.
Publication date:	1991
Test cost:	$30
Test length:	Variable
Test materials:	Test cards, score sheet
Test format:	Varied—interviews, situation role plays, question and answer, monologues and retelling, object and picture identification, simple descriptions
Scoring method:	Holistic

This test is based on the new course of study recently adopted by Columbus Public Schools. It is proficiency oriented to determine what students can do with the language but, at the same time, is achievement based so that it can measure to what extent course objectives have been met and facilitate assigning letter or numerical grades rather than ratings or proficiency levels. Test items are situation based and attempt to test only what the student realistically can be expected to say. The test is administered to small groups or teams. The members of each team are allowed 2–4 minutes to accomplish their task. Teachers uses score sheets to assign grades to each member of the team. Using this method, 24 students can be tested and graded within 25 minutes. The kit includes a midyear checklist. Similar kits exist for levels 2 and 3.

The test was developed by the Columbus Public Schools Level I Foreign Language Oral Assessment Project over a three-year period.

The test is appropriate for all foreign languages.

Contact Address:
Dr. Robert E. Robison
Foreign Language Supervisor
Columbus Public Schools
52 Starling Street
Columbus, OH 43215
(614) 365-5024

Sample 2. Student Self Assessment of Foreign Language Performance (All Languages)

Availability:	Restricted
Current users:	Prince George's County Public Schools, Maryland
Type of FL program:	Immersion, FLES, middle school and high school sequential foreign language
Intended grade level:	6–9
Intended test use:	Proficiency, achievement, self-evaluation
Skills tested:	Speaking, reading, writing, listening
Test author:	Pat Barr-Harrison
Publication date:	1993
Test cost:	Contact Pat Barr-Harrison
Test length:	15 items, 2 of which require a written response
Test materials:	One copy per student of self-assessment checklist
Test format:	Checklist
Scoring method:	Student rates his or her knowledge and production ability using a three-point scale: yes (no assistance), yes (with assistance), or no

This self-assessment checklist asks the students to rate their own language ability in reference to 13 curriculum objectives. The student is also asked to describe additional tasks that he or she is able to perform and to indicate which of these tasks he or she is willing to demonstrate. This assessment provides the teacher with an idea of the students' understanding and ability to use material taught in the class.

For test development and technical information, contact Pat Barr-Harrison.

The test is appropriate for all languages; it is currently used for French, German, Italian, Japanese, Russian, and Spanish.

Contact Address:
Ms. Pat Barr-Harrison
Supervisor of Foreign Languages
Prince George's County Public Schools
9201 East Hampton Drive

Capitol Heights, MD 20743
(301) 808-8265
FAX: (301) 808-8291

High School Samples

Sample 1. San Antonio Independent School District: Oral Proficiency Assessment (Spanish)

This assessment instrument was developed over a 30-month period as part of a project undertaken by the San Antonio (Texas) Independent School District. The project aimed to (1) increase teacher familiarity with oral language assessment techniques; (2) develop a tape-mediated assessment instrument of French, German, and Spanish at the end of level 2 and for Japanese at the end of level 3; and (3) administer this test to the district's language students. The final product, after field testing and revision, tests students' oral abilities by asking them questions related to themselves, family, school, and leisure activities. Each topic follows the ACTFL-OPI sequence of warm-up, level check, probes, and wind-down. This tape-mediated interview is scored using an assessment grid that includes categories of response measured on a 0–5 scale, with the addition of a + for an exceptionally good response. As a follow up to this assessment, similar assessments for level 3 (French, German, and Spanish) and Japanese level 4 were developed.

A full description of the San Antonio project and the resultant assessment instrument can be found in: Manley, J. (1995). Assessing students' oral language: One school district's response. *Foreign Language Annals*, 28(1), 93–102.

Contact address:
Dr. Joan Manley
University of Texas at El Paso
Department of Languages and Linguistics
El Paso, TX 79968

Sample 2. Commands through Craft Making (German)

A number of interesting classroom assessments have been developed by Deloris DeLapp and her colleagues for use with grade 9–12 German students in Aurora (Colorado) Public Schools. These are alternative assessments that are scored by teachers and student(s) using a teacher-developed rubric. The assessment tasks are based on content or proficiency benchmarks that have been established for each level of foreign language. For example, one assessment task, entitled "Commands through Craft Making," gives students the opportunity to demonstrate their ability to give and follow directions in a foreign language. Students use a standardized decision-making process (the district requires the inclusion of a complex thinking skill with each assessment) to choose a simple arts and crafts project to describe to the other groups in class, such as a macramé belt or a beaded necklace. Each group gives directions on how to make the craft, either orally or in written form, to the other groups. They use the *ihr* command form. The groups are then responsible for making the craft. Assessment is conducted by observing how well the groups were able to make the craft, thus showing how well the directions were given and how well they were understood. This task relates directly to a grade 9 content or proficiency benchmark, which states that the student speaks for a variety of purposes and audiences.

Contact Address:
Ms. Deloris DeLapp
Hinkley High School
1250 Chambers Rd.
Aurora, CO 80011
(303) 340-1500 x252

As we have seen in this sampling, a wide variety of assessment instruments are being used at the state, district, and local levels. Instruments such as the New York State Second Language Proficiency Examination reflect the more traditional, standardized testing format, whereas assessment instruments such as the COPE reflect the recent trend toward proficiency-based, holistically scored formats. Other trends to note include a move toward technology-mediated assessment (North Carolina and Texas), situationally based or context-based assessment (Louisiana and Oklahoma), and self-assessment (Maryland). This wide range of assessment instruments is equally reflective of the particular circumstances and needs of each state, district, or local area where they were developed. The use of audiotape-mediated or videotaped assessment may be for the purpose of simplifying administration and scoring procedures rather than an eagerness to employ technology.

NATIONAL STANDARDS AND ASSESSMENT

The national foreign language standards, which were released to the public in early 1996, define standards for content (what students should know and be able to do) in foreign language education. The federally funded foreign language standards project was a joint effort among the American Council on the Teaching of Foreign Languages, the American Association of Teachers of French, the American Association of Teachers of German, and the American Association of Teachers of Spanish and Portuguese. The standards are designed to be used in conjunction with state and local standards and curriculum frameworks to determine reasonable expectations for students in individual districts and schools. They are not a curriculum guide, although they suggest the types of curricular experiences needed to enable students to achieve the standards. The standards task force identified five goal areas that encompass all of the purposes and uses of foreign languages: (1) communication, communicate in languages other than English; (2) cultures, gain knowledge and understanding of other cultures; (3) connection, connect with other disciplines and acquire information; (4) comparison, develop insight into the nature of language and culture; and (5) communities, participate in multilingual communities at home and around the world.

While the standards document does not include performance standards or assessments, it indicates the importance of linking standards to curriculum, curriculum to objectives, and objectives to instructional and assessment practices. The National Academy of Education's panel on standards-based education reform (McLaughlin, Shepard, & O'Day, 1995) recommends that assessment should be compatible with and exemplify the content standards; be accompanied by evidence of validity, reliability, and fairness; and allow students to demonstrate proficiency by multiple methods. Assessment is seen as an integral and inseparable part of the instructional process.

Liskin-Gasparro (1996) urges that, in spite of the promise of new assessment models for raising standards for student achievement, increased collaboration among teachers, and forging stronger links between teaching and assessment, numerous issues must be addressed at the local and national levels before authentic assessment programs can be implemented in states, districts, or schools. She suggests that technical (e.g., validity and reliability) and professional (teacher involvement) issues need to be addressed as alternative assessment projects increase in larger and more diverse school districts. In addition, research will be needed on ways that schools can make the most productive use of assessment information to improve instruction (Kean, 1992, as quoted in Liskin-Gasparro, 1996).

To help educators see the connection between the content standards and assessment practices, the National K–12 Foreign Language Resource Center (Iowa State University and Center for Applied Linguistics) is coordinating a teacher-based research project that is drafting assessment scenarios that link the standards with sample objectives, instructional activities, and subsequent assessment strategies. The overall goal of the project is to help foreign language teachers develop sample scenarios, based on the national standards, for assessing the language of students in their classrooms. The targeted level for the guidelines is grades 4 and 8, building on the first two levels of the three levels of the national standards (grades 4, 8, and 12). The project is a first step in developing performance standards, which can be used to define the level of accomplishment expected for single tasks or for an entire course of study.

The specific goals of the project are to (1) improve the ability of foreign language teachers to assess their own students, (2) facilitate collaboration among foreign language teachers and educational researchers, and (3) integrate assessment practices with the new foreign language standards. Working collaboratively, teachers, district and state foreign language supervisors, and researchers are developing scenarios and then documenting how they use the scenarios to develop assessment strategies for their own students.

The scenarios have the following format: a description of a theme-based class activity (e.g., a literature-based project on a Puerto Rican story), the targeted grade level, the objectives for the lesson (e.g., students will read the story, use story vocabulary, dramatize the story, make connections with how people celebrate holidays), a listing of the targeted standards (e.g., interpersonal communication, presentational communication, language comparison), and suggested forms of assessment appropriate for each objective. Some of the assessments included are strategies that can be used continuously throughout the year, such as oral assessment inventories, holistic checklists with criteria for oral and written language evaluation, learning logs, dialogue journals, "hard data" portfolios with structured rating systems, and "can-do" self-assessment statements. Additional reflections on standards, objectives, and assessment conclude each scenario. Future project activities include finalizing the scenarios, testing them in classrooms around the country, and disseminating them to the public. This project is one example of an initiative addressing how teachers can assess student achievement of the standards.

Another project underway addressing assessment and foreign language standards is the three-year, federally funded national school–college collaborative project, Making Connections in Foreign Language Instruction Project. The intent of this project, coordinated by a partnership of ACTFL, the College Board, and the New England Network of Academic Alliances, is to strengthen and energize the relationship among the articulation and achievement initiative (a previous initiative of the partnership), the National Standards for Foreign Language Education, individual state frameworks, and curricular models such as the College Board's Pacesetter Spanish. The innate coherence of these initiatives will be stressed, and the project will seek to institutionalize, at grades K–16 nationally, the adoption of consistent instructional practice through the development of concrete examples of classroom-based standards, curricular and instructional models, and embedded assessment strategies.

A handful of other initiatives are underway that address the assessment of the standards, and more need to be initiated. The critical aspect of assessment that must be considered in relation to the standards is that the primary purpose of assessment is to improve instruction and student learning. To help others with this goal in relation to the standards, teachers need to develop a thorough understanding of the standards, adapt their curriculum to better reflect the standards, and then develop assessment activities that are integrated into the curriculum.

CONCLUSION AND FUTURE DIRECTIONS

Foreign language assessment practices at the elementary and secondary levels have mirrored the evolving philosophies and practices in the field throughout this century. As new approaches to teaching foreign languages have become accepted practice, assessment of student learning in the classroom has reflected that change. The traditional approaches to assessment that had been commonly used, however, have never been abandoned.

Yet, this coexistence of traditional and alternative assessment practices presents a challenge to the classroom teacher. Teachers report dissatisfaction with their current classroom assessment practices and frustration in not knowing how to improve them. Just as teachers need preservice and inservice professional development opportunities in new instructional strategies, they also need opportunities to learn how to develop forms of performance assessment that reflect the new strategies and the evolving curricular content.

Teachers are eager to explore the use of assessment as a way of improving instruction and student learning. In spite of the limited opportunities that most teachers have had for learning about classroom-based assessment, it is evident that innovative assessment practices are being explored in today's foreign language classrooms at all levels. The examples of assessment instruments presented in this chapter attest to this fact.

A historical event in the field of foreign language education, which will have important ramifications for future instructional strategies, curriculum design, and assessment practices, is the definition of content standards for foreign language learning. As the profession examines, explores, and reflects on these standards, we will need to devise assessment instruments for measuring progress toward the content standards. These tasks will take time and require long-term collaboration of both classroom teachers and university researchers. The re-evaluation of our assessment practices represents an important challenge to the foreign language profession in the coming years.

References

American Association of Teachers of German, Inc. (AATG) (1994, Fall). Testing and awards program infoblatt. Cherry Hill, NJ: Author.

Baker, E. L. (1990). *What probably works in alternative assessment.* Los Angeles: UCLA Graduate School of Education; National Center for Research and Evaluation, Standards, and Student Testing.

Baker, E. L. (1994, March). Making performance assessment work: The road ahead. *Educational Leadership, 51*(6), 58–62.

Bartz, W. H. (1991). Are they learning what we're teaching? Assessing language skills in the classroom. In *Focus on the foreign language learner: Priorities and strategies. Selected papers from the 23rd Central States Conference on the Teaching of Foreign Language, Indianapolis, IN, March 21–24, 1991* (pp. 69–82). Lincolnwood, IL: National Textbook Company. (ERIC Document Reproduction Service No. ED 344 495)

Campbell, C. M. (1995). Results of November's questionnaire: Format changes in the national Spanish examination. *Enlace*, 9(3), 2.

Center for Applied Linguistics. (1995). *National profile: United States. Language education study.* (Report to the International Association for the Evaluation of Educational Achievement). Washington, DC: Author.

Clark, J. L. D. (1979). Direct vs. semi-direct tests of speaking ability. In E. J. Briere & F. B. Hinofotis (Eds.), *Concepts in language testing: Some recent studies* (pp. 35–39). Washington, DC: TESOL.

College Board. (1986). CLEP *Test Information Guide. College Spanish (Levels 1 and 2).* Princeton, NJ: Author.

College Board. (1990). CLEP *Test Information Guide. College French (Levels 1 and 2).* Princeton, NJ: Author.

College Board. (1995a). CLEP *Test Information Guide. College level German language examination.* Princeton, NJ: Author.

College Board. (1995b). *A guide to the advanced placement program: May 1996* (Brochure). New York: Author.

College Board. (1995c). *Taking the SAT II: Subject tests, 1995–1996.* Princeton, NJ: Author.

Curtain, H. A., & Pesola, C. A. (1989). Elementary school foreign languages: Perspectives, practices, and promises. In K. Muller (Ed.), *Languages in elementary schools* (pp. 1–13). New York: American Forum. (ERIC Document Reproduction Service No. ED 356 672)

Gabet, L. (1986). 'Espirit Français,' ou comment le concept d'enseignement d'une langue étrangère, au niveau élémentaire, divint une réalité en Californie du Nord. *French Review*, 60(2), 175–179.

Genesee, F. (1994). Assessment alternatives. TESOL *Matters*, 4(5), 3.

Group two: Language B guide. (1994). (p. 44). Geneva: International Baccalaureate.

Herman, J. L., Aschbacher, P. R., & Winters, L. (1992). *A practical guide to alternative assessment.* Alexandria, VA: Association for Supervision and Curriculum Development.

Hewitt, C. B., Ryan, J. M., & Kuhs, T. M. (1993). *Assessment of student learning in foreign language.* Columbia: South Carolina Center for Excellence in the Assessment of Student Learning. (ERIC Document Reproduction Service No. ED 358 162)

Japan Foundation Language Center. (1995). *The Japanese language proficiency test* (Brochure). Santa Monica, CA: Author.

Kean, M. H. (1992). Targeting education and missing the schools: A consideration of national standards. NASSP *Bulletin*, 76, 17–22.

Lewis, A. C. (1992). No shortcuts for alternative assessment. *Research and Development Review*, 7(4), 2–3.

Liskin-Gasparro, J. E. (1987). The ACTFL proficiency guidelines: A historical perspective. In T. Higgs (Ed.), *Teaching for proficiency, the organizing principle* (pp. 11–42). Lincolnwood, IL: National Textbook.

Liskin-Gasparro, J. E. (1996). Assessment: From content standards to student performance. In R. Lafayette (Ed.), *National standards: A catalyst for reform* (pp. 169–196). Lincolnwood, IL: National Textbook.

Lorenz, E., Met, M., Artman, J., Amin, I., Cardona, V., & Russell, G. (Eds.). (1994a). *Teaching culture in grades K–8: A resource manual for teachers of French.* Rockville, MD: Montgomery County Public Schools.

Lorenz, E., Met, M., Artman, J., Amin, I., Cardona, V., & Russell, G. (Eds.). (1994b). *Teaching culture in grades K–8: A resource manual for teachers of Spanish.* Rockville, MD: Montgomery County Public Schools.

Louisiana State Department of Education (1989). Bulletin 1734—French as a Second Language Program Curriculum Guide, Grades 4–8. Baton Rouge, LA: Author.

McLaughlin, M. W., Shepard, L. A., & O'Day, J. A. (1995). *Improving education through standards-based reform.* (A report by the National Academy of Education Panel on Standards-Based Education Reform). Stanford, CA: National Academy of Education.

McTighe, J., & Ferrara, S. (1994). *Assessing learning in the classroom.* Washington, DC: National Education Association.

Montgomery County Public Schools. (1995). IB program ranks among top in world. *The Bulletin*, 38, 1, 4.

Omaggio, A. (1986). Teaching language in context. Boston: Heinle & Heinle.

Rosenbusch, M. H. (1995). *Foreign language teachers' views of assessment.* Unpublished manuscript.

Singerman, A. (Ed.). (1996). *Acquiring cross-cultural competence: Four stages for American students of French.* Lincolnwood, IL: National Textbook.

Stansfield, C. W. (1989). *Simulated oral proficiency interviews.* ERIC Digest. Washington, DC: ERIC Clearinghouse on Languages and Linguistics.

Stansfield, C. W. (1990, April). *A comparative analysis of simulated and direct oral proficiency interviews.* Paper presented at the annual meeting of the Regional Language Centre Conference, Singapore.

Stansfield, C. W. (1992). ACTFL *speaking proficiency guidelines.* ERIC Digest. Washington, DC: ERIC Clearinghouse on Languages and Linguistics.

Thompson, L. (1995). K–8 *foreign language assessment: A bibliography.* Washington, DC: ERIC Clearinghouse on Languages and Linguistics.

Thompson, L., Christian, D., Stansfield, C. W., & Rhodes, N. (1990). Foreign language instruction in the United States. In A. Padilla, H. Fairchild, & C. Valadez (Eds.), *Foreign language education: Issues and strategies* (pp. 22–35). Newbury Park, CA: Sage Publ.

CHAPTER 14

A User-Friendly Guide to Assessment in Visual Arts

DENNIS DAKE and JOHN WEINKEIN[1]
Iowa State University

WHAT DOES ASSESSMENT MEAN IN
THE VISUAL ARTS?

This chapter proposes that assessment in the visual arts must have a special character based on the unique nature of the discipline itself. For any assessment system to be effective and useful it must prove workable under real-world conditions and it must be be deemed user friendly over an extended period of time. This approach will be called *assessment consumerism*.

The truths that assessment attempts to unearth are seldom simple and never absolute. In the visual arts, the special, complex nature of visual perception means that assessment takes on a special set of characteristics. Visual perception is a continual interaction with the environment, and therefore, assessment of the visual arts must also be an ongoing dialogue rather than a final summation.

Much of the focus of this chapter will be on the assessment of studio activity in the visual arts, because that is the dominant type of activity present in K–12 visual arts programs. There is an increasing emphasis within the

[1]With contributions by: Enid Zimmerman, Indiana University, Bloomington, IN; Ann Joyce, Kings College, Wilkes-Barre, PA; and Jerome J. Hausman, Urban Gateways, Chicago, IL.

art education profession on nonstudio activities, focusing on art history, art criticism, and aesthetics. This new emphasis further complicates the picture for assessment practices in the visual arts. It is the contention in this chapter that these nonstudio activities, which depend upon traditional, testable outcomes, can be effectively assessed with procedures already in place in social science and humanities education. No further disciplinary-specific response seems to be required for assessing "paper–pencil" learning in art. Studio activities, however, do require a unique and creative response to the unique and creative nature of the discipline. Consideration of several questions may help to clarify the uniqueness of assessment practices in the visual arts.

Since diversity is inherent in the approach used in this chapter, material is presented in an anthology format. This approach provides for the multivocality (many voices) that can better address the richness of alternative assessment in the visual arts. The contributions to this chapter, although not exhaustive, present a sense of the range of investigation into assessment within the visual arts discipline. Contributors include Enid Zimmerman, Indiana University, Bloomington, Indiana; Ann Joyce, King's College, Wilkes-Barre, Pennsylvania; and Jerome Hausman, Urban Gateways, Chicago, Illinois. Additionally, examples are cited from Iowa State University's curriculum development project, New Art Basics. Two Iowa State University master's program graduates, Lois Lamansky (an elementary art teacher, Ankeny, Iowa) and Brent Knoot (a middle school art teacher, Ottumwa, Iowa) have each contributed original assessment models.

If assessment of educational outcomes within the visual arts is to be successful, it is the contention of these authors that assessment methodology must be primarily visual in focus, holistic in content, and integrative rather than analytic in conclusion. Assessment processes and conclusions must be viewed as authentic by both the teachers who design and administer them and the students who receive and contribute to assessment. To be effective within the visual arts discipline, assessment must be both effective in assessing learning and growth and accepted by art teachers and their students as helpful and nonintrusive.

Means of Representation: Quantitative vs. Qualitative

While the dominant modes of educational assessment are quantitative in symbolization and scientific in methodology, visual arts education is more compatible with qualitative forms of visual inquiry. This preference grows less out of a rejection of traditional quantitative forms of assessment than principled design based on inherent understanding of the qualitative nature of the visual arts discipline.

> The meanings that are engendered through choreography, through music, and through visual arts are unique or special to their forms. There are some meanings

that can be grasped through visual form that cannot be described in language or in quantitative form. (Eisner, 1995)

The visual arts are inherently holistic, non-reductionist, and organic in character, requiring assessment methods that differ from academic disciplines based on words, numbers, and quantifiable knowledge. Quantitative methods are, of necessity, mechanistic and linear in their reasoning. The inherent differences between artistic and scientific methods lead naturally to differing means of inquiry and representation.

Visual perception is simultaneous and not sequential. It is configurational and not linguistic in nature. The relationships between visual elements within the art work, and between the visual art object and the world around it, must be considered in assessment. The understanding and transformation of spatial patterns and relations through critical visual thinking leads to concrete perceptual insights that can't be standardized. Artistic production and learning are based on the creative visual thoughts of the individuals. The contexts in which students create their ideas and judge their worth must also be considered part of learning experience.

In the Jerome Hausman article later in this chapter, for example, reference is made to taking into account the whole context of black inner city students' lives in assessing their artistic progress. For these reasons artistic assessment methodology needs to be based on visual and holistic principles (much like qualitative, educational research methodology.)

The Role of Aesthetics and Artistic Standards

For teachers and students alike, life provides the opportunity to make ever finer discernments of quality. An endless array of these assessments takes place every day, in the marketplace, communities, schools, and homes. These qualitative assessments actively engage people as consumers in a cultural environment.

The qualitative decisions people make, both individually and communally, find their expression through the physical senses. Through responding to the particular experiences of the senses, increasingly sophisticated choices can be made about all the available goods and services, from tennis shoes to textbooks, in the collective marketplace. Collectively humans participate in creating the cultural value system and are, in turn, shaped by it. A culture created by informed decisions is perhaps the most visible product of education.

Without visual education people cannot see the forest for the trees. If a teacher's assessment decisions are specific only to his or her own studio artist context, they may be of no particular educational value to the student. A teacher's individual perspective is not necessarily transferrable in meaning to the student. An authentic assessment approach considers the personal and concrete experiences of the student equally with those of the teacher. Student's and teacher's perceptions must be mutually understood and contextual to the time and place of their creation. Humans come to know their world through contextualized experiences, not decontextualized, isolated objects and experiences. (See Illustration 1)

One effective model for helping art teachers contextually assess learning is provided by the New Art Basics (NAB) cooperative staff development and curriculum research project, which is cooperatively operated by the Art Education Area of the Art and Design Department at Iowa State University and hundreds of midwestern K–12 art teachers. The content areas promoted and assessed by the NAB program include visualization, visual thinking, metaphoric thinking, and human, cultural and historical contexts. These areas are crucial visual thinking skills within art education. A prototype assessment system developed within this program will be presented later in this chapter.

Understanding the importance of the psychological and social functions of art works, within appropriate and applicapable cultural aesthetic systems,

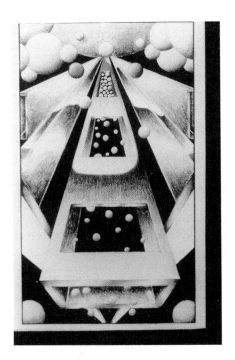

ILLUSTRATION 1
Visual logic strategy, avoid the dot, high school student example (courtesy of New Art Basics Project).

involves a global visual legacy. A contextual orientation is primary to visual arts education and should precede a more traditional orientation to formalistic qualities (i.e., elements such as line, shape, value, texture, and color and principles such as balance, unity, variety, and rhythm).

Until recently, in American culture, education in the art classroom has been geared to the white middle-class student assessed exclusively from a white, European model of artistic and aesthetic quality. The art teacher may not have clearly perceived the diversity of alternative aesthetic models from a variety of cultures available to him or her. The continuing honest, critical seeing necessary for visual arts assessment leads to in-depth reflection on the entire visual and environmental (human, cultural, and historical) contexts an art work both embodies and suggests. As students now operate in a pluralistic culture, it is especially pertinent that cultural diversity and forms of less traditional art expression be included in visual arts programming and assessment.

For too long, a process of omission has occurred in our schools providing a narrow selection of images in terms of the entire world production of art forms. The decision of what aesthetic standards to use for assessment is not a neutral, value-free issue. It is value laden and has political, ethical, and socioeconomic implications. The disciplinary nature of the visual arts makes this a natural arena for expressions of such complex human content. Teachers should ask themself the kind of questions that raise ethical, social, cultural, and ecological issues pertinent to assessment of the visual arts.

Action Orientation

Inherent in the visual arts is the process of making objects, doing the work, taking the necessary action through a disciplinary experience with physical materials. Each student artist is continually confronted throughout the art experience with a multi leveled self-assessment process that involves attention and intention. Does this art object meet my personal criteria? Will others like it? Students, like the one shown in Illustration 2, must continually assess and assign value to their work as it occurs. Often unexpected, undetermined, and unanticipated qualities occur naturally, which could not be predicted in advance. These emergent qualities contribute to the uniqueness of each art making experience, but they make prespecifying objectives and learning goals difficult for the visual arts educator.

Art students may have very different levels of engagement in their art making and reflect a wide diversity within their classroom and school. Their own intentions and motivations will vary by degree and constancy with social, cultural, and emotional factors, contributing to the uniqueness of each art making experience. In the art classroom, a student beginning a drawing may make a mark on his or her paper, erase it, and repeat this process multiple times until the level of frustration is either great enough to force

ILLUSTRATION 2
Student participating in visual brainstorming activity (courtesy of New Art Basics Project).

resignation or the student arrives at a satisfactory response. This is the student's own self-assessment process at work.

Within this action orientation, the role of the visual arts teacher is to intervene and provide a variety of assessment "tools" for the student. These may range from intangible preproduction strategies, such as visualizing the first intended lines, to attentively exploring the physical relationships between materials and techniques, to suggesting historical exemplars and approaches, to oral comments on affective attitudes and emotional states. Each type of assessment "tool" is helpful to the student or consumer in developing self-guidance.

Both formatively and summatively, student self-assessment is of fundamental importance for understanding the artwork's origin, its evolutionary progress, and the quality of the final product. Lois Lamansky, an Ankeny, Iowa, elementary art teacher, has developed one self-assessment model that has been shown to work quite well. This model also provides teacher mediated pre- and post-tests that help with the assessment of the transfer of knowledge, skill, and experience, (see the methods and processes section for both tests and self-assessment instruments).

Assessment or Measurement?

Visual and creative learning can be assessed in multiple dimensions and raise continuing contextual issues for extended dialogue. Rather than attempting to remove all ambiguity, assessment in the visual arts must be tolerant of an irreducible ambiguity ever-present in the visual world. Value can be assigned to a visual learning experience without definitive closure and final measurement. While measurement implies quantities that can be standardized and compared across samples, such analytical activities are antithetical to the nature of the visual arts discipline. It is possible to appraise the worth of art learning without measuring the quantity of any individual element.

Reflection vs. Propositional Thought

The ability to formulate propositions (objectives and student outcomes) is commendable only when the desired outcome is predictable, statable, and knowable in advance. The type of learning that makes definitive propositions possible must be a closed system. The arts are an open learning system, based on divergent thinking rather than convergence and closure. In visual arts learning, emerging qualities are important and desirable. Preset learning objectives can blind the assessor to important emerging qualities that were unanticipated during lesson planning.

How Can Assessment Be Conducted?

If predetermined objectives and outcomes and quantification are inappropriate, how then can assessment be conducted? The literature on assessment in the visual arts suggests three contexts for evaluative comparisons (Eisner, 1971). Each of these contexts offers the teacher opportunities for unique perspectives on student achievement and each is problematic in differing ways.

First, given the visual art's traditional Euro–American emphasis on individual and original achievement, the most prevalent form of assessment is to compare each student with his or her achievement in the past. Using portfolio systems and self-assessment measures, many art educators have found methods for compiling, maintaining, and utilizing visual and other records of student progress and achievement as holistic benchmarks for assessing growth.

Two problems attach themselves to this approach to assessment. First, it is difficult and time consuming to compile and maintain a portfolio of sufficient depth and duration to make possible accurate self-comparison. Second, creative artistic growth is not uniform or sufficiently predictable to always assess whether any particular student achievement represents the most significant step toward greater growth. Accurate perception of an individual's growth, in any case, always is colored by the assessor's personal aesthetic and stylistic biases, his or her past experiences with the student, and an individual sense of appropriate artistic standards.

A second, related context involves comparing individual student artists to the achievement of other students. Although individual artistic excellence has an idiosyncratic nature, general levels of creative and artistic ability, by age level, can be determined using the broad outlines of professional theories and the personal experience of individual teachers. Classwide standards of achievement are a natural outgrowth of patterns determined by teachers as they strive to set high-quality learning goals. Two problems associated with assessment by group comparison are (1) a gradual lowering of achievement standards to the lowest common denominator, thereby eliminating the excellence on which art is based, and (2) overlooking individual differences that are the very basis of original achievement in the visual arts. It is also possible, while asserting the common standards of the group, for the teacher to gradually drift into an overdependence on impersonal formalistic assessment criteria that reduce and simplify the complex nature of expression and achievement in the visual arts.

The third and final context for assessment comparisons is to formulate goals and standards based on established aesthetic and artistic criteria and compare individual student achievement with these norms. Within the recent history of art education, this has provided a seemingly objective and observer-neutral option for assessment. However, in an increasingly multiculturally diverse and complex postmodern world, such use of exclusively formal criteria has come under justifiable criticism for being culturally biased toward Western European, male-dominated aesthetics. A wealth of different aesthetic systems are now accessible through modern technologies from throughout world cultures. Overly narrow sets of criteria limit creative expression and achievement rather than promote sound arts learning. Additionally, postmodernism enlists eclectic and appropriated imagery worldwide as a legitimate artistic tool. The other extreme on the continuum is equally problematic: overly broad criteria and artistic standards threaten to weaken the sense of excellence without which the visual arts quickly deteriorate into just another minor manual skill.

To maximize the assessment accuracy and minimize the associated problems, it is suggested that an advanced, user-friendly assessment system in the visual arts utilize a mixture of each of the three contexts. Relying on comparisons, using only one of the three contexts, increases the problems associated with that context. This could be unfair to either the individual, the group, or the traditions of the aesthetic standards. The standards used in visual arts assessment must take the individual into account within the context of peer group ability levels. The specific student group with which assessment is taking place always exists within a cultural context.

THEORY: WHAT IS THE NEED FOR ASSESSMENT?

It has been said that only that which can be assessed is worthy of being included in the curriculum. In practice many art teachers, however, question the need for rigorous assessment in the face of potential threats to individual creative freedom. Standardization and overly close scrutiny have been shown to deaden creative thought.

One way to avoid the deadening effect of rigorous scrutiny on the creative process is to base instruction and assessment on discipline-specific higher-order thinking skills (HOTS), which represent basic thinking styles within the visual arts discipline. These visual thinking skills are the unique contributions of the visual arts to the general mental development of students. Determining such basic thinking skills and setting-appropriate achievement assessment standards focused on these thinking skills is a primary task of the visual arts educator.

The New Art Basics Project has been exploring thinking skills for mental visualization, disciplined visual thought, metaphoric thinking, and contextual and relational thinking leading to visual logic and multicultural understanding. In assessing learning in this thinking skills approach, specific visual evidence for each thinking skill is necessary to assure that judgment is not merely a matter of personal opinion on the part of the teacher. Assessment in the visual arts must continually be related to actual visual examples and image experiencing behavior by the student. The importance of being able to provide convincing evidence of educational effectiveness through assessment is vital for any academic discipline in this age of accountability. The need, however, is not for massive expenditures of time and effort to pile up mountains of standardized evidence to prove the worth of visual learning without first considering whether content and structure of the discipline is worthy of inclusion in the educational curricula. Karen Hamblen has pointed out this importance of thinking skills that the visual arts provide to children.

> Memorization of facts and application exercises are proving to be inadequate in preparing students for participation in our Information Society. With a proliferation of information and rapid social changes, skills to analyze information, clarify meaning and evaluate significance become essential.

The New Art Basics evaluation system described later in this chapter provides an example of an assessment system that attempts to provide accurate assessment methodology for the visual arts without being destructive to the discipline itself. This system's visual analysis of specific thinking skills and concepts provides the art teacher with a compatible assessment system.

Who Benefits from Assessment?

Any assessment system involves many groups of educational professionals and students in ongoing activities. On one level, these activities are an exercise in political power. If the administration of a state or local district is the group to insist on extensive assessment, it is likely that the primary beneficiary of this activity will be those same officials. Top-down directives for assessment, whether dutifully implemented or perfunctorily complied with, usually benefit the individuals who want a paper trail of accountability. In this top-down approach little benefit and all the work accrues to teachers or students. In a worse case scenario, assessment is used as a club to force compliance. This approach has more negative consequences for educational reform than it has benefits. Assessment activities in the visual arts are best generated from art teachers themselves, with significant input from students. Art teachers are visually and creatively oriented people. They are by disciplinary training inclined toward visual phenomena as evidence for assessment. Allowing them to generate their own forms of assessment conveys the message that their hard-earned disciplinary expertise is valuable even though it is not based on a scientific, quantitative model. There are three positive reasons to assess learning in the visual arts.

The primary reason to assess learning in the visual arts is to give students feedback on their achievements and address the deficiencies that need to be overcome to promote self-directed growth in the future. This reason empowers the students to direct their own educational development and has the potential to increase ongoing student motivation.

Two additional reasons to assess visual arts learning are of direct benefit to the art teacher who is the all-important interface between the student–learner and the content of the discipline. First, accurate feedback from assessment can aid the teacher in improving his or her instructional abilities. Discovering what is currently being effectively learned and what is not gives the teacher an opportunity to modify and improve instructional methodology. A second reason to assess accurate information is to aid in program development. Modifications in art curricula need to be made in response to carefully established needs for greater emphasis or selective focus on some specific art content.

A final need for assessment in the visual arts grows out of the current emphasis in education on interdisciplinary learning. If the visual arts are to participate as an equal educational partner in learning that breaks down disciplinary barriers, then goals and outcomes need to be carefully defined and rigorously assessed to determine whether significant learning is taking place. Without disciplinary integrity and substance, the visual arts quickly degenerate into illustrational service projects without serious educational merit. Communication between disciplines requires clarity of understanding and respect for the inherent nature of each discipline. Serious assessment contributes greatly to defining the learning possible within the visual arts discipline.

What Is the Role of Standards?

While the most effective educational assessment grows out of grassroots design and personal motivation, the education profession continues to generate educational standards at the school district, state, and national levels. Part of being a well-informed consumer as a professional educator involves being aware of the professional standards suggested by the larger professional community. Art educators with only individual standards become increasingly isolated academically. The wisdom of thoroughly discussed and defined sets of standards can be beneficial in helping teachers set higher goals for student learning and program performance. In 1994, the National Art Education Association, in conjunction with other professional organizations, developed the National Visual Arts Standards as broad goals and guidelines for individual teachers and local schools in their school reform efforts. The six content goals suggested by the National Standards are

- Understand and apply visual arts media, techniques and processes.
- Use knowledge of visual arts structures and functions.
- Choose and evaluate a range of subject matter, symbols, and ideas.
- Understand the visual arts in relation to history and cultures.
- Reflect on and assess the characteristics and merits of their work and the work of others.
- Make connections between visual arts and other disciplines.

Under each of these content standards are numerous achievement standards specifying the understanding and levels of achievement that students are expected to attain for grades K–4, 6–8, and 9–12. These national standards along with integrated state frameworks, curriculum guidelines, and local school district requirements are valuable tools for art teachers in determining the learning objectives and outcomes that are most appropriate in their classroom.

It is important that visual arts assessment activities take into account the guiding goals suggested by national, state, and school district standards and frameworks. The shared professional vision the standards suggest is a vital foundation for building art programs, instruction, visual arts content, and assessment appropriate to local circumstances. The objectives, goals, and student outcomes that are the target of assessment of learning will be most firmly stated when they partake of this shared professional vision.

National and state standards must never be considered as top-down mandates that dictate assessment activities. In asking for standardized compliance from the classroom art teacher, the administration is violating the basic nature of the visual arts discipline and removing true creative incentive from the artist–teacher to regard assessment as a benefit to art learning. Such an attitude will not help improve and update visual arts education.

The visual arts in recent history, have suffered from idiosyncratic standards developed by each teacher. In an age of assessment, this state of affairs can no longer be a valid use of individual artistic freedom. Disciplines that are not assessed will probably never be accepted as basic educational programming. Art teachers must learn to creatively develop successful assessment programs within state, national, and school district standards and goals.

ASSESSMENT CONSUMERISM

Assessment can be understood only in the context of the persons who will use the results. In the social setting of the school, the fruits of assessment are the qualities of growth, refinement, and discrimination gained during the educational experience (see Illustration 3). Several years ago the saying "you are what you eat" came into popular usage. This might now be extended to "you are what you buy". Like the consumer in the marketplace, one must consider the type of assessment that will produce results worth buying?

Assessment in the visual arts involves a process of perceiving and experiencing finer and finer discernments in our knowing. Students and teachers alike, as direct or indirect consumers of education, are engaged in varying degrees of self-cultivation regarding aesthetic and artistic decision making. Everyone needs to make informed and advised choices about his or her environment. Through these choice experiences, doors continue to open and can lead to further refinement and increasingly discerning connoisseurship (Eisner, 1991). In effect, students and teachers need to be continually evolving as expert consumers of assessments.

Assessment systems in the visual arts should also be open to the same type of evolutionary development as the growth of individual aesthetic deci-

ILLUSTRATION 3
Consumers (students and teacher) working interactively on visual thinking
activity (courtesy of New Art Basics).

sion makers. For example, the portfolio, a educational consumer product, is not only the thing itself, the object, "a flat, portable case" (Webster, 1977) or a container to hold images, drawings, or prints. The portfolio has been transformed and recontextualized into an evolutionary process in use across the disciplinary map. There are, for example, personal portfolios, political portfolios, and financial portfolios. Perhaps these dramatic examples reflect a shift to consumerism, as an outcome of quality product orientation?

Portfolios for art educators provide something visual and tangible to stand for the students' experiences. An approach based in concrete, perceivable qualities is teleologic to the visual arts. Starting from these concrete elements teachers can assess the visual relationships that are the basis of qualitative structures.

In the marketplace of educational assessment, a wide array and diversity of assessment models is available. No one methodology, system, or set of criteria will work in all classrooms. How is the teacher to make a choice that will best serve his or her needs, those of students, the school, district, and society at large?

Included in this chapter, are exemplars of consumer-sensitive assessment systems for use within different contexts. These are classroom-tested models, which give insight into the nature of authentic assessment from the standpoint of those who must use them. While these classroom contexts may differ from one's own, it is hoped that they will better help each reader to understand students' learning and outcomes.

Implementation of Assessment Consumerism

If assessment consumerism is to be effectively implemented in visual arts education it must have an integrally designed implementation procedure. The authors of this chapter suggest a system based upon total quality education (TQE) principles. TQE requires teachers to become accountable for designing effective assessment systems that will be consistently maintained, utilized, and valued. Only if empowered teachers as consumers of educational material continue to value assessment activities and what they learn from them will educational assessment in and of the visual arts be possible.

In a TQE approach to implementing assessment, art teachers must be valued as professionals. They must be actively engaged in quality circles teamwork and group decision making, both in determining goals and objectives and in designing assessment systems that must work in practice. Teamwork between teaching professionals will in turn be mirrored in closer teamwork between teachers and students as a vital component of assessing visual arts learning. Both students and teachers need to be solidly focused on qualitatively superior standards and evaluation criteria. Final judgment needs to be delayed until sufficient critical thinking has been done about the entire holistic visual experience. A sensitivity to emergent qualities that can not be predictable in advance of the learning experience is also an important part of this cooperative learning experience. All models and processes that are developed under the consumer assessment model need to be extensively field tested before they can be considered effective. Theory and practice must be brought together to create an effective assessment model for the visual arts.

What Types of Assessment Are Appropriate in the Visual Arts?

General Principles

All the assessment models and procedures adopted in the visual arts should be based on the principles of assessment consumerism. If the art teacher and his or her students are regarded as the ultimate consumers of any assessment product, that system must be deemed both efficient and not overly burdensome on the visual experimentation and playful, creative thought required in the visual arts. It is suggested that a variety of assessment procedures be combined to produce an effective system that is responsive to the holistic nature of the visual arts. It is probably best if any record keeping be of a visual nature (where overall assessments can be grasped as a visual whole).

Three major types of assessment (paper–pencil, observation, and performance) have been identified as applicable and appropriate to public school education. Carmen L. Armstrong's *Designing Assessment in Art*, a 1994 publication by National Art Education Association, addresses all three types of assessment at greater length. The first type, available in many forms, has briefly been mentioned and identified as not discipline specific to the visual arts, it will remain outside the domain of this chapter. Our focus will be on the second and third types, which necessitate the teacher being directly engaged in the entire context of the learning activity. Observation and performance meet the criteria of alternative assessment methods, alternative to traditional assessment techniques of objective testing, especially involving written performance.

Authentic assessment must be meaningful and relevant to real life. It should be noted that several variables need to be considered prior to embarking on any alternative forms of assessment. They all require significant time and may often be quite labor intensive. On the teacher's part they will require a commitment to follow through over an extended period of time, employing as much continuity and consistency as possible. From the outset, a thorough and realistic appraisal of one's resources to facilitate this commitment will be imperative. This includes all manner of resources at the teacher's disposal, physical facilities, equipment, support staff, level of non-teaching assignments, to name a few. All of these will affect the teacher's ability to implement and document the alternative assessment practices.

Documentation of student learning and performance outcomes need to take tangible concrete form. Documentation helps monitor consistency and serves as the permanent student record and a resource for reflection, both for teaching and curricular change. Traditionally, documentation occurred through the student's grade record and occasionally supplemented with student visual examples, often collected by chance, or default, or for school exhibition. Currently, many teachers using alternative assessment are exploring multiple processes for data collection and documentation. The following are examples of several alternative means by which this is being accomplished.

Examples

Portfolios can represent individuals, small focus groups or classes of student work. They may include individual lesson products, units of work, and thematic groups. They may span varying time periods, from a unit or grading period to longitudinal collections over multiple years. For example, one elementary art teacher has established a portfolio for each student that includes a self-portrait from each year K–6. The Arts PROPEL program, tested in the Pittsburgh, Pennsylvania, public schools, is one of the most notable applied research projects using the portfolio format. Portfolios can naturally extend into exhibitions of formative and summative student work. While portfolios typically focus on art production, multidisciplinary examples may be included (see illustration 4). The following forms may be part of a portfolio or stand singly as student documentation.

Videotaped performance, especially of multimedia events, may include several art forms representing several lesson outcomes and culminate in this specific form of visual evidence. With less or limited equipment, an alternative may be to use color slides or photographs to visually record such events.

Additionally, student journals, including visual and written components, may become part of the portfolio record. Student journals have been used effectively in grades from upper elementary through high school and include a variety of anecdotal records. This same format has proven helpful for teachers in keeping their own classroom observation journals. Teachers have found that a journal can be a mnemonic device to review the classroom experiences over a period of time. Such records may be especially helpful when planning cross- and interdisciplinary curricular organization. For example, if an interdisciplinary visual arts approach is developed that includes aesthetics, art history, and art criticism further assessment, including critiques in various formats, may become appropriate. In the authors' experience it is best to consistently vary the critique form to accommodate different learning styles. Alternative critique forms include using oral, written, and visual responses to students' own work, that of peers and other artists. Any or all of these documentation forms may be supplemented with audiotapes, interviews, logs, or journals of class activities.

ILLUSTRATION 4
Elementary art student preparing portfolio
(courtesy of New Art Basics Project).

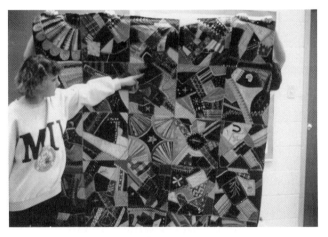

ILLUSTRATION 5
Student discussing quilt brought from home
(courtesy of New Art Basics Project).

Finally, within both observation and performance assessment, the use of checklists, worksheets, questionnaires, and self-assessment forms can be effective forms of documentation of authentic assessment.

An example of teacher-designed assessment procedures that follow one class over an extended period of time was designed by Ankeny, Iowa, elementary art teacher Lois Lamansky. As part of her graduate program at Iowa

Student Name: _____
Homeroom Teacher: _____

STORY QUILT PRETEST

1. What is a quilt? _____
_____
2. What was a quilting bee? _____
_____
3. What do Faith Ringgold, Lillian Beattie, and Harriet Powers have in
   common? _____
_____
_____
_____

4. Describe how you can do storytelling when making a quilt. _____
_____
_____
_____
_____

5. Applique is
   ___the name of a famous quiltmaker
   ___a type of quilt
   ___a special paper used for quilt patterns
6. What is a folk tale? _____
_____

7. What is a folklorist's job? _____
_____
_____

FIGURE I
Elementary story quilt art activity pretest, designed by Lois Lamansky
(courtesy of New Art Basics Project).

State University, she developed a yearlong interdisciplinary program with her
upper elementary students in Storytelling and Art: A Link to Understanding
(one aspect of which is shown in Illustration 5).

Figures 1 to 4 are examples from one strategy lesson in a series of storytelling activities for fifth graders. These include a pretest (Figure 1), a post-
test (Figure 2), and a double (teacher and student) assessment form (Figure
3). Additionally, at the close of the school year, a summative questionnaire
(Figure 4) was provided for student response to the overall program experience of storytelling.

Whatever the particular accumulation of portfolio content, storage space
is an immediate concern. With the continued development and access to
electronic technology, computer disks will become an increasingly effective

Student Name: _____
Homeroom Teacher: _____

STORY QUILT POSTTEST

1. What is a quilt?_____

2. What was a quilting bee?_____

3. What do Faith Ringgold, Lillian Beattie, and Harriet Powers have in
   common?_____
   _____
   _____

4. Describe how you can do storytelling when making a quilt._____
   _____
   _____
   _____

5. Applique is
   ___the name of a famous quiltmaker
   ___a type of quilt
   ___a special paper used for quilt patterns
6. What is a folk tale?_____
   _____

7. What is a folklorist's job?_____
   _____

FIGURE 2
Elementary story quilt art activity posttest, designed by Lois Lamansky
(courtesy of New Art Basics Project).

means for storage and retrieval. The particular combination of components can be designed by the individual teacher yet reflect input from students, fellow teachers, and other resource professionals. For in the final analysis, what is important is the ability to effectively use for interpretation, what one has collected.

THE NEW ART BASICS SYSTEM OF EVALUATION

The New Art Basics system of assessment involves looking critically at ongoing student achievement in the areas of art content, media knowledge, thinking skill development, and affective growth. Selecting appropriate learn-

Name: _____
Homeroom: _____ Grade Level: __4th__   Grading Scale: 10 Excellent
Art Assignment: ____Story Quilt Square_____   9 Very Good
                                                                             8 Good
                                                                             7 Satisfactory
                                                                             6 Poor
                                                                             5 Very Poor
                                                                             4 Unacceptable

  1. Success of my square
     accurately telling my
     share of the folktale: 10   9   8   7   6   5   4

  2. Cooperation with my group: 10   9   8   7   6   5   4

  3. Craftsmanship: 10   9   8   7   6   5   4

  4. Quality of my quilt square: 10   9   8   7   6   5   4

  5. Daily work habits: 10   9   8   7   6   5   4

Student comments: _____

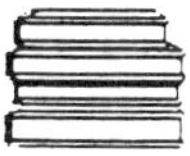

_____

_____

_____ Total student points

Name: _____
Homeroom: _____ Grade Level: __4th__   Grading Scale: 10 Excellent
Art Assignment: ____Story Quilt Square_____   9 Very Good
                                                                             8 Good
                                                                             7 Satisfactory
                                                                             6 Poor
                                                                             5 Very Poor
                                                                             4 Unacceptable

  1. Success of my square
     accurately telling my
     share of the folktale: 10   9   8   7   6   5   4

  2. Cooperation with my group: 10   9   8   7   6   5   4

  3. Craftsmanship: 10   9   8   7   6   5   4

  4. Quality of my quilt square: 10   9   8   7   6   5   4

  5. Daily work habits: 10   9   8   7   6   5   4

Teacher comments: _____

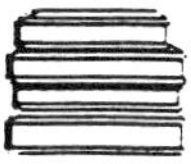

_____

_____

_____ Total teacher points

_____ Total student points

_____ Overall grade

FIGURE 3

Elementary story quilt teacher and student assessment form, designed by
Lois Lamansky (courtesy of New Art Basics Project).

STUDENT QUESTIONNAIRE

Student name_____
Homeroom   14   15   16
Date____May 1995_____

1. Did you enjoy the storytelling and art activities that we did this year?
          yes_____   no_____   sort of_____

2. Rate the following art activities that Mrs. Lamansky designed:

	Excellent	Good	Average	Poor
Clay Storytellers	_____	_____	_____	_____
Flower Legend Paintings	_____	_____	_____	_____
String Stories	_____	_____	_____	_____
Cinderella Tales	_____	_____	_____	_____
Trickster Tales	_____	_____	_____	_____
Quilt Stories	_____	_____	_____	_____
Bird Masks	_____	_____	_____	_____
Personal Collages	_____	_____	_____	_____

3. Evaluate the different ways that you told stories with your art:

	Liked	Disliked	I Didn't Do
By writing	_____	_____	_____
By orally telling into a tape recorder	_____	_____	_____
By orally telling within a cooperative group	_____	_____	_____
By using string and orally telling to others	_____	_____	_____

FIGURE 4
Summary student questionnaire for fourth grade storytelling activities, designed by Lois Lamansky (courtesy of New Art Basics Project).

	Liked	Disliked	I Didn't Do
By typing stories on the typewriter or computer	_____	_____	_____
By using visual images in my art to tell a story	_____	_____	_____
By using words or statements written on my art	_____	_____	_____
By performing a play in front of the class	_____	_____	_____
By talking about my art in front of the class	_____	_____	_____

4. Did you mind that Mrs. Lamansky took pictures of you or your artwork with her camera or camcorder?

   No_____   Yes_____   Sometimes_____

5. Did you mind pre-tests and post-tests?

   No_____   Yes_____   Sometimes_____

6. Did you like grading yourself on assignments?

   No_____   Yes_____   Sometimes_____

7. What did you learn this year about Native American artists? (Use their names if you can or describe what they made)

FIGURE 4 (*Continued*)

ing objectives for visual art activities is the most difficult aspect of making an assessment. Because activities in the visual arts are holistically organic, any single objective will be too atomistic to gain a sufficiently holistic picture of achievement. Therefore, it is suggested that several objectives or goals be formulated for each learning activity (see Illustrations 6 & 7 as examples). These would be stated as concepts to be gained or behavioral goals that can be observed.

   In the NAB system illustrated in Figure 5, all achievement and learning is assessed by either the teacher or student based on individual expectations of growth. Authentic individual assessments are recorded for each learning activity or strategy on a simple form (as positive or negative growth units

8. What did you learn this year about African-American artists? (Use their names if you can or describe what they made)

9. What did you learn this year about Native American people in general?

10. What did you learn this year about African-American people in general?

11. What did you learn about the ways in which our storytelling is the same as the other cultures that we studied? (Native Americans and African-Americans)

12. What did you learn about the ways in which our storytelling is different than the other cultures that we studied? (Native Americans and African-Americans)

THANKS 4TH GRADERS!!!

FIGURE 4 (*Continued*)

above or below expectations). Averages of student performance over an instructional unit are then visually determined and recorded on the chart. This system is designed to be user friendly and cost effective.

Although it is apparent that these growth averages (Figure 6) could be converted into a quantitative measurement for assigning grades, the most educationally significant purpose for the growth averages is to promote a

ILLUSTRATION 6

Elementary student's (two-dimensional) portraiture activity (Courtesy of
New Art Basics Project). Student examples from a unit on portrait drawing.
Each learning activity has designated content objectives or behavioral goals
in four areas: academic art content, media knowledge, thinking skills, and
affective growth.

focused, continuing dialogue between teacher and student. This dialogue
could productively relate not only to discussions of student performance
(Figure 7) but also to discussions about the viability of instructional methods
and curriculum design. A critical analysis, by teachers (Figure 8) of the adequacy of their baseline, 0, expectations could also lead to instructional improvement and program reform. This system of assessment is currently
under field study by teachers in the New Art Basics Project.

A MODEL FOR EVALUATING THE PROCESS
OF VISUAL ABSTRACTION

The assessment model in Figures 9 to 13 was developed by art educator
Brent Knoot for evaluating student performance related to learning the pro-

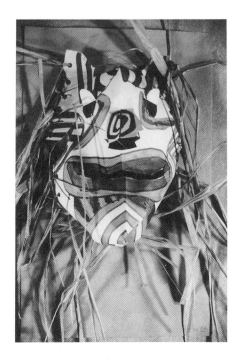

ILLUSTRATION 7

Elementary student's (three-dimensional) mask activity. (Courtesy of New
Art Basics Project). Student examples from a unit on portrait drawing. Each
learning activity has designated content objectives or behavioral goals in
four areas: academic art content, media knowledge, thinking skills, and
affective growth.

cess of visual abstraction. The final objective was to identify student achievement in learning the abstraction process on a five-stage scale of artistic
growth. This model was adapted from the writings of Michael Parsons.

The primary argument we put forth is that assessment systems for use in
the visual arts discipline must be designed and implemented with the individual user/consumer in mind. This assessment consumerism should

- Be qualitative rather than quantitative in nature.
- Apply the principles of authentic assessment.
- Be conducted, recorded, and communicated as much as possible in a
  visual medium.
- Take into account a variety of cultural aesthetic systems.
- Use a variety of assessment methods in concert.

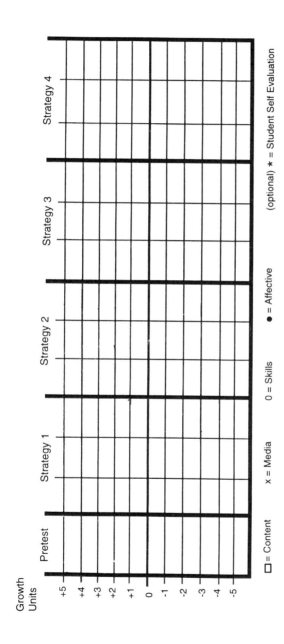

FIGURE 5

The NAB record chart is a simple grid rectangle that allows both teacher and student to enter assessments with a single mark, in a horizontal column (for pretest activity or any of four teaching/learning unit activities). On the vertical dimension each mark represents s growth unit, in plus or minus increments of 5 steps, centered on the "0" or expectation line.

Growth
Units

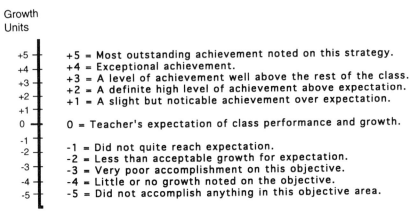

+5 = Most outstanding achievement noted on this strategy.
+4 = Exceptional achievement.
+3 = A level of achievement well above the rest of the class.
+2 = A definite high level of achievement above expectation.
+1 = A slight but noticable achievement over expectation.

0 = Teacher's expectation of class performance and growth.

-1 = Did not quite reach expectation.
-2 = Less than acceptable growth for expectation.
-3 = Very poor accomplishment on this objective.
-4 = Little or no growth noted on the objective.
-5 = Did not accomplish anything in this objective area.

FIGURE 6

A growth unit is defined as an arbitrary unit of measurement that refers directly to either concrete elements and relationships within the visual art work or to some observable behavior of the student. By making individual marks for each objective or outcome, the teacher creates a holistic visual pattern of student achievement and learning immediately visible on the chart.

- Be used for the improvement of instruction and student learning, not as a standardized set of rules.

In general, assessment consumerism may turn out to be the best contribution the visual arts can make to assessment practices.

AUTHENTIC ASSESSMENT OF A PAINTING CLASS: SITTING DOWN AND TALKING WITH STUDENTS

In recent years, there has been an active interest by educators in using methods that more adequately assess the progress and achievements of students across a wide variety of disciplines than do traditional standardized testing procedures. These assessment measures, which are concerned with students acquiring knowledge and skills and solving authentic or realistic problems the same way as in the world outside school, have come to be known as *authentic assessment*. Authentic assessment involves examination of processes as well as products of learning. In such assessment, students are given opportunity to engage in tasks that are integrated, complex, and challenging. They are active participants in creating and constructing their own responses to tasks and demonstrating processes by which they solve problems to audiences in public arenas (Armstrong, 1994; Boughton, 1994; Herman,

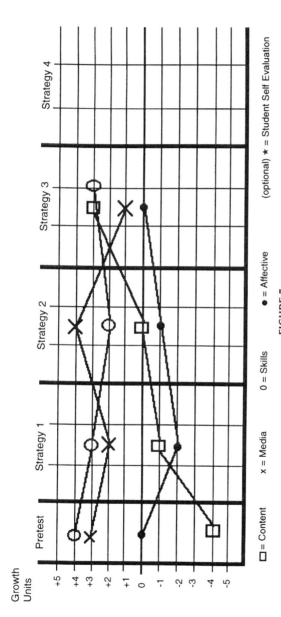

FIGURE 7

This shows an evaluation chart filled out by the teacher with marks in each of the four assessment areas for three student unit activities and a pretest. Connecting lines can be used to graph the general pattern of achievement in each assessment area.

□ = Content   x = Media   0 = Skills   ● = Affective   (optional) ★ = Student Self Evaluation

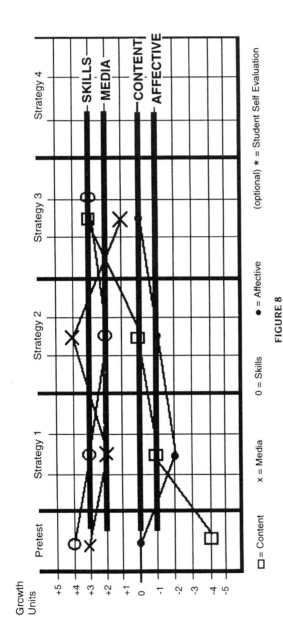

FIGURE 8

At the conclusion of a unit of study (composed of at least one pretest activity and three or four teaching–learning strategies), the student's overall pattern of achievement can be visually estimated. This is done by visually assessing the highs and lows of performance for any one objective over the entire unit and drawing a dark or colored horizontal line that indicates average achievement in that area. Student self-assessment over the course of the unit can also be charted for comparison with the teacher assessment.

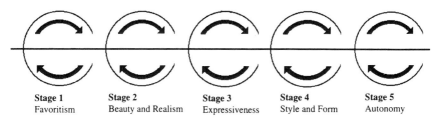

Stage 1	Stage 2	Stage 3	Stage 4	Stage 5
Favoritism	Beauty and Realism	Expressiveness	Style and Form	Autonomy

FIGURE 9

Five-stage recording chart, designed by Brent Knoot, to record student achievement in learning the process of visual abstraction.

NAME #603
PERIOD 6TH

SHARDS OF ME

OBJECTIVE: Complete a Cubist self-portrait by thoroughly "looking" at their reflection in a shattered mirror, and developing a complete composition with shattered Cubist form in using effective use of shading to define forms.

COMPOSITION: — NEARLY ALL AREAS DEVELOPED

10	(9)	8	7	6	5	4	3	2	1	0

shows Cubist influence within portrait and background with all areas developed

only some areas are developed or partially developed

portrait floats in middle of paper, no background, or only "filled" in

FORM:

10	9	8	7	6	5	4	3	2	1	0

shows Cubist shattered forms in portraiture, excellent "looking" at mirror, shows facial features

only "looking" at mirror half of the time, working from memory

no Cubist influence, not "looking" at mirror

SHADING/RENDERING: — CONTINUE TO WORK ON HATCHING/CROSS-HATCHING

10	9	(8)	7	6	5	4	3	2	1	0

uses hatching/cross-hatching and use of light/dark shading to define shattered forms

limited use of hatching/ cross-hatching and light/ dark shading, outline

a lot of "white" areas no hatching/cross hatching or shading

GENERAL ARTISTIC QUALITIES:

(10)	9	8	7	6	5	4	3	2	1	0

drawing is neat, free of smudges, wrinkles and tears; shows creativity, challenge

drawing has a few smudges, wrinkles, and/or tears; shows some individuality

drawing is very smudged with wrinkles and/or tears, looks very ordinary

EFFECTIVE USE OF TIME/DEADLINE:

10	(9)	8	7	6	5	4	3	2	1	0

student used every available minute of class time working on project and completed it to the best of ability

student used majority of class time working on project, simply completing it but not to the best ability

student required continual prodding to keep on task; project incomplete

FIGURE 10

The first stage of this assessment process involves the use of a teacher constructed rubric for each learning activity. In this example, the student (whose work is shown in Figure 11) is evaluated on a full-page rubric on a number of specific criteria.

$$
\begin{array}{r}
9 \quad \text{(composition)} \\
10 \quad \text{(form)} \\
+ \quad 8 \quad \text{(shading/rendering)} \\
\hline
\end{array}
$$

$$3 \mid \overline{27}$$

9 = Rubric Average

FIGURE 11

The series of assessments from the rubric shown in Figure 11 are averaged into a single number called the *rubric average*. In this example a rubric average of 9 is the result.

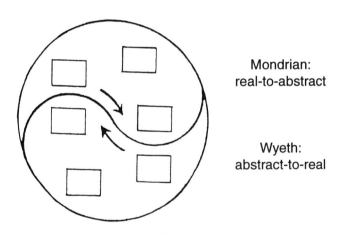

Mondrian:
real-to-abstract

Wyeth:
abstract-to-real

FIGURE 12

This diagram indicates the two learning styles for abstraction identified in a detailed review of the visual record of art history. Artists such as American Andrew Wyeth naturally prefer to work out their ideas with very abstract sketches of compositional structure before adding the precise, observed detail necessary to develop a final painting with convincing optical naturalism. Other artists, such as Dutch Piet Mondrian, begin their visual thinking with representational forms and gradually, over a period of time, abstract down to the essence of a scene. The two individual learning styles, abstract to real and real to abstract, are viewed as interlocking aspects of the same process of visual abstraction.

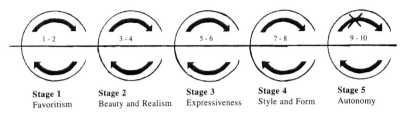

Stage 1	Stage 2	Stage 3	Stage 4	Stage 5
Favoritism	Beauty and Realism	Expressiveness	Style and Form	Autonomy

FIGURE 13

The rubric average of 9 is recorded in the State 5 (autonomy) circle on the abstraction learning scale consisting of five circular stages. The mark is placed in the upper half of the circle to indicate that the student is working with a process of realism to abstraction.

A glance at the chart provides multiple information on the student's achievement. The student, in this example, is deemed to be at the most advanced stage of learning the process of abstraction and has adopted a personally authentic learning style, moving from real toward abstract.

ILLUSTRATION 8

Sixth grade student example, abstract "cubism" strategy: Shards of Me. Students were asked to create a self-portrait from the broken images they perceive in a purposely shattered mirror (artwork courtesy of the New Art Basics Project).

Aschbacher, & Winters, 1992; Marzano, Pickering, & Tighe, 1993; Rudner & Boston, 1994; Zimmerman, 1994, in press).

Good authentic assessment can be viewed as a process in which students are actively engaged in learning, and instruction is an integral part of determining their achievements. Classroom assessment that is authentic, according to Shepard (1989), should be designed to support instruction and should be informal, teacher initiated, adapted to local contexts, sensitive to changes in student learning, meaningful to students, capable of supplying immediately detailed feedback, and requiring tasks that have instructional value in and of themselves. Such assessment also should take into consideration that learners differ in their interests, cognitive styles, rates of learning, patterns of development, abilities, motivations, work habits, and temperaments as well as ethnicity, sex, and social class membership (Zimmerman, 1992c, 1994).

The Indiana University Summer Arts Institute[2]

I would like to describe, and provide examples of, how authentic assessment measures were employed in a program Gilbert Clark and I codirected for over a decade, commencing in 1981. The Indiana University Summer Arts Institute was a residential two-week program for students talented in the visual arts that took place on the university campus. Principle goals set for the institute were to extend knowledge, skills, and understanding about all aspects of the visual arts and provide opportunities for students to interact and work with others with similar and differing backgrounds, interests, and abilities as well as professionals in the visual arts (Clark & Zimmerman, 1988; Zimmerman, 1992a).

Authentic assessment procedures at the institute provided feedback about teaching and learning processes, demonstrated to what extent students and teachers had met their objectives, informed students and their parents about student progress and achievements and where improvements were necessary, and encouraged changes in the current program. To be nominated, students had to meet criteria set by the institute staff (Clark & Zimmerman, 1987). The advanced painting class will be described as an example of how authentic assessment was conducted at the classroom level. This class met for 11 instructional days, from 10:00 A.M. to noon. The 20 students in this class were to enter grades 8 through 11 the following fall.

A number of researchers have suggested that authentic assessments should employ a variety of assessment measures over time to assess students' use of multiple strategies on a wide range of educational tasks (Herman et al., 1992; Rudner & Boston, 1994; Zimmerman, 1992a). They caution

[2]Section contributed by Enid Zimmerman.

about relying on portfolio work alone to judge a student's progress and achievements in art. In assessing the painting class at the institute, 12 different measures were used to determine student and teacher progress and achievements.

Class Assessment

As part of a larger research study, I observed every advanced painting class at the institute and interviewed the teacher of that class (Zimmerman, 1991, 1992b). My information was collected using notes; tapes of five teaching sessions that included individual and group critiques by the painting teacher; slides of classroom activities and student portfolios that contained sketches, related resources, artwork in process, and completed pieces; students' sketchbook journals; taped teacher interviews; and two art teacher-observer journals. I also held three focus group meetings with 6–8 students in each group; two doctoral students individually interviewed all 20 students in the class with respect to their reflections about their artwork, experiences in the painting class, and the institute in general. In addition, I observed the final exhibition of student work and evaluations were collected, after the institute concluded, from students, teachers, and parents.

Teacher Assessment

Jeff was the painting teacher, and his philosophy was that teachers are responsible for helping students learn about themselves and their artwork. To capture student attention he told me, "a teacher needs to be dynamic to keep them interested and challenged . . . and should teach with intensity and compassion." He said,

> art teachers should enable their students to be self-generating by making them aware of contexts for their artwork and stimulating them to widen and deepen that context. Often the teaching process begins when the teacher supplies a context as a starting point that is more complex than a student's original conception. This more complex; context contains mechanisms for stimulation and self-criticism that lead to further growth.

Jeff planned his curriculum around creating self-portraits. First the students would paint, in blacks, whites, and grays, a simple sphere, then "big eyes, big lips, and big noses" (see Illustration 9). Next, the students would interpret, through color paintings, a portrait by an artist of their own choosing. Finally they would make a pencil sketch and then complete an acrylic painting of a self-portrait. One of Jeff's goals for this unit was to help students learn what it is like to be an artist (see Illustration 10) who experiences "energy shifts of alternating feelings of something starting to happen with feelings of frustration." Another goal was to have the students paint adequate self-portraits.

ILLUSTRATION 9

This student is painting a "big eye." He wrote in his journal, "We are doing features of our faces like our eyes and our noses, but we are painting them very large. I never looked at an eye so long and noticed so much about it, like highlights, shapes, tones, and especially how eyes can express things."

He felt that painting is a skill that can be taught and that "Kids want control . . . they want to paint like Rembrandt not Pollack."

Jeff employed many strategies to help students learn, including sketching diagrams on the board, providing them with clear performance targets and agreed-upon standards, conducting group and individual oral critiques at each phase of the painting unit, and providing written responses to reflections in the students' journals or sketchbooks about the processes they were experiencing in creating their self-portraits. One of most successful student assessments that this teacher provided was through critiquing student work in progress and as a finished product. In fact, he spent almost half the class time critiquing student work. Assessment can be taken to mean (Latin, *ad* + *sedere*) to sit down together (Ross, Radnor, Mitchell, & Bierton, 1993) or (French, *assidere*) to sit beside the learner to find out (Marshall, 1993).

Jeff was most successful in "sitting down beside" his students in regular shared acts of assessment through "talk." He was able to provide immediate

ILLUSTRATION 10
Interpreting a portrait by Rembrandt was a challenge for this student who wrote in his journal: "I thought this would be easier than it was. This is more than copying. Besides getting the colors, shapes, and textures right you have to figure out Rembrandt's techniques for making it look like a real person."

feedback to students so that they could engage in meaningful learning experiences and reflect on their own progress and achievements. Praise statements usually preceded corrections and suggestions for improvement. This teacher's ability to have his students solve expressive problems through painting techniques and media (Illustration 11), as well as being able to empathize with his students as young artists, was evident when he told one student who was struggling with her self-portrait: "Get yourself together . . . you have a lot of strength . . . you can do it." Then, teacher and student discussed how the student could solve some of the problems she was confronting.

Teacher-Observer Responses

The painting class served as a field site for two art teachers enrolled in practicum experience in a class. These teachers were observers for all sessions of the painting class and kept journals with their observations and reflections about the class. Their journals were based on their written observation notes in which they raised questions and concerns and identified and described dilemmas they witnessed and how these problems were resolved. In addition, they were required to write summary reflections after each class observation and a final summary about their entire practicum experience.

ILLUSTRATION 11

A great deal of time was spent by this student mixing colors similar to those found in a reproduction of a portrait by Cezanne. She noted in her journal, "Getting the colors right was really difficult. It took a long time and I had to look at other paintings by Cezanne to make sure the colors in the reproduction were true."

One of the two observers noted that Jeff focused on problem-solving skills and introduced other art disciplines into his curriculum. She wrote,

> Jeff noticed that some of the kids were bored with their paintings and he pointed out that the reason people get bored when they paint is that they are not convinced that their work is "real." For him, painting involved problem solving and using analysis to figure out what the problem was in one's own work. He said not to assume the whole painting is "wrong" and told them to analyze exactly where the problem lies. I thought this was a great way to introduce critical thinking skills.

She added, "I love the way he introduces art history, art criticism, and aesthetics into a studio class! It is a perfect example how this can be done informally and not in a lecture situation." This observer also noted one problem she had with the teacher's strategies: "This man has a lot of power and these children could easily fall under his spell and take some of his remarks literally, when what he really wants to do is make them think."

The other observer noted that when a student was frustrated, the teacher told her to solve her painting problems and "don't just dump the work . . . stand back and coolly analyze . . . what do you need to do to make this work better? Remember anyone can do this . . . this is just a skill . . . like brushing your teeth." This observer also commented, "The teacher used portraits by artists from many different cultures and compared the different moods, textures, atmospheres, etc. created in their works and had the students contrast these qualities with their own works." He also noted that the teacher concluded the last class with these words: "You all did extremely well . . . remember painting is filled with stress and frustrations, but you can succeed." This observer felt the individual student critiques were valuable, although during class critiques, even though the teacher encouraged students to add comments, "the teacher dominated the discussions and did not pose many questions that might have encouraged further discussion."

Both observers commented on the final exhibition in which work was chosen and hung by the students. Both work in progress and completed pieces were included as well as excerpts from journals that accompanied the work. One of the observers wrote in her journal about the educational value of the final exhibit and how participating in the painting practicum would affect her future teaching experiences:

> When everything was up, in its entirety, I could see what these kids accomplished in a short period of time. I talked to several parents at the exhibit and they seemed proud of their kids and said they learned a lot about art and the processes their children went through to create their "masterpieces." I learned a lot of things that I can take back to my own art classroom, especially, I know I will keep a reflective journal for all my teaching experiences.

Student Assessment

Authentic assessment was conducted to determine student progress and achievement in the painting class through students' sketchbooks and journals, photographs and slides of their work in progress and completed portraits, interviews, focus groups, and final institute evaluation forms. In the interviews and focus groups, students were unanimous in their approval of the painting class. They said they learned a lot in the class about painting techniques (Illustrations 12 and 13), how to look at art in a "different way," and expressing themselves through paint media. A number of students reported they gained more confidence as they progressed throughout the class. Group critiques were cited as a means of "learning about our own mistakes and someone else's too." One student said about the painting teacher: "He gives you an idea about what he wants you to do. He makes you go off on your own, too. If he sees you are getting bored he diverts your attention to something else by telling stories. I think he is a really good

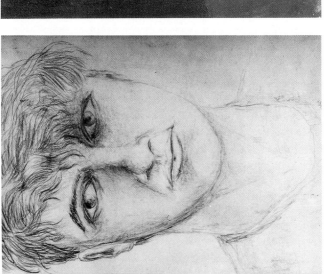

ILLUSTRATION 12 and 13

This student made a preparatory sketch that was the basis for his self-portrait painting. He reflected in his journal: "Every time I put a brush to the canvas, it looks awful. It's really hard to blend colors. Pencil I can work with, it's much harder to control paint."

teacher and a good person, too." Another student described what she was learning about painting techniques: "I could never get noses right. I learned how to do that and how to make highlights, the tones, the darks and lights; now I understand how to do it." Still another student expressed his feelings about his frustrations and accomplishments: "I enjoyed meeting the other students and being with people like myself. The classes were hard and I had to push myself to make my self-portrait look alive and real. But, I didn't enjoy the work, but I enjoy knowing I will enjoy what happened here in the future."

Following is an excerpt from a student's journal concerning her feelings about pushing her art talent and abilities in the painting class:

> It is kind of good that we do different projects, because I get tired after two days painting the same thing. I get frustrated at myself. It looks so bad and it looked so good before. I have to paint now because it is one of the best times to paint when I am frustrated. Even though I am down and bored I need to push myself through it. I know I will realize afterward that it looks good again. I can see the light at the end of the rainbow.

Another student summarized her reactions to the painting class, with a few, well conceived words: "This class has done a lot for my person and for me. I know I will be able to take what I learned in the painting class and apply it to my painting experiences in the future."

Parent Assessment

After the 1988 institute concluded, parents or guardians of students in the painting class were sent Jeff's open-ended written evaluations of their children's progress as well as evaluation forms to fill out. On the forms that were returned to the institute, parents reported that their children enjoyed the experience, learned about painting techniques and skills, were able to reflect on their experiences, matured socially and emotionally, learned to accept criticism, and appreciated Jeff's teaching strategies. An example of one parent's response to questions on the evaluation form follows: (1) What were your child's overall impressions of the painting class? "Rebecca loved her experience—every aspect. She used words such as *great, learned so much, never boring*, and *learned so much about myself too*"; (2) What experience was talked about the most? "The painting teacher and the way he constructively criticized and appreciated her work. His respect for the students as young artists was evident when he invited them to his studio and to see how he worked"; (3) What else was remembered about the painting class? "The teacher's manner, kind, but with specific suggestions for improvement"; (4) On the back of this form, please describe your reactions to the program. "My daughter is a farm girl and she enjoyed socializing. . . . There are a lot of kids from different backgrounds and it's a good experience for kids to meet other kids with different lifestyles."

ILLUSTRATION 14

[Self-portrait]. "My goal," this student wrote, "is to paint my insides out. I'm interested in getting out how I feel at certain times when I'm struggling to stay on top of things. I really exaggerated my eyes which tell how I feel. I made the other parts of my face smaller and less important."

Another parent's response to question (4) also involved opportunities her son had to socialize with others with similar interests: "Abe throughly enjoyed the intense instruction and a social setting where he was able to get to know a group of kids with similar inclinations and forge friendships in a short period of time." A few suggestions were made by parents for improving the painting classes, such as "Send out a list of resources to students before they attend the institute. A few readings could be sent as well." Student suggestions for improvement included allowing participants to take more than one painting class during the institute, adding an art careers class, and lengthening the program to three weeks to allow for "more in-depth advancement of individual art work. This would also contribute to a more relaxed atmosphere. We could also have a greater number of rest periods or catch up days for completing artwork." A number of these suggestions were discussed with the painting teacher along with his own suggestions for change. Several of these suggestions and critiques from the teacher-observers were incorporated into the painting class that Jeff taught at the institute the following summer.

ILLUSTRATION 15
This student's journal contained the following observations: "Almost everyone else is painting heads. I feel I can paint the way I want to in my own style and in my own way. Jeff came over and showed me a few techniques and that helped me see how the background should go with the rest of the painting. I really like the results and feel like I accomplished a lot this summer."

Reflections on the Assessment Process

Most of the goals for the institute, and specifically the painting class, were met as determined by the authentic assessment procedures just described. Students in the painting class did gain new knowledge, skills, and under-standing about the visual arts (Illustration 14). They also had many opportunities to interact with others who had similar interests and abilities. In the painting class, they also became proficient in critiquing their own artwork and that of others, developed vocabulary to discuss works of art, and expanded their ability to make informed decisions about their own artwork and that of others (Illustration 15). The painting teacher's goals for the students to learn about themselves and their artwork and to experience what "it is like to be an artist" also were achieved. In the assessment, both products and processes were taken into consideration and the teacher "sat down" with his students and collaborated with them to solve difficult technical, expressive, and cognitive problems. General authentic assessment goals were (1) demonstrating to what extent teacher and students met their objectives; (2) informing students about what they needed to do to improve; (3) providing the teacher with information that helped him to recognize his successes and make revisions when appropriate; (4) establishing a valid assessment system with tasks that are worthwhile, meaningful, and significant; (5) providing a vehicle for helping parents to understand their children's growth; and (6) requiring a final public exhibition where students demonstrated skills of inquiry and expression and their abilities to respond effectively and imaginatively to a topic (Archbald & Newmann, 1988; Taylor, 1991; Wiggins, 1989). All these are evident in the variety of measures used in the authentic assessments conducted at the institute.

The authentic assessments reported here were specifically designed for the context in which the institute took place and the variety of students who participated in experiences in the painting class taught by Jeff. Conducting authentic assessment can empower teachers and provide them with effective instructional tools and new emphases on teaching-relevant problem-solving skills. According to Rudner and Boston (1994), the emphasis of authentic assessment should be to improve teaching and learning at the classroom level. Although authentic assessment makes additional demands on teachers, students, and resources than would normally be expected and requires extra time to plan and develop materials and arrange meetings between teachers and students (Zimmerman, 1993), the wealth of information gleaned by "sitting down next to our students" and engaging in meaningful dialogues that result in better teaching and learning is more than worth the effort.

CLASSROOM ASSESSMENT RESEARCH[3]

Classroom assessment in art encompasses two dichotomous categories, formative assessment and summative assessment. With the long-standing use of portfolios, art educators may find summative assessment the more familiar of the two. Specifically, summative assessment is evaluation at an end of instruction, at the completion of an instructional span of time, or after the conclusion of the process of learning about or making art. Summative assessment can occur with an activity such as grading student papers, tests, artwork, projects, and performances.

Additionally, art educators use summative assessment at the end of a marking period, semester, or academic year with reviewing and grading a final portfolio. These summative assessment points provide feedback to stu-

[3]Section contributed by Ann Joyce.

dents in the form of a number or a letter, which may or may not include written or verbal comments. Unfortunately, this feedback comes when it is generally too late to mend gaps in learning.

In summative assessment, grading functions as a worth standard. This represents a quality level compared and contrasted with the criteria of an established performance standard. An underlying assumption here is that the educational process changes students. Therefore, grading acts as a benchmark, a point in measuring progress toward those anticipated changes.

But, what real opportunity exists for students to learn from that feedback and make constructive changes that range from major reforms to minor revisions when the process, for all intents and purposes, has come to an end? What real opportunity exists for growth and development when art teachers may never again see those students or when those students may care about only a final grade and moving on? Concurrently, how do art educators evaluate students relative to all components of the art curriculum? And, finally, how do teachers know if students grasped and synthesized the history, aesthetics, philosophy, and production portions of the art learning experience?

Conversely, formative assessment allows art educators to holistically evaluate any or all components of the art curriculum. This type of evaluation can occur at any point in the instructional process. Furthermore, it can occur as many or as few times as a teacher would like before the process ends. Historically, this is familiar ground for studio teachers, as they traditionally offer feedback and initiate discussions with students concerning work in progress. An inherent pitfall exists when teachers disseminate feedback in a top-down style with the instructor as the bearer of knowledge and student as a vessel to be filled. But, there are methodologies that teachers can use to assay the level and quality of student learning at any point in the learning process. This is where formative assessment comes into play. And, the feedback can originate from any source, including the art educator, other teachers, peers in the class, or self-reflection and self-assessment.

As Diane Halpern and associates (1994) notes, classroom assessment is an intervention at various phases of the traditional educational cycle of first teach, next study and learn, and then test and apply. The aim of formative assessment is to effect temporary pauses in this sequence for refinement and improvement of student learning while there is time to explore new paths or make changes in a previously planned course of action. Specifically, formative assessment techniques can increase teacher awareness of learning that is or is not occurring in or out of the classroom, which, in turn, can positively affect student growth and development. Moreover, formative assessment allows students and teachers to look at the journey of making art and value the process as well as the product. Ultimately, formative assessment can improve both teaching and learning.

Formative assessment may not provide educators with rigid statistical data. Rather, the purpose of formative assessment is to take the pulse of students. It allows teachers to glean indicators of what learning is happening or not happening. These assessment outcomes might include significant information, meaningful insights, and weighty indicators of student learning. As an ongoing activity, formative assessment measures can provide a series of momentary snapshots of the big picture. Using a medical analogy, some students ask if a specific assessment during a class will "just take a small X ray or provide a comprehensive MRI." As a process, formative evaluations can focus on individual students, classes of students, or larger groups of students. Ultimately, classroom research information is valuable for discerning patterns or making broad deductions.

Formative assessment results can deliver rude awakenings to art educators, especially when classroom assessments reveal serious problems in learning. For instance, when a teacher considers a class session outstanding but an assessment yields less than 25% accomplishing the stated objectives of the class, an educator can view the experience a personal failure. A healthier stance is to view the event as a wonderful opportunity to not just cover material but to help students to learn from a sequential art curriculum. Art educators must realize that some feedback may sting. In fact, didactic feedback, or direct and indirect student comment on various aspects of the teaching process [as proffered by Lawrence Rudner and Carol Boston in A Look at Performance Assessment for Art Education (1994)], may be the most difficult to deal with as it directly correlates with the performance of the art teacher. On the other hand, art educators need not share the results with anyone. The beauty of classroom assessment is that this research is self-directed and self-paced. It is not mandated by anyone. It is for a teacher and by the same teacher. And, since it is usually ungraded, it is akin to a series of confidential communications between teacher and student. Additionally, each teacher maintains complete control and decides how often, when, and what to assay.

An important caveat when attempting formative classroom research is to start out slowly. Try one of the simplest assessment methods, such as one-sentence summaries or concept maps, as described by Cross and Angelo (1988), or one-minute papers or muddiest point, as offered by Angelo and Cross (1993). After a first trial of an assessment, reflect on it to determine any revisions for improvement such as allowing more or less time for students to complete the assessment. Then try the revised assessment with students. Homegrown assessment vehicles tend to work best with continual fine-tuning depending on the class personality and the individual students involved. And, remember, what works beautifully with one class may fizzle with another.

One of the most important things teachers can do is show enthusiasm. When the teacher's energy is contagious, most students become genuinely excited about assessment. Moreover, students must understand the importance of this research in their learning process. For this reason, consider linking formative assessment to a class participation grade. Most important, it is not enough to use formative assessment methods and gather indicators from students. Respond to students with feedback. If half a class confused Magritte with Dali, reteach that the very next class before doing anything else. Come prepared to class to rework it in a new way, as you already know the first way was ineffective. The overall goal in active learning and formative assessment is not to cover material, but to learn it—to make meaningful connections from it. Encourage students to read, write, talk, interact, engage, perform, listen, and reflect.

Experiment and learn to adapt formative assessment vehicles to various age groups. For instance, while secondary students might rate a class using a scale from highly effective to totally ineffective, early elementary students might rate it by coloring or circling line drawings of children's faces with a continuum of different expressions from broad smiles to sad frowns. Another formative assessment exercise, fence sitting, elicits dialogue from students and helps them take a definite stance on an issue. Select two dichotomous examples of an artist's work. Instruct students to decide which of the two images or solutions is better. For example, Milton Glaser's *Zabriskie Point*, a 1972 movie poster shows the graphic designer's skills as a draftsman, includes a narrative dimension, and represents the conclusion of the film when an American house is blown up and its contents scatter into a desolate landscape. Contrast this with Glaser's *One Print One Painting* poster, an atypical 1968 poster that portrays image and meaning exclusively with type and its manipulation within an isometric cube. The time frame for this assessment is at least an entire class period or as an out-of-class assignment for debate during the next class session.

Whenever students prepare portfolio pieces, instruct them to also write a critical narrative to annotate or supplement the artwork. For junior high, secondary, and higher education students, the commentary can furnish an explanation of the significance of the work, clarify how the student dealt with problems encountered in the process of making art, elucidate how the student interpreted a theme, and so on. Instruct elementary students to write about their art. With younger children, begin with one prompt, such as to explain what everything is in their work. When students develop a comfort level with one prompt, add another, such as to give reasons for using the colors they did.

Figure 14 represents a formative assessment class exercise that attempts to introduce art phobic students to communicating visually. To some degree, most students can use words or writing to communicate. Students attempt that in step 1 where they write about a horrific scene and in step 3 where they write about an idyllic or peaceful scene. In steps 2 and 4, students must visually illustrate those same scenes using sketches, drawings, or magazine clippings. This may panic half the class as they equate this with realistic drawing ability and argue that they cannot do that successfully. This exercise forces students to sit up in their seats, if only to complain, and eventually move into action. Figure 14 demonstrates responses from a freshman college

**Comm 211– Introduction to Mass Communications – Mrs. Ann Joyce – King's College
Class Exercise "Verbal and Visual Images"**

Name   Section   Date

Images pervade our societies. We use them to communicate on many levels including icon, index and symbol. We receive approximately 80 percent of our information through our eyes.

1. Create a verbal image of a horrific scene. Use words to make your vision come to life.

The wreckage was strewn over both sides of the street. Bodies were being pulled out of the way of the flames. There was blood everywhere. One person lay impaled on a metal fence. The person had been thrown from one of the cars that had been involved in the accident. There was nothing anyone could do to help. A child stood screaming for her mother who had been killed. No one could calm her.

2. Create a visual image of the same horrific scene. Sketch or draw to make your vision come to life.

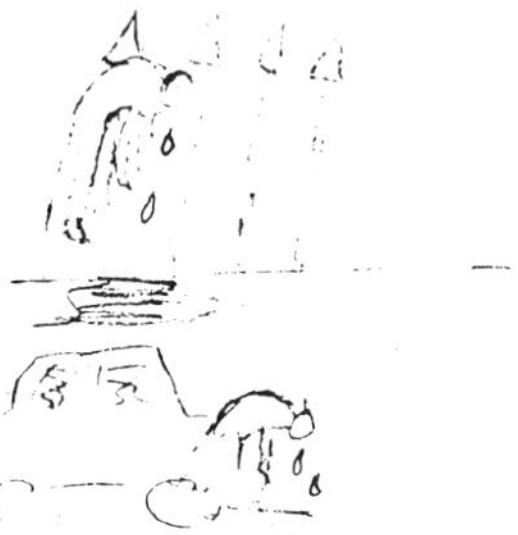

3. Create a verbal image of an idyllic or peaceful scene. Use words to make your vision come to life.

The sand was still warm from the afternoon sun and you could smell the sweet, saltyness of the water. The waves broke softly, gently, against the shore. The sun was setting into the blue water and throwing its radiant color over the water, wrapping it in a soft orange, and pink glow. The light bounced off the clouds and made them appear dark and gray but also beautiful. Then, as quickly as it started it was gone.

4. Create a visual image of the same idyllic or peaceful scene. Sketch or draw to make your vision come to life.

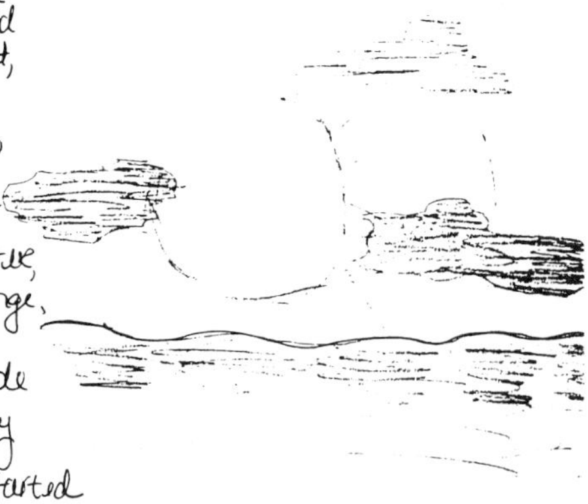

FIGURE 14

Class exercise, verbal and visual images, designed by Ann Joyce.

student who shows ease with words contrasted with a limited vocabulary for creating visual images. Of the many possible outcomes from this type of formative assessment with nonartist students, the most common is less difficulty with words and more difficulty with images. When a student performs in this manner, it allows the art educator to deal with student feelings of inadequacy and possible performance anxiety in the first weeks of contact with a student.

The in-class critique portion of this exercise always elicits exuberant discussion. As students critically examine and unpack the wide range of effective and ineffective ways to communicate both verbally and visually, they take first steps in assimilating the language of visual communication and mastering visual schemata. In this exercise, students perform, talk, listen, interact, write, and reflect upon their learning.

To adapt this exercise for elementary students, limit the exercise to one written response and one sketch for each student. Give students lined paper for writing and sturdy drawing paper for sketching. Show a print or slide of a work in your curriculum, keep it projected, then ask students to write about it and draw it. Field tested with slides of Deborah Butterfield's horse sculptures, a group of first grade Cub Scouts clamored to talk about the horses and to show each other their drawings, but not to share their minimal writing abilities.

The class exercise in Figure 15 is for an introductory class where students learn the elements and principles of visual design, the building blocks of visual literacy. This exercise provides word problems for critical reflection. Student can respond individually or in small groups. Group discussions encourage peer teaching when one student just does not understand a concept or relationship. Others in the group each explain in their own words until the student successfully understands. Question 5 has no wrong answer, only a faulty substantiation of an answer. Groups can banter back and forth for 20 minutes on this question alone. Figure 15 shows an assessment as completed, incorrectly in part, by a small group of students. Beginning a class with an assessment of this type can reveal when students did not read assigned material or when students had difficulty comprehending reading assignments.

The ethics of visual communications class exercise in Figure 16 takes the form of case studies that present students with scenarios that may pose ethical dilemmas. These case studies generally elicit much dialogue, even from those shy students reticent to participate in class; they have written something on their paper that they can say. For some of the cases, divide students into groups of those who agree, those who disagree, and those who are neutral. A debate of the issues involved then begins. Many students do not grasp accepted standards or rules of conduct for artists and designers even though they may have read a code of conduct and copyright laws, both cloaked in legal jargon. This assessment furnishes a jump-start to move directly to the issues.

**Communications 233 – Graphics for Mass Communications – Mrs. Ann Joyce
Class Exercise – Design Elements and Principles – King's College**

Name _____,_____   Date _____

Respond on the lines provided with brief answers.

1. _Symmetrical_____

For sighted individuals, visual balance applies to all
natural and creature-made compositions. Viewed in
aggregate, boulders, rocks and crushed stones at the base
of a rock slide exemplify one type of naturally occurring
balance. Architecture represents human-made balance.
Study the architectural illustration at right. What is the
name for the kind of visual balance it represents?

2. _Contrast_____

Compare and contrast the following type passages. Decide what design elements both possess.
Among those choices, discern the one design element that both have but that differs significantly
in each. In other words, what one design element is profoundly visually illustrated?

The honing of ability in graphic design involves both lengthy study and intense investigation and experimentation. Good graphic communication is difficult to achieve but never looks it. Excellent graphic communication is a master challenge but looks effortless.	**The honing of ability in graphic design involves both lengthy study and intense investigation and experimentation. Good graphic communication is difficult to achieve but never looks it. Excellent graphic communication is a master challenge but looks effortless.**

3 _personification_____

The big bad wolf lives in the forest and paints as a hobby. Throughout fairy tale land big bad
wolf exhibits oil paintings of pig houses. His favorite composition is a 1993 triptych entitled,
"Straw House, Wood House, Brick House." In a recent *Grimms Gazette* Sunday feature wolf
elucidates, "For me, straw, wood and brick conjure rich visual images and create a wonderful
interplay of pattern." What design element most accurately aligns with wolf's description?

4. _implied shapes_____

A chain link fence generally forms a regular pattern. The holes formed by the meshed wires
result in the perception of a distinct shape. Just like the hole in a doughnut, these shapes do not
exist as actual entities. What is the design term for this type of shape?

5. ____No_____

As you backpack through Bangor, Maine, you encounter author Stephen King. He invites you
into his gargoyle festooned living compound to discuss the possibility of creating the title
graphics and theater poster for the movie interpretation of *Needful Things*. He instructs you to
portend, above all, ineffable pain. Will you use the design principle harmony? (Respond on line
above.) Why or why not?

_____Because everything should be different_____

FIGURE 15

Class exercise, Design elements and principles, designed by Ann Joyce.

In Figure 17, a crossword puzzle serves as a pretest during the first class
of a term. Administer the same crossword in the form of a post-test during
your last class meeting. The post-test in Figure 17 demonstrates a less than

**Communications 233 – Graphics for Mass Communications – Mrs. Ann Joyce – King's College
Class Exercise – " The Ethics of Visual Communications"**

Name   Date
_____   _____

Read each case study and rate each using the following scale. You may want to underline key words
or jot notes in the margins.

    1   unequivocally disagree
    2   strongly disagree
    3   moderately disagree
    4   slightly disagree
    5   neither disagree or agree
    6   slightly agree
    7   moderately agree
    8   strongly agree
    9   unequivocally agree

___ 1. Last month, a small retail hardware store called "Nuts and Bolt" ran an ad in a small newspaper that
       circulates only within a twenty-five mile radius in northern California. You happened to see the ad on a
       trip to that area to visit relatives. You thought the ad had a great idea and a very clever design. Your
       client has a similar type store in Wilkes-Barre and advertises in the *Citizens Voice*. You checked carefully
       and the ad did not have a copyright symbol or copyright notice in it. Therefore, it is OK for you to copy
       the ad as long as you alter it slightly such as changing the Helvetica typeface of the original ad to an Avant
       Garde typeface in your ad.

___ 2. Martha is a junior student with a 3.82 GPA, a goal to become editor of a college publication in her senior
       year, and aspirations of highest average in the department at commencement. Unfortunately, she cannot
       seem to get a handle on graphics. After two average projects she decides to insure a great grade on the
       third project. After some casual conversation, she discovers that the professor is ignorant concerning rap
       music. Martha is no Rembrandt so she illustrates her CD cover project with a drawing that she traced
       from the CD cover of a more obscure rap group. The typography and color were her own invention, but
       the illustration was not. The CD cover project looked great and she received an "A" as a grade. During
       the critique she said she will put the project in her portfolio. You feel what she did was wrong.

___ 3. A group of four students from King's decide to open a retail novelty store named "Wild & Crazy." The
       store location is a rented space on the first floor of the Margarida building. The product line includes gag
       gifts, posters, t-shirts, and trendy merchandise. These entrepreneurs plan a biweekly ad campaign in *The
       Crown* using two cartoon characters similar to something you might see in "The Far Side" comic strip. In
       each ad "Wild" (who is male) and "Crazy" (who is female) engage in a dialogue about a piece of
       merchandise the store has on sale. Each cartoon begins with Crazy shopping in the store and ends with
       Wild laughing hysterically about the product and lamenting "That's retarded!" You think this is a great
       concept to create awareness and attract the target audience of college students into the store.

___ 4. When your employment search ended, you did not land the Madison Avenue agency job you coveted.
       But, you were fortunate to land a wonderful entry-level position at one of the three ad agencies in your
       home town of fifty thousand people. After six months on the job, the agency account executive who
       handles "North South East West Bank" tells you the bank has decreased by half their work with your
       agency. The exec informs you to temporarily pad your job sheets where you record how much time you
       spend working on an account. The exec tells you to add one hour for every two that you actually work on
       the bank account. That amounts to an extra $50 every time you charge $100. That way, your ad agency
       can recover some of its lost billings while the account exec scrambles to muster new business and fill the
       void. You comply with this request.

___ 5. In a project, your college graphics professor asks you portray a rich visual tapestry for viewers to feast
       their eyes upon. The professor assigns each student a real dud of an industrial product where it seems
       virtually impossible to "Sell the sizzle, not the steak." Since the customer for your gizmo is 98.852 percent
       white, male, blue-collar, age 55 to 61, you solve the problem by designing an ad with a color photograph
       of a 21-year-old, very attractive, blond female holding the product.

FIGURE 16

Class exercise, the ethics of visual communications, designed by Ann Joyce.

average performance with only 13 responses with 1 error out of 32 possible
responses. For any course, design a group crossword puzzle assessment that
student teams attempt to solve at the beginning of class. Allow groups to
use their text, additional readings, and handouts as simple recall is not the
intended outcome. The goal is additional contact with the materials in a
different manner for the benefit of students with different learning styles. It

Communications 233 – Graphics for Mass Communications Posttest – Spring 1994
Mrs. Ann Joyce – King's College

Name _____ Section _____ Date 5/3

© 1993 Ann Joyce

ACROSS
1. Design principle that is the opposite of harmony
4. Printing process using depressed wells that fill with ink
2. Errors or omissions that a printer makes
9. A preliminary sketch or plan of a design
11. Invented movable metal type in Germany
12. "Red" in four/color printing
14. A type of early full-size layout
15. The lightness or darkness of a color or black
16. A press using a continuous roll of paper
17. Used to cut shapes in paper by a printer
18. Type is measured in this increment
19. A competitive process to solicit costs of printing jobs
22. Type without serifs
23. A binding method using staples
26. The intensity of a color
27. A screened continuous tone image

DOWN
1. A color scheme using opposites on the color wheel
2. Design element that shows surface pattern such as smooth
3. A term for white space or empty portions of a design
5. A color scheme using 3 colors next to each other on the color wheel
6. Blue in four/color printing
8. Four sheets of film each encoded with one of four colors necessary for process color printing
10. The study of type
13. A miniature preliminary sketch of a design
14. A primary color
18. Column width is usually stated in this measurement
19. Layout format shaped like a single straight column
20. Computerized page composition and design is ___ publishing
21. A layout format with one main column or thrust and smaller perpendicular "branches" or projections
24. Two color printing of an image is a ___ tone
25. To adjust letter or word spacing
28. Changes made by a client at typesetter or printer

FIGURE 17

Class posttest Graphics for Mass Communications, designed by Ann Joyce.

also can reinforce connections to other areas of the curriculum such as English and history.

Another pretest might include an open-ended questionnaire to help art teachers learn more about their students and what will help them to succeed in the course. Query students as to why they want to learn art, desktop publishing, or whatever the course is about; when they feel most creatively stimulated in a course; what kinds of assignments they find most beneficial; and so on. If a student often replies "hands-on" or "apply what I've learned," this provides valuable insights. Other responses sometimes reveal a high-achieving student who the art educator may lose without careful attention to the high degree of challenge the student thrives on.

Figure 18 demonstrates another portion of a course pretest, where introductory desktop publishing students attempt to name computer icons. As shown in this sample, many will guess even when instructed not to do so. Another variation of this pretest could show pictures of art from the planned curriculum and instruct students to name the title, the artist, explain what the art is about, or all of these. For elementary students, use illustrations of art tools and tell students to name each or tell what it does. Also hold the art tool in plain view so that students have a second reference with the actual tool. Include some easy responses such as scissors and crayons so that the assessment does not frustrate students.

In another assessment pretest, students construct a concept map or web by brainstorming or writing anything that comes to their minds when given a word. Place a word such as art, modern art, postmodern art in a circle in the center of the page. Practice one example first, using the name of your school on the chalkboard with the entire class. Ask students to call out anything that comes to mind using free association. Write all the responses on the board in related clusters. Students generally come forward with all types of connections from academics to sports to cocurricular activities. Make sure that your demonstration reveals layers of rich brainstorming and connections and tell students that is the expected level.

Self-assessments provide indicators of areas students may not feel comfortable discussing in a critique. It is critical to tell students only the teacher will see the results. Ask students to respond to questions such as, "When I compare my design with the designs of others in this course, my design shows . . ." on a scale from "much more creativity and imagination" through "neither more nor less creativity and imagination" to "much less creativity and imagination." With advanced students, ask them to assay their progress using more advanced criteria as in Figure 19. Have students plot their progress on the thermometer as they test the wellness of their project. Always provide a brief definition of all criteria. Using frequent classroom assessments subtly encourages students to prepare for class and work on assigned projects between classes as they face accountability. In Figure 19, the student attempts to evaluate herself along the scale and provides explanatory comments in the margins.

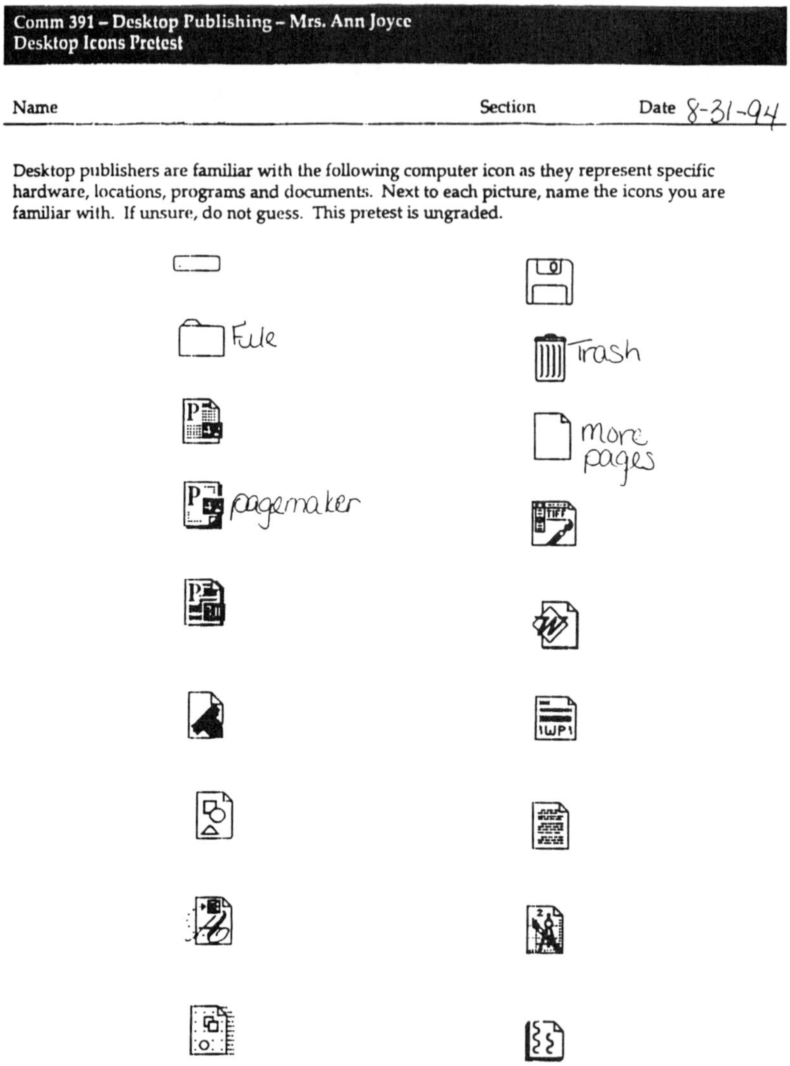

Comm 391 – Desktop Publishing – Mrs. Ann Joyce
Desktop Icons Pretest

Name ______ Section ______ Date 8-31-94

Desktop publishers are familiar with the following computer icon as they represent specific hardware, locations, programs and documents. Next to each picture, name the icons you are familiar with. If unsure, do not guess. This pretest is ungraded.

File
Trash
more pages
pagemaker
TIFF
WP

FIGURE 18
Class pretest Desktop Icons, designed by Ann Joyce.

Teachers can develop assessment forms with criteria, a rating scale, and an area for additional comments for assaying the quality of oral presentations. Early in the course, students may simply explain a piece of work extemporaneously to the class. At the end of the course, students may formally present a portfolio of artwork from the course with a prepared presentation.

Comm 391 – Advanced Desktop Publishing – Mrs. Ann Joyce – King's College
"Thermometer" Formative Assessment of Work in Progress

Name _____ Date ⊘/₦/95

To test the "wellness" of your work in progress, plot any of the following design considerations on
the thermometer below. Not all will be applicable to your design. The rating scale is: 10 = most
effective, successful or "healthy" and 0 = least effective, least successful or "in intensive care." Use
the space to the left and right of the thermometer to briefly explain your rating choices.

✓Alphasignal	Objective part of the message without any inflection or rhetoric
✓Parasignal	The mode of the signal including shape and color designations
×Infrasignal	Subtleties of information underlying or beneath the message
✓Icon	A representation, copy or imitation such as your photo as an icon for you
×Index	A factual or causal connection such as smoke as an index for fire
×Symbol	A learned connection or relationship such as spoken or written word
×Metasymbol	When meaning transcends a simple one-to-one relationship such as a dove with an olive branch as a metasymbol for peace
×Correspondence	When design components have similar or corresponding visual properties and develop a relationship or correspondence
×Graphic Resonance	The reverberation, echo or subtle quality of tone or timbre that intensifies the message and enriches the receptivity/experience for the viewer. When connotation and expressive power interact to create an aesthetic dimension
×Field of Tension	Taut relationships between the elements of the design and the edges of the shape in which the elements reside (paper edges) that provide the viewer with a complex, multilayered experience
×Historicism	Copying of historical precedents
Eclecticism	Selecting elements from diverse sources and combining them into an acceptable style
Pluralistic Reinvention	Extracting from many sources of form & expression to create graphic resonance

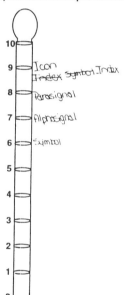

FIGURE 19

Class exercise, thermometer, a formative assessment of work in progress,
form designed by Ann Joyce.

Providing students with written criteria helps to allay fears and improve quality as they work through each point of consideration.

Teachers can also create classroom assessment vehicles that students can
use to self-assess their art, vehicles that other students can use to assess

the work of their peers, and vehicles that art educators can use to assess the work of their students. Include all the criteria for grading such as visual impact, feeling response, problem solving, meaning, and craftsmanship as well as a rating scale from very high to not apparent. These kinds of assessments are effective as both formative and summative vehicles.

Specifically designed as a peer assessment, the guidelines in Figure 20 allow students to evaluate another student's writing about art. Evaluation categories include language, connections and relationships, emotive elements, movement, and interpretation. Raters evaluate each category as to its quantity or presence, its quality, and its overall rating.

Finally, Figure 21 portrays a formative classroom research model, where teachers utilize "interceding points," which are opportunities to solicit feedback to guide students through meaningful learning. This model involves three distinct stages or steps forming a continuous loop of assay stage, interpretation stage, and return stage.

In the assay stage, educators determine what feedback to collect. For instance, do art educators want evidence or indicators on simple recall? Are teachers looking for the ways in which students synthesize a battery of complex ideas? Next, how should teachers collect this data? Should teachers use a pencil–paper assessment, case study, opinionnaire, and so on? When should teachers collect it? Should teachers collect it before class begins regarding the previous class, midway through each class meeting, or at the end of each session? How often should they collect it? Should they do so daily, weekly, quarterly, or at longer intervals?

In the interpretation stage, educators distinguish and codify student feedback. They may rate the quantity and quality of it. They also may assay the honesty or dishonesty of it. In the return stage, educators express, dispense, or in some way impart a range of feedback to students. This is critical to complete the research cycle and reap a higher level of benefits from the activity.

As with any type of research, formative classroom assessment does not always produce sound data. It might include complete dishonesty, "snow jobs," from students. Educators need to develop a keen eye and sometimes follow a gut reaction when they read something that just does not sit right.

When we examine the triumphs of formative classroom assessment, educators examine the artifacts or products of the research. What connections occurred? What surprise results occurred? When were art educators able to reteach students who did not comprehend? When were teachers able to open other avenues of awareness to students who failed to experiment and explore? What personal problems did students disclose—bulimia, depression, suicide attempts, abuse, rape, addiction—enabling teachers to guide students away from suffering alone and into professional care? These are but a few of the classroom assessment techniques that help teachers guide students through meaningful learning.

Comm 391 – Design History & Philosophy – Mrs. Ann Joyce – King's College
"Writing About & Interpreting Visual Communications Peer Assessment"

Title of Work _____

Name of Student Writing & Interpreting Work _____ Date _____

Name of Student Evaluator _____

Criteria	Quantity or Presence	Quality	Overall Rating
Language Vivid / Descriptive Use of Icon / Index / Symbol Explain:	VeryHigh High Moderate Low VeryLow Not Apparent VeryHigh High Moderate Low VeryLow Not Apparent	VeryHigh High Moderate Low VeryLow Not Apparent VeryHigh High Moderate Low VeryLow Not Apparent	VeryHigh High Moderate Low VeryLow Not Apparent VeryHigh High Moderate Low VeryLow Not Apparent
Connections & Relationships Metaphor / Simile / Personification History / Culture / Personal Experience Explain:	VeryHigh High Moderate Low VeryLow Not Apparent VeryHigh High Moderate Low VeryLow Not Apparent	VeryHigh High Moderate Low VeryLow Not Apparent VeryHigh High Moderate Low VeryLow Not Apparent	VeryHigh High Moderate Low VeryLow Not Apparent VeryHigh High Moderate Low VeryLow Not Apparent
Emotive Element Aesthetic Response or Reaction Explain:	VeryHigh High Moderate Low VeryLow Not Apparent	VeryHigh High Moderate Low VeryLow Not Apparent	VeryHigh High Moderate Low VeryLow Not Apparent
Movement Decoding or Unpacking of Graphic Explain:	VeryHigh High Moderate Low VeryLow Not Apparent	VeryHigh High Moderate Low VeryLow Not Apparent	VeryHigh High Moderate Low VeryLow Not Apparent
Interpretation Discerning a Main Theme Supporting a Main Theme Stating a Meaning or Meanings Explain:	VeryHigh High Moderate Low VeryLow Not Apparent VeryHigh High Moderate Low VeryLow Not Apparent VeryHigh High Moderate Low VeryLow Not Apparent	VeryHigh High Moderate Low VeryLow Not Apparent VeryHigh High Moderate Low VeryLow Not Apparent VeryHigh High Moderate Low VeryLow Not Apparent	VeryHigh High Moderate Low VeryLow Not Apparent VeryHigh High Moderate Low VeryLow Not Apparent VeryHigh High Moderate Low VeryLow Not Apparent

FIGURE 20

Writing about and Interpreting Visual Communications Peer Assessment form, designed by Ann Joyce.

Formative Classroom Research
A Working Model

1. ASSAY STAGE

- What feedback to collect
- How to collect it
- When to collect it
- How often to collect it

2. INTERPRETATION STAGE

- Distinguish student feedback
- Codify student feedback
- Rate the feedback quantity
- Rate the feedback quality
- Rate the feedback honesty

3. RETURN STAGE

- Express, dispense or impart a range of feedback to students

© Ann Joyce 1995

FIGURE 21

Formative classroom research, a working model chart, designed by Ann Joyce.

AUTHENTIC CLASSROOM ASSESSMENT IN AN INNER CITY HIGH SCHOOL PROGRAM[4]

I will begin my account of a project dealing with "authentic classroom assessment" with more generalized observations. The project that I will describe was conducted in an inner city Chicago High School (the Paul Robeson High School in the Englewood section of Chicago). Racially, this has an all black student body coming from an economically depressed neighborhood. The project Is the Civil War Really Over? was conceived and conducted by three teachers (social studies, English, and visual arts); three Urban Gateways Artists (music, theater, and visual arts); and me, the director of Arts Curriculum Planning and Evaluation for Urban Gateways, the Center for the Arts in Education.

We began with the assumption that program planning and evaluation are inextricably linked. For us, it was obvious that what and how we evaluate is connected to what and how we teach. Beyond this generalization, we conceived of this project as developing and documenting an approach to instruction that involved (1) cooperative and coordinated planning for instruction in English, social studies, and the visual arts; (2) linking and cross-referencing work in each of the classes; (3) the use of artists as resources in

[4]Section contributed by Jerome J. Hausman.

each of the classes; (4) the use of portfolios (including video portfolios) as primary means for describing and uating student learning.

One can observe that the process of portfolio review, so common in professional art instruction, has now become a popular assessment methodology in education, a means for evaluating learning in the general curriculum as well as the visual arts. Indeed, the idea has been expanded to include the idea of a teaching portfolio: a collection of teacher- and student-generated materials that provide evidence about a teacher's effectiveness. Like the art portfolio, a variety of items can be included for review: student writing as well as visual examples, lists of books read by students with their commentaries, video- and audiotapes, unit plans, student and teacher evaluations, teaching resources, and the like. In short, the portfolio brings together the tangible "stuff of instruction" to help reconstruct the dynamics of what teachers and students have done in the classroom. From this evidence, evaluative judgment can be made as to the content and effectiveness of that classroom. Assessment then carries with it actual "things" said and done by the students.

Lest anyone think that the introduction of portfolio assessment in lieu of more traditional testing will provide an immediate panacea, be disabused of this idea. For all of its methodological attractiveness, portfolio assessment still leaves us with many dilemmas and complications: rater, reliability and validity, scoring rubrics, values, and criteria. Making judgments based on a portfolio review and interview is time consuming. Nuanced judgment is required. There are no quick and easy ways to scan portfolios and then produce shorthand summaries or statistical comparisons that will communicate with clarity and effectiveness. Despite these observations, it should be emphasized that portfolio assessment involves looking directly at what students have done. Something is powerful and persuasive about the actual things that the student has done or the precise words and phrases used to express ideas or feelings. What is evaluated grows directly from the concrete behaviors of the student.

Returning to my description of the project, each of the three classes was organized around themes leading to the culminating question: is the Civil War really over? An underlying assumption was that the Civil War should not be understood as an isolated, irrelevant event of the past. Many of its issues (human rights, economic priorities, governmental versus private controls, etc.) are alive today. The students were helped to identify these issues and find their own place in relation to shaping constructive solutions. The lessons of history should inform us as to decisions and actions in the present. It was intended that students be helped to think critically about the past and how ideas of the past help to structure our sense of the present. They were encouraged to reflect on their personal perspectives and approaches to history. Of course, we wanted the students to know more about and understand the Civil War as a major event in American history. It follows that our criteria for evaluation and our documentation centered on what we wanted students to understand and do.

Seen from afar, it is possible to nod approvingly at generalizations that argue for greater commitment and accomplishment on the part of all students. A rhetoric, using terms like *discipline, responsibility, freedom, intelligence, creativity,* and *inquiry,* fills our literature. Policy statements about what we hope will happen abound; yet, the tactics of implementation and assessment must be carried out at the level of daily student–teacher interaction. We need to look at each student as the primary source for our data and generalizations. Here a great strength of portfolio assessment can be realized. We focus upon individuals—the processes in which they have engaged and the products of their efforts. For better or worse, the persuasive rhetoric of what we want to happen faces head-on the realities of "things done."

In school, as in life, each student needs to be seen as an individual struggling to make sense of the myriad of factors (obstacles as well as nurturing elements; things given approval by our society as well as things forbidden or illegal) that make up human experience. Given the harsh realities of inner city neighborhoods, it is as if most of individual student energy goes into an improvisational orientation, fending off immediate crises and seeking to gain momentary or more immediate gratification. This pattern of "coping" soon becomes a way of life—short-term solutions lacking in planning or sustained caring. Why plan for a bleak future?

For many attending Robeson High School, "school" is seen as a necessary "requirement." On the one hand, school provides an escape from some of life's trauma and unpredictable elements; but on the other, school is seen as a "gigantic waste of time," where what is being taught has little or nothing to do with what it will take to survive on the streets.

Formalist approaches to art education offer a kind of "academic respectability." We can speak or write of formal, technical, sensory, and expressive qualities in works of art. We can place works of art in particular historical or stylistic categories. However, in the lives of Robeson High School students, these elements have low priority. Teachers working on this project spoke of wanting to have their students "care about what they were doing." They wanted them to develop the ability to engage in "intelligent criticism," to be able to focus on information and develop a means for responsible and informed decision making and action.

The work of the Robeson High School Project was greatly influenced by the writings of Resnick (1987). In this work, the question was raised as to whether schools can do a better job of teaching "higher-order skills." The emphasis was on relating the problem-solving abilities that mathematicians, scientists, and engineers use in the task of educating students. Interestingly enough, the definition offered for *higher-order thinking* coincided with the desired orientation for instruction on this project: the desired path of action in student learning could not be fully specified in advance; the "total path" for learning needed to be seen from multiple vantage points; we anticipated that there would be multiple solutions, requiring nuanced judgment and interpretation; evaluation would involve multiple criteria and would be directed at student ability to engage in effortful activity, self-regulation, and generate the kinds of elaboration and judgment associated with higher-order thinking. These, then, became the very points we looked for in evaluating the student portfolios.

Specific criteria used in evaluating the students were adapted from the work done in Project Arts Propel, a collaboration between Project Zero, the Harvard Graduate School of Education; Educational Testing Service; and the Pittsburgh Public Schools. The criteria were as follows:

- *Student perception.* Perception of the students' environment (both in and outside of school): the ability to notice details and analyze factors contributing to environmental conditions; ability to grasp factors as they influenced thought and actions during and following the Civil War; ability to perceive and understand conditions as they influenced perceptions of the Civil War; ability to identify works of artists (writers, composers, visual artists, etc.), past and present, that deal with issues of personal freedom, economic conditions, and the like.

- *Student production.* Craftsmanship: evidence of skillful and appropriate use of tools and materials; attention to technique and detail; follow-through in completing tasks; understanding of the consequences of actions; grasp of processes and issues; ability to make "connections"; ability to grasp and retain factual information; inventiveness: evidence of creative ideas; strategies or solutions; commitment, the ability to pursue and stay with ideas; ability to complete work; expression, the extent to which work done reflects personal strength and interest.

- *Student reflection.* Self-understanding: students ability to articulate personal goals and working approach; ability to assess personal strengths and limitations; critical approaches: ability to assess strengths and weaknesses in work and actions of others; use of feedback, the ability to accept and incorporate new ideas; capacity to make informed and critical judgment to modify future behaviors.

Staff conferences were held, in which the work of each student was discussed in relation to these criteria. Our evaluations consisted of comparing each student with himself or herself over the period of the project. In addition, comparisons were made among the students. Overall, what we sought to identify was changes in behavior and learning outcomes related to the priorities and criteria of the project.

Three Urban Gateways' artists were assigned to this project: Mwata Bowden, a jazz musician; Cynthia Weiss, a visual artist; and Dale Young, a director and actor. All are experienced teachers, have engaged in numerous Urban Gateways projects, residencies, and special projects. Each of the artists worked in the three classes: English, social studies, and visual arts; each made eight visits to the school. The artists did not come to the situation with a series of "planned lessons"; rather their task was to observe and then bring what ideas and suggestions they had that would focus upon an aesthetic and artistic dimension to what was being done. Obviously, each artist came to the situation with particular skills, strengths, and interests. Mwata Bowden, for example, had extensive training and knowledge that enabled him to discuss the origins and forms of music in both the North and South during the Civil War period. His experience as a jazz musician extended and enriched student experiences as they constructed their own musical instruments and created compositions to accompany presentation of personal histories in a video format. Cynthia Weiss, a visual artist, worked extensively in the development of a ceramic tile mural. She also had designed a series of student lessons in which they did photo collages, using images of themselves set in Civil War contexts. Dale Young worked with students in making them more aware of voice quality and body movements in their presentations. Each of the artists attended to those dimensions of choice and control that give form and content to student presentations.

For the teachers (Guadalupe Barajas, the art teacher; Etta Claiborne, the English teacher; and Markie Hancock, the social studies teacher), the task of cooperative and coordinated instruction proved interesting and informative. In the beginning, they each focused on themes of perspective and multiple points of view. In the visual arts, the initial emphases were on drawing—selecting and focusing on visual elements, qualitative decisions, and controls in constructing an image. From the drawing activities, the students moved to collage activities, with emphases on multiple perspectives, the juxtaposition of visual elements, the manipulation of factors of scale, space, and sequence in conveying meaning. All of this served as background for researching images and themes that would be used in the construction of the mural: Is the Civil War Really Over? Here it is interesting to note that the physical and technical requirements in doing a mural made necessary the progressive focusing upon the task of production. A particular kind of planning, thinking, and cooperative activity was necessary. Individual needs and predispositions had to give way to a communally designed outcome. By contrast, activities in the English and social studies classes allowed for more individualized and personalized outcomes. In the beginning, students focused on the development of personal narratives. They conducted interviews and developed written accounts of the lives of family members and friends. The question "What is history?" was raised and discussed. Students were made more sensitive and aware of particular points of view and biases in the reporting of history. Indeed, they began to see how some things were noted and emphasized while others were not noted and perhaps consciously or subconsciously ignored. The fundamental assumptions of this approach was noted by Markie Hancock, the social studies teacher:

History is about inquiry. Historical inquiry is when we ask questions that are of interest to us about any past event. History changes each time it is retold. It is the relationship of historian to the event which more than anything determines how history will be recorded. There is no "absolute" history—no certain way that any event occurred. There are not objective facts that exist apart from the historian and his or her version of the event. Of utmost significance, then, is the awareness, to the greatest extent possible, of one's perspective and approach to historical sources. It is more important to objectively know one's political and personal relationship to events than to be falsely in pursuit of "objective truth."

The analysis of issues surrounding the Civil War were examined in three units: politics and economics, women during the Civil War, and the African-American experience. Source material included biographies and narrative accounts of Civil War events—the writing of women, slaves, soldiers in the Confederate and Union Armies, political leaders, and so on. Student read and discussed poetry and literature; they analyzed newspaper accounts. As part of the documentation process, Jeff Spitz, a professional cameraman, used a camcorder to record activities in each of the classes. Initially his documentation was general, picking up examples of classroom discussion, student activities, as well as general views of the school and its community. These general tapes were screened and served as the basis for discussions and analysis of student learning. As the project and this process evolved, we began to focus more on individual students as sources for case studies. We referred to this as the development of video portfolios. What we wanted to do was to create in-depth case studies of individual students as they dealt with the wide range of learning activities that made up the Is the Civil War Really Over? unit. Along with the portfolios of work done in the art, English, and social studies classes, we were able to review our general videotaped accounts and "pull off" segments pertaining to each of three students (Tressa Williams, Robasia Wright, and Dametries Holmes) and create separate tapes containing vignettes of their actions over a 10-week period.

Ten weeks is a relatively brief period for discerning fundamental change in student attitudes, values, and learning outcomes. We did find that our criteria for evaluation (student perceptions, student production, and student reflections) was a useful format for engaging in our evaluations. Discussions and analyses of each of the students used multiple perspectives (the vantage points of three teachers). There was a breaking down of "departmental barriers." Using actual work from each class provided a concrete frame of reference for the discussions that were held. The video documentation proved invaluable for reflecting on the dynamics of student interaction with teachers, artists, and fellow students.

The bottom line in our efforts has always been the growth and enrichment of attitude, knowledge, and values by each student. Evaluation and instruction are inextricably linked. The process of evaluation informed instruction; conversely, the goals and purposes of instruction served to structure the criteria and methodologies for evaluation. Our teachers viewed discrete instances in ways that fit them into a larger, more comprehensive rubric of student performance.

We have come away from this pilot effort with stronger and more supportive feelings regarding the need for longitudinal data. Dealing with high school students is dealing with young adults whose lives already have felt the impact and been shaped by many factors and circumstances. Viewing portfolios, screening videotapes, and drawing on direct observations helped us construct our hypothesis of what made each student "tick." We used our evaluation data to identify characteristic modes of thought through which each of the students seemed to "make sense" of his or her world. Each person became a "model" that we then used to explain how they were dealing with their world. The process of portfolio review validated and refined the models through comparative analysis of subsequent observable behavior and additions to the portfolios. At any given point in time, each student could be seen as acting in a coherent pattern that reflects his or her "style" and represents the dimensions of a certain rationale. The "sense" made out of the world imposes itself on perceptions and actions. This was a pilot project. Observing and evaluating students over a 10-week period is insufficient for identifying dramatic and fundamental changes in a student's life. As we proceeded we were painfully aware of the weaknesses as well as the strengths of the methodologies being employed. Attending to multiple details and simultaneous events makes it difficult to isolate singular variables. Indeed, our project is ladened with confounding variables. We can never fully know the underlying factors in students' lives that influence their perceptions and actions. This is the reality of teaching in any school. Yet, while the limitations are apparent, we have come to recognize a great potential in dealing with student evaluation in a holistic way. Our more in-depth studies of Tressa, Robashia, and Dametries served to strengthen our resolve to pursue an approach to evaluation that centers on "meaning and processes and transactions involved in the construction of meanings." We are here indebted to the work of Jerome Bruner (1990) and his call for a new emphasis on folk psychology dealing with "the nature, causes and consequences" of intentional states (p. 14). He has called for our developing stories of how and why people "organize views of themselves, of others and of the world in which they live" (p. 137).

As we have viewed it, we sought to develop portfolios augmented by videotaped documentation (video portfolios) for telling these stories and evaluating the students. This is an approach to evaluation that we feel has great promise.

References

Angelo, T. A., & Cross, K. P. (1993). *Classroom assessment techniques: A handbook for college teachers* (2nd ed.). San Francisco: Jossey-Bass.

Archbald, D. A., & Newmann, F. M. (1988). *Beyond standardized testing: Assessing achievement in the secondary school.* Reston, VA: National Association of Secondary School Principals.

Armstrong, C. (1994). *Designing assessment in art.* Reston, VA: National Art Education Association.

Boughton, D. (1994). *Evaluation and assessment in visual arts education.* Geelong, Victoria, Australia: Deakin University.

Bruner, J. S. (1990). *Acts of meaning.* Cambridge, MA: Harvard University Press.

Clark, G., & Zimmerman, E. (1987). *Resources for educating artistically talented students.* Syracuse, NY: Syracuse University Press.

Clark, G., & Zimmerman, E. (1988). Views of self, family background, and school: Interviews with artistically talented students. *Gifted Child Quarterly,* 32(4), 340–346.

Cross, K. P., & Angelo, T. A. (1988). *Classroom assessment techniques: A handbook for faculty.* Ann Arbor, MI: National Center for Research to Improve Postsecondary Teaching and Learning.

Eisner, E. (1971). How can you measure a rainbow? Tactics for evaluating the teaching of art. *Art Education,* 24(5), 36–39.

Eisner, E. (1991). *The enlightened eye qualitative inquiry and the enhancement of educational practice.* New York: Macmillan.

Eisner, E. (1995). In *Visual arts education reform handbook: Suggested policy perspectives on art content and student learning in art education* (p. 14). Reston, VA: National Art Education Association. 1st ed., foreword by Lee R. Kerscher & Jacquelyn Ann K. Kegley.

Halpern, D. F. & Associates. (1994). Changing college classrooms: New teaching and learning strategies for an increasingly complex world. *The Jossey-Bass Higher and Adult Education Series.*

Hamblen, K. (1988, September). If it is to be tested it will be taught: A rationale worthy of examination. *Art Education,* pp. 59–62.

Hamblen, K. (1992–1993). Deconstructing developmental models of artistic expression and aesthetic response. *American Educational Research Association Arts and Learning Research* 1992–1993, 10(1), 184–196.

Herman, J. L., Aschbacher, P. K., & Winters, L. (1992). *A practical guide to alternative assessment.* Alexandria, VA: Association for Supervision and Curriculum Development.

Marshall, S. P. (1993). Forward. In J. L. Herman, P. R. Aschbacher, & L. Winters (Eds.), *A practical guide to alternative assessment* (pp. v–vi). Alexandria, VA: Association for Supervision and Curriculum Development.

Marzano, R. J., Pickering, D., & McTighe, J. (1993). *Assessing student outcomes: Performance assessment using the dimensions of learning model.* Alexandria, VA: Association for Supervision and Curriculum Development.

Resnick, L. B. (1987). *Education and learning to think.* Washington, DC: Committee on Mathematics, Science, and Technology Education, Commission on Behavioral and Social Sciences and Education, National Research Council.

Ross, M., Radnor, H., Mitchell, S., & Bierton, C. (1993). *Assessing achievement in the arts.* Buckingham, UK: Open University Press.

Rudner, L. M., & Boston, C. (1994). *A look at performance assessment for art education.* Reston, VA: National Art Education Association.

Shepard, L. (1989). Why we need better assessments. *Educational Leadership,* 46(7), 4–8.

Stiggins, R. (1985, September/October). The challenge of measuring artistic performance. *Design for Arts in Education,* pp. 40–43.

Taylor, P. (1991). *In the process: A visual arts portfolio assessment pilot project.* Carmichael: California Art Education Association.

Webster (1977). New World Dictionary of the American Language, N.Y. The World Publishing Co., p. 465.

Wiggins, G. (1989). Toward more authentic and equitable assessment. *Phi Delta Kappan,* 70(9), 703–713.

Zimmerman, E. (1991). Rembrandt to Rembrandt: A case study of a memorable painting teacher. *Roeper Review,* 13(Z), 76–81.

Zimmerman, E. (1992a). Assessing students' progress and achievements in art. *Art Education*, 45(6), 34–38.

Zimmerman, E. (1992b). A comparative study of two painting teachers of talented adolescents. *Studies in Art Education*, 33(2), 174–185.

Zimmerman, E. (1992c). How should students' progress and achievements be assessed? A case for assessment that is responsive to diverse students' needs. *Visual Arts Research*, 20(1), 29–35.

Zimmerman, E. (1994). Authentic assessment does not always mean equitable assessment. *Insea News*, 1, 3.

Zimmerman, E. (in press). Authentic assessment in art education. In S. LaPierre & E. Zimmerman (Eds.), *Research methods in art education*, Reston, VA: National Art Education Association.

Zimmerman, J. (1993). Student Portfolios: Classroom uses. *Consumer Guide* (OERI), 8, 1–4.

PART

IV

Developing Standards

Kindergarten through Grade 12 Standards: A Philosophy of Grading

BRENDA H. LOYD and DOUGLAS E. LOYD
University of Virginia

INTRODUCTION

Grades and grading have been used for a variety of purposes. Primarily, grades and the grading systems provide systematic and formal procedures for communicating evaluations made by teachers regarding a student's academic achievement to guardians, parents, institutions of higher education, employees, as well as many others (Judd, 1983). However, grades and grading are also used directly or indirectly to motivate and reward students for displaying appropriate academic learning behavior and attitudes. They have also been used as a means of punishment for inappropriate classroom behavior, lack of effort, and lack of consistency (Canady & Hotchkiss, 1989; Hills, 1991). Given the variety of purposes, it is not surprising that there are almost as many grading systems as there are teachers.

As students progress from kindergarten through 12th grade (K–12), they are presumed to be continually in a process of growth. Growth is expected across physical, social, and academic (skills and content) domains. As students move through grades K–12, they are expected by teachers to progress in all these things simultaneously, and the degree to which expected growth in a given domain is emphasized in the classroom differs considerably as the student progresses through school. For the early primary years, the development of social skills may be considered important and relevant goals by teachers, parents, and administrators. During the middle level years, social skills, particularly as they relate to peers and adults, receive considerable focus. At the high school level, emphasis shifts to the goals of complex integration of academic content and skills.

It is probably not possible to describe one grading process that addresses such diverse goals. However, it is reasonable to suggest principles of grading that can guide the development of a grading system at any level. The four common principles are as follows:

1. The system of grading should be clear and understandable (to parents, other stakeholders, and most especially students).
2. The system of grading should be communicated to all stakeholders (e.g., students, parents, administrators).
3. Grading should be fair for all students regardless of gender, class, race, or socioeconomic status.
4. Grading should support, enhance, and inform the instructional process.

Principle 1. The System of Grading Should Be Clear and Understandable

It is not enough for teachers to know what they expect or recognize quality or high-level work when they see it. For a grading system to be effective, the expectations for student achievement and performance need to be clear and explicit. For example, it is not sufficient for a teacher to be able to recognize an outstanding "A quality" essay or a satisfactory "C quality" essay. What is critical is that the teacher be able to articulate the criteria that define an outstanding essay or a satisfactory essay to the students who are writing the essay, to the parent who sees the grade on a paper, or to an employer who sees a grade on a transcript.

It is not sufficient for teachers to describe what they expect from students by using the term *appropriate scientific observations*; instead, the teacher needs to specify what those words mean in the context of the particular assignment. This might mean something like "The student will use descriptive words to record the color, texture, smell, and location of a tree" or "The student will use three different senses to examine a rock and will record the results using descriptive words." Examples, illustrations, and samples provide further means of helping students and their parents understand the criteria and levels of success in attaining the criteria.

Principle 2. The System of Grading Should Be Communicated to All Stakeholders

For only the teacher to know and understand the criteria is not sufficient. The student must also know what the teacher expects, how to demonstrate satisfactory completion of the requirements, and how to achieve outstanding performance. The communication of these expectations must be clear and unambiguous and appropriate to the level of the student. For example, for primary-age students an oral explanation of the grading system along with examples of the various grades should be given. For older students, a written explanation describing the grading system should be given.

Whatever the level of the student or the content of the class, the student should always be able to expect that there will be no hidden rules. The expectations on which the grade will be based, and the means of determining whether the expectations have been met, must be communicated to the student in an understandable and age-appropriate fashion.

Similarly, parents, administrators, employers, and others who make judgments about the student's performance should have clear information about the basis on which the grading decision is made.

Principle 3. Grading Should Be Fair to All Students Regardless of Gender, Class, Race, or Socioeconomic Status

It may seem obvious to state that grading should be fair, but in fact, lack of fairness is probably the most common complaint about particular implementations of grading systems in the classroom (Archer & McCarthy, 1988; Stiggins, Frisbie, & Griswold, 1989). At a minimum, two apparently divergent factors are involved in fairness. The first is the perception by students that they are being treated fairly; this perception is created or reinforced by not changing the rules in the "middle of the game" and not "playing favorites" by favoring one student over another. However, fairness does not necessarily mean sameness; a second factor to be considered is that once the expectations are set, it is possible for students to produce different types of evidence indicating that they have met them. In other words, student performance does not have to be the same for the grading system to be fair and perceived as fair.

For example, if a teacher's goal is to assess whether students have discerned the theme of a short story and whether they can provide evidence that supports the statement of that theme, students may elect to present their response orally, in a written essay, through a picture or graph, a poem, as well as many other possible modes.

Finally, evidence indicates that some tasks are gender biased or race biased, and some are unfair because students from impoverished environments have not had similar exposure as those from privileged environments. Often projects, for example, reflect the parent's educational level, resources, or access to computer facilities. Tasks on which students are to be graded must be carefully structured to rule out these biases or scoring rubrics (i.e., guidelines) must be structured so that the playing field is level for all.

Principle 4. Grading Should Support, Enhance, and Inform the Instructional Process

Whatever the primary goals of instruction are, those goals should receive the greatest emphasis in the grading system. Secondary goals should receive secondary emphasis. It should be clear from the grading system what is most important. For example, if a goal is to integrate content and skills, but evidence used in the grading process emphasizes discrete skills and knowledge (e.g., rote memorization) then the grading system is not supporting and enhancing the instructional process; rather, it is actually encouraging behavior that may be contrary to the stated purpose of the learning activity. Similarly, if the goal of instruction is academic achievement, but the grade is based largely on compliant or disruptive classroom behavior, then the grading system is not supporting and enhancing the instructional process, but rather is being used to encourage or discourage certain socially acceptable behavior that may or may not be related to the learning goals of the classroom.

It is important to realize that students perceive that we value what we assess. If our assessment reflects our primary goals, our students will see our goals as the important goals; if we assess lesser goals, our students will elevate these to the important focus of their learning. The grading process will also be most effective if the process yields information to the teacher about what has been successful and what has not been successful in the teaching and instructional process.

COMPONENTS OF A GRADING SYSTEM

Individual grading systems will differ substantially depending on the age level of the students, the emphases placed in the instructional process, and a variety of other factors (e.g., the ability level of students). At a minimum, however, the grading system should consist of several significant stages that occur either consciously or unconsciously whenever grades are assigned in a classroom context. These stages generally follow one another in sequence, but are intimately interrelated:

Setting goals of instruction.
Establishing parameters for evidence relevant to goals.
Measuring, or collecting the evidence.
Judging and evaluating the evidence.
Combining judgments for summative statements of
    accomplishment.
Reporting.
Re-evaluating goals and modifying instruction.

Goals of Instruction

The formulation and statement of the goals of instruction lays the foundation not only for effective instruction but also for appropriate evaluation of student achievement (Terwilliger, 1989). It is particularly important that the goals include all expectations, to the extent possible, for the students. The statement of goals should be explicit but not trivial. Instructional goals developed for the class should include both short-term goals that express expectations specific to the unit of study (i.e., minimal objectives) and long-term goals that indicate how these skills and content fit into the larger developmental process (i.e., developmental objectives).

Instructional goals may relate to academics, but they may also convey expectations regarding classroom behavior, attitudes, or social behavior. Whatever the true expectations are for instruction, they should be formulated as goals. To be effective as a foundation for the grading system, however, these goals must adhere to the four principles discussed earlier: they must be clear and understandable; communicated; fair regardless of gender, class, race or socioeconomic status; and support, enhance, and inform the instructional process.

Evidence Relevant to Goals

Evidence of progress or attainment of goals can come from a variety of sources: written examinations, quizzes, individual projects, oral presentation, group projects, observation, student reports, class participation, homework, and the like. There are many different types of evidence, and it is usually important to collect a variety of types to provide for fairness, as some students may be better able to demonstrate proficiency in one mode than in another (see Gardner, 1993, for a further discussion of the issue). It is frequently also the case that multiple modes of evidence are necessary to completely represent different facets of the instructional goals. Therefore, use of multiple sources of evidence is not simply a matter of fairness but also necessary to ensure an appropriate match between types of evidence and instructional goals. Some types of evidence will seem to relate more directly to some goals than other goals. For example, if the goal is mastery of a basic skill, then a quiz or comprehensive exam that measures that specific skill might be quite appropriate. However, if the goal is the integration of content, concepts and skills, then a project or report might be a more appropriate form of evidence. A basic tenet of the identification of the most appropriate sources of evidence is to try to assess as directly as possible; that is, match the task to the goal. Following these guidelines will contribute to validity of the assessment and grading process.

Whatever the type of evidence to be collected, it should be relevant to the goals and should conform to the principles for grading: (1) the teacher should be able to communicate to the students what kinds of evidence (e.g., written assignments, lab work) will be used to evaluate achievement of the goals, (2) the teacher should make sure that students understand the full range of evidence to be used (e.g., if classroom behavior will "count" as well as performance on quizzes, this must be communicated), (3) the teacher should be certain that the expectations regarding evidence are fair, and (4) the types of evidence used should support, enhance, and inform the instructional process.

Measuring, or Collecting the Evidence

Whichever type of evidence is judged to be most appropriate for the specific goal(s), one of the most important things to achieve is *reliability*. The teacher must gather enough evidence to be confident that it is a true indicator of student performance or achievement and not just a chance occurrence. For example, a set of math problems rather than a single problem is probably a better indication of math performance or achievement. With only a single problem there is the possibility that some unique characteristic of the problem may keep a student from displaying his or her true math ability. Similarly, a single observation is not enough to be convinced of a student's behavior or accomplishment. Each observation should involve a series of systematically observed events. The series of events to be observed and recorded should be clear and unambiguous to the students, so that the collection of the evidence will be communicable, communicated, fair, and support and enhance the instructional process.

Judging and Evaluating the Evidence

Measurement is the systematic assignment of numbers to evidence or observations. However, the meaning of the assigned numbers is not inherent in the numbers themselves. For example, in converting test scores to percentages, 50% may not necessarily indicate an unsatisfactory performance and 90% may not necessarily indicate an outstanding performance. The meaning of the numbers comes from judgments that reflect the values, goals, and standards of the individual making the judgments in the context in which the judgments are made. Such judgments may come then directly from teachers or may reflect a confluence of the values of students, students' peers, or a number of other stakeholders. These meanings are sometimes set beforehand, to identify the elements and indications of a satisfactory answer or successful performance. Sometimes meanings are set after the evidence is collected to identify an outstanding performance and a satisfactory performance on the particular measure. If standards are set after the evidence collection, the meanings have to be clearly consistent with general expectations that have been communicated.

The means by which the evidence is evaluated must be made explicit, both in the teacher's understanding and in the understanding of the students. The evaluation process must be fair and must support, enhance, and inform the instructional process. This is the point in most grading systems where teachers tend to diverge from the basic principles in two quite different ways. Teachers may become so rigidly committed to the goals and expectations they have communicated to students that they cannot find ways to apply their own professional judgment to the evidence before them when a student uses an unusual, creative, or nontraditional means for solving a problem, communicating achievement of a goal, and so forth. Rigid "sameness" of evaluation is not always "fair." Or teachers may rely so heavily on intuitive judgment or peer judgment about students that the evidence collected is simply arranged or evaluated in a manner that suits a preconceived notion of a student's achievement level or performance, which may have been developed and applied apart from the formal evidence explicitly collected.

Combining Judgments for Summative Statements of Accomplishment

Usually grades formally communicate, through report cards or other official communication for the school, academic achievement and performance for a given period of time (six weeks or semester grades are perhaps the most common). Therefore, a summative statement for the time period usually requires the teacher to be extremely concise in expressing an overall student evaluation in the "shorthand" form of a single letter or number, which indicates the student's overall achievement or performance in a given subject area. The construction of that summation is one of the most important factors in the grading process. The means by which the teacher calculates or assigns a summary grade must support the overall primary goal of instruction; therefore, as the grade is devised, computed, or constructed, factors that are primary should have more influence and factors that are secondary should have less influence in the letter or number assigned.

Simply combining or averaging the numbers that result from the series of observations or measurements will not always produce the results the teacher intends. For example, scores with greater variability will have a greater influence on the final distribution of grades than is obvious from just the weighting of the scores. If a teacher assigns grades by examining student score distributions, and if all students score 90 on every test except one, and there is a wide range of scores on that one test, then a simple averaging of grades would have the effect of using that single test to assign final grades.

At this point in the grading process, all the principles elucidated earlier must again be kept in mind: the process by which the summative grade is determined must be clear and understandable, communicated, fair, and support and enhance the instructional process. With this in mind, it may be that, after scores are combined, there is still a need for the teacher's professional judgment to evaluate what is satisfactory performance and what is outstanding performance.

Reporting

The reporting of grades must be timely, confidential, clear, and take into account the different audiences to which grades are reported. Teachers can talk to students directly, especially if there is any question about a particular grade; parents need communication from teachers about the meaning of final grades; administrators are also a relevant audience, as teachers need to be able to articulate how their grading process meets the goals of the school system.

Different grade levels and schools may require different forms for the reporting of grades. Generally, from kindergarten through first or second grade, performance evaluations are expressed in written statements from the teacher. Beginning at about third or fourth grade, students begin to become aware of the importance of the summative grade (systems using O for "outstanding," S for "satisfactory," and N for "needs improvement" serve as a sort of bridge to the A–B–C–D–F system in the upper grades). By the time the student reaches high school, the descriptive part of the report has frequently disappeared and the entire grading period's work is represented as a single letter, with no comment from the teacher. This progression is traditional but often misunderstood. To avoid misunderstandings, any grade-related reporting strategy should be accompanied by supporting description or documentation. These descriptors should always be an important part of the overall grading process to avoid misinterpretation by outsiders, who may impose their own interpretations based on their own values.

Regardless of the form in which grades are reported, they function as communication between the teacher and the various "audiences" (student, parent, administrator). The process of communication itself must be fair, timely, confidential, and clear. For early primary school children, descriptions of the things they can do (e.g., recognize consonants, create simple sentences) is a clearer communication of progress than just a number or letter. Clear description also provides information that can be useful for continuing educational development and achievement, both at school and at home. For older students, documentation of how evidence is judged and scores are combined makes explicit the goals of instruction and provides students with a framework they can use to guide their own academic accomplishments.

Re-evaluating Goals and Modifying Instruction

As evidence is collected regarding achievement of instructional goals, the teacher will almost always find it necessary to modify expectations and reformulate goals so that they more closely reflect both what is desirable and what is realistically possible in the specific learning environment. By the time final grades are assigned and reported, the teacher should have enough evidence for a more thorough re-evaluation of the goals on which the instruction and grading were based. The grading process is not just a means of assigning value to student achievement; it also provides the opportunity to learn about the effectiveness of the instructional process. The grading process therefore should be viewed as an integral part of the instructional process, so that, even though the steps of grading may be described separately, grading can be viewed as a system and not as a set of unrelated events. The final component of the grading system or process is an explicit re-examination of how the information gathered informs the instructional process. This re-evaluation includes consideration of what students have accomplished, what they have only partially accomplished, and what they have failed to understand. Based on this consideration of student progress in conjunction with the context of the classroom, short-term and long-term instructional goals may need to be refined, modified, or expanded.

CONCLUSION: FROM PRINCIPLES TO PRACTICE

Throughout the primary and secondary school years (K–12), the four principles of grading (clear and understandable, communicable, fair, and support, enhance, and inform the instructional process) can provide a framework for understanding and improving the grading systems of individual teachers and schools. The components of the grading process, leading from instructional goals through collection of evidence of student achievement to the assignment and reporting of grades, correspond naturally to the flow of the instructional process as well. Therefore, the implementation of an effective grading system that flows from these four principles provides an opportunity for improving many other aspects of the educational process.

References

Archer, J., & McCarthy, B. (1988). Personal biases in student assessment. *Educational Research,* 30(2), 142–145.
Canady, R. L., & Hotchkiss, P. R. (1989). It's a good score! Just a bad grade. *Phi Delta Kappan,* 71, 68–71.
Gardner, H. (1993). *Multiple intelligence: A theory in practice.* New York: Basic Books.
Hills, J. R. (1991). Apathy concerning grading and testing. *Phi Delta Kappan,* 72, 540–545.
Judd, C. H. (1983). On scientific study of high school problems. *American Journal of Education,* 91, 419–434.
Stiggins, R. J., Frisbie, D. A., & Griswold, P. A. (1989). Inside high school grading practices: Building a research agenda. *Educational Measurement: Issues and Practice,* 8, 5–14.
Terwilliger, J. S. (1989). Classroom standard setting and grading practices. *Educational Measurement: Issues and Practice,* 8, 15–19.

chapter 16

Using Portfolios for Large-Scale Assessment

BRIAN M. STECHER
RAND *Corporation*

JOAN L. HERMAN
UCLA/CRESST

INTRODUCTION

In recent years, educational policy makers have expressed growing concern about the quality of traditional large-scale testing programs and their possible negative effects on curriculum and instruction (Kellaghan & Madaus, 1991; Koretz, Linn, Dunbar, & Shepard, 1991; Shepard, 1991; Smith & Rottenberg, 1991). Increasing numbers of educators believe greater emphasis on portfolios (and other types of performance assessments) rather than multiple-choice tests can improve state testing efforts (Wiggins, 1989, 1993; Wolf, 1992, 1993). Portfolio advocates argue that such a change will both increase the validity of state testing programs and improve their value to schools. They believe the addition of genuine student work products into the formal assessment system will increase confidence in the inferences drawn from testing results and satisfaction with the actions that flow from these inferences. In this chapter, we examine current research on portfolio assessment and consider the strengths and weaknesses of portfolios for large-scale assessment.

Recent research suggests that educators' concerns about the quality and effects of large-scale testing are well founded; over the past decade researchers have accumulated ample evidence of the limitations of standardized multiple-choice tests in high-stakes settings. The most significant problems are that the results are not always trustworthy and the tests can lead to undesirable consequences. For example, researchers discovered that student scores in high-stakes testing programs were increasing artificially due to test preparation rather than changes in the students' underlying knowledge and ability (Koretz et al., 1991). Such corruption means that scores no longer generalize to the larger domain from which the individual items were drawn. Researchers also have reported persistent differences between population groups on state tests, and some people argue, as a result, that the scores generated by standard testing programs are biased. Research also shows that high-stakes testing programs have had undesirable consequences at the classroom level, including narrowing the curriculum, overemphasizing decontextualized bits of information, limiting the types of instructional strategies used, and devoting undue time to test preparation (Kellaghan & Madaus, 1991; Shepard, 1991; Smith & Rottenberg, 1991).

One solution to these problems may be the use of portfolios of student work for assessment. Advocates of portfolios believe they have many advantages over multiple-choice tests. First, portfolios provide more complete, thorough, and meaningful information about student performance. Having such richer information about what students have done, permits people to make more accurate inferences about what students can do. Second, believing that "you get what you assess . . . [and] you do not get what you do not assess" (Resnick & Resnick, 1992), advocates of portfolios hope that their use will lead to positive changes in curriculum and instruction. For example, portfolios focus teachers' and students' attention on complete tasks rather than disconnected bits of information and on learning in context rather than decontextualized knowledge. Portfolios also emphasize self-reflection, which helps cement meta-cognitive strategies. Third, advocates argue that portfolios are fairer to students from different population groups. The work that goes into portfolios are fully realized products produced in natural classroom settings not artificial choices made in a constrained testing situation. This may be fairer to all students. Current research supports some of these claims but not others, and this chapter explores the strengths and weaknesses of portfolios as tools for large-scale assessment.

Features of Portfolio Assessment

To determine the accuracy of these claims we need a clear understanding of what is meant by *portfolio assessment*. The term *portfolio* is borrowed from the domain of art, where it represents a diverse collection of work produced over an extended period of time, including early sketches as well as finished products. An assessment portfolio, by analogy, is a folder or file containing the products of students learning, including such things as written materials (both drafts and final versions), tabular or pictorial representations, computer programs, and video- and audiotapes documenting performance. Portfolios may also contain self-evaluations and reflections about the work that has been included. What marks a portfolio as an assessment rather than simply a collection of work is that its contents are judged. Criteria are applied to reach a judgment about the value or quality of performance and, more specifically, to aid decisions about individual students, programs, schools, or other entities.

In practice, the conditions under which student work is produced and assembled into a portfolio can vary. For example, in Vermont the choice of assignments and the rules for producing, reviewing and revising student work are set by the teachers. In Kentucky, writing portfolios are somewhat more constrained—each must include specific genres of writing—but the conditions under which the work is performed vary from teacher to teacher. Some portfolios may contain group products, others are limited to work done by an individual student. The work itself usually reflects the normal interactive efforts of students in class—coached by the teacher, kibitzed by peers, and assisted by parents and other adults.[1] However, it is possible to require that pieces be done without assistance or collaboration. To date, each large-scale implementation of portfolios has unique features, and it is somewhat difficult to comment on portfolios in general because of the variations that exist.

Equally important, the nature of the performance to be included in portfolios is different than those captured in multiple-choice and short-answer types of assessment. One of the advantages of portfolios over multiple-choice tests is the ability to include extended, constructed work, such as a critical essay or an explanation of a solution to a novel mathematics problem. As a result, portfolio assessments usually are implemented in conjunction with curriculum reform. For example, the Vermont mathematics portfolios were designed to drive changes in curriculum and instruction, placing greater emphasis on problem solving and mathematical communication (Mills & Brewer, 1988). Similarly, the Kentucky portfolios were part of a major overhaul of the educational system that included a new set of valued outcomes for students (Kentucky Department of Education, 1993a). Consequently, it is often difficult to disentangle portfolios as assessment tools from portfolios as elements of curriculum reform.

Nevertheless, many current assessment portfolios have in common four features. These features contribute to the strengths of portfolios but they also can pose problems for their use as assessment tools. Most portfolios are

- Cumulative, collected over an extended period of time,
- Embedded, derived from regular instructional events not "on-demand" tasks,

[1]Students may or may not be required to identify the type and level of assistance they received.

- Self-selected, students are responsible for selecting at least some of the entries,
- Reflective, students comment on the choice of work, its quality, and its production.

As a final note, it is important to point out that *this chapter will not examine portfolios from the perspective of classroom assessment.* Our focus is on district and state testing programs for accountability and other aggregate purposes. Portfolios may have great potential for classroom assessment (an issue to which we will return at the end of the chapter), but portfolio quality and utility for large-scale assessment purposes are the focus here.

Essential Qualities of Large-Scale Assessment

We use the term *large-scale assessment* to mean a measurement activity that is prescribed by political entities and used to support their accountability and decision-making needs. Based on the performance of individual students, the activity provides aggregate measures of the performance of educational units (such as classes, schools, or districts); it may or may not be used to make decisions about individual students, as well. The prototypical large-scale assessment is a statewide testing program, and occasionally we will use these terms synonymously. However, our concept of large-scale assessment can also include district and regional testing programs, and the conclusions we draw apply to these assessment activities as well as to state testing programs.

The purposes of large-scale assessment should determine the characteristics that assessment instruments possess. Most large-scale assessment programs are designed to serve the information needs of policy makers related to one or more of the following purposes:

1. To describe the status of the educational system.
2. To permit comparison between individuals and units for selection or evaluation.
3. To serve as criteria for accountability.
4. To signal desired outcomes.
5. To inform program planning and improvement.

To achieve these purposes, assessment systems must be built from components that produce accurate, meaningful information that is relevant to the goals of education. We refer to this as *technical quality.* It is important that an assessment have adequate technical quality to ensure that policy makers' judgment is reasonable and their actions are well-informed, particularly since such judgment and actions have important consequences for students and schools. The first part of our review summarizes research on the technical quality of portfolios.

Policy makers also must be concerned about feasibility when thinking about large-scale assessment. They cannot ignore the practical demands imposed by the development and implementation of a large assessment system, including the human resources and expertise needed for support. In addition, the fiscal resources available for assessment are limited, so costs are a serious consideration. Nor can policy makers ignore the acceptability of portfolio assessment to educational stakeholders at the local and state levels. This aspect of feasibility has often been overlooked, but recent citizen actions in opposition to assessment systems in California and Arizona point out the importance of public understanding and acceptance. The second part of our review summarizes research on the feasibility of portfolio assessment.

Finally, because they enact assessment policies to serve multiple purposes, policy makers must also be concerned with the consequences and impact of their assessment mandates. Assessment systems are created with beneficial purposes in mind; however, they may have unanticipated negative consequences. For example, they may send the wrong signals to educators about what is valued and where they should put their energy. An evaluation of large-scale assessment alternatives is incomplete without consideration of the potential impact of these systems on schools. In fact, contemporary theories of measurement include such consequences as an aspect of validity (Messick, 1992). Our review concludes with evidence regarding the potential effects of portfolios, both positive and negative.

How well is large-scale portfolio assessment working? In the following section, we review the research literature to see how portfolios measure up with regard to criteria of technical quality and feasibility. We also examine the literature regarding the effects of portfolios and draw conclusions about their usefulness for large-scale assessment purposes.

THE RESEARCH BASE

In this section we review the research on portfolios to learn how well they meet the quality and feasibility demands of large-scale assessment and what their likely impact will be on schools. Because portfolios are a recent innovation in assessment, the literature is somewhat thin (Herman & Winters, 1994). Few operational testing programs include portfolios and fewer still have been evaluated. Among the states, only Vermont and Kentucky use portfolios as regular components of their statewide assessment systems in mathematics or science [Consortium for Policy Research in Education (CPRE), 1995], and we know of no other states using portfolios in other subjects. Fortunately, both of these states have been thoroughly evaluated. Portfolio experiments also have occurred at the district level, but we know of only one district, the Pittsburgh Public School District, that uses portfolios as formal assessment tools. There have been a number of other portfolio prototypes and small-scale implementations, but not all were the subject of independent research. As a result, most of our information regarding the technical quality, feasibility, and impact of portfolios for large-scale assessment comes from a small number of sources.[2] We occasionally draw on relevant findings from research on other forms of open-ended or performance-based assessment to supplement this research base.

Construct Validity

Technical quality is a general term we use to refer to the accuracy and meaningfulness of test results. In common terms, how good is the assessment? Does it in fact measure what it is intended to measure? Deceptively simple, these questions grow more and more complex as new forms of assessment and new uses for assessment data provoke technical debates and challenge traditional psychometric approaches for assessing technical quality (Baker, O'Neil, & Linn, 1993; Linn, Baker, & Dunbar, 1991). Despite debate about specific methodologies, current thinking subsumes most aspects of technical quality under the broad heading of construct validity. The primary issue is whether test results provide accurate inferences for specific decision-making contexts, such as decisions about whether a student is ready to graduate or about how well a school is performing. A test in and of itself is neither valid nor invalid; rather, current theory requires that we accumulate evidence of the accuracy of inferences made on the basis of that assessment for particular purposes. For purposes of this chapter we focus on three as-

[2] The most extensive evaluation of a large-scale portfolio assessment comes from Vermont. In the late 1980s, Vermont embarked on the development of an innovative statewide assessment program where none had existed previously. The purpose of the new assessment system was twofold: to provide information about student performance for school-level accountability and to promote curriculum reform. The cornerstone of the assessment system was nonstandardized portfolios of student work in mathematics and writing. Vermont implemented its portfolio assessment system in 1991–1992 after a year of planning and a yearlong pilot test. The system includes portfolios in writing and mathematics in grades 4 and 8 as well as on-demand uniform tests in these subject areas. The Vermont assessment system was evaluated over a three-year period by researchers from RAND.

Writing portfolios became part of the Kentucky statewide assessment (KIRIS, the Kentucky Instructional Results Information System) in grades 4 and 8 in 1991–1992, and mathematics portfolios were added the following year. KIRIS also includes interdisciplinary performance assessments and noncognitive indicators of school success. The assessment system is one element in a sweeping state educational reform (Kentucky Educational Reform Act) enacted in 1990. KIRIS has been evaluated by researchers from Western Michigan University under the auspices of the Kentucky Institute for Education Research (KIER) and by other organizations.

The Pittsburgh program focuses on student writing in grades 6 through 12. Beginning in 1991–1992 the district produced a public accounting based on randomly selected student portfolios. Research results have been published by the district as well as by the district's research partners at Educational Testing Service.

pects of construct validity that have relevance in current studies of portfolio use: reliability, meaningfulness,[3] and comparability.

Reliability of Scores

Elementary statistics tests are quick to point out that reliability is a necessary but not sufficient prerequisite to validity. And, of course, this is the case: a measure that does not retain its meaning and yield consistent results in the face of superficial changes in the assessment situation cannot provide accurate information for decision making. A reliable assessment, in short, is one that is relatively free from errors of measurement and one that provides an accurate picture of capability. In the case of portfolios, these two aspects of reliability reflect the consistency of the rating process (reliability of ratings) and the lack of error in the overall score (score reliability).

Reliability of Ratings.   A first premise of measurement is that the "yardstick" used be a consistent one. Therefore, raters judging student performance should be in basic agreement as to what scores should be assigned to students' work, within some tolerable limits (which measurement experts report as "measurement error"). Do raters agree on how a portfolio ought to be scored? Do they assign the same or nearly similar scores to a particular student's work? If the answers to these questions are not affirmative, then student scores are a measure of who does the scoring rather than the quality of the work. Because interrater agreement is accepted as the foundation on which all other decisions about portfolio quality are made, consistency of scoring has received the most empirical attention in large-scale portfolio assessment programs to date. It also is an essential first step that has presented significant challenges as the following examples show.

Results from Vermont's pioneering statewide portfolio assessment program, perhaps the most visible example in the country, have been disheartening. Here, fourth and eighth grade students kept portfolios in both writing and mathematics. Writing portfolios contained six to eight pieces representing various writing genres, with one designated as a "best piece." Mathematics portfolios contained five to seven "best pieces." Although scoring criteria and procedures for the two types of portfolios differed, both used analytic scoring in which student work was rated on a number of different dimensions using a four-point scale. Samples of student portfolios from each participating classroom were sent to a central location for scoring by volunteer teachers. Based on the second year of full implementation, Koretz, Stecher, Klein, and McCaffrey (1994a) report interrater reliabilities for writing portfolios total

---

[3] To avoid confusion with the broad term *construct validity*, we use the word *meaningfulness* to represent the narrower, more traditional sense of validity, which is based on appropriateness of content and similarity to other measures of the same construct.

scores of .56 and .63, at grades four and eight, respectively, a trivial increase from the first year's scoring; and for mathematics portfolios .72 and .79, respectively, an appreciable increase in consistency from the previous year's scoring. These levels of agreement were insufficient to permit reporting many of the aggregate statistics the state had planned to use: Vermont could not accurately report the proportion of students in the state who achieved each point on the scoring dimensions, and it could not provide accurate data on the comparative performance of districts.

Recent results from the Kentucky statewide program also show the challenge of achieving reliable scoring (Hambleton et al., 1995). In Kentucky, students are provided general guidelines regarding the types of pieces to include in each of math and writing portfolios. For example, at grade 12 writing portfolios must include a personal narrative; one short story, a poem or play; and three pieces of writing that achieve at least one of seven possible purposes. All Kentucky portfolios are scored locally by teachers using a holistic scoring guide; and there is an elaborate auditing system for monitoring consistency of scoring through rescoring samples of classes and students at the district level and centrally at the state level (Kentucky Department of Education, 1993a).

Comparisons between the writing portfolio scores assigned locally (by teachers in students' home schools) and those assigned in the independent state level scoring were moderately correlated, with coefficients of .70 and .67 at the fourth and eighth grade levels, respectively.[4] However, despite this moderate consistency in how the two groups of scorers ranked students, Hambleton et al., report significant inconsistency in how the standards were applied. Teachers in students' home schools rated students considerably higher than the state level scoring. For example at grade 8, while only 28% of the student sample was rated as "novice" by their home teachers, 51% was rated in the independent scoring.

In contrast, Pittsburgh Public Schools' writing portfolio assessment program obtained high interrater agreement (LeMahieu, Gitomer, & Eresh, 1994). Collected over a year following Arts Propel program and subsequent Pittsburgh staff development, Pittsburgh portfolios required students to compose, revise, and reflect on their writing and to select evidence of these processes for their portfolios. Portfolios contained at least six pieces selected to meet such general categories as "a satisfying piece," "an unsatisfying piece," "an important piece," and "a free pick." Raters were asked to rate the portfolios on each of three dimensions: (1) accomplishment in writing, (2) use of process and resources, and (3) growth and engagement. Despite the amount of latitude raters had in selecting pieces to rate and the broad scope of the scoring criteria, interrater agreement correlations ranged from

[4] Spearman rank-order correlation coefficients.

.60 to .70, and the generalizability estimate of interrater agreement when two raters reviewed each piece was in the .80 range.

Other examples of large-scale portfolio assessment that used a select group of scorers also have had success in achieving scorer consistency. For example, the National Assessment of Educational Progress trial of portfolios achieved interrater reliabilities of .76 to .79 (Gentile, 1992).

Score Reliability. Interrater agreement provides an upper bound on the reliability, but is only one of several sources of error in measurement in a student's overall portfolio score. Errors of measurement introduced by the variable nature of portfolio content have seldom been examined to date but they are likely to be an important issue for large-scale portfolio assessment. Rather than standardized tasks (like items in a test), portfolio entries typically are highly variable across individual classrooms and individual students. For example, two different students in the same classroom may include as best pieces responses to different assignments, and the nature and interrelationships between portfolio tasks in one classroom are likely to vary from those in another. The key issue is the extent to which a portfolio score represents a stable capability, and we examine that issue by analyzing the variability of student performance across portfolio tasks, among other factors. (This variability also presents a challenge to the comparability of scores, which we consider later.)

In Vermont, one of the few places to score portfolio tasks individually rather than just scoring the portfolio overall, found very substantial variability in performance across different pieces within a portfolio (Koretz et al., 1994a). In fact, there was greater variability within students than across students—meaning that students varied with themselves overall more than they varied from other students. A standard strategy to improving the generalizability of scores is to increase the number of tasks on which the scores are based. However, Koretz et al. found that more than 25 tasks would be necessary to achieve a modestly reliable total score. Further, it would have been almost impossible to achieve reliable dimension scores.

Meaningfulness of Scores

More than consistency of measurement (reliability) is needed to assure that test results are meaningful. *Validity* refers to the degree to which an inference made on the basis of a test or assessment is justified—does the test result have the meaning it is intended to have? An answer to the question "What does a test score tell you about whether an individual meets the standards for a particular content area?" is a judgment about the validity of the test for ascertaining standards attainment in that area. If there is evidence that the test has high validity, then the test user should be relatively confident that one can generalize from the test scores to capability on that standard.

Traditionally, the concern for meaningfulness has been divided into a number of distinct aspects, including content validity, concurrent validity, and predictive validity. Each aspect signals different types of evidence and different features of an assessment that might threaten the validity of its results for particular purposes. For example, the issue of content validity focuses attention on the extent to which the content of an assessment actually represents the domain that is intended to be assessed. If the test uses only a narrow range of problems, for instance, then it might not reflect the test taker's ability to do other types of problems, such as a grammar test that asked students only to find mistakes might not provide the best measure of a person's ability to produce grammatically correct paragraphs and certainly not the best measure of that person's ability to write a convincing, persuasive essay. Content validity might be threatened if an assessment is based on a narrow slice of a larger domain, such as a science test that includes only biology and physics might not permit strong inferences about a person's knowledge of science.

While establishing content validity is a process of garnering expert judgment about the nature of the domain to be assessed and the match between the actual assessment and its goals, concurrent validity relies on empirical evidence. Here, the relationship between test results and other valued indices of performance are the primary foci. To have confidence that a new reading test provides a good measure of reading, we want to see evidence that its results are consistent with student performance on other, trusted indicators of the construct, in this case, reading, and not highly related to measures of unlike constructs, for example, mathematic problem solving. We look for patterns of evidence that show that assessment results are consistent with what we would expect if the assessment is a good measure of the intended construct and distinct from measures of other, unlike constructs.

Content Validity.   Content validity is a raison d'être in portfolio assessment. Yet, its existence appears to have been assumed rather than directly judged or empirically verified. In the case of portfolios, essential issues in content validity include whether there is a match between portfolio content and curriculum goals, or in the case of states or districts that have them, a match with specific standards; whether the portfolio tasks represent significant learning goals for students; and whether the tasks are the foci of classroom instruction. While having content and curriculum experts and teachers involved in establishing required portfolio content is the first step in documenting content validity, subsequent steps in judging the content, depth, breadth, and quality of classroom tasks vis-à-vis intended curriculum goals and specific standards has yet to be accomplished. We return to these curriculum and instruction issues in the implementation and impact sections that follow.

Concurrent Validity. Very little study has been done of the concurrent validity of portfolio assessments, and the scant evidence that does exist raises more questions than answers. In Vermont, for example, Koretz, Stecher, Klein, McCaffrey, and Deibert (1993) looked at the relationships between portfolio assessments and standard, on-demand assessments in language arts and mathematics. They expected to find at least moderate relationships between portfolio and on-demand assessments within each subject area and little or no relationship between scores from different subjects. While the correlations between writing portfolios and the writing uniform test seemed reasonable, the correlations between subjects were not. After taking differences in reliability into account, mathematics portfolio scores showed about the same relationship to the uniform test in writing as to the uniform test in mathematics. More recently, similar analyses involving Kentucky's writing portfolios were similarly ambiguous. Scores from the writing portfolios were related highly to both multiple-choice and open-ended tests of reading, correlated relatively weakly with scores from the on-demand writing assessment, and related quite strongly to scores from the multiple-choice mathematics test.

Similarly, Herman, Gearhart, and Baker (1993) found virtually no relationship between scores for writing portfolios and for standard writing assessments. Two-thirds of the students who would have been classified as competent based on the portfolio assessment score would not have been so classified on the basis of the standard assessment. Thus, it was not the case that a student classified as a capable writer on the basis of the portfolio would necessarily do well when given a standard writing prompt. Furthermore, students classified as capable on the basis of an overall quality score were not always so classified when each piece in the portfolio was scored separately. Which assessment best represents students' skills? Does one assessment approach overestimate or another underestimate students' skills? Or do the different assessment instruments simply tap different parts of the assessed domain? These questions remain open, and debates about the meaning of portfolio scores are unresolved.

Comparability

A third aspect of construct validity that is relevant to portfolio assessment is comparability—that the results of an assessment have the same meaning for different students. If two students achieve the same score on an assessment, then we want to be able to say that those two students are equally capable. Alternatively, if one student scores substantially higher than another, we want to draw accurate inferences about the first student's greater capability. This is essential both at the individual level if portfolio scores are used for selection purposes (such as college admission) and at the aggregate level if the results of portfolio assessment are used to evaluate school quality. In traditional assessment, tasks are identical for every person, as are the conditions of administration and scoring—hence, the term *standardized*. Standardized test scores can be compared directly because they were based on exactly the same problems or tasks, administered in the same manner, and scored the same way, regardless of geographical location or time'(even year) of scoring. Without such standardization, scores given by different raters, at different times, for different years may not be comparable, recalling the reliability issues we raised earlier.

Portfolio assessment adds an additional twist to the comparability challenge: in many portfolio assessments test takers may be given a choice of problems; so in effect, they are taking different tests. Under these circumstances, one might be concerned that the test scores do not represent the same set of performances for all students (Mislevy, 1994). In addition, because students often select which pieces of work will be judged, no two portfolios may contain the same pieces. Furthermore, as the following discussion will show, there may be substantial variability in the conditions under which a portfolio is produced. All this uncontrolled variability (in measurement terms) leads to serious questions about the comparability of results from different students, classes, and schools.

Whose Work Is It?   One reason for thinking that portfolios may overestimate individual performance for some students comes from portfolios' very strengths: they are integrated with instruction. In good classroom instruction, students often get support in planning, drafting, and revising their writing. But does this additional support from peers, teachers, or others constitute learning for an individual student or does it simply make an individual's portfolio work look better than it would without such assistance? When portfolios are used for classroom assessment, this question is not a major issue. Teachers, after all, have many indicators of student capability and are intimately aware of the conditions under which work is produced. In large-scale assessment settings where the question is what can an *individual* do, the issue becomes important indeed.

An important fairness issue is at work here as well. If some students get more help and support than others with their work, are they not unfairly advantaged during the assessment? Research in Vermont clearly reveals differences in teachers' classroom policies toward revision and support for collaboration on portfolio pieces (Koretz, Stecher, & Deibert, 1992; Koretz et al., 1993; Koretz, Stecher, Klein & McCaffrey, 1994a,b). Some teachers encouraged revision, others discouraged it, still others required it. Policies on feedback and support similarly were variable; in some classrooms, obtaining feedback from others was permissible; in other classrooms it was explicitly forbidden. Classroom conditions under which the portfolios were produced thus have an unknown effect on students performance.

A small, exploratory study by Gearhart, Herman, Baker, and Whittaker (1993) suggests that the problem is not simply one of variation by classroom. Adding to the complications is unknown variability within classrooms. The researchers asked teachers such things as how much structure or prompting they provided individual students, what type of peer or teacher editorial assistance occurred, and what were the available resources and time for portfolio compilation. Research results showed that there were differences in the amount of support given to individual students within classrooms as well as differences between classrooms participating in the study. When students have different levels of assistance, how do we assess their work to determine what they actually can do individually? How do we provide equitable assessment settings? And what do scores mean about the relative capability of the students?

The popularity of group work and recommendations to include it in portfolios add additional complications to the "Whose work is it?" question. How is a rater to judge a student's competence on the basis of collaborative work? Webb (1993) found substantial differences in students' performance when judged on the basis of cooperative group work compared to that done individually. Not too surprisingly, low-ability students had higher scores on the basis of group work than on individual work; and indeed an important rationale for group work is that groups may be able to come up with better solutions than individuals working alone, providing more students with better and more equitable opportunities to learn. But group learning opportunities may not translate well into assessment opportunities: a group product may not help us assess the capabilities of individual members. Saner, Mc-Caffrey, Stecher, Klein, and Bell (1994) found that work done with a partner on a science performance assessment did not provide a good estimate of individual ability.

Still, additional complications arise when classwork merges with "homework." In this case, the amount of help students get from parents, other family members, and friends becomes an additional threat to the validity of interpretations about individual student scores. Consider the student whose ambitious and overzealous parent helps him or her to embellish a composition compared to the student who receives no assistance whatsoever. Will portfolio assessments disadvantage the latter student? And what of the school whose community is populated by highly educated professionals, highly involved in their children's schooling and able to give lots of help with work done at home? If student portfolios are used for school accountability, is this school likely to look like it is doing a better job of educating students than a school where students receive substantially less help? Differential support issues become important when student work is scored remotely and scores are used to make high-stakes decisions about students or schools.

Despite the claims of some advocates that portfolios will be fairer assessments of students' accomplishments than traditional measures, the equity of portfolio assessment deserves continuing scrutiny. Research to date suggests that patterns of performance on portfolios mirror those on traditional measures in terms of the *relative* performance levels of disadvantaged or minority groups. P. G. LeMahieu and D. H. Gitomer (personal communication, October 5, 1993), for example, in a study of writing portfolios, found that females do better than males and that white students show higher levels of performance than African-American students. Hearne and Schuman (1993) similarly found the same demographic patterns of performance for traditional standardized and portfolio assessments.

Overall, the demands of construct validity present serious challenges for large-scale portfolio assessment. Although there is some evidence that initial problems with the reliability of ratings can be overcome, other quality concerns endure. The issues of score reliability, meaningfulness, and comparability remain obstacles to the use of portfolios for the purposes of large-scale assessment.

Feasibility

In this section we examine practical and logistic questions about the use of portfolios in large-scale assessment. How difficult will it be to develop and implement this form of assessment? What resources will be required? How will parents, teachers, and other stakeholders react to the results of a portfolio assessment?

Assessment Development

The familiar components of test development—preparing content specifications, writing items, conducting pilot tests and item analysis, and assembling test forms—are absent in a portfolio assessment, but other assessment preparation activities must be conducted. In the case of portfolios, assessment development includes specifying the nature of the work desired from students, the conditions under which it is to be performed, and the manner in which it is to be scored. All these tasks may require substantial time and expertise, and it is important to examine whether it is practical to develop large-scale portfolio assessments.

One prerequisite for a portfolio assessment is the existence of curriculum and performance standards (or their equivalent) to enable teachers and students to understand the nature of the work that should be included in the portfolio. For example, should a language arts portfolio contain spelling tests, timed writing assignments, drafts of creative writing exercises, library research notes, or class projects? Should a mathematics portfolio contain math worksheets, computational exercises, or essays about mathematics? There must be a content framework or a set of "academic expectations" to give direction to the portfolio effort. Beyond that there must be guidelines about the purpose of the portfolio and the aspects of the framework that are to be represented. For example, the Vermont portfolios contain "best pieces" illustrating optimum performance. In Pittsburgh, writing portfolios contain "an important piece," "a satisfying piece," "an unsatisfying piece," "a free pick," and an "optional negotiated free pick" at the teacher's discretion (LeMahieu, Gitomer, & Eresh, 1994, p. 3). Kentucky places greater emphasis on representing the curriculum; mathematics portfolios include "a breadth of entries (types, tools, and core concepts)" (Kentucky Department of Education, 1993b, p. 2). A large-scale portfolio assessment could embody any of these perspectives on content, as well as others.

Participating teachers and students also must understand the conditions under which work is to be produced and portfolios are to be assembled (e.g., Can students revise their work? Is group work acceptable? How long can students devote to work products? Can they receive assistance from peers, parents, or other adults? Who selects the pieces to be included in the portfolios?). In Kentucky, the state guidelines indicate that students are supposed to be the "sole creators, authors and owners of their work" (Kentucky Department of Education, 1993b, p. iii). Vermont places greater emphasis on local adaptability, letting teachers decide how portfolio products are to be created. If the results of portfolio assessment are to be used for comparison of students, schools, or districts—as is the case with many forms of large-scale assessment—then standardization of conditions is an important consideration, and formal rules and procedures may have to be developed.

Creating a scoring system may be the most difficult developmental activity associated with portfolio assessment. The scoring system must translate the conceptual framework and production guidelines into explicit criteria for awarding points or classifying students or both. This task is difficult because frameworks are often written in very general terms, the products to be judged are so complex and varied, and where portfolio assessment is coupled with curriculum reform, people may be less familiar with the aspects of performance that are to be rewarded. Scoring becomes the arena in which battles about curriculum priorities and the nature of student performance are fought. In some instances, the scoring rubrics can become the defining elements of the curriculum reform for teachers (Stecher & Mitchell, 1995a).

How great is the assessment development burden? Although good estimates are scarce, it appears to be far greater than might be anticipated. Educators in Vermont worked on the project for two years before they implemented it on a statewide basis, and the development process did not end once the system was implemented. As Koretz et al. (1994b) note, "Development in the first two subject areas undertaken is still continuing during the third year of statewide implementation and is clearly very costly." Much of this effort went into aligning the goals of the portfolio assessment with recent curriculum reform efforts (e.g., the National Council for Teachers of Mathematics). Similarly, LeMahieu et al. (1994) note that the successful implementation of the Arts Propel writing portfolios in Pittsburgh was based on "several years of discussions of student writing," involving teachers, researchers, and language arts supervisors. The development of the Kentucky assessment system involved content advisory committees for each subject area, who met five times the first year and continued to meet regularly thereafter (Kentucky Department of Education, 1993a, 1994). Similar observations were made by Gitomer and Duschl (1994) about scope of reform required to support science portfolios,

> Successful science portfolio is not merely an interesting assessment technique that simply can be placed within a traditional science classroom. Instead, good portfolio practice requires fundamental changes in conception of science and science teaching, in ideas about learning and instruction, and of course, in the practice and function of assessment.

Such change does not come easily or quickly. Policy makers should anticipate four- or five-year time frames for assessment development (CPRE, 1995, p. 10).

It is worth noting that some of the assessment development burden can fall at the local level, as well. The Vermont portfolio assessment was decentralized, giving teachers greater flexibility to tailor the reform to the needs of their classrooms. As a consequence, teachers were responsible for activities, including finding appropriate tasks to prompt student work, that might be done centrally had the assessment reform been conceptualized differently.

Implementation

The literature suggests that implementing a new assessment system or modifying an existing system can require significant resources at the state and the local levels. The state-level start-up process must include informing schools and teachers, distributing guidelines and materials, training teachers, monitoring operations, providing support, and occasionally troubleshooting. As Aschbacher (1993) describes, "Even quite modest implementation of alternative assessment takes a tremendous amount of time and externally-provided professional development."

As an example, Vermont provided many staff development opportunities for teachers while implementing its portfolio assessment. During the pilot year, the state sponsored a statewide orientation meeting in the fall and a series of regional workshops during the school year. In subsequent years in-service training was expanded to include summer and fall institutes and workshops during the year. All teachers were provided with a *Resource Book* with examples of instructional tasks and a *Teacher's Guide* explaining procedures. In addition, regional networks were established with consultants to provide supplemental training and support at the grassroots level (Koretz et al., 1993).

Even with this level of sustained training, teachers' knowledge of some key elements of the reform was incomplete. After the first year, three-quarters of the Vermont fourth and eighth grade teachers were "occasionally" or "frequently" confused about what they were supposed to do with portfolios or how they were supposed to do it (Koretz, Stecher, & Deibert, 1992). After three years, although teachers had mastered many of the concepts inherent in the portfolio assessment, they still did not share a common understanding of mathematical problem solving, a key element of the reform (Stecher & Mitchell, 1995b). Implementation also was slow in Kentucky. After three years, evaluators still observed that "performance assessment has not been integrated into instructional processes across the grade levels, as envisioned by the legislation" (Pankratz, 1995, p. 2). These findings are consistent with other observations about the difficulty teachers have implementing alternative assessments and the need for sustained support (Aschbacher, 1993).

The implementation burden associated with portfolio assessment is felt strongly at the local level as well as the state level. In Vermont almost all schools provided release time for teachers to attend portfolio institutes and workshops. In addition, more than one-fourth of principals provided release time for teachers to work on preparing lessons, selecting pieces, and organizing final portfolios (Koretz et al., 1993). Moreover, teachers spent considerable extra time preparing for the portfolio assessment in addition to their attendance at the state workshops. During the first year, Vermont teachers spent 17 hours each month (on average) *outside of class* finding portfolio tasks, preparing lessons, and evaluating the contents of portfolios. Of the teachers, 60% said they often lacked the time to prepare portfolio lessons (Koretz et al., 1992). Although there was some evidence that the time demands on teachers declined in the second year, the change was only slight. Less than one-third of the Vermont teachers said that portfolios were less of a burden the second year (Stecher & Hamilton, 1994). (There also were dramatic changes in classroom practices to accommodate the portfolio assessment, which will be addressed in the section on impact.)

However, the Vermont and Kentucky experiences may not tell the whole story. Researchers in Pittsburgh, "did not observe the levels of discomfort . . . and additional work associated with the [portfolio] assessment" (LeMahieu et al., 1994, p. 20). Pittsburgh teachers acknowledge that there is work involved in the development of portfolios, but prefer that it not be characterized as an "add-on." Instead, they see it as "part and parcel of curriculum and instruction." For them the characterization of portfolios as "embedded" assessment is more accurate. The time devoted to portfolios was not attributed to the demands of assessment but to the needs of learning and instruction. (It is worth noting Vermont math teachers reported spending 13 hours per month of *class time* on portfolio activities, such as doing lessons and helping students organize and manage their work, in addition to the 17 hours outside of class that we attributed to implementation.) Kentucky superintendents and district assessment coordinators identified staff development as one of the three most positive benefits of the state reform (Pankratz, 1995).

It is difficult to resolve these conflicting points of view about the burdens of portfolio assessment. Over time, the attitudes of teachers in Vermont and Kentucky may come to resemble those of teachers in Pittsburgh if the process of generating portfolio pieces becomes more integrated with regular instructional activities. Others think that "the time devoted to revising and polishing final pieces can run into weeks rather than hours if the stakes are high" (CPRE, 1995).

In contrast, the scoring component of portfolio assessment is more likely to be perceived as an external activity, which can be difficult and time consuming. Because the scoring system is based on judgment, it is essential that there be shared standards and a common evaluative framework. However, it is difficult to develop shared understanding and train teachers to apply scoring rubrics consistently. Even after the second year of implementation, interreader agreement in Vermont was too low to permit the use of the scores for accountability purposes (Koretz et al., 1994b). LeMahieu et al. (1994) reported greater success in scoring writing portfolios reliably in the Arts Propel project. They attributed this success to "long-standing institutional effort to develop a common interpretative framework for examining and considering student writing; that is, extensive, long-term, focused staff development. The difficulty of establishing a shared interpretive framework was noted by researchers studying the advanced placement studio art assessment (Myford & Mislevy, 1994), and the lesson for large-scale portfolio assessment seems to be that successful scoring requires efforts to engage all teachers in in-depth, extended, thoughtful discussions of the desired features of student work.

In Vermont, teachers were encouraged to score the portfolios of their own students both to learn more about the scoring process and the nature of student work and to produce information for local classroom use. Most devoted considerable time to this activity; on average they spent five hours per month scoring and evaluating their own students portfolios during the first year (Koretz et al., 1993).[5] The burden did not lessen in subsequent years, with over 80% of the teachers reporting that scoring was still too time consuming (Stecher & Hamilton, 1994).

On the other hand, benefits accrued from this careful examination of student work that have not been quantified. Overall the Vermont assessment required considerable effort on the part of teachers and principals and generated both enthusiasm and stress. The principals and teachers in Vermont characterized the portfolio assessments as a "worthwhile burden" (Koretz et al., 1994b). Similar mixed reactions were found in Kentucky, where a poll of superintendents and district assessment coordinators revealed stress and

---

[5] These 5 hours are included in the 17 hours reported above for all activities outside of class.

increased paperwork to be the most negative aspects of the reform and high expectations and more writing to be the most positive aspects (Pankratz, 1995).

Cost

Estimating the cost of alternative assessment, such as portfolios, is difficult. Portfolio assessment costs are difficult to study because they are spread out across many levels of the educational system, because the assessment activities occur throughout the school year, and because the activities that make up the assessment (classroom tasks and student work products) also are part of instruction and staff development. Disentangling the contribution to assessment is problematic. Nevertheless, there are conceptual models for analyzing the cost of alternative assessments and for conducting cost–benefit analyses that address both the operation of the assessment the benefits that it generates (Catterall & Winters, 1994; Picus, 1994. However, no thorough cost analyses of operating portfolio assessment programs have been conducted. Most partial analyses conclude that development, administration, scoring, and reporting costs are higher for performance-based assessments than for multiple-choice tests (Hardy, 1995; Hoover & Bray, 1995; Stecher, 1995). Overall, portfolio assessment is perceived to be "time consuming and very expensive" (Pankratz, 1995, p. 2).

The one component whose cost is easiest to estimate is scoring. For example, Catterall and Winters (1994) estimate the cost of scoring a 45-minute essay as part of the California assessment system is between $3 and $5. Stecher (1995) estimates the cost of scoring one class period of hands-on science tasks at between $4 and $5 per student for large groups of students. By comparison, the Iowa Test of Basic Skills complete battery can be scored for about $1 per student. RAND researchers reported that Vermont spent approximately $13 per pupil just for honoraria and room and board costs to score the math portfolios (Koretz et al., 1994b). The actual costs for scoring a large-scale portfolio assessment probably will depend on the procedures used to generate the portfolios, the number of pieces, and the nature of the scoring rubrics.

Acceptability

Because they are widely publicized and used for accountability purposes, large-scale forms of assessment are carefully scrutinized by educators, community members, legislators, and other groups. These people must feel comfortable that the assessment focuses on appropriate skills and presents results that are fair and accurate. If judgment is made about proficiency, then audiences must understand and accept the standards used for classifying student work (LeMahieu et al., 1994).

Unfortunately, such acceptance is not automatic. For example, recent challenges from citizens' groups and legislators led to dramatic changes in statewide testing programs in California and Arizona (Merl, 1994). As a result, educational agencies must be concerned that large-scale assessment instruments are acceptable to stakeholders, including legislators, community members, parents, and students. In 1995 evaluators in Kentucky concluded that "stakeholders have too little understanding and confidence in KIRIS" even after almost four years of implementation (Pankratz, 1995, p. 2). This does not necessarily mean they lack confidence in portfolios, because KIRIS is much more than just portfolios, but it suggests that it is difficult to convince the public about the efficacy of alternative assessment for large-scale assessment. This reluctance may be due to allegiance to multiple-choice tests, fear of change, or to the small proportion of students able to meet higher standards (CPRE, 1995).

Another aspect of acceptability is reporting. In Kentucky there is research to suggest that most audiences approve of the general goals of educational and assessment reform, but they may grow dissatisfied with the process as it is implemented. Kifer (1994) reports that a huge majority of the general public supported the six goals of KERA (71 to 84%). However, the approval for the actual reform process was much lower. In fact, over four years, disapproval had risen from 13 to 33%, while approval had dropped from 82 to 41%. Kifer offers no explanation for these trends but notes that they are troubling. One reason for the decline in support may be a failure to communicate findings clearly. An independent technical review committee appointed by the General Assembly to study KIRIS found room for improvement in the public reporting documents associated with the assessment (Hambleton et al., 1995). Furthermore, a statewide survey revealed that more than one-half of the general public and 40% of parents in Kentucky "know very little or nothing about" the state educational reforms (Pankratz, 1995, p. 16).

Overall, the development and implementation of a large-scale portfolio assessment appears to be a complex and expensive task. Considerable resources—including personnel, expertise, and time—are needed to overcome the practical problems associated with this form of assessment. Some of the same features that make portfolios attractive from an instructional perspective—their close relationship with curriculum, their integration into instructional activities—make them difficult to use on a large-scale basis. Furthermore, stakeholders in the educational system are unfamiliar with portfolios, and they have been reluctant to embrace other new forms of assessment.

Impact

Assessment portfolios have had dramatic effects on attitudes and practices where they have been used. In Vermont, portfolios were the cornerstone of the first-ever statewide assessment program, which may have contributed to their dramatic impact (Koretz et al., 1994a). Over one-half of the teachers reported that they were more enthusiastic about mathematics most of the time. Forty percent reported that their goals for mathematics had improved as a result. In terms of classroom practices, mathematics teachers reported spending more time on problem solving and communication, which were the major foci of the portfolio assessment. For example, about 70% reported devoting more time to making charts, graphs, and diagrams and to writing reports about mathematics. Similarly, about three-fourths reported having students spend more time applying mathematical knowledge to new situations, and about one-half reported spending more time on exploration of mathematical patterns. Teachers also reported changes in instructional practices, such as increasing the time students worked in pairs or small groups (Koretz et al., 1994a). Furthermore, the scoring rubrics, which translated the general curriculum goals into concrete operational terms, had marked influence on curriculum and instruction (Stecher & Mitchell, 1995a).

However, both principals and teachers perceived portfolios to be burdensome (Koretz et al., 1993). Many teachers grew frustrated in the second year because they did not perceive a lessening of the time demands associated with the portfolios. The reform was designed to give teachers considerable flexibility, and as a result there was considerable variation in the changes they made to curriculum and instruction (Koretz et al., 1994b).

Kentucky teachers also reported considerable changes in classroom practices, although these must be attributed to the KERA reform as a whole, which included portfolios as one component along with on-demand tasks and noncognitive elements. As Pankratz (1995) summarized, "KIRIS has helped to improve instruction and student achievement in writing." There is evidence that principals are enthusiastic about the portfolios; 90% of Kentucky principals "agreed" or "strongly agreed" that "writing portfolios have great instructional potential" (Pankratz, 1995, p. 5).

In Pittsburgh, the portfolio assessment was not implemented as an independent assessment reform, rather it was part of a long-term effort to influence teaching practice and curriculum development through discussion of the goals of writing. Observers believe it has been successful in this regard (LeMahieu et al., 1994).

Overall, researchers have reported changes in principals' and teachers' attitudes and practices. On the positive side, portfolios have been associated with greater enthusiasm for teaching, higher expectations for students, and changes in educational goals, content, and instructional procedures. On the negative side, they have been perceived to be burdensome, teachers have had a difficult time understanding the underlying concepts, and there are inconsistencies in their impact on curriculum and instruction. There is no strong evidence yet about changes in student performance.

POTENTIAL FOR PORTFOLIO USE
IN LARGE-SCALE ASSESSMENT

The utility of portfolios for large-scale assessment is directly related to the purposes of the assessment. In the introduction, we outlined five potential uses for large-scale assessment: describing the status of the educational system, comparing individuals and units for selection or evaluation, holding schools and districts accountable, signaling desired outcomes, and providing information for program planning and improvement. Our review of the literature suggests that portfolio assessments are well suited to some of these purposes but poorly suited to others.

At their present state of development, portfolios have limited value for the purposes of evaluation and accountability because of unresolved technical problems and large resource demands. For these purposes, policy makers and the public demand succinct and trustworthy information about student performance. Their "bottom line" seems to be relatively simple, uncontextualized answers to broad questions about the educational system. Is instruction effective? How well are the schools working? What value do schools add to students? Educational policy makers are more interested in the relative performance of groups of students and in changes in group performance over time. How are the students within their educational setting performing on valued outcomes compared to other students in the district, state, nation, or even the world? At present, portfolio assessment cannot provide information about student performance with adequate reliability and validity for these purposes. Nor is it clear that states could afford the resources necessary to develop and implement portfolio assessment on such a large scale if the technical hurdles could be overcome.

Similarly, portfolios currently lack the reliability and validity they need to be effective tools for individual selection or certification. Although it might be feasible for students to assemble portfolios for selection or certification purposes—such as promotion, attainment of graduation standards, or admission to college—it does not appear that portfolio scores are currently of sufficient technical quality to be used as a sole or determining factor in such decisions. Portfolio scores do not meet the minimum standards for reliability, validity, or comparability needed to support these uses.

In contrast, current research on portfolio assessment suggests that portfolios can be powerful tools in support of instructional reform and school improvement. Available evidence indicates that portfolios do serve a strong signaling function by focusing teachers' conversations on the desirable features of student work and their expectations for students. In this way, portfolio assessments can support thoughtful planning and program improvement efforts. Evidence from large-scale implementations of portfolio assessment indicates that schools and teachers alter both their goals for students and their instructional practices. While these changes come at a price (in terms of time and stress), they appear to be meaningful rather than superficial. In response to portfolio assessments teachers have initiated new teaching strategies and increased the frequency of assignments that enable students to demonstrate complex thinking and problem-solving skills.

Overall, this review paints a mixed picture of the utility of portfolios for large-scale assessment. Portfolios unevenly serve the purposes policy makers hope to achieve with large-scale assessment systems, providing relatively strong signals about desired student outcomes and classroom activities but relatively weak quantitative indicators of individual and group performance. However, such a mixed review should sound familiar, because a mismatch between the characteristics of assessment and the demands of large-scale testing is not unique to portfolios. Multiple-choice tests also unevenly serve the diverse purposes of large-scale assessment, as do other forms of performance-based assessments. In this regard, no assessment tool is perfectly suited to the complex goals policy makers hope to achieve with statewide testing programs.

The mismatch between individual assessment tools and the purposes of assessment systems suggests an effective strategy may be fashioned by combining assessments techniques in ways that capitalize on their strengths. In the case of portfolio assessment, their current strength is clearly in support of curriculum and instruction. Eventually, it may be possible to improve the measurement value of portfolios, using stronger designs and tighter controls to enhance their validity, reliability, and comparability. At present, there already is a good match between portfolios and certain policy goals for large-scale assessment. The problem becomes finding a way to realize this value in a multifaceted assessment system. The design of such a system is beyond the scope of this chapter, but we raise the possibility to indicate that we are not closing the book on portfolios as tools for large-scale assessment. As policy makers consider innovative approaches to large-scale assessment, such as portfolios, they need to think about innovative system designs to fulfill the multiple purposes they hold for assessment. Because portfolios contain direct evidence of classroom practice, they provide a unique window on the quality of classroom instruction. Might there be a way to capture that quality economically at the school level? Might there be a way to bring parents into the assessment and evaluation process based on portfolios? We believe it is worth exploring the possibilities of designing large-scale assessment systems that utilize portfolios for the purposes they serve well.

In the final analysis, portfolio assessment's greatest strength may be for a different purpose—as a tool for classroom assessment. In the classroom, the teacher is engaged with his or her students and knows them well from daily classroom contact. She or he has numerous opportunities to build and confirm a judgment of their capabilities and is not particularly concerned with comparing the abilities of students in one class with students in other classes or with their performance in previous years. The teacher's demands for technical quality in a single assessment are much less than in the large-scale testing context. Consequently, errors in measurement from a single source do not have such grave consequences because they can be moderated by the teacher's knowledge and experience with individual students. At the classroom level, a teacher's primary motivation for assessment is to obtain information that can be used to improve curriculum and instruction, to understand and diagnose students' needs and progress, and perhaps to contribute to grading. These needs play into the strengths of portfolios, and it may be as classroom assessment tools that portfolio assessments realize their greatest potential.

References

Aschbacher, P. R. (1993). *Issues in innovative assessment for classroom practice: Barriers and facilitators* (CSE Tech. Rep. No. 359). Los Angeles: UCLA Center for the Study of Evaluation.

Baker, E. L., O'Neil, H. F., & Linn, R. L. (1993, December). Policy and validity prospects for performance-based assessment. *American Psychologist*, 48(12), 1210–1218.

Catterall, J. S., & Winters, L. (1994). *Economic analysis of testing: Competency, certification and "authentic" assessments* (CSE Tech. Rep. No. 383). Los Angeles: UCLA Center for the Study of Evaluation.

Consortium for Policy Research in Education (CPRE) (1995). *Tracking student achievement in science and math: The promise of state assessment programs* (RB-17, p. 10). New Brunswick: Rutgers, the State University of New Jersey.

Gearhart, M., Herman, J. L., Baker, E. L., & Whittaker, A. (1993). Whose work is it? A question for the validity of large-scale portfolio assessment (CSE Tech. Rep. No. 363). Los Angeles: CRESST/UCLA.

Gentile, C. (1992, April). *Exploring new methods for collecting students school-based writing: NAEP's 1990 portfolio study.* Washington, DC: National Center for Education Statistics, Office of Educational Research and Improvement, U.S. Department of Education.

Gitomer, D. H., & Duschl, R. A. (1994). *Moving toward a portfolio culture in science education* (MS No. 94-07). Princeton, NJ: Educational Testing Service.

Hambleton, R. K., Jaeger, R. M., Koretz, D., Linn, R. L., Millman, J., & Phillips, S. E. (1995). *Review of the measurement quality of the Kentucky Instructional Results Information System, 1991–1994.* Frankfort: Kentucky General Assembly.

Hardy, R. A. (1995). Examining the costs of performance assessment. *Applied Measurement in Education*, 8(2), 121–134.

Hearne, J., & Schuman, S. (1993). *Portfolio assessment: Implementation and use at an elementary level* (Tech. Rep. No. 143). (ERIC Document Reproduction Service No. ED 349 330)

Herman, J. L., Gearhart, M., & Baker, E. L. (1993, Summer). Assessing writing portfolios: Issues in the validity and meaning of scores. *Educational Assessment*, 1(3), 201–224.

Herman, J. L., & Winters, L. (1994, October). Portfolio research: A slim collection. *Educational Leadership*, 52(2), 48–55.

Hoover, H. D., & Bray, G. B. (1995, April). *The research and development phase: Can a performance assessment be cost-effective?* Paper presented at the annual meeting of the American Educational Research Association, San Francisco.

Kellaghan, T., & Madaus, G. (1991). National testing: Lessons for America from Europe. *Educational Leadership*, 49(3), 87–93.

Kentucky Department of Education (1993a). *Kentucky instructional results information system: 1991–92 technical report.* Frankfort: Author.

Kentucky Department of Education (1993b). *Kentucky mathematics portfolio: Teacher's guide.* Frankfort: Author.

Kentucky Department of Education (1994). *Kentucky instructional results information system: 1992–93 technical report.* Frankfort: Author.

Kifer, E. (1994). Perceptions, attitudes, and beliefs about the Kentucky Education Reform Act (KERA). In *A review of research on the Kentucky Education Reform Act* (KERA) (pp. 202–211). Frankfort: Kentucky Institute for Education Research.

Koretz, D., Linn, R., Dunbar, S., & Shepard, L. (1991). *The effects of high stakes testing on achievement.* Presentation at the annual meeting of the American Educational Research Association, Chicago.

Koretz, D., Stecher, B., & Deibert, E. (1992, August). *The Vermont portfolio assessment program: Interim report on implementation and impact, 1991–92 school year* (CSE Tech. Rep. No. 350). Los Angeles: CRESST/UCLA.

Koretz, D., Stecher, B., Klein, S., & McCaffrey, D. (1994a, July). *The evolution of a portfolio program: The impact and quality of the Vermont program in its second year* (1992–93) (CSE Tech. Rep. No. 385). Los Angeles: CRESST/UCLA.

Koretz, D., Stecher, B. M., Klein, S., & McCaffrey, D. (1994b, Fall). The Vermont portfolio assessment program: Findings and implications, *Educational Measurement: Issues and Practices, 13*(3), 5–16.

Koretz, D., Stecher, B., Klein, S., McCaffrey, D., & Deibert, E. (1993, December). *Can portfolios assess student performance and influence instruction? The 1991–92 Vermont experience* (CSE Tech. Rep. No. 371). Los Angeles: CRESST/UCLA. (Reprinted as RAND, RP-259, 1994)

LeMahieu, P. G., Gitomer, D. H., & Eresh, J. T. (1994). *Portfolios beyond the classroom: Data quality and qualities* (MS No. 94-01). Princeton, NJ: Educational Testing Service.

Linn, R. L., Baker, E. L., & Dunbar, S. B. (1991). *Complex performance-based assessments: Expectations and validation criteria* (CSE Tech. Rep. No. 331). Los Angeles: CRESST/UCLA.

Merl, J. (1994, May 6). Furor continues to build over state's CLAS exams. *Los Angeles Times*, A1,18.

Messick, S. (1992). Validity of test interpretation and use. In M. Alkin (Ed.), *Encyclopedia of educational research* (6th ed., pp. 1487–1495). New York: Macmillan.

Mills, R. P., & Brewer, W. R. (1988, October 18/November 10). *Working together to show results: An approach to school accountability in Vermont.* Montpelier: Vermont Department of Education.

Mislevy, R. J. (1994). Evidence and inference in educational assessment. *Psychometrica, 59,* 439–483.

Myford, C. M., & Mislevy, R. J. (1994). *Monitoring and improving a portfolio assessment system* (MS No. 94-04). Princeton, NJ: Educational Testing Service.

Pankratz, R. (1995). *Summary of research related to KERA.* Frankfort: Kentucky Institute for Education Research.

Picus, L. O. (1994). *A conceptual framework for analyzing the costs of alternative assessment* (CSE Tech. Rep. No. 384). Los Angeles: UCLA Center for the Study of Evaluation.

Resnick, L. B., & Resnick, D. P. (1992). Assessing the thinking curriculum: New tools for educational reform. In B. Gifford & M. C. O'Connor (Eds.), *Changing assessments: Alternative views of aptitude, achievement, and instruction* (pp. 37–76). Boston: Kluwer.

Saner, H., McCaffrey, D., Stecher, B., Klein, S., & Bell, R. (1994). The effects of working in pairs in science performance assessment. *Educational Assessment, 2*(4), 325–338.

Shepard, L. (1991). Will national tests improve student learning? *Phi Delta Kappan, 71,* 232–238.

Smith, M. L., & Rottenberg, C. (1991). Unintended consequences of external testing in elementary schools. *Educational Measurement: Issues and Practice, 10*(4), 7–11.

Stecher, B. M. (1995). *The cost of performance assessment in science.* Invited symposium presented at the annual meeting of the National Council on Measurement in Education, San Francisco.

Stecher, B. M., & Hamilton, E. G. (1994, April). *Portfolio assessment in Vermont, 1992–93: The teachers' perspective on implementation and impact.* Paper presented at the annual meeting of the National Council on Measurement in Education, New Orleans, LA.

Stecher, B. M., & Mitchell, K. J. (1995a). *Portfolio driven reform: Vermont teachers' understanding of mathematical problem solving* (CSE Tech. Rep. No. 400). Los Angeles, CA: CRESST/UCLA.

Stecher, B. M., & Mitchell, K. (1995b). *Vermont teachers' understanding of mathematical problem solving and "good" math problems.* Paper presented as part of the symposium "The impact of alternative assessment on teachers' knowledge and practice" at the annual meeting of the American Educational Research Association, San Francisco.

Webb, N. (1993). *Collaborative group versus individual assessment in mathematics: Group processes and outcomes* (CSE Tech. Rep. No. 352). Los Angeles: CRESST/UCLA.

Wiggins, G. (1989, May). A true test: Toward more authentic and equitable assessment. *Phi Delta Kappan,* 70(9), 703–713.

Wiggins, G. (1993, November). Assessment: Authenticity, context, and validity. *Phi Delta Kappan,* 75(3), 200–208, 210–214.

Wolf, D. P. (1992, May). Good measures: Assessment as a tool for educational reform. *Educational Leadership,* 49(8), 8–13.

Wolf, D. P. (1993). Assessment as an episode of learning. In R. Bennett & W. Ward (Eds.), *Construction versus choice in cognitive measurement* (pp. 213–240). Hillsdale, NJ: Erlbaum.

CHAPTER

17

The National Assessment
of Educational Progress

ALBERT E. BEATON
Boston College

The National Assessment of Educational Progress (NAEP) is a continuing federally mandated national survey of educational achievement. NAEP is also known as the "Nation's Report Card." NAEP is not a typical standardized testing program. Usual testing programs are intended to test or evaluate individual students; instead, NAEP is intended primarily to estimate the performance of populations of students and to report their aggregated performance and trends in their performance to educational policy makers and the general public. NAEP produces reliable results for the nation as a whole, for participating states, and for important subpopulations such as different genders and racial or ethnic groupings. It measures performance over a large range of tasks and topics in subject areas such as reading, writing, and mathematics. NAEP measurements of individual students are not reliable enough for evaluations or decisions about them.

The difference in the goals of NAEP from other testing programs has led to rather unusual features in its design. Since individual students do not receive test scores, NAEP uses well-selected samples of students to represent the populations and subpopulations it measures. Without the need to compare individual students, NAEP uses different assessment forms with different items to collect data from its sample, thus extending the content coverage of any subject area. Since the aggregation of the best estimates of individuals' performance is not in general the best estimate of a population's performance, NAEP does not even make estimates of individual student scores. How these differences from the usual standardized testing programs

Handbook of Classroom Assessment

and other NAEP innovations meld into a coherent assessment program will be the discussed in the remainder of this chapter.

It is helpful for students of testing to understand the design and implementation of NAEP, since by contrast, NAEP may show the assumptions and limitations of standard testing. NAEP is built on the basic ideas of test theory and, more particularly, item response theory or IRT (see Lord, 1980). However, the fact that NAEP needed a broad coverage of the subject matter being tested and did not need reliable individual scores has led to innovations and deviations from standard practice. Examining these differences will help the student better understand the basics of testing.

NAEP data are available to the educational research community, including graduate students, who may use the data to investigate educational and social issues not addressed by NAEP or, perhaps, to reproduce and modify the psychometric models used by NAEP. An NAEP *Primer* for users of NAEP data has been written by Beaton and Gonzalez (1995). User guides for the NAEP database are also available (Rogers, Kline, Johnson, Mislevy, & Rust, 1990, 1992).

NAEP is a particularly well-documented testing program. The intended design of NAEP has been described by Messick, Beaton, and Lord (1983). The actual implementation is described in a number of technical reports (Beaton, 1987, 1988; Johnson & Allen, 1992; Johnson & Carlson, 1994) and in special issues of the *Journal of Educational Measurement* (1990) and the *Journal of Educational Statistics* (1990).

In this chapter, the general design of NAEP will be described. Since NAEP is a continuing program, its design is constantly changing to meet new information demands and budgetary restraints. Although the design details may vary, the components of a testing program are relatively fixed. The reader is referred to Allen and Zwick (1992), Beaton and Zwick (1992), and Johnson (1992a, 1992b) for other overviews of NAEP and to the technical reports for more detailed information.

POPULATIONS AND SAMPLING

When NAEP started in 1969, it defined its populations as all youth in the United States who were 9-, 13-, and 17-years-old and also young adults. Private and parochial school students were considered part of the populations. Age, rather than grade, was chosen to define populations because age has the same meaning in all states; whereas the meaning of grade might differ from state to state because of differences in the age of entry to school or because of school retention policies. Students 9- and 13-years-old could be readily found in school classrooms, but 17-year-olds were more difficult to assess, since although many were in school, substantial numbers had already left. Young adults, of course, generally were not in school. Due to the extreme costs of assessment, regular assessment of the young adult population was dropped in 1974 and the out-of-school 17-year-old population was dropped in 1980.

As NAEP developed over the years, it reconsidered its decision to sample age populations instead of grade populations. Although age was more clearly defined, grade was more important in educational decision making since school policies are generally made by grades. For this reason, NAEP extended its population definitions to include students in the grades most commonly attended by the 9-, 13-, and 17-year-old students. The NAEP populations were changed to students who were 9-years-old *or* in the 4th grade, students who were 13-years-old *or* in the 8th grade, and students who were 17-years-old *or* in the 12th grade. From the NAEP data, population estimates can be made either for 9-year-olds or 4th graders, 13-year-olds or 8th graders, or in-school 17-year-olds or 12th graders.

In 1990, NAEP began, on a trial basis, the assessment of student populations in individual states. This innovation led to simpler population definitions for state samples; that is, state populations were defined as 4th, 8th, and 12th graders without concern for their age. The schools subjects and grade levels in the trial state assessments are determined by the National Assessment Governing Board (NAGB). These state data have been used to compare the performance of students in various states and territories. The state assessments are done voluntarily; that is, each state or territory may choose to participate or not.

The sampling of students from these populations is extremely important, since a poor sample would affect the quality of NAEP results. To assure appropriate national samples, the entire United States is divided into primary sampling units (PSUs), which generally correspond to Census Bureau Metropolitan Statistics Areas or counties. A number of these PSUs are sampled, and an exhaustive list of all public and private schools is prepared and checked for these PSUs. Schools are randomly selected with probability proportional to size. Private schools and schools with large minority populations are oversampled to assure the precision of estimates. Within each school, a list of students is prepared who are in either an appropriate grade or at an appropriate age. A sample of these students is selected for assessment.

The changes in the population definitions over time has posed a challenge for the estimation of the trends in student performance. To maintain continuity, a separate national sample is selected using the original population definitions, and these students are assessed in reading, mathematics, and science using the same time limits and procedures as in the earlier assessments. These samples are used to estimate the long-term trends in student performance.

The sampling for states is somewhat simpler. A list of all schools in the state is prepared and schools are selected with probability proportional to

TABLE I
NAEP Subject Area Coverage

Year	Subject areas (grades in parentheses)
National Samples	
1970	Science, Citizenship, Writing
1971	Reading, Literature
1972	Music, Social Studies
1973	Science, Mathematics
1974	Career and Occupational Development, Writing
1975	Reading, Art, Index of Basic Skills
1976	Citizenship/Social Studies, Mathematics
1977	Science, Reading, Health
1978	Mathematics, Consumer Skills
1979	Writing, Art, Music
1980	Reading/Literature, Art
1982	Science, Mathematics, Citizenship/Social Studies
1984	Reading, Writing
1985	Adult Literacy
1986	Reading, Mathematics, Science, Computer Competence
	U.S. History, Literature
1988	Reading, Writing, Civics, U.S. History, Geography
	Document Literacy
1990	Reading, Writing, Mathematics, Science
1992	Reading, Writing, Mathematics, Science
1994	Reading, Writing, Mathematics, Science
	U.S. History, Geography
State Samples	
1990	Mathematics (8)
1992	Mathematics (4,8), Reading (4)
1994	Reading (4)

Note. Only the last part of the academic year is presented. Thus, 1970 should be read as 1969–1970.

size. Within each school, all students at the appropriate grade levels are listed and a random sample is selected without replacement. These students are administered the NAEP assessment instruments.

The details of the sampling in NAEP are described by Rust (1992) and Rust and Johnson (1992). More detailed information about sampling is given in Kish (1965) and Frankel (1983).

SUBJECT COVERAGE AND ASSESSMENT INSTRUMENT DEVELOPMENT

Over the years, NAEP has assessed many subject areas; foremost have been the basics—reading, writing, mathematics, and science—but NAEP has also assessed such diverse subject areas as citizenship, civics, art, music, history, and geography (see Table 1 for a list of all subject areas). The subjects to be assessed are determined by the National Assessment Governing Board within the constraints of the NAEP enabling legislation and the available funding.

Assessment development involves a consensus process (Foertsch, Jones, & Koeffler, 1992; Mullis, 1992). An Assessment Development Committee of teachers and subject matter experts in a particular subject area is appointed and then given the task of accepting existing specification, modifying them, or developing new specifications for an assessment. The result of this is an assessment grid that specifies the topics that will be covered and the way that they will be assessed. Professional item writers prepare more than enough items to fill the grid. The items are pretested on a large sample of students before the final items are selected. The Assessment Development Committee and the NAGB approve of the final version of the assessment.

This process leads to a broad coverage of each subject area and many different types of items. NAEP has some multiple-choice items but also has many open-ended items and items that require extended response by the students. NAEP has also experimented recently with hands-on performance assessments. The collection of items for a subject area in any assessment is quite large, larger than NAEP is willing to ask any student to do.

In addition to subject matter items to measure student proficiency, there are also questionnaires for the students, some of their teachers, and their school principals. The student questionnaires are short, taking around 10 minutes to complete, and contain questions about a student's background and attitudes to the subject area being assessed. The teacher questionnaire asks about the teacher's background and teaching methods. The school principal questionnaire asks about the school's neighborhood and its facilities.

NAEP has had to balance its need for information against the cost of the interruption of a student's workday. If NAEP asks for too much student time, schools and students may refuse to participate, thus introducing an unknown bias into NAEP estimates. NAEP attempts to keep an individual student's time to about one hour to avoid refusals. However, one hour of assessment time is not sufficient for a student to answer all of the items that are necessary for the broad coverage of the subject area. To keep the assessment time short and still cover the subject area, NAEP has introduced balance incomplete block (BIB) spiraling.

BIB spiraling is a method of assigning items to booklets in such a way that each item is administered to a reasonably large probability sample of students and each pair of items is also administered to a somewhat smaller sample of students. The need for a large sample of students to respond to each item is obvious: NAEP wants a reliable estimate of how the population of students would do on each item. The need for the pairing of items is more subtle: NAEP wants to be able to estimate the correlation coefficients among all the items to study the dimensionality of the subject area. If a subject area has only one dimension, then only one index is necessary to describe the population's proficiency; if the subject area is multidimensional, then more that one indicator is necessary.

BIB spirally works by dividing the item pool into blocks that are assigned the same amount of time to complete. In NAEP, the blocks are usually assigned about 15 minutes. These blocks are then assigned to booklets using a balanced incomplete block design. For example, let us assume that the item pool consists of 1 hour and 45 minutes of questions; this pool can be divided into seven blocks, each of which is rated at 15 minutes. We will number these blocks 1 to 7. Seven booklets, each containing three blocks, can then be assembled as follows:

	Block A	Block B	Block C
Booklet 1	1	2	4
Booklet 2	2	3	5
Booklet 3	3	4	6
Booklet 4	4	5	7
Booklet 5	5	6	1
Booklet 6	6	7	2
Booklet 7	7	1	3

Note that each block occurs in three booklets: once in the first block, A; once in the second, B; and once in the third, C. Note also, each pair of blocks occurs in one, and only one, booklet. For example, blocks 4 and 6 are both in Booklet 3. The spiraling is accomplished by sorting the booklets into a random sequence.

Using BIB spiraling, therefore, each sampled student receives a booklet at random, containing a part of the item pool. Any student may receive an "easy" or "hard" booklet, depending on how the items were assigned to blocks and the luck of the draw. However, over all students, not only are all items administered but all pairs of items are administered to a probability sample of students.

Detailed information on the assessment instruments is given by Kline (1992).

FIELD ADMINISTRATION

The field administration of the national NAEP is a complex operation. Before the assessment begins, it is important to attain the permission and support of the educational administrators. This is done using a top-down approach in which the chief state school officer is approached, then the district superintendent, and the school principal. Each must agree to allow the assessment to proceed. The students also have the opportunity to refuse to participate but seldom do.

After a school agrees to participate in the national sample, a trained assessment administrator meets with the school to develop a list of eligible students and to sample from that list. The selected students are administered the assessment in a separate room by the trained administrators to minimize the disruption of other school activities and to assure uniform timing and assessment procedures.

In state assessments, the state school system provides the assessment administrators, who are carefully trained by NAEP central staff. To assure uniform assessment conditions, a substantial sample of schools are visited by quality control monitors on the day of assessment to evaluate the correspondence of the assessment procedures to NAEP rules.

The field administration in NAEP is described in Caldwell, Slobasky, Moore, and Ter Maat (1992).

SCORING THE NAEP EXERCISES

A NAEP administration now generates millions of open-ended and extended response items that must be scored by trained individuals. Scoring may be simply right or wrong or may be on a graded scale. This scoring is done centrally, item by item, with carefully trained graders. Quality control checks are made regularly to assure the reliability of the scoring. NAEP's scoring procedures are described in Latham (1994).

THE NAEP DATABASE

All of the NAEP data are collected into a database (Rogers, Freund, & Ferris, 1992). The different age and grade combinations are kept separate. The database includes sampling information; sampling weights; data from the principal, teacher, and student questionnaires; and the student responses to subject matter questions. The sampling weights are necessary in making population estimates, since some subpopulations are oversampled, and also to adjust for nonresponse. Some derived variables are added to the database, such as parents' education, which is derived from separate questions about the students mother's and father's education. As will be discussed, student "plausible values" will be added to the database.

SCALING

As stated already, the aim of NAEP is to report the proficiency of populations and subpopulations of students and trends in their proficiencies to the policy makers and the public. The question here is how is this done, given the complex database just described with students being administered different items. The earliest NAEP assessments published population estimates for many individual items, but this method failed because there was too much information for the reader to examine and evaluate. Publishing individual items also made it difficult to measure trends in proficiency, which requires that items be kept secure. Another method of summarizing the data was necessary.

The answer to data summarization came from extensions of item response theory (IRT). Item response theory is a way of estimating a student's proficiency from a set of item responses. Basically, IRT takes advantage of regularities in the data; that is, easy items are answered correctly by almost everybody and hard items answered by only a few students with high proficiency. Low-proficiency students will very seldom be able to answer a difficult item correctly. Middle-level students will answer easy and middle-difficulty items correctly but seldom answer the difficult items correctly. Using this regularity in the data, item response theory can describe the properties or parameters of items; NAEP uses the three-parameter logistic model (Wingersky, 1983; Wingersky, Barton, & Lord, 1982), which describes items in terms of difficulty, the item's ability to discriminate between high- and low-proficiency students, and a guessing parameter for multiple-choice items.

The regularity in the data will vary depending on the data's dimensionality. For example, the NAEP mathematics assessment has five subscales (number and operations, measurement, geometry, data analysis and statistics, and algebra and functions), which are estimated for publication. It is important that each subscale be unidimensional; that is, behave in a regular manner as described previously. Educational data are never perfectly unidimensional, especially with multiple-choice items, where there often a few low-scoring students will get difficult items correct by chance. NAEP routinely examines each item to assure that it is contributing to its IRT scale.

With the item parameters estimated, it is usually possible to estimate a scale or subscale value for each student. For NAEP, this is problematic. For each subscale in NAEP, students will vary in the number of items administered, and some student may be administered very few items for a subscale such as algebra. In this case, the student's proficiency will be unreliably estimated and, perhaps, not estimable at all. If the item parameters of the three-parameter logistic model are estimated using maximum likelihood methods, the usual procedure, then students who get all items correct or score below the chance level will not receive finite proficiency estimates. Using poorly estimated proficiency values would result in poorly estimated proficiency distributions, which would frustrate NAEP's aims. Clearly, these student proficiency estimates would not be satisfactory for individual student reporting or decision making.

Instead of making estimates of an individual student's proficiency (called *point estimates*), NAEP estimates a distribution of reasonable estimates for an individual's proficiency, which are called *plausible values*. The estimation procedure faces up to the fact that the data cannot specify an individual's proficiently accurately and so gives the probability of each possible proficiency value actually happening. In statistical terms, this is the posterior distribution for an individual's proficiency given the individual's item responses and other collateral data. NAEP then represents an individual by taking a random sample from that individual's posterior distribution. Typically, NAEP draws five plausible values at random for each individual.

Note that NAEP uses more than the item response data in developing the plausible values. The use of collateral data comes from missing data theory (Rubin, 1987; Rubin & Schneker, 1986). The idea is as follows: basically, the student's actual proficiency and how the student would have done on the items that were not administered are considered missing data. To infer the value of the missing data, one should use all the data available. The best available estimate is made from knowledge of what a student did on the items that were administered and what other similar students did on the missing information. Using collateral information about a student in making proficiency estimates is known as *conditioning*.

At the end of the scaling process (Beaton & Johnson, 1992; Mislevy, 1987, 1992; Mislevy, Beaton, Kaplan, & Sheehan, 1992; Mislevy, Johnson, & Muraki, 1992; Mislevy & Sheehan, 1987, 1989), NAEP is left with five plausible values for each student on each scale or subscale. One plausible value for a student is as good as another; the only difference is the random number used in selection. If the five plausible values are close together, then one may infer that the proficiency is measured fairly accurately; if the plausible values are quite different, the measurement is inaccurate. The plausible values encompass not only probable values for the estimation of proficiency but also the amount of error in the estimation.

It can be shown that using these plausible values produces consistent estimates of population parameters, which is what NAEP is aiming for. By *consistent*, we mean here that the sample estimates will approach the population values as the sample size grows without limit. Using plausible values requires some extra work in data analysis but produces consistent parameter estimates and also estimates of their accuracy. For more information about using plausible values, see Beaton and Gonzalez (1995).

As mentioned earlier, NAEP estimates plausible values for each of the several subscales in a subject matter area. NAEP uses a weighted average of subscale plausible values to create overall plausible values for subject areas such as mathematics.

INTERPRETING NAEP SCALES

The scores of most standardized tests are interpreted by norm referencing; that is, by comparing the performance of a student to that of other students, using percentiles or other such statistics. NAEP has tried to avoid this interpretation by scale anchoring and standard setting (Beaton & Allen, 1992).

First, NAEP has arbitrarily decided to place its population distributions on a scale that runs from 0 to 500 on the first year of an assessment and then let the distribution rise or fall depending on the progress or regress of student proficiency. This choice leads to a theoretical interpretation of a NAEP scale. Let us assume that we could make a ideal test with the following properties: the test had 500 items and the difficulty of the items were spread evenly across the ability levels of the students. All of the items have high and equal discrimination, and there is no opportunity for guessing. This test would fit the assumptions of the Rasch model. The plausible values would then be estimates of the number of items that a student would get correctly on this ideal test.

By construction, most students score within the range 100–400 on the NAEP scales. It behooves us to try to state what students know and can do at certain points on the scale. To this end, NAEP has selected several "anchor" points and tried to do just this. These anchor points usually have been selected at 200, 250, 300, and 350. Using several methods of anchoring, NAEP locates a group of items that students at an anchor level can probably answer and that a student at the next lower level cannot. These groups of items have been interpreted by subject matter experts to form general statements about what students know and can do at the selected scale points.

More recently, NAEP has experimented with standard setting for NAEP results. This has been approached by having expert panels review the NAEP items and estimate the proportion of students at the basic, proficient, and advanced levels of proficiency who should be able to answer the items correctly. These item decisions have been converted into points on the NAEP scale that represent basic, proficient, and advanced levels of achievement.

The scaling and analysis of NAEP data are described separately by subject area; for example, reading (Donoghue, 1992), mathematics (Yamamoto & Jenkins, 1992), and science (Allen, 1992). Writing (Grima & Johnson, 1992) has used a different method of scaling, called the *average response method* (Beaton & Johnson (1990).

MAKING THE POPULATION ESTIMATES

The student plausible values can be used to make estimates of population parameters and distributions in ways similar to ordinary test scores but with some distinct differences. A single plausible value can be used to estimate a population parameter but another plausible value will make a somewhat different estimate. With plausible values, the proper way is to estimate that population parameter separately using each plausible value and then average the results of the five estimates.

Estimating the accuracy of the parameter estimates requires consideration of the sampling error, the measurement error, and their combination
(Johnson and Rust, 1992a, 1992b; Mislevy, Beaton et al., 1992). As for sampling error, NAEP does not have simple random samples; as already noted,
NAEP uses a multistage sampling procedure, sampling PSUs, schools, and
students. For this reason, the standard errors computed in most statistical
systems, which assume simple random sampling, are inappropriate. Instead,
NAEP uses the jackknife method (see Beaton & Gonzalez, 1995, for examples
of using the jackknife method with NAEP data).

The measurement error is characterized by the differences between the
parameter estimates made from different plausible values. It is possible to
compute the variance of these estimates. Mislevy, Beaton et al. (1992) have
given a formula for combining the variance of the parameter estimates with
the sampling error to produce an estimate of the total error in a population
estimate.

REPORTING

Reporting is the last step, where NAEP fulfills its aim of informing policy
makers and the public. As we have seen, NAEP includes a substantial
amount of innovative and complex technology. Fortunately, this technology
contributes to NAEP's ability to produce readable, informative reports that
include not only the required population estimates but also estimates of the
accuracy of its results.

NAEP reports are typically written by a few persons who have subject
matter expertise and knowledge about the important policy issues that the
NAEP data can address. They are involved from the beginning, including the
design of the assessment instruments and the administration of the survey.
They review the NAEP output, often asking for additional information from
the database. The statistical significance of reported results is of major concern. Special care is taken to avoid misinterpretation of results by policy
makers and the public.

Each draft manuscript is carefully reviewed by editors, subject matter experts, and statisticians to assure that the writing is clear, the issues discussed are relevant, and that the statistical limitations of the results are
addressed. The final result is another "nation's report card."

It is important to realize that NAEP also produces reports for more specific
audiences including teachers, subject matter experts, and testing specialists.

References

Allen, N. L. (1992). Data analysis for the science assessment. In E. G. Johnson & N. Allen (Eds.),
    The NAEP 1990 Technical Report (Report No. 21-TR-20, pp. 275–287). Princeton, NJ: Educational
    Testing Service.

Allen, N. L., & Zwick, R. (1992). Overview of Part II: The analysis of 1990 NAEP data. In E. G. Johnson & N. Allen (Eds.), The NAEP 1990 Technical Report (Report No. 21-TR-20, pp. 143–157). Princeton, NJ: Educational Testing Service.

Beaton, A. E. (Ed.), (1987). The NAEP 1983–1984 Technical Report (Report No. 15-TR-20). Princeton, NJ: Educational Testing Service.

Beaton, A. E. (Ed.) (1988). Expanding the new design. In The NAEP 1985–1986 Technical Report (Report No. 17-TR-20). Princeton, NJ: Educational Testing Service.

Beaton, A. E., & Allen, N. L. (1992). Interpreting scales through scale anchoring. Journal of Educational Statistics, 17(2), 191–204.

Beaton, A. E., and Gonzalez, E. (1995). NAEP Primer. Chestnut Hill, MA: Boston College Center for the Study of Testing, Evaluation, and Educational Policy.

Beaton, A. E., & Johnson, E. G. (1990). The average response method of scaling. Journal of Educational Statistics, 15(1), 9–38.

Beaton, A. E., & Johnson, E. G. (1992). Overview of the scaling methodology used in the national assessment. Journal of Educational Measurement, 29(2), 163–176.

Beaton, A. E., & Zwick, R. (1992). Overview of the national assessment of educational progress. Journal of Educational Statistics, 17(2), 95–109.

Caldwell, N., Slobasky, R., Moore, D., & Ter Maat, J. (1992). Field operations and data collection. In E. G. Johnson & N. L. Allen (Eds.), The NAEP 1990 Technical Report (Report No. 21-TR-20, pp. 89–106). Princeton, NJ: Educational Testing Service.

Donoghue, J. R. (1992). Data analysis for the reading assessment. In E. G. Johnson & N. Allen (Eds.), The NAEP 1990 Technical Report (Report No. 21-TR-20, pp. 215–225). Princeton, NJ: Educational Testing Service.

Foertsch, M. A., Jones, L. R., & Koffler, S. L. (1992). Developing the NAEP objectives, items, and background questions for the 1990 assessments of reading, mathematics, and science. In E. G. Johnson & N. Allen (Eds.), The NAEP 1990 Technical Report (Report No. 21-TR-20, pp. 29–49). Princeton, NJ: Education Testing Service.

Frankel, M. (1983). Sampling theory. In P. H. Rossi, J. D. Wright, & A. Anderson (Eds.), Handbook of survey research. San Diego, CA: Academic Press.

Grima, A. W., & Johnson, E. G. (1992). Data analysis for the writing assessment. In E. G. Johnson and N. Allen (Eds.), The NAEP 1990 Technical Report (Report No. 21-TR-20, pp. 303–321). Princeton, NJ: Education Testing Service.

Johnson, E. G. (1992a). Overview of Part I: The design and implementation of the 1990 NAEP. In E. G. Johnson and N. Allen (Eds.), The NAEP 1990 Technical Report (Report No. 21-TR-20, pp. 9–28). Princeton, NJ: Educational Testing Service.

Johnson, E. G. (1992b). The design of the national assessment of educational progress. Journal of Educational Measurement, 29(2), 95–110.

Johnson, E. G., & Allen, N. (Eds.), (1992). The NAEP 1990 Technical Report (Report No. 21-TR-20, pp. 115–126). Princeton, NJ: Educational Testing Service.

Johnson, E. G., & Carlson (Eds.). (1994). The NAEP 1992 Technical Report (Report No. 23-TR-20). Washington, DC: U.S. Dept. of Education.

Johnson, E. G., & Rust, K. F. (1992a). Population inferences and variance estimation for NAEP data. Journal of Educational Statistics, 17(2), 175–190.

Johnson, E. G., & Rust, K. F. (1992b). Weighting procedures and estimation of sampling variance. In E. G. Johnson & N. Allen (Eds.), The NAEP 1990 Technical Report (Report No. 21-TR-20, pp. 159–193). Princeton, NJ: Educational Testing Service.

Kish, L. (1965). Survey sampling. New York: Wiley

Kline, D. L. (1992). Assessment instruments. In E. G. Johnson & N. Allen (Eds.), The NAEP 1990 Technical Report (Report No. 21-TR-20, pp. 71–88). Princeton, NJ: Education Testing Service.

Latham, A. S. (1994). Professional scoring. In E. G. Johnson and Carlson (Eds.), The NAEP 1992 Technical Report (Report No. 23-TR-20). Washington, DC: U.S. Dept. of Education.

Lord, F. M. (1980). *Applications of Item Response Theory to Practical Testing Problems.* Hillsdale, NJ: Erlbaum.

Messick, S. J., Beaton, A. E., & Lord, F. M. (1983). *NAEP reconsidered: A new design for a new era* (NAEP Report No. 83-1). Princeton, NJ: Educational Testing Service.

Mislevy, R. J. (1987). The reading data analysis: Introduction. In A. E. Beaton (Ed.), *The NAEP 1983–1984 Technical Report* (Report No. 15-TR-20, pp. 239–244). Princeton, NJ: Educational Testing Service.

Mislevy, R. J. (1992). Scaling procedures. In E. G. Johnson & N. Allen (Eds.), *The NAEP 1990 Technical Report* (Report No. 21-TR-20, pp. 199–213). Princeton, NJ: Education Testing Service.

Mislevy, R. J., Beaton, A. E., Kaplan, B., & Sheehan, K. M. (1992). Estimating population characteristics from sparse matrix samples of item responses. *Journal of Educational Measurement,* 29(2), 133–162.

Mislevy, R. J., Johnson, E. G., & Muraki, E. (1992). Scaling procedures in NAEP. *Journal of Educational Statistics,* 17(2), 131–154.

Mislevy, R. J., & Sheehan, K. M. (1987). Marginal estimation procedures. In A. E. Beaton (Ed.), *The NAEP 1983–1984 Technical Report* (Report No. 15-TR-20, pp. 293–360). Princeton, NJ: Educational Testing Service.

Mislevy, R. J., & Sheehan, K. M. (1989). Information matrices in latent-variable models. *Journal of Educational Statistics,* 14(4), 335–350.

Mullis, I. V. (1992). Developing the NAEP content area frameworks and innovative assessment methods in the 1992 assessments of mathematics, reading and writing. *Journal of Educational Measurement,* 29(2), 111–132.

Rogers, A. M., Freund, D. S., & Ferris, J. J. (1992). Database creation quality control of data entry and database products. In E. G. Johnson & N. Allen (Eds.), *The NAEP 1990 Technical Report* (Report No. 21-TR-20, pp. 127–133). Princeton, NJ: Educational Testing Service.

Rogers, A. M., Kline, D. L., Johnson, E. G., Mislevy, R. M., & Rust, K. F. (1990). *National Assessment of Educational Progress 1988 public-use data tapes version 2.0 user guide.* Princeton, NJ: Educational Testing Service, National Assessment of Educational Progress.

Rogers, A. M., Kline, D. L., Johnson, E. G., Mislevy, R. M., & Rust, K. F. (1992). *National Assessment of Educational Progress 1990 public-use data tapes version 2.0 user guide.* Princeton, NJ: Educational Testing Service, National Assessment of Educational Progress.

Rubin, D. B. (1987). *Multiple imputations for non response in surveys.* New York: Wiley.

Rubin, D. B., & Schneker, N. (1986). Multiple imputation for interval estimation from simple random samples with ignorable non response. *Journal of the American Statistical Association,* 81, 366–374.

Rust, K. F. (1992). Sample Design. In E. G. Johnson & N. Allen (Eds.), *The NAEP 1990 Technical Report* (Report No. 21-TR-20, pp. 51–68). Princeton, NJ: Educational Testing Service.

Rust, K. F., & Johnson, E. G. (1992). Sampling and weighting in the national assessment. *Journal of Educational Statistics,* 17(2), 111–130.

Wingersky, M. S. (1983). LOGIST: A program for computing maximum likelihood procedures for logistic test models. In R. K. Hambleton (Ed.), *Applications of item response theory* (pp. 45–56). Vancouver, Canada: Educational Research Institute of British Columbia.

Wingersky, M. S., Barton, M. A., & Lord, F. M. (1982). *LOGIST user's guide.* Princeton, NJ: Educational Testing Service.

Yamamoto, K., & Jenkins, F. (1992). Data analysis for the mathematics assessment. In E. G. Johnson & N. Allen (Eds.), *The NAEP 1990 Technical Report* (Report No. 21-TR-20, pp. 243–256). Princeton, NJ: Educational Testing Service.

CHAPTER

18

Epilogue: Classroom Assessment—Looking Forward

GARY D. PHYE

Iowa State University

INTRODUCTION

When talking with teachers, I am often asked *why* there is such an increased emphasis on classroom assessment. This question is often immediately followed by the comment that assessment takes away from "learning time." At this point, if I can get a word in edgewise, my response is "How do you know that learning is occurring?" This question has served as the impetus for a renewed interest in teacher-developed assessment activities. Academic learning is unique in that each subject area has a formal knowledge base. Outside the classroom, to be successful, one needs both formal knowledge that is classroom situated and informal knowledge that is not situated in the schools. The learning of a formal knowledge base is frequently referred to as the *schooling process*. In today's technological society, a formal knowledge base, loosely defined as content literacy, is a critical tool for successfully coping with a changing environment. Consequently, as teachers, *what* we are being held accountable for is fostering the learning of academic knowledge.

Classroom learning (Phye, 1986), involves a change in a student's knowledge base as a result of classroom instruction. Learning is the process responsible for the observed changes. Change can be determined only if there are a minimum of two assessment points (at the beginning and end of instruction). Ideally, assessments that fall between these two points will monitor the learning process. Having identified change as a central characteristic of any definition of learning, a second critical characteristic must also be considered: "permanence of change" or what may be called the *maintenance of learning*. Consequently, any definition of classroom learning must articulate these two characteristics. Phrased differently, classroom learning and retention are not two separate processes. Classroom learning can be demonstrated only when information being processed has been retained. In the classroom, this means that instructional objectives and assessment objectives must be integrated in a manner consistent with the curriculum goals identified by the school.

This is not a radical view of classroom assessment. Rather it reflects the overall view of individuals who have contributed chapters. The overall view of classroom assessment taken in this volume is but a reflection of emerging standards for classroom assessment that are being developed and refined. These standards are a work in progress, not a finalized template for classroom assessment. However, a formal attempt to establish *national* standards for classroom assessment systems has been undertaken by the National Forum on Assessment. Because it is timely and because the basic theme proposed is consistent with the views expressed in this handbook, a brief review follows.

PRINCIPLES FOR ASSESSMENT

The National Forum is cochaired by Monty Neill of Fair Test and Ruth Mitchell of the RAND Corporation (Gong, 1995). The principles consist of statements highlighting what the National Forum views as critical elements of a system designed to assess student progress. These principles are couched in terms of elements for a fair (reliable and valid) assessment system. Thus, each principle introduces an issue that must be addressed when evaluating a student assessment system at the school or school district level.

1. The primary purpose of assessment is to improve student learning. Classroom assessment is organized around the primary purpose of improving student learning and therefore employs methods consistent with learning goals, curriculum, instruction, and current knowledge of how students learn.

2. Assessment for other purposes support student learning. This principle applies at both ends of the continuum of assessment, either high-stakes assessment or individual student placement. In other words, the assessment system should not use one criterion for school accountability and improvement, a second criterion for special needs placement, and a third criterion for parent–teacher conferences. Regardless of the question being addressed, the various criteria must in some way reflect or support student learning. This principle provides the basis for an integrated assessment system at a school site.

3. Assessment systems are fair to all students. This principle identifies those elements of an assessment system that must be monitored to provide all students with optimum opportunities for learning. These elements include assessment policies, assessment practices, assessment instruments, and uses of assessment information. Principle 3 is met when assessment results accurately reflect a student's actual knowledge, understanding, and achievement.

4. Professional collaboration and development improves assessment practices. The system is no better than the teachers and other professionals that develop, maintain, and operate the assessment system. Thus, teacher educators are the key to making the assessment system a successful element in the schooling process. Given the information provided by Plake and Impara in Chapter 3, school districts and state organizations must provide resources (both time and money) for staff development. Staff development must involve substantive opportunities for collaborative professional development that includes discussions of assessment, actual student work, and the integration of instructional and assessment objectives to attain curriculum goals.

5. The broad community participates in assessment development. The definition of *community* is critical to the success of this principle. In a physical sense, this includes the teacher educators, parents, students and school district personnel that are viewed as stake holders at the school district level. In a professional sense, the educational community includes local teacher educators, state educational professionals, and educational experts typically located at universities, educational research and development centers, or private organizations devoted to educational consulting.

6. Communication about assessment is regular and clear. Assessment practices and standards for success must be periodically communicated in a manner appropriate for student, family, and community consumption. The communication process must include means and opportunities for public response and dialogue. This principle also includes the opportunity for feedback to parents and students, using examples to show how high-quality performance and local students' work are alike and how they are different.

7. Assessment systems at any level must be open to ongoing, systematic review and improvement. This last principle simply recognizes the complexity involved with meeting principles 1 through 6. In other words, because of elements such as shifting student populations, modified curriculums and goals, new assessment activities, and the like, the development of an assessment system is an ongoing "work in progress." An assessment system cannot be developed and then remain unchanged when the curriculum, instructional techniques and our current knowledge of how students learn is in a state of flux.

PROFESSIONAL COLLABORATION
AND DEVELOPMENT

This handbook of classroom assessment was developed with the goal of enhancing collaboration and communication among all professionals within the educational community. In too many instances, professionals functioning in the schools are not in direct communication with professionals developing policy and educational practices that affect the daily classroom practices of learning, instruction, and assessment. This handbook, along with other handbooks in the Educational Psychology Book Series, is being developed to serve this purpose. Communication among theorists has its place, as does communication among teacher educators. However, when the lines of communication become rigid and theory no longer provides guidance for practice and practice no longer influences theory development, everyone suffers. This includes not only the professional educator but the students who are the beneficiaries of our combined efforts. To many of us in the education profession, this is what makes our profession unique. Without practice (classroom teaching), there is no need for theory. Without theory, classroom practices become stagnant and nonproductive as measured in terms of our primary objective, the improvement of student learning.

Many of us are involved with the development of activities and techniques in addition to theoretical models. This combination of endeavors characterizes the chapter authors contributing to this volume. Consequently, they are valuable resources to be drawn on for professional development activities involving classroom assessment and student learning.

An epilogue is defined in my *Webster's Second International* (1984) *Dictionary* as "a short concluding section at the end of a literary work, often discussing the future of its characters." Having already discussed their views of future directions for classroom assessment practices and activities, I want to introduce you to the *main* characters responsible for individual chapters. Each has voiced his or her view of theory and practice as it relates to specific areas of student assessment. The following sketch is provided to further identify areas of expertise that can be drawn on for collaborative efforts and professional staff development activities.

MEET THE AUTHORS

Gregory J. Cizek is associate professor of educational research and measurement at the University of Toledo. His interests include standard setting, assessment formats, and home education. Currently, he applies his research interests and experience assisting with national projects such as the National Assessment of Educational Progress and various licensure and certification programs. He also collaborates with various state-level testing programs, works to implement district-level planned assessment systems, and helps home schooling families assess the educational progress of their students.

Barbara S. Plake is the W.C. Meirhenery Distinguished Professor and director of the Oscar and Luella Buros Center for Testing at the University of Nebraska. She has served as president of the National Council on Measurement in Education and the Midwest Educational Research Association. Barbara has consulted with numerous school districts in Nebraska, the Missouri Department of Education, and served on the technical advisory board for the National Board of Professional Teacher Standards. She is cofounder and coeditor of *Applied Measurement in Education*. In her spare time, she has written over 90 articles, published in nationally refereed journals and several books and book chapters.

Robert C. Calfee is a cognitive psychologist with research interests in the effects of schooling on the intellectual potential of individuals and groups. He earned his degrees at UCLA, did post-graduate work at Stanford, and spent five years in Psychology at the University of Wisconsin, Madison. In 1969, he returned to Stanford University to join the School of Education, where he is presently a professor in the committee on Language, Literacy, and Culture and the committee on Psychological Studies.

Bob's interests have evolved over the past two decades from a focus on assessment of beginning literacy skills to a concern with the broader reach of the school as a literate environment. His theoretical efforts are directed toward the nature of human thought processes and the influence of language and literacy in the development of problem solving and communication. Research activities include Project READ, The Inquiring School, The Text Analysis Project, and Methods of Alternative Assessment. These projects all combine theoretical and practical facets directed toward understanding and facilitating school change. He has also written critical papers in recent years on the effects of testing and educational indicators, ability grouping, teacher assessment, and the psychology of reading. Bob is a former editor of the *Journal of Educational Psychology*, current editor of the journal *Educational Assessment*, and has recently coedited the *Handbook of Research in Educational Psychology*.

Edys Ouellmalz is a senior educational researcher in the Center for Technology in Learning at SRI International. She served as the key consultant on the design and evaluation of the Multicultural Reading and Thinking Project and worked with schools and districts in California to design higher-order thinking projects. Edys has had over 25 years of experience in project leadership and the design of assessment systems. She directed SRI's project for NSF to enhance the quality of the third International Mathematics and Science Study. As director of the RMC Research California Office, she supervised evaluation and research projects and also directed a Chapter 1 Technical

Assistance Center that provided technical assistance to nine Western states in the areas of assessment, evaluation, advanced skills, and program improvement. Over the past 15 years, she has consulted extensively with state departments of education in Arkansas, California, Colorado, Connecticut, Delaware, Illinois, and Maryland on their statewide assessment programs. Edys has been a faculty member at Stanford University's School of Education, UCLA's Center for the Study of Evaluation, and has taught English and social studies at the junior high school level. She is former associate editor of the *Journal of Educational Psychology* and is currently on the Advisory Board of *Educational Assessment*. She has numerous publications on assessment and is frequently an invited speaker on the topic.

Herbert Marsh is professor of education and acting pro vice chancellor of research at the University of Western Sydney Macarthur in Campbelltown, Australia. Herb is one of the foremost authorities in the world on the development of academic self-concept. In addition to being one of the most prolific writers for research journals, Herb has been at the forefront in maintaining that self-concept cannot be adequately understood if its multidimensional, domain-specific nature is ignored. This position, which is backed up by extensive research data based on intervention studies, must be acknowledged by the educational establishment in the United States. Marsh's systematic, internationally based research findings must be acknowledged by educators proposing programs in the schools aimed at the enhancement of self-esteem or general self-concept. At a time when many educators and psychologists are questioning the self-esteem programs found in many schools, Marsh's approach provides valuable insight into the assessment of affective and motivational variables loosely aggregated under the rubric of self-concept.

Timothy Bender is professor of psychology at Southwest Missouri State University. Tim is heavily involved with the preparation of teachers seeking certification in middle school or secondary education. Tim's research interests include students' use of classroom exam feedback, subjective well-being in children, and computer applications in college instruction. He has written in the areas of student use of feedback and is currently initiating a research program focusing on "subjective well-being." In addition to being active in national and regional professional organizations, Tim is heavily involved in local educational service activities.

Cheryl E Sanders obtained her Ph.D. in developmental psychology from Iowa State University. She currently teaches child development courses at Metropolitan State University and has taught in the Child Development Department at the University of Colorado. Cheryl's research interests include moral reasoning development of gifted children and the training of inductive reasoning and problem-solving skills. She has also written in the area of problem solving and transfer with college-age students.

Tim Ansley is associate professor of educational measurement and statistics at the University of Iowa. He codirects the Iowa High School Testing

Program and is director of the Iowa Algebra Testing Program. Tim is a former high school mathematics teacher. Contact with the public schools is maintained through workshops, where he provides teachers, counselors, and administrators with information on the interpretation and use of standardized test scores. He also provides, on a regular basis, staff development workshops on testing and grading. Tim has authored or coauthored numerous articles related to educational measurement in addition to coauthoring several standardized aptitude and achievement tests. Tim's current professional interests are in the valid measurement of student achievement, particularly achievement in mathematics problem solving.

Frank Lester holds the rank of professor of mathematics education in the School of Education at Indiana University—Bloomington. He joined the faculty in 1972, immediately following the completion of a Ph.D. in mathematics education at the Ohio State University. Since 1992, he has been the editor of the *Journal for Research in Mathematics Education*. Frank has been a Fulbright Fellow and lectured widely in Europe, South America, and the United States on mathematical problem solving, alternative assessment, and research in mathematics education. His primary research interests lie in the areas of mathematical problem solving and meta-cognition, especially with respect to problem-solving instruction at the elementary and middle school levels. Frank is responsible for the development of research-based instructional materials for grades 1–8 that emphasized mathematical problem solving several years prior to the development of the widely acclaimed Curriculum and Evaluation Standards of the National Council of Teachers of Mathematics. He is currently involved with two National Science Foundation projects, one on mathematical modeling in secondary mathematics and the other addressing university mathematics experiences of prospective elementary teachers.

Janet Alleman is a professor in the department of teacher education at Michigan State University. She is author and coauthor of a range of publications including an elementary social studies textbook series, a social studies methods text, and numerous journal articles. Janet has been a contributor to the Stanford Achievement Tests and a consultant to the Educational Testing Service. She has served as the chair for the National Council for the Social Studies Testing Committee and currently is a member of the NCSS Committee for advanced certification of social studies teachers. Janet's most recent publication is a book coauthored with Jere Brophy, *Powerful Social Studies for Elementary Students*.

Fred M. Newmann is professor of curriculum and instruction at the University of Wisconsin—Madison. Fred directed the National Center on Effective Secondary Schools and the Center on Organization and Restructuring of Schools. With 30 years experience in school reform research, curriculum development, and teacher education, he has contributed new curriculum in the analysis of public controversy and community-based learning and innovative ways of conceptualizing and scoring authentic instruction and assessment tasks. In addition to these topics, his publications deal with curriculum for citizenship, higher-order thinking in social studies, education and the building of community, and student engagement in secondary schools. His recent research focuses on the content areas of mathematics and social studies and asks how nationwide efforts at restructuring affect authentic student achievement. Two worthwhile publications that can be obtained by directly contacting Fred Newmann are A *Guide to Authentic Instruction and Assessment: Visions, Standards, and Scoring* (with W. Secada and G. Wehlage) and *Successful School Restructuring: A Report to the Public and Educators* (with G. Wehlage).

Nancy Rhodes is codirector of the Foreign Language Education Testing Division at the Center for Applied Linguistics in Washington, D.C. She has been involved in language research for the past 15 years. She is especially interested in oral language assessment and working with teachers to develop assessment strategies. Nancy is also serving as the associate director for the National K–12 Foreign Language Resource Center, a federally funded project administered by Iowa State University. This project involves the cooperative efforts of teachers and researchers, who are developing guidelines for assessing student's classroom language. She holds a master's degree in sociolinguistics from Georgetown University and has taught Spanish and English as a second language at the elementary, high school, and adult levels. Nancy has written extensively in the field of foreign language learning. She was a founding member and chair of the National Network for Early Language Learning, an organization of elementary school foreign language teachers, program supervisors, administrators, and teacher trainers. She currently serves as executive secretary for the organization and also serves on the Board of Directors of the Joint National Committee for Languages.

Dennis Dake holds the rank of professor in the Department of Art and Design at Iowa State University (ISU). Dennis has been responsible primarily for the preparation and training of art teachers at ISU. In addition to numerous art exhibitions and showings, Dennis, in collaboration with John Weinkein, developed the New Art Basics in Art Education program at ISU. This is a consortium of art teachers through out the state of Iowa that are networked via computer and share innovative curriculum, instruction, and assessment ideas and techniques. The network has become a major force in providing leadership in instruction and assessment of art education in K–12 classrooms in Iowa. These efforts have recently been extended to include the development of a model for computer-based distance learning via the statewide fiber optic network.

Brian Stecher is associate corporate research manager and social scientist at RAND. He is known for his research on the implementation of statewide assessment and accountability systems in education. He recently served as a consultant on performance measures and standards to the National Assessment of Vocational Education. Recent research activities include evaluation studies of large-scale assessment reforms in Vermont, Kentucky, and

Maryland and a study of the impact of federally mandated standards and measures of performance on vocational education programs nationally. Brian is currently working on a National Science Foundation study of the feasibility of using hands-on performance measures in science for large-scale assessment programs. Brian holds an elementary teaching credential and for seven years taught algebra and abstract mathematics to elementary school students in urban school districts.

Albert Beaton is currently professor of education at Boston College. After receiving his doctorate in educational measurement and statistics from Harvard, Albert was involved with research, teaching, and administration. From 1983 until 1990, he was director of design, research and data analysis for the National Assessment of Educational Progress. During this time (1981–1991) he also held the position of director of research at Educational Testing Service (ETS). This followed his administrative tenure as director of the Division of Measurement, Statistics, and Data Analysis Research at ETS. Currently Albert is international study director for the Third International Math and Science Study. In addition to writing in the areas of statistics and psychometrics, he has contributed to the research literature in computer science, education, and psychology. In addition to his current teaching activities at Boston College, he has taught at Stanford, Princeton, Harvard, Dublin Trinity College, and NUFFIC in the Hague.

CONCLUSION

With such a distinguished cast, the editing of this handbook has been a pleasurable and rewarding experience. I encourage the readers to contact individual authors if they have further questions or need professional assistance. The addresses of all authors are listed in the front of the handbook. Also, I would encourage readers to contact me if you have a particular topic that would fit the format I am trying to establish with the handbooks. If the topic appears to have widespread appeal among teacher–educators in the field, I will try to develop a handbook on that topic as part of the book series.

References

Gong, B. (1995, November). Emerging standards for classroom assessment. *Occasional newsletter of the AERA Special Interest Group on Classroom Assessment*, 1, 1.

Phye, G. D. (1986). Practice and skilled classroom performance. In G. D. Phye, & T. Andre (Eds.), *Cognitive classroom learning: Understanding, thinking, and problem solving* (pp. 141–168). Orlando, FL: Academic Press.

Index